Regional and Urban Economics and Economic Development

Regional and Urban Economics and Economic Development

Theory and Methods

Mary E. Edwards

Auerbach Publications
Taylor & Francis Group
Boca Raton   New York

Auerbach Publications is an imprint of the
Taylor & Francis Group, an informa business

Auerbach Publications
Taylor & Francis Group
6000 Broken Sound Parkway NW, Suite 300
Boca Raton, FL 33487-2742

© 2007 by Taylor & Francis Group, LLC
Auerbach is an imprint of Taylor & Francis Group, an Informa business

No claim to original U.S. Government works
Printed in the United States of America on acid-free paper
10 9 8 7 6 5 4 3

International Standard Book Number-10: 0-8493-8317-X (Hardcover)
International Standard Book Number-13: 978-0-8493-8317-5 (Hardcover)

Visit the Taylor & Francis Web site at
http://www.taylorandfrancis.com

and the Auerbach Web site at
http://www.auerbach-publications.com

Dedication

To my husband,

Chester

Foreword

A basic principle among geographers is that everything is somewhere, and where it is matters. Far from being random, the spatial distribution of phenomena over the earth's surface has causes, and it also has effects. An important part of both causes and effects relates to cost, or in other words, economic factors. Regional and urban economics explore these cost-related causes and effects of the location of many kinds of phenomena.

Understanding these economic factors has important practical uses, both in personal lives and in the establishment of public policy. *Regional and Urban Economics: Theory and Methods* addresses these topics from both points of view. People make many decisions in their lives, even unconsciously, on the basis of relative costs. Particularly in these days of high and rising fuel prices, how far away a potential destination is can greatly impact its attractiveness. Similarly, business firms must locate their facilities somewhere. The inputs needed and the market are also located somewhere, and firms must somehow bring those factors together or bridge the gaps between them. Thus, they face transportation expenses—the cost of relative locations—and factor these expenses into location decisions. Their choices will, in turn, influence other locational decisions.

Public policy decisions are a major factor in locational decision-making. They involve the siting of public facilities, which in turn may make a particular location more or less attractive to enterprises. Firms bring jobs and purchase goods and services locally, thereby influencing how attractive the region is to people. In other words, attracting firms to a region is a key to its economic development, raising the standard of living for residents.

These principles also apply to urban areas, where the vast majority of North Americans live. Periurban zones, those rural areas that border cities, have been especially attractive to Americans, leading to greater wealth but also to the spread of urban features that have been dubbed "sprawl." Issues of housing affordability, loss of green space, and increased traffic congestion have been particularly controversial, leading to various proposals and calls for "sustainable" or "smart" growth of cities. Economics faces the emotional component of these issues with hard analysis, which brings new perspectives even though it may not have final answers. The issue becomes political, and in such policy disputes, economics offers a less emotional perspective. It also introduces the spatial perspective of impacts on neighboring places, as one jurisdiction considers a particular policy alternative that may seem especially attractive for its residents but may exacerbate problems elsewhere in the wider region.

Urban economics also addresses locational questions of public facilities, especially as cities attempt to deal with problems that concentrated there, such as poverty and crime. Cities contain diverse populations that contend for resources, and municipal governments face the challenge of an equitable distribution of costs and benefits.

Regional and Urban Economics: Theory and Methods introduces students to these principles that will impact their lives. They make daily decisions as consumers and as residents, and the book regularly invites them to consider these questions. Furthermore, if only as voters, they participate in collective decisions on various questions of public policy, including the all-important issue of where. Where it is matters in terms of economic causes and effects.

Elizabeth J. Leppman
Lexington, Kentucky

Preface

This book provides a solid approach to analyzing the economy of a region or urban area. The aim is to first study firm location analysis and then to investigate why regions grow. Once regional growth is understood, it is possible to envision how growth affects the various-sized cities within an area and the use of land in and around its cities. After determining where households will locate, it is then possible to analyze the effectiveness of local governments in solving problems endemic to an urban area.

It is important for students to have hands-on experience in evaluating regional data. Provided are straightforward directions for delineating market areas, for identifying the economic base of a region, and for decomposing regional employment data to determine why it is expanding or contracting. This text also describes methods for calculating and interpreting various indicators of social welfare, such as standard-of-living indices, dependency ratios, employment and unemployment indicators, inequality indices, and migration rates.

Finally, herein lies a framework for evaluating public policy based on efficiency and equity concerns. This framework uses analyses based on traditional public finance models as well as on public choice models. Several definitions of "equity" are investigated, and these definitions are incorporated throughout the text in the policy analyses.

Intended Audience
The audience of this textbook includes students of economics, real estate, public administration, and economic development. It is assumed that students have studied principles of macroeconomics and microeconomics. The book is accessible to students whose understanding of economics is limited; however, techniques unique to regional analysis will also interest advanced undergraduate students and master's degree students of economics.

Pedagogy

Not everyone will be interested in studying the entire book in one semester, nor will they need to. Students of a regional and urban course will be primarily interested in the first three parts: Market Areas and Firm Location Analysis, Regional Growth and Development, and Urban Land Use and Urban Form. The instructor may feel free to add topics from Part IV based on current local issues and problems.

The appendices to Chapter 3, Chapter 7, and Chapter 15 provide detailed analyses of regions or cities. Real estate students or future entrepreneurs will benefit from determining the market areas for retail or service industries (Chapter 3). The economic base analyses and shift-share analyses of Chapter 7 do require a basic knowledge of spreadsheets, but the activities benefit students by giving them a perspective of what makes their specific regions unique. The exercise on estimating social welfare indicators in Chapter 11 provides students with both the equations for the indicators and an idea of how to interpret them. The Web site for the textbook will include updated links to the data sources at the county and state levels.

Courses that focus primarily on urban economics will benefit more from the following chapters:

- Chapter 3 (Market Areas and Systems of Cities)
- Chapter 5 (Agglomeration Economies and Entrepreneurs' Preferences)
- Chapter 9 (Core-Periphery Models—Distance Counts)
- Chapter 10 (Regional Labor Markets and Migration)

With the information contained in these four chapters, urban economics students may proceed to Parts III and IV (Urban Land Use and Urban Form, and Urban Problems and Policy).

Students whose primary objective is policy evaluation may consider first looking at Chapter 16. Chapters that focus primarily on policy topics include (along with Parts III and IV):

- Chapter 6 (Spatial Pricing Decisions), which delves into the welfare impacts of distance on pricing and spatial price discrimination. Such topics are important for students interested in antitrust and industrial organizations
- Chapter 11 (Can Government Change a Region's Growth Path?), which critiques the various and sundry place-based methods of economic development
- Chapter 15 (Growth Controls, Smart Growth and Zoning)

Acknowledgments

This book has benefited from suggestions and comments from students as well as professors. Earlier versions of the manuscript have been tested by undergraduate and graduate students at St. Cloud State University and master's level students at the University of Minnesota-Twin Cities campus. I gratefully acknowledge assistance from King Banaian, Örn Bodvarsson, Sarah Dorger, Daniel Gallagher, Richard Gleisner, Ann Grossman, Philip Grossman, Eric Hampton, Patricia Hughes, Shawn Jarvis, Yasuko Kamada, Eungmin Kang, Catherine Lafon, Ming Lo, Hal Lofgreen, William Luksetich, Mana Komai, Masoud Moghaddam, Mark Partridge, Attawet Prougestaporn, Ken Rebeck, Luz Triana-Echeverria, and Michael White. I also thank Joan O'Driscoll, and the interlibrary loan staff at St. Cloud State University, as well as other former and current colleagues and students of St. Cloud State University, without whom this book would not be possible. I also thank Natalie Artha for providing the meticulous illustrations for the textbook and the accompanying PowerPoint slides. I also thank the anonymous referees for their comments.

Special thanks goes to Guy Levilain, who has read several versions of the manuscript and who has contributed significantly to the readability of the entire text.

A Web site for the book is found at *http://web.stcloudstate.edu/meedwards/*. The Web site includes links to current news articles that deal with regional and urban economics and economic development topics, as well as current links to data sources.

About the Author

Mary E. Edwards is a Professor of Economics at St. Cloud State University, where she has taught courses in regional and urban economics for many years. She currently directs the Master of Science Program in Applied Economics at the university. She also has been a visiting professor at the Department of Applied Economics at the University of Minnesota and at the Université Toulouse I in Toulouse, France.

Mary E. Edwards was president of the Minnesota Economics Association and has served on the board of that association. She has also been involved with the Minnesota Economic Development Center and the Economics Research Institute at St. Cloud State University, and a member of the Research Committee for St. Cloud Area Economic Development Partnership. She has done numerous regional analyses for these agencies. She has also published in the *Journal of Regional Science, Nonprofit and Voluntary Sector Quarterly, Atlantic Economic Journal, American Journal of Economics and Sociology*, and other journals.

List of Figures

List of Tables

Contents

PART II: REGIONAL GROWTH AND DEVELOPMENT

Chapter 1

Nature and Scope of Regional and Urban Economics

Every economic activity has a location, but dissimilar activities flourish in different areas. The fields of regional and urban economics consider the impact of location and distance on economic activity. Regional economics helps to determine where different types of economic activity will prosper. For instance, if regional economists look at a photograph of the Earth at night (Figure 1.1), want to know which economic activity locates where; why firms or households locate in some places but not in others, and why some activities thrive in areas that are toxic to other pursuits. Regional economists are curious about migration patterns—they ask why some households and firms choose to locate in the midst of large urban centers and others in the suburbs or rural areas. Regional economics combines tools from microeconomics, macroeconomics, and international economics to analyze location patterns and other components of regional growth rates.

Urban economists, on the other hand, are interested in the relation of the peripheral urban areas to the city itself as well as land use patterns within a city. They study the location of employment centers relative to residential districts or green spaces (Figure 1.2). Because people often live next to other people of the same income level or those who share the same tastes,

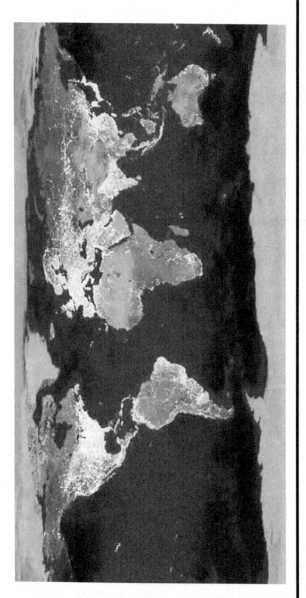

Figure 1.1 The earth at night. (Photo courtesy of Mayhew, C. and R. Simmon. NASA/GSFC, NOAA/ NGDC, DMSP Digital Archive. From http://antwrp.gsfc.nasa.gov/apod/ap001127.html.)

Figure 1.2 Skyline of Houston, Texas. (Retrieved from http://commons.wiki-media.org/wiki/Image:Houston_Skyline11.jpg.)

urban economists are particularly interested in land use, land rents, local government and local education policies, and housing, as well as social problems relating to poverty and crime.

Roots of Spatial Economics

The economic analysis of spatial problems can be traced to a 1755 treatise of Richard Cantillon, an Irish banker who lived in Paris. Cantillon examined the relationship of the cities to the surrounding countryside. Wealthier cities were located in areas that had more productive farmland. If farmers produced large amounts of surplus products, the cities bustled with economic activity.[1]

Between 1800 and 1950, German scholars were at the forefront of spatial economic thought. The early German works were not known to most English-speaking economists until they were translated in the middle or late 20th century. Johann Heinrich von Thünen's (1826) model of

---

[1] Cantillon (1755).

agricultural land use was briefly mentioned in Alfred Marshall's *Principles of Economics* (1892), but Thünen's book *Der isolierte Staat* (*The Isolated State*) was not fully translated into English until 1966. His agricultural land-use model forms the foundation for all urban land models today. Von Thünen's goal was to answer the question, "I have a piece of land, what is the best use for that land?"[2]

In 1885, mathematician Carl Wilhelm Friedrich Launhardt pioneered the relation between land use and land rents in what are called "bid-rent functions." He also explored the concept of market area analysis and spatial demand curves. His primary work, *Mathematische Begründung der Volkswirtschaftslehre* (*Mathematical Underpinnings of Economics*), was not translated into English until 1993.[3]

Alfred Weber's *Über den Standort der Industrie* (*Theory of Industrial Location*) followed Thünen's example by asking: "I have an industry, where do I locate it?" Walter Christaller developed a model showing how cities are linked in a hierarchical network in his 1933 work, *Die zentralen Orte in Süddeutschland* (*Central Places in Southern Germany*). Finally, in 1944 August Lösch expanded on this network with his work *Die räumliche Ordnung der Wirtschaft* (*The Economics of Location*), where he developed a formal model of market areas to complement Christaller's system of cities. Because of World War II, Lösch's work could not be translated into English until 1954. Even though American Economist Harold Hotelling's (1929) article, "Stability in Competition", is one of the most cited in current literature, most of the writings on regional and urban economics in the United States appeared after 1950.

What Makes up a Region?

The two major categories of regions are **functional** (operational) and **administrative** (political). Ideally, but rarely, these signify the same geographical area. The functional regions depend on some type of homogeneity within the area. The administrative regions are determined by political subdivisions and often become the area in which policy decisions are implemented.

The primary issue of regional economics concerns the appropriate delineation of a region. The traditional response was fairly easy. Siebert (1969), for example, defined a region as a "subsystem of a national economy." Historically, regional economic analysis has been limited to one country, but no longer. National frontiers are not always adequate to define spatial units of analysis because functional regions transcend political

---
[2] Blaug (1979).
[3] Shieh (2004).

boundaries. The Red River Valley Region, for instance, extends from the border between North Dakota and Minnesota into Manitoba, Canada. Maine's economy is more similar to that of New Brunswick, Canada, than to that of Nebraska.

The Blue Banana and the European Boomerang are also examples of such functional regions. As shown in Figure 1.3, Europe's Blue Banana encompasses the southwest of England, Lille (France), Brussels (Belgium), Luxembourg, The Netherlands, the Ruhr and the Rhine Valleys, Switzerland, and the north of Italy. Similarly, Central European cities of Gdansk,

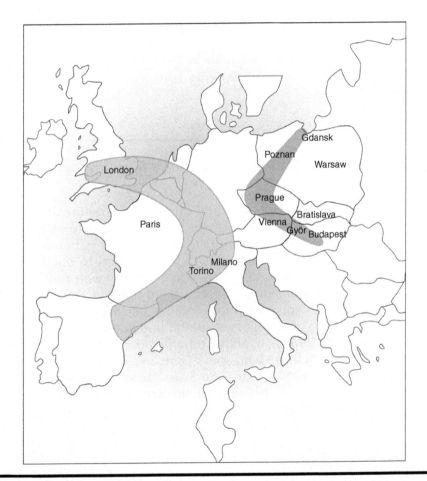

Figure 1.3 Europe's Blue Banana and the corresponding Boomerang. (Map courtesy of Borsi Balazs, GKI Economic Research Co. and the Office for Official publications of the European Communities 2005. The RECORD Experimental Map Innovative Research Organizations in European Accession Country, http://www.zsi.at/attach/RECORD_experimental_map.pdf, January 2004.)

Poznan, Wroclaw, Prague, Brno, Bratislava/Vienna, and Budapest form what Gorzelak (1996) calls the Central European Boomerang. The Central European Boomerang is predicted to become the core of this part of Europe because of the greater number of connections its cities have with the West. A final example of a European functional region is the proposed Mediterranean Arc in Europe includes the contiguous areas that border the Mediterranean Sea in Italy, France, and Spain.[4]

Classifying Regions

Classifying regions is the most basic task in spatial analysis, but at the same time, it can be one of the most controversial problems for both administrative and functional regions. For example, much controversy comes from redistricting political boundaries of the congressional districts to dilute the strength of the opposing party (gerrymandering) in the United States.[5]

Regional Boundaries within a Multilingual Country

Language or other cultural differences delineate market areas that are contained within and between country boundaries. Rossera (1990) analyzed patterns of telephone calls within Switzerland in 1985 to trace informal economic boundaries in a country with four distinct national languages. He found that the French and German sections phone each other infrequently because the two languages are quite different. People who speak Romansh, on the other hand, communicate as often with those who speak German as they do with those who speak Italian. The Swiss-French and Swiss-Italians, probably because of the common linguistic root, connect much more often with each other than with their German compatriots.

---

[4] Dictionnaire des mots et expressions de couleur du XXe siècle, http://www.ciril.fr/INALF/inalf.presentation/bleu/bleu-exemple.htm#banane bleue (accessed on January 6, 2000; site now discontinued). Club A. M. M. (1991), http://www.marseille-innov.org/AMM/cr311091.html.

[5] Leung (1983); Lane (1993).

The territories of Switzerland's four languages are as follows: 1: French; 2: German; 3: Italian; 4: Romansh.

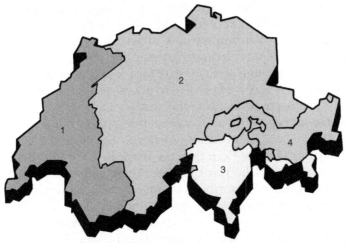

Rossera (1990); Map courtesy of *Encyclopedia of Linguistics* from an article by from Ray Harlow, entitled, Switzerland. http://strazny.com/encyclopedia/ sample-region.html

Think About It...

List the different administrative regions in which your city or neighborhood is included. On the Internet, search for the name of your city along with the word "region" or "district."

State (province, prefecture)_____

County, borough, or parish_____

Congressional district_____

Smaller cities may be part of a township within a county or a "census delineated area"_____

Counties may be part of metropolitan areas_____

Watershed district_____

School district_____

Economic development region_____

Judicial districts_____

Police precinct_____

County commissioner district_____

Other: _____

Often, secondary data are created and made available by administrative regions. With the growing availability and precision of various Geographic Information Systems (GIS) in providing information specific to areas smaller than counties, the definition of a region based on the geographic level of available data may soon become less of an issue. Unfortunately for the researcher, most economic data are currently available only at the county or the state level. Generating accurate data for areas smaller than those at the county or state level is very expensive to obtain and potentially invades the privacy of the firms or residents in the area.

A *functional region* requires a greater degree of commonality than an administrative region. Examples of functional regions in the United States include the Bible Belt, the Corn Belt, the Black Belt, the Rust Belt, the Jello Belt, the Snow Belt, and the Tornado Alley. These regions are homogeneous relative to a specific descriptor, but they are seldom administrative regions in that they do not have their own governing bodies.

Functional regions are not necessarily contiguous. Homogeneous economic regions may transcend political and national boundaries or be subsets within a given jurisdiction. National boundaries may become natural, economic boundaries of a region to the extent that they reflect the social, linguistic, cultural, or psychological space. The ideal classification assumes that the region can be precisely identified. For example, not all areas within Texas, Florida, or Kansas, for instance, are dominated by conservative, evangelical Protestants, and thus, not all people in those areas would consider themselves part of the Bible Belt (Figure 1.4). In reality, there are few precise boundaries for functional regions. A continuum, rather than a direct true/false type of response, characterizes most attributes that classify functional regions. The Bible Belt is an example of a functional region superimposed on a map of the individual states or administrative regions. Note that the more darkly shaded areas taper off to lighter areas at the perimeter. Observe that at the edge of this region on the map the color starts fading. How gradual a specific characteristic tapers off is subjective. For this reason it is seldom possible to delineate regions to please everyone.

In addition, other regions are created by the proximity of an urban center: market areas, emergency medical service regions, or areas served by electrical companies. The limits as well as the characteristics of these regions can change with time. For example, (1) before the 1970s, the Rust Belt was an area called the Manufacturing Belt. (2) Because of climatic changes, a map of Tornado Alley (Figure 1.1 through 1.5) will vary from year to year.

Methods of classifying regions generally involve a combination of educated guesses and statistical analyses that aggregate communities with other political subdivisions and portray them as single homogeneous unit. Cluster analysis, factor analysis, and principal components are some of the statistical procedures that are used. For examples of how regions are

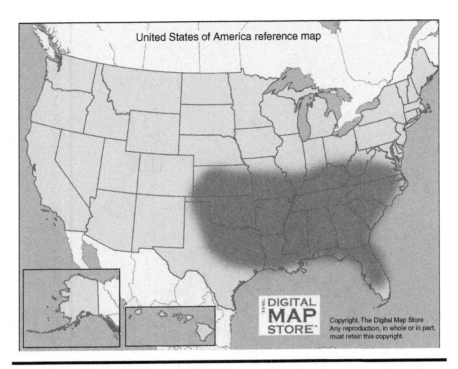

United States of America reference map

Figure 1.4 Bible Belt. (Courtesy of Maponics, LLC (www.maponics.com) and map retrieved from http://en.wikipedia.org/wiki/Image:Map_of_USA_high-lighting_ Bible_Belt.png#file.)

delineated, see Miller (1976); Shields and Deller (1996); Karlsson and Olsson (2006). Miller classifies the counties in Nebraska into various regions by the local industries. Shields and Deller use a cluster analysis to define comparable regions for Wisconsin counties. Karlsson and Olsson use labor market data to delineate functional regions in Sweden.

Think About It...

List the different functional regions in which your city or neighborhood is included. You may benefit from searching the Internet for the term "region" or "belt" dealing with an important aspect of your culture, climate, heritage, or location.

Geographic location as determined by the Census Bureau (East, Midwest, Atlantic States, etc.)

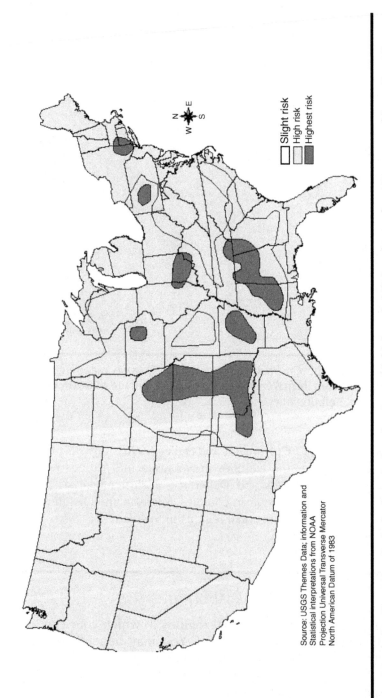

Source: USGS Themes Data; information and
Statistical interpretations from NOAA
Projection Universal Transverse Mercator
North American Datum of 1983

Slight risk
High risk
Highest risk

Figure 1.5   Tornado Alley. Note the lack of contiguity of regions with high probabilities of tornados. (Courtesy of State Data Center, University of Arkansas-Little Rock.)

"Belts" designating your area:

Market area of which major store, hospital, or weather radio center:

_____

_____

_____

How Does Space Affect Traditional Economics?

Regional economics focuses on proximity and transportation costs, increasing returns to scale and externalities. These components change the face of traditional economic theory. Traditional economic models assume a perfectly competitive market structure, with constant returns to scale. Externalities are of concern, but only as examples of market failure. However, externalities permeate the majority of regional and urban economic analyses.

Spatial Market Structures

The major effect of distance on microeconomic theory is that it changes the types of possible market structures. When we include distance in the model, the only type of market structure that makes sense is the oligopoly. The main assumption of perfect competition is that many buyers and sellers of a homogeneous product act so that no one can influence price. This assumption is violated immediately when we consider spatial locations. Distance differentiates goods, and transport costs increase the price that the consumers pay. A dozen fresh eggs from the convenience store next door is not the same good to a hungry consumer as a dozen eggs from a farmer on the other side of the county. Even if egg prices are identical, the consumer pays transportation costs to bring the eggs home.

Similarly, a spatial monopolist does not have license to act like a monopolist in the traditional sense. The only dry cleaner in town may consider itself a local monopolist. However, if dry cleaners in neighboring towns decrease their prices substantially, the local dry cleaner will be forced to do likewise. Spatial monopolists have to keep tabs on what their competitors in the neighboring towns are doing. Firms that react to what their rivals are doing are in essence oligopolists, not monopolists.

Finally, monopolistic competition is untenable in a spatial context. The monopolistically competitive market structure has a great many firms selling differentiated products. The number of businesses is supposedly so large that no firm is concerned about the competition. However, an urban market structure that resembles a monopolistically competitive industry conforms more precisely to a **chain oligopoly**. If a firm in one part of a city decreases its prices, the firms adjacent to it are also forced to lose sales or decrease their own prices, as do their neighbors. Like falling dominos, the chain reactions from a price decrease by one firm eventually affects all firms of that type in the metropolitan area.

Regional Growth Policies

Distance (space) also disrupts macroeconomic theories as they are applied to a regional economy. Macroeconomic models that seem robust on a national or international scale are not as solid at a regional level. For example, monetary policy is a less effective local policy instrument. Because money flows easily within a country, it is difficult to increase loans to one area while stopping the funds from spilling over into nearby regions.

Short-run macroeconomic models specify that the problem of unemployment can be corrected by increasing "spending" in that area, but these models do not specify what should be purchased or from whom. When it comes to actually implementing such policies, this detail becomes critical in determining their overall success. Long-run macroeconomic models suggest that if we wait long enough, and if no legislation interferes with trade and migration, the "law of one price" will apply. Wages, growth rates, and prices everywhere will equilibrate. Such models do not explain persistent economic growth and income disparities among regions where no legislation has ever interfered with migration or trade. We will see what modifications must be made for macroeconomic policies to be successfully applied to regions in Part II of this textbook.[6]

Local Public Finance

Pure public goods are defined as goods that are nonrival and nonexcludable. An unlimited number of people can enjoy a public good without lowering the quality for anyone else or without increasing its cost. In addition, excluding anyone from using a specific public good is difficult if not impossible. However, most public goods produced and consumed locally can become congested (club goods). Congestion decreases the quality while increasing the social cost of using the good, making it more

---

[6] Perroux (1950); Greenhut (1978).

rival than a pure public good is supposed to be. Similarly, local public goods can be partly excludable. Students can be excluded from attending a school if their families do not live in that district. Likewise, libraries may exclude people from borrowing their books or using their facilities, and fire departments can refuse to put out the fire in a neighboring jurisdiction. As we will see in Part IV, it is not clear whether local government or the private sector is more efficient at providing club goods.

In addition, goods provided by one jurisdiction affect neighboring jurisdictions, as do restrictions imposed within one jurisdiction. Crime control for a central city keeps its daytime population safer, even though much of the daytime population lives and pays taxes in the suburbs. Families from both the inner city and the suburbs may enjoy events and public goods of the central city equally. However, the family from the inner city is often charged as much as 5% more of its income in taxes than an otherwise similar family living in the suburbs to pay for the crime prevention within the central city.[7]

Plan of the Book

This book contains four parts. Our study of location theory in Part I leads directly to regional growth analysis in Part II. Firms start up and an area thrives; firms leave and the area withers. Firms influence the shape and activities in their area for years to come. Thus we ask, "what makes some regions grow faster than others?" as well as, "What can a region do to bridle its growth?" We will study reginal disparities, and try to explain why one segment of a country grows at a different pace than another. We will also investigate why some rural areas surrounding a city benefit while others are harmed by the growth of that city. Finally, we will explore the regional labor markets and migration before examining the result of various roles of government in determining regional growth.

We then turn our attention to urban land use and urban form (Part III). We observe where firms and households locate in areas within and surrounding cities. We investigate why some cities house their poor near their central business district, while in others, the lower-income people live outside the central urban area. We consider first the traditional monocentric model, where there is one "downtown," before studying the polycentric urban models, where there are many employment centers and shopping areas throughout the entire metropolitan area. As a city grows, transportation becomes essential to its vitality. Transportation networks make housing and employment locations feasible and thus influence the urban landscape.

---

[7] Scotchmer and Thisse (1992).

In Part III, we also examine why segregation in the United States in 2000 was more pronounced than it was 120 years earlier, what can be done to make housing more affordable, and ways that a city can most efficiently increase the free-flow of traffic in and out of the city.

Part IV concentrates on urban problems and policy evaluation by first introducing a strategy for evaluating policy that takes both equity and efficiency into consideration. We focus on the efficiency and equity concerns of implementing growth controls and "smart growth" concepts for a city, as well as the effectiveness of local governments to provide public goods and raise revenues to pay for these goods. The last three chapters consider three specific public goods that local governments provide their citizens: poverty relief, education, and crime control.

To the extent that economic growth increases the demand for labor, thus creating jobs and increasing wages, the entire course could be construed as a course on alleviating poverty. Understanding firm location may increase the probability of creating an environment conducive for firms to create jobs in an area. Realizing what triggers regional economic growth could help raise the standard of living for people within that region. The result of recognizing (1) where within a city people and firms locate, (2) that transportation patterns ascertain easier access to jobs, and (3) that quality education and training improve the productivity of workers will help people rise out of poverty.

Regional and urban economics are interdisciplinary subjects. They borrow and adapt ideas and analytical methods from geography, physics, social psychology, public administration, sociology, ecology, and history. Within economics itself, the fields of regional and urban economics link microeconomic and macroeconomic analysis. Since economic regions can traverse political boundaries, regional economics models are starting to influence international trade theory.

Appendix: Data Sources

As we analyze different topics, it is useful to apply the analyses locally. Web sites that will be helpful for the research assignments will have updated links on the book's Web site. These include:

- Census population, estimates and forecasts, age distributions, educational attainment, income and race, home values, and ownership rates. http://www.census.gov through American Factfinder.
- Earned income by industry, per capita personal income: Regional Economic Information System (REIS) data. These data are now available not only by county, borough or parish but also by metropolitan and micropolitan statistical areas. Choose CA05 at

http://www.bea.gov/bea/regional/reis/.

■ Income distribution for after-tax income, effective buying income series: sales and marketing management; ***Annual Survey of Buying Power***.

■ Number of people who are employed and unemployed as well as the unemployment rates by state, county, and for some metropolitan areas are found in the Local Area Unemployment Statistics (LAUS) data http://www.bls.gov/lau/.

■ Employment and wages by industry are available through the Quarterly Census of Employment and Wages ES202 for the county, MSA, state and national levels at http://www.bls.gov/cew/. Otherwise, check your state's workforce center or Department of Labor affiliate.

■ Retail and service sales data are available in economic censuses conducted in years ending in two and seven from the census bureau: http://www.census.gov/.

■ Crime rates are available through http://fbi.gov/ucr/ucr.htm by county or through your state Bureau of Criminal Apprehension.

In addition, note that city data available through the State of the Cities Data Systems (SOCDS) can be found at the Web site of the Department of Housing and Urban Development (http://socds.huduser.org/SOCDS_Home.htm). Check data sources available from your state in the ***Statistical Abstract of the United States*** at http://www.census.gov/compendia/statab/. There is also a ***Statistical Abstract of the World*** published by Thomson Gale. Finally, check the agencies in charge of the various administrative regions overseeing your area for sources of secondary data for your area.

Research Questions

Choose a city to study throughout the term. For that city or its county (borough or parish), find out information that will be useful for analyzing your region this term:

■ The population from the last decennial census, current estimated population, and the forecasted population.

■ The age distribution, racial composition, and median educational attainment.

■ Land area and population density of your city and surrounding civil divisions.

■ Employment by industry.

■ The per capita personal income of the county.

■ Income distribution for after-tax income and median income.

■ Unemployment rate estimates for the county.

- Average annual wages by industry for your county.
- Median housing values for your city and contiguous regions.
- Crime rates.

Use data from state or census sources, but beware of using data from the city's advertising page. Those data are often out-of-date.

1. How does your city differ from those that your classmates are studying with respect to these statistics?
   a. Do per capita personal incomes, median housing values, educational attainment, and crime rates seem positively or negatively correlated?
   b. Which of your industries employ the most people? Why do you think those industries are located in your region?
2. From your findings, write a one-page advertisement aimed to attract a retail firm to your region. What attributes does your region have to offer?

References

Blaug, M. 1979. The German hegemony of location theory: a puzzle in the history of economic thought. *History of Political Economy* 11 (1):21–29.

Cantillon, R. 1755. *Essai sur la Nature du Commerce en Général*. Edited with an English translation and other material by H. Higgs, C. B. Reissued for The Royal Economic Society by Frank Cass and Co., Ltd., London. 1959. http://oll.libertyfund.org/Home3/Book.php?recordID=0611 (accessed on May 22, 2006).

Club, A. M. M. 1991. A propos de la situation actuelle et de l'avenir international de l'aire métropolitaine marseillaise. (31 October 1991): http://www.marseille-innov.org/AMM/cr311091.html (accessed on January 6, 2000).

European Commission. 2004. The RECORD experimental map innovative research organizations in European accession countries. (January 2004): http://www.zsi.at/attach/RECORD_experimental_map.pdf (accessed on April 15, 2006).

Gorzelak, G. 1996. *The Regional Dimension of Transformation in Central Europe*, London: Regional Studies Association, as cited in Taylor, P. J. and M. Hoyler, 2000. The Spatial Order of European Cities under Conditions of Contemporary Globalization. *Tijdschrift voor Economische en Sociale Geografie*, 91 (2): 176–189.

Greenhut, M. L. 1978. Impacts of distance on microeconomic theory. *Manchester School of Economic and Social Studies* 46 (1):17–40.

Harlow, R. Switzerland. *Encyclopedia of linguistics*, http://strazny.com/encyclopedia/sample-region.html (accessed on July 17, 2005).

Hotelling, H. 1929. Stability in competition. *Economic Journal* 39 (153):41–57.

Karlsson, C. and M. Olsson. 2006. The identification of functional regions: theory, methods, and applications. *The Annals of Regional Science* 40 (1):1–18.

Lane, T. 1993. Is there a future for regional science in economics? *Annals of Regional Science* 27 (3):285–293.

Leung, Y. 1983. A linguistically-based regional classification system. In *Measuring the Unmeasurable*, editor-in-chief, Peter Nijkamp, co-editors, Helga Leitner, Neil Wrigley. Boston: M. Nijhoff 451–485.

Mayhew, C. and R. Simmon. *The earth at night.* (NASA/GSFC), NOAA/ NGDC, DMSP Digital Archive. From http://antwrp.gsfc.nasa.gov/apod/ap001127.html (accessed on July 19, 2006).

Miller, A. R. 1976. A taxonomy of Nebraska county economies: an application of the optimization approach to identifying a system of regions. *Journal of Regional Science* 16 (2):225–236.

Perroux, F. 1950. Economic space: theory and applications. *Quarterly Journal of Economics* 64 (1):89–104.

Rossera, F. 1990. Discontinuities and barriers in communications: the case of Swiss communities of different language. *Annals of Regional Science* 24 (4):319–336.

Scotchmer, S. and J.-F. Thisse. 1992. Space and competition: a puzzle. *Annals of Regional Science* 26 (3):269–286.

Shieh, Y.-N. 2004. Wilhelm Launhardt and bid-rent curves: a note. *Journal of the History of Economic Thought* 26 (4):537–542.

Shields, M. and Deller S. C. Clustering Wisconsin counties for analytical comparisons. CCED Department of Agricultural and Applied Economics. University of Wisconsin-Madison/Extension. Staff Paper 96.7, 1996.

Siebert, H. 1969. *Regional Economic Growth: Theory and Policy*, Scranton, PA: International Textbook Company.

Thünen, J. H. von. 1966 [1826] *The Isolated State; an English edition of Der isolierte Staat*. Translated by Carla M. Wartenberg. Edited with an introduction by Peter Hall. Oxford, New York, Pergamon Press.

Weber, A. 1929 [1909] *Theory of the Location of Industries*. [Translated by C. J. Friedrich from *Über den Standort der Industrie*]. Chicago: The University of Chicago Press.

MARKET AREAS AND FIRM LOCATION ANALYSIS

The success or failure of many urban professionals hinges on their understanding of why firms locate where they do. Location can make or break a business. Realtors who know location theory sell and present properties more effectively. Public officials and economic developers recognize that enticing firms to an area creates jobs and increases wages, incomes, local tax bases, and property values. A firm's location choice thus affects a region's quality of life.

What factors does a firm consider when it decides where to locate? The answer is very simple: business owners will locate where they can maximize the return on their investments. For some entrepreneurs, a good location is where they will maximize profits or just minimize costs. For others, proximity to specific inputs or customers will thus be the primary criterion for the choice of a location. For a final set of business owners, the optimal place depends on the amenities offered.

Transportation costs play a fundamental role in this choice. Firms that pay more to transport their output are defined as market oriented. Market-oriented firms produce goods with short shelf lives or goods that are expensive to transport, such as newspapers, fresh vegetables, bakery goods, or products that gain weight in the production process. In contrast, input-oriented firms pay more to transport inputs. Some firms cluster in a region and thus influence the cost structure of all enterprises in the same area, generally by lowering the production costs. Then, even more firms will be attracted to the region because of the cost advantages resulting from the agglomeration. Lower production costs that benefit firms clustered together are called **agglomeration economies**.

This part examines various models of firm location behavior. Chapter 2 and Chapter 3 focus on what Fujita and Thisse (1997, 2002) call "shopping models." Shopping models are appropriate for studying the competitive behavior among firms that sell consumer goods, as opposed to shipping models, which describe competition among producers. Shopping models assume that the costs of labor and other inputs are the same everywhere. The only factors that change with the location are the number of consumers that the firm can attract and the number of rival firms.

A model of urban hierarchy that determines which cities more efficiently provide what services stems from the simple model of market areas. Chapter 3 explores theories that explain the relationships among neighboring cities of different sizes, that is, theories of hierarchies, networks of cities, and central places. The concept of a central place is rooted in the fact that each type of product requires a market area of a certain size. The combinations of products sold in a city changes with its size. Consumers in smaller cities need to travel to an urban center to find specialized products.

Chapter 4 and Chapter 5 explore "shipping models." In Chapter 4, when we relax the assumption that the costs of production are equal everywhere, we discover that the costs of the inputs and transportation costs produce a predictable effect on the location of enterprises. Chapter 5 concentrates on the effects of agglomeration economies on firm location. Agglomeration economies, along with the theory of cumulative causality, help shape the foundation of the endogenous growth theory, (New Growth Theory) that is supported by development economists, international economists, and macroeconomists.

Chapter 6 concentrates on spatial pricing patterns. These pricing patterns refute the myth that monopoly is the only market structure capable of practicing price discrimination. Price discrimination consists of selling the same product at different prices and to different consumers without incurring any increase in cost. The chapter also reveals the ineptitude of some antitrust laws, such as the Robinson-Patman Act, which actually create and sustain local monopolies while claiming to encourage competition. Chapter 6 highlights the inconsistency between a basing-point pricing system—which is now illegal but which the American steel companies used until 1924—and the "legal by definition" basing-point pricing system that the U.S. federal government uses to establish prices. The steel mills in Europe currently use a basing-point pricing system despite Article 85 of the Treaty of Rome that, in principle, forbids commercial restrictions in the European Union.

Chapter 2

Linear Market Areas

To determine where a firm will locate, we will start by delimiting a market area for a spatial monopolist. By delimiting the potential market area, we find the optimal location for a firm depending on the consumers' pattern of dispersal and the product's elasticity of demand. The underlying assumption in these models is that all inputs are sold everywhere for the same price. According to Fujita and Thisse (1997, 2002), the models in this chapter and in Chapter 3 are known as *shopping models*. Shopping models allow us to study the competitive behavior of firms that sell directly to consumers. They apply principally not only to the retail trade and service industries, but also to the manufacturing firms if input costs are identical wherever a firm locates. Shopping models assume that the consumers pay all transportation costs, that is, if all firms use *free on board (f.o.b.) pricing* policies.

In this chapter, we first note that if a firm starts as a spatial monopolist, it may not remain so for long if the local market is profitable. Profits attract entry. Entry changes a monopoly into a duopoly or an oligopoly. We will next determine where the new enterprises will locate, and then we consider pricing strategies and other games that duopolists or oligopolists play. Finally, we will expand the theory to explore commuter shopping, multi-purpose, and multi-stop shopping behavior.

The distance consumers are prepared to travel to buy a product determines the market area. The traditional demand curve for a product shows the quantity of a good that people are willing and able to buy at a specific price. However, the real amount that consumers pay is more than the sum they pull out of their wallets. The *delivered price (full price)* equals the store price, also called the mill price (or gate price for agricultural products), plus the transportation costs that are incurred in traveling to the store. This **transportation cost** includes more than the cost of gas, oil, insurance, and depreciation for an automobile, or than the cost of bus, taxi, or subway fares. The most important component of transportation cost is the opportunity cost of the time involved in traveling to and from the store.

We assume that the spatial monopolist imposes an **f.o.b. mill price**, which means that consumers pay the mill price (the price that the store charges) plus all transportation costs. Under f.o.b. pricing, if the consumers do not go to the store to buy the product, they can order the product from the dealer and pay all shipping charges. The opposite of f.o.b. pricing is **uniformed delivered pricing**, also known as cost, insurance, and freight (**c.i.f.**) **pricing**. Under uniform delivered pricing, the firms pay all transportation costs. Firms that offer free delivery (for goods such as flowers, pizzas, prescriptions, or groceries) employ a uniform delivered pricing strategy, and thereby become price discriminators.

From Demand Functions to Price–Distance Functions

One way to determine the distance that consumers are prepared to travel to shop is to examine transportation costs in light of the demand curve. Economists generally start with the most restricted, and the simplest models that still explain the effects of the variable under study. Little by little, we relax the stringent assumptions, making the model more realistic. The simplest models in spatial economics require the following assumptions:

First, the transport costs are constant and consist of both out-of-pocket costs and psychic costs, that is, costs that represent the additional stress or the opportunity cost of the time. Second, assuming that the transportation costs per unit of distance are constant, the price-distance function shows the total cost incurred by the consumers in traveling from their residences to the store. Finally, we assume that each of them only buys one article, that they do not stock up or buy in bulk, that they have no other reason to go to the store, and that they have no other errands to do along the way.

The **delivered price (full price)** that consumers pay is the mill price plus transport costs. The **limit price** is the maximum price that the consumers are willing and able to pay for a good. It is the price at which a linear demand function intersects the *y*-axis. For the demand curve in Panel B of Figure 2.1, the limit price is $10. Note that the demand curve represents a typical household, regardless of its location. A market demand is the summation of all the individual demand curves. Because the goal of this exercise is to determine the maximum distance that individuals or households will travel to shop, the market demand curve would not be appropriate.

Think About It...

Determine your "full price" for going to get ... (substitutions are possible)

1. An ice cream cone
2. A single loaf of bread, or
3. A cup of "designer" coffee

Store price   #1. ———

Transport costs (for drivers)

Distance to store (in miles) multiplied by 40.5¢ per mile	2a _____
Parking fees	2b _____
Time to drive there, park, and return home multiplied by hourly wage	2c _____

or (for users of public transportation)

Roundtrip fare	3a _____
Time to ride there and return home, including any transfers, multiplied by hourly wage	3b _____

Total transport costs (either 2a+2b+2c or 3a+3b)

                                               #2. ———

Full price of purchased item   (#1+#2) ———

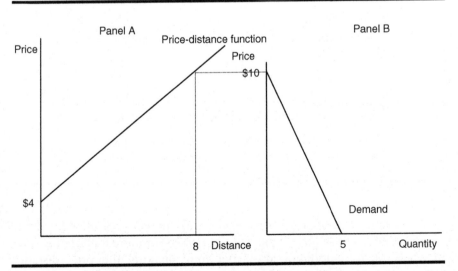

Figure 2.1 Price-distance function and demand function.

Figure 2.1 shows the distance that a consumer is prepared to travel. Panel A is a price-distance function. The slope of the price-distance function is the transport cost per unit of distance (block, mile, or kilometer). In Figure 2.1, consumers who live eight miles from the store do without the good or service rather than travel that far because the delivered price is higher than their limit price ($10). Those who live just fewer than eight miles away will patronize the store in town, albeit rarely. (Calculations associated with Figure 2.1 are in the Mathematical Appendix.)

Dynamics of Market Areas

The market area for a spatial monopolist is a function of its demand curve and the price-distance function. The radius of the market area varies when a store changes its prices or when transportation costs change for consumers. When a store changes the price of its product, the price-distance function will shift upward or downward, parallel to the original function. If the mill price increases, say from $4 to $6, as in Figure 2.2, the radius of the market area drops to 5.33 miles. A decrease in the price to $2 increases the radius of the market area to 10.67 miles. (See Appendix for details.)

Think About It…

Consider again your trips to just get an ice cream cone, a loaf of bread, or a cup of coffee. How would the following affect your full price and your decision to go for the items?

1. Store price doubled (mill price increases)
2. Gas prices (or fares) went up 25 percent (transportation costs increase)
3. Congestion increased the time to get to the facility by 25 percent (transportation costs increase)
4. You want to celebrate your best friend's birthday with this good (demand increases)

The spatial monopolist cannot control all market area changes. Road construction, considerably higher gasoline prices, or more traffic congestion increase the transportation costs per mile, making the price-distance function steeper. In Figure 2.3, for example, if the price of the product is

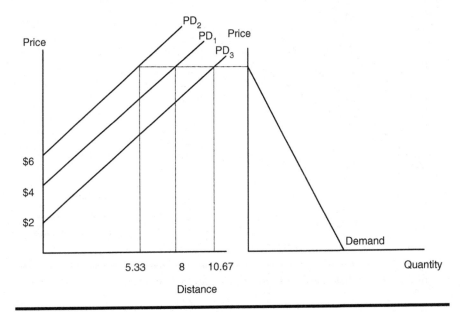

Figure 2.2 Price-distance functions and demand when the mill (store) price changes.

$4, but the transportation costs per mile double to $1.50, the market area radius shrinks from 8 to 4 miles. However, if one constructs a more efficient road system that cuts down the time needed to drive to the store and the transportation costs per mile fall by 50¢, then the market area radius expands to 12 miles. (Details are in the Appendix.)

The Debilitating Effect of Decreased Transportation Costs for Small Banks

Rosser (1991) blames the decline in the number of banks at the end of the 1920s on the proliferation of the automobile. As more people owned automobiles, their marginal transportation cost fell because consumers could go farther in less time, which increased the market area of banks. Greater competition from banks in neighboring cities forced inefficient banks out of business.

Rosser (1991)

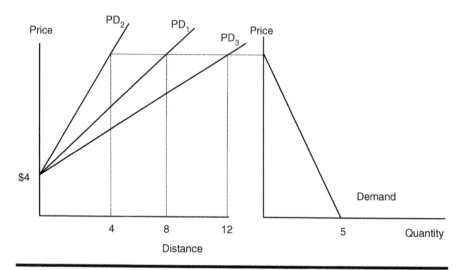

Figure 2.3 Price-distance functions and demand when transport costs change.

Finally, the market area changes when the demand curve shifts. If demand for the product increases, pushing the limit price to $12 (rather than $10), the market area boundary will increase from 8 miles to 10.67 miles. If instead the limit price falls to $6, the boundary decreases to 2.67 miles. The graph of this instance is left for the reader to draw and analyze. (See the Appendix for a hint.)

In summary, the mill price, the cost of transportation, and the demand for the firm's product determine the market boundary for a spatial monopolist. Market boundaries shrink if the firm charges a higher price, if travel costs increase, or if demand decreases. Market area boundaries expand when the firm lowers its price, when travel costs decrease, or when demand increases.

Price Elasticity of Demand and Distance

The price elasticity of demand for a product increases with distance to the store. Consumers who live farther from the store are more sensitive to price changes. They have more elastic demand curves than those living closer to the store. The price elasticity of demand measures the responsiveness of consumers to price changes. The formula for elasticity of demand is

$$\left| \frac{\%\Delta Q}{\%\Delta P} \right| \tag{2.1}$$

Along a linear demand curve, the absolute value of the elasticity of demand ranges from ∞ (at the limit price) to zero (at a price of zero).

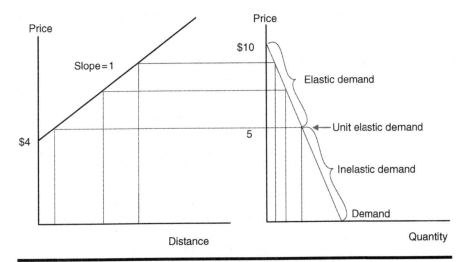

Figure 2.4   Price-distance function and elasticity of demand.

The midpoint on a demand curve is the point of **_unit elasticity_** because the percent change in quantity equals the percent change in price. Above this point, the elasticity coefficients are greater than one, and the demand is called "**_elastic_**." The demand is "**_inelastic_**" when the elasticity coefficients are less than one, on the lower portion of the demand curve.

Because the limit price is ten and half of ten is five, at a price of $5 the demand curve of Figure 2.4 is unit elastic. Therefore, because consumers who live right next to the firm pay $4 for the product, their demand is inelastic. If customers living 1 mile from the point of sale incur $1 in transportation costs, they face a delivered price of $5, and consequently, have a unit elastic demand. Consumers who live farther pay yet a higher delivered price and have an even more elastic demand. Those who live 8 miles from the firm are the most responsive to price changes and face a nearly perfectly elastic demand. Knowing this, firms try to decrease delivered prices for distant consumers for whom the demand is elastic, while increasing prices for local customers who have inelastic demand. We will see in chapter 6 some examples of spatial price discrimination conditional upon distance from the point of sale.

Hotelling's Linear Markets

Market area analysis is traced to a model developed by Harold Hotelling (1929). Economic theory asserts that excess profits invite entry. Hotelling tried to determine whether a firm that enters a market endowed with excess profits would locate close to the original firm or away from it. The traditional answer from Hotelling's theory is that the location depends on the elasticity of demand.

To understand Hotelling's answer, let us assume that consumers are equally spaced along the linear market area. To picture this market area, think of the main street of a town with individual houses on equally sized lots. This assumption means that as market area changes, sales change proportionally. Let us then, assume that the demand curve for the homogeneous product is perfectly inelastic. Perfectly inelastic demand curves are vertical and thus have no limit price. An example of a good with a perfectly inelastic demand would be insulin. If the price of insulin increases, diabetics cannot substitute a cheaper medicine. In contrast, if the price of insulin drops, firms do not increase sales. Diabetics cannot consume more insulin and other patients will not substitute insulin for another prescription.

Think About It...

Look at a detailed map of your city or neighborhood. Pick out the locations of the following types of stores:

1. Convenience stores
2. Video stores
3. Gas stations
4. Large grocery stores
5. Used car shops
6. Major employers
7. Restaurants
8. Clothing and apparel stores

Which stores cluster together and which stores are dispersed? Is there a pattern of dispersal along a transportation network?

Spatial Duopolies with Perfectly Inelastic Demand

Besides a perfectly inelastic demand, Hotelling assumed that consumers are equally distributed along the linear market area and every consumer buys only 1 unit of the product. He also assumed that they incur all transport costs. According to Hotelling, firms behave like lemonade stands on wheels—they move up and down the street *costlessly*. A single firm can locate anywhere, and because of perfectly inelastic demand, it will not lose any customers because they are ready to pay any expense to obtain their good. However, when the consumers have a choice between two firms, they buy from the firm with the lowest delivered price. Finally, Hotelling assumed that consumers don't have any reason to prefer one store over another for better quality products or better service.

Firm A in Figure 2.5 is a spatial monopolist located at the first quartile. If Firm B decides to enter the market, that firm will locate just to the right of the original firm. Firm A would retain all consumers located to the left of the store (the entire first quartile) and half of the consumers between it and Firm B. The market area of Firm A is the small region on the left. Firm B controls the large area on the right.

Because consumers purchase from the firm with the lowest delivered price, Firm B controls three-fourths of the market. However, to increase its market share, all that Firm A has to do is to move just to the right of B. Firm B retaliates and moves to the right of A.

Because moving is costless, the two firms continue leapfrogging until they reach an equilibrium location in the middle of the market area. In this

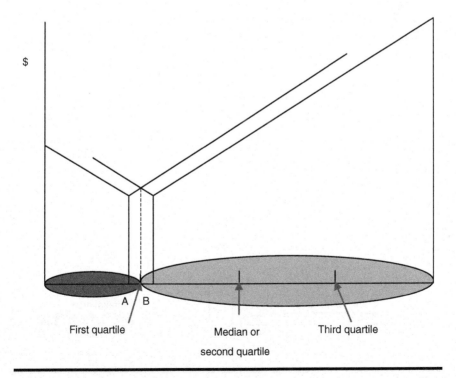

Figure 2.5 Unstable market areas for a duopoly.

fashion, every firm will control half the entire market. Consumers in quartiles one and two will shop at A and consumers in quartiles three and four will shop at B, as shown in Figure 2.6. Both firms face the same transportation and production costs.

Notice that according to Hotelling's model, when the firms locate together in the center of the market, neither firm thinks to lower its price. This price stability is the key to a stable equilibrium in this model. Once they locate in the market center, there is no other place where either firm can relocate and increase its revenues.

Hotelling called the tendency for the firms to cluster in the middle of the market area the ***principle of minimum differentiation***. He used this principle to explain not only geographic advantages, but also the behavior of candidates in electoral campaigns and the absence of radical innovations in retail goods.

Hotelling justified the difficulty in distinguishing one politician from another during election time by using locations along a continuum of preferences for or against specific issues. Politicians from the far left or the far right will collect fewer votes that those who agree with the median voter. Therefore, Hotelling observed,

> Every candidate '*pussyfoots*,' replies ambiguously to questions, refuses to take a definite stand in any controversy for fear of losing votes. (Hotelling 1929). (The italics are in the original.)

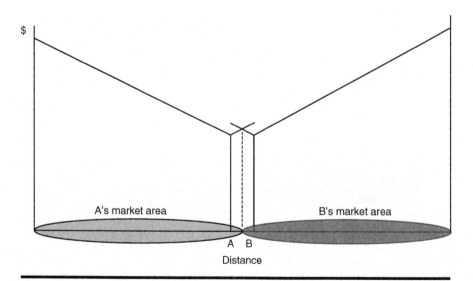

Figure 2.6 Market areas for a duopoly under perfectly inelastic demands.

Hotelling also used the principle of minimum differentiation to justify why "buyers are confronted everywhere with an excessive sameness" in retail products. If we consider "location" with respect to the attributes of a product, the principle of minimum differentiation establishes that firms producing heterogeneous products can alienate certain groups of consumers. Retailers, consequently, will tend to

> make only slight deviations in order to have for the new commodity as many buyers of the old as possible, and to get, so to speak, *between* one's competitors and a mass of consumers (Hotelling 1929). (The italics are in the original.)

Think About It...

When you find you lack a key ingredient for tonight's dinner, you have two choices: (1) change your menu, or (2) buy the ingredient.

If you decide to purchase the good, under what conditions do you go to the closest store? When do you go to a more distant one?

Spatial Duopolies with Elastic Demand

Hotelling's theory continues by supporting the hypothesis that most firms will locate far from each other because the demand for most goods is not perfectly inelastic. Firms that sell goods with an elastic demand tend to disperse. Figure 2.7 shows that our spatial monopolist "A" is located in the center of Main Street. If the limit price is $10, the spatial monopolist will have a market area just under 8 miles in either direction from the store. Because all the consumers have identical demand curves and because they are spaced equidistant from one another, our monopolist could locate anywhere within 8 miles of either end of Main Street and maintain the same quantity of sales.

Figure 2.8 shows that if two firms are located at the first and third quartiles along a linear market area, if these duopolists sell identical products for $4, and if transportation costs are 75¢ per mile for both firms, they will divide the market equally. In this way, no consumer will pay more than the limit price of $10. The consumers will frequent the store that offers them the lowest delivered price. Consequently, a customer at

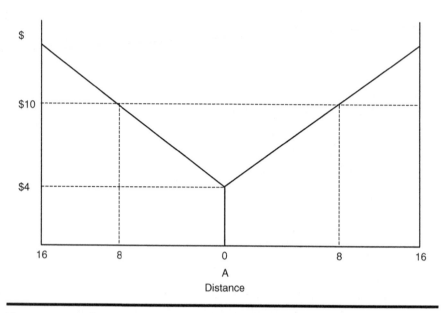

Figure 2.7 **Market area for a monopoly when the demand has a limit price.**

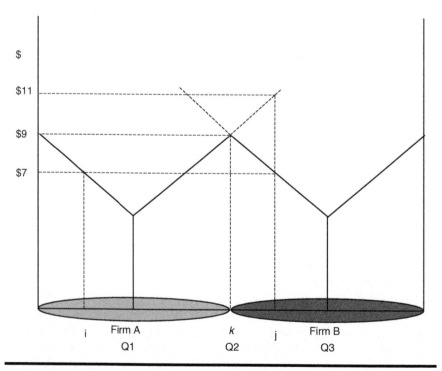

Figure 2.8 **Market areas for duopolists when their demand curves have a limit price.**

point *i* shops at Firm A. The consumer at point *j* prefers to shop at Firm B and pay a delivered price of $7 rather than $11 at Firm A. Customers located at the median point of the market area (point *k*) are indifferent between A and B. Point *k* is therefore referred to as the ***break-even location***. At either store, the delivered price for consumer *k* is $9. The market area for Firm A is on the left of the market and Firm B's market area is on the right.

From the previous diagram, it seems that consumers always shop at the nearest establishment. This assertion is true if the stores sell identical products at the same price and if their consumers face identical transportation costs. However, Figure 2.9 shows one situation where consumers may wish to avoid the nearest store and shop at a store farther from their house. Why?

Firms C and D are located on quartiles of the bounded market area. Both stores charge the same price ($4) for identical products. Transportation costs for Firm D are $1.50 per mile, but only 25¢ per mile for C. Firm D may have either inadequate parking or difficult access. Because of the high transportation costs, only consumers within approximately 2 units of distance around Firm D will shop there. Consumers who reside more than 2.34 units of distance to the right of D will actually save on transportation costs by shopping at C. The market area of Firm D resembles an island inside C's market area. (Calculations are in the Mathematical Appendix.)

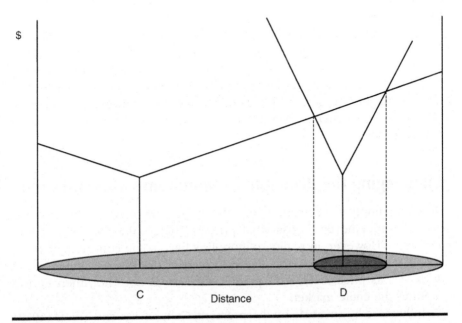

Figure 2.9 Demand curves for a duopoly when one has higher transport costs.

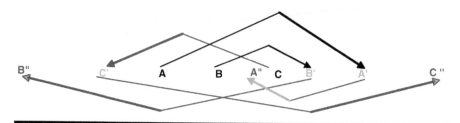

Figure 2.10 How three firms relocate to share the market.

Three's a Crowd

Hotelling's model was extended by Lerner and Singer (1937) and Eaton and Lipsey (1975) to explain how more than two firms (carts on wheels) compete for the same market. If more than two firms sell identical products in a linear market, competition forces them to eventually disperse. If three firms try to locate next to one another, the firm in the center will have too narrow of a market for survival. Because moving is costless, the firm in the middle of the trio will move down the street, leapfrogging over the other firms until the three share one-third of the market area equally (Figure 2.10). In the same way, four firms would share one-fourth of the market, and so forth. Entry will continue as long as each firm's share of the market permits it to cover its costs including a normal rate of return. The minimum market area needed to limit a firm to a normal profit is called its *threshold size*.

What happens to entry if each of the firms faces a slightly greater than normal rate of return but the sum of the excess profits is not enough to sustain the coexistence of one more firm? The excess profits continue until (1) the market grows large enough to permit an additional firm to eke out a living, (2) a new firm benefits from lower production costs, or (3) a new firm benefits from an owner who is content with less than a normal profit.

Challenging the Principle of Minimum Differentiation

Hotelling implicitly assumed that the firms only have to choose the location—they never choose what price to charge. Price was exogenous and fixed. However, in reality, oligopolists have some control over price. For example, if Firms A and B are located at the market center and A decreases its price, even by a penny, but Firm B does not, then Firm A captures the entire market.

Influenced by an article by d'Aspremont, Gabszewicz, and Thisse (1979), researchers now question the principle of minimum differentiation for spatial

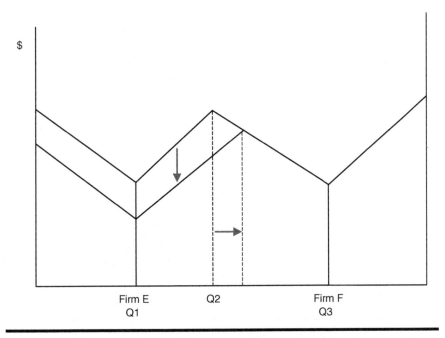

Figure 2.11 Duopoly when one firm lowers its price.

duopolists producing homogeneous products. d'Aspremont, Gabszewicz, and Thisse (1979) concluded that Hotelling's model will have a stable equilibrium only if the established firms are certain that their competitor (competitors) will adopt the same established price when they enter the market.

If the firms can change both their locations and their prices, the principle of minimum differentiation does not result in a stable equilibrium. The stores are spatial monopolists to be sure, but to keep their market share, they must worry about the prices that the other firms charge. Figure 2.11 shows Firms E and F. This time, both firms have the same transportation costs. If Firm E lowers its mill price from $4 to $2 and Firm F keeps the same price, F's market area will decrease. Conversely, if Firm E increases its prices, F's market area will expand.

However, if, we see in Figure 2.12, Firms E and F sold products with an inelastic demand and if they were jux\taposed in the center of the market area, one firm (e.g., Firm E) could theoretically lower its price by 1 cent to capture the entire market.

In the **Bertrand model** of oligopoly behavior, when one firm lowers its price, it does so assuming that its rival's price won't change.[1] The Bertrand

---

[1] For more information about subgame perfect Nash equilibrium concepts in game theory, Drew Fudenberg and Jean Tirole, *Game Theory* (and London: MIT Press, 1991).

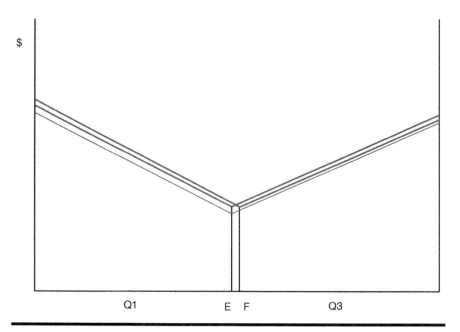

Figure 2.12 Price shading.

model assumes that all goods are homogeneous and that all consumers buy from the seller with the lowest price. Firm A chooses its price assuming that Firm B will not react. Once Firm A sets a new price, Firm B has three options. (1) It could keep a higher price (and lose all sales); (2) it could set an equal price (and share the market), or (3) it could set an even lower price and capture the entire market itself. In Figure 2.12, the last choice is the most profitable and the one that Firm B will choose—again, assuming that Firm A will not respond.

Of course, Firm A reacts and faces the same three choices, Firm A is going to surprise Firm B by choosing to set an even lower price. The price wars wage on until the point where all prices equal the marginal cost of production. Prices may even dip below the marginal cost for short periods of time if one firm tries to drive its rival out of business.

As the Bertrand theory suggests, stores along a well-traveled route practice *price shading*, that is, they set a price just below that of their competitors. Price shading increases market share as long as the price charged is higher than the marginal cost. The store that begins this price war hopes that in the end some firms will go out of business and others will not dare to enter the market. As rival firms leave the market, demand for the remaining firms temporarily increases until the supernormal profit attracts other entrants.

Firms will realize above normal profits, according to d'Aspremont, Gabszewicz, and Thisse (1979), only if they locate as far away from each other as possible. The greater the distance separating firms the more control they have over their own price because a longer distance makes comparison shopping more difficult. The resulting dispersion is by no means nirvana, however. Firms farthest from the market center discover that their customer base is smaller and are lured back toward the center. At the market center, they will again be pressured to disperse by fierce price wars. Firms will never be satisfied with their location.

Think About It...

Do you always shop at the store offering the lowest delivered (full) price for each good you purchase? What besides price influences your decision to shop at a particular establishment?

One way for firms to achieve equilibrium in a linear market is to produce heterogeneous products (products for which there are different models, styles, colors, etc.) Firms that differentiate their products tend to cluster in the market center. The prices will not be identical because the products are not identical. The clustering of firms results in a retail agglomeration that decreases search costs for consumers, thus creating **economies of retail agglomeration**. These lower search costs increase the **probability** that consumers will buy from one of the firms in the cluster. Thus, equilibrium now exists in the form of a possibility ('that the consumers will choose to shop at a certain store) rather than a prediction from an exact mathematical relationship.[2]

The proximity of firms selling similar **but not identical goods** gives consumers the chance to comparison shop. Retail agglomeration economies explain why clothing stores, used car lots, and antique dealers locate close to one another. They also explain why many shopping malls have food courts where food vendors group together.

Consumer Search Behavior and Firm Location

Vendors selling identical products tend to disperse, but product differentiation creates overlapping market areas. In contrast, a large variety of choices forces consumers to pay more attention to specific attributes of

---

[2] de Palma et al. (1985); Claycombe (1991).

products rather than transportation costs.[3] Consumers may not purchase a good with the lowest delivered price if they are willing and able to pay more for a good with a specific attribute. For example, a shopper looking for a pair of shoes to exactly match the color of an evening gown will search where there is a large number of shoe stores. The result will be larger selections and lower prices.

Travel to Shop Behavior

Traditional location theory assumes that the manufacturers sell directly to the consumers and that consumers buy one and only one product per trip. In reality, determining the delivered price of a good is more complicated than adding the transportation cost to a mill price. Transportation costs accrue per trip and cannot be equally and consistently allocated among various goods and services. The marginal transportation costs incurred by a consumer bringing home one more compact disk or one more apple are effectively zero. Consumers who stop at a store on their way home from work pay virtually no additional transportation costs except for the opportunity cost of their leisure time.

Three's Company: Multipurpose and Multi-Stop Shopping

The value of a consumer's time is the largest component of transportation costs. When a shopper stops at several places on the same trip, the trip is defined as a *multi-stop shopping trip*. *Multipurpose shopping*, on the other hand, occurs when the consumer reduces transportation costs by grouping purchases into only one stop.[4] Why stop to see the hair stylist and then the dry cleaner, pay the light bill, cash a check at the bank, and finally get groceries at the supermarket if all errands could be completed at one location? Anything that makes a shopping trip more pleasing or less time-consuming will either add to the marginal benefit or decrease the marginal cost of shopping. Consumers will frequent the facility that gives them the largest net marginal benefits.

Agglomeration and Dispersion in Action

Fischer and Harrington (1996) investigated interindustry variations in the tendency for firms to

---

[3] Dudey (1990).
[4] Thill (1992).

agglomerate. Antique dealers, shoe stores, and used car dealerships tend to cluster together. Antiques are objects that are very difficult to compare, and collectors are often open to all possibilities and any good deal. Likewise, finding the correct pair of shoes requires physically inspecting them and trying them on. Used automobiles are heterogeneous and a costly investment. Determining their quality requires both visual inspection and testing.

On the other hand, Fischer and Harrington found that video stores, movie theaters, gasoline stations and supermarkets are more widely dispersed. For these, there is little product differentiation and no reason to comparison shop. Video stores may differentiate themselves by specializing in a specific type of film, but all of them carry the same new releases. As for cinemas, consumers who chose their movie, see it in the closest theater. Customers who merely want to fill up their gas tanks consider all vendors of gasoline as sellers of homogeneous products. Likewise, those who just need a gallon of milk will treat all stores that sell dairy products, including service stations, as homogeneous.

Fischer and Harrington (1996)

Empirically, Multipurpose Shopping Predominates

Multipurpose shopping behavior is much more common than single-purpose shopping. In Upsala, Sweden, 61 percent of all shopping trips are multipurpose. Likewise, between 63 percent and 74 percent of all shopping trips in Hamilton, Ontario, Canada, are multipurpose, depending on whether the primary errand was for grocery or nongrocery items.

Hanson (1980); O'Kelly (1981)

Commuter Shopping Behavior

Competing stores are not necessarily adjacent. Commuters are equally likely to shop in any store along the entire commute from work to home, *ceteris paribus*. They will avoid stores with difficult access or limited parking in favor of those with easier access. Those who live close to their workplace might pass by only one store, if any, on their way home; while others who have longer commutes could choose from a dozen or more stores with equal probability. The number of stores in competition depends on the commuting distance of the potential customer. The larger number of stores for consumers with long commutes increases the number of substitute products, hence demand becomes increasingly more price elastic.

Commuters Increase Congestion but Decrease the Price of Beef

One would think that prudent retailers would adjust their prices to those of their rivals. Thus longer commutes should lead to greater competition between grocery stores and lower grocery prices. Claycombe and Mahan (1993) tested this hypothesis by tracking the retail prices for beef in various MSAs in the United States. To explain these price variations, they analyzed the effects of mass transit and carpooling, average commuting distance, average wage, and a four-firm concentration ratio on retail prices of beef.

Their results support the hypothesis that in cities where a greater proportion of workers use mass transit, retail stores charge more for beef. This is because people who use mass transit are not as inclined as those who commute by automobile to shop at any store along the commute. In contrast, a longer commute by automobile causes the retail price of beef to fall, presumably due to competition among a larger number of stores.

Claycombe and Mahan (1993)

Shopping Centers and Retail Agglomeration

The first suburban shopping mall in the United States opened in 1956 in Bloomington, Minnesota, near where the Mall of America is now. Dayton's and Donaldson's department stores jointly constructed an enclosed shopping center to reduce construction costs. Rather than compete for a portion of the customers who shopped at the mall, the two rivals (who sell heterogeneous goods) both discovered increased sales as the same customers bought goods from both stores.

By reducing search costs for consumers, stores in a shopping mall can prosper, as in the case of Dayton's and Donaldson's, or perish because of externalities generated by the other stores. Externalities include prices in rival stores as well as the possibility that the ***anchor stores*** (the large department stores that dominate a shopping center) succeed in attracting consumers. If one store in a shopping mall increases its price, neighboring stores benefit in the short run because of an increase in their sales if they offer similar products. In the long run, however, consumers will equate this price increase to an increase in the total cost of shopping at this center. Consumers will shop where they can take care of all their errands with the least total cost. Of course, the opposite will happen if a store lowers its prices.

Anchor stores generally pay very low rents if they pay rent at all because they generate positive externalities for neighboring firms. The anchor stores act as magnets for the shopping center. If an anchor store in a mall closes, the smaller specialty stores endure significantly lower sales.

Summary and Conclusions

This chapter examined market areas and shopping models—models that highlight the rivalry among firms that sell consumer goods. The first set of models concerned linear market areas. The linear market areas were obtained by combining the demand function with the distance between the customer's house and the store. Consumers pay the delivered price, that is, the mill price plus transportation costs.

A firm's market area will expand if the firm lowers its price, if the transportation costs decrease, or if demand for the product increases. Similarly, a contraction of the market boundary occurs if the firm increases its price, if transportation costs increase, or if demand falls.

The elasticity of demand for the product increases with the distance that the consumer needs to travel. Consumers who live farther from the store are much more responsive to changes in price than consumers who live nearby. Thus, if a firm would decrease transport costs only for distant customers, it would expand its market area as we will see in Chapter 6.

With Hotelling's model we examined why some firms group together and other firms disperse. The traditional response, according to the principle of minimum differentiation, is that firms with perfectly inelastic demand for their product aggregate in the middle of the market area. Firms that face demand curves that are not perfectly inelastic (those that have limit prices), tend to disperse. The principle of minimum differentiation also explains why rival politicians all say the same things as Election Day approaches. This principle justifies why retail products are so similar.

D'Aspremont, Gabszewicz, and Thisse (1979) introduced game theory into Hotelling's model, and contested the principle of minimum differentiation. In Hotelling's model, the existing firms do not change their price when a new firm enters the market. If firms cluster, game theory asserts that they tend to undercut one another's price and thus expand their markets. Prices fall to or even below marginal cost in this conflict. Accordingly, firms cluster at the market center if they sell heterogeneous products rather than homogeneous ones.

When firms that sell similar products cluster together, they create retail agglomeration economies. The consumers can comparison shop more easily. Certain types of retail industries are more likely to group together than others. Firms that sell heterogeneous products like used cars, shoes, and garden supplies tend to cluster while firms that sell homogeneous products tend to disperse.

The assertion that consumers purchase each good with the lowest delivered price has also been modified by models of multi-stop, multi-purpose, and commuter shopping behavior. Most shopping trips are for more than one purpose. Consumers combine many errands in one trip, either stopping at a number of places or finishing several errands at one location. A consumer's highest cost is the opportunity cost of time. Any agglomeration of stores that decreases the number of stops or a store that improves its ambiance creates a more pleasant shopping experience, thereby attracting more consumers. Many errands are taken care of on the way to and from work. All stores selling the same product that locate along commuting routes are in direct competition with one another regardless of their proximity to residential areas.

Commuters who travel by automobile expand the number of rivals if they pass more stores along their commute. Cities where commuters travel long distances by automobile benefit from lower prices for grocery or other daily necessities because many stores are in competition over a long route.

Each store in a shopping center potentially influences the number of customers for every other firm in that center. If a firm lowers its price, that particular firm attracts more customers. These customers then tend to do their errands in the same place. Overall, consumers equate a decrease in the price of one good with a decrease in the overall cost of shopping at that center. The opposite result happens if a firm in a shopping mall increases its prices.

Chapter Questions

1. Determine the market area radius from the following price-distance function/demand curve relationship:
   a. List three ways that the firm could increase its market area and draw each of these on a graph similar to the one below.
   b. If demand decreases so that the limit price is $7 rather than $9, draw what happens to the market area radius of the firm.
   c. Which is more elastic, demand from a consumer 10 blocks from the store or demand from a consumer one block from the store? Show graphically.

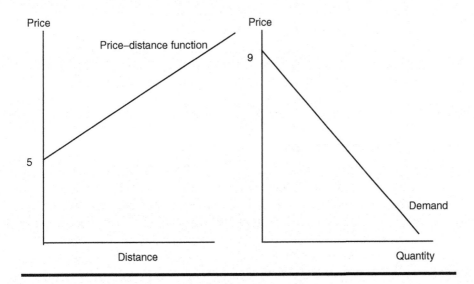

2. Frank and Jessie James have started up convenience stores that are almost identical. They are located at quartiles in a linear market area. The only difference is that Frank's prices are higher than Jessie's, and Frank's transportation costs are also greater than Jessie's. Diagram this case and determine the market areas for both Frank and Jessie.
3. According to Harold Hotelling, in an election campaign "Every candidate '*pussyfoots*,' replies ambiguously to questions, and refuses to take a definite stand in any controversy for fear of losing votes." Depict this phenomenon graphically using Hotelling's model.

4. Pat Jevons from Hardly Burgers has decided that because a large enough market exists, it would be profitable to open a kiosk-restaurant next to the university. Pat's problem is that Chris Señior of Windful Sandwiches had also chosen a site in the same market area. The demand for fast food around campus at noon is perfectly inelastic, and surveys conclude that consumers consider Hardly Burgers and Windful Sandwiches to be basically the same thing. Changing locations is costless. Production costs for both firms are equal.

   a. Using Hotelling's traditional theory, where should Pat locate? Diagram and briefly explain your answer.

   b. According to the argument made by d'Aspremont, Gabszewicz, and Thisse (1979), is this location a stable equilibrium? If not, what if anything could Pat and Chris do to make their existence in the market more stable?

5. Differentiate between multipurpose and multi-stop shopping. How does commuting influence these shopping patterns? If you were designing a shopping mall, where in your city would you suggest it be located and what types of stores would you require to take advantage of travel-to-shop behavior?

6. Claycombe and Mahan (1993) determined that beef prices are lower in areas where commuting by automobile is highest. Would you predict the same type of behavior for clothing, furniture sales, and automobile sales? Why or why not?

Research Assignments

1. Check out the Web site for travel times to work and means of transportation to work for your city or county through the census at http://www.census.gov (QT-P23; from ST-3 data) and compare these data to others in your class.

   a. When do most people leave home to go to work in your area?

   b. What is the mean travel time to work?

   c. What proportion of commuters drive alone?

   d. If your city is in a metropolitan statistical area (MSA), check out the American Chamber of Commerce Research Associates (ACCRA) *Cost of Living Index* for the average price of a T-bone steak in your area and compare it with other MSAs that the class is studying. Do you notice a trend in beef prices and "proportion of commuters who drive alone" when comparing your data to that of others in the class?

2. Describe a retail center in the city that you are studying. Which stores sell complementary goods? Which stores sell substitute goods? How

could your retail center increase the marginal benefit for its customers?

Mathematical Appendix

Algebraically, Panel B of Figure 2.1 is a demand function for the product. The limit price, the maximum price that consumers will pay for any quantity of the good, is $10. The equation for the demand function for this example is $Q=5-\frac{1}{2}P$, where Q is the quantity demanded and P is the price. By solving for P, we will get the inverse demand function: $P=10-2Q$. The ***inverse demand function*** allows one to easily graph a demand function with price on the vertical axis. If the mill price is $4 and transport costs are 75¢ per mile, the price-distance function as graphed in Panel A of Figure 2.1 is $P=4+0.75D$, where D is the distance from the store to the consumer's residence. To find the radius of a market area, set the price-distance function equal to the limit price of the demand function and solve for D. In this example, where $10 is the limit price, $4+0.75D=10$ and $D=8$. Thus, the farthest distance that people will travel at the current mill price is eight units.

The equation for PD_1 in Figure 2.2 is $P=4+0.75D$. When the mill price increases to $6, the equation for PD_2 becomes $P=6+0.75D$. A drop in the mill price to $2 changes the equation for PD_3 to $P=2+0.75D$. Setting each of these three equations equal to the limit price of $10 generates the market area radii of 8, 5.33, and 10.67, respectively.

In Figure 2.3, the equation for the price-distance function for PD_1 remains at $P=4+0.75D$, but the equation for PD_2 becomes $P=4+1.5D$ because transport costs per mile are $1.50 and people will no longer travel even 4 miles to the store. However, if transport costs per mile decrease to 50¢, the equation for the price-distance function becomes $P=4+0.5D$, as in PD_3. The market area radius expands to 12 miles.

Market areas also change with demand. When the equation for the price-distance function ($P=4+0.75D$) equals a limit price of $12 instead of $10, the radius of the market area extends to 10.67 [(12−4)/0.75]. But when the limit price is $6, the radius drops to 2.67 [(6−4)/0.75].

The price-distance function for the monopolist in Figure 2.7 is still $P=4+0.75D$. Setting this equation equal to $10 limit price, $4+0.75D=10$, creates a market area radius of 6/0.75=8 units of distance.

In Figure 2.9, if the price-distance functions for C and D intersect at $6.55, then the break-even point is 10.2 units of distance right of C (where $4+0.25D=2.55$ or $D=2.55/0.25=10.2$) and 1.7 units to the left of D (where $4+1.5D=2.55$ or $D=2.55/1.5=1.7$). Similarly, the price-distance functions equate to the right of D at $7.57, a point 2.38 units to the right of D, and 14.28 units right of C.

Questions to Mathematical Appendix

1. Assume that the demand curve is $Q = 5 - \frac{1}{4}P$. The mill price is $5 and transportation costs are 50¢ per mile.
   a. Find the inverse demand function.
   b. Find the price-distance function.
   c. Find the radius of the market area.
2. What is the new radius of the market area in Question 1 if the transportation costs increase to $1.00 per mile? What if they decrease to $0.25 per mile?
3. What is the new radius of the market area in Question 1 if the mill price drops to $2.50? What if it increases to $7.50?
4. What is the new radius of the market area in Question 1 if demand changes to $Q = 7.5 - \frac{1}{4}P$?
5. What is the new radius of the market area if demand for the firm in Question 1 changes to $Q = 2.5 - \frac{1}{2}P$?

References

Claycombe, R. J. 1991. Spatial retail markets. *International Journal of Industrial Organization* 9 (2):303–313.

Claycombe, R. J., and T. E. Mahan. 1993. Spatial aspects of retail market structure: beef pricing revisited. *International Journal of Industrial Organization* 11 (2):283–291.

d'Aspremont, C., J. J. Gabszewicz, and J. F. Thisse. 1979. On Hotelling's "Stability in competition". *Econometrica* 47 (5):1145–1150.

de Palma, A., V. Ginsburgh, Y. Y. Papageorgiou, and J.-F. Thisse. 1985. The principle of minimum differentiation holds under sufficient heterogeneity. *Econometrica* 53 (4):767–781.

Dudey, M. 1990. Competition by choice: the effect of consumer search on firm location decisions. *American Economic Review* 80 (5):1092–1104.

Eaton, B. C., and R. G. Lipsey. 1975. The principle of minimum differentiation reconsidered: some new developments in the theory of spatial competition. *Review of Economic Studies* 42 (1):27–49.

Fischer, J. H., and J. E. Harrington. 1996. Product variety and firm agglomeration. *RAND Journal of Economics* 27 (2):281–309.

Fudenberg, D., and J. Tirole. 1991. *Game Theory*. Cambridge, Mass: MIT Press.

Fujita, M., and J.-F. Thisse. 1997. Economie géographique, problèmes anciens et nouvelles perspectives. *Annales d'Economie et de Statistique* 45 (37):87.

Fujita, M., and J.-F. Thisse. 2002. *Economics of Agglomeration: Cities, Industrial Location, and Regional Growth*. New York: Cambridge University Press.

Hanson, S. 1980. Spatial diversification and multipurpose travel. *Geographical Analysis* 12:245–257.

Hotelling, H. 1929. Stability in competition. *Economic Journal* 39 (153):41–57.

Lerner, A. P., and H. W. Singer. 1967. Some notes on duopoly and spatial competition. *The Journal of Political Economy* 45 (2):145–186.

O'Kelly, M. E. 1981. A model of the demand for retail facilities, incorporation multi-stop multipurpose trips. *Geographical Analysis* 13:134–148.

Rosser, J. B. Jr. 1991. *From Catastrophe to Chaos: A General Theory of Economic Discontinuities*. Norwell Mass: Kluwer Academic.

Thill, J. C. 1992. Spatial duopolistic competition with multipurpose and multi-stop shopping. *Annals of Regional Science* 26 (3):287–304.

Chapter 3

Market Areas and Systems of Cities

The layout of most cities is not delineated by a main street because all but the smallest cities have a street system that moves in more than one dimension. Unless the city is wedged against sheer rock cliffs, people travel from many directions to shop there. The models in Chapter 3 give a second dimension. In this chapter we will follow a logical analysis that goes from the market area of a firm to city settlements and from city settlements to a hierarchical system of cities. As we will see, the implications of the central place theory on economic development, especially for rural areas, differ considerably from economic development for urban areas.

. To understand the concept of central places, imagine yourself in an open, flat agricultural area dotted with farms equidistant apart and of equal-sized hamlets, villages, towns, and cities, each sized place also equidistant apart. The central place theory describes shopping patterns between these different settlements. It also determines the types of retailers who will serve each place and the nearby residents by extending the shopping models of spatial competition. The theory of central places explains the systems of cities and shopping areas for traditional economies in which the smallest towns only serve an agricultural population. Generally, this model depicts the market areas for local goods and services such as newspapers, hairdressers, dentists and doctors, movies, and grocers, as well as nonmarket services like places of worship, post offices, or courthouses, which are also primary functions of cities.[1]

Location on a Plain

August Lösch (1938) modeled a world consisting of a flat, homogeneous plain. The plain is equally fertile everywhere, with evenly distributed resources. Self-sufficient farms are spread evenly about the plain. His example was that one farmer excels in brewing beer. If that farmer/brewer offers to trade beer with one neighbor in return for veterinary assistance and with another neighbor in exchange for bread, the brewer can thus procure larger vats and other specialized equipment for beer making. In doing so, production costs would fall because of economies of scale. Economies of scale, also known as increasing returns to scale, are observed when larger firms can produce a good at a lower average cost.

One way to picture a market area for a spatial monopolist, such as our brewer, is to generate a quantity–distance function. The quantity–distance function is derived from the demand curve and the price–distance function. The analysis of the price–distance function is shown by the top half of Figure 3.1 that we studied in Chapter 2 (Figure 2.1). We find in the first and second quadrants of Figure 3.1 that at the limit price of $10, consumers travel a maximum of just under 8 miles to purchase the good. Those who live adjacent to the retail outlet will purchase 3 units at the mill price of $4.

The key graph in this figure is the quantity–distance function in Quadrant III. To find the quantity–distance function, first we extend the dashed line that shows the limit of the market area from the price–distance function in Quadrant II down to Quadrant III. Consumers located at a distance of exactly 8 miles from the outlet will purchase a quantity just equal to zero from that outlet. This is point α.

To find out the quantity purchased by consumers who live adjacent to the store, (Point β), we use a reflexive 45° line in Quadrant IV. To find Point β in Quadrant III, start with the demand curve in Quadrant I. At the mill price of $4, the quantity demanded is 3 units. This quantity of 3 units is reflected off the 45° line in Quadrant IV and echoes to the vertical axis of the quantity distance function in Quadrant III. Consumers living adjacent to the retail outlet purchase 3 units (Point β). As distance increases, the quantity purchased declines until a distance of 8 miles from the outlet, where the consumers purchase nothing.

---

[1] Polèse (1994).

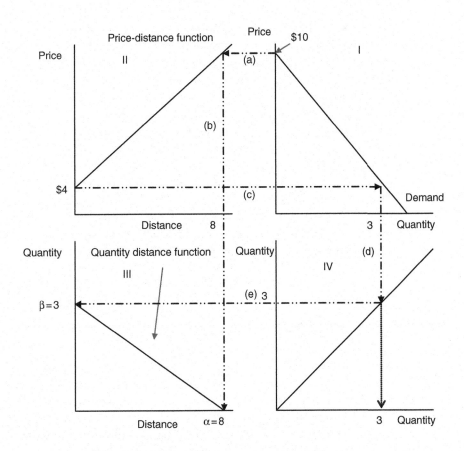

Figure 3.1 Derivation of the quantity–distance function.

Define "Nearest"

The assumption that drives the hierarchy of central places is that consumers patronize the nearest place that offers the good. But do they? Clark and Rushton (1970) asked this question of 521 households in Christchurch, New Zealand. The answer depended on what goods were purchased as well as how one measured distance. Of those surveyed, 57 percent generally patronized the nearest center for groceries if distance was measured along the route. However, when the researchers used "crow-fly" distance, the percentage fell to 39 percent. They also found that householders have a zone of indifference wherein the consumer has no particular spatial preference if the stores are a small distance apart. Further, they calculated that only 35 percent of rural Iowa households patronized the nearest town for major grocery purchases.

Olfert and Stabler (1994) surveyed rural households of Saskatchewan, Canada and found that most (75 percent) used the services of the post office, 72 percent used the local grain elevator and 65 percent used the elementary school—which are furnished by first-order centers. However, only 20 percent of those who lived near order-one centers purchased groceries locally. Grocery shopping is regularly combined with other errands taking place in the larger central places.

Clark and Rushton (1970),
Olfert and Stabler (1994)

We assume that consumers are still evenly distributed about the market area. They travel to shop for one good and only for that one i.e., to purchase goods like ice cream cones or for services like haircuts—things that they cannot buy in bulk or stockpile at home. The analysis from Figure 3.1 is easily applied to a linear to a planar market area by spinning the quantity–distance function in a circle. The resulting diagram (Figure 3.2) is called a ***demand cone***. A demand cone shows the quantity that a spatial monopolist sells to people who live at each distance from its location. Most importantly, the base of the demand cone shows the maximum boundary of the market area of a firm.

Our brewer is able to make beer at a lower cost than the other farmers can and soon will become the monopoly supplier of beer to neighbors. Neighboring farmers travel to the brewer's establishment as long as the amount that they save from buying their beer there is more than the sum of the cost of traveling plus the opportunity cost of the time and effort needed to make their own brew.

Soon other breweries will start up at some distance from the original brewer. However, Figure 3.3 shows that if everyone who establishes a brewery has a circular market area, farmers who reside in the "gap" marked by the arrow are not served by the newly established industry. The possibility of a profitable market continuously attracts entry, so firms will jostle about and encroach on their competitors' markets.

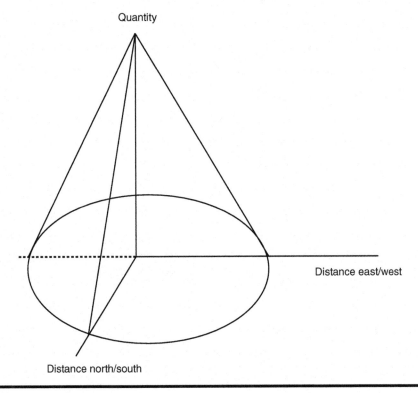

Figure 3.2 Demand cone.

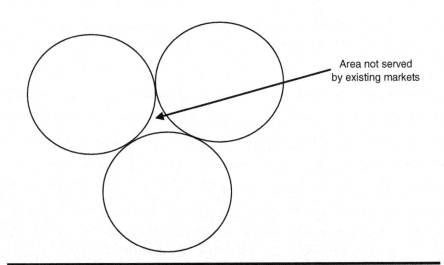

Figure 3.3 Market areas of spatial monopolists.

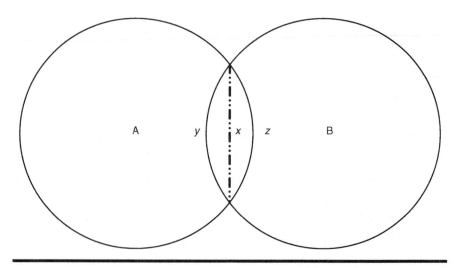

Figure 3.4   Overlapping market areas of two spatial monopolists.

This encroachment on the competitors' market areas will "flatten out" the sides of the original markets. Consider the repositioning of two brewers A and B in Figure 3.4. Firm A, located in the center of one market, will initially sell to consumers located at farmsteads x, y, and z. As firm B moves closer to A, their market areas overlap. Consumers at location y will still buy from A. However, because both A and B sell identical products, the consumers at z buy beer at a lower delivered price from firm B. Consumers at x buy as much beer from A as they do from B because both stores offer them the same delivered price.

New firms continue to enter this market until the entire plain is covered with a lattice of hexagons similar to the honeycomb developed in Figure 3.5 and Figure 3.6.

Why Hexagons?

In long-run equilibrium, market area configurations must have three characteristics. First, there cannot be gaps in economic space. Gaps indicate that potential consumers are not served. All areas of the plain must be in the market area of one firm or another. Second, in equilibrium, the market areas of the same level good cannot overlap. Finally, the market areas have to equal the threshold size market for the firm. In long-run equilibrium, the potential market area configurations are the hexagon, the square, and the triangle. Circles, pentagons, or octagons do not cover the markets completely without leaving gaps.

For a threshold-size market configuration to be efficient, the distance from each corner to the center of the market area needs to be the shortest. Consumers who live at the corners of the hexagonal market area are closer to market than those who live at the corners of a square or a triangle of the same size. Compared to a hexagon of the same area, the distance from a corner to the center of a triangle is 32 percent longer, and for a square it is 13 percent longer. Hexagons keep transportation costs lowest and are therefore the most efficient shape.

Greenhut (1971)

In competing for business, firms eventually drop their prices until they reach the level where marginal cost equals marginal revenue and supernormal profits are zero. The graph generally described as the long-run equilibrium in monopolistic competition, is identical to the one given for long-run equilibrium for a spatial monopolist. See Figure 3.7. The size of the

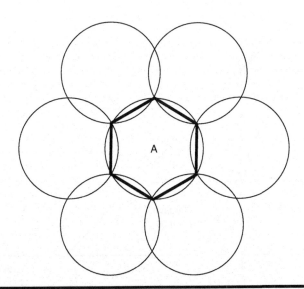

Figure 3.5 Evolution of circular market areas into hexagonal market areas.

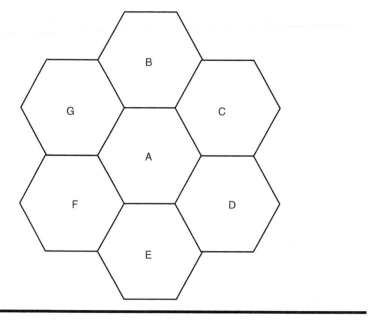

Figure 3.6 Honeycomb of long-run equilibrium market areas.

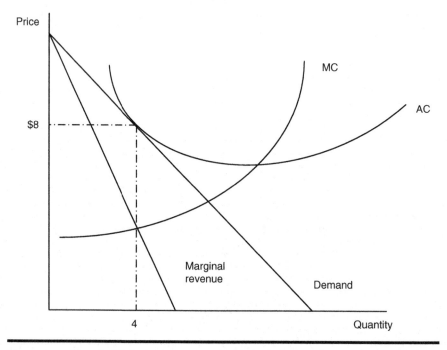

Figure 3.7 Threshold size market area for a spatial monopolist.

market area that allows no excess profits is known as the **threshold size market area**. Firms do earn a normal profit, however.

Different industries require different threshold sizes; hence they will command different sizes of hexagonal market areas. Firms with market areas smaller than threshold size make losses and cannot survive in the long run. Market areas larger than threshold size invite entry because of the existence of supernormal profits. Places where the production of several different types of goods overlaps eventually become cities. As the number of activities within a city increases, costs of production continue to decrease because of agglomeration economies. For example, our brewer attracts bottle producers and grain farms. Grain farmers attract flour mills. Employees will want to live nearby, triggering a market for retail goods and services.

How Large Is a Threshold Size

Several studies estimate the threshold size for certain retail and service firms. In the United States, for example, a druggist or a tire dealer needs a minimum of about 500 people to break even, dentists need 700, general practitioners need 900, and plumbers need 1400. Because it is not a linear progression, two tire dealers need a population of 1800, two druggists need a population of 2000, and a second general practitioner needs a population of 3500 to break even.

A minimum population of around 4000 can support one food store, a building and gardening store, and an eating and drinking establishment. The market area population would need to grow to 9500 for an apparel store to subsist.

Bresnahan and Reiss (1991),
Deller and Harris (1993)

Systems of Cities and Central Places

The market area analysis of Lösch (1938) is based on the geographer Walter Christaller's (1933) description of central places and the functional hierarchy of cities in southern Germany. Christaller started by generating market areas for individual goods and services on a homogeneous plain, where each market area is the threshold size. His one condition is that every consumer must have access to every good. Level-one goods, the lowest order goods and services, are available at the smallest villages of order one. Firms with a slightly larger threshold size produce level-two goods and locate in slightly larger, order-two towns. All goods and services that are available in order-one centers are also available in order-two centers. The highest order goods are provided in one and only one city. The entire nation is the market area of highest-order goods, according to Christaller. Cities of each rank are equidistant from one another.

Each size central place offers a different assortment of goods and services. The smallest central places that provide goods for basic needs which do not need a large threshold size are of order-one. These are the agricultural villages that have a gasoline station combined with a convenience store, and perhaps a bar, a post office, and a church.

Think About It...

What order place do you live in? Compare your answers with Table 3.1.

Where do you go to buy bread? Dairy products? Fresh produce? For your weekly shopping trip? To purchase an engagement ring? To buy dress shoes or a pair of jeans?

Where can you go for a cup of coffee? For a beer? For a sit-down lunch? For a formal dinner? To stay overnight in a hotel or a motel? To visit the nearest five-star hotel? To host a convention for 1500 people?

Where is the nearest primary school, secondary school, two-year higher education institution? University? Major research university?

Where is the nearest church, synagogue, or mosque? Cathedral?

Where is your local bank? Is it a branch bank or a single bank? Where can you purchase foreign currency? Where is the closest financial advisor? Brokerage house?

Where is the clinic where you get your annual check-up? Where is the closest pharmacy? Maternity ward? Where can you find a specialist? Have gall bladder surgery? Have a heart transplant or brain surgery?

Where is the closest post office? Police station? Court house? Where do you take your driving test? Where is your congressperson's regional office located?

Where can you rent videos or DVDs? Go to the cinema? Go to a rock concert? See live jazz? A symphony orchestra concert? See live theater? Go to the opera?

Where is the nearest inter-city bus terminal? Train station? Airport? International airport?

What type of manufacturing is in your area? Firms with fewer than 25 workers? 26–100 employees? 101–250? 251–500? 501–1000? More than 1000 workers?

The hierarchical system of cities asserts that every place of a higher order also provides all the goods offered in the lower-order places. In long-run equilibrium, the whole face of the economy will be covered with several lattices of different sized hexagons. See Figure 3.8. The ***small*** hexagons

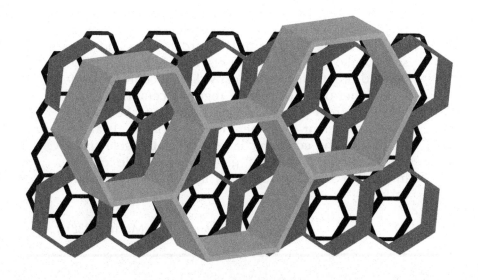

Figure 3.8 Overlapping market areas for three different industries.

depict market areas for order-one places (and show the market area for convenience stores, small cafés, primary and middle schools, and post offices). The ***medium-sized*** hexagons are for order-two places (full, weekly shopping, building materials, hotels and restaurants, secondary schools, banks, court house, or cinemas). ***Large*** hexagons are market areas for order-three places (specialized retail, 2-year higher educational facilities, hospital, business services, and bus or train terminals). Note that the centers of the medium-sized hexagons coincide with centers of the small hexagons and the centers of the large hexagons coincide with centers of both. This overlapping of central places for goods of different levels exists because every central place of a higher order sells all of the goods that are sold in the lower-order places.

Live performing arts, fine arts, and museums are almost exclusively found in large cities. Live performances cannot be shipped to buyers at other locations. These services must be consumed on the spot, so they must locate where a financially well-off arts audience is large enough to support them. In general, this audience is found only in metropolitan areas.[2]

Central Places in Turkey

Many researchers have generated typologies of functions by the size of the central place. For example, in one of the more recent descriptions, Mutlu (1988) set up six orders of central places for Turkey that are nearly identical to central place hierarchies of other countries. The smallest orders, orders zero and one, serve only their own residents thus is not a center. Second-order places are mostly district centers. Third- and higher-order places are regional centers. Fourth- and fifth-order places are large enough to be able to create sufficient agglomeration economies. Istanbul dominates the economic landscape as the sole sixth-order center. Table 3.1 gives an example of the increasing scope of functions in cities of increasing orders.

Mutlu (1988)

[2] Heilbrun (1992).

Table 3.1 Functions Available in Central Places in Turkey

	Zero-Order Center	First-Order Center	Second-Order Center	Third-Order Center	Fourth-Order Center	Fifth-Order Center	Sixth-Order Center
Number of places	35,812	650	504	58	11	4	1
Retail goods	Partial convenience	Convenience goods	Full shopping; weekly market; gas stations; building materials	Specialized retail	Specialized shopping	Luxury shopping	
Hospitality industry	Coffee shop	Eatery	Hotel and restaurant			Luxury hotels and restaurants	
Education	Primary school	Middle school	Secondary schools	Two-year higher education institution	University	Major university; research center	
Religious centers	Mosque						
Financial services		Credit cooperative	Bank			Financial services	Specialized financial services
Health and medicine		Dispensary	Doctors; medical services	Hospital, specialized medical services	Major hospital		

(continued)

Table 3.1 (Continued)

	Zero-Order Center	First-Order Center	Second-Order Center	Third-Order Center	Fourth-Order Center	Fifth-Order Center	Sixth-Order Center
Government		Post office; subdistrict level government offices	Court house, district-level government offices; military offices; police station	Specialized courts; Province-level government offices	Regional offices of public works agencies		
Legal services			Legal services				
Other services			Repair services; partial business services	Business services; design bureaus			Specialized business services
Entertainment			Cinema			Theater, concert hall	
Transportation			Bus and minibus terminal service	Inter-city bus terminal	Major bus and train terminal; airport	Major airport	International airport
Manufacturing			Artisan workshops	Limited manufacturing	Manufacturing	Headquarters of firms; major manufacturing	Headquarters of major firms; diverse manufacturing

Note that all higher-order centers also offer all goods and services offered from the lower-order centers.
Source: Adaptation of Mutlu, 1988. Reprinted with permission from Blackwell Publishing.

Intra-City Shopping Centers Follow Central Place Hierarchies

West, von Hohenbalken, and Kroner (1985) found that shopping centers within a city conform to the central place theory. Not only do shopping centers come in different sizes, but they are also organized in a hierarchy and have properties similar to those suggested by the travel-to-shop models of Chapter 2. The authors classify three types of commercial centers: small neighborhood centers, community centers (which are a little larger), and the largest centers, the central retail districts.

Neighborhood centers include stores that primarily serve convenience shoppers, such as drug stores, grocery stores, and gasoline stations. Consumers of these stores engage in little search or comparison-shopping. Quality and price variations are insignificant.

Community centers accommodate the same stores, but because they cater to multipurpose shoppers they also contain stores that need a larger consumer base such as book stores, music stores, and gift shops in addition to shoe and clothing stores, and camera shops.

Central retail districts house the same stores as the community centers plus a wide variety of stores for comparison shoppers who want to purchase large--ticket items such as automobiles and appliances. They also contain stores that can provide or benefit from externalities of other stores. Movie theaters use the parking lots in off-peak times. Both arcades and movie theaters serve as temporary baby sitters for slightly older children.

West, von Hohenbalken, and Kroner (1985)

Economies of agglomeration result from the concentration of art activities in the larger cities. The largest cost decrease comes from the presence of a pool of highly specialized inputs, like labor, wanting to work in the industry. For example, New York City became the most logical center for radio and television production in the 1920s because the new industry could draw from the vast pool of actors, directors, and writers centered in the Broadway theater industry.

Where the Jobs Are

Burns and Healy (1978) tested the hypothesis that occupational patterns vary with city size. Urbanization increases the demand for different types of products. Because the demand for labor is a derived demand, the demand for different products manifests itself in the demand for different types of occupations.

Larger cities have more pollution. Therefore, the demand for dry cleaners is higher there than in smaller towns. People in larger cities on average earn higher real incomes, and thus they purchase what economists call "normal goods" (goods for which demand increases with rising incomes). Higher incomes boost the demand for urban occupations such as taxi drivers, pharmacists, bartenders, bus drivers, police officers, firefighters, janitors, and house/office cleaning services. Occupations that are more predominant in the smaller cities, according to Burns and Healy, are librarians, nurses, servers, barbers, teachers, and clergymen.

Burns and Healy (1978)

Rank-Size Distribution of Cities and Zipf's Law

According to Zipf's law (Rank-Size Rule), if one ranks the cities in a country (1 for the largest city, 2 for the second largest city, etc.) and multiplies the rank (R_j) by a measure of its size (S_j), the product is a positive constant. Zipf's law applies to almost all countries and periods for which there is data.

Why? Two types of explanations exist. Urban economists have suggested intricate patterns of productivity differences, transportation costs, and externalities to understand Zipf's Law. The problem is that such a fragile and complex relationship can hardly exist everywhere and through time. A second explanation is based on Gibrait's law, which postulates that a random city growth rate with the same average and the same standard deviation within the distribution will, in the limit, converge to Zipf's law.

Although the rank-sized distribution may be constant, the ranking of specific cities is not constant over time. Structural changes in the individual economies influence the growth or decline of individual cities.

Brakman et al. (1999), Gabaix (1999)

The Instability of Urban Hierarchies

Although the hierarchy of urban areas is a stable phenomenon, the position of each city within a hierarchy is unstable and unpredictable from one census to another. The volatility is due to changes in transportation and communication systems. Improved transportation and communication leads to the growth of larger cities and the decline of smaller towns. With decreases in transportation costs, various retail functions consolidate into higher-order centers. When the highway systems improve, more and more consumers bypass the small centers to shop in larger cities where the number of functions and the variety of goods and services offered are larger. Improved transportation systems cripple the retail and service sectors in small towns.[3]

Approaches for Studying Competing Centers

There are two problems with Christaller's and Lösch's methods for determining market area boundaries. First, neither method accounted for price differences affecting market boundaries. We know from Figure 2.2 that when firms lower their prices, their market boundaries expand, everything else equal. Second, with these methods there is not really a way to account for differences in population, in demographics, or in the variety of goods sold. Two other methods of analyzing spatial choice models deal with these problems: Fetter's Law of Market Areas and Reilly's Law of Retail Gravitation.[4]

---

[3] Guérin-Pace (1995); Huff and Lutz (1995).
[4] Parr (1995).

Fetter's Law of Market Areas

Fetter's law of market areas says that the market area boundary between two competing centers that sell the same good is a line along which the delivery prices of the goods are equal. The advantage is that it allows for differences in prices and transportation rates.[5]

Pricing Cocaine and Marijuana in Central Places

Because of increased competition and economies of scale, central places are supposed to have lower priced retail goods. Caulkins (1995) was able to study prices of illegal drugs in the mid-Atlantic and Great Lakes States. He found that the larger cities on the East Coast—New York/Newark, Philadelphia, Baltimore, Washington DC— and middle-sized cities close to these had lower prices for cocaine. Much of the cocaine that is sold in this part of the country comes in via the ships or airplanes to the large cities. Cocaine sells for higher prices in smaller cities and inland.

However, marijuana production is predominantly domestic, concentrated on the West Coast, the Midwest, and Appalachia, but not on the East Coast. Marijuana prices are not related to market size, but are positively related to the distance between Appalachia and the East-Coast market.

Caulkins (1995)

Between centers A and B, the market boundary is found where

$$p_A + D_A t_A = p_B + D_B t_B$$

where p_A and p_B are the prices of the goods at the centers, A and B, D_A, and D_B are the distances from A and B to the market boundary, and t_A and t_B are the transport rates per unit of distance of shipping the good from A or B.

---

[5] Fetter (1924).

If transport rates and product prices are the same in both centers on a flat plain without roads, the market area delineation will be identical to the hexagons of the central place theory. Higher-order centers have greater economies of scale and more competition to keep prices lower. Thus prices must differ between two centers of different levels.

Reilly's Law of Retail Gravitation

The law of retail gravitation depends on empirical observations rather than on a theoretical model. The law holds that two competing centers will attract consumers from a third location in direct proportion to their respective sizes and in inverse proportion to the relative distances to the residences.

The law of retail gravitation also allows the existence of a wider market area for goods sold in larger cities. This formula captures the fact that longer hours of operation, a larger variety of goods, and better opportunities to comparison shop in a higher-order center may draw consumers away from the closer but smaller places in favor of the larger central places. Some consumers will bypass the closer centers if they think that the advantages gained by going the extra distance are greater than the additional transportation costs incurred.

However, the law of retail gravitation cannot directly account for price differences if, for some reason, the lower price occurs in the lower-level center. A diagram of market areas on a plain without roads, based on Reilly's law, would also show the hexagons of central place theory. However, given the existence of roads, swamps, lakes, hills, and other obstructions, the resulting diagram looks more like an amoeba than a hexagon. For an example, see Figure 3A.1 in the Appendix.

Rural Health Care and Central Places

The hierarchy of cities limits the types and the quality of health care for rural inhabitants. Because of the lack of jobs for young people in rural areas, the population is decreasing and aging. Rural hospitals close because of declining populations, the large number of employees per patient, and neighboring hospitals that may offer more services. On average in the United States, a closed rural hospital is 19 minutes away from another hospital, but a closed urban hospital is only 3.5 min. away from another hospital.

On the face of it, people living in the more sparsely populated rural areas are at risk of not receiving timely medical care because the population is below the threshold size for a small hospital. Rural hospitals not only have fewer beds and a lower occupancy rate, but they also treat less complex medical conditions. Patients who need specialists are forced to commute to the larger urban hospitals. More than 60 percent of the vulnerable patients go elsewhere for their medical care. Either they have to travel a considerable distance or their entire household moves to a larger city, further decreasing rural populations.

Samuels, Cunningham, and Choi (1991), Lille-Blanton, et al. (1992), Goody (1993)

Rural Cities and Economic Growth

Central place theory supports the hypothesis that economic growth and development for cities differs according to a city's rank within the system of cities. Unless cities reach a certain level in the hierarchy, they do not become good catalysts for growth and development on their own.

The proportion of goods produced for local consumption grows with city size. Thus, the ***multiplier***—an estimate of the increase in spending and respending in a community due to an initial autonomous injection of spending—is greater for larger cities than for smaller ones. Autonomous injections of spending come from four sources: (1) consumers or businesses spending more money locally, (2) increases in goods made in the area but sold elsewhere, (3) tourism, or (4) government spending.[6]

People from larger towns do not generally go to smaller places to buy lower-order goods. Because of the multiplier effect, rural economic developers will generate more local economic activity if they focus on larger towns than on small hamlets. Spending focused on small rural hamlets benefits the larger central places that serve that hamlet rather than the businesses in the hamlet itself. In Chapter 9, we will study the recent discussions about location of firms and residences in the rural periphery and deep rural areas relative to an urban core.

---

[6] Ahn and Nourse (1988); Mutlu (1988).

Multipliers Increase as Communities Grow

Olfert and Stabler (1994) estimated the community-level multipliers for different orders of cities in Saskatchewan, Canada. The smallest multiplier of 1.09 is for what they call minimum convenience centers, or cities of order 1. This means that for every $1 spent in a city of order 1, only 9¢ is respent within that community. However, in the highest-order places the multiplier is 1.43.

Thus, increasing local incomes by $100 would require an injection of $91.74 in a center of order 1 because the injection multiplied by the multiplier equals the growth in income: $91.74 \times 1.09 = $100. For the same increase in incomes for the largest centers, only $69.93 would need to be injected into the local economy.

Olfert and Stabler (1994)

Do You Want Fries with Your Car Loan?

The level of retail sales in a community should increase when banks lend to consumers. Henderson and Wallace (1992) asked whether rural borrowers spend the loan in the community where it originates or somewhere else. They found that rural consumers generally use consumer loans to buy automobiles from businesses located in larger places, thus benefiting larger cities within the local hierarchy. Loans to rural consumers also benefit building material stores and furniture stores in the largest communities within the hierarchy, but not to the same extent.

A final industry that benefits from rural consumer loans is the eating and drinking industry in the mid-sized and larger towns. Rural consumers celebrate by having a nice dinner during their trip to spend the loan.

Henderson and Wallace (1992)

Limitations of the Central Place Theory

It is amazing that urban hierarchies conform as well as they do to the predictions of the central place theory. Urban hierarchies exist in all countries of the world, but they never conform perfectly to the model. Homogeneous plains without rivers, mountains, or roads are rare—if they exist at all. Buying power, tastes, and preferences are not homogeneous. Institutional obstacles such as administrative or cultural frontiers limit the market areas at country borders, thus permitting gaps or allowing some market areas to constantly have supernormal profits.[7]

The theory of central places explains the pre-Industrial Revolution urban systems extremely well. It applies to activities where the size of the market is only limited by transportation costs. The model mainly applies to shopping models or models of local manufacturing rather than shipping models. The textile or automotive industry has no reason to follow a hierarchical model because their goods are not primarily produced for local consumption.

Some researchers regard the central place theory as the cornerstone of location economics, but the theory is not fully specified, and thus it cannot be an equilibrium theory. Neither increasing returns to scale nor agglomeration economies for manufacturing firms, two other cornerstones of location economics, are accounted for in this model.

Central place theory ignores the supply channels in the system. All interactions are assumed to take place between clients in the hinterland and the specific central place. Cities from different hierarchies never trade with one another in this model. Similarly, trade never flows upward from smaller to larger places.

Central place theory ignores the artificial barriers of doing business, such as cultural or linguistic barriers, political boundaries, or local regulations that limit trade in one form or another. This assumption is also unrealistic. For example, Helliwell (1996) determined that the economic linkages within Canada are tighter than those between the provinces and neighboring states of the United States. Quebec sells more goods to the more distant Anglophone provinces than it does to the United States.

Local trade restrictions, such as blue laws (laws that restrict trade of certain goods on Sunday or the Sabbath), could change a market area if consumers find that they prefer another, more convenient store slightly farther from home. If consumers who live close to another political jurisdiction cannot purchase extra wine for Sunday dinner on Sunday

---

[7] Ahn and Nourse (1988); Pedersen (1992); Polèse (1994); Helliwell (1996); Bennett and Graham (1998).

morning or if they cannot buy a scrub brush until Monday at their local store, the store may lose out on sales to desperate customers.

Finally, the traditional theory of central places does not allow for the effect of pollution, traffic congestion, high crime rates, or high rents that will cause people to want to disperse to lower-order places in the hierarchy.

Summary and Conclusions

The central place theory and its resulting hierarchical system of cities are logical extensions of the shopping models of Chapter 2. August Lösch started his model of a homogeneous plain with resources and self-sufficient farmsteads being evenly dispersed. As the self-sufficient farmers decide to specialize and produce only one good rather than everything that their farm needs, they are able to trade with the neighboring farms. The increased production of specific goods decreases average production costs because of increasing returns to scale. The decreased cost lowers the price of the good, thereby increasing the distance that households are willing to travel to buy it.

As other farmers start producing the same good, the original circular market area of the monopolist shrinks and ultimately conforms to a hexagonal shape. In the long run the market area for each producer shrink to the threshold size—just large enough to allow them to earn no more than a normal profit.

With specialization in producing even just one good, a farmer/entrepreneur attracts other artisans and manufacturers, and eventually small cities appear. Production costs drop even more as agglomeration economies take hold. A homogeneous plain dotted with self-sufficient farmsteads evolves into a landscape with a logical and predictable system of cities of various sizes.

Christaller's description of central places is also dependent on market areas of threshold size and it generates a hierarchy from the functions provided by the cities. Goods with sufficient demand within relatively small market areas are level-one goods, and are provided at every center. Other slightly more specialized goods are provided only at higher centers. Undeniably, some goods are so specialized that only one center in the country (or the world) provides them. These are the highest-level goods.

Urban hierarchies are unstable because modifications of transportation and communication systems change the position of a city. For example, improved highway systems cripple the retail and service sectors of small towns, pushing them to an even lower rank in the hierarchy.

When the traditional central place theory is modified to take account of lower prices in the larger centers, the hexagons for these higher-order centers will be slightly larger than for the smaller centers. Multipliers are larger in cities that are higher up the hierarchy. To increase incomes in a small village by $100 would require an initial injection very close to $100. However, because of greater amounts of spending and respending, a substantially smaller injection in the large cities will achieve the same result.

Central place theory is far from perfect. It is not fully specified because it ignores all supply and production. All goods are assumed to flow from large cities to small towns. Trade from the bottom–up does not exist, nor does trade between cities of equal rank or cities in different hierarchies. Central place theory has no way of accounting for the outflow of people from crowded, crime-ridden, polluted cities seeking peace and tranquility in the smaller towns with lower housing costs.

Economists are generally a pragmatic lot. If a theory predicts well, it is maintained regardless of the validity of the assumptions. Theories that do not predict well are only disposed of when a better theory takes their place. Central place theory predicts the behavior in many urban hierarchies fairly well, despite the fact that few, if any, places conform to its assumptions. The predictions hold mainly for cities in economies with a large agricultural base.

Chapter Questions

1. "The reason that Duelm, Minnesota (population around 25, located 12 miles east of St. Cloud, Minnesota) is smaller than Minneapolis is that Minneapolis was settled before Duelm. In about 50 more years, Duelm will be as large as Minneapolis and will be able to provide the same set of goods and services to its residents." Comment.
2. Why do rural hospitals not have the same quality facilities as the large urban hospitals? Explain in terms of hierarchy of cities and central place theory.
3. (Mathematical question) Assume that the demand curve is $Q = 5 - 1/4P$. The mill price is $5 and transportation costs are 50¢ per mile.
   a. Find the inverse demand function.
   b. Find the price–distance function.
   c. Find the radius of the market area.
   d. Find the equation for the quantity–distance function.

e. Given that the volume of a cone is 1/3(area of base×height), or $1/3\pi r^2 h$, estimate the quantity of sales.

Research Assignments

1. Find the population for your county and for your state. From the ***County Business Patterns*** (http://www.census.gov/epcd/cbp/view/cbpview.html), determine for your county the number of firms by retail and by service industry using the detailed NAICS (North American Industry Classification System) industry code. For select industries, compare the population per firm for your county with that of your state.

   If you are willing to assume that the industry in your state is in equilibrium and the majority of retailers are at their minimum threshold size, you can deduce how many more retail or service industries your county's population could support.
2. Check the Help Wanted ads in your city for the types of occupations needed. Compare those to the Help Wanted advertisements for a larger city and for a smaller town in your region.
3. Consult a road map and a telephone book (or the Internet) for the area surrounding your city.
   a. Note which larger cities serve your city and which smaller ones your city serves. First, note from the map the largest city in your area. For now, define "area" as either your county or places within about 55 miles of your city (about an hour's drive). Classify the cities according to population, determining for your region what size city would be considered a hamlet, village, town, or city. How would your city be classified?

	Type of Place		
Hamlets (First-Order Centers)	Villages (Second-Order Centers)	Towns (Third-Order Centers)	Cities (Fourth-Order or larger Centers)
Number of places per classification			
Average population			

   b. Using the yellow pages of a telephone directory (or the Internet), fill in the following table by indicating the types of each of these industry groups that are located in the first-order places, second-order places, etc., in your region. (Your results may loosely follow Table 3.1.)

	Type of Place			
	Hamlets	*Villages*	*Towns*	*Cities*
Retail goods				
Hospitality industry				
Education				
Religious centers				
Financial centers				
Health and medicine				
Government				
Legal services				
Other services				
Entertainment				
Transportation				
Manufacturing				

Appendix: Delineating Markets

Comparing the trade area of one gasoline station with that of its rival across the street makes no sense either empirically or theoretically. Both establishments in essence share the same market area. Everything else equal, the service station on one side of the street captures customers going to work, whereas the other attracts customers going home. On the other hand, accessibility, ease of parking, quality products, store popularity, or lower prices induces some consumers to choose a specific store over others regardless of proximity.

However, it is useful and fairly easy to estimate the market area for a retail industry or a service industry in a city. Such an analysis would determine the optimal geographic area for a specific firm's publicity campaign. An estimate of potential sales by location would be useful in determining whether a retail or service firm should locate in one city or another.

Market areas of specific retail and service industries are of different sizes, depending on whether the good is frequently consumed or a consumer durable good. **Frequently consumed goods** such as gasoline, food, and haircuts are bought and used regularly. Consumer **durable goods** such as clothing, furniture, appliances, automobiles, and physicians' services are bought irregularly. Trade areas for convenience goods are smaller than those for consumer durables.

This appendix starts with a description of several informal methods of analyzing market areas. A more formal method requires estimating (1) the retail trade area of a city for a specific retail or service industry, (2) the service or trade area population, (3) the pull factor, and (4) the potential sales of that industry in the area. To demonstrate the more formal method, we analyze the market area for a retail furniture industry in the imaginary city of Adamsville. The final section outlines explicitly where one can find the appropriate data and maps to analyze a specific industry within a specific city.

Informal Methods of Market Area Analysis

Several methods can be used to informally estimate market areas for a city or shopping center. These methods include a "survey" of automobile license plates, collecting addresses of regular customers, or an assumption that circulation patterns of local newspapers determine the geographic range of potential customers.

Shopping centers sometimes ask employees to scan the parking lot and list the quantity of cars licensed in each area. In some states and countries, license plates clearly show the counties or districts where the license was purchased. This technique loses its usefulness if (1) the counties are extremely large, (2) if the area is a tourist magnet like the Mall of America or Disneyland, or (3) if the area is a stop on the freeway on the way to a popular site.

A second way to informally evaluate market areas consists of the retailers and service providers collecting the addresses of customers from checks. In the United States, to get a general idea of annual purchasing patterns, samples of these addresses are ideally collected three times: before Thanksgiving, during the Christmas season, and sometime in the spring. This method is more precise than just listing the county of origin. An underlying assumption is that individuals who pay cash or use credit cards have the same spatial distribution as those who use checks. When retailers refuse to accept out-of-town checks, they lose one method of knowing the true extent of their market area.

In the third method, retailers and service providers assume that the market area of the newspaper or the service area of the local radio or television station delineates their own market area. This assumption begs the question of how far out the retailer should advertise.

Formal Market Area Analysis

The informal methods may be useful to see who is currently attracted to the industry in a specific city, but they do not predict the locations of people who could be interested. A more formal analysis uses Reilly's Law of Retail Gravitation to calculate the ***market area boundaries***. Once the boundaries are computed, the analysis requires approximating the number of people who live within the boundaries, or the ***trade area population***. Next, one calculates the ***trade area capture (TAC)*** to determine the number of "customer equivalents" served by that industry. With the ***pull factor***, one can find out whether the area is attracting people from outside its region or if its "logical" customer base is purchasing the goods from outside the area. Finally, knowing the ***potential sales*** gives an estimate of the total industry sales that the area could expect to receive.

Implementing Reilly's Law of Retail Gravitation

Reilly's law of retail gravitation helps determine the trade area for a community or for a spatial monopolist. Reilly's law estimates the farthest distance that consumers will commonly travel to shop in a certain city. This procedure describes a basic economic trade-off for comparison shoppers. The decision is between the attraction of a larger, more diverse shopping area and the deterrence of distance. The trade-off between size of shopping areas and distance is measured using a ***gravity model***. A gravity model simulates the idea that shopping areas act like magnets, attracting consumers as if they were little steel balls located various distances away from several magnets. More powerful magnets attract the steel balls from a farther distance than the weaker magnets can. For a concise discussion of the many variations of the gravity model that have been developed since Reilly's (1931) work, see O'Kelly and Miller (1989), Brown (1992).

Reilly's Law is most useful for rural shopping areas. Commuting patterns in larger metropolitan areas decrease the effectiveness of this method in determining the market area for a suburban shopping center. Finding the boundary area for a specific retail or service industry in a city requires several steps. One must first identify the closest cities that sell the same product or service and the distance from those cites to the urban center under study. Larger populations generally indicate more variety and lower prices because of greater competition. Thus, we would expect cities with larger populations to have larger market areas.

According to Reilly's Law, the distance from a smaller city to a trade area boundary with a larger city is as follows:

$$\frac{\text{Distance between the two cities}}{1 + \sqrt{\dfrac{\text{Population of the larger city}}{\text{Population of the smaller city}}}}.$$

Once we determine the appropriate cities for the analysis, we need the population of each of the cities and the distance between them as in Table 3A.1. Note that in this example, Elmquist and Calhoun do not have furniture stores. Therefore, these cities are passed by when determining the market area boundaries for Adamsville's furniture dealers. Adamsville is larger than DeWitt and Florence. Thus, we estimate the market boundary for

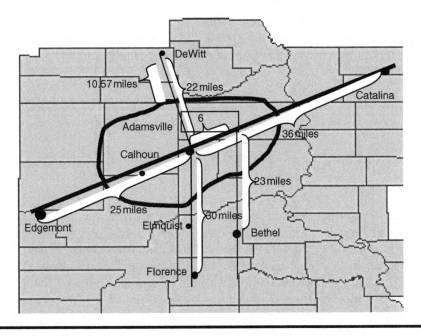

Figure 3A.1   Map of Adamsville and surrounding minor civil divisions.

these cities, as follows:

$$\text{DeWitt}: \frac{22}{1 + \sqrt{\frac{4161}{3553}}} = 10.57 \quad \text{Florence}: \frac{30}{1 + \sqrt{\frac{4161}{2990}}} = 13.76$$

The market area for furniture between Adamsville and DeWitt would then be 10.57 miles from DeWitt, or 11.43 (22 − 10.57) miles from Adamsville. Between Florence and Adamsville, the market area is 13.76 miles from Florence, or 16.24 (30 − 13.76) from Adamsville.

Table 3A.1   Population and Distance Data Needed to Implement Reilly's Law

Cities	Population	Distance from Adamsville	Calculated Distance to Market Boundary	Calculated Distance to Market Boundary from Adamsville Using Reilly'S Law
Adamsville	4161	0	—	—
Bethel	4674	6+23=29	14.08	14.08
Catalina	4864	36	17.30	17.30
DeWitt	3553	22	10.57	11.43
Edgemont	5215	25	11.09	11.09
Florence	2990	30	13.76	16.24

Because Adamsville is smaller than Bethel, Catalina, and Edgemont, Reilly's Formula determines the distance between Adamsville and its market boundary in the direction of each of these three cities:

$$\text{Bethel}: \frac{29}{1+\sqrt{\frac{4674}{4161}}} = 14.08; \quad \text{Catelina}: \frac{36}{1+\sqrt{\frac{4864}{4161}}} = 17.30;$$

$$\text{Edgemont}: \frac{25}{1+\sqrt{\frac{5215}{4161}}} = 11.09$$

Notice first that the estimated market area for Adamsville resembles the form of an amoeba more than a hexagon. Market areas for Adamsville slide closer to the smaller cities like Florence, but farther from the larger cities like Edgemont. If all cities had exactly the same population and were evenly spaced about the plain, the amoeba would have a more regular shape.

Next, notice that the market area between Bethel and Adamsville is closer to Adamsville because there is no direct route to Bethel. Residents of Bethel have to travel 23 miles on the secondary road before reaching the principal road to Adamsville. Adamsville's market area would be closer to Bethel if a direct route between the two cities existed. Notice also that the entire city of Calhoun is in Adamsville's market area, whereas we presume that everyone in Elmquist shops in Florence for furniture.

Applying this method to analyze the market area for a retail furniture industry assumes that all furniture stores are identical and sell the same products. To the extent that some people prefer to decorate their homes with "distinctive" furniture, this exaggerates the number of potential customers. This method also underestimates the number of potential customers in your market to the extent that people who live outside the area find their "unique" goods.[8]

Applying Reilly's Law

The Retail Trade Committee of the Bemidji Area Chamber of Commerce used Reilly's Law to generate an initial estimate of the market area for Bemidji, a sparsely populated city in northwest Minnesota. Survey teams went door-to-door along the roads to ask the households where they actually did most of

[8] Hustedde, Shaffer and Pulver (1984).

their shopping for particular items. The teams started from the estimated market boundary until it was clear that all households within a certain distance from the market boundary shopped in Bemidji at least occasionally. That point became the market boundary between Bemidji and the closest city.

The survey team found that the total trade area for Bemidji was in reality larger than Reilly's law suggested. Neither the radio station nor the print media covered the entire trade area for the city. Clothing, grocery, hardware stores, and restaurants exercised the greatest drawing power on shoppers.

Bemidji Area Chamber of Commerce
Retail Trade Committee (1981)

Trade Area Population

To determine the trade (market) area population, copy the trade area of the city on a map that specifies minor civil divisions, such as one found in the back of the *Census of Population and Housing Summary Statistics* publications. From the population data, determine the population within the trade area. The estimated trade areas could include parts of rural townships. When this happens, estimate the proportion of the area included in the trade area and assume the population is proportional to the area by assuming that the population density is the same throughout the minor civil division. See Figure 3A.2 and Table 3A.2 for an example.

Trade Area Capture

The total population in the trade area gives an idea of how many people are living in this market area, but there are two other questions to address. First, how do the local sales compare with the state's sales per person (per capita), and second, how does this translate into potential sales? We must remember also that most goods are normal goods, that is, as people's incomes increase, they purchase more. This means that areas with higher than normal incomes are expected to generate higher than normal sales. If we divide the total sales of the city by the per capita sales for the state (adjusted according to income differences), we will have a rough idea of the *customer equivalents*. This calculation will not yield the total number of customers

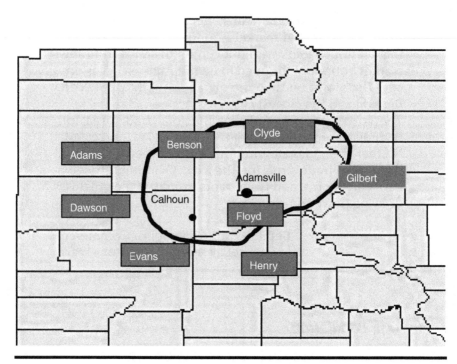

Figure 3A.2 Minor civil divisions within the trade area for Adamsville.

Table 3A.2 Calculating Total Trade Area Population

Minor Civil Division (Column 1)	Population (Column 2)	Estimated Share of Land Area in Market for Adamsville (Column 3)	Total Population in Market Area by Minor Civil Division (Multiply Column 2 by Column 3)
Adams township	936	33%	308.88
Adamsville	4161	100%	4161.00
Benson township	591	100%	591.00
Clyde township	1545	80%	1236.00
Calhoun	830	100%	830.00
Dawson township	953	33%	314.49
Evans township	3654	1%	36.54
Floyd township	5583	87%	4857.21
Gilbert township	1730	25%	432.5
Henry township	1766	10%	176.6
Total trade area population			12,944.22

because some people, children younger than five, for instance, will not themselves purchase anything, but they are enumerated in the population.

The ***trade area capture*** (TAC) generates a statistic that is comparable to the number of consumers attracted to a specific community to shop for a certain product. The trade area capture is a measure of the merchants' capability to capture sales at a rate proportional to the growth rate of incomes in the entire area.

The TAC is an index with which one can compare potential sales between areas, among industries, or over time. The TAC multiplies the state's per capita expenditures for industry j by income levels of the local area proportional to the state.

The TAC is calculated as follows:

$$\frac{\text{Actual retail sales for industry j in city i}}{\frac{\text{Total state expenditures for industry j}}{\text{State population}} \times \frac{\text{County (or city) per capita income}}{\text{State per capita income}}}.$$

By using the TAC, we assume, moreover, that consumers throughout the state have consistent buying habits concerning goods sold in industry j. A TAC of 6890 indicates that the local sales for industry j will be equal to the expenditures generated by a population of 6890.

By comparing the TAC over time, we can estimate whether the number of people shopping in a community is trending upward or downward. If the TAC trends downward for firms in industry j, retailers may wonder why consumers are shopping elsewhere. However, large demographic changes may explain changes in the TAC.[9]

For Adamsville, the TAC for the retail furniture industry is

$$\frac{\$\ 6{,}789{,}012}{\frac{\$\ 123{,}456{,}789}{178{,}210} \times \frac{\$\ 25{,}321}{\$\ 20{,}435}} = 7908.925,$$

much less than the estimated trade area population of 12,944.22.

Pull Factor

The TAC is the key ingredient in determining the ***pull factor***. The pull factor is used to determine the proportion of consumers who come from outside the trade area to shop. It can also estimate the proportion of sales lost to other areas. The pull factor for industry j would be

$$\text{Pull factor for industry j} = \frac{\text{Trade Area Capture for industry j}}{\text{Trade area population}}.$$

---

[9] Yanagida et al. (1991).

If the pull factor equals 1, the city is drawing all the customers for its industry j from within the trade area boundary. Pull factors greater than 1 mean that the city pulls customers from outside its natural trade area boundaries. This results in a "surplus" of spending over what was predicted. A pull factor of 1.25 suggests that "customer equivalents" equal to 25% of the trade area population come from outside the trade area. Pull factors of a community are a positive function of the community's age, the distance to the nearest larger trade center, and the extent of rural depopulation.

Pull factors less than 1 either indicate that the local shoppers are spending less than the state average because of demographic reasons or a large number of people living in the trade area are traveling to nearby cities to shop. An area with a median age population of 63 is not going to sell as many baby items as an area with the median age population of 23. According to Stone (2004), local stores may struggle, (that is, have pull factors less than 1) especially in rural areas, if a discount store such as Wal-Mart is located within 25 miles of the town.

For our example, the pull factor for furniture sales in Adamsville is $(7,908.925)/(12,944.22) = 0.61$. Because the pull factor is substantially less than 1, either the customers in Adamsville are purchasing significantly less furniture than consumers statewide or they are purchasing their furniture outside the Adamsville market area.

Potential Sales

Potential sales are estimated with the following formula:

$$\text{Trade area population} \times \text{State per capita expenditures for industry j}$$

$$\times \frac{\text{County (or city) per capita income}}{\text{State per capita income}}.$$

To estimate potential sales, multiply the trade area population by the denominator of the TAC. The formula allows local sales to differ from state sales by the level of income. It is possible to adjust this equation by other measures of community demographics. For example, older people may have less discretionary income to spend on retail goods because they spend more on health care. Areas with higher housing costs may experience lower than average retail sales. According to the formula, the calculation of potential sales is independent of the pull factor. When the pull factor is greater than 1, the equation predicts that future sales will be less than current sales. Thus, if the pull factor is greater than 1, it is preferable to multiply potential sales by the pull factor.

A pull factor that is less than 1 would overestimate potential sales, but a growth in the number of stores can create a retail agglomeration economy that could increase sales. In our example, projected furniture sales in Adamsville total

$$12,944.22 \times \frac{\$\ 123,456,789}{178,210} \times \frac{\$\ 25,321}{\$\ 20,435} = \$\ 11,111,303.00,$$

which is significantly more than the actual sales of $6,789,102.

Summary and Conclusions

This analysis identifies other questions to be considered. Why is this pull factor closer to 0.50 than 1.0? Why are sales higher than expected for the retail furniture industry in Adamsville? Could another furniture store in the area create sufficient economies of retail agglomeration to stimulate the industry? Answers to these are the domain of marketing experts.

Now It's Your Turn

The calculation of the trade area for a specific retail or service industry in a city requires several steps:

1. Find a good road map or use one of the Internet map sites.
2. Ascertain that sales data exist for the retail or service industry that you would like to study.
3. Find the closest cities that have firms in the same industry. (Note: you do not need the sales figures for these cities.)
4. Use a map that depicts minor civil divisions and draw the market area for your city.
5. Gather the following data:
   a. Population of the closest cities that have firms in the subject industry.
   b. State population.
   c. Actual retail sales in your city.
   d. Actual retail sales in your state.
   e. State per capita income.
   f. County (or city) per capita income.
   g. Population of minor civil divisions and cities in your market area.

6. Follow the example for the retail furniture industry in Adamsville.

From **Census of Retail Sales or Census of Services**, a state agency that collects sales tax data, or a private firm providing data:[10]
—— Actual retail sales for the subject industry.
—— Actual retail expenditures in the state for the subject industry.

From Regional Economic Information Systems, CA05:[11]
—— Per capita income for the county in which the subject city is located.
—— Per capita income for the state in which the subject city is located.

From **Regional Economic Information Systems, CA05**, the state's Demography Department, or Bureau of Economic Analysis's **Regional Economic Information System** (REIS) series:
—— State Population.

References

Ahn, J. K., and H. O. Nourse. 1988. Spatial economic interdependence in an urban hierarchy system. *Journal of Regional Science* 28 (3):421–432.

Bemidji Area Chamber of Commerce Retail Trade Committee. 1981. *The retail trade area of Bemidji*, Minnesota Retail Research Report #1.

Bennett, R. J., and D. J. Graham. 1998. Explaining size differentiation of business service centres. *Urban Studies* 35 (9):1457–1480.

Brakman, S., H. Garretsen, C. Van Marrewijk, and M. van den Berg. 1999. The return of Zipf: towards a further understanding of the rank-size distribution. *Journal of Regional Science* 39 (1):183–213.

Bresnahan, T. F., and P. C. Reiss. 1991. Entry and competition in concentrated markets. *Journal of Political Economy* 99 (5):977–1009.

Brown, S. 1992. The wheel of retail gravitation? *Environment and Planning A* 24 (10):1409–1429.

Burns, L. S., and R. G. Healy. 1978. The metropolitan hierarchy of occupations: an economic interpretation of central place theory. *Regional Science and Urban Economics* 8 (4):381–393.

---

[10] See Isaki (1990) regarding the use of the ratio-correlation method to estimate a county's retail sales figures for years not covered by the censuses. These publications come out for years ending in 2 or 7. States that collect sales taxes sometimes have adequate sales data for industries that are subject to the sales tax. Private data sources such as *Sales and Marketing Management* also give estimates of sales data.

[11] The REIS dataset includes per capita income estimates for the same times by county and micropolitan statistical area. Median income would be a more accurate income figure to use, but generally it is only published every 10 years with the Census of Population.

Caulkins, J. P. 1995. Domestic geographic variation in illicit drug prices. *Journal of Urban Economics* 37 (1):38–56.

Christaller, W. 1966. [1933]. *Central places in southern Germany.* Translated from *Die zentralen Orte in Süddeutschland* ed. C. W. Baskin, Prentice Hall, Englewood Cliffs, NJ.

Clark, W. A. V., and G. Rushton. 1970. Models of intra-urban consumer behavior and their implications for central place theory. *Economic Geography* 46 (3):486–497.

Deller, S. C., and T. R. Harris. 1993. Estimation of minimum market thresholds for rural commercial sectors using stochastic frontier estimators. *Regional Science Perspectives* 23 (1):3–17.

Fetter, F.A. 1995. [1924]. The economic law of market areas. *The economics of location.* Vol 1: Location., eds. Melvin L. Greenhut, George Norman, 189-198. Elgar Reference Collection: International Library of Critical Writings in Economics, Vol. 42. Aldershot, U.K.: Elgar; distributed in the U.S. by Ashgate, Brookfield, VT.

Gabaix, X. 1999. Zipf's law and the growth of cities. *American Economic Review* 89 (2):129–132.

Goody, B. 1993. Sole providers of hospital care in rural areas. *Inquiry* 30 (1):34–40.

Greenhut, M. L. 1971. *A Theory of the Firm in Economic Space.* Austin, TX: Austin Press, Educational Division, Lone Star Publishers.

Guérin-Pace, F. 1995. Rank-size distribution and the process of urban growth. *Urban Studies* 32 (3):551–562.

Heilbrun, J. 1992. Art and culture as central place functions. *Urban Studies* 29 (2):205–215.

Helliwell, J. F. 1996. Do national borders matter for Quebec's trade? *Canadian Journal of Economics* 29 (3):507–522.

Henderson, D., and G. Wallace. 1992. Retail business adjustment in rural hierarchies. *Growth and Change* 23 (1):80–93.

Huff, D. L., and J. M. Lutz. 1995. Change and continuity in the Irish urban system, 1966-1981. *Urban Studies* 32 (1):155–173.

Hustedde, R., R. Shaffer, and G. Pulver. 1984. *Community Economic Analysis, A How To Manual.* Ames, Iowa: North Central Regional Center for Rural Development, Iowa State University.

Isaki, C. T. 1990. Small-area estimation of economic statistics. *Journal of Business and Economic Statistics* 8 (4):435–441.

Lillie-Blanton, M. 1992. Rural and urban hospital closures, 1985-1988: operating and environmental characteristics that affect risk. *Inquiry* 29 (3):332–344.

Lösch, A. 1995 [1938]. The nature of economic regions. *The economics of location. Volume 1: Location,* Melvin L. Greenhut, George Norman eds., 329-336. Elgar Reference Collection: International Library of Critical Writings in Economics, vol. 42. Aldershot, U.K.: Elgar; distributed in the U.S. by Ashgate, Brookfield, Vt.

Mutlu, S. 1988. The spatial urban hierarchy in Turkey: its structure and some of its determinants. *Growth and Change* 19 (3):53–74.

O'Kelly, M. E., and H. J. Miller. 1989. A synthesis of some market area delimitation models. *Growth and Change* 20 (3):14–33.

Olfert, M. R., and J. C. Stabler. 1994. Community level multipliers for rural development initiatives. *Growth and Change* 25 (4):467–486.

Parr, J. B. 1995. Alternative approaches to market-area structure in the urban system. *Urban Studies* 32 (8):1317–1329.

Pedersen, P. O. 1992. The structure of small service centers under conditions of uncertain supplies. *International Regional Science Review* 14 (3):307–316.

Polèse, M. 1994. *Économie urbaine et régionale, logique spatiale des mutations économiques*. Paris: Economia.

Samuels, S., J. P. Cunningham, and C. Choi. 1991. The impact of hospital closures on travel time to hospitals. *Inquiry* 28 (2):194–199.

Stone, K. E. 2004. Impact of the Wal-Mart Phenomenon on Rural Communities Iowa State University, Department of Economics, Staff General Research Papers.

West, D. S., B. Von Hohenbalken, and K. Kroner. 1985. Tests of intraurban central place theories. *Economic Journal* 95 (377):101–117.

Yanagida, J. F., B. B. Johnson, J. Young, and M. Lundeen. 1991. An analysis of economic and noneconomic factors affecting retail sales leakages. *Review of Regional Studies* 21 (1):53–64.

Chapter 4

Industrial Location

Manufacturing firms face slightly more complicated location decisions than retail or service firms because the cost of their inputs is different at each location. Manufacturers also must account for the transport of the input(s) as well as the output(s). Chapter 4 and Chapter 5 explore **shipping models** that explain the competitive behavior of manufacturing firms. Oligopoly is the major industry structure that applies to shopping models. By contrast, shipping models often assume a worldwide market for the good. In the resulting perfectly competitive product market, firms have little or no control over price. Hence, to maximize profits, they must minimize cost.

Starting in this chapter, we relax the assumption that resources are equally distributed over a homogeneous plain. We assume pockets of dense population, as well as immovable resources such as lakes, rivers, mountains, forests, and coal mines. In this chapter, we will study several models of least-cost location. First, we will investigate what a least-cost location entails. Because firms can substitute various quantities of each input for one another, finding a **least-cost location** involves more than a comparison of the cost of inputs at different potential sites. As the example of Urban Center and Pine Grove illustrates, firms will use different proportions of inputs depending on their costs at various locations.

Second, a firm's cost structure depends on its size. The concept of increasing returns to scale is vital in explaining where economic activity locates, so we will examine the influence of **internal economies of scale** on location choice.

Third, from the ***transportation models***, we discovered that there are a limited number of potential locations that can minimize total costs. Firms might decrease total transportation costs by bringing inputs to the plant and selling the product locally. Instead, they may consider shipping their output to a distant market and locating close to their inputs. To see the distinction, we to examine Hoover's (1971) theories of how transportation influences manufacturing firm location.

Think About It...

What are the principal industries in and around your city? What attracted the industries to that location?

Least-Cost Location with Variable Inputs

Weber's (1929) theory of industrial location starts with this question: where is the best place to locate an industry given that the market, the needed fuel, labor, and raw materials are all in separate places? According to the least-cost theory of industrial location, the producer chooses a site that minimizes the sum of total production plus transportation costs. A perfectly competitive product market means that the firm has no control over price and that it will sell everything that it produces at the going rate.

Production costs vary depending on the local market for the inputs. Firms that decide to locate in areas with labor shortages may need to offer higher wages to attract enough workers. These higher wages have two effects on a local labor market. First, the firm's higher wages bid workers away from other companies, thereby increasing the production costs for all local employers. Second, the higher wages draw workers who live farther away by increasing the distance they are willing and able to commute. Firms will find inexpensive labor costs either in areas where a large plant has recently closed or in areas near a large pool of qualified, well-paid, and very productive workers.

At first glance, one may think that deciding the location that will minimize costs should be easy. First, one could determine the necessary amount of capital, labor, land, and raw materials. Then, by multiplying the quantities by the local input prices, one chooses the location where the sum is minimized. However, this simplified model ignores the fact that most entrepreneurs can vary the proportions of inputs they used. Because entrepreneurs can generally use many different combinations of inputs, they will base the location decision on the relative cost of inputs and the combination that they would purchase at each location.

Firms that locate in a sparsely populated area may enjoy lower costs of raw materials but face higher labor costs compared to firms that locate next to densely populated urban areas. The rural firms may adopt a production technology that uses fewer workers but more land and raw materials than their city cousins to produce the same level of output.

We used isoquant and isocost curves to illustrate how firms choose among locations according to input costs. **Isoquants** show all possible combinations of two inputs (per unit of time) that are necessary to produce a certain level of output (per time), depending on the existing technology. Isoquants are derived from the firm's production function. As long as the available technology is the same in each location, the isoquants are identical. Isoquants differ by location only if local regulations ban certain production processes or if needed resources such as electricity are unreliable.

Without loss of generality and only for ease of exposition, we assume two inputs, x_1 and x_2. Figure 4.1 shows three types of isoquants for two inputs. Isoquant a depicts a production process with perfect substitutability of resources. For example, for some tasks, a robot could easily replace a human. When this is possible, there is a perfect substitutability between capital (robots) and labor.

Isoquant b shows a "normal" isoquant with imperfectly substitutable inputs. One example of imperfect substitutability is found in farming. One farmhand, using a large tractor and plow that costs approximately $280,000, could plow 160 acres per day. To plow 160 acres, one could also hire 160 farmhands, each equipped with a horse and a single-bottom plow worth $3200. Because a unit of capital is defined in terms of dollars, the quantity of 160 acres could be plowed by one farmhand and 280,000 units of capital. On the other hand, 160 units of labor could plow 160 acres with 3200 units of capital. The profit-maximizing combination depends on the cost of salaries

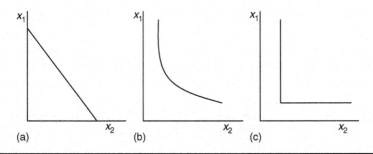

Figure 4.1   Three isoquants.

relative to the cost of capital (interest rate, depreciation rate, and other costs of maintaining capital).[1]

Finally, isoquant *c* allows no substitutability of resources. This "Leontief" production function describes bicycle production. Two wheels and one frame make a bicycle, and no number of extra wheels will take the place of a second frame. Input-output analysis, a technique that we will present in Chapter 7, measures the impact of changes in one industry on various sectors of an economy and assumes all production functions are of the Leontief type.

With any production function, a change in output is equal to the sum of the changes in inputs used, each multiplied by its marginal product. The **marginal product of x (MP$_x$)** is the extra output generated by adding one more unit of the input *x*. Therefore, for a production function with two inputs,

$$\Delta \text{Output} = \text{MP}_{x_1} \Delta x_1 + \text{MP}_{x_2} \Delta x_2. \tag{4.1}$$

Along an isoquant, the change in output is zero, so

$$0 = \text{MP}_{x1} \Delta x_1 + \text{MP}_{x_2} \Delta x_2. \tag{4.2}$$

With a slight rearrangement of terms, we found that the slope of the isoquant function is equal to the negation of the ratio of the marginal products.

$$\frac{\Delta X_1}{\Delta X_2} = -\frac{\text{MP}_{X_2}}{\text{MP}_{X_1}}. \tag{4.3}$$

The **isocost** curve shows all possible combinations of two goods that a firm can purchase for a given total cost; thus it represents a firm's budget constraint. Isocost curves are linear functions that depend on the total amount a firm can spend on production (total production cost) and local input prices. Figure 4.2 depicts an isocost curve. The intercepts for the isocost curve represent the total budget if it were allocated solely to purchase either input x_1 or input x_2. The slope of the line is the ratio of the prices of the two inputs.

The optimal combination of inputs is the one that produces the desired quantity of output at the lowest possible cost. The optimal combination is found at the point where the isoquant is tangent to the isocost line. Figure 4.3 depicts three isoquants and an isocost curve.

The slopes of the isocost and isoquant are equal at the point of tangency. Thus when the firm is in equilibrium with respect to input usage, $\text{MP}_{x_2}/\text{MP}_{x_1} = P_{x_2}/P_{x_1}$, or $\text{MP}_{x_1}/P_{x_1} = \text{MP}_{x_2}/P_{x_2}$. This relationship demonstrates

---

[1] John Deere Co., E-mail correspondence 26 April 2001; Rockwood Tack and Seed, Sauk Rapids, Minnesota. Interview 26 April 2001.

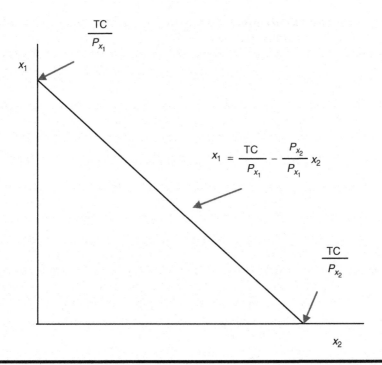

$$x_1 = \frac{TC}{P_{x_1}} - \frac{P_{x_2}}{P_{x_1}} x_2$$

Figure 4.2 Isocost curve.

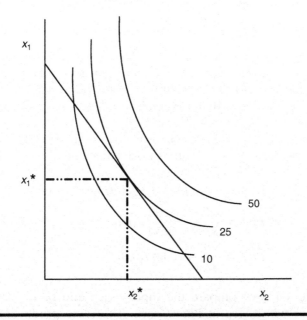

Figure 4.3 Isocost curve and isoquant map showing a firm's equilibrium.

the **equimarginal principle**. It implies that in equilibrium, the extra output generated by the last dollar spent on x_1 will equal the extra output generated by the last dollar spent on x_2. In other words, one more dollar spent for another unit of any input—be it capital, labor, or even paper clips—will produce the same quantity of output.

The following exercise adapted from Nourse (1968) uses isoquants and isocosts to clarify the fact that multiplying a fixed input combination by local input prices will not provide an adequate estimate of production costs in a locality. Different input prices result in distinct combinations of inputs used in production.

Assume that someone wants to start a firm that makes wreaths from pine boughs. The new design for the wreaths will appeal to households throughout the entire year. The firm considers two potential locations for the plant. Assume that the cost of equipment, land, and buildings in both locations is identical and that consumers pay all shipping costs.

The first location is at Pine Grove, a small town in the middle of a lush pine forest. The pine boughs are plentiful and cost a mere $150 per load; but because the population is sparse, labor is expensive. A going wage of $400 per week will attract enough workers to the facility. Thus, the budget constraint at Pine Grove will be

$$TC = \$150 \, Pine + \$400 \, Labor,$$

$$Pine = \frac{TC}{\$150} - \frac{\$400}{\$150} Labor, \quad or$$

$$Pine = \frac{TC}{\$150} - 2.67 \, Labor,$$

where TC is the total cost of production, $Pine$ is the loads of pine boughs and $Labor$ is the amount of labor measured in hours per week.

The second location, Urban Center, is a college town with an abundant labor force but few pine trees. The firm can hire all the necessary labor for $200 per week. Because the firm needs to ship the boughs, the cost for the pine is $250 per load. Urban Center's isocost becomes

$$TC = \$250 \, Pine + \$200 \, Labor,$$

$$Pine = \frac{TC}{\$250} - \frac{\$200}{\$250} Labor, \quad or$$

$$Pine = \frac{TC}{\$250} - 0.80 \, Labor.$$

Using Figure 4.4, we compare the input usage and production costs at Urban Center with those at Pine Grove. The same production function applies regardless of location, thus the same isoquant map holds true for

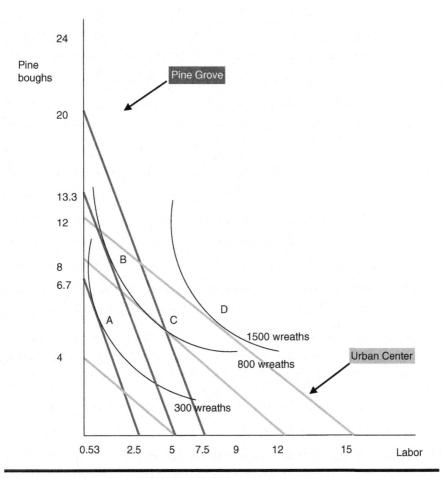

Figure 4.4   Resource use based on location. (Adapted from Nourse, H.O. *Regional Economics,* McGraw-Hill, New York, 1968.)

both places. Figure 4.4 combines the isoquant map with the dark steep isocost curves for Pine Grove and the light flatter isocost curves for Urban Center. Note that for each place the three isocost curves represent total costs of $1000, $2000, and $3000.

If the firm were in Pine Grove, it could produce 300 wreaths per week using approximately 5.253 loads of pine and 0.53 units of labor for a total cost of $1000 because $TC = \$1000 = (\$150 \times 5.253) + (\$400 \times 0.53)$. For $2000, the firm can make 800 wreaths in Pine Grove using eight loads of pine boughs and two units of labor [$2000 = (\$150 \times 8) + (\$400 \times 2)$]. These combinations will ensure that the firm's choice of inputs is one that maximizes output given the isocost constraints. The optimal quantities of inputs are found at the point where the isoquant is tangent to the isocost curve.

Similarly, if an isocost curve limits total production costs to $2000, a firm located at Urban Center could produce 800 wreaths using 4.4 loads of pine and 4.5 units of labor [$2000 = ($250 × 4.4) + ($200 × 4.5)]. To make 1500 wreaths, the firm needs 5.6 loads of pine and eight full-time workers for a total cost of $3000 [$3000 = ($250 × 5.6) + ($200 × 8)].

Figure 4.4 also derives four least-cost combinations of inputs. If the maximum number of wreaths expected to be sold per week will be around 300, the plant will locate in Pine Grove. Three hundred wreaths will be produced using combination A on the diagram (5.253 loads of pine and 0.53 units of labor) for a total cost of $1000. Producing 300 wreaths in Urban Center will cost more than $1000 per week for any possible input combination.

If, however, the firm believes it can sell 800 wreaths, the production cost will be $2000 in Pine Grove or Urban Center. In Pine Grove, where labor is more expensive, the firm will use eight loads of pine boughs and two units of labor (Point B). In Urban Center, the firm will purchase just 4.5 loads of boughs and hire 4.4 workers (Point C).

Finally, if the firm needs to supply 1500 wreaths to the market, the cost would surpass $3000 in Pine Grove. Thus, firms that foresee sales of 1500 wreaths will locate in Urban Center, hire 8.5 units of labor, and purchase 5.2 loads of pine boughs (Point D) for a total cost of $3000 per week.

The example of Pine Grove and Urban Center underscores a substitution between transport costs and nontransport costs. The firm must choose to either pay the cost to transport the pine boughs to a location where labor is plentiful or pay a higher salary to attract workers who will need to commute.

Increasing vs. Constant Returns to Scale

The concept of internal increasing returns to scale is essential in explaining where economic activity locates. The long-run average cost curve (LRAC) illustrates returns to scale. By finding the lowest total cost necessary to produce each quantity of output, one can generate the LRAC for a firm at a specific site. The average cost would be the total cost (represented by the isocost curve) divided by the quantity produced (from the isoquant). This cost curve is long-run because both inputs (x_1 and x_2) are variable.

The long-run is the required time frame when analyzing location theory because in the long run, all inputs are variable, including the size of the plant. When the size of a plant changes, so does its short-run average cost curve (SRAC). The LRAC is merely the envelope of the lowest possible costs needed to produce each level of output, regardless of the size of the firm. Figure 4.5 shows the SRACs of three firms enveloped into a LRAC.

Increasing returns to scale, sometimes called ***economies of scale***, exist if, as the size of the firm increases, the average cost of production declines. If, however, as the size of the firm increases average costs do not

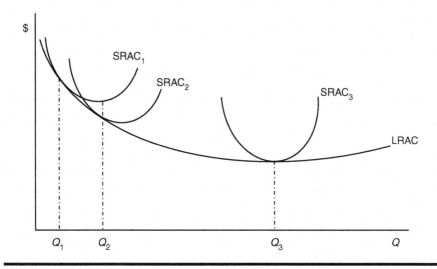

Figure 4.5 Long-run average cost curve.

change, the firm has ***constant returns to scale***. Less often, ***decreasing returns to scale*** or ***diseconomies of scale*** appear if, as a firm increases the size of the plant, the average production cost increases.

Firms that exhibit constant returns to scale for each quantity produced have a horizontal LRAC curve. Firms with constant returns to scale become increasingly smaller and they spread out so they can provide goods to more consumers at lower delivered prices. Pushed to the extreme, this model results in the end of specialization and trade because each household will be entirely self-sufficient—just like the farmers at the beginning of Lösch's model (Chapter 3).

Examples of these ***Robinson Crusoe goods*** are those which are exclusively produced by a household. The cost of producing a slice of fresh, hot toast, for example, is the same for everyone—a slice of bread, the electricity to run a toaster, the opportunity cost of purchasing a toaster in terms of interest income foregone, and the opportunity cost of the few minutes waiting for the toast to pop up. Regardless of how many pieces of toast are made, the average cost is approximately the same (with a slight adjustment for two or four slice toasters, perhaps). Toast is generally produced in the individual household, so transportation costs are zero. Hot, fresh toast is never delivered door-to-door like pizza because there are not enough increasing returns to scale in its production. Finally, the choice of the optimal location of "toast factories" is never an issue.

However, increasing returns to scale are evident in the production of toasters. This production requires the skills and technology needed to create an "ideal" slice of toasted bread. Each household that would have the capabilities and the equipment needed to produce its own toaster would do so at a very high cost. However, if it already has the tools and the knowledge, the production of many toasters will decrease the average cost. As the "firm" grows, average costs of production will keep declining, and this story continues in a fashion similar to that of Lösch's brewers. When each household produces its own, transportation costs are zero, but the long-run average cost is high for such a small quantity. As the quantity produced increases, long-run average costs decrease, and the firm will sell to an increasingly larger market area. Eventually, shipping costs will outweigh the cost-savings from increasing returns to scale and a different branch or a new firm will be profitable. The resulting economy is not a perfectly competitive market with many buyers and sellers, but a Löschean market of spatial monopolists who act as oligopolists.

In addition, when the assumption of equally dispersed consumers is relaxed, we find that firms in densely populated areas benefit most from the internal economies of scale because they are selling more. They are not necessarily more profitable because the price of land is also high.

This seemingly innocuous concept of increasing returns to scale undermines the traditional general equilibrium analysis, international trade models, and neoclassical growth theories, all of which produce equilibrium among perfectly competitive markets endowed with constant returns to scale.

Transport-Oriented Models

Neither the isoquant–isocost analysis nor the contribution of increasing returns to scale addresses transportation costs. Transportation costs are more than just a marginal cost of production because they differ depending on the firm's location relative to its inputs and its market. Firms are classified as one of the three types: resource-oriented, transport-oriented, or footloose. Transport-oriented firms are further subdivided as either input-oriented or market-oriented. Firms that are not tied to the site of a resource and face minimal transport costs are defined as *footloose*. See Figure 4.6.

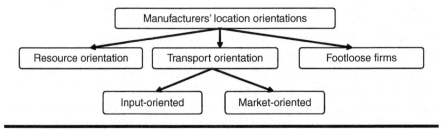

Figure 4.6   Location orientation chart.

Resource Orientation

The easiest location decisions are for resource-oriented firms because they have few choices regarding where they can locate. Lumberjacks must work in forests. Coalmines should be in the vicinity of coal deposits. The city of International Falls, Minnesota holds a copyright on the phrase "Icebox of the Nation" to attract businesses that need to produce or test items used in cold weather.

Transport Orientation

The more interesting location decisions involve distance. In this section, we will establish the concept of long-haul economies, where the transportation rates over long distances are nonlinear. Second, we introduce a model where one input and one output are to be transported, and finally, we consider the movement of many inputs and outputs.

Think About It...

Determine the modes of transportation (including walking, bicycling, driving, rail, boat, and airplane) that you could use to go to each destination from the center of your city:

Distance	Walk	Bicycle	Drive/Bus/ Taxi/Truck	Rail	Boat	Air
1 block						
1 mile						
10 miles						
100 miles						
1000 miles						
To another continent						

For distances with several transport modes, how many transportation providers serve your area? What mode would result in the lowest cost of going that distance for yourself? For a 10-lb. package? For 2000 lbs. of freight?

Long-Haul Economies

The price-distance functions of Chapter 2 and Chapter 3 assume a constant transportation rate. In reality, the longer the distance required to travel, the lower the cost of going an extra unit. According to Hoover (1971), **long-haul economies** exist if the marginal transportation costs decline as distance increases.

The decline in marginal transport costs due to long-haul economies comes from two sources. First, as distance increases, different types of carriers compete to transport goods. The increased competition keeps prices competitive. For very short distances, say one-half mile, one could go by foot, car or truck, but never by airplane. For distances of 400 miles, besides automobiles and trucks, we add rail and airplanes as possible carriers. For 1000 miles or more, barges, boats, and ships are possibilities if the site is next to water.

North Dakota Hostages

North Dakota is a captive market for railroad pricing because inter- and intramodal competition is extremely limited. The major markets for North Dakota's grain are on the east and west coasts and the Gulf of Mexico. Rail transport is more efficient than trucking for such long distances. St. Paul, Minnesota, which has the nearest barge-loading facility, is over 200 miles from the North Dakota silos, and the Port of Duluth in Minnesota is over 250 miles. Trucks deliver the grain to these centers where it is loaded on barges or ships.

Burlington Northern (BN) and Soo Line are the only two rail carriers that serve North Dakota, and BN owns the majority of the track. Rail transport costs for wheat and barley are higher than for corn and soybeans because of the lack of intermodal competition. Corn and soybeans grow chiefly in the eastern part of the state where trucks can efficiently carry the grain to Duluth or St. Paul. The wheat and barley grown in western North Dakota are hostages of the two rail lines because trucks do not carry these commodities to their west-coast markets.

Koo, Tolliver, and Bitzan (1993).

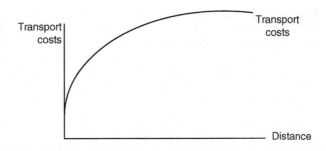

Figure 4.7   Long-haul economies.

A second reason that long-haul economies exist is that for each trans-portation mode, the marginal cost of going one more mile decreases as distance increases. Large trucks have to shift at least eight times after they stop at a traffic light before they can reach a speed of 30 miles per hour. Thus, trucks take more time and use more fuel to go one more mile in town than on the freeway. For these two reasons—increased competition between transport modes and decreased marginal cost—transport costs over long distances have a logarithmic shape rather than a linear shape, as shown in Figure 4.7.

Transporting One Input and One Output

The most elementary transportation model of location analysis is one where a firm needs to transport either one input or one output. Labor and other necessary resources are ubiquitous (located everywhere) at the same price. So to maximize profits, the firm must find the place where transportation costs are minimized. To do this, the firm must determine the total transportation cost at every possible location. ***Total transportation cost*** is the sum of the ***cost of procuring the inputs*** plus the ***cost of distributing the output***. Determining where to locate will result in a "tug-of-war" between the input source and the market.

The transport cost includes not only the cost of the truck drivers and the loaders, but also fuel, licenses, and insurance. In addition, Paul Samuelson (1983) observed that firms incur costs because some of the output, in effect, melts away like an iceberg: produce deteriorates, dries up, or starts to rot. Fragile items break. Time-sensitive items such as newspapers lose rel-evance. Table 4.1 lists procurement costs (of inputs), distribution costs (of outputs), and total transport costs for a hypothetical firm. The sum of the procurement costs (Column A) and the distribution costs (Column B) gives total transportation costs at each distance from the input source (Column C). In this example, at a distance of four units from the input source, transportation costs are maximized. Because total transportation costs are lowest at the market, this firm is classified as ***market-oriented***.

Table 4.1 Hypothetical Transportation Costs

Distance from the Input Source	Distance from the Market to Inputs Source	Column A Cost of Procuring Inputs	Column B Cost of Distributing Output	Column C Total Transport Costs (A + B)
0	10	4.00	6.00	10.00
1	9	4.48	5.95	10.43
2	8	4.92	5.80	10.72
3	7	5.32	5.55	10.87
4	6	5.68	5.20	10.88
5	5	6.00	4.75	10.75
6	4	6.28	4.20	10.48
7	3	6.52	3.55	10.07
8	2	6.72	2.80	9.52
9	1	6.88	1.95	8.83
10	0	7.00	1.00	8.00

Figure 4.8 shows the procurement, distribution, and total transport costs from Table 4.1. If input prices are the same everywhere, the firm will locate where transportation costs are lowest—in this case, at the market. If, on the other hand, the input source has lower total transport costs, the firm will locate there and be classified as input-oriented. Unless the transportation route includes a transshipment point, no firm will minimize transport costs

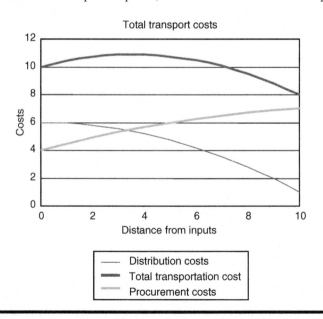

Figure 4.8 Total transport costs.

by locating at a point between its input source and market. ***Transshipment points*** occur where the shipped good needs to change modes of transportation. For instance, when North Dakota grain is trucked to port elevators in Duluth, Minnesota, where the supply is then loaded onto ships, Duluth is the transshipment point for the grain.

Think About It...

For which industry/industries would your city be a viable location (given only the transportation costs of inputs/outputs)? Explain why or why not each industry is a viable option.

Firewood chopping   Gasoline refinery
Soda pop bottling
Dynamite   Vegetable processing
Holiday wreaths   Baseball bats
Gold mine   Casino
Flour mill   Coupon redemption
Telemarketing   Headquarters for political
                             lobbyists

Some input-oriented firms engage in ***weight-losing*** activities, which are activities where the output weighs less than the input. Other input-oriented firms use inputs that are fragile or spoil quickly. Firms tending to locate near the input source include those in the canning industry, those that make palates, lumber, chipboard, and chemicals.[2]

Transshipment Point between Ore and Automobiles

One firm that transforms the iron ore mined in northern Minnesota into taconite pellets is located at Silver Bay, on the North Shore of Lake Superior. The raw ore comes by train to the plant that is located on the lake. At the plant, the raw ore is crushed, separated from the waste material, ground into powder, and mixed with bentonite (an absorptive and colloidal

---

[2] Funke (1984).

clay used especially as a sealing agent http://www.
merriam-webster.com) before it is formed into pellets
and baked in ovens. The taconite pellets are then
loaded onto ore boats and shipped to steel mills
throughout the Great Lakes.

Market-oriented firms engage in ***weight-gaining*** activities. The term
"weight-gaining" applies to goods for which the production process uses
inputs that are available everywhere. Bottling soft drinks is a weight-gaining
activity because the firm adds water at the market site rather than at the
place where the syrup is mixed. Firms that tend to locate near the market
generally produce output which, because it is heavier, bulkier, more
delicate, perishable, or more dangerous than its inputs, is more expensive
to ship. These activities are generically termed "weight-gaining."

Think About It...

Which of the principal industries in your area engage in
weight-losing activities?

Which of them engage in weight-gaining activities?

Do the shipments in your area seem to consist more of
inputs coming in or output leaving?

Is your city a transshipment point for any industries?
Which ones?

Location of Weight-Gaining and Weight-Losing Activities in Poland

Nowak and Romanowska (1985) studied the location
patterns of the food processing industry in Poland.
They discovered that sugar beets, potatoes, and food
preservation are input-oriented industries. The sugar
content in beets diminishes if they are transported long
distances. The starch content in potatoes also

diminishes over time. The food preservation industry needs to locate next to the perishable inputs.

Factories producing beverages high in water content locate next to the market to decrease distribution costs. However, breweries do need a source of water that is suitable for brewing. Baking industries are market-oriented because baking increases the perishability of the grain and yeast.

Plants making pasteurized milk or producing butter, cheese, or condensed or powdered milk locate near the raw material because raw milk is perishable and heavier than the final products. However, firms producing fresh milk products and soft cheeses locate near the market. Fresh milk products and soft cheese are as perishable as raw milk, but also more fragile to transport.

Slaughterhouses in Poland are situated near the input source because transporting live animals over long distances involves losses. Some animals die or lose weight in transit. However, butcher shops are market-oriented. Firms that produce fodder or mill grain are footloose. Their location depends more on the availability of hydro-energy sources.

Nowak and Romanowska (1985).

Three-Way Tug-of-War

The ideal weight helps us determine whether a product is market-oriented or input-oriented. The *ideal weight* of an input is the transport cost per ton per mile multiplied by the number of tons of input the firm uses during each period. Likewise, the ideal weight of the output is the transport cost per ton per mile multiplied by the number of tons of output the firm ships during each time.

Table 4.2 shows a combination of two inputs that a firm uses to produce one output. In this example, input A costs 10¢ more to ship than input B, but the firm uses more input B than input A. This firm will be input-oriented even though the output costs the most per unit to ship. It will be tempted to locate near input B, where the ideal weight is the largest. However, the final decision depends on the location of the other inputs and the market in relation to the source of input B.

Table 4.2 Calculation of Ideal Weights for Two Inputs and an Output

	Input A	Input B	Output
Transport cost per ton per mile	30¢	20¢	50¢
Number of tons per week	30	50	10
Ideal weight	9	10	5

We can analyze firm location along a nonlinear route, using ideal weights. Figure 4.9 shows three potential routes that link the locations of two inputs and one output. Sites A, B, and C are associated with ideal weights of 2, 3, and 4. For Route *i*, the cost minimizing location is at B, even though C's ideal weight is larger. A firm originally located at A finds that it decreases its transport costs by $5 ($3+$4−$2) for each mile that it approaches B. Similarly, a firm at C decreases its transportation costs by $1 ($2+$3−$4) for every mile it moves toward B. The optimal location is therefore B.

For Route *ii*, however, the firm will locate at C because the ideal weight at point C (6) is more than the sum of the ideal weights at A and B (2+3). The diagram of Route *iii* shows that an area with no inputs, no market, and no transshipment point can be a profitable site if it is at a junction. Moving one mile from A toward the junction would save the firm net transportation costs of $5, ($3+$4−$2). Moving one mile from B toward the junction would save $3($2+$4−$3). Likewise, moving one mile from C toward the junction would save the firm $1($2+$3−$4).

Footloose Firms

Footloose firms are firms for which the transportation cost is not very important. These firms are not tied to any location because they do not

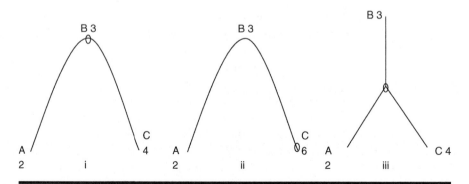

Figure 4.9 Firm location on nonlinear routes.

require an immobile natural resource. However, because transportation costs are of no consequence in a firm's location decision does not imply that it will locate haphazardly. Footloose firms locate where they can take advantage of agglomeration economies (Chapter 5).

Access to information about what consumers want could cause footloose firms to cluster near the market. At one time, printing and publishing and high-tech industries were considered footloose. However, firms in both of these industries need to locate near the market to be able to quickly adapt to changing needs of the end user. Footloose firms also cluster together when they find that despite high land prices and higher wages, their overall costs decrease if they locate in a city or where others in their industry locate.[3]

Summary and Conclusions

This chapter started by looking at least-cost locations from an isoquant and isocost perspective. By analyzing isoquants and isocosts, firms determine the best place to locate given substitutability of inputs, input prices, and the production function. From this, the chapter reviewed the importance of the concept of internal economies of scale to location theory. Without internal economies of scale, location is not an issue because households will be self-sufficient, Robinson Crusoe economies.

A final method of location analysis assumes that inputs cost the same everywhere, so minimizing costs necessitates minimizing transportation costs. Firms are classified as resource-oriented, transport-oriented, or footloose. Resource-oriented firms have to locate near the resources. Transport-orientation places firms next to the inputs or market, depending on whether the input or the output is more costly to transport. Footloose firms seem at first to locate anywhere they please, but other factors such as agglomeration economies dictate where footloose firms can effectively locate.

Chapter Questions

1. "When my furniture-making business was new, I located near a beautiful oak forest. However, as the firm grew, I preferred to locate near the city where my market was." Graph this in terms of isocost and isoquant curves.

---

[3] Thisse (1993); Justman (1994).

2. From the following table of distribution and procurement costs:

Hypothetical Transportation Costs				
Distance from the Input Source	Distance from the Market to Input Source	Column A Cost of Distributing Output	Column B Cost of Procuring the Input	Column C Total Transport Costs
0	10	6.00	4.00	
1	9	5.95	4.48	
2	8	5.80	4.92	
3	7	5.55	5.32	
4	6	5.20	5.68	
5	5	4.75	6.00	
6	4	4.20	6.28	
7	3	3.55	6.52	
8	2	2.80	6.72	
9	1	1.95	6.88	
10	0	1.00	7.00	

    a. Determine total transport costs.
    b. To maximize profits, should this firm be located at the market, at the input source, or at a transshipment point?
    c. Graph these transportation cost curves.

3. Cole Younger makes baseball bats exclusively for the Northfield Bandits, a little-known baseball team. The only inputs are wood and labor. The price of labor is the same in Twig (northern Minnesota) as it is in Northfield, where the bats are sold. Where should Cole locate the plant? Diagram this case of one input and one output and briefly explain your decision.

4. Since 9/11, transportation costs have increased substantially because of the heightened security precautions.
    a. What will this do to the market areas of firms?
    b. What actions could firms take to change the market area back to where it was? Only suggest things that firms can actually control. Show this using price-distance functions and demand functions.
    c. If the cost of sending dangerous cargo by air doubles (it did) so that airlines are no longer a viable transport mode for such cargo, what is an alternative transportation mode? What might this suggest for traffic safety given that fewer travelers are going by air also?

5. Based solely on ideal weights of inputs and outputs, determine whether these industries would locate at the market site or input site. Briefly defend your responses.
   a. Local newspapers
   b. Food dehydration
   c. Granite gravestones
   d. Cement blocks
   e. Lumber
   f. Beer
   g. Bread
   h. Hazardous waste

6. Given the ideal weights in each of the graphs below, where will you locate—A, B, C, or elsewhere? Circle your preferred location or location segment.

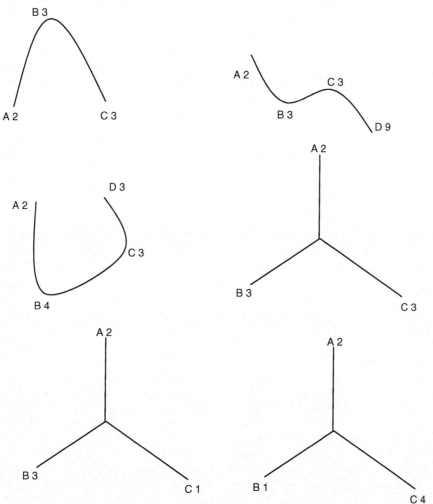

Research Assignments

1. Using data from the MCD/County-To-MCD/County Worker Flow Files, in the Journey to Work and Place of Work data sets, (http://www.census.gov/population/www/socdemo/journey.html), determine:
    a. The counties where the people who live in your county work.
    b. The counties where the people who work in your county live.
    c. Compare the "average wage and salary disbursements" from the CA30 REIS data sets (http://www.bea.gov/regional/reis/) for your county with the other county or counties from which most workers reside. Which county shows higher disbursements?
    d. Compare the "average wage and salary disbursements" for your county with the other county or counties where most workers work. Which county shows higher disbursements?
2. Using data from the ***County Business Patterns***, determine the average employment per firm for the largest manufacturing industries in your county. Compare that statistic to your state.
    a. Does it look like, on average, the firms in your industries are smaller, about the same size, or larger than those in your state?
    b. From the ***Census of Business data***, compare output per worker for these same industries in your county with the output per worker in the state. Do these numbers seem to suggest economies of scale (greater output per worker in industries with more average workers per firm), constant returns to scale (constant output per worker), or diseconomies of scale (lower output per worker with firms that have more average workers per firm)?
3. Using data from the ***Census of Business*** or ***County Business Patterns*** and your knowledge of your area, decide if the largest firms in your area are resource-oriented, transport-oriented, or footloose. If they are transport-oriented, are they located close to their inputs, close to their market, or both?

References

Funke, U. H. 1984. The locational behavior of the chemical industry in the United States after World War II. In *Operations Research and Economic Theory: Essays in Honor of Martin J. Beckmann*, eds. H. Hauptmann, W. Krelle, and K.C. Mosler, Tokyo: Springer, 151–161.

Hoover, E. 1971. *Introduction to Regional Economics*. New York: Knopf.

Justman, M. 1994. The effect of local demand on industry location. *Review of Economics and Statistics* 76 (4):742–753.

Koo, W. W., D. D. Tolliver, and J. D. Bitzan. 1993. Railroad pricing in captive markets: an empirical study of North Dakota grain rates. *Logistics and Transportation Review* 29 (2):123–137.

Nourse, H. O. 1968. *Regional Economics*. New York: McGraw-Hill.

Nowak, J., and H. Romanowska. 1985. Locational patterns of the food-processing industry in Poland. *European Review of Agricultural Economics* 12 (3):233–246.

Samuelson, P. A. 1983. Thünen at two hundred. *Journal of Economic Literature* 21 (4):1468–1488.

Thisse, J.-F. 1993. Oligopoly and the polarization of space. *European Economic Review* 37 (2–3):299–307.

Weber, A. 1929 [1909]. *Theory of the Location of Industries*. [Translated by C.J. Friedrich from *Über den Standort der Industrie*], The University of Chicago Press, Chicago.

Chapter 5

Agglomeration Economies and Entrepreneurs' Preferences

Firms group together initially to minimize transportation costs or to take advantage of internal economies of scales by selling to a larger market. When they do locate together, they also benefit from lower costs that are not passed on to firms outside the cluster. When this happens, the firms in the cluster are benefiting from agglomeration economies. On the other hand, when too many firms locate in an area, they could cause diseconomies of agglomeration, which will result instead in increased production costs.

Not all firms locate to maximize profits. Some locate to maximize the utility or minimize the stress of their owner. An entrepreneur may choose a site because it is endowed with desirable amenities. Such entrepreneurs value their utility functions over their bottom lines. The appendix to this chapter presents decision making under uncertainty, a subject that further underscores the role of the decision maker's personality in determining the location of the enterprise. This chapter will analyze the roles of agglomeration and diseconomies of agglomeration, as well as the part that the entrepreneurs' preferences and tastes for risk play in their location decision.

Agglomeration Economies

The mere existence of a cluster of firms in an area generates **agglomeration economies**, also known as external economies or cluster economies. Agglomeration economies promote grouping together and thus create centripetal forces that entice economic activity to congregate. When the clusters get too large, **diseconomies of agglomeration** set in, triggering a *centrifugal force* that repels economic activity.

Think About It...

What are the predominant industries in your area? Choose one industry and determine how firms in the industry benefit from clustering together in your area (localization economies). Is there a source of qualified labor? Other inexpensive inputs? A research center?

Check the yellow pages of your telephone book. What business services can firms in your city find that are not available in smaller cities? Examples of such business services are accounting and bookkeeping services, business consultants, advertising specialists, copy centers, trucking companies, specialized janitorial firms, business records storage, architects, or specialists in business litigation and transactional law (urbanization economies).

If none of these categories seem to fit a large local firm, find out where the owner grew up.

Firms locating in proximity trigger two types of **agglomeration economies**: localization and urbanization. **Localization economies** decrease the cost of production for every firm in a *specific industry* that locates within an area. **Urbanization economies** decrease the cost of production for every firm that locates in a particular city, *regardless of industry*. Both localization and urbanization economies influence labor supply, specialized resources, and technological spillovers. In addition, clusters of firms in cities potentially increase product demand, thereby allowing urban firms to benefit from internal economies of scale. Firms within such agglomerations benefit from a lower cost of doing business or an increase in their creativity.

Mickey Mouse and Agglomeration Economies

Theme parks generally group together to take advantage of retail agglomeration economies. The presence of several sources of entertainment in an area will supposedly decrease the time and travel costs for consumers, and thereby increase sales for all of the theme parks in that area. If this were true, theme parks would be complementary goods.

Localization economies in production exist in central Florida because the theme parks have access to a large number of experienced entertainers. In addition, Disney's national advertising generates external benefits by increasing the pool of visitors. Because of this, new entrants into the industry will be more successful if they locate close to a dominant firm and if they offer a large number of activities.

However, Braun and Milman (1990) found that theme parks in central Florida are really substitute goods. The degree of substitutability of a theme park decreases both with distance and with the number of attributes offered in the alternate park. Take the case of Walt Disney World: this giant has created spillover benefits for the less prestigious parks. Two reasons explain this phenomenon. First, over 78 percent of the tourists who drive and 72 percent of those who fly to central Florida to attend a theme park have been to the area before. For them, the entertainment industry has a more price elastic demand, because once they visit Walt Disney World, the other parks can offer a few hours of leisure for a lower admission price. Second, because of similar events in each park, groups and families are likely to consider an alternative as long as it offers enough activities to interest everyone.

Braun and Milman (1990)

Localization Economies

Alfred Marshall (1920) identified three types of externalities generated by spatially concentrated firms. First, a cluster of firms in the same industry attracts a **pool of specialized labor**. Second, a large enough cluster generates a market that sustains **specialized firms** that focus on only one facet of the production process. These specialists lower the production costs for the other local firms of that industry. Finally, firms in the area can benefit from sharing ideas or **technological spillovers**.

Pools of Specialized Labor

Easy access to specialized labor as well as the formal and informal communication between specialists motivates firms to cluster. Firms' access to knowledgeable employees lowers the costs of on-the-job training and heightens productivity. The increase in productivity boosts wages, which entices professionals who are even more qualified. New employers drawn to the area because of a competitive labor pool, often must poach labor away from other firms, again increasing local wages.[1]

A large concentration of skilled professionals increases access to specialized training. Workers invest more readily in industry-specific human capital if they have a future in that industry. Firms that produce related products use employees with similar skills. If the business cycles of related industries are not correlated, area workers will be better off than those outside of the area because the likelihood that a worker will be unemployed for very long is reduced.

As we mentioned before, the effects of formal and informal communication between specialized workers benefit all firms because it is essential for innovation. Informal conversations are an important source of up-to-date information about competitors, customers' wants, new trends in technology, and the industry overall. Social relationships and even gossips become a crucial aspect of doing business. Specialists who do the same work but for different firms may have trained together and probably move in the same social circles. They naturally talk shop with one another, and thereby help one another solve technical problems. By helping their friends, they in turn find out what the competition is doing.[2]

Specialized Resources

A second type of localization economy takes place when access to and communication with owners of specialized nonlabor resources is possible. Thus, firms locate next to one another to minimize transportation costs. Those that locate next a supplier of inputs

---

[1] Fujita and Thisse (1997).
[2] Oakey and Cooper (1989); Saxenian (1996); Fujita and Thisse (1997).

take advantage of **backward linkages** (or firms that produce **upstream products**). Enterprises that locate next to their market take advantage of **forward linkages** (or firms that produce **downstream products**).

Industries for which a backward linkage is primary include food processing, shoe and leather glove factories, clothing producers, and paper mills: the output is less expensive to ship than the input. Industries that gain from forward linkages include textile mills, saw mills, typesetters, steel mills and foundries, shipbuilders, machine shops, communications equipment, cement, scientific professional equipment, and signs and displays.[3]

A proximity to backward and forward linkages is important first of all because it encourages firms to engage in face-to-face communication. A noted psychologist, Albert Mehrabian (1972), estimated that 7% of total communication involves the dictionary definitions of words; 38% involves the way that these words are pronounced; and 55% of communication comes these from facial expression and body language. It is impossible discern body language over telephone or through e-mail. Face-to-face contact is the driving force behind the spatial concentration of office firms. It establishes trust between firms. Thus, trust is built by learning about the idiosyncrasies of the individuals involved through interactions.[4]

By clustering, firms also decrease transportation costs. Not all of a firm's inputs or outputs reach their destination because of Samuelson's (1983) iceberg phenomenon that we discussed in Chapter 4. Firms decrease transportation costs by locating next to their suppliers and adopting a just in time (JIT) method of managing inventories. Toyota Motor Corporation of Japan started practicing the JIT inventory system in the 1950s to eliminate warehousing costs. Geographic proximity decreases the response time of parts suppliers so that inputs can be supplied to a factory almost immediately.

The JIT inventory system attempts not only to eliminate waste, but to also remove safety nets that firms count on to minimize mistakes and calamities that befall individual suppliers. On the other hand, firms that provide parts at a moment's notice need strict quality control to minimize the number of defective parts. These firms become vulnerable and must depend on the loyalty of their sole buyer.

Strikes or natural disasters at one plant harm the entire system. According to Kremer's (1993) O-Ring Theory of Economic Development, any network is only as strong as its weakest link. Just as faulty O-rings caused the crash of

---

[3] Oksanen and Williams (1984).
[4] Harrison (1992); Mun and Yoshikawa (1993).

New Epoch for the Jurassien Arc

The Jura region of Switzerland is an old region with strong industrial traditions in horology. Small- and medium-sized firms specializing in watchmaking have long dominated the region. For thirty years (1945-1975), a rigid, hierarchical structure caused its stagnation. This industry structure survived because of a product standardization which lead to a decline in the need for skilled labor. Repetition and high productivity became the primary objective in producing mechanical watches. The intense competition pushed firms to become over-specialized: entire firms focused on one action, like mounting precious stones in the watch works.

But starting in 1975, competitors from Japan, Germany, and Hong Kong adopted the new quartz technology and watchmaking components became extremely price-elastic. A one cent difference in price was enough to lose a sale, and the Swiss horology industry plunged. Skilled workers migrated to the United States. Long-standing localization economies had resulted in unduly structured production rules that led to inefficiency.

Thanks to new technology introduced in the mid 1970s, a microtechnology industry emerged from the Swiss watchmaking cluster. This industry specializes in micromechanic and microelectric products like photo equipment, sensors of all types, and medical equipment such as endoscopes. Most workers in these firms came from watchmaking. The mingling of two industries increased production in both. The remaining horologists concentrated on producing fashion watches. By 1980, Switzerland produced 29 percent of the quantity and 35 percent of the total world revenue in watches. By 1991, the Swiss watch industry supplied only 15 percent of the quantity but attracted 53 percent of world sales revenues. The rigidities of the past have been replaced by an efficient decentralization strong enough to withstand yet another horological assault:

around 2003, the Chinese started exporting inexpensive watches and by 2005, China exported 56 percent of the world's watches, but attracted 10 percent of the global sales revenue, while the Swiss supplied only 2 percent of the world's watches for 50 percent of the revenues.

Maillat and Léchot (1992), Crevoisier (1994),
Young (1999), and Glasmeier (2000),
Federation of the Swiss Watch industry (2006)

the Space Shuttle Challenger in 1986, inefficient firms within a JIT organization decrease the quality of final output if firms cannot benefit from the free competition among suppliers.

How JIT Saved Harley–Davidson

Cost decreases experienced by Japanese competitors who practiced JIT drove Harley–Davidson to the verge of bankruptcy. Harley–Davidson lobbied for a temporary trade barrier. While the barrier was in place, Harley-Davidson also adopted JIT. The JIT inventory system contributed to Harley–Davidson's recovery and reemergence as a strong competitor on the international market.

(Huh, 1994)

Face-to-Face Communication in the Financial Sector

Pryke and Lee (1995) are convinced that the Internet will not undermine international financial centers like the City of London. Electronic communication cannot execute the essential communication and interpretation needed in the finance industry. Creating networks of contacts between employees of diverse firms is a crucial part of the work in financial centers. In effect, individuals are constantly being reassessed regarding their trustworthiness, status, and the possibility of becoming prospective partners.

Financial market participants need information quickly

To create a new financial instrument, a firm must simultaneously design and package the product while gauging interest among potential customers. Face-to-face contact permits the agent to tone down a marketing pitch that is too aggressive. Aggressive marketing raises suspicions about the true risk of a new instrument.

Once a product is launched, it is necessary to continue the social contacts (invitations to lunch or for a drink). Informal meetings allow everyone to judge each other by their body language and voice inflections, and permit a more accurate assessment of the speaker on the telephone. These encounters reinforce the feeling of trust among traders in financial centers. Financial markets rely heavily on trust, so face-to-face contacts are *sine qua non*.

Pryke and Lee (1995)

Producer Services

Firms either within or outside of a cluster might prefer to subcontract (outsource) different production steps rather than hire employees to do the work. Outsourcing will be cost effective if the outsourced process benefits from scale economies or lower input prices (especially wages and fringe benefits).

Both Prayers and Technology Jobs Outsourced to India

Outsourcing of IT jobs to technology centers in Bangalore, India is explained by their inexpensive, skilled labor. However, technology is not the only service being outsourced. Because of the shortage of Roman Catholic clergy in North America and Europe, the Vatican, bishops, and religious orders often send requests via e-mail to Kerala, located southeast of Bangalore.

Each mass is said in Malayalam, the local language, in front of a public congregation. During mass, the prayer for the soul of the deceased relative, a sick friend, a newly baptized baby, or the thanksgiving for a favor received is announced. Most of the requests from the United States include donations from $5 to $10 (about 220 to 440 Indian rupees) while prayers for locals average about 40 rupees. To spread the wealth, bishops in Kerala limit the priests to just one mass a day. Such outsourcing has been going on for decades and has only been controversial recently because of the corporate outsourcing of IT jobs from the West.

Newindpress (2004), Sify (2004)

By subcontracting, (1) firms avoid the relatively high cost of an underused specialist, (2) firms avoid investing in costly but rarely used equipment, (3) firms are not affected by technology changes nor with potential changes in regulation and environmental standards associated with that one aspect of production.[5]

Capital Markets

Industry-specific information in an area where many firms of that industry aggregate provides all firms with easier access to capital markets. Bankers who specifically deal with certain industries are more likely lend to a firm than are bankers who are not industry experts.

Technological Spillovers

Technological spillovers, sometimes called technological externalities, stimulate innovation. **Innovation** involves the creation, development, and distribution of an invention, whereas, according to Schumpeter, **imitation** ensures that benefits from this innovation are maximized for all society. Face-to-face contact is again important to gain access to information and feedback about ideas and to quickly adopt the new technology.

Poaching skilled labor from competitors is one way to benefit from knowledge spillovers. Regions dominated by large firms owning branch production plants are less likely to have the exchange of information, the research and development, and state-of-the-art technology. Fewer spin-off firms survive where large companies have contracts to buy and sell.

Innovation takes place more easily in small firms that subcontract nonexclusively with one another. Small firms operate on an efficient network of forward and backward linkages and thus lower production

---

[5] Chon (1996).

costs. Competition pushes these clusters of firms to increase their capability and their drive to innovate. Poaching skilled labor from competitors is one way to benefit from knowledge spillovers.

This situation does not exist in regions dominated by large firms and where production is limited to standardized goods. The large firms are more apt to have the same exchange of information, the research and development, and state-of-the-art technology. Innovation is not a priority because of their standardized goods. A climate of false confidence leads the large firms to think that the competition is dormant, giving birth to a Rust Belt.

How Far Does a Technological Spillover Spill?

Krugman (1991b) wondered: How far does a technological spillover spill? Determining the distance that knowledge flows is difficult because there is no paper trail. Anselin, Varga, and Acs (1997) looked at data for 43 states and 125 metropolitan statistical areas in the United States and determine that a university research center increases innovation in private firms within fifty miles, but the private innovation does not influence university research and development activities. Based on Austrian data, Fischer and Varga (2003) noted the negative effect of distance on the dissemination of ideas. These authors also found that factual knowledge travels farther than intuitive knowledge common to people of the same culture (in the largest sense of the word.)

Rosenthal and Strange (2003) found that the effect of localization economies in the first mile is from 10 to 1000 times larger than the effect two to five miles away. Beyond five miles, the decrease in localization economies (as measured by industry employment) is less evident.

Head, Ries, and Swenson (1995) asked about the spillover of cultural knowledge by studying Japanese firms that located in the United States. Physical proximity decreases the cost of casual conversation. Japanese industrial groups (*keiretsu*) have formal agreements between suppliers of inputs and buyers of their output. They note that the Japanese firms do not mimic the geographical pattern of the U.S. firms. Initial investments by Japanese firms in one industrial *keiretsu* attract Japanese firms from the same group to locate nearby. The geographic extent of manufacturing agglomeration goes just slightly beyond state borders. One state becomes more attractive because of increases in Japanese industrial activity in neighboring states.

Krugman (1991b), Head, Ries, and Swenson (1995), Anselin, Varga, and Acs (1997), Maurseth and Verspagen (2002), Fischer and Varga (2003), Rosenthal and Strange (2003)

Foxy Lemmings?

Small firms who want to take advantage of localization economies will sometimes locate in an area just because other small firms prosper there. In essence, firms start up where firms start up. The logic of this strategy assumes that entrepreneurs are risk-averse. Knowledge mitigates risk, but searching for answers to the appropriate questions is costly.

Young firms must make prudent locational choices to survive. Pascal and McCall (1980) compare these young firms to swimmers in the ocean: "Adrift in a sea of uncertainty, what could be more logical than heading toward those islands which have demonstrably provided salvation to similar and earlier swimmers?"

Pascal and McCall (1980)

Urbanization Economies

Urbanization economies are the advantages connected with the size of an urban area, regardless of the industry involved. Benefits from urbanization also reflect Marshall's three external economies: (1) access to specialized labor, (2) access to other resources, and (3) technological spillovers.

Specialized Labor

Urbanization economies come from the "Law of Large Numbers." Sales of output and purchases of inputs fluctuate for many firms because of seasonal, cyclical, or even random events. In an urban area, the workers are better off. The agglomeration of firms reduces the likelihood that they will have a long bout of unemployment—*if* they are willing and able to change industries. In addition, their spouses have fewer problems finding employment in a large city. An area with many employers has a better probability of keeping a labor force fully employed than one with few companies.[6]

Further, urbanization decreases labor costs because special services are more easily accessible there than in rural areas. A rural manufacturing firm may need to operate its own fleet of trucks to deliver its product to the market. If so, the owners of the firm have to be cognizant of the regulations concerning not only their own products, but also intrastate and interstate trucking. Keeping current on trucking rules represents a loss of time that the owners could use to further their own production.

The firm may also need to hire a mechanic if there is no one locally who specializes in maintaining large trucks. The company mechanic would have to stay on track of the latest technological and regulatory changes. Unless the manufacturing firm is extremely large, the mechanic will not have enough work to stay in the garage full time. That employee will be a part-time mechanic—a part-time assembly line worker, thereby underemployed, given the specialized training.[7]

Specialized Resources

Cities also provide a greater number of public services and more adequate infrastructure. For example, urban areas offer wastewater processing upfront, something that a rural area simply cannot afford. Larger cities can provide better infrastructure such as adequate water supply and sanitation facilities, quality roads, and fire and police protection at a lower average cost than can rural areas.

Readily available financing makes urban areas more attractive. Urban banks send to diverse investment projects. If a project fails, the bank repossesses the asset. Banks are more willing to lend in urban areas because the second-best use of a unique piece of real estate in a large city is more valuable than in a small city. In the large city, the range of possible uses for atypical building specifications is higher. Because there are more ways to reprocess failed projects, assets in large cities have a greater salvage value. The increased salvage values mean more collateral, decreasing the

---

[6] Goldstein and Gronberg (1984).
[7] Goldstein and Gronberg (1984).

risk of an individual loan. Because of the lower risk levels, urban bankers will undertake projects that would be too risky in smaller, rural towns.[8]

Technological Spillovers

New products are the outcome of the process of "novelty by combination," that is, random collisions of technical possibilities and consumer needs. The sheer variety of goods in a city generates ideas for even more products outside the same industries. A series of videos titled "***Connections***," written and produced by science historian James Burke, chronicles many innovations generated from seemingly unconnected inventions. (See Burke's website at http://www.k-web.org).[9]

Diseconomies of Agglomeration

Empirical studies corroborate the hypothesis that city workers are more productive than those in the rural areas. Productivity levels and thus incomes are higher in large cities because new technologies benefit the urban firms first. Workers learn more quickly from nearby practitioners than from books or the Internet, thus new technology spreads more quickly in an area with skilled workers.[10]

But here is a paradox: an urban location is much more efficient for firms. Productivity is higher and the effect of innovations is much more powerful. The variety provided in larger centers boosts the consumers' utility functions. Given this, why does the world not just turn into one giant city?[11]

Diseconomies of urbanization predominate if cities are too big. These ***diseconomies of agglomeration*** become a centrifugal force, repelling economic agents from one another. Congestion increases transportation costs. Influxes of people and firms all bid for land, increasing its price. More smokestacks coupled with escalating traffic increase pollution. Large numbers of newcomers lower the probability that criminals will get caught, causing a higher crime rate. When the increases in costs due to congestion, pollution, land rents, and crime cancel the cost savings due to agglomeration economies, firms leave.

---

[8] Helsley and Strange (1991).

[9] Karlsson (1997).

[10] See Moomaw (1985); Sveikauskas, Gowdy, and Funk (1988); Eaton and Eckstein (1997); Lee and Zang (1998) for example.

[11] Goldstein and Gronberg (1984).

Which Type of Agglomeration Is Profitable for Whom?

Do industries benefit more from localization or urbanization economies? Lee and Zang (1998) concluded that localization economies are important for Korean manufacturers, but these industries receive little benefit from urbanization economies. Henderson (1986) also determined that localization economies prevail for US and Brazilian firms, and urbanization economies have little effect.

Moomaw (1988) estimated that the food and apparel industries only benefit from urbanization economies, whereas paper products, stone, clay, and glass, and fabricated metals only profit from localization economies. Chemicals and primary metals also benefit from localization economies, but they are worse off if they locate in cities. Urban diseconomies force out heavy industries that rely on unprocessed materials, and produce output that is either bulky to ship or that pollutes. Finally, the printing, plastics, and electrical machinery industries benefit from both localization and urbanization economies. These flourish in cities with industry clusters.

Henderson (1986), Lee and Zang (1998), and Moomaw (1988)

Accidents, History, and Circular and Cumulative Causality

Clusters can be caused by an accident of history or by a self-fulfilling prophecy. Whatever the reason a firm locates in an area, once clusters are established, increasing returns along with localization and urbanization economies will cause the clustering to persist even when the original reason for that location is no longer there. An example of *circular causality* is in the box entitled ***Foxy Lemmings***. Firms want to locate where similar firms have located. Growth brings agglomeration economies that in turn foster growth.[12]

---

[12] David (1985); Krugman (1991a); Fujita and Mori (1996); Venables (1996).

In addition, economic development may be irreversible because of the hypothesis of **cumulative causality** (Myrdal, 1939). Fujita and Mori (1996) point out that Chicago and Paris were initially port cities. Even though cheap access to water is no longer important, both cities continue to prosper because of a chain of self-reinforcing events that locked in the agglomeration effects. Cumulative causality also works in reverse. If key firms leave an agglomeration, reversing the actions that caused the flight will not necessarily bring the firms back once they trigger a new agglomeration elsewhere.[13]

The Death of a Steel Mill

Strohmeyer (1985) details the demise of steelmaking in Lackawanna, New York in 1983. In the 1960s, Bethlehem Steel Company built a new steel mill at Burns Harbor, Indiana. However, increases in imports and competition from non-unionized minimills started to hurt the traditional steel companies. To solve the problem of excess capacity, Bethlehem Steel was forced to close one of its plants. The closure decision was made on the basis of labor problems and property tax rates.

Labor hostility at the Lackawanna plant was infamous. According to Strohmeyer, more labor grievances were filed in that plant than in all other Bethlehem plants combined. For instance, one grievance cited the plant for flying a flag with 48 stars the day after Hawaii was admitted to the union. A union worker once filed a grievance for four extra hours of pay because a manager carried a board across the room. The work rules at that plant were not flexible enough to allow that plant to be as technologically efficient as necessary to survive.

In addition to the labor problems, twice the city officials in Lackawanna had arbitrarily increased property taxes on that plant. Strohmeyer alleges that the Lackawanna branch paid more than five times the average amount of property tax per ton of steel than the five other major Bethlehem plants together. Bethlehem Steel paid as much as 73 percent of the total property taxes of the city of Lackawanna.

---

[13] Fujita and Mori (1996); Venables (1996).

After the plant closed, the city agreed that the property tax assessment was unfair and cut taxes from $17 million to $2.5 million, yet Bethlehem did not reopen the Lackawanna plant. In addition, local employers refused to hire the unemployed steelworkers who had a history of poor work habits.

Strohmeyer (1985)

Utility Maximization and Plant Location

Entrepreneurs who maximize their own utilities locate in areas with pleasant scenery, lovely parks and recreational facilities or other amenities, and accept a lower than normal profit to do so. Perhaps an "accident of history" was not really an accident. Many studies that have surveyed entrepreneurs asked why they chose their location. A majority of responses include the personal preference of the founder. For example, the natural resources found in Hershey, Pennsylvania did not lower costs of making chocolate for Milton Hershey, the founder of Hershey's Chocolate Factory. His family was from Lancaster, Pennsylvania, just south of Hershey.

Greenhut (1971) adds *psychic income* and personal preferences as possible factors for firm location. Some entrepreneurs start a business to maximize their psychic incomes (utilities), not their taxable incomes. From this premise, Greenhut demonstrates that the imperfectly competitive firms can be just as efficient as perfectly competitive ones.

In the long run, perfectly competitive firms produce that quantity where the marginal cost equals marginal revenue at the minimum of the average cost curve, as Figure 5.1 shows. The perfectly competitive model is the economist's utopia because it is allocatively and technically efficient. Consumers pay only the marginal cost of producing the last item demonstrating allocative efficiency. They are also paying the lowest possible cost to produce the item, proving technical efficiency. Firms are only making a normal profit and there is no excess capacity. All firms, in the long run, are the most efficient size because they are producing at the minimum of the average cost curve.

Both distance and increasing returns to scale produce imperfect competition. Under imperfect competition, firms face downward-sloping demand curves. Their marginal revenue (MR) is always higher than the marginal cost, and firms can neither produce nor price at the lowest point on the average

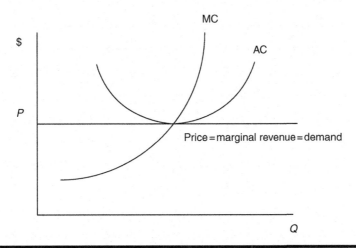

Figure 5.1   Perfectly competitive firm in long-run equilibrium.

cost curve. An example of the cost and demand curves of an imperfect competitor in long-run equilibrium is shown in Figure 5.2. The firm produces the quantity where MR=MC, and determines the price from the demand curve. This firm is only making a normal rate of return because the price is equal to the average cost of producing the optimal quantity Q^*.

Cost functions cover the direct costs of production plus a "normal" rate of return. The normal rate of return includes compensation sufficient to cover

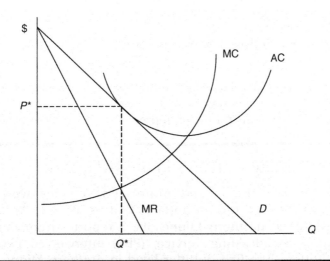

Figure 5.2   Imperfect competitor with normal profit.

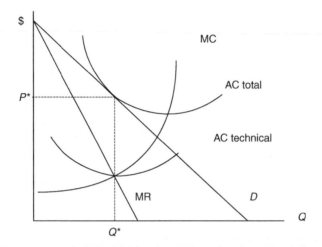

Figure 5.3 Technical average cost and total average cost curves of imperfect competitor. (Printed with permission from Melvin L. Greenhut.)

the opportunity costs of the entrepreneurs. The normal rate of return must also compensate the entrepreneurs for the amount of risk they undertake for investing in a small business rather than something less precarious.

Greenhut suggests a division of the imperfect competitor's cost curve into two components: a **technical cost curve**, which covers all the direct costs (accounting costs) of production, and a curve showing **opportunity cost**. Opportunity costs include:

- Compensation for risk.
- Income that the entrepreneurs would have earned in their next best alternative.
- Adjustment for psychic income.

The result is shown in Figure 5.3. In the long run, the technical average cost curve will reach a minimum at the quantity where MC = MR. We assume that the opportunity costs for the entrepreneurs are fixed costs rather than

Utility vs. Profits in the Wilderness

When motorboats and motorized vehicles were banned from the Boundary Waters Canoe Area (BWCA) in northern Minnesota, a reporter from the Public Broadcasting Service, (PBS) interviewed two outfitters. The first outfitter lived in northern Minnesota his entire life. His investment in motorboats was significant. He could do nothing but moan and grumble about how unfair the ban was and about his imminent loss of income and potential bankruptcy.

The second outfitter was a couple that came from the East Coast. They both left high-pressure jobs with six-digit salaries for the peace and tranquility of rustic living in the Boundary Waters. The second outfitter seemed therefore genuinely relieved that motorized vehicles and motorboats would be banned, and foresaw no possibility of bankruptcy. The decrease in household income that the second outfitter was willing to forego is one measure of psychic income—the dollar value of the increase in utility from the new location.

---

variable costs. This makes sense if opportunity costs do not change with the quantity of output that the firm produces. An increase in fixed costs slides the average cost curve up the marginal cost curve.

By splitting the average cost curve in this fashion, we find that in equilibrium the firm is efficient because output is at the minimum of the technical average cost curve and the compensation to entrepreneurs is just the amount necessary to keep the firm in business. A person's opportunity cost and valuation of psychic income are subjective. Entrepreneurs with lower opportunity costs will gladly enter this market, thereby decreasing the demand curve for the established firms. With entry, some established entrepreneurs will determine that the location is no longer profitable for them and they will leave the local industry.

Eventually, entrepreneurs with the same opportunity cost, taste for risk, and psychic income will run similar industries because of this market-driven self-selection mechanism. For example, wildcatters who live for the excitement of finding oil or SWAT team members who crave the adrenaline rush of raiding and combating drug lords will not do well debugging computer programs day after day. Saxenian (1996) reported that executives of high-tech industries in Silicon Valley wore clothes and supported an ambiance much less formal than their counterparts along Route 128 in Boston preferred.

Summary and Conclusions

In a spatial setting, agglomeration economies divide themselves into localization and urbanization economies. Localization economies affect clusters of firms within the same industry and within the same area. Urbanization economies shape clusters of firms in the same city, regardless of industry. The externalities come from the accessibility and communication among three major sources: large pools of specialized labor, specialized resources, and technological spillovers. Agglomeration acts as a centripetal force, pulling firms and consumers toward an urban location.

As cities grow, the forces of agglomeration are met with opposing forces of dispersion. Urban growth creates congestion, longer commutes, more crime, and pollution. When the increased costs of locating in the city negate the benefits, firms and people will move. Diseconomies of agglomeration act as a centrifugal force repelling economic activity away from the city.

Circular causality and cumulative causality can sustain an industry cluster that started up because of random chance, an accident, or history rather than because of any savings in production costs or access to markets. Once the agglomerations take root, they may become irreversible.

Greenhut's theory allows entrepreneurs to maximize utility rather than just monetary profits. They forgo accounting profits in lieu of psychic income. In this theory, the technical costs of production are separated from the opportunity costs of the entrepreneur. When an industry is in long-run equilibrium, production will be at an output level coincident with the minimum of the technical cost curve and entrepreneurs will be compensated at the minimum amount required to keep them in business.

Increasing returns, economies of agglomeration, and cumulative causality form the foundation of the new theory of endogenous growth. This long-run growth theory revolutionized ideas concerning economic development. In Chapter 8, we will further explore the impact that the theory of endogenous growth has on regional economies.

Chapter Questions

1. Differentiate between localization and urbanization economies. Give examples of each in your city. Justify your classification.
2. What is the largest industry in your area in terms of employment? What forward or backward linkages could that industry have responded to when firms located there? For what other industries is this industry a forward linkage? For what industries is it a backward linkage?
3. Explain Greenhut's argument that imperfectly competitive firms can be as efficient as perfectly competitive firms.
   a. Use a graph to substantiate your argument.
   b. How can this argument be used as an economic development tool for the area that you are studying?

Research Assignments

1. Might your metropolitan area be prone to diseconomies of agglomeration? To justify your response:
   a. Check the American Chamber of Commerce Research Associates (ACCRA) Cost of Living Index in your library to compare the index of housing prices with those of other metropolitan areas.
   b. Compare violent crime reports for your city or county with that of the nation through the Uniform Crime Reports or your state's Bureau of Criminal Apprehension.
   c. Search the EPA's site for environmental information about your community at http://www.epa.gov/epahome/whereyoulive.htm.
2. Explore the economic history of your city. What were the first major employers to locate in your city? What industries followed? Do they seem to have located because of forward or backward linkages? Which may have been more important—localization or urbanization economies?

Appendix Location under Uncertainty

Uncertainty poses its own dilemma for entrepreneurs. Of course, they may maximize expected profits, and the analysis will be similar to what we have done thus far; but location decisions are often more complicated.

Risk and uncertainty are distinct concepts because risk involves objective probabilities. A chain with many franchises may be able to determine the objective probability of a certain profit level. However, the expected profit for most location decisions depends on subjective probabilities for which situations are all different. These figures are grounded as firmly as possible in estimates, but the estimates depend on some *state of nature* over which the decision maker has no control—the economic business cycle, the stability of world politics, and input price fluctuations, for example.

Say for instance that a firm is considering four sites, each with a different expected profit level for the next 5 years depending on whether the nation is in a recession, experiencing moderate growth, or a significant expansion. As we will show in Chapter 7, regions respond differently depending on the reaction of the dominant industries to the national economy. A firm may benefit from lower wages during economic expansions if the industries of the surrounding firms are counter-cyclic, or face higher wages during recessions. On the other hand, if the firm is located in an area dominated by pro-cyclic industries, it would encounter the opposite pattern.

Table 5A.1 shows a hypothetical payoff matrix for our firm. Profits corresponding to each of the four sites will be different according to the

Table 5A.1 Payoff Matrix (in Millions)

	Recession	Moderate Growth	Boom
Site 1	60	40	25
Site 2	30	45	60
Site 3	20	50	70
Site 4	20	67	30

national business cycle. The columns correspond to each of the three states of nature: recession, moderate growth, and significant expansion. The rows show the expected profits in each of the four potential sites under each state of nature.

The first thing that our decision maker would want to determine is the probability that each of these states of nature might occur in the next 5 years. If the decision maker had no idea, the final choice might be the site where the average payoff would be highest. This Laplace Criterion is equivalent to assigning the same probability to each state of nature. As Table 5A.2 shows, Site 3 would provide the highest average payoff.

The decision maker will choose a different site, however, under a hunch that the economy is headed for recession and that the probability of recession is 50%, the probability of moderate growth is 40%, and the probability of a boom is 10%. The Bayesian Criterion depends on a weighted average of the probabilities that each state of nature will occur. The sum of the assigned probabilities must equal 100%. The decision maker will choose the site with the maximum weighted average payoff, given by $E(X) = \sum_{i=1}^{n} p_i X_i$, where i signifies each state of nature, p_i is the probability that each state of nature will occur, and X_i is the payoff associated with each state of nature.

The Bayesian payoff for Site 1 in Table 5A.3 is calculated as follows: $0.5 \times 60 + 0.4 \times 40 + 0.1 \times 25 = 48.50$. Because Site 1 has the greatest profitability during recessions, the weighted payoff for this site is larger than for any other site in the payoff table. Decision makers facing the same payoffs

Table 5A.2 Laplace (Equal Probability) Payoff Matrix (in Millions)

	Recession	Moderate Growth	Boom	Average Payoff
Site 1	60	40	25	41.67
Site 2	30	45	60	45.00
Site 3	*20*	*50*	*70*	*46.67*
Site 4	20	67	30	39.00

Table 5A.3 Bayesian (Weighted Probability) Payoff Matrix (in Millions)

	Recession (50% Probability)	Moderate Growth (40% Probability)	Boom (10% Probability)	Weighed Payoff
Site 1	*60*	*40*	*25*	*48.50*
Site 2	30	45	60	39.00
Site 3	20	50	70	37.00
Site 4	20	67	30	39.80

but who assign a higher probability to an economic boom or moderate growth will choose Site 3 or Site 4 over Site 1, according to this criterion.

Other criteria exist for decision makers who do not try to determine the probabilities of each state of nature. For instance, a pessimistic decision maker would be interested in following the ***Maximin Criterion***. Decision makers who prefer this criterion choose the site where the maximum payoff would be the best of the worst possible results. For Site 1, the worst will be a gain of 25; 30 for Site 2; and 20 for Site 3 and Site 4. Rather than lose sleep worrying if a recession will happen that would exclude the possibility of meeting other obligations and goals at the lowest possible profit, Site 2 is preferred. Site 2 has the best of the worst possible gains; it will be a relatively safe decision (Table 5A.4).

Some entrepreneurs may prefer a ***Maximax Criterion*** and will choose the site with the largest possible payoff. Because Site 3 provides the largest payoff, the optimistic, risk-loving Maximax entrepreneur will choose Site 3.

Finally, those decision makers who are hyperpessimists can minimize their fears by choosing their site according to a ***Minimax Regret Criterion***. By this criterion, the decision maker determines the potential regret associated with each decision and will choose the site that will give the minimum possible regret. The decision maker who follows this strategy first transforms the payoff matrix into a regret matrix.

Table 5A.4 Payoff Matrix (in Millions)

	Recession	Moderate Growth	Boom
Site 1	60	40	25
Site 2 (Maximin)	30	45	60
Site 3 (Maximax)	20	50	70
Site 4	20	67	30

Table 5A.5 Regret Matrix (in Millions)

	Recession	Moderate Growth	Boom
Site 1	0	27	45
Site 2	30	22	10
Site 3	40	17	0
Site 4	40	0	40

In constructing the regret matrix (Table 5A.5), the pessimist decides that if a recession will be the state of nature, Site 1 provides the maximum payoff of $60 million. Thus, if the decision maker is located at Site 1 just before a recession, the regret would be zero (60–60). However, if Site 2 were chosen, the regret would be 30 (60–30). Likewise, the regret associated with Site 3 would be 40, and at Site 4 it would be 25.

Under the state of nature corresponding to moderate growth, the optimal location (and consequently the location with no regret) would be Site 4. Site 1 would be associated with a regret of 27 (67–40); 22 for Site 2 (67–45); and Site 3 is associated with a 17 amount of regret (67–50). Similarly, during an economic expansion, the decision maker would have no regrets had Site 3 been chosen, but a regret of 45, 10, and 40 for Site 1, Site 2, and Site 4, respectively.

Once the regret matrix is constructed, the decision maker identifies the maximum potential regret for each decision: for Site 1, the maximum potential regret is 45; 30 for Site 2; and 40 for Site 3 and Site 4. Thus, to minimize the maximum regret, this decision maker will choose Site 2.

In summary, although most firms do locate to maximize profits, an uncertain future leads decision makers to choose sites according to subjective or behavioral criteria. In the example, a person who follows the Laplace criteria assigns equal probabilities for each state of nature and chooses the site with the largest average payoff (Site 3). Entrepreneurs who subjectively believe that a specific state of nature will occur will put more emphasis on payoffs associated with the state of nature that they foresee. In our example, if the recession has a higher probability, Site 1 is preferred; if moderate growth, it is Site 4; if an economic boom, Site 3. Site 2 is the ideal place for those who adopt a Maximin criterion because this site has the best among the worst possible payoffs (30 million). Optimists who are of a Maximax nature prefer Site 3 because it has the maximum possible payoff. Finally, the Minimax decision makers who worry about the stress associated with decisions prefer Site 2, which procures the lowest maximum regret.

References

Anselin, L., A. Varga, and Z. Acs. 1997. Local geographic spillovers between university research and high technology innovations. *Journal of Urban Economics* 42 (3):422–448.

Braun, B. M., and A. Milman. 1990. Localization economies in the theme park industry. *Review of Regional Studies* 20 (3):33–37.

Chon, S. 1996. Small and medium-sized enterprises in the republic of Korea: implications for the development of technology-intensive industries. *Small Business Economics* 8 (2):107–120.

Crevoisier, O. 1994. Dynamique industrielle et dynamique régionale: l'articulation par les milieux innovateurs. *Revue d'Economie Industrielle* 0 (70):33–48.

David, P. A. 1985. Clio and the economics of QWERTY. *American Economic Review* 75 (2):332–337.

Eaton, J., and Z. Eckstein. 1997. Cities and growth: theory and evidence from France and Japan. *Regional Science and Urban Economics* 27 (4–5):443–474.

Federation of the Swiss watch industry. 2006. The Swiss and world watchmaking industry in 2005. http://www.fhs.ch/statistics/watchmaking_2005.pdf, accessed 18 November 2006.

Fischer, M. M., and A. Varga. 2003. Spatial knowledge spillovers and university research: evidence from Austria. *Annals of Regional Science* 37 (2):303–322.

Fujita, M., and T. Mori. 1996. The role of ports in the making of major cities: self-agglomeration and hub-effect. *Journal of Development Economics* 49 (1):93–120.

Fujita, M., and J.-F. Thisse. 1997. Economie géographique, problèmes anciens et nouvelles perspectives. *Annales d'Economie et de Statistique* 0 (45):37–87.

Fudenberg, D., and J. Tirole. 1991. *Game Theory*, Cambridge, MA: MIT Press.

Glasmeier, A. K. 2000. *Manufacturing Time: Global Competition in the Watch Industry* 1795–2000. Perspectives on economic change, New York: Guilford Press.

Goldstein, G. S., and T. J. Gronberg. 1984. Economies of scope and economies of agglomeration. *Journal of Urban Economics* 16 (1):91–104.

Greenhut, M. L. 1971. *A Theory of the Firm in Economic Space*, Austin, TX: Lone Star Publishers, Inc./Austin Press, Educational Division.

Harrison, L. E. 1992. *Who Prospers? How Cultural Values Shape Economic and Political Success*, New York: Harper Collins/Basic Books.

Head, K., J. Ries, and D. Swenson. 1995. Agglomeration benefits and location choice: evidence from Japanese manufacturing investments in the United States. *Journal of International Economics* 38 (3–4):223–247.

Helsley, R. W., and W. C. Strange. 1991. Agglomeration economies and urban capital markets. *Journal of Urban Economics* 29 (1):96–112.

Henderson, J. V. 1986. Urbanization in a developing country: city size and population composition. *Journal of Development Economics* 22 (2):269–293.

Huh, C. 1994. Just in time inventory management: has it made a difference? *FRBSF Weekly Letter Number* 94 (18).

Karlsson, C. 1997. Product development, innovation networks, infrastructure and agglomeration economies. *Annals of Regional Science* 31 (3):235–258.

Kremer, M. 1993. The O-ring theory of economic development. *Quarterly Journal of Economics* 108 (3):551–575.

Krugman, P. 1991a. *Geography and trade*, Gaston Eyskens Lecture Series. Cambridge, MA/Louvain, Belgium: MIT Press/Louvain University Press.

Krugman, P. 1991b. Increasing returns and economic geography. *Journal of Political Economy* 99 (3):483–499.

Lee, Y. J., and H. Zang. 1998. Urbanization and regional productivity in Korean manufacturing. *Urban Studies* 35 (11):2085–2099.

Maillat, D., and G. Léchot. 1992. Système de production territorial et rôle de l'espace urbain: le cas des villes de l'arc jurassien. *Schweizerische Zeitschrift fur Volkswirtschaft und Statistik/Swiss Journal of Economics and Statistics* 128 (3):339–354.

Marshall, A. 1920. *Principles of Economics*, 8th ed., London: Macmillan.

Maurseth, P. B., and B. Verspagen. 2002. Knowledge spillovers in Europe: a patent citations analysis. *Scandinavian Journal of Economics* 104 (4):531–545.

Mehrabian, A. 1972. *Nonverbal Communication*. Chicago: Aldine Atherton.

Moomaw, R. L. 1985. Firm location and city size: reduced productivity advantages as a factor in the decline of manufacturing in urban areas. *Journal of Urban Economics* 17(1): 73-89.

Moomaw, R. L. 1988. Agglomeration economies: localization or urbanization? *Urban Studies* 25 (2):150–161.

Mun, Se-il, and K. Yoshikawa. 1993. Communication among firms, traffic congestion and office agglomeration. *Annals of Regional Science* 27 (1):61–77.

Myrdal, G. 1939. *Monetary Equilibrium*. London: Hodge.

Newindpress. *When Schumi won, Thanksgiving Prayers were Outsourced to Kerala*, http://newindpress.com/, 28 April 2004.

Oakey, R. P., and S. Y. Cooper. 1989. High technology industry, agglomeration and the potential for peripherally sited small firms. *Regional Studies* 23 (4):347–360.

Oksanen, E. H., and J. R. Williams. 1984. Industrial location and inter-industry linkages. *Empirical Economics* 9 (3):139–150.

Pascal, A. H., and J. J. McCall. 1980. Agglomeration economies, search costs, and industrial location. *Journal of Urban Economics* 8 (3):383–388.

Pryke, M., and R. Lee. 1995. Place your bets: towards an understanding of globalization, socio-financial engineering and competition within a financial centre. *Urban Studies* 32 (2):329–344.

Rosenthal, S. S., and W. C. Strange. 2003. Geography, industrial organization, and agglomeration. *Review of Economics and Statistics* 85 (2):377–393.

Samuelson, P. A. 1983. Thünen at two hundred. *Journal of Economic Literature* 21 (4):1468–1488.

Saxenian, A. 1996. *Regional Advantage: Culture and Competition in Silicon Valley and Route 128*, 2nd ed., Cambridge: Harvard University Press.

Sify. *U.S. Outsourcing Prayers to India*, http://sify.com/news/othernews/fullstory.php?id=13498514, 15 June 2004.

Strohmeyer, J. 1985. Agonizing ordeal of a one-company town. *Business and Society Review* (54):45–49.

Sveikauskas, L., J. Gowdy, and M. Funk. 1988. Urban productivity: city size or industry size. *Journal of Regional Science* 28 (2):185–202.

Venables, A. J. 1996. Localization of industry and trade performance. *Oxford Review of Economic Policy* 12 (3):52–60.

Von Neumann, J., and O. Morgenstern. 1967. *Theory of Games and Economic Behavior.* Princeton University Press.

Young, A. 1999. Markets in time: the rise, fall, and revival of Swiss watch-making. Reprinted from *The Freeman* 49 (1). (http://www.libertyhaven.com/countries-andregions/swiss/marketstimes.html)

Chapter 6

Spatial Pricing Decisions

By definition, transport costs cause **delivered prices** (store price +
transport costs) to change with distance. But if a firm delivers its product
to the residence, customers living far from the firm do not necessarily pay
more than those living nearby. The price of sending a letter to a neighbor is
the same as sending it to someone living on the other side of the country.
Pizzerias offer free delivery if the customer is within a certain distance of
their establishment. Some Internet retailers and catalogue distributors offer
free delivery. If you buy used products from an enterprise such as Amazon.
com, you are charged a flat fee for shipping regardless of where you are in
relation to the seller's location.

These are examples of **uniform delivered pricing**. All consumers pay
the same price regardless of where they are located. This chapter will
compare free on board (f.o.b.) mill pricing to four discriminatory pricing
strategies where the firm pays a portion of the cost of transporting the
product. In doing so, this chapter will provide examples of the impact of
spatial economics on antitrust legislation and other topics within the
industrial organization literature.

Perfect spatial price discrimination, uniform delivered pricing, zonal
pricing, and basing-point pricing are all examples of price discrimination.
Some spatial price discrimination practices are unlawful in the United States
under antitrust laws, but they may be quite acceptable in other countries.
Are these practices socially irresponsible? How do spatial pricing practices
affect market areas and output? Who in society gains or loses with these
pricing innovations? This chapter will examine these questions.

Think About It...

Have you purchased anything lately where you paid more or less than what someone else was charged?

Which firms give student discounts? Do you frequent these establishments more than their competitors who do not give students "a break?"

Which businesses give senior citizen discounts?

Which firms offer home delivery?

What Is Price Discrimination?

A firm price discriminates if it sells its product at different prices to distinct markets when the price differences are not associated with cost differences. For example, students sometimes get discounts on haircuts, beverages, pizza, and gas by showing their student IDs. If senior citizens are willing to admit their age, they pay less than the younger customers do for the same meals. Businesspersons who purchase tickets only two weeks before a flight or who are not willing to stay over Saturday nights pay more.

Firms that practice ***spatial price discrimination*** often deliver their products themselves. Firms that deliver goods have lower operating costs than retail stores because they need less room to stockpile the inventory and they do not need a storefront to display their wares. Their "storefront" consists of the door-to-door sales force, their catalogs, or their Web pages. However, firms don't always have to deliver their products to absorb transportation costs. Walibi, the Belgian version of Disneyland, price discriminates by giving visitors rebates on their train tickets.

Why would a firm price discriminate? Firms charge different prices in different markets to increase profits. To be able to price discriminate:

- A firm must have market power, that is, some control over price.
- The different markets must have different price elasticities of demand.
- Customers of each market must be separable and easily identifiable.
- Administrative costs of charging different prices must be less than the potential gains.
- Arbitrage cannot be possible or profitable.

Firms always produce the quantity where their marginal cost equals marginal revenue. If they price discriminate, they will choose that quantity

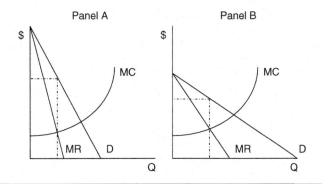

Figure 6.1 Price discrimination.

where the marginal cost of producing the next unit equals the marginal revenue of selling the next unit in each market. Markets with more elastic demand pay lower prices than those with less elastic demand. For example, business customers have few choices if tomorrow they must suddenly attend a meeting 1000 miles away. They have a relatively inelastic demand for air travel. On the other hand, tourists have many choices when planning their vacations, so they are more responsive to price differences.[1]

In Figure 6.1, the market in Panel A has a less elastic demand than the market in Panel B. The firm equates the marginal cost of production with the marginal revenue within each market. Consumers in Panel A pay a higher price than those in Panel B. The firm is thus said to discriminate in favor of Market B and against Market A.

International Price Discrimination

Bryan (1990) looked at Canadian exports to determine whether spatial price discrimination (freight absorption) occurs in international trade. She observed that freight absorption exists in the aluminum, asbestos, copper, and newsprint industries. Firms had a tendency to spatially price discriminate when either the prices of their own commodities increased rapidly or in the late 1970s when Canada's oil prices soared.

Bryan (1990)

---

[1] Anderson and Neven (1990); Schuler (1991); Tabuchi (1999).

Spatial Price Discrimination

Spatial price discrimination means that some amount of freight cost is absorbed by the firm. Freight absorption is widespread. Greenhut, Norman, and Hung (1987) estimated that more than two-thirds of a sample of 174 firms in the United States practiced price discrimination over part or all of their market area. In Germany, 79% of firms and in Japan 82% of firms discriminated in price. Because of the Robinson–Patman Act, which is designed to prevent "unfair" price discrimination, United States firms hesitate to price discriminate, even though consumers may benefit from such a practice.

Any spatial pricing that is not f.o.b. mill pricing is discriminatory. Spatial price discrimination generally leads to larger market areas, greater production, and larger profits than f.o.b. pricing. Furthermore, spatial price discrimination is sometimes considered a sign of market power.

The Robinson–Patman Act of the United States and Great Britain's Price Commission appear to favor mill pricing and oppose some forms of spatial price discrimination. Rather than protect the consumer from being gouged by lack of competition, the Robinson–Patman Act actually stifles competition and forces consumers who live farther from the store to pay higher prices. The landmark decision of the Supreme Court of the United States in 1967 in favor of Utah Pies (see below) illustrates the problems created by policies for which the logic is based on neither spatial pricing nor location theory.[2]

Fiery Competition in the Frozen Pie Market

In the Utah Pie case, the Supreme Court declared that competing firms were guilty of discriminatory pricing because their delivered prices were higher closer to their market than in the Salt Lake City, Utah, market. Continental Baking, Carnation, and Pet Milk Companies engaged in such fierce price competition that the Supreme Court determined this was harmful to Utah Pie, a local competitor, even though Utah Pie maintained 45 percent of the Salt Lake City frozen pie market.

Utah Pie entered the frozen pie business in 1967, selling its pies for $4.15 per dozen while the already established Pet, Carnation, and Continental companies sold their pies at an average of $4.91 per dozen. Forty-four

---

[2] Phlips and Thisse (1982); Anderson and de Palma (1988); de Palma and Liu (1993).

months later, Utah Pie sold its pies for $2.75 in response to an average price of $3.27 from the competitors. When it became evident that all four firms were selling under cost, Utah Pie sued the others, charging price discrimination.

Citing the Robinson–Patman Act, the Supreme Court ruled in favor of Utah Pie. Thus, it "protected" Salt Lake City consumers from getting good deals on frozen pies and safeguarded the competitor rather than competition, according to the dissenting opinions of Mr. Justice Stewart and Mr. Justice Harlan.

Utah Pie Co. v. Continental Baking Co. 386 United States 685 (1967) at http://www.ripon.edu/faculty/bowenj/antitrust/upievcon.htm

Delivered Pricing Schedules

Price discrimination means lowering prices for consumers with more elastic demands. Because the demand for nearby consumers is less elastic than for those who live farther away (Chapter 2), firms can more readily discriminate against nearby consumers. Figure 6.2 shows the differences in pricing patterns for firms that use f.o.b. mill pricing and perfect discriminatory spatial pricing. The f.o.b. mill price–distance function is the solid line. If Firm A uses discriminatory spatial pricing (the dotted line), the mill price increases and customers close to the plant subsidize delivery to the distant customers. This increases the market area for Firm A, if we assume that

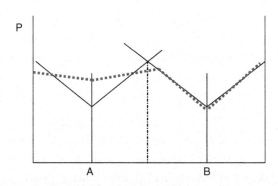

Figure 6.2 Perfect discriminatory spatial pricing and free on board (f.o.b.) mill pricing patterns.

Firm B does not retaliate. However, if Firm A practices perfect discriminatory spatial pricing, it also competes by lowering prices in Firm B's market.

Perfect Discriminatory Spatial Pricing

Under perfect discriminatory spatial pricing, the spatial monopolist maximizes profits on each separate local market. Each market is charged a different price. If Firm A were to use discriminatory spatial pricing while Firm B kept f.o.b. mill pricing, Firm A's market area would increase. Its nearby customers would be subsidizing the market expansion.

Because each market is treated differently, there is no logical reason why a delivered price schedule needs to be linear and upward sloping over the entire market. Under perfect discriminatory spatial pricing, the sizes of cities along the route or the aggressiveness of the competition in a city could cause dips in the delivered price schedule, as shown in Figure 6.2.[3]

Think About It...

What businesses in your city spatially price discriminate?

Do firms that offer free delivery charge the same prices for their goods as the firms that do not offer free delivery?

Uniform Delivered Pricing

Under uniform delivered pricing, the firm provides the good to all its consumers at the same price regardless of distance, as shown by the dashed line in Figure 6.3. Industries that practice uniform delivered pricing are those that offer "free delivery" for goods such as pizza and flowers. Internet companies and catalogue promotions often do the same thing. In addition, some food processing industries (e.g., almonds, canning peaches and pears, rice, sugar beets, processing tomatoes, and wine grapes) regularly use uniform delivered pricing. This form of pricing is very simple to administer. The firm does not need to calculate prices as a function of distance from the plant. Under this pricing strategy, however, the firm may

---

[3] Greenhut, Hwang and Shwiff (1984); Thisse and Vives (1988).

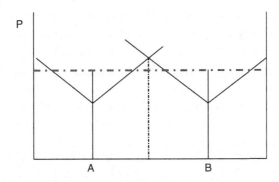

Figure 6.3 Uniform delivered pricing and free on board (f.o.b.) mill pricing patterns.

refuse to supply potential customers who are located too far away—to do so would decrease profits.[4]

Firms might choose uniform delivered pricing over discriminatory spatial pricing even if profits are not maximized because under discriminatory spatial pricing:

1. Administration and implementation costs are high;
2. Arbitrage is very likely; and most importantly,
3. Antitrust authorities tolerate uniform delivered pricing more than they do discriminatory spatial pricing.

Antitrust authorities tolerate uniform delivered pricing because it seems more "fair." Spatial discriminatory pricing gives more flexibility against the competition, but the prospect of litigation keeps firms from pricing aggressively.

Zonal Pricing

Zonal pricing is a compromise between uniform spatial pricing and discriminatory spatial pricing. Under a zonal pricing system, all customers in a given region pay the same price. Zones can correspond to distances from a plant, entire countries, economic regions like the Pacific Rim, or natural areas such as east of the Mississippi River. The United States Postal Service, for instance, implements eight zones to determine rates for parcel post. Most other delivery firms follow their lead. Any firm in Zone 1 pays the same rate to send a package that weights 10 lbs. across the street or to any

---

[4] Norman (1981); Cheung and Wang (1996); Durham, Sexton and Song (1996).

other firm in the same zone. Sending the same package even a mile into the next zone costs more and takes longer to ship.[5]

Uniform Delivered Pricing and Coca-Cola Plants

The price of soft drinks does not vary with distance from the bottling plant. Osleeb and Cromley (1978) studied the location of Coca-Cola plants in Canada. Distribution costs are important for this type of firm because it must absorb all delivery costs. Because the bottlers of the same product do not want to compete with one another using price, the uniform delivered price is the most sensible pricing option.

For firms that sell large volumes of output in relatively small shipments to a large number of widely dispersed buyers discriminatory spatial pricing would be extremely difficult to administer. With uniform delivered pricing, the firm imposes a single price that includes the production costs and an average transportation cost and thereby saves money.

Osleeb and Cromley (1978)

Figure 6.4 compares f.o.b. mill pricing (dark solid line), spatial price discrimination (light solid line), and zonal pricing (dashed line). As one can see, zonal pricing has several advantages for a firm. First, even with a small number of zones, the firm can capture a large amount of the profit it would make under spatial discriminatory pricing with a much lower administration cost. Second, zonal pricing deters entry because the original firm only needs to lower prices in zones where potential rivals are about to invade. Firm A in Figure 6.4 is the price discriminator. As in Figure 6.2, this firm assumes that Firm B will not be aware of its pricing policies, or if it is aware of them, Firm B will neither retaliate nor change its own pricing.

The major problem with zonal pricing is determining how to prevent arbitrage among consumers. If the jump in transport costs between zones is

---

[5] Peeters and Thisse (1996); Hansen, Peeters, and Thisse (1997).

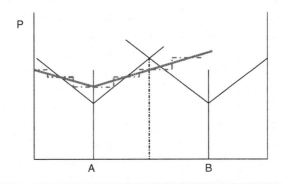

Figure 6.4 Zonal pricing, spatial price discrimination and free on board (f.o.b.) mill pricing patterns.

large enough, a consumer could profitably set up an enterprise adjacent to the next zone and resell the delivered goods to consumers in the next zone, thereby cutting the firm from collecting the more lucrative transportation costs from the next zone. For example, before the European Union was organized, the automobile market in Europe used zonal pricing where each country was a unique zone. Because of severe competition in Belgium, French cars were sold at significantly lower prices there than in France. French consumers could import French cars from Belgium at a lower delivered price than they would have paid for the same car at home.

Basing-Point Pricing

Under the basing-point pricing system, if Firm A is the base point, all transportation costs are calculated as if they were sold by Firm A. In Figure 6.5, Customer Z pays less for the product than Customer X (P_x) because Z is closer to Firm A than is X. However, X pays P_x regardless of whether the good is purchased from A or B. If B sells the good, B charges what is known as phantom freight—an amount much greater than the actual transport cost. For example, see the section titled "Costly Phantoms" below.[6]

Costly Phantoms

Before 1963, all plywood in the United States was made in the Pacific Northwest from Douglas fir trees and sold

---

[6] Stocking (1954) in Espinosa (1992); Espinosa (1992); Hughes and Barbezat (1996).

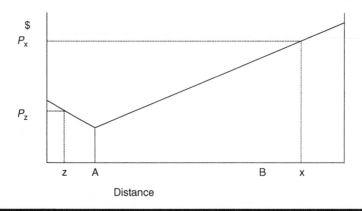

Figure 6.5 Basing-point pricing.

based on freight rates computed from Portland, Oregon. New laminating techniques permitted South-eastern plants to produce plywood using local pine trees. By the mid 1970s, nearly 40 percent of total plywood production in the United States came from the Southeast.

According to a 1978 FTC report, a lumberyard in New Orleans, Louisiana bought 50,000 square feet of plywood from a mill located 60 miles away in Holden, Louisiana. The actual cost to deliver the plywood was $80, but the New Orleans lumberyard was charged the cost of rail shipment from Portland to New Orleans ($764). The Holden mill collected a phantom freight amount of $684 ($764−$80).

Gilligan (1992)

Examples of basing–point pricing are plentiful. Until 1924, every steel producer in the United States calculated transportation rates as if the producer was located in Pittsburgh, Pennsylvania. Steel producers located west of Pittsburgh absorbed freight charges if they shipped to customers east of Pittsburgh. The pricing system was known as the Pittsburgh-Plus system. Basing-point pricing of steel contributed to the slow growth of industrial-ization in the American South.

Historical German Steel Cartel and Basing-Point Pricing

Hughes and Barbezat (1996) observed that between the two World Wars, German steel cartels established base points at the sites of firms with significant bargaining power. In this way, they secured high prices of steel relative to the going international rates. In 1925, the German government reimposed tariffs on steel. German, Belgian, Luxemburg, and French steel firms signed international accords that strictly limited the importation of steel.

Control for steel products was in the hands of the *Stahlwerksverband*, a German governmental agency that set production quotas and administered the basing-point pricing system from 1926–1939. It succeeded in maintaining a price that was about 30 percent greater than the world steel price.

Hughes and Barbezat (1996)

Current European Steel Cartel and Basing-Point Pricing

A multiple basing-point price system for steel is in place in Europe despite Article 85 of the Treaty of Rome, which outlines the antitrust policy of the European Union (Phlips 1988). The reason for this pricing system is to maintain the traditional steel markets of France, Germany, Belgium, Luxembourg, and Italy. Before 1951, German and French steel producers set national prices according to a single basing–point pricing system. Germany's base was at Oberhausen and France's base at Thionville. The big northern steel producers could sell anywhere in France, but the smaller southern producers could only afford to sell to local customers because of the amount of freight absorption needed to sell farther north.

In trying to formulate a common steel market in 1957, the goal was to define a common pricing policy so that the market shares did not change. The agreement, Article 60 of the European Coal and Steel Community (ECSC) treaty, allowed a delivered price to be quoted by all producers that was equal to the lowest combination of base point plus freight for the multiple basing points.

Phlips (1988)

But If the Government Sets Prices...

In 1948, basing-point pricing systems were outlawed in the United States. Nevertheless, since the 1960s, the Federal Milk Marketing Order (FMMO) set prices of fluid milk as if it were all shipped from Eau Claire, Wisconsin. As of 1998, dairy farmers receive prices for fluid milk that range from a low of $1.20 per hundredweight (ctw) in Eau Claire to a high of $4.10/ctw in Miami, Florida. The price is based on the average price in the Minnesota/Wisconsin area, and it increases with distance from Eau Claire, Wisconsin, by about 20¢/ctw per mile. Regulators do not consider this practice as a violation of antitrust pricing policy because the prices vary by zone with distance from Eau Claire, and zonal pricing is legal.

The FMMO originated to ensure that bottled milk would be available in grocery stores in all parts of the country. The highway system was not developed enough in the 1960s, so it was difficult to transport milk from the dairy states of Minnesota and Wisconsin. Florida's dairy farmers face higher costs because its warm and humid climate is more amenable to orange groves than dairy herds.

In the 1960s, legislators decided that a strong dairy industry in Florida guaranteed that children in Miami would have a stable supply of fresh milk every day. To promote their dairy industry, these legislators felt that

Florida's dairy farmers should be compensated more than dairy farmers in the upper Midwest. Now that the highway system has improved and shipping fluid milk from Wisconsin to Florida is reliable, dairy farmers in the upper Midwest consider the FMMO out-of-date and inefficient. However, it is politically impossible to get rid of the dairy pricing structure. Some farmers in the upper Midwest still wait in vain for price supports to start orange groves that would guarantee the children of Minnesota their fresh orange juice every day.

Florida dairy farmers are not perfectly happy with the FMMO regulation, either. Between the hot months of July to November, Florida's dairy producers cannot produce enough and they have to import milk to meet the demand. However, they export milk for the other seven months of the year. This exported milk is sold at prices lower than those imposed in Florida, which results in a loss of income when they sell their surplus outside the state.

Robert Cropp, Dairy Marketing
and Policy Specialist, telephone interview,
April 17, 1992; Nubern and Kilmer (1997)

Most evidence suggests that basing–point pricing is the work of well-organized cartels and not a result of competition.[7] Basing-point pricing helps the firms in the cartel by providing extra profit from phantom freight, and it makes customers indifferent about which producer to order from because price differences are eliminated.

The firms within the cartel decide on the location of the base—that is, which location will be "A" in Figure 6.5. During the 1930s, the cement producers chose the plant of a certain indomitable owner to be the base point. They then slashed the price of cement by half. Losses to the other producers were slight, but the involuntary base firm was not only forced to sell cement at half its former price, but it received no phantom freight whatsoever. After 6 weeks of this punishment, the recalcitrant owner voluntarily joined the Portland Cement Association.

In 1948, the United States antitrust legislation declared the basing–point pricing system to be unlawful. It lessened competition and caused inefficient locations of firms by mitigating the benefits of decentralization.

---

[7] Haddock (1982), for instance, does not concur.

Cross-hauling, the purchase of goods from more distant factories, was common albeit an inefficient practice.

United States court cases that challenged basing–point pricing policies have involved steel, cement, corn products, conduit, plywood, gypsum board, and lead products. In 2001, Minnesota farmers unsuccessfully sued to have the zonal basing–point pricing system for milk declared illegal.[8]

The questions remain: Are these practices socially irresponsible? Who benefits and who loses under these pricing strategies?

Welfare Analysis of Pricing Decisions

To answer the question of whether these spatial pricing policies are socially beneficial or not, one must first set a standard for measuring social welfare. One method of measuring social welfare is to determine whether society as a whole will gain or lose. This is done by estimating the amount of consumer and producer surplus under the various policy options.

Think About It...

Do you always pay the maximum price you are willing to pay and are you always able to pay for every product you purchase?

What price does a gallon of gas have to be before you no longer fill up the tank and actually find alternative transportation?

Similarly, would those of you who are employed work just as hard if you were paid 1¢ less per hour? If pressed, would you accept a decrease in pay of 2¢? How low would your wage have to fall before you change jobs or occupations?

Consumer and Producer Surplus

Consumer surplus is the difference between the maximum price that consumers are willing and able to pay and the actual price. Because the demand curve shows the quantity of a good or service that consumers are

---

[8] United States v. Gypsum Co. (1940, 1950); Corn Products Refining Company v. FTC (1945); FTC v. Cement Institution (1948); Triangle Conduit and Cable Co. V. FTC (1948); FTC v. National Lead Co. (1957); Boise Cascade Corp. et al. v. FTC (1978).

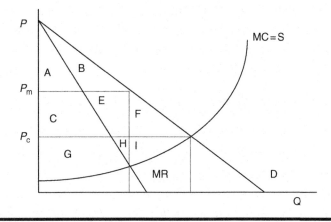

Figure 6.6 Producer and consumer surplus.

willing and able to purchase at each price, consumer surplus is the area between the demand curve and the price P_c or area ABCEF in Figure 6.6.

Producer surplus is the difference between the minimum price for a product that producers are willing and able to accept and the actual price. For a perfectly competitive market, producer surplus is the area above the marginal cost curve and below the price—sections GHI. Producer surplus includes the industry profit plus the amount that the firms pay for fixed costs. The area under the marginal cost curve is the total variable cost that the industry incurs to produce a specific quantity of output.

When firms have even a modicum of market power, they set their own prices to sell that quantity for which marginal cost equals marginal revenue. For industry structures that are not perfectly competitive, the consumer surplus shrinks to area AB. Producer surplus increases to CEGH. Area FI is the amount of welfare lost to society, called the **deadweight loss**.

Society is better off having perfectly competitive markets because there is no deadweight loss. However, as we know, spatial models are not compatible with perfect competition. Under imperfect competition, consumers are worse off because consumer surplus drops by area CEF. Welfare from area CE is redistributed from consumers to producers; so for that area, society as a whole is no worse off. However, because of the deadweight loss (area FI), social welfare is diminished.

If firms could perfectly price discriminate, that is, if they can sell their goods to each consumer at the maximum price the consumer is willing and able to pay—then the output will again be at the quantity where marginal cost equals demand. Social welfare under perfect price discrimination will equal social welfare under perfect competition because there is no deadweight loss. The difference is that under perfect price discrimination, the firm has usurped the entire consumer surplus. Producer surplus would be the entire area below the demand curve and above the supply curve.

Who Gains Under Spatial Price Discrimination?

The answer to this question depends on the type of spatial price discrimination and the conditions under which it is practiced. According to Beckmann (1976), f.o.b. mill pricing is the only spatial pricing strategy that does not price discriminate. However, f.o.b. mill pricing is the most expensive for distant buyers. Spatial price discrimination of any sort, practiced by a spatial monopolist, can temporarily increase social welfare because the market area of the firm increases. Yet, when rivals switch to the same pricing system, that advantage is lost; f.o.b. mill prices are easy to administer and they constitute a safe policy against a charge of discrimination. When the mill price reflects the marginal cost of production and market areas are fixed, as in long-run equilibrium, this pricing system provides the highest consumer surplus and greatest welfare benefits because it mirrors the perfectly competitive solution in traditional economics.[9]

However, in the case of isolated spatial monopolists, price is set above marginal cost. Discriminatory monopolists can serve larger markets and sell more total output than monopolists who use f.o.b. mill pricing. In this case, consumers would gain more under spatial price discrimination than under mill pricing.

Discriminatory pricing generates a welfare loss for consumers located close to the plant but a welfare gain for those farther away. Firms need to compete vigorously in distant markets—a practice that benefits distant consumers at the expense of those nearby.

Discriminatory "Park in the Heart"

The Downtown Business Association in Edmonton, Alberta, Canada wants to lure suburban shoppers into shopping downtown rather than in suburban stores. They mail parking coupons to residences and place parking coupons in local newspapers. The parking discounts are only valid during noncommuting hours from 6:00 pm to 1:00 am or between 3:00 and 6:00 pm on

---

[9] Beckmann (1976); Hamilton and Thisse (1992).

weekends. In this way, they encourage off-peak travel. The downtown merchants discriminate against people who work close by and consumers who live within walking distance of the facility. Downtown residents subsidize distant shoppers because a price increase for the merchandise covers the reduction in parking costs for suburbanites.

This program is profitable for all downtown stores, but some stores refuse to subsidize the parking costs of their customers. These free riders have thus increased their profits at the expense of other stores. In fact, according to Lindsey and West (1997), the profits of the downtown merchants increased under the "Park in the Heart" program while the profits of suburban stores dwindled.

Downtown Business Association,
http://lots.impark.com/Edmonton/faq.html,
retrieved April 2001, Lindsey and West (1997)

The welfare analysis of perfect spatial price discrimination is similar to the analysis of perfect price discrimination in traditional economics. Output increases, so more people will have access to the product than under mill pricing for an isolated spatial monopolist. However, producer surplus may not totally engulf consumer surplus. In markets with vigorous competition, consumer welfare is larger than in markets with less competition. Social welfare is also at a maximum, but antitrust authorities will have the industry under their microscope if the competition gets too brutal.

Under a uniform delivered pricing rule, consumers near the plant are worse off because they subsidize transportation costs for those at the edge of the market area. Problems might come about if consumers are refused service because the delivered price does not cover transportation costs. Generally, antitrust authorities do not target industries that use uniform delivered pricing because it seems "fair" to charge everyone the same price, regardless of distance. In fixed market areas, a uniform price system yields the lowest consumer surplus because uniform delivered prices are always higher than any other type of pricing.

Summary and Conclusions

This chapter compares the effects of f.o.b. mill pricing to four discriminatory spatial pricing strategies: uniform delivered pricing, perfect spatial price discrimination, zonal pricing, and basing–point pricing. Basing-point pricing is illegal in the United States and Great Britain, but it is still used for steel prices in parts of Europe and for milk in the United States. The Supreme Court of the United States decided that perfect spatial price discrimination practices were illegal under the Robinson–Patman Act, and the legality of zonal pricing has been questioned. This chapter asks if these practices are socially irresponsible. The response is "not necessarily."

Firms that price discriminate offer lower prices to consumers who have a more elastic demand. Because the distant consumers have more elastic demands than those who are nearby, the transportation costs of distant consumers are subsidized by the closer consumers. In this way, the firm's market area increases, as does its production and profits. Because spatial price discrimination in all its forms is one sign of market power, some types violate antitrust laws. Basing-point pricing, for instance, is the result of well-organized cartels that can bully outside firms to join them or face bankruptcy.

The f.o.b. mill pricing could signal a lack of price discrimination under a perfectly competitive market, but only if the local prices mirror the marginal cost of production and the market areas cannot expand. When this happens, output and social welfare are maximized and profits are minimized. For this reason, f.o.b. pricing becomes the standard by which to judge the other spatial pricing mechanisms.

Perfect spatial price discrimination allows the firm to price according to the market conditions at each point. Prices will not follow a linear formula that increases at a constant rate with distance from the plant. Consumers are better off under this type of pricing than with any other, but it is illegal in the United States under the Robinson–Patman Act. Zonal pricing is similar to perfect spatial price discrimination, but it is easier to administer. Court cases have challenged zonal pricing, but it is still considered legal.

Under uniform delivered pricing, everyone pays the same price for the good regardless of their locations relative to the seller. Prices are always higher than for any other type of pricing, forcing consumers near the plant to subsidize those farther away. Uniform delivered pricing is considered "safe" because antitrust authorities think that everyone is treated equally.

Chapter Questions

1. Determine what pricing policy each of these scenarios depicts and draw price–distance functions similar to diagrams in Figures 6.2 through 6.5 showing the following scenarios:
   a. Albruzzo's Pizza breaks from tradition and offers free delivery anywhere within 10 miles of their store. The other pizza places in town charge per mile to deliver hot pizza.

b. To cut down on the cost of owning delivery vehicles, Abigail's Health Spa and Grooming Center sends a taxi to pick up and deliver Pooch or Tabby. The customer pays for the pet's day at the spa plus the transportation cost from the taxi meter.

c. Flourishing Flowers, an online florist, charges its consumers 1¢ less than the flower shops in their own city and offers free delivery.

d. To purchase exotic "Crawfish Jerky" from Crawlin' Crawfish Farms in Louisiana, the consumer is charged the price plus transportation costs calculated by the post office.

e. The dandelion oil industry of North America decided to create a cartel and set prices as if all dandelion oil came from the city of Dandelion, Illinois. Consumers who want relief from aching muscles will pay the same price irrespective of where they live or which firm sells them their dandelion oil.

Research Assignment

Check out the prices for raw milk in your state through the USDA Web site: http://www.ams.usda.gov/dairy/orders.htm. Compare these prices with the price of whole milk for metropolitan areas in your state as listed in the ACCRA Cost of Living Index. Do consumers pay more for milk in states where milk producers receive a higher price per cwt?

References

Anderson, S. P., and A. de Palma. 1988. Spatial price discrimination with heterogeneous products. *Review of Economic Studies* 55 (4):573–592.

Anderson, S. P., and D. J. Neven. 1990. Spatial competition à la Cournot: price discrimination by quantity-setting oligopolists. *Journal of Regional Science* 30 (1):1–14.

Beckmann, M. J. 1976. Spatial price policies revisited. *Bell Journal of Economics* 7 (2):619–630.

Bryan, I. A. 1990. Spatial pricing in international trade: some limited evidence. *Weltwirtschaftliches Archiv* 126 (3):494–510.

Cheung, F. K., and X. Wang. 1996. Mill and uniform pricing: a comparison. *Journal of Regional Science* 36 (1):129–143.

Corn Products Co. V. Comm'n, 324 United States 726. Villanova Center for Information and Policy. http://www.vcilp.org/Fed-Ct/Supreme/Flite/opinions/ 324US726.htm (accessed 19 July 1998; site now discontinued).

de Palma, A., and Q. Liu. 1993. The welfare aspects of spatial pricing policies reconsidered for a monopoly case. *Journal of Regional Science* 33 (1):1–12.

Downtown Business Association. http://lots.impark.com/Edmonton/faq.html, retrieved April 2001.

Durham, C. A., R. J. Sexton, and J. H. Song. 1996. Spatial competition, uniform pricing, and transportation efficiency in the California processing tomato industry. *American Journal of Agricultural Economics* 78 (1):115–125.

Espinosa, M. P. 1992. Delivered pricing, FOB pricing, and collusion in spatial markets. *RAND Journal of Economics* 23 (1):64–85.

Federal Trade Commission v. National Lead Co., 227F.2D825 Reversed. Villanova Center for Information and Policy, http://www.vcilp.org/Fed-Ct/Supreme/ Flite/opinions/352US419.htm (accessed 19 July 1998; site now discontinued).

Gilligan, T. W. 1992. Imperfect competition and basing-point pricing: evidence from the softwood plywood industry. *American Economic Review* 82 (5):1106–1119.

Greenhut, M. L., M. Hwang, and S. Shwiff. 1984. Differences in spatial pricing in the United States: a statistical analysis and case studies. *Annals of Regional Science* 18 (3):49–66.

Greenhut, M. L., G. Norman, and C. S. Hung. 1987. *The economics of imperfect competition: a spatial approach.* Cambridge: Cambridge University Press.

Haddock, D. D. 1982. Basing-point pricing: competitive vs. collusive theories. *American Economic Review* 72 (3):289–306.

Hamilton, J. H., and J.-F. Thisse. 1992. Duopoly with spatial and quantity-dependent price discrimination. *Regional Science and Urban Economics* 22 (2):175–185.

Hansen, P., D. Peeters, and J.-F. Thisse. 1997. Facility location under zone pricing. *Journal of Regional Science* 37 (1):1–22.

Hughes, J. W., and D. P. Barbezat. 1996. Basing-point pricing and the *Stahlwerksverband*: An examination of the new competitive school. *Journal of Economic History* 56 (1):215–222.

Lindsey, C. R., and D. S. West. 1997. Spatial price discrimination: the use of parking coupons by downtown retailers. *Review of Industrial Organization* 12 (3):417–438.

Norman, G. 1981. Uniform pricing as an optimal spatial pricing policy. *Economica* 48 (189):87–91.

Nubern, C. A., and R. L. Kilmer. 1997. Impact of spatial price discrimination within Florida dairy cooperatives. *Agricultural and Resource Economics Review* 26 (1):94–105.

Osleeb, J. P., and R. G. Cromley. 1978. The location of plants of the uniform delivered price manufacturer: a case study of Coca-Cola Ltd. *Economic Geography* 54 (1):40–52.

Peeters, D., and J.-F. Thisse. 1996. Zone pricing. *Journal of Regional Science* 36 (2):291–301.

Phlips, L. 1988. Price discrimination: a survey of the theory. *Journal of Economic Surveys* 2 (2):135–167.

Phlips, L., and J.-F. Thisse. 1982. Spatial competition and the theory of differentiated markets: an introduction, In *The Economics of Location. Volume 3: Spatial Microeconomics*, eds. M. L. Greenhut, and N. George, *Elgar Reference Collection: International Library of Critical Writings in Economics*, Vol. 42, Elgar/Distributed in the U.S. by Ashgate, Aldershot, U.K./Brookfield, VT, 319–327.

Schuler, R. E. 1991. Differentiated prices over space, time, style, and quality: The importance of the distribution network, In *Spatial Analysis in Marketing: Theory, Methods, and Applications*, eds. A. Ghosh, and C.A. Ingene, *Research in Marketing, Supplement no. 5 Greenwich*, JAI Press, London, 13–34.

Tabuchi, T. 1999. Pricing policy in spatial competition. *Regional Science and Urban Economics* 29 (5):617–631.

Thisse, J.-F., and X. Vives. 1988. On the strategic choice of spatial price policy. *American Economic Review* 78 (1):122–137.

United States v. Gypsum Co., 340 United States 76. Villanova Center for Information and Policy, http://www.vcilp.org/Fed-Ct/Supreme/Flite/opinions/ 352US76.htm (accessed 19 July 1998; site now discontinued).

United States v. Gypsum Co., 333 United States 364. Villanova Center for Information and Policy, http://www.vcilp.org/Fed-Ct/Supreme/Flite/opinions/ 333US364.htm (accessed 19 July 1998; site now discontinued).

Utah Pie Co. V. Continental Baking Co. 386 United States 685 (1967) in http://www. ripon.edu/faculty/bowenj/antitrust/upievcon.htm

REGIONAL GROWTH AND DEVELOPMENT

Economic growth generally causes increased standards of living. But how is growth—especially sustainable growth—created? This part focuses on growth from a regional viewpoint. As we will see, a regional perspective of optimal growth is more complex than one from a macroeconomic perspective.

The economic literature on regional growth and development is based on one of the two distinct concepts: location at an isolated point or proximity to some focal point. The earliest regional economic models were adaptations of macroeconomic models. These adaptations, like most macroeconomic models, analyze the region as if it were merely a point, unrelated to other points and devoid of any concept of space. Models, such as the economic base model or input–output, could be applied to an entire country as well as to a geographical subset of the country with little change in interpretation. Likewise, international trade models and neoclassical growth theory allow for movement of goods or production factors from one point to another, ignoring transport costs.

Endogenous growth models, to some extent, incorporate agglomeration economies and proximity, but the intraregional dynamics will only be important in the determination of regional growth when a model explains the core-periphery relationships. Core-periphery models (Chapter 9) integrate elements of demand, supply, and proximity in explaining regional growth.

This part starts by introducing a series of regional economic models and continues by discussing the roles of technology, production factors, and proximity in determining a region's growth. Chapter 7 will introduce demand-based models such as the Keynesian model, the economic base, and the input–output models as well as the shift-share analysis. This method determines the demand factors that affect changes in regional employment. Chapter 8 will examine the supply-based, long-run growth models— neoclassical and endogenous growth (new growth). Chapter 8 will continue with the role of growth and the dissemination of technology in regional analysis. Because technology is spread by entrepreneurs who decide the optimal quality of capital and the necessary skill levels for their employees, the chapter also discusses the roles of entrepreneurs, physical capital, and human capital in regional growth. Chapter 9 will examine several core-periphery models to determine the effect of the proximity to a metropolitan area on a region's growth. Chapter 10 will explore regional labor markets and migration. Growth is a panacea for some regions but a scourge in others. Some community leaders spend their time designing policies to stimulate economic growth, whereas others strive to restrain it. The question that Chapter 11 will ask is: what can a government do to trigger growth in an economy? Chapter 15 examines the effectiveness of growth controls and "smart growth" for a city because the arguments for restricting growth are heard more often in densely populated urban areas.

Part II also explores the various prescriptions for economic growth. Given the various models, fashions, and trends in the economic development industry, how do we know if a specific model, and therefore the proposals that come from it, is valid? Models are useful if they (1) are consistent with what one observes; (2) give a better understanding of the subject; (3) predict well, especially when the present and the future differ from the past; and (4) are relevant regardless of time or place.[1] The culmination of models that are presented in this part, as well as the examples from many diverse regions, provides the insight needed to understand and appreciate the intricacies of regional growth.

Even before Adam Smith published *An Inquiry into the Nature and Causes of the Wealth of Nations* in 1776, philosophers tried to determine the causes of economic growth. Most of the economic growth literature is based on macroeconomic models. Originally, regional economics tried to adapt these theories to a subnational region (mesoeconomy). However, as we saw

---

[1] Miernyk (1979).

in Chapter 1, the term "region" can consist of countries, groups of countries, and subsets of states and minor political subdivisions with some type of commonality. The key to a functional region of this sort requires not only that the areas have something in common, but also that the different sectors of this region are relatively homogeneous and function cohesively. But in reality, a region is most often defined and analyzed using administrative boundaries because data are most easily available under this form. Nonetheless, administrative jurisdictions do not guarantee homogeneity. Larger jurisdictions tend of course to be less homogeneous than smaller ones.

Macroeconomic growth theory generally targets individual countries. A country has a closed economy if it does not trade with other countries. If it does trade, it has an open economy. These economies have their own currency and a monetary authority that controls the interest rates and bank loans, thereby influencing aggregate demand. Exports or increases in demand that come from outside the economy are either stimulated or tempered by exchange rate fluctuations. Any technological change generated within a country helps that country first because ideas propagate slowly due to political, cultural, and linguistic boundaries.

Conditions that foster regional growth differ somewhat from those that macroeconomic models assume. First, because regional theories have traditionally been applied to subnational regions, all regions are open economies. Second, regional banking authorities have little or no control over the amount of loans to their residents because financial capital flows freely across regions. Third, the exchange rate between these regions is usually fixed at a one-to-one ratio because everyone uses the same currency. Therefore, fluctuating exchange rates do not interfere with trade. Fourth, because of a lack of national, political, cultural, or linguistic differences, technological innovations flow more freely. Finally, relatively few obstacles impede the migration of labor and capital. These five characteristics are the necessary foundations of any mesoeconomic analysis.

Reference

Miernyk, W. H. 1979. A note on recent regional growth theories, *Journal of Regional Science* 19 (3):303–308.

Chapter 7

Short-Run Income Models

This chapter starts our journey through the mesoeconomic theories with a simple production possibilities model. We will then visits the concepts that affect regional aggregate demand: the Keynesian and economic base theories. Next, we will investigate the input–output framework to determine exactly how the increased demand for one industry affects many more industries. We will finish by learning how to decompose a region's growth in employment, or lack thereof.

Production Possibilities Curves and Economic Growth

The first model for students of economics summarizes the essence of economic growth theory. The production possibility curve introduces the role of constraints and the concept of opportunity cost. Because resources are scarce, to produce more of one good requires a decrease in the production of another. Growing economies, on the other hand, overcome their initial constraints and are more productive in all sectors.

Figure 7.1 shows a typical production possibility curve. The economy produces two goods, X_1 and X_2. If all resources are used to produce X_1, the maximum X_1 is at Point A. Likewise, if all the resources are devoted to producing X_2, B is the maximum that the economy can produce. An economy can choose combinations of X_1 and X_2, such as Points C and E. At Point D, the resources are not fully used. The economy does not yet have the capability to produce the combination of goods at Point I.

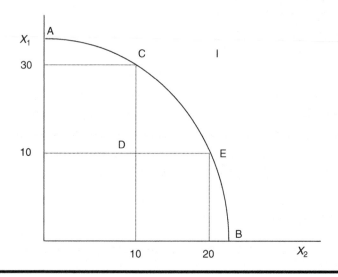

Figure 7.1 Production possibilities curve.

Short-run growth policies based on Keynesian theory stress job creation or unemployment reduction by increasing demand for locally produced goods. Job creation of this nature is not a true "growth policy." Policies that merely create jobs by increasing demand move the economy from Point D toward some point nearer to the production possibilities curve. Economic growth comes about either by increasing the quality or quantity of resources or by technology and innovation. We will examine these supply-based models in Chapter 8.

Comparative Advantage

A region is said to have ***comparative advantage*** in producing a certain good, X, if its opportunity cost is lower than that of the regions with which it trades. The concept of comparative advantage originated in international trade theory. Regions have a variety of resources at their disposal, such as land and natural resources, capital, labor, and technological expertise. The costs of production differ among regions because resources are not distributed equally. Efficiency requires that areas with lower opportunity costs of producing a good such as textiles export that good to areas where production costs are higher. Similarly, if a second area produces electronic components at lower cost, this second area should specialize in electronics and import its textiles. Because Florida is more efficient at producing oranges and Wisconsin is more efficient at producing cheese, world production increases if Wisconsin trades cheese for Florida oranges.

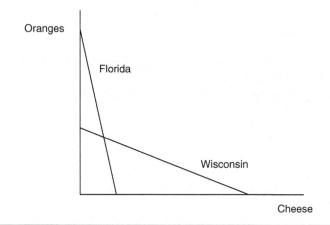

Figure 7.2 Two linear production possibilities curves showing comparative advantage.

As population increases, regions diversify. The diversification influences the area's comparative advantage. A region's comparative advantage could also be modified by an investment in infrastructure, education, and training, or by providing cultural and social amenities to attract skilled workers.

Production possibilities curves can demonstrate the concept of comparative advantage. For simplicity, we will assume a world of two regions, Florida and Wisconsin, each having identical amounts of capital and labor. We also assume that this world only produces two goods, cheese and oranges. Finally, we assume linear production possibility curves for each region, as shown in Figure 7.2.

The opportunity cost of cheese production in Wisconsin (the absolute value of the slope of its production possibilities curve) is less than it is in Florida, so Wisconsin has comparative advantage in producing cheese. Similarly, Florida has comparative advantage in citrus groves. International trade theory suggests that if regions specialize in producing goods for which they have comparative advantage and exchange those goods for products for which they lack comparative advantage, world output and income will increase.

Think About It...

What goods are produced in your area and sold (exported) to other regions? Would you say that you have comparative advantage in producing those goods? If so, what do you expect is the source of your comparative advantage?

What goods must your area import from other regions?

Absolute advantage exists if a region can produce a much larger quantity of a given good than another region of a similar size while using the same amount of resources. Even when a region has no absolute advantage in producing any product, efficiency demands that it should specialize in producing and exporting the good for which it has a comparative advantage.[1]

Demand-Based Models (Short-Run)

Keynesian economists assert that insufficient demand is the primary cause of unemployment. Economies can be in equilibrium despite very high unemployment rates. Only changes in *exogenous spending*—that is, spending generated outside the region—can propel the economy to full-employment equilibrium. This model does not allow labor and capital to migrate to more lucrative markets.

The Keynesian model is as follows: The total income (Y) is equal to the amount of output produced. Expenditures come from four sources: the amount of consumer spending (C); investment [spending by businesses] (I); government spending (G); and the amount of exports (X). In regional analysis, exports are goods sold outside the region as well as outside the country. To identify net exports, subtract the region's imports (M) from its exports ($X-M$). Incomes are generated only by producing output, so output and income are identical. In equilibrium, total expenditures $[C+I+G+(X-M)]$ equal total income (Y):

$$Y = C + I + G + (X - M) \tag{7.1}$$

The amount that consumers purchase is determined by the consumption function

$$C = a + bY_d, \tag{7.2}$$

where Y_d is disposable income:

$$Y_d = Y - T, \tag{7.3}$$

---

[1] Schmidt (1993).

and T is the amount of tax. Variable a is the amount of autonomous consumption that does not depend on income and b is the marginal propensity to consume—the increase in consumption that results from an increase in disposable income of $1. Similarly, the import function,

$$M = d + mY_d \qquad (7.4)$$

describes the volume of imports. Variable d designates the amount of autonomous imports that a region uses even when incomes are zero, and m is the marginal propensity to import or the increase in imports that results from an increase in disposable income of $1.

The amount $(a+I+G+X-d)$ is exogenous spending determined outside the model. Increases in the exogenous variables boost regional income via a multiplier process. The income multiplier describes the change in income generated by changes in expenditures. The **regional income multiplier** is found by using the formula $1/[1-(b-m)]$, where $(b-m)$ is the **marginal propensity to consume locally**. Any shock in an exogenous variable will change income by a multiple of the original shock in a predictable fashion, that is,

$$\Delta Y = \frac{1}{1-(b-m)} \Delta \text{ Exogenous spending.} \qquad (7.5)$$

For example, if on average consumers spend 80¢ of every dollar that they receive, their marginal propensity to consume is 0.8. But if they spend 60¢ (of the 80¢) on goods made outside the area, the marginal propensity to consume locally is $0.8-0.6=0.2$ and the local income multiplier is

$$\frac{1}{1-(0.80-0.60)} = \frac{1}{1-0.2} = \frac{1}{0.8} = 1.25. \qquad (7.6)$$

In the traditional Keynesian model, an area's low wages will not attract new firms (capital) because capital does not migrate. Instead, lower real wages only exacerbate an unemployment problem by reducing consumption. Symmetrically, higher wages increase consumption and thereby stimulate local employment. Firms (investment) might migrate to areas with lower interest rates, but because these interest rates are invariant within a nation, capital does not migrate.[2]

Consumption is primarily a function of the household's current or expected income, and therefore by itself it cannot pull an economy out of a recession. Business investment is primarily a function of "animal spirits," according to Keynes, and thus it cannot be trusted to alleviate a recession. By tying investment to "animal spirits," Keynes meant that businesses do not base their spending decisions on what is best for the region, but what is best

---

[2] McCombie (1988a).

for their own survival. When a regional economy is in a recession, businesses cut back spending and thereby worsen the local recession. Similarly, bankers are less inclined to lend to businesses in a depressed area because such loans are risky. Alternatively, when the economy is booming, rather than cut back their spending to lessen inflationary pressures, businesses spend even more and thus intensify the potential inflation. Bankers are also inclined to lend when a region is growing because the recovery of their money is more certain.

Because investment tends to be procyclical, we cannot rely on it to alleviate a region's unemployment problem. Proponents of Keynesian theory promote regional exports as well as federal government spending. They use regional multipliers to find the total impact of a given increase in expenditures. Stimulating employment creation in this type of model means either promoting export industries with rapidly expanding demand or attempting to increase market shares of industries in a less resilient market.[3]

Economic Base Theory and Analysis

Economic base theory, popularized by Charles Tiebout in the 1960s, is a combination of Keynesian and international trade theories. In this model, the primary engines of regional economic growth are local firms that produce goods for export because these industries inject income into the economy. Economic base techniques are more accurate and thus more appropriate for small, isolated regions than for diversified metropolitan regions. Likewise, they are more appropriate for short-term rather than long-term impact analyses.[4]

According to the economic base theory, two types of local industries exist: **basic industries** that produce goods or services for export and **nonbasic industries** that produce goods or services for local consumption. Economic base theory assumes that an increase in exports will stimulate not only employment and income in basic industries but also the demand for nonbasic goods and services. We can identify the basic industries by estimating location quotients.

Location Quotients

Location quotients compare the relative concentration of employment in a given industry of a region to that of a benchmark. Location quotients are often used to identify the export base of an area and estimate the number of employees directly linked to exports. To calculate location quotients from

---

[3] Winger (2000).
[4] Klosterman and Xie (1993).

state employment figures, the benchmark is generally the country; for county-level employment, the appropriate benchmark is the state. The location quotient formula for industry i is

$$\frac{e_i}{e} \bigg/ \frac{E_i}{E} \tag{7.7}$$

where e_i is the employment in industry i within the subject region; e is total employment in that region; E_i is employment in industry i for the benchmark area; and E is total employment in the benchmark area.

Interpreting Location Quotients

If the location quotient for a particular industry is greater than 1, the industry is classified as an export industry. The region's industry uses a greater proportion of employment than does that of the benchmark, thus it must produce more goods than local residents consume. Large location quotients reflect local comparative advantages of that industry.[5] On the other hand, if the location quotient is less than 1, the industry does not produce enough goods or services for local consumption and it is considered an import industry. Finally, if the location quotient for an industry equals 1, the industry produces just enough to satisfy local consumption.

It is tempting to assume that if a location quotient is less than 1, then more firms from that industry would thrive in the region. Although this may be true, small location quotients more than likely reflect a lack of comparative advantage. For instance, the location quotient for cotton production in Alaska is almost zero because cotton does not grow in too many parts of that state.

Assumptions Underlying Location Quotient Analysis

Three assumptions that deal with identical tastes, similar productivity levels, and homogeneous products are important in interpreting location quotients. First, we assume that consumption patterns are the same in the region as the rest of the benchmark area. This means, for example, that Floridians and Michiganders have the same desire to own snowmobiles. A violation of this assumption biases the location quotient upward for areas that produce a good to satisfy specific local preferences.

A second assumption states that labor is equally productive everywhere. Value added per manufacturing production worker hour, a common measure of productivity, averaged $105.34 for the United States in 2004. New Mexico's

---

[5] Hildebrand and Mace (1950).

productivity per worker was the highest of all states ($270.63), and Mississippi's ($67.12) was the lowest. If it were true that all states produce the same types of goods, location quotients would underestimate the amount of export activity in New Mexico because fewer workers are needed to produce the same quantity of output as in other areas. At the same time, Mississippi's export activity would be overestimated because the workforce is only 64% as productive as the country's average.

Finally, the location quotient method assumes that each industry produces a single, perfectly homogeneous good. This assumption leads to two problems. First, firms that produce several products have only one North American Industry Classification System (NAICS) code.[6] If a firm produces goods that could be classified under several codes, the firm usually chooses the code that provides them lower workers' compensation insurance premiums.

Second, industries are aggregates of slightly varied rather than perfectly homogeneous economic activity. For example, lutefisk producers are classified as NAICS 3117.[7] This classification includes varied activities such as canning, smoking, salting, drying, and freezing seafood, as well as shucking and packing fresh shellfish. Total employment in the NAICS 3117 industry (E_i) was 41,307 nationally in 2002 when total national employment (E) was 166,699,000. Employment in this same industry in Minnesota (e_i) was around 375 in 2002, when total Minnesota employment (e) was 3,359,670.[8] The calculated location quotient for the industry in 2002 is approximately 0.45, which suggests that Minnesota's fish processing sector does not satisfy local consumption. This is despite the fact that they export lutefisk to places as far away as Illinois and even Norway. Because of the data aggregation and disclosure problems, the location quotient cannot show the uniqueness of the lutefisk industry in Minnesota.

Employment Multipliers

Because data on income and consumption expenditures are not collected on a local level, regional analysts generate multipliers using

---

[6] The NAICS replaced the Standard Industry Classification system (SIC codes) beginning in 1997. The NAICS provides common industry definitions for Canada, Mexico, and the United States.

[7] Lutefisk is dried codfish that has been soaked in a water and lye solution before cooking, according to the Merriam-Webster Dictionary, http://www.m-w.com, accessed 9 October 2002. Lutefisk is a traditional food brought by the first Norwegian immigrants. Minnesota exports it to North Dakota, Wisconsin, and even to Norway, but few communities in the United States have heard of this ethnic delicacy.

[8] The stated employment was in the range 250–499, so we chose the midpoint of 375 to estimate the location quotient. The actual value of the location quotient is somewhere between 0.30 and 0.60.

employment data, which are available after a lag of one to three years. The base multiplier is

$$\frac{\text{Total Employment}}{\text{Basic Employment}} \qquad (7.8)$$

where **basic employment** is the total employment needed to produce goods for export and **total employment** is the sum of basic and nonbasic employment. If the base multiplier is 2.7, each worker in a basic industry generates 1.7 jobs in nonbasic industries. The next step is therefore to identify the amount of basic employment.

Table 7.1 shows the employment, location quotients, basic employment, and economic base multipliers for Ohio and Wayne County, Ohio, using 2003 data. The first and second columns of numbers show the 2003 employment data for the State of Ohio and Wayne County. The third column shows the location quotients for Wayne County using data from the State of Ohio as a benchmark. The fourth column presents basic employment for the export industries.

The analysis shows that in 2003, Wayne County exported products from farming, forestry, fishing, construction, mining, manufacturing, educational services, and state and local government. Construction will be an export industry either if the industry within that county is growing faster than the state's average or if construction firms located in that county work in other areas. However, because the location quotients for both government and government enterprises and state and local government are slightly greater than one, those sectors just satisfy local consumption. The remaining sectors are classified as import sectors because their location quotients are less than one. Proportionally fewer workers are employed in these sectors in the county compared with the state.

Calculating Basic Employment

Equation 7.9 gives the formula for estimating export employment, X, for each industry:

$$X_i = \left(\frac{e_i}{e} - \frac{E_i}{E}\right) \times e. \qquad (7.9)$$

The sum of the export employment for industries having location quotients greater than one gives the regional basic employment. All other employment is nonbasic.[9]

---

[9] Sasaki (1963); Isserman (1980).

Table 7.1 Employment for the State of Ohio and Wayne County, Ohio, Location Quotients and Basic Employment, 2003

	Ohio	Wayne County	Location Quotients	Basic Employment
Total employment	6,674,406	62,029	—	—
Farm employment	96,488	2496	2.783	1599
Forestry, fishing, related activities	13,358	226	1.820	102
Mining	18,287	656	3.860	486
Utilities	22,967	(D)	—	—
Construction	347,175	3649	1.131	423
Manufacturing	869,999	14,650	1.812	6565
Wholesale trade	253,840	2266	0.961	—
Retail trade	766,418	6,380	0.896	—
Transportation and warehousing	209,126	(D)	—	—
Information	108,428	420	0.417	—
Finance and insurance	305,584	1944	0.685	—
Real estate and rental and leasing	198,946	1163	0.629	—
Professional and technical services	354,293	1923	0.584	—
Management of companies and enterprises	93,438	473	0.545	—
Administrative and waste services	376,629	2068	0.591	—
Educational services	118,657	1620	1.469	517
Health care and social assistance	734,961	4783	0.700	—
Arts, entertainment, and recreation	118,699	599	0.543	—
Accommodation and food services	444,199	3613	0.875	—
Other services, except public administration	374,729	3197	0.918	—

Government and government enterprises	848,185	7905	1.003	22[a]
Federal, civilian	77,706	270	0.374	
Military	39,063	308	0.848	
State and local	731,416	7327	1.078	530[a]
State government	178,806	1645	0.990	
Local government	552,610	5682	1.106	546
Total basic (export) employment:				10,768

Data are from the BEA Regional Economic Information System (REIS) CA 25: http://www.bea.gov/bea/regional/reis/, Date accessed 26 July 2005.

[a] In this example, to avoid double counting, we ignored the 22 and 530 for Government and government enterprises and State and local, respectively. We only used the 546 from Local government in our calculation of total basic employment.

Note that when the location quotient is less than one, the calculated "export employment" would be negative. Because import industries do not export anything by definition, their amount of export employment is equal to zero. Note also that the government and government enterprise sector consists of federal, civilian, military, and state and local employees. One must be sure to only count them once. In this example, we only kept the basic employment from the local government sector. Finally, note that data are not available for the Utilities or Transportation and Warehousing sectors. If either of these sectors is in truth an export industry, our estimate of basic employment is too low.

Estimating Employment Multipliers

From Table 7.1, we can calculate the employment multiplier. Divide the total employment figure by the sum of export employment (Column 4) to estimate the multiplier: $62,029/10,238 = 6.059$. Note that this estimate *may* be biased upward. The lack of employment for two sectors (Utilities and Transportation & Warehousing) requires that we treat these as import sectors. If the sectors are indeed importers, there is no bias. However, if these sectors produce goods for export, our denominator is smaller than it should be, causing the potential upward bias in the multiplier. The input–output technique gives more precise estimates of multipliers because it estimates multipliers for each individual industry based on the expected interindustry linkages. IMPLAN, a popular input–output software program, estimates several types of multipliers for a maximum of 528 sectors of a specific county. The Bureau of Economic Analysis (BEA) created the Regional Input–Output Modeling System (RIMS II) that can produce multipliers for over 400 sectors in each county. Multipliers calculated using the economic base method are generally larger than those calculated by an input–output program for diverse, metropolitan areas. However, for rural areas, the multipliers are often approximately the same size.

Size and Stability of Multipliers

An increase in demand for goods from an area affects (1) the industry producing these goods, (2) the suppliers of intermediate goods, and (3) the expenditures of employees in the affected industries. The *direct effect* of an increase in demand in one industry is an increase in employment in that industry. The *indirect effect* entails an increase in demand for intermediate goods needed to produce this increased demand. Finally, the *induced effect* comes from the spending of employees who work in both the original industry and the auxiliary industries. Both the direct and indirect effects increase the amount of basic goods produced whereas the induced effect primarily increases the demand for nonbasic goods. In and of itself, increasing the demand for basic goods will not shift the production

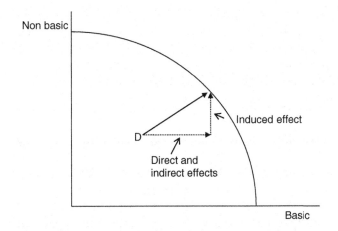

Figure 7.3 Direct, indirect, and induced effects on a production possibilities curve.

possibilities curve outward, but it will move the economy from a point within the curve (such as Point D in Figure 7.3) to some point closer to the curve. The increases in direct and indirect effects do not shift out the production possibilities curve because they are caused only by an increase in demand. Aggregate supply is fixed in this short-run framework.

The size of the multiplier depends on the number of local backward linkages and the degree of import substitution. Larger urban areas with more localization and urbanization economies will have larger multipliers than those in less populated, rural areas. In addition, more markets can attain threshold size in urbanized areas. Consumers import fewer goods from outside the area if they have a greater choice in local products. More backward linkages mean a larger local multiplier. However, a larger propensity to substitute imports for locally made goods decreases the marginal propensity to consume locally, and thus shrinks the multiplier (because the denominator, $[1-(b-m)]$, is larger).

Higher regional incomes can have either a positive or a negative effect on the size of the multiplier. Higher incomes mean an increased demand for all normal goods and suggest a larger multiplier. However, this tendency is met with two opposing effects. First, higher incomes are also associated with a greater propensity to purchase luxury goods. If the luxury goods are imported, ***import substitution*** decreases the marginal propensity to spend locally. Second, the marginal propensity to consume tends to decrease as incomes increase because consumers with higher incomes also save greater proportions of their income. The resulting lower marginal propensity to consume will also diminish the size of the multiplier.[10]

---

[10] Martin and Miley (1983); Vias and Mulligan (1997).

Note that in international trade analyses, a large import substitution is generally considered a plus for a low-income area because the inhabitants now have sufficient earnings to purchase imports rather than having to rely on local production. What such analyses do not recognize is that the local manufacturers of these products lose sales and have to lay off workers because of the substitution of imports for locally manufactured goods.

Rural Services as Economic Development Tools

Gilmer, Keil and Mack (1989) used location quotients to identify the existence, direction, and nature of the supply of services according to a hierarchy of central places in the rural southeast United States. They found few basic exports or imports of rural services and not one service industry that was both basic and footloose. The diversity of supply of services follows this rural hierarchy.

However, arbitrarily embedding services in lower-order places as an economic development initiative reduces their overall efficiency because the cost reduction predicted from agglomeration economies prevails only in higher-order places.

Gilmer, Keil and Mack (1989)

Another factor that influences the size of the multiplier is the speed of regional economic growth. Any rapid expansion in regional output that leads to shortages of labor or other inputs forces the local economy to look outside the area for its inputs. If this happens, the marginal propensity to consume locally shrinks for two reasons: (1) nonlocal suppliers sell goods to local firms and (2) commuters who fill temporary jobs are apt to spend a large proportion of their earnings at or around their places of residence. As the marginal propensity to consume locally shrinks, so does the multiplier.

Finally, multipliers ignore any feedback effects between regions. A strict interpretation of the Keynesian model asserts that increases in exports will boost the economy and equilibrium income, but increases in imports will lower equilibrium income. However, when Region A purchases more from Region B, employment and income in Region B both increase. In turn,

Region B's prosperity increases its demand for exports coming from Region A.

Regional Income Multipliers in Sub-Saharan Africa

Hazell and Hojjati (1995) used a farm survey in Eastern Province, Zambia to estimate the regional income multipliers for agriculture. Their calculations show that the multipliers for the valley and plateau are 2.57 and 2.48. That means that each kwacha of additional value added due to increased agricultural production generates about 1.5 kwacha of additional income. However, because farm production and investment linkages are still quite weak, most of the income multiplier rises from spending in the agricultural sector itself.

Hazell and Hojjati (1995)

Nontraditional Economic Bases

Traditionally, agriculture, mining, and manufacturing were the only driving forces in the economic base literature. All services were considered nonbasic. However, services, tourism, and people who receive income transfers can constitute a region's economic base.

Services

Current research stresses the fact that there are several types of services: consumer and producer services, health services, educational services, and tourism. The majority of consumer services and tourist industry jobs lead to the low-wage jobs with no future that are typically associated with the service industry. However, producer services as well as most health and educational services entail professional, productive, and high-wage positions similar to those in manufacturing.

Producer services are exportable in three ways. First, a service such as advertising, insurance, or computer software may be exported directly to consumers. Second, specialized medical care or tourism services are "exported" when the consumer comes from another region. Third, a service may be exported indirectly because it is embodied in exported manufac-tured goods. Products are bundles of many different processes. Some of the processes come from services and others from manufacturing. Even steelmaking is becoming more service oriented. Through outsourcing, service providers inspect, slit, coat, store, and deliver the materials to customers.[11]

Tourism

By definition, tourists are nonresidents, and thus tourism becomes a pipeline through which money flows into a region. However, there is no NAICS code for a "tourism industry," and jobs created by tourism are extremely difficult to identify. Except for airlines, travel agencies, insurance companies, and aircraft manufacturers, few industries rely on tourist expenditures. Backward linkages exist in the form of the hospitality industry and gasoline service stations. Most tourists stay in hotels or motels, but occasionally, so do local residents. Tourists eat at restaurants and fill up their gas tanks, as do local residents. Similarly, tourists stand in lines of super-markets and banks along with residents.

Unlike most producer services, tourism employment is generally limited to part-time and seasonal work requiring entry-level skills. In addition, the work provides wages, benefits, and advancement potential which in fact are more generous in the manufacturing or resource extraction industries. Sometimes a government decides to create jobs by promoting tourism and by preserving natural amenities. Such programs are often funded by additional taxes imposed on an existing manufacturing or extraction industry. The tourism agenda may also require additional regulations imposed on the manufacturing or extraction industries. The impact of such policies may indeed create a larger number of (low-wage) jobs. However, the cost of such a program in terms of employment opportunities includes the number of higher paying occupations foregone.[12]

Retirees and Other Sources of Income Transfers

The presence of retirees is another alternative economic base. Rural areas that succeed in attracting retirees outperform others in such economic development measures as income, population, and employment growth. Retirees are drawn to rural areas that are accessible, low cost, and attractive. They prefer areas endowed with natural amenities, "small-town values," and

---

[11] Groshen (1987); Harris (1987); Hansen (1994).

[12] Blank (1989); Williams (1997).

good medical facilities. Retirees purchase a community's nonbasic goods and thus create jobs similar to those found in tourism. Salaries providing employment created by the retirees are on average 87% lower than the average earnings in other rural areas, even though retirees support higher-wage jobs in the health industry.[13]

Financial Markets and Regional Growth

From a macroeconomic viewpoint, bank lending plays an important role in determining or controlling the growth of a nation. Bank lending should cause increases in regional economic activity either by increasing local demand or by increasing the types of goods and services available to consumers. However, as Mark Twain once said, "A banker is a fellow who lends you his umbrella when the sun is shining, but wants it back the minute it begins to rain." Bankers hesitate to lend to depressed areas because such areas have high default rates.

Monetary policy is an efficient tool for increasing aggregate demand in a national economy, but it is not an effective regional development policy tool. As soon as countries of the European Union adopted the euro, they sacrificed the use of monetary policy as an economic stabilization tool. In the United States, two characteristics restrict the capability of the Federal Reserve to use monetary policy to assist one state. First, financial assets flow freely across state borders and investors will purchase securities from whichever source pays the highest yields. The lack of barriers to the flow of financial assets means that the interest rates on securities of equal risk will equilibrate everywhere within a country.

Second, because California, for example, uses the same currency as the rest of the United States, its exchange rate with respect to other states is permanently fixed at one. If the Federal Reserve Board tries to improve economic conditions in California, it will generate inflationary pressures in parts of the country that are experiencing full employment.

The lack of information about the borrower also impedes inter-regional capital flows, and thus restricts lending. The cost of monitoring loans increases with distance, so the content of a bank's loan portfolio depends on its location. In addition, distance from the borrower is also an obstacle for lenders who limit their financial activity to a specific local area.

Although, as we saw in Chapter 5, rural banks may have more knowl-edge of the local entrepreneurs and their projects, they are also less likely than larger urban banks to finance more innovative and thus riskier investment projects. Local banks cannot encourage very much risky

---

[13] Sastry (1992); Reeder, Schneider and Green (1993); Deller et al. (2001).

innovation, so dynamic entrepreneurs approach larger urban financial markets to finance their dreams.[14]

Input–Output Analysis

Input–output analysis is a way of quantifying the structure of an economy in a given year. According to this model, the economy has three components: interindustry transactions, final demand, and value added. Interindustry transactions are the sales and purchases of intermediate products. Consumption, investment, government spending, and regional exports constitute the final demand sectors. Value-added sectors account for inputs such as labor and capital provided by households (babysitting, housecleaning or lawn mowing services).

Input–output traces the sales of one sector to all other sectors within the economy. Because the input–output table is actually a double-entry accounting system, input–output also determines the inputs purchased from each sector that are used to produce its final product. The TABLEAU ÉCONOMIQUE of François Quesnay and the seventeenth century French Physiocrats was the first attempt at explaining the concept of circular flow in terms of inputs required to produce each good and receipts needed to maintain their employment levels. Input–output analysis is a detailed extension of the TABLEAU ÉCONOMIQUE created by 1973 Nobel Prize winner Wassily Leontief in 1936. Researchers have since developed more technical, supply-based models (Ghosh, 1958, for example) and some that combine supply and demand into an extremely complex model.

Uses of Input–Output Analysis

Input–output analysis is a popular technique for (1) regional forecasting and planning, (2) developing potential scenarios for an economy if an industry were to expand, contract, or disappear, and (3) evaluating the impact of government regulations or changes in fiscal policy. Wundt and Martin (1993) used input–output analysis to point out the mix of industries in Connecticut that would minimize employment instability when the defense industry's budget was cut in the 1990s. With input–output analysis, Wolff et al. (1995) highlighted the potential impacts of an electric-vehicle manufacturing if such a complex were to locate in Los Angeles.

Extensions of input–output analysis also measure environmental impacts. For example, Siegel and Johnson (1991) investigated the impact

---

[14] Cogley and Schann (1994).

of the Conservation Research Program on a rural economy. Waters, Holland, and Weber (1994) determined the number of jobs lost in Oregon and California when the northern spotted owl was listed as an endangered species. Most estimates of the impact of a university on a local economy are based in part on input–output analysis. This tool can also generate allows an estimate of the regional impact of the elusive tourist dollar.

The Antismoking Campaign and the Scottish Economy

A study by McNicoll and Boyle (1992) used input–output analysis to estimate the effect on the Scottish economy if everyone stopped smoking. The authors ignored health and productivity effects of smoking-related disease and focused on the expenditure effects of smoking cessation. They estimated the number of smokers along with the spending habits by age group and determined that if these smokers stopped smoking, they would have an additional £122.2 million that they currently spend on cigarettes that can be used for spending in sectors endowed with larger multipliers. The net effect was that for each £1 million reduction in cigarettes purchased, Scottish output would rise by £1.1 million. Employment would increase by 64.4 full-time jobs. Moreover, the £89.9 million reduction in tobacco tax payments will be compensated by gains in taxes from other sales with a resulting net loss of only £42.6 in tax revenue.

Boyle and McNicoll (1992)

Recent input–output models by Polenske and Hewings (2004) extended the research possibilities in international trade using by adjusting for feedback between trading regions. Macroeconomic analysis benefits from estimations of commodity trade flows. In addition, regional and global supply chain theories come from input–output techniques. Supply chains analyze where firms acquire their raw materials, how they convert the raw materials and other inputs into final products, and the method by which they transport their products to the retail stores.

Measuring the Impact of the Grateful Dead

Gazel and Schwer (1997) estimated the economic impact of three Grateful Dead concerts on the Las Vegas economy. Benefits from the concerts come from goods and services sold to nonlocal fans and the expected expenditures of the local public, who would have gone elsewhere to see the Grateful Dead had the group not performed in Las Vegas. Over 2000 expenditure surveys were completed from a total of 111,554 and the researchers used RIMS II multipliers to estimate the average impact coming from different expenditure groups.

The employment impact on Las Vegas was 324.9 jobs— 219.9 were created by outside tourists. Spending to coordinate and run the shows created 57.6 jobs. Spending by residents of Las Vegas who would have gone elsewhere to see the Grateful Dead supported 47.4 jobs.

Gazel and Schwer (1997)

Mathematics of Input–Output Analysis

Mathematically, one can divide the economy into n sectors. The transactions table accounts for the dollar value of transactions between one sector and every other sector of the local economy. Rows show distribution of sales by sectors. X_i is the total output produced by sector i; z_{ij} represents all sales of intermediate products from i to other industries; and Y_i is the total final demand for output from sector i. $X_i = z_{i1} + z_{i2} + \ldots + z_{ii} + \ldots + z_{in} + Y_i$. Columns indicate the amount of the product that each sector purchases from all the other sectors to make its product. Specifically, $X_j = z_{1j} + z_{2j} + \ldots + z_{nj} + V_j = \sum_i^n z_{ij} + V_j$, where X_j is the total spending of sector j and V_j are the payments to a factor of production in sector j. The basic assumption is that the sum of all inputs in the economy should equal the sum of all outputs, or $\Sigma X_i = \Sigma X_j$. A hypothetical **transactions table** is depicted in Table 7.2.

Horizontally, the numbers in the transactions table identify the buyer of output produced by each sector. In Table 7.2, Sector A sells $12 worth of goods to other firms in Sector A, $35 to Sector B, $85 to C, $22 to D,

Table 7.2 Hypothetical Transactions Table

| | Buyers | | | | | | Gross |
| | Interindustry Flows of Goods | | | | | Final | Regional |
Sellers	A	B	C	D	E	Demand	Output
A	12	35	85	22	12	540	706
B	25	34	25	1	26	350	461
C	45	25	32	11	5	338	456
D	155	42	44	56	25	266	588
E	24	255	25	4	251	563	1122
							3333
Value added	445	70	245	494	803	—	—
Imports	25	3	20	25	35	—	—
Total spending	706	461	456	588	1122	—	3333

$12 to E, and $540 to final demand. The gross output of Sector A is $706. **Vertically**, the table shows from which other sector each sector bought the inputs needed to produce its output. For Sector C to make its $456 worth of goods, it spent $85 for products made in Sector A, $25 for B, $32 for products from other firms in its own Sector C, $44 for D, and $25 for E. In addition, $245 goes to households in the form of wages, interest paid to capital, and profits, all of which constitute value added. Finally, $20 goes to the purchase of imports.

Technical (or direct) coefficients (a_{ij}) are calculated by dividing each cell of the transactions table by the sum of the column figures, which represent total spending for that sector. Each cell of the table of technical coefficients gives the percentage of total expenditures that is allocated to each sector because of the first (or direct) transaction. In matrix notation, $[A] = a_{ij} = z_{ij}/X_j$. Table 7.3 gives the **Table of Technical Coefficients** associated with Table 7.2.

Each cell in the matrix shown in Table 7.3 represents the proportion of every dollar that must be paid by the column sector to every other sector to produce $1 worth of output. Thus to produce $10 worth of output, Sector B purchases 76¢ of output from Sector A, 74¢ from B, 54¢ from C, 91¢ from D, and $5.53 from E. In addition, Sector B allocates $1.45 in wages, interest, and profits and 7¢ for imported goods.

Technical coefficients only show the quantity of output from each industry needed to produce final demand (the first round effect). The amount of output from each industry needed to produce both the original output and each intermediate good is shown in a table of multipliers. Imagine that the direct effect of an increase in final demand is

Table 7.3 Table of Technical Coefficients

Industries	Industries				
	A	B	C	D	E
A	0.017	0.076	0.186	0.037	0.011
B	0.035	0.074	0.055	0.002	0.023
C	0.064	0.054	0.070	0.019	0.004
D	0.220	0.091	0.096	0.095	0.022
E	0.034	0.553	0.055	0.007	0.224
Value added	0.595	0.145	0.493	0.798	0.684
Imports	0.035	0.007	0.044	0.043	0.031
Total spending	1.000	1.000	1.000	1.000	1.000

like a drop of water falling into a still pond. The initial impact produces the most intense effect, but each successive round will be less and less intense up to the point where there is scarcely any effect felt.

Each successive round is represented by higher powers of the **A** matrix (the matrix of a_{ij}). In matrix notation, the direct effect is represented by $\mathbf{I}-\mathbf{A}$, where I is the identity matrix. An identity matrix is a square matrix with a value of 1 on the diagonal and 0 in the off-diagonal cells. The matrix $[\mathbf{I}-\mathbf{A}]$ is called the Leontief matrix. Both the direct and indirect effects are represented by the series $\mathbf{I}-\mathbf{A}+\mathbf{A}^2+\mathbf{A}^3+\ldots+\mathbf{A}^n$. As the power of **A** increases, it will approach a zero matrix. To generate the multiplier matrix and approximate the power series, one must invert the Leontief matrix, $[\mathbf{I}-\mathbf{A}]^{-1}$. The production needed to satisfy an increase in final demand (X) is calculated by multiplying the vector of final demand (**Y**) by the inverse of the Leontief matrix, $X=[\mathbf{I}-\mathbf{A}]^{-1}\mathbf{Y}$. This calculation is analogous to that used in finding the traditional Keynesian multiplier (Equation 7.2). The result is a **Table of Multipliers** (Table 7.4).

According to Table 7.4, an increase of $1 in the final demand of Sector B requires a total of 11.6¢ spent in Sector A. Besides the original $1, an additional 10.9¢ is spent in B, 8¢ in C, etc., for a total of $2.276. Sector B has the largest multiplier. Sector D purchases fewer intermediate products locally and thus it has a much smaller multiplier. Therefore, at first glance, an efficient jobs program might target Sector B because that sector provides the largest "bang for the buck." However, first glances can be misleading. Multipliers go both ways. A large multiplier for a declining industry such as agriculture spells economic disaster if agriculture is the region's mainstay.[15]

---

[15] Leontief (1936, 1970); Miernyk (1965); Miller and Blair (1985); Chappelle, D. E., et al. (1986); Adamou and Gowdy (1990); DRI/McGraw-Hill (1994).

Table 7.4 Table of Multipliers

	A	B	C	D	E
A	1.047	0.116	0.223	0.048	0.021
B	0.047	1.109	0.078	0.006	0.034
C	0.080	0.080	1.100	0.026	0.011
D	0.270	0.168	0.183	1.121	0.042
E	0.088	0.803	0.144	0.018	1.315
Type I multipliers	1.533	2.276	1.727	1.219	1.422

Input–Output Multipliers

The Type I multiplier is the sum of the direct and indirect effects divided by the direct effect. Because the multipliers generated by a simplified Leontief inverse matrix exclude employee spending, these are Type I multipliers. The Type II multipliers come from more complex programs that add the induced effects to the numerator. Mathematically,

$$\text{Type I Multiplier}: \frac{\text{Direct} + \text{Indirect}}{\text{Direct}}$$

$$\text{Type II Multiplier}: \frac{\text{Direct} + \text{Indirect} + \text{Induced}}{\text{Direct}}. \quad (7.10)$$

The multipliers vary by sector because of the strength of the backward linkages associated with each specific sector. The Type II multiplier is always larger than the Type I multiplier for the same sector because it includes spending by employees of all firms associated with making the final product.

Note that an industry's forward linkages play no part in estimating its impact on an economy. A local airport may be the key determinant if a firm decides to settle some distance from the major trade center; but the economic impact of the airport estimated by input–output analysis ignores everything but the direct, indirect, and induced effects from the amount of fuel, parts, and labor purchased locally by that facility. Similarly, a university's impact would include only the amount of spending generated by the university, its employees, and its students, but not the technical innovation provided by professors or the supply of educated labor provided by students, professors, and spouses.

Assumptions Implicit in Input–Output Analysis

There are a large number of assumptions implicit in an input–output analysis. Assumptions become limitations only when they compromise the integrity of the conclusions of the study. The key is to make the appropriate policy decisions from the results of the analysis while keeping in mind the limitations of the technique. Ten "families" of these assumptions are:

First, the model assumes a linear production function. This is not a major problem when analyzing small impacts, but it will overestimate the effects of large events. There are no capacity constraints or threshold size effects, and thus industries are treated as if they could expand indefinitely to meet demand. Similarly, industries will never fold if demand tumbles below a certain level. Finally, there are no bottlenecks. All resources are always readily available, but at the same time, they are neither unemployed nor underemployed.

Second, all production is made from a recipe that strictly forbids input substitution. Leontief's isoquants are L-shaped, as we saw in Chapter 4.

Third, the model assumes homogeneous output within each sector. The less aggregation in a sector, the more reliable the result. This requires that much more data be collected to create sectors that are as homogeneous as possible.

Fourth, there is no cross-hauling (simultaneously shipping the same product in opposite directions over the same route). If a local sector produces a necessary input, the model assumes that the input is indeed purchased locally.

Fifth, because it is a static model, it ignores interregional feedbacks or any dynamics such as changes in technology over the period of analysis.

Sixth, there are no internal or external economies of scale. That is, each firm has constant returns to scale and no agglomeration economies. In addition, there are no central place effects.

Seventh, any loss of employment means no further consumption in the region. The unemployed workers pack up and leave as soon as they get their layoff notices. The induced effect does not account for spending by laid-off workers who temporarily receive unemployment benefits.

Eighth, any increased demand for labor lures new households to move to the area. These households will start consuming products as soon as they start work, but not until then.

Ninth, in most input–output programs, an industry's inputs are imputed from a national input–output matrix. This assumes that Coca-Cola producers in Kansas City, Missouri use the same ingredients as producers in Miami, Florida, which may be true. But it also assumes that all electricity is produced by the same "recipe," whether it comes from the Grand Coulee Dam in Washington State, nuclear powered plants, wind generators, or thermal plants whether they burn coal, natural gas, or garbage.

Finally, for researchers who prefer parametric approaches to data analysis, input–output analysis offers no confidence intervals, no t-statistics, and no way to test proximity to the "truth." Because of this, the vast amount of data used in input–output models must be as up-to-date as possible, especially when describing or analyzing a rapidly growing economy.

Decomposing Regional Employment

The economic base concept argues that insufficient demand is the principal cause of employment rate differences among regions. Taking the idea a step further, we can decompose the demand to identify the causes of employment differences. Several major components of demand affect a region's employment rate: national (or state) factors, the cyclical nature of predominant industries, and the mix of industries. Per-unit wage rates and the proportion of urban to rural areas are also important in determining regional employment.

Changes in national aggregate demand affect the employment rate of a region. If a country exports more, this increase will directly or indirectly affect all regions of that nation. Because the national unemployment rate includes the unemployment rates of all regions, national recessions and regional unemployment rates are interdependent by construction. However, the severity and timing of national recessions varies among regions by their mix of industries.

"Tell me what your industries are and I will tell you your future." A region's industry mix affects its employment level in several ways. First, different regions specialize in diverse commodities, each with distinct income elasticities. This means that the reaction of a region over the national business cycle will depend on which industries are in that region. When the country is in a recession, countercyclical industries expand and cyclical industries contract. Areas dominated by countercyclical industries ride out a national recession with relatively low unemployment rates. In addition, firms that have not modernized their capital stock cannot compete in a depressed national market. Thus the older industrialized regions suffer more severely during national recessions than the rest of the country does.

Second, employment in different industries waxes and wanes with the demands for output in each industry. For example, energy-producing regions react much differently to a fall in crude oil prices than the energy-consuming regions do.

Other factors influence a region's employment rate, such as the ***per-unit labor costs*** (the ratio of real wage to labor productivity). Differences in unit labor costs affect local demand and supply, and consequently, the employment rate. If the real wage falls or if labor productivity increases, the region becomes more competitive and employment increases.[16]

Shift-Share Analysis

The classical shift-share approach trisects the change in employment (d_{ij}) into a growth component (g_{ij}), an industry mix component (m_{ij}), and a competitive effect (c_{ij}). The growth and industry mix components are usually referred to as the share portion; the competitive effect is the shift portion of the technique.

Mathematically, the classical shift-share approach uses the following equations:

$$d_{ij} = g_{ij} + m_{ij} + c_{ij}, \tag{7.11}$$

$$g_{ij} = E_{ij0}\, r_B, \tag{7.12}$$

$$m_{ij} = E_{ij0}(r_{iB} - r_B) \tag{7.13}$$

$$c_{ij} = E_{ij0}(r_{ij} - r_{iB}) \tag{7.14}$$

where E_{ij0} is the number of employees in industry i within region j during time 0,

$$d_{ij} = E_{ij1} - E_{ij0} \tag{7.15}$$

is the regional change in employment in industry i, because E_{ij1} is the number of employees in industry i within region j in the new period.

$$r_B = \frac{(E_{B1} - E_{B0})}{E_{B0}} \tag{7.16}$$

is the overall growth rate of the benchmark area (country or state). E_{B0} and E_{B1} are the total number of employees in the benchmark area during period 0 and period 1, respectively.

$$r_{iB} = \frac{(E_{iB1} - E_{iB0})}{E_{iB0}} \tag{7.17}$$

is the growth rate of industry i in the benchmark. E_{iB1} and E_{iB0} are the total number of employees in industry i in the benchmark area during period 0 and period 1, respectively.

---

[16] Howland (1984); Schweitzer and Roberts (1996); Taylor and Bradley (1997).

$$r_{ij} = \frac{(E_{ij1} - E_{ij0})}{E_{ij0}} \tag{7.18}$$

is the growth rate of industry i in region j. E_{ij1} and E_{ij0} are the total number of employees in industry i in region j during period 0 and period 1, respectively.

Besides estimating employment growth, this technique is used to decompose rural retail trade patterns, crime rates, sales of insurance by types, and poverty rates. Shift-share analysis is one of the more controversial techniques used by regional economists. Many articles have either questioned or applauded its usefulness.[17]

Stability of the Competitive Effect

The nature of the competitive effect is the principal cause of most of the disagreement concerning shift-share analysis. Shift-share was originally promoted as a method of forecasting regional employment growth. As a possible forecasting tool, regional forecasts would depend on forecasts of the benchmark (national or state) growth and the expected growth of the region's predominant industries. The competitive effect would be merely white noise. But because the competitive effect was significant in regression analyse designed to explain employment growth, researchers explored the possibility that it was a measure of the regional comparative advantage. If the competitive effect were stable and predictable, it could refine a regional forecast.

Past empirical tests tried to measure both the stability and possible determinants of the competitive effect, but without much success. For example, Buck (1970) followed up his analysis of data in Merseyside and the northwest of England by going from firm to firm with surveys that would reveal the "real causes" and the statistical significance of the competitive effect. He found no example in which the competitive effect was due to locational advantages. Firms "grew" more than the national average for three principle reasons: (1) there were problems with the data—firms were either classified incorrectly or they produced nonhomogeneous products and their employees were allocated incorrectly to certain industries; (2) some firms were reorganized; or (3) others relocated to the region to profit from government inducements. However, not one single firm gave a "spatial explanation" for a more rapid growth rate in their area.

---

[17] Blair and Mabry (1980); Stevens and Moore (1980); Halperin and Mabry (1984); Senf (1989); Wright (1996).

Data problems aside, although the competitive effect may measure a region's competitive advantage, it provides no hint concerning the capability of a region to retain the growth-sector industries. It does not identify the specific factors that give some regions—but not others—a comparative advantage.[18]

Esteban-Marquillas Extension

Esteban-Marquillas (1972) noted that the competitive effect is actually a combination of the concentration of regional employment by industry and the growth rate of that industry. Esteban-Marquillas was the first to correct this problem by calculating "homothetic employment." Homothetic employment is the level of employment that sector i of region j would be expected to have if this region had the same structure as the nation or state. In other words, location quotients calculated with a region's homothetic employment would equal 1. In this way, homothetic employment ties the shift-share analysis to the location quotient method. This technique adds reliability to the shift-share model because the location quotient is a reliable indicator of the structure of an area compared to its base.

Esteban-Marquillas redefined the competitive effect and added a fourth component—the allocation effect (a_{ij})—so that the shift-share analysis remains a tautology (true by definition). The redefined competitive effect is as follows:

$$c'_{ij} = E'_{ij0}(r_{ij} - r_{iB}) \tag{7.19}$$

where E'_{ij0} is homothetic employment:

$$E'_{ij0} = E_j(E_{iB}/E_B) \tag{7.20}$$

The component a_{ij} consists of a specialization effect $(E_{ij0} - E'_{ij0})$ and a measure of comparative advantage $(r_{ij} - r_{iB})$:

$$a_{ij} = (E_{ij0} - E'_{ij0})(r_{ij} - r_{iB}) \tag{7.21}$$

The resulting four possible combinations of specialization and comparative advantage imply different policy prescriptions. A positive allocation effect, where the specialization effect and the comparative advantage are either both positive or both negative, signifies an efficient allocation of resources. This will exist if either the region is specialized $(E_{ij0} - E'_{ij0}) > 0$ and has comparative advantage $(r_{ij} - r_{iB}) > 0$ or if it is not specialized $(E_{ij0} - E'_{ij0}) < 0$ and does not have comparative advantage

---

[18] Brown (1969); Buck (1970); Stilwell (1970); Brown (1971); Berzeg (1978); Shaffer (1979); Hustedde, Shaffer and Pulver (1989).

$(r_{ij} - r_{iB}) < 0$. The positive allocation effect suggests that the market is working efficiently without outside intervention.

A negative allocation effect suggests an incorrect industry mix for the region. This will happen if a region is specialized $(E_{ij0} - E'_{ij0}) > 0$ but does not have comparative advantage $(r_{ij} - r_{iB}) < 0$ or if the region is not specialized $(E_{ij0} - E'_{ij0}) < 0$ but does have comparative advantage $(r_{ij} - r_{iB}) > 0$. The incorrect industry mix suggests that perhaps the market is not working efficiently and further study is necessary to determine how best to remedy the problem.[19]

> If the industry is specialized
>
>> And if it demonstrates comparative advantage
>>
>>> The industry is healthy and intervention is unnecessary.
>>
>> But if there is discernable comparative advantage
>>
>>> Intervention may be useful, but further study is needed.
>
> If the industry is not specialized
>
>> But if it demonstrates comparative advantage
>>
>>> Intervention may be useful, but further study is needed.
>>
>> However, if there is discernable comparative advantage
>>
>>> The sustainability of intervention is questionable. The industry cannot efficiently expand.

The signs (+ or −) of specialization or comparative advantage are strongly affected by the choice of the base year. The interpretations of these two effects are also sensitive to the amount of local industry employment. For example, if regional employment grows from two to four workers (100%), while employment in the benchmark region increases from 300 to 350 (16.7%), the region gives the illusion of a disproportionate comparative advantage. This situation can falsely lead researchers and policy makers to want to intensify the specialization in that industry.

The results of a shift-share analysis for Lincoln County, Nebraska between 2001 and 2003 are shown in Table 7.5 through Table 7.7. The benchmark for Lincoln County is the State of Nebraska. Table 7.5 shows the employment and the growth rates in each of the two regions. Note that because of disclosure problems with data, there are no employment figures for Lincoln County in forestry, fishing and related activities, mining, utilities, wholesale trade, and transportation and warehousing

---

[19] Herzog and Olsen (1977); Arcelus (1984); Loveridge and Selting (1998).

for both 2001 and 2003. Between 2001 and 2003, employment in Lincoln County grew faster than anywhere in the entire state thanks to the dynamics of the following sectors, which grew more rapidly than those in the entire state:

Information
Finance and insurance
Real estate and rental and leasing
Professional and technical services
Administrative and waste services
Educational services
Health care and social assistance
Arts, entertainment, and recreation
Accommodation and food services
Other services, except public administration

During these two years, Nebraska's employment grew by 0.2% while Lincoln County's employment grew by approximately 1.1%.

To compare the calculations in Table 7.5 with the Equation 7.10 through Equation 7.13, note that $r_B = 0.002$ from the last row of Column 3. The r_{iB} figures for each of the industries are the remaining figures in the third column. Similarly, the figures by industry in Column 6 corresponding to Column 3 are the r_{ij} for the industries of Lincoln County.

Table 7.6 shows a traditional shift-share analysis without the Esteban-Marquillas extension. According to the **growth component** (Column 1 in Table 7.6), employment in each industry would have increased employment by 0.2% if they each increased at the same rate as the state. However, some industries in Nebraska declined during this period, and not all of those that grew did so at the same rate. The **industry mix effect** (Column 3) adjusts the expected employment change upward or downward according to whether that industry grew faster or slower than the average in the state. The sectors that grew at a rate greater than 0.2% have a positive industry mix. The rest have a negative industry mix.

Similarly, the sectors in Lincoln County that grew at a faster rate than the state's counterparts show a positive **competitive effect** (Column 4). A negative competitive effect means that the state's industry grew faster than its counterpart within Lincoln County. For the remaining industries, the state's growth surpassed that of the county. Their competitive effect is therefore negative.

As an example, we interpret the employment decomposition of the health care and social assistance sector for Lincoln County as follows: In 2001, Lincoln County had 2567 employees in that industry. If employment

Table 7.5 Employment and Growth Rates for the State of Nebraska and Lincoln County, Nebraska, for 2001 and 2003

	Nebraska			Lincoln		
	2001	2003	Growth Rate	2001	2003	Growth Rate
Farm employment	62,362	60,084	−0.037	1362	1305	−0.042
Construction	65,442	67,243	0.028	1204	1140	−0.053
Manufacturing	113,892	105,363	−0.075	435	359	−0.175
Retail trade	139,535	137,296	−0.016	3334	3257	−0.023
Information	25,384	23,114	−0.089	234	256	0.094
Finance and insurance	65,427	66,684	0.019	780	803	0.029
Real estate and rental and leasing	26,038	27,128	0.042	476	500	0.050
Professional and technical services	51,565	52,342	0.015	566	636	0.124
Management of companies and enterprises	13,350	14,020	0.050	60	31	−0.483
Administrative and waste services	62,465	56,966	−0.088	404	407	0.007
Educational services	19,242	20,110	0.045	136	147	0.081
Health care and social assistance	112,387	119,216	0.061	2567	2748	0.071
Arts, entertainment, and recreation	18,084	18,918	0.046	245	260	0.061
Accommodation and food services	70,928	72,220	0.018	1800	1857	0.032
Other services, except public administration	61,850	66,523	0.076	1164	1258	0.081
Government and government enterprises	164,160	166,722	0.016	2933	2891	−0.014
Total employment	1,182,375	1,184,678	0.002	21,258	21,497	0.011

Employment data from http://www.bea.gov/bea/regional/reis

Table 7.6 Shift-Share Decomposition for Lincoln County, Nebraska, 2001–2003

	Lincoln Co 2001	Growth Component	Industry Mix	Competitive Effect
Farm employment	1,362	2.653	−52.405	−7.248
Construction	1,204	2.345	30.790	−97.135
Manufacturing	435	0.847	−33.423	−43.424
Retail trade	3,334	6.494	−59.992	−23.502
Information	234	0.456	−21.382	42.926
Finance and insurance	780	1.519	13.466	8.014
Real estate and rental and leasing	476	0.927	18.999	4.074
Professional and technical services	566	1.102	7.426	61.471
Management of companies and enterprises	60	0.117	2.894	−32.011
Administrative and waste services	404	0.787	−36.352	38.565
Educational services	136	0.265	5.870	4.865
Health care and social assistance	2,567	5.000	150.979	25.021
Arts, entertainment, and recreation	245	0.477	10.822	3.701
Accommodation and food services	1,800	3.506	29.282	24.212
Other services, except public administration	1,164	2.267	85.677	6.055
Government and government enterprises	2,933	−2.218	101.557	−121.339

Table 7.7 Results of Esteban-Marquillas Extension

	Lincoln County 2001	Homothetic Employment	Specialization	Comparative Advantage	Intervention
Farm employment	1,362	1,121.211	240.789	−0.005	Possibly useful
Construction	1,204	1,176.586	27.414	−0.081	Possibly useful
Manufacturing	435	2,047.672	−1,612.672	−0.100	Useless
Wholesale trade	3,334	2,508.709	825.291	−0.007	Possibly useful
Retail trade	234	456.381	−222.381	0.183	Possibly useful
Information	780	1,176.316	−396.316	0.010	Possibly useful
Finance and insurance	476	468.139	7.861	0.009	Unnecessary
Real estate and rental and leasing	566	927.091	−361.091	0.109	Possibly useful
Professional and technical services	60	240.021	−180.021	−0.534	Useless
Educational services	404	1,123.062	−719.062	0.095	Possibly useful
Health care and social assistance	136	345.953	−209.953	0.036	Possibly useful
Arts, entertainment, and recreation	2,567	2,020.613	546.387	0.010	Unnecessary
Accommodation and food services	245	325.133	−80.133	**0.015**	Possibly useful
Other services, except public administration	1,800	1,275.219	524.781	0.013	Unnecessary
Government and government enterprises	1,164	1,112.005	51.995	0.005	Unnecessary

in the health industry grew at the same rate as the state's overall employment (r_B) between 2001 and 2003, Lincoln County should expect a gain of five employees. However, this sector in Nebraska actually increased at a faster rate than the state's 0.2% growth. Therefore, because of the size of its health care industry, Lincoln County could expect to gain an additional 150.979 health care jobs due to the industry mix effect. For some reason, this industry in Lincoln County grew even faster than it did in the rest of the state. This competitive effect accounted for an additional 25.021 jobs. According to Equation 7.11 and 7.15, the sum of columns 3, 4, and 5 for each industry must equal the difference in employment between the two years for Lincoln County. If not, check the calculations again.

Table 7.7 shows the results of the Esteban-Marquillas extension by calculating the homothetic employment, the specialization effect, and comparative advantage. The sign (+ or −) of the specialization effect and comparative advantage figures in Column 3 and 4 are what is important. The number itself is of no significance.

Industries classified under "intervention unnecessary" and "intervention useless" are those for which the market is working efficiently without outside intervention. For the first industries (health care and social assistance and other services except public administration), specialization and comparative advantage are positive. For the latter industries (manufacturing and educational services), the county is not specialized nor does it have comparative advantage. On the other hand, industries that are classified as "possibly useful" imply that they do not function efficiently. Such industries may be specialized but lack comparative advantage (farm employment, construction, retail trade, real estate and rental and leasing, accommodation, and food services). The subject of a secondary report could explain why these export industries are growing slower than their counterparts in the rest of the state. Likewise, industries that have comparative advantage but are not specialized (wholesale trade; information; finance, insurance, and real estate; professional and technical services; arts, entertainment and recreation; and government and government enterprises) are equally inefficient. Their secondary report could further investigate why the industries which seem to be growing faster than their counterparts in the rest of the state have proportionally fewer workers.

Summary and Conclusions

The economic base analysis stems from the traditional Keynesian theory applied to regional demand. Within the economic base analysis, industries are classified as either basic (export) industries or nonbasic (import) industries. Basic industries are the engines that drive regional economic growth. The magnitude of the effect of increasing exports depends on the size of the employment multiplier. The employment multiplier is calculated by dividing total employment by basic employment, and it reveals the number of jobs that result when an additional worker is employed in an export industry (including the new export job itself).

The impact of increasing export employment can be divided into three parts: the direct effect is the initial increase in the demand for the export good, the indirect effect includes the necessary local purchases of intermediate products, and the induced effect consists of spending of employees who work in the export industries as well as in the auxiliary industries. Location quotients measure the regional concentration of employment in a given industry.

Larger multipliers come from stronger backward linkages supporting the export industries and larger numbers of threshold-size industries that allow consumers to purchase goods and services locally. However, the marginal propensity to consume locally and thus the income multiplier tends to decrease as local per capita incomes grow. This is because consumers save more or substitute imported luxury goods for local products. Finally, multipliers ignore feedback effects with the trading partners.

Input–output analysis accounts for interindustry transactions when estimating the impact of final demand on a locality. By accounting for these backward linkages, this technique estimates different multipliers for changes in final demand for each sector of the economy. However, neither input–output nor economic base analysis accounts for supply effects nor do they adjust for distance or proximity between production facilities.

Finally, the shift-share technique decomposes employment changes into a growth component, industry mix, or competitive effect that is probably due to the area's comparative advantage. Comparing what are essentially the regional location quotients with the relative growth rate of each industry permits us to evaluate the efficiency of intervention within specific industries.

Chapter Questions

1. Why is high regional unemployment depicted by a point inside the production possibilities curve rather than by an inward shift of the production possibilities curve?
2. Draw a production possibilities curve for a region with the basic

industry on the horizontal axis and the nonbasic industry on the vertical axis, showing:

a.   A 20% out-migration of the working age population
b.   A 15% unemployment rate compared to the national unemployment rate of 5.4%
c.   Three-month extension of unemployment compensation in the region
d.   The region at full employment when the federal government places a new order for $1.5 million new lawnmowers from an area firm
e.   An influx of skilled labor

3.   Say that the world consists of two equally endowed regions, Wibbleton and Wobbleton. Say further that the only two goods produced are bitter butter and pickled peppers. The maximum output of the two goods in each of the two regions is shown in the following table:

a.   Draw the linear production possibilities curves for both regions

	Bitter Butter	Pickled Peppers
Wibbleton	2	4
Wobbleton	3	3

with Bitter Butter on the horizontal axis and Pickled Peppers on the vertical axis.

b.   Which region has comparative advantage in producing bitter butter? Pickled peppers?
c.   Which region has absolute advantage in producing bitter butter? Pickled peppers?
d.   Can trade take place? If so, which region should specialize in producing bitter butter? Pickled peppers?

4.   Calculate the regional multiplier under these scenarios:

a.   The marginal propensity to consume (MPC) is 0.9 and the marginal propensity to import (MPM) is 0.4.
b.   Import substitution increases the MPM to 0.6 while the MPC remains at 0.9.
c.   The MPC drops to 0.75 because local workers are wary about the future of the regional economy, but the MPM stays at 0.4.
d.   A "buy local" campaign reduces the MPM to 0.2 while the MPC stays at 0.9.

5.   For each of the scenarios in question 4, what would be the total increase in expenditures (incomes) if the federal government purchases $1.5 million new lawnmowers from a local firm?

6.   If residents of St. Ives spend $50 of every extra $100 in income on

locally produced goods and $20 on goods produced in other areas,

a. What is their marginal propensity to consume?_____
b. What is their marginal propensity to consume locally?_____
c. If local firms increase imports by $1 million, by how much will local incomes increase?_____

7. Say that 100 people work in Muffet County: 25 produce tuffets, 20 make curds, and 55 manufacture spider repellant. Within the state, 25% of the workers produce tuffets, 2% make curds, and 60% produce spider repellant.

a. Calculate the location quotients for the three industries in Muffet County.
b. Identify which, if any, are import industries, export industries, or producing for local consumption.
c. Estimate the basic multiplier for Muffet County.

8. If an increase in demand of $1.5 million worth of lawnmowers causes demand for intermediate products to rise by $300,000 and $500,000 more to be spent by employees, calculate the Type I and Type II multipliers.

Research Assignments

1. Estimate the location quotients and basic employment for your county (or MSA) using your state as the benchmark. Estimate your economic base multiplier.

a. Now assume that the basic employment in your region consists of all employees in the following sectors:

   Farming
   Forestry
   Mining
   Manufacturing
   Federal civilian
   Military sectors

   All other employment is nonbasic. Recalculate your economic base multiplier using this "assignment method."
b. If possible, compare these multipliers with the industry multipliers from an input–output program.

2. Estimate and interpret the growth component, the industry mix, and the competitive effect for your county.

3. Given the Esteban-Marquillas extension, classify your industries according to the feasibility of government intervention. From your knowledge of these industries, would you argue that those under "intervention possibly useful" need outside assistance or do they fall

into the "fallacy of small numbers," in which moderate changes in small numbers turn into exceptionally large percentages?

Appendix: Short-Run Model of an Open Economy

The traditional Keynesian model adapted to a region is as follows:

$$E = C + I + G + (X - M) \qquad (7.1a)$$

where E=Desired Expenditures, C=Consumption, I=Investment, G=Government Spending; $X-M$=net exports (Exports − Imports).

In equilibrium, income (or output or actual expenditures)=Desired Expenditures, or

$$Y = C + I + G + (X - M) \qquad (7.2a)$$

and

$$C = a + bY_d, \qquad (7.3a)$$

$$Y_d = Y - T \qquad (7.4a)$$

$$T = tY \qquad (7.5a)$$

$$M = d + mY_d. \qquad (7.6a)$$

A part of consumption and imports increases with income and the rest is constant. Thus, a and d are, respectively, autonomous portions of consumption and imports. The coefficient b is the amount of consumption that changes with income (the marginal propensity to consume). Likewise, m is the change in imports stemming from a change in income, or the marginal propensity to import. Subtracting $b-m$ gives the marginal propensity to consume locally.

Solving for a generic formula for the multiplier:

$$E = a + b(1-t)Y + I + G + X - (d + m(1-t)Y), \qquad (7.7a)$$

or

$$E = (b-m)(1-t)Y + (a + I + G + X - d) \qquad (7.8a)$$

Because this is in equilibrium,

$$Y^e = E, \qquad (7.9a)$$

and the following equation can be written:

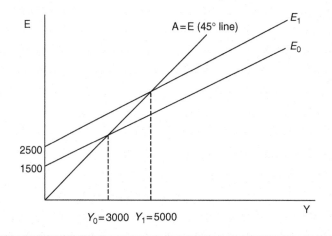

Figure 7A.1   Keynesian Cross.

$$Y = \left(\frac{1}{1-(b-m)(1-t)}\right)(a + I + G + X - d) \qquad (7.10a)$$

where Y^e is the equilibrium income level.

This method permits us to see the impact of change in exports on a region. Any of the exogenous variables (a, I, G, X, or d) will have the same multiplier effect.

$$\Delta Y = \left(\frac{1}{1-(b-m)(1-t)}\right)\Delta X \qquad (7.11a)$$

where $1/[1-(b-m)(1-t)]$ is the multiplier.

The impact of a change in an area's income tax rate decreases the amount of consumption of goods purchased locally as well as those purchased from outside the area.

Figure 7A.1 depicts the following problem: expenditures in the economy are as follows:

a or autonomous consumption$=100$ and $b=0.9$; so that $C=100+0.9(Yd)$,

d or autonomous imports$=150$ and $m=0.186$ so that,

$$M = 150 - 0.186(Yd),$$
$$t = 0.30, \quad \text{so that} \quad Yd = 0.70Y,$$
$$I = 500, \quad G = 400, \quad \text{and}$$
$$X = 650.$$

Consequently, in this economy,

$$E = C + I + G + (X - M),$$

$$= 100 + 0.9 + (1 - 0.3Y) + 500 + 400 + 650 - 150 - 0.186(1 - 0.3Y),$$

$$= 100 + 0.27Y + 500 + 400 + 600 - 150 - 0.13Y,$$

$$= (0.9 - 0.186)(1 - 0.3)Y + (100 + 500 + 400 + 650 - 150),$$

$$= 0.5Y + 1500.$$

In equilibrium, $Y = E$, so $Y^e = [1/(1 - 0.5)]1500 = 3000 =$ the equilibrium level of income. The equilibrium level of income/output is not necessarily associated with full employment. However, if the level of output at full employment is 5000, the economy will not reach full employment without a change of 1000 in exogenous expenditures. An increase in exports (or autonomous consumption, investment, or government spending) by 1,000 will increase equilibrium income by 2,000 because $[1/(1 - 0.5)] = 2 =$ the regional multiplier.

Modeling Interregional Dependencies

Expanding on McCombie (1988b), this short-run model of an open economy could be extended to analyze two trading regions, but it becomes problematic in the presence of more than two regions. Assume there are two regions, core (*c*) and periphery (*p*).

$$Yi = Ci + Ii + Gi + (Xi - Mi) \tag{7.12a}$$
$$Ci = ai + bYd_i, \tag{7.13a}$$
$$Yd_i = Yi - Ti \tag{7.14a}$$
$$Ti = tiYi \tag{7.15a}$$
$$Mi = di + mYi. \tag{7.16a}$$

Assume that each region has the same marginal propensity to consume and to import. Assume further that

$$Xc = Mp \tag{7.17a}$$

and

$$Xp = Mc \tag{7.18a}$$

The income level of one region (the core, for instance) is a function of imports and consequently a function of the income level of the periphery. Any increase in exogenous spending of the core affects the periphery by its marginal propensity to import. Likewise, an increase in taxes in the core could decrease the amount of imports and thus affect the exports of the periphery as well as the income in the periphery.

References

Adamou, N., and J. M. Gowdy. 1990. Inner, final, and feedback structures in an extended input–output system. *Environment and Planning A* 22 (12):1621–1636.

Arcelus, F. J. 1984. An extension of shift-share analysis *Growth and Change* 15 (1):3–8.

Berzeg, K. 1978. The empirical content of shift-share analysis *Journal of Regional Science* 18 (3):463–469.

Blair, D. W., and R. H. Mabry. 1980. Regional crime growth: an application of the shift-share technique. *Growth and Change* 11 (1):48–51.

Blank, U. 1989. *The community tourism industry imperative: The necessity, the opportunities, its potential.* State College, Pa: Venture Publishing Inc.

Brown, H. J. 1969. Shift and share projections of regional economic growth: an empirical test *Journal of Regional Science* 9 (1):1–18.

Brown, H. J. 1971. The stability of the regional-share component: reply *Journal of Regional Science* 11 (1):113–114.

Buck, T. W. 1970. Shift and share analysis—A guide to regional policy? *Regional Studies* 4 (4):445–450.

Chappelle, D. E., Heinen, S. E., James, L. M., Kittleson, K. M., and Olson, D. D. 1986. *Economic impacts of Michigan forest industries: A partially survey-based input–output study.* Research Report 472., Natural Resources, Michigan State University Agricultural Experiment Station, East Lansing, Michigan.

Cogley, T., and D. Schaan. 1994. Should the central bank be responsible for regional stabilization? *FRBSF Weekly Letter*, No 94-25.

Deller, S. C., T.-H.Tsai, D. W. Marcouiller, and D. B. K. English. 2001. The role of amenities and quality of life in rural economic growth *American Journal of Agricultural Economics* 83 (2):352–365.

DRI/McGraw-Hill. 1994. *An assessment of input–output multipliers,* Report provided for Tom Keane, Contracting Officer Technical Representative, U.S. Department of Transportation.

Esteban-Marquillas, J. M. 1992. A reinterpretation of shift-share analysis. *Journal of Regional Science* 2 (3), (1972):249–255.

Gazel, R. C., and R. Schwer. 1997. Beyond rock and roll: The economic impact of the Grateful Dead on a local economy. *Journal of Cultural Economics* 21 (1):41–55.

Ghosh, A. 1958. Input–output approach in an allocation system. *Economica* 25(97):58–64.

Gilmer, R. W., S. R. Keil, and R. S. Mack. 1989. The service sector in a hierarchy of rural places: potential for export activity. *Land Economics* 65 (3):217–227.

Groshen, E. L. 1987. Can services be a source of export-led growth? Evidence from the Fourth District, *FRB Cleveland Economic Review* Quarter 3.

Halperin, S. B., and R. H. Mabry. 1984. Property and casualty insurance lines comparison: a shift-share analysis *Journal of Risk and Insurance* 51 (3):524–535.

Hansen, N. 1994. The strategic role of producer services in regional development *International Regional Science Review* 16 (1–2):187–195.

Hazell, P. B. R., and B. Hojjati. 1995. Farm/non-farm growth linkages in Zambia *Journal of African Economies* 4 (3):406–435.

Herzog, H. W., Jr. and R. J. Olsen. 1977. Shift-share analysis revisited: The allocation effect and the stability of regional structure. *Journal of Regional Science* 17 (3):441–454.

Hildebrand, G. H., and A. Mace. 1950. The Employment multiplier in an expanding industrial market: Los Angeles County, 1940–1947. *Review of Economics and Statistics* 32 (3):241–249.

Howland, M. 1984. Age of capital and regional business cycles. *Growth and Change* 15 (2):29–37.

Hustedde, R., R. Shaffer, and G. Pulver. 1989. *Community Economic Analysis: A How to Manual*, Ames Iowa: North Central Regional Center for Rural Development.

Isserman, A. M. 1980. Estimating export activity in a regional economy: a theoretical and empirical analysis of alternative methods. *International Regional Science Review* 5 (2):155–184.

Klosterman, R. E., and Y. Xie. 1993. ECONBASE:economic base analysis. Spreadsheet Models for Urban and Regional Analysis.eds. R. E. Klosterman, R. K. Brail, and E. G. Bossard , New Brunswick, NewJersey: Center for Urban Policy Research, 161–182.

Leontief, W. 1936. Quantitative input and output relations in the economic system of the United States. *Review of Economics and Statistics* 18 (3):105–125.

Leontief, W. 1970. Environmental repercussions and the economic structure: an input–output approach. *Review of Economics and Statistics* 52 (3):262–271.

Loveridge, S., and A. C. Selting. 1998. A review and comparison of shift-share identities. *International Regional Science Review* 21 (1):37–58.

Martin, R. C., and H. W. Miley, Jr. 1983. The stability of economic base multipliers: Some empirical evidence. *Review of Regional Studies* 13 (3):18–25.

McCombie, J. S. L. 1988a. A synoptic view of regional growth and unemployment: I—the neoclassical theory. *Urban Studies* 25 (4):267–281.

McCombie, J. S. L. 1988b. A synoptic view of regional growth and unemployment: II—the post-Keynesian theory. *Urban Studies* 25 (5):399–417.

McNicoll, I. H., and S. Boyle. 1992. Regional economic impact of a reduction of resident expenditure on cigarettes: a case study of Glasgow. *Applied Economics* 24 (3):291–296.

Miernyk, W. H. 1965. *The Elements of Input–Output Analysis*. New York: Random House.

Miernyk, W. H. 1979. A note on recent regional growth theories. *Journal of Regional Science* 19 (3):303–308.

Miller, R., and P. Blair. 1985. *Input–Output Analysis: Foundations and Extensions*. Englewood Cliffs, New Jersey: Prentice Hall.

Polenske, K. R., and G. J. D. Hewings. 2004. Trade and spatial economic interdependence. *Papers in Regional Science* 83 (1):269–289.

Reeder, R. J., M. J. Schneider, and B. L. Green. 1993. Attracting retireesas a development strategy. In *Economic adaptation: alternatives for nonmetropo-litanareas, in Economic adaptation: Alternatives for nonmetropolitanareas,* ed. D. L. Barkley In Rural Studies Series, Boulder and Oxford: WestviewPress, 127–144.

Sasaki, K. 1963. Military expenditures and the employment multiplier in Hawaii. *Review of Economics and Statistics* 45 (3):289–304.

Sastry, M. L. 1992. Estimating the economic impacts of elderly migration: an input–output analysis. *Growth and Change* 23 (1):54–79.

Schmidt, R. H. 1993. Regional comparative advantage, *FRBSF Weekly Letter* Number, 93-37.

Schweitzer, M. E., and K. M. Roberts. 1996. State employment 1995: slowing to a recession? *FRB Cleveland Economic Commentary*, 1–4 .

Senf, D. R. 1989. Measures of shifts in regional retail trade. *Review of Regional Studies* 19 (3):18–23.

Shaffer, R. 1979. Determinants of the competitive share in Wisconsin counties 1962–1972: the role of government policy. *Annals of Regional Science* 13 (2):67–80.

Siegel, P. B., and T. G. Johnson. 1991. Break-even analysis of the conservation reserve program: the Virginia case. *Land Economics* 67 (4):447–461.

Stevens, B. H., and C. L. Moore. 1980. A critical review of the literature on shift-share as a forecasting technique. *Journal of Regional Science* 20 (4):419–437.

Stilwell, F. J. B. 1970. Further thoughts on the shift and share approach. *Regional Studies* 4 (4):451–458.

Taylor, J., and S. Bradley. 1997. Unemployment in Europe: a comparative analysis of regional disparities in Germany, Italy and the United Kingdom. *Kyklos* 50 (2):221–245.

Tiebout, C. M. 1962. *The Committee for Economic Base Study.* Supplementary Paper no.16, Committee for Economic Development.

Vias, A. C., and G. F. Mulligan. 1997. Disaggregate economic base multipliers in small communities. *Environment and Planning A* 29 (6):955–974.

Waters, E. C., D. W. Holland, and B. A. Weber. 1994. Interregional effects of reduced timber harvests: the impact of the northern spotted owl listing in rural and urban Oregon. *Journal of Agricultural and Resource Economics* 19 (1):141–160.

Williams, C. C. 1997. *Consumer services and economic development.* London: Routledge.

Winger, A. R. 2000. Regional growth in the "new" economy. *Review of Regional Studies* 30 (1):27–41.

Wolff, G., D. Rigby, D. Gauthier, and M. Cenzatti. 1995. The potential impacts of an electric vehicle manufacturing complex on the Los Angeles economy. *Environment and Planning A* 27 (6):877–905.

Wright, R. E. 1996. Standardized poverty measurement. *Journal of Economic Studies* 23 (4):3–17.

Wundt, B. D., and L. R. Martin. 1993. Minimizing employment instability: a model of industrial expansion with input–output considerations. *Regional Science Perspectives* 23 (1):81–99.

Chapter 8

Supply-Based Regional Growth Analysis

Long-run regional growth models concentrate on factors that shift the production possibilities curve outward. The changes in employment analyzed in Chapter 7 could result from a shifting production possibilities curve, but short-run theories give no reason for such a shift to take place.

How can an economy prepare itself for long-run sustainable growth? Two macroeconomic models underlie long-run regional economic growth analysis: the neoclassical growth model of Solow (1956) and Swan (2001), and the "new" or endogenous growth theory. The two models are not only the foundations for different concepts of long-run sustainable growth, but they also support different policy prescriptions for achieving this growth. The neoclassical model analyzes regional growth as if all economic activity were located at a point, as do most macroeconomic models; but the new growth theory acknowledges, among other things, that a location relative to some focal point is important in determining a region's growth potential. These theories are characterized by their focus on the dynamics or the process of change more than on the change itself.[1]

This chapter will first review the neoclassical growth model and evaluate its policy implications. We will then focus on the endogenous growth theory. This theory highlights the importance of innovation and the

---

[1] Johnson (1994).

diffusion of technology as the factors determining growth. Finally, we will explore how agglomeration economies can foster innovation; and how capital, entrepreneurship, and labor combine to create innovation and transmit technological advances.

Neoclassical Growth Theory

Solow's (1956) and Swan's (2001) neoclassical growth theory applies production theory to an entire region or country as if it were a firm producing only one type of output.

Output is a function of labor, capital, and exogenously acquired technology, that is,

$$Y = f(K,L,\phi) \tag{8.1}$$

where Y, K, and L are the levels of output, capital, and labor, respectively. The production function exhibits constant returns to scale. The level of technical progress, ϕ, does not vary across space. The technology available to cities and developed economies is immediately available to rural, low-income areas. Capital and labor are equally productive everywhere. The rate of return to capital is constant and equal to the national interest rate. The marginal product of labor equals the wage paid in a perfectly competitive market.

According to the aggregate production function models, regional output is a function of aggregate capital and labor. Researchers have also added spending on energy or government spending on infrastructure as inputs. Growth occurs when the amount of resources increases or when technology changes shift the production function upward (Figure 8.1). If labor is the input under consideration, increasing the amount of capital shifts the aggregate production function upward because labor is more productive if the capital/labor ratio is high.

Increases in regional productivity come about (1) by technological progress, (2) from an increased amount of capital per worker, or (3) from correcting a misallocation of resources (spatial mismatch). In equilibrium, over time, the growth of wages as well as the growth of the rate of return to capital is everywhere equal to the national average rates.

Unlike the Keynesian model, there is no investment function per se in the neoclassical growth theory. Instead, regional savings are a constant proportion of regional output and all savings are invested in capital. The marginal propensity to save is the same in every region.

In the Keynesian-based model, resources are immobile. Only goods flow from one area to another. However, in the neoclassical model, capital and labor also migrate to where their rates of return are the highest. In this way,

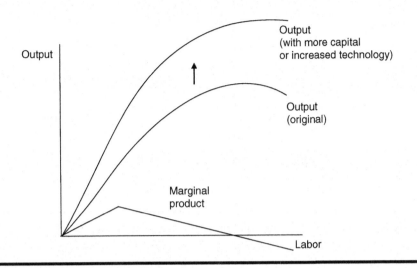

Figure 8.1 Production function.

the market corrects any resource misallocation. An increase in regional output can exceed the national average because of variations in the growth of regional labor force. When this happens, the rate of return to capital will be higher than normal and the region will import capital. This influx of capital (firms) will increase the ratio of capital to labor, decrease the rate of return to capital, and increase the wage rate until the entire economy is again in equilibrium.

Neoclassical firms always sell their outputs in a perfectly competitive market. Perfect competition implies that the firms are input-oriented or footloose, but never market oriented. This is because market-oriented firms are by nature imperfectly competitive (Chapter 2). Therefore, in the neoclassical model, entrepreneurs maximize profits by minimizing costs, as in Weber's location model.

The neoclassical theory asserts that the free movement of capital and labor corrects any misallocation of resources, causing a convergence of incomes, growth rates, and capital intensity among regions. The logic is as follows: Say Urbania and Pine Grove are two subareas of an economy. Urbania has greater employment and population density, more capital, and higher wages because of the greater labor demand. Pine Grove is agrarian, with fewer workers earning relatively low wages and large amounts of inexpensive land.

Under these conditions, firms from Urbania want to relocate in Pine Grove, bidding up factor prices there while depressing factor prices in Urbania. More goods will be produced in Pine Grove and sold in both the regions. The greater the differences in factor prices, the faster the firms migrate to Pine Grove. In this way, Pine Grove will ***catch up*** to (grow more

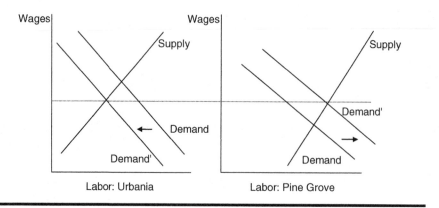

Figure 8.2 Neoclassical wage equilibration via capital migration.

quickly than) Urbania. Firms stop moving to Pine Grove when the cost of inputs in both areas is the same. Figure 8.2 demonstrates this scenario for the labor markets in Urbania and Pine Grove.

If, for some reason, not enough firms (therefore capital) relocate in Pine Grove, the high wages of Urbania will attract workers from Pine Grove, increasing both labor supply and the demand for land in Urbania while decreasing them in Pine Grove. As labor supply increases, wages plummet. As the demand for land increases, lands rents rise, further decreasing the real wage of workers in Urbania. In Pine Grove, the opposite occurs. The process will continue until real wages in both the areas converge, as shown in Figure 8.3.

Because there is no standardized measure of technology, in this model, the share of growth due to technological progress is measured as the residual after explaining the growth due to the other production

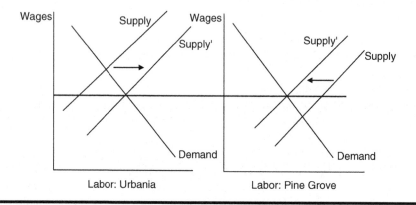

Figure 8.3 Neoclassical wage equilibration via labor migration.

factors. According to Denison (1985), this "Solow residual" represented more than 33% of the economic growth in the United States between 1929 and 1982.

Chinese Rural Industry and Neoclassical Production Functions

The growth of Chinese rural industry has been triple the growth of national GDP and now represents nearly half the total Chinese economy. Using county- (xian-) level data, Peng, Zucker, and Darby (1997) estimated a Cobb–Douglas production function that explains over 80 percent of the cross-county variation in per capita rural industrial output. Technology is transferred from urban to rural areas via urban residents commuting to work in rural firms. The savings from past agricultural income provided the start-up capital needed for rural enterprises.

Peng, Zucker, and Darby (1997)

Criticisms of the Regional Neoclassical Growth Model

Everyone agrees that economies cannot grow without capital and labor. If migration more efficiently allocates resources to their most profitable use, with ***everything else equal***, wage rates, growth rates, land rents, and rates of return to capital will unquestionably all equilibrate. However, the list of "everything else" that needs to be held constant is extensive in an economy composed of multiple regions.

If land rents were equal everywhere, lower wages alone would attract firms. Low-wage regions would see a faster increase in growth rates and wage rates than higher-wage areas. However, this "catch-up" does not always happen. Researchers then try to identify the impediments to this expected convergence. Two main obstacles, free trade and migration, should induce low-income regions to catch up and converge with high-income areas, whereas restricted trade and migration should result in diverging economies.

However, a survey by Barro (1991) of cross-country or cross-region studies finds no correlation among growth rates of per capita income and the initial per capita income level, as one would expect if low-income countries were to grow faster to catch up to the high-income countries. Moreover, few studies of growth rates of countries or of sub-national regions can establish any type of consistent convergence process.[2]

Furthermore, where trade and migration have always been free, as in almost all subnational studies, the neoclassical model cannot explain the persistence of regional income differences. For example, firms are not fleeing Santa Clara County, California, the heart of Silicon Valley, where the average annual wage per job was $69,288 in 2004, to flock to Garfield County, in eastern Montana which has much lower land prices and an average wage of $17,012. It is evident that something besides low factor prices must be involved.

In neoclassical growth theory, differences in per capita income and growth rates across regions cannot persist without market interference. Wages that are artificially high—perhaps because of some minimum wage imposed by government or a labor union—cause regional unemployment. Thus, to reduce unemployment, workers must accept a sufficient decrease in their real wage to permit the regional labor market to equilibrate. If not, they will leave to work in another area.

If the convergence hypothesis is valid for countries, for what level of disaggregation does the hypothesis remain valid? Should all states, provinces, or prefectures be expected to eventually enjoy the same wage rates? If so, what about counties, townships, and households?

Production Stew

Leijonhufvold (1986) compared the neoclassical production function to a recipe for bouillabaisse (a flavorful fish stew). Put capital and labor into a pot. Place the pot on the "heat" via the production function, and output magically appears. How do capital and labor combine to create output? No clue. How do production and growth take place? It is a mystery.

Leijonhufvold (1986)

A final problem is that the "Solow Residual," which is the amount of growth that is not explained by the quantity of inputs (the residual of the regression equation), is interpreted as a measure of technological innovation. This technological innovation sprinkles across an economy like rain,

---

[2] Barro (1991); Gundlach (1993).

landing everywhere equally and instantaneously. Ideas, knowledge, and technology are essentially global public goods, that is, goods that are nonrival and nonexcludable to the entire world. In this model, knowledge and ideas are never generated within an economy itself. Agglomeration economies such as technological spillovers or even entrepreneurial ability, both of which facilitate the dispersion of knowledge and technology, have no role in economic growth.[3]

The paradox is that as soon as the new technology appears in the economy, neoclassical workers know precisely what to do with it. If they come to work and find that someone substituted a state-of-the-art computer along with all the latest software for their manual typewriter, and they know instantaneously how to boot up, their output immediately jumps to a new level. There is no learning curve, but at the same time, these astute workers are neither capable of modifying the existing technology to come up with better instruments nor capable of re-creating the technology that falls into their hands.

Policy Prescriptions from Neoclassical Theory

Policy suggestions proposed by the neoclassical growth theory often mask a moral requirement that low-income areas *should* grow at a faster rate than developed areas. Implementing such a practice requires taxes be levied on the developed regions and used to assist growth in low-income areas.[4]

However, government expenditures designed to boost growth in a specific region are ineffective on two accounts. First, they crowd out private investment because entrepreneurs will not compete with government in providing the same goods or services. Second, the increase in employment in one region resulting from the increase in spending comes at the expense of jobs lost in the taxed areas. Market forces will effectively lead to convergence of regional productivity.

Endogenous Growth Theory

Theodore Schulz, 1979 Nobel Prize winner for his pioneering research in economic development, said of neoclassical growth theory: "In retrospect it seems odd that early growth models treated technology as exogenous." Most economists now agree that almost all technical change is endogenous, resulting from the aims and ambitions of economic actors.[5]

---

[3] Nelson and Winter (1974); Fagerberg and Verspagen (1996).

[4] McCombie (1988).

[5] Schultz (1990).

According to Romer's (1986) endogenous growth theory, output$=f$ (Capital, Labor, and Knowledge). The production function with respect to capital and labor is standard with diminishing marginal productivities, but the marginal product of knowledge is increasing.

- There is no automatic equilibrating mechanism that requires low-income areas to grow faster than developed areas.
- Per capita output can grow at an ever-increasing rate over time. Convergence is not necessary. In fact, growth in some regions can be slower than it is in others or it can even be stagnant.
- Growth is a function of key elements of location theory: externalities and increasing returns to scale combined with decreasing returns to producing new knowledge.

Input and output markets are not necessarily perfectly competitive. The production function for output can exhibit either constant or increasing returns to scale. However, the production function for knowledge, the most basic form of capital, must exhibit diminishing returns. That is, once we have a certain stock of knowledge, doubling inputs devoted to research does not double the amount of new knowledge.[6]

Most endogenous growth models assume some form of production based on:

- Technology and innovation.
- Unskilled and skilled labor.
- Physical capital.
- Infrastructure and public services.

Technology and innovation are first and foremost in the new growth theory. Labor can flow from unskilled to skilled markets, with a time lag. Investments in human capital potentially lead to constant learning. Physical capital always incorporates the latest technology.

Infrastructure includes both physical and social infrastructure. Physical infrastructure includes the provision and maintenance of utilities, roads, highways, and bridges, as well as mail and telephone systems. Social infrastructure includes the existence and respect for property rights as well as nonobstructive bureaucracies. Costs involved in trying to circumvent antiquated red tape or bureaucratic blunders, as well as social costs resulting from distorted incentives, lead to negative side effects that impede growth. The government's only roles are to provide and maintain infrastructure and to enforce property rights. Theory and evidence pertaining to what

---

[6] Romer (1986, 1990, 1995); Stern (1991); Amable and Guellec (1992); Podrecca (1993).

determines growth are not yet sufficiently developed, as needed to base confident policy advice.[7]

Innovation and the Diffusion of Technology

Technology is the saving force for all economies everywhere. However, there is no consensus about just how technology saves us. It is most definitely not a salvation from uncertainty. For example, some studies stress the technological change that causes what has been termed a "deskilling" of jobs, that is, a simplification of complex tasks. Other studies emphasize that new technology requires higher skills. "Solid proof" exists that net employment could increase, decrease, or remain stable in firms that adopt the latest technologies; sometimes all occurring simultaneously within the same firm.

Two major classifications of technological innovations explain this supposed inconsistency: ***process innovations***—the new production processes or improvements on existing technology, and ***product innovations***—the creation of new products or improvements on existing products. Process innovations result in the deskilling of jobs whereas product innovations require higher skills that lead to invention and testing of new products.

Innovation is defined as using knowledge to invent and introduce a new product, process, or service into the marketplace. Researchers classify an industry as innovative in one of the two ways: (1) the ratio of its spending on research and development to its total sales or (2) the industry's ratio of research and development employment to total employment. Firms that innovate grow faster than those that introduce few or no innovations either because innovations cause more rapid growth or because the faster-growing firms have a greater ability to innovate.

The focus on technology requires a third concept of time: the ***very long run***. In the very long run, technological change is necessary, but not a sufficient condition for economic growth. Diffusion of the technology also must take place.[8]

Knowledge, Innovation, and Technological Progress

As long as access to new knowledge is easy, timely, and inexpensive, the more that is known, the easier it is to invent and discover even more. Major

---

[7] Stern (1991); Amable and Guellec (1992).
[8] Butler (1990); Flynn (1993); Carlsson (1994); Goss and Vozikis (1994); Vaessen and Keeble (1995).

discoveries, especially from engineering and chemistry, increase productivity for any industry that makes use of them. Some economies prosper while others decline solely because of differences in creativity, labor skills, and the diffusion of innovations. Highly innovative regions increase the technological gap, leaving behind those regions that do not innovate. On the other hand, imitation and diffusion reduce technology gaps.[9]

Knowledge Is a Public Good

Knowledge fits within the traditional categories of private and public goods. Private and public goods represent two extremes in a dual continuum of nonrivalry and nonexcludability. **Nonrivalry** means that several people can use the same good simultaneously. **Nonexcludability** means that it is difficult to prohibit people from using the good. **Pure private goods** are both rival and excludable, whereas **pure public goods** are nonrival and nonexcludable. Figure 8.4 shows a dual continuum with rival/nonrival on one axis and excludable/nonexcludable on the other axis. Pure private goods are rival and excludable; pure public goods are nonrival and nonexcludable.

Within this framework, knowledge could start as a private good if it is privately funded. Private research is temporarily **rival** because of confidentiality agreements and patents. Government-funded research is theoretically nonrival from the start because the results of such research are supposed to be public knowledge. Similarly, knowledge is partly **excludable** for a short time because of obstacles such as language, distance, or political embargoes. Copy protection for computer software also creates excludable goods.

Romer (1996) describes **technology** as a set of ideas combined with "physical things" used in production. An idea (knowledge) is a nonrival good, but physical things are rival goods. Economic growth comes from the discovery of (producing knowledge about) new uses for the same things. Generating knowledge produces positive externalities when the knowledge is diffused. Firms try by any means possible to guard their secrets, but they do so in vain because knowledge is always accessible in the long run. Knowledge will eventually become a nonrival, nonexcludable good.

Once researchers incur the cost of creating a set of instructions, others may use the procedures several times with no additional social cost. For example, no matter how many times a recipe is used, the quality of the recipe never deteriorates. Knowledge is never used up in production; therefore, many people can access it simultaneously. Knowledge starts as a locally nonrival and potentially excludable good. The exchange of ideas

---

[9] Batten and Kobayashi (1993); Lazaric and Lorenz (1998).

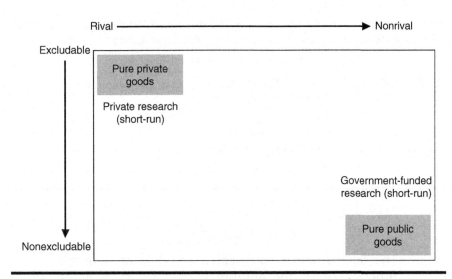

Figure 8.4   Dual continuum showing rival/nonrival and excludable/nonexcludable goods.

(knowledge spillovers), even by chance, circulates information until it eventually becomes entirely ***nonexcludable***.[10]

A Firm's Investment in Research and Development

The market will not allocate enough resources to the "ideas" sector because of externalities and spillovers in producing knowledge. Thus, without intervention, growth rates will be suboptimal. Intellectual property rights reward producers of knowledge with supernormal profits and thereby give an incentive to create more knowledge, but these rights also forbid disclosure of "sensitive" information, and thus they become the major obstacles to its diffusion.

When a good is ***nonrival***, the marginal cost of one more user is zero, thus the allocatively efficient price is also zero. At first glance, economic efficiency seems to suggest that all knowledge should be made available to anyone. However, over time, a policy that does not protect intellectual property rights would have unfortunate consequences. Innovation is the result of investment in research and development. Such expenses involve

---

[10] Butler (1990); Batten and Kobayashi (1993); Podrecca (1993); Romer (1995, 1996); Podrecca (1993); Lazaric and Lorenz (1998); Carlino (2001).

substantial uncertainty because they precede the creation of a new product. The expected rate of return on research and development

$$\left(\frac{\text{the present discounted value of the stream of net operating profits}}{\text{the present value of R \& D costs}}\right)$$

has to be at least equal to the expected rate of return of another project.[11]

Why Would Private Firms Invest in Research and Development?

The rate of return on research and development is a function of (1) the amount that must be spent on research and development before a new product is discovered and developed, (2) the demand that can be created for the new product as well as the estimated production costs, and (3) the amount of time the firm can produce the product exclusively and thereby earn supernormal profits. The second component explains the paucity of research that goes into orphan drugs (drugs for which usage is limited). The third component demonstrates how intellectual property rights affect the incentive to innovate. If no exclusive production rights exist, the expected rate of return decreases and the firm may need to abandon its research.

Butler (1990)

Exactly How Does Knowledge Spill Over?

The economic value of a technology is directly proportional to the speed and the range of dissemination as well as the varied ways it can be used. Knowledge could be exchanged among people in the same industry (localization economies) or among many industries in geographic proximity (urbanization economies). By sharing inputs, backward linkages facilitate

---

[11] Butler (1990); Brander (1992).

innovation because they decrease the cost of using new ideas. Some researchers follow Perroux (1950) and insist that suppliers and producers do not have to be geographically concentrated to foster innovation. Input suppliers need not even be on the same continent to be influential.

Then again, other researchers follow Boudeville (1966), claiming that spatial proximity and agglomeration economies are fundamental for innovation. If easy, timely, and inexpensive access to knowledge facilitates innovation, being surrounded by a well-functioning system of inventors and scientists promotes creativity and results in highly productive research and development activities. Nevertheless, innovation requires more than the proximity of innovators, the presence of research institutions, and a highly trained workforce. Key components interact and maintain a viable, dependable, and high-quality network.

Brandenburger and Nalebuff (1996) coined the term "co-opetition" to describe the propensity of firms to cooperate so that an industry's market size expands while each firm competes for market share. Co-opetition includes joint ventures and government lobbying efforts favoring the industry rather than a specific firm. The firms engage in strategies where they and their competitors benefit.

Collaboration stimulates creativity through potential synergies of ideas, and because it decreases the average cost of experiments, especially of those that involve expensive equipment. An environment that seems to have all the elements favorable to innovation is called by many names: ***innovative milieu, industrial district, technopole***, and ***science park***. Silicon Valley is the universal benchmark for an innovative environment.

A milieu is an industrial culture that promotes collective learning. According to Maillat and Kebir (1999), learning is in permanent evolution, interacting among various actors within the group, within the formal and informal institutions in the economy, and within the organization itself. Knowledge itself must be acquired, maintained, and reproduced. "Creative forgetting" must be practiced so that technical change can move forward. Such a milieu consists of what Pascallon (1991) calls a ***golden triangle*** of high-tech industries, research universities, and public or private research centers. A successful milieu requires solid infrastructures of training and research combined with an attitude of "co-opetition" shared by professionals.[12]

---

[12] Rallet (1991); Brandenburger and Nalebuff (1996); Helsley and Strange (2002); Fritsch (2002) as described by Rossell and Walker (1999); Pascallon (1991); Andersson and Persson (1993); Camagni (1993); Crevoisier (1994); Fischer and Varga (2003).

Proximity is essential for an innovative milieu. A milieu creates a public image of prestige. The skilled labor force is geographically immobile, but professionally mobile, thereby permitting a rapid dissemination of knowledge. Also, the possibility of informal contacts builds an industrial atmosphere that encourages casual information flows and cooperation between the customer and the supplier. Finally, this common industrial culture tolerates risk. Although some researchers believe in the necessity of a dynamic innovative milieu that balances cooperation and competition,[13] others think that a relatively hostile business environment encourages innovation.[14]

Community Colleges and Regional Growth

Industry agglomerations influence community colleges, which in turn can influence industry agglomerations and regional economies. Rosenfeld (2000) lists two-year colleges throughout the world that both influence and are influenced by their local economic bases.

Because 60 percent of the seafood processing and exporting industry of New Zealand is located in Nelson, several neighboring polytechnic institutes target fisheries and marine technology. Their presence attracts students from throughout the South Pacific. Moreover, Hickory, North Carolina, which provides 60 percent of the United States hosiery production, operates the only hosiery technology center in the United States. Alabama Southern Community College trains employees for that region's chemical processing and pulp-and-paper industries. De Anza and Mission Community Colleges in California are the "training partners" of electronics and computer industries in Silicon Valley just as EUC-Syd (*Erhverves Uddannelses Center Syd*) trains the technicians of the electronics industry in Southern Jutland, Denmark.

Galway–Mayo Institute of Technology's Furniture College in Letterfrack, Ireland and Itawamba

---

[13] Brusco (1986), for example.
[14] Vaessen and Keeble (1995), for example.

Community College in northeast Mississippi both train craftsmen within a program created by community leaders to try to jumpstart their respective areas' dormant furniture industries.

When the initiatives are taken by local industry, the majority of students have guaranteed employment. However, when community leaders request the training programs, the results are not as positive. Graduates from either Galway–Mayo's or Itawamba's furniture program either have to leave the area to find work, persuade local firms to modernize, or start their own companies.

Rosenfeld (2000)

Human Capital and Technical Change

Educated labor is a key predictor of the richness and diversity of a regional economic base because it enhances productivity. The construction of the Brooklyn Bridge (shown in Figure 8.5) took 14 years to complete in the late 1800s; but 80 years later, the Verrazano-Narrows Bridge from Brooklyn to Staten Island (Figure 8.6) was built in 5 years. This improvement in productivity comes from (1) advances in physical technology integrated

Figure 8.5 Brooklyn Bridge. Courtesy of Simone Roda http://commons.wikimedia. org/wiki/Image:Brooklyn_Bridge_-_New_York_City.jpg.

Figure 8.6 Verrazano-Narrows Bridge. (Courtesy of Aram Dulyan http://en.wikipedia. org/wiki/Image:Verrazano-Bridge-Dawn.jpg. With permission.)

in newer capital, (2) increases in the knowledge of bridge building, and most importantly, (3) incorporation of human capital in individual workers. The pace of economic growth depends on the speed of diffusion of new production techniques. The ability to acquire and apply these techniques increases with the level of formal schooling of the labor force (human capital).

Theodore Schultz first introduced the concept of ***human capital*** in 1963. Schultz observed that people not only purchase goods for current consumption, but they also invest in themselves to receive future monetary and nonmonetary compensation. Technically, the term "human capital" includes health care, education, job search time, job search costs (e.g., newspapers, agencies, and moving), and on-the-job training. Empirically, however, because of a lack of data, human capital is measured only by the length of time in the labor force or by various measures of formal educational attainment. Formal schooling, along with on-the-job training, promotes economic growth because it continuously enriches human capital and consequently the stock of society's knowledge. Learning-by-doing fosters human capital accumulation. Learning-by-doing means that the more often a worker carries out a process, the better it is done. With repetition, workers learn shortcuts or develop the skills needed to streamline a task.[15]

---

[15] Blaug (1976); Tallman and Wang (1992).

Converging Educational Attainment

Canals, Diebolt, and Jaoul (2003) asked whether higher education is the convergence mechanism by which regions within a country can catch up to each other. By studying the French system of higher education between 1964 and 2000, they found that until recently the proportion of people continuing in higher education was low in the north and northeast (Rust-Belt) of France and higher in the west/southwest research and service-oriented part of the country.

Enrollment in higher education depends on the number of **bacheliers** (i.e., students who pass the **baccalauréat** exam) who continue their studies and the duration of these studies. Because few students migrate when they enroll for the first time in higher education, the recruitment efforts of regional institutions as well as the number of such institutions are an important determinant of the spatial distribution of educational attainment. The spatial distribution of educational attainment tends to persist because children of highly educated families, which are generally found in dynamic regions, are proportionately greater consumers of university education than others.

In spite of this, regional educational attainment levels are starting to converge due to the socioeconomic goals of the population, increased number of institutions of higher education, increased number of tracks that students can follow, local government policies that subsidized training, and the unemployment/underemployment phenomenon, which makes the pursuit of education not a necessity from an increased rate of return on investment but also a way of living.

Canals, Diebolt, and Jaoul (2003)

Measures of Formal Education

Endogenous growth theory promotes human capital accumulation as a determinant of economic growth. The proponents of this relatively new theory continue experimenting to determine the optimal measure of the concept. Data restrictions limit researchers to three measures of human capital: enrollment rates, literacy rates, and average educational attainment.

Enrollment rates refer to the proportion of school age children enrolled in school at the beginning of the academic year. In theory, enrollment rates should predict the future stock of human capital. However, the predictive value does not account for students who have left or those who have chosen not to work after they graduate.

The ***literacy rate*** is a more accurate measure of current educational attainment than the enrollment rates because it represents a basic level of human capital acquired by individuals at a point in time. For example, Coronado and Vargas (2001) measured literacy rates around El Paso, Texas, with a questionnaire written in English. The respondents need to sign their names, locate tidbits of information in news articles, locate the expiration dates on a driver's license, and total a bank deposit entry. A major problem in estimating literacy rates in the United States in this manner is that for 18% of the households in 2000, English was not the primary language. A lack of proficiency in one language does not exclude knowledge in other fields. If the workplace is a multilingual environment for its employees, then productivity should not suffer. Nonetheless, proficiency in the primary language of the region does increase productivity and potential earnings of the individual workers by statistically significant amounts.

Quebec's Obstinate Unemployment Problems

Job creation in Quebec has long been a priority for the Canadian government. Because of persistent unemployment, the Quebecois have invested in lower amounts of human capital. Migration to other provinces is exceptionally costly because almost 60 percent of the population is unilingual in this Francophone province. To migrate, these workers have to learn a second language, and even then, their difficulty with English leads to underemployment and lower than expected wages given their qualifications.

Lacroix (1984)

Think About it…

How literate are you… in another language?

Escriba su nombre y apellido: —————————

Por favor, resuma el artículo del periódico de hoy, el Universal en http://www.eluniversal.com.mx/noticiash. html

¿Cuándo expira/caduca licencia de manejar?

Si el saldo de su cuenta corriente es originalmente 500 pesos y Ud. escribe un cheque por 200 pesos, ¿Cuál es su saldo?

Écrire votre prénom et nom: —————————

Quelle est la date d'expiration de votre permis de conduire? ——————————

Lire les manchettes dans *Le Nouvel Observateur* d'aujourd'hui à http://permanent.nouvelobs.com/

Si le solde de votre compte est 500**€, et vous écrivez un chèque pour le montant de 200€, quel est votre nouveau solde? ——————————

Schriben Sie Ihr Vorname und Nachname:
——————————

Fassen Sie die Schlagzeilengeschichte heutiger Zeitung zusammen, *Berliner Morgenpost* bei http://morgenpost. berlin1.de.

Wenn Ihr Kontostand ursprünglich 500€ ist, und sie schreiben einen Scheck für 200€, was ist Ihr neu Kontostand? ——————————

あなたの氏名を下線上に書いてください。 ——————————

下記アドレスから今日の朝日新聞記事、トップニュース・ヘッドライン（一面）の記事を一つ抜粋し、
その概要を書きなさい。
（http://mdn.mainichi-msn.co.jp/）

あなたの運転免許書き換え日を下線上にかいてください。——————————

次の問題に答えなさい。該当する答えを下線上にかいてください。

あなたが500円で口座を開設したとします。後日200円下ろしました。今ある預金高は幾らですか？
——————————円

Lawyers, Engineers, and Economic Growth

The field is as important as the average educational attainment level. For instance, United States lawyers have, at the margin, a negative impact on real national income. Enrollments in law schools have a negative and significant effect on growth, while the same enrollments in engineering have positive and significant effects. Engineers increase the capacity of an economy to innovate, while lawyers...

Magee, Brock, and Young (1989)
as cited in Murphy, Shleifer, and
Vishny (1989) and Barro (1991)

Literacy is only the first step in human capital acquisition. Higher levels of education measured by *average educational attainment* provide a more valuable set of skills and knowledge to workers. The United States Census classifies the number of people aged 25 and older by educational level. However, these data implicitly assume that, for example, workers with master's degrees in elementary education or social work are perfect substitutes in the labor market for people with degrees in computer science, engineering, or nursing. Workers with the same level of education are implicitly assumed to possess the same skills. Despite these criticisms of this human capital measure, Murphy, Shleifer, and Vishny (1989) determined that an increase in the average educational attainment by 10% leads to an average 8% increase in a state's aggregate output.[16]

Rates of Return to an Investment in Education

Can we have too much schooling? Much research on human capital involves calculating the rates of return to formal schooling. Rates of return vary from a high of 80% for elementary school education in low-income countries to a low of −3% for some graduate education in the United States. The rate of return for a quality preschool is between 7 and 16%. Current estimates pin the average rate of return for a bachelor's degree at 8% and from 7 to 12% for a graduate degree.[17]

---

[16] Murphy, Shleifer, and Vishny (1989); Romer (1989); Tansel and Güngor (1997); Carlino (1995); Sala-i-Martin and Mulligan (1995); Coronado and Vargas (2001).

[17] Blaug (1976); Tallman and Wang (1992); Khan (1993).

Unequal Rates of Return to Education

Rates of return to education are significantly lower in rural areas than in urban areas. The increase in income dispersion between rural and urban areas since 1970 is for the most part due to spatial differences in human capital. The proportion of high school and college graduates has been growing faster in urban areas than rural areas.

Rural returns are different for Blacks, Whites, and Native Americans. Whites and American Indians in rural areas experience very weak returns. For all three races, females enjoy much higher returns. The rural labor force tends to be older and less mobile; therefore, it is more vulnerable to negative labor market shocks than the younger, urban labor. Thus, rural unemployment is consistently higher than urban unemployment.

Renkow (1996) and Kimmel (1997)

In general, private rates of return decline constantly (i.e., monotonically) as years of schooling are added. Overinvestment tends to occur when an individual's main goal in furthering his or her education is to earn more money. Conversely, individuals will underinvest in human capital if they lack confidence and doubt their abilities.

Think About it...

What is the rate of return on your human capital investment?

To estimate the financial benefits, determine the average annual salary for your intended profession from http://www.bls.gov/oes/current/oes_nat.htm. Multiply that average salary by the number of years you plan to work. Subtract from that amount the life-time salary you would receive had you stayed in your current (or former) occupation for the same number of years to get your net benefit from completing your degree. ————————

To estimate the cost of your education: Multiply the number of credits you need to graduate by the price per credit. Add to this figure the salary you could have earned had you worked full time instead of attending a university. —————————————

Your rate of return on investment will be the ratio of the net benefit divided by the cost of the degree.

From society's viewpoint, however, individuals underinvest in their education because they do not consider the positive externalities associated with it. Educated workers learn cognitive skills. They acquire the self-reliance and the dynamism needed for success. They are more patient toward bureaucracies, comply more with organizational rules, and are essentially easier to train. Employers use educational attainment to screen workers not only in terms of ability, achievement, and motivation, but also ethnic origin.

Think About it…

How is your social capital network?

To what extent do you agree with the following statements?

		Strongly Agree	Agree	Disagree	Strongly Disagree
1	Sometimes I do things for others when I don't feel like doing them	(4)	(3)	(2)	(1)
2	Other people often call on me for help	(4)	(3)	(2)	(1)
3	Most of my friends know one another	(4)	(3)	(2)	(1)
4	At my friends' birthday parties there are many people I hardly know	(4)	(3)	(2)	(1)
5	My good friends also know my family members	(4)	(3)	(2)	(1)
6	At work I meet completely different people than during leisure time	(4)	(3)	(2)	(1)

		Strongly Agree	Agree	Disagree	Strongly Disagree
7	My neighbors come to my birthday parties	(4)	(3)	(2)	(1)
8	My colleagues come to my birthday parties	(4)	(3)	(2)	(1)
9	I do not easily ask for help when I need it	(4)	(3)	(2)	(1)
10	You can't expect your neighbors to help you with serious problems	(4)	(3)	(2)	(1)
11	You can't expect your colleagues to help you with serious problems	(4)	(3)	(2)	(1)
12	I would like to have more friends	(4)	(3)	(2)	(1)
13	I easily make contact with others	(4)	(3)	(2)	(1)
14	I would like to have more contact with my neighbors	(4)	(3)	(2)	(1)
15	I would like to have more contact with my colleagues	(4)	(3)	(2)	(1)
16	I send my neighbors Christmas and holiday cards	(4)	(3)	(2)	(1)
17	I have experienced being disappointed in placing my trust in others	(4)	(3)	(2)	(1)
18	Before I trust someone I have to be sure of his or her intentions	(4)	(3)	(2)	(1)

These 18 questions summarize 4 components of social capital:

1.   Satisfaction with the present network (Items 8, 12, 14, and 15)

2.   Integration of different types of relationships in the network (Items 3, 5, 7, and 16)

3.   Expectation and propensity to use social resources (Items 6, 9, 10, 11, and 18)

4.   Ease of making new contacts (Items 1, 2, 4, and 13).

Flap et al. 1999/2000 http://www.xs4all.nl/~gaag/work/SSND.pdf. Reprinted with permission of Dr. Henk Flap.

Social Capital

Human capital includes social capital. **Social capital** consists of a network of informal social relations, family and community connections, common values, and respect for norms that encourages information spillovers and becomes an "informal safety net." This form of human capital emphasizes the value of connections between individuals and groups. A person's ability to make use of informal social networks depends on the availability of the necessary resources. Social capital produces positive and negative effects on a community. People do favors for others if they believe that there will be reciprocity. The more "social debts" a person holds, the more social capital is available to improve his or her own welfare in time of need. However, using "old-boy networks" instead of hiring the best person, social intolerance, and discrimination against "outsiders" limit knowledge dissemination and illustrate the negative effects of such networks.

Social capital also includes knowledge of local customs and institutions. Local knowledge describes how to adapt to a climate and a community, the workings of local networks, the identification of the true decision maker—who consistently has the most accurate information and disseminates it—and in general, all elements necessary to determine how the community shapes its own destiny.[18]

Social Mindset in Regional Growth

The predominant social institutions affect the dissemination of knowledge and ideas as well as human capital development. A striking example is that of the relationship between the dominant religious establishment and long-run economic growth of a region. Economic historian Richard Easterlin (1981) determined that colonialism, absolute monarchy, the Roman Catholic Church, and Islamic fundamentalism deter mass schooling and the free circulation of ideas. On the other hand, Protestantism and Humanism positively influence economic growth, scientific progress, pure reason, and the conviction that humanity is the master of its own destiny.

The new growth theory emphasizes the role that externalities play in the growth process through enhancing labor productivity. More productive individuals work with other high-skilled workers. Incomes in poorer regions cannot converge because these regions lack human capital, and they are resigned that this is their fate. For those who try to change the intellectual climate of their region, an insufficient market for skilled labor creates a brain drain as children leave for university and never return.

---

[18] Gunderson (1998); Malecki (2000).

Cities with higher average levels of human capital experience faster employment growth. Employment growth in one city is positively related to the stock of human capital elsewhere in the same metropolitan area, but some of the effects of human capital are limited to the city level. Differences in human capital attainment determine most of the differences in city employment rates. According to Simon (1998), cities in which firms hire people to absorb, create, transmit, and implement knowledge grow more quickly and are more productive than others. Cities with high concentrations of educated people generate more localized spillovers.[19]

The Role of Capital and Entrepreneurship in Regional Growth

When economists speak of capital, they refer to plant and equipment or tangible, physical capital. Increasing "plant" means expanding existing firms or attracting new ones. Attracting new firms involves investing in new technology. Because the current technology is embodied in the newest plant designs and the current models of equipment, attracting new firms implies technological investment.

In the traditional neoclassical growth model, increases in capital cause growth merely because capital is a factor of production. Empirically, however, an increased use of capital explains only a small proportion of growth in these models. Investment in capital is measured as some aggregated dollar value of capital minus an aggregated depreciation rate. Investment increases productivity because it supplies larger amounts of capital per worker. Even temporary increases in investment can enhance permanently productivity the because of permanent increases in capital stock. The incentives inherent in the type of ownership of capital determine the impact of capital on regional growth.

Private Capital

Arrow's (1962) ***vintage model of capital*** assumes that capital embodies the technology of the time that it was constructed. Analyzing vintage models of capital is difficult because ideally, each piece of equipment needs to be catalogued by its construction date. Instead of having 25 computers as components of capital in a production function, a firm would have five computers that are 1 year old, 10 that are 2 years old, etc., and would

---

[19] Easterlin (1981); De Long (1988); Lucas (1988).

soon run into statistical problems when estimating its production function. The newer the computer is, the greater is the amount of technology incorporated into that piece of equipment. The frequency of investment thus affects the dispersion of technology.

A large capital stock increases the marginal and average product of labor, but not all of the added output increases living standards. Larger stocks of capital mean that a greater share of current output must replace worn-out capital or maintain existing capital.[20]

Three types of depreciation affect capital:

- Physical depreciation (the wear and tear on equipment).
- Depreciation due to obsolescence.
- Depreciation due to reduced demand for an outmoded product.

Entrepreneurship and Innovation

According to the vintage theory, new production methods and improved techniques are devised according to a sequential process of innovations. For each new period, entrepreneurs can identify the current "best practice" technique. They may replace old vintages by adapting the current best practice, continue with the existing production methods, or introduce a new production method themselves. Eventually, obsolete techniques disappear.

New firms with all new equipments respond more readily to new technologies and specific market changes. According to Schumpeter's (1942) theory of creative destruction, innovating entrepreneurs lead the most important firms. These entrepreneurs struggle and flourish in a competitive, dynamic environment. Through relentless innovation, they continuously create disequilibrium. Trial and error drives the economy to increasingly higher productivity levels.

Capital Mobility

Capital migrates to where its return is highest. The level of capital mobility varies by industry. The two most important determinants of regional investment at the aggregate level are expected profitability and aggregate demand. If profits are higher than normal and capital requirements are modest, other firms enter the market

---

[20] Johansson (1991); Bacchetta (1994).

and the increased competition quickly decreases both prices and profits. A neighborhood grocery store will invest in capital proportionally to the size of the local market. The expect rates of return to capital invested in grocery stores do not vary noticeably across regions.

On the other hand, auto assembly plants can use either local or imported inputs, but they effectively export all of their output to a national or international market. The cost of capital is determined nationally, but wages are determined locally. Wage differences cause regional differences in rates of return to capital. For these assembly plants, local market size is inconsequential. Standardized production does not benefit from agglomeration economies, and labor—the main local input—is ubiquitous. Auto assembly plants are therefore truly footloose, and more mobile than any market-oriented firm.

Ford and Poret (1991)

Economic actors control neither the exact nature nor the timing of innovations. For short periods, the first to adopt an innovation becomes a monopoly, but such monopolies do not last because the market will force all firms to adopt the better technologies to survive. Innovations enhance a firm's productivity only during their diffusion. Unless a technique is shown to be quite profitable early on, dissemination will take time. Thus the economy creates new technologies superimposed on the top of past technology, and combined with the most avant-garde technologies, all of which compete simultaneously for dominance.

Future technologies consistently threaten economic profits (rents) created by current research, but this threat should not stop research. The tendency of curtailing future research to protect a process of production creates a no-growth trap. No research, no innovations. The economy stagnates.[21]

Private Investment and New Firms

Chapter 2 through Chapter 5 of this text studied firm location decisions from a microeconomic perspective. Recent empirical studies have investigated

---

[21] Nelson and Winter (1974); Whittington (1984); Aghion and Howitt (1992); Young (1993); Silverberg and Lehnert (1994); Eberts and Montgomery (1995); Gladstone and Lee (1995).

causes of new firm formation (firm births) in different countries from a macroeconomic perspective. In general, the most significant variable describing firm births is a growth in demand (measured by a lagged change in population). Urbanization and localization economies as well as the presence of small, specialized firms also encourage firm births. In addition, persistent high unemployment rates boost the creation of new firms. Unemployed people who cannot find jobs will in effect start their own businesses. This tendency is known as ***unemployment desperation***. The small service firms that result from unemployment desperation increase start-up as well as failure rates because of the inexperience of "apprentice entrepreneurs."[22]

Government Incentives and New Firm Formation

Until the late 1960s, low wages were the principal incentive for new manufacturers. Since then, these firms worry more about the growth potential of the labor supply, frequency and duration of local labor disputes, and existence of right-to-work laws, which ban the monopoly of unions on workplaces. In addition, intangible factors (e.g., amenities and work ethic) and historical accident figure prominently in the location of manufacturing capital.

Researchers consistently find no statistically significant indication that local government aid to new firms actually increases the number of firm births. Most new firms would have chosen their locations anyway without government intervention. Local government initiatives more often only improve the survival rates of existing firms.

Browne, Mieszkowski, and Syron (1980),
Keeble and Walker (1994) and Davidsson,
Lindmark, and Olofsson (1995)

---

[22] Browne, with Mieszkowski and Syron (1980); Nakosteen and Zimmer (1987); Ford and Poret (1991); Keeble and Walker (1994); and Davidsson, Lindmark, and Olofsson (1995); Kottman (1992).

Manufacturing Capital and Business Cycles

Firm size and market concentration influence innovative behavior and research and development expenditure. Small, new firms introduce a larger number of low-value innovations than larger firms do, and they sell their innovations mainly to small niche markets. Such firms are crucial in innovation and production networks involving both small and large firms. Despite the large risks, innovative and high-tech firms are no more likely to fail than other small firms. This may result from better educated and more experienced entrepreneurs.

The older a firm is, the less apt it is to innovate. Old industrial areas host fewer innovations because the investment in older vintage capital decreases their innovative capability. These "***rust belts***" are dominated by mass production industries. Large plants have strong internal labor markets that limit the entry of new ideas. The predominance of large firms impedes new firm formation. Potential leaders with entrepreneurial talents leave.

Older capital stock condemns an area to be vulnerable to the business cycles. Layoffs due to national recessions hit harder because firms are less profitable. Plants using old capital face higher average production costs for three reasons. First, an older vintage of capital does not use complementary factors of production as efficiently as new capital. Anyone who has attempted to use new software on an older computer can attest to this. Second, because of technological change, older facilities are less cost effective than newer ones. For example, multistory plants that rely on gravity to move components from one section to another are less efficient than automated assembly lines. Third, sources of raw materials and transportation modes change over time. Older plants that are prudently located adjacent to a railroad depot are no longer cost minimizers when trucks become the major transportation mode.[23]

Does Firm Size Matter? The Weak Helping the Strong

The rate of new firm formation depends on the level of specialization of the local industrial system and the proportion of existing small- to medium-sized firms. Areas with many small manufacturing firms validate a social structure that fosters an entrepreneurial spirit and facilitates the start-up of new businesses. In contrast, areas with a few very large firms have low rates of new firm formation. Areas such as Pittsburgh, Pennsylvania, before United States Steel closed its mills, lack productive networks because the firms make most of their own inputs.

---

[23] Howland (1984); Camagni (1986); O'Farrell and Oakey (1992); Fielding (1994); Tether (2000).

The economic contribution of small businesses is understated according to empirical evidence. Schwalbach (1994) and others consistently find that small businesses outperform large ones in industries dominated by technical change, especially if we count informal research and development activities. Profitable large firms have downsized and now outsource some of their functions to small- or medium-sized businesses. Other large firms really consist of hundreds of business units, each of which runs as a separate entity. Modern technology industries are among the most prosperous in small business sectors.

Our discussion of the advantages of economies of scale seems contradictory. In Chapter 5, we asserted that increasing returns to scale was essential to understanding location theory. We expect survival rates for large businesses due to cost and technological advantages. Besides, large firms can more easily protect their market shares. On the other hand, empirical studies praise the small, flexible establishments rather than the larger plants. Regions with large businesses do not grow as fast as those with small firms. The suspected disadvantage that small businesses are not able to exploit scale economies is questionable unless the economies of scale are present even for moderately small firms or the benefits of (external) agglomeration economies outweigh the lack of internal scale economies.

High barriers to entry exist in industries dominated by large firms. Large unionized firms effectively establish a regional minimum wage such that small firms or potential start-ups cannot successfully bid for workers. In addition, large-scale factories and assembly plants hire greater proportions of manual workers who have low probabilities of becoming entrepreneurs. Large companies determine the growth rate of the regions that they influence. Local economies that are dominated by large firms become slaves to the cyclical nature of the dominant industry.[24]

French Experiences with New Firm Formation

One reason that the rate of job growth in France lagged other European countries and the United States during the 1980s is because French policy makers preferred the "Fordist" production model, a model composed of multi-sector assembly line plants. The "Fordist" production entails stamping out large quantities of homogeneous products, and benefits greatly from

---

[24] Rondi and Sembenelli (1991); Garofoli (1994); Schwalbach (1994).

internal economies of scale. Now that the government is allowing the creation of a large number of small- to medium-size establishments, new firm formation is escalating. The smaller size firms thrive because they are flexible, innovative, and adaptable to markets that require limited, diversified, or specialized products.

The majority of new firms start in very dense urban areas. Highly concentrated urban zones provide personal "start-up insurance" for new entrepreneurs. Starting firms are practically guaranteed a qualified work force, suppliers, clients, necessary services, access to networks of physical or information infrastructures, and capital markets to help fund some of the risk.

Thus, French firms that started in rural areas generally did so in rural manufacturing districts where development, specialization, and modernization of activities favor only limited firm creation. On the other hand, technological districts facilitate technology transfer within manufacturing districts and they thrive in proximity to an active urban region.

Savy and Veltz (1993) as noted in Guesnier (1994)

Foreign Direct Investment: Does Ownership of Capital Matter?

Foreign ownership of firms is on the rise in developed countries as well as in developing countries. Assembly or maquiladora plants in Mexico, Haiti, and Columbia are predominantly, but not entirely, owned by United States firms. In northern United Kingdom, over 80% of manufacturing employment is externally managed. Many "foreign" cars sold in the United States are made by American employees who work for Japanese or German firms. Although almost all of the literature on foreign direct investment defines the word "foreign" to mean ownership by investors based outside the country, the same analysis and conclusions apply to anyone from outside a locality owning local capital.[25]

---

[25] Glickman and Woodward (1988); Swamidass (1990); Coughlin, Terza, and Arromdee (1991); Tomaney (1994); Ó'Hualacháin and Reid (1997).

How to Lure Foreign-Owned Capital

Research shows that agglomeration economies are more important to foreign firms than to national firms. Labor market conditions as well as local fiscal conditions are also important in the location decisions of foreign-owned firms. Specifically, higher wages discourage foreign direct investment while high unemployment rates attract it. On the other hand, the effect of union membership on levels of foreign direct investment within states in the United States is inconclusive. In addition, higher taxes dissuade foreign investment unless the higher taxes fund the development of transportation infrastructures.

Glickman and Woodward (1988),
Swamidass (1990), Coughlin,
Terza, and Arromdee (1991), and
O'Huallacháin and Reid (1997)

Cultivating Foreign Direct Investment

Foreign direct investment takes place in one of two ways—either the parent firm builds an entirely new branch in the area (***Greenfield investment***) or it acquires existing facilities. Greenfield investments are strictly controlled branches of the parent organization, but the acquired firms may preserve some degree of autonomy.

Two competing theories explain international production: the internalization theory and the network theory. According to the ***internalization theory***, an outside area would have a scarce asset that the firm's multinational organization needs. The parent firm invests in foreign assets instead of assets in its own region when the host region offers an advantage not available in the home region. These advantages include local resources or markets, investments that develop another area's resources rather than import them from that area, or an advantageous supply of labor. The internalization theory assumes that (1) the creation and use of assets are essentially internal activities of the firm and (2) spatial differentiation gives a geographical dimension to production. This theory best fits situations where the home region and host regions each have unique sets of production advantages.

Firms that illustrate the ***network theory*** try to acquire complementary assets by expanding their networks. Network expansion comes about by either buying an existing plant or embarking in a joint venture strategy. This theory stresses the importance of competitive local assets, especially the technological spillovers and strong, preestablished production networks. According to this scenario, internalization is impossible because it requires a firm to have vast experience on a global scale.[26]

Telecoms Cluster in a Texan Network

The Telecom Corridor®* in Richardson, an affluent suburb north of Dallas–Fort Worth, is one of the highest concentrations of innovative telecommunications and technology-based companies in the world. A survey of telecom companies provides three principal reasons why companies clustered in the area. First, firms wanted to be near their suppliers or customers. Firm MCI, for example, was drawn there because of the local start-ups of two of its major suppliers: DanRay and Collins Radio. Second, firms came to the area because they purchased a local company. For example, Nortel purchased DanRay and Alcatel bought Rockwell International's Network Transmission Systems Division, which itself had acquired Collins Radio. Finally, newcomers, such as Samsung, chose this suburb because it wanted to join a prestigious telecom region.

About the Telecom Corridor.® http://www.telecomcorridor.com/tc/ (accessed on January 4, 2002, site now discontinued); Rossell and Walker (1999).

* Telecom Corridor® is a registered trademark of the Richardson Chamber of Commerce.

Virtuous and Vicious Cycles

Multinationals can stimulate a specific host region as well as regions within countries and the global economy. The concepts of virtuous and vicious cycles of technological development are used to analyze potential effects of external investment. Multinationals play a critical role in the ***virtuous cycle*** of developing the technological capability of host regions if they develop or

[26] Lagendijk and van der Knaap (1993).

maintain solid local networks. The major impacts of multinationals and nonindigenous firms affect local suppliers. Because of cumulative causation (Chapter 5), areas develop rapidly due to foreign investment if the firms devote resources to encourage indigenous technological development. The region will subsequently attract internal investment and encourage agglomeration economies. This trend illustrates the network theory.

For host regions, foreign investment can heighten comparative advantage and improve global allocative and technical efficiencies if the foreign firm is more efficient than indigenous competitors. The increase in foreign involvement in an area and the associated increase in production attract even more foreign investment from assembly plants and component manufacturers. However, because the multinationals are more sensitive to relative changes in technology, demand conditions, and local taxes, they risk leaving a host region if the initial advantages disappear.

In contrast, a *vicious cycle* linked to the decline of technological capability takes place when an assembly plant imports the majority of its components. Foreign firms that acquire indigenous businesses may abandon the existing supply networks. This initiates lower sales for indigenous enterprises and a reduction in local technological capability. Rather than acting as centers of regional growth, the foreign firms create an illusionary "capital-intensive mirage in the desert" which, because of the absence of skilled labor, will never create an industrial complex or any type of sustainable regional development. This tendency illustrates the internalization theory.

If foreign firms outsource less frequently than domestic firms, there are no local benefits to nonindigenous investment. Nonindigenous firms can actually delay the region's growth potential by aggravating labor shortages or high rates of employee turnover for local firms.[27]

"One" Is a Hazardous Number

The oil industry in Aberdeen, Scotland, created well-paid jobs, but it also displaced jobs in nonpetroleum industries. Moreover, it protected the area from a severe national recession, but its predominance accelerated the decline of traditional manufacturing and became an obstacle to the start-up of new, fast-growing industries. As a result, Aberdeen's economy

---

[27] Ashcroft and Love (1992); Higson and Elliott (1994); Young, Hood, and Peters (1994); Lagendijk (1995).

is highly dependent on a single industry dominated by foreign-owned capital. Such an economic structure does not promote long-term growth.

Harris (1987)

Maquiladora Controversies

Assembly plants such as maquiladoras in Mexico and other Latin American countries are universal. Because of specific treaties between Mexico and the United States, the maquiladoras have been able to "import" components and "export" finished goods since 1965. In 1998, nearly 3000 plants were located in Mexico and they employed over 1 million workers. The maquiladora industry absorbed almost 8 percent of Mexican farm employment and 28 percent of its manufacturing employment.

In 1998, maquiladoras were Mexico's top source of foreign exchange after the drop in oil prices. The assembly plants are concentrated in Mexico's northern border states. Before the plants were built, Mexico's northern border cities had among the highest unemployment rates in the country. Now these rates are among the nation's lowest. American suppliers have relocated to cities such as El Paso. Some of the highest state-of-the-art production technology is now found in Mexican maquiladora companies, including research and design centers. The Delphi Mexico Technical Center in Ciudad Juárez is the most advanced of 27 such centers around the world for designing auto parts used by General Motors. The literacy rate of Ciudad Juárez is the highest in the nation because of the need for skilled workers. This pattern is consistent along the United States-Mexican border.

Consumers as well as United States firms benefit from relatively low prices and production costs. Through their extensive use of United States suppliers, maquiladoras are far from stealing American jobs—in fact, they increase the possibility of their very existence. In addition, if the operations moved to East Asia, the backward linkages (i.e., American suppliers) would risk disappearing. Some parent companies avoided bankruptcy thanks to the maquiladoras.

Even though their working conditions vary greatly, the maquiladoras offer salaries higher than the local norm. For example, for the apparel maquiladoras we find clean modern facilities as well as sweatshops, while the electronics maquiladoras tend to be large, modern operations that use up-to-date machinery and have various amenities: cafeterias, continuing education programs, and lobbying of the local government to build adequate and affordable housing for workers and assist them with financing. If a maquiladora generates no forward or backward linkages with firms in that country and if its workers spend their earnings elsewhere (e.g., the case of Mexicans who choose to shop in the United States), then this assembly plant cannot create economic growth for the host region.

Economists who argue against maquiladoras accuse the American companies of moving their operations because the host regions have lax environmental regulations. In Mexicali, for instance, the evidence leads us to conclude that the maquiladoras generate significant amounts of hazardous waste. As there is no proof that the waste is re-exported to the United States or treated in Mexicali, the probability is high that the waste is illegally dumped in the Mexicali area.

Grunwald (1983), Sanchez (1990),
Tiano (1990), Vargas (1999),
Coronado and Vargas (2001)

Summary and Conclusions

This chapter reiterated the application of two macroeconomic growth models for regional economic analysis. The neoclassical growth model assumes that regional output can be estimated as if it were a microeconomic production function, in which output is a function of capital and labor, and the effect of technological innovation is the unexplained (Solow) residual. Labor and capital are able to migrate freely between regions. Following the model to its logical conclusion, we could imagine a world governed by long-run equilibrium where growth rates, wages, and land rents in all regions are the same. Any disequilibrium is eliminated by flows of labor or capital (new firms).

All analysts agree that growth is not possible without capital and labor acting together. If free migration is possible and if everything else is held constant, wage rates, growth rates, land rents, etc., will be the same everywhere. However, the list of "everything else" that needs to be "held constant" is very long. The failure of the neoclassical growth theory is evident when the analysis of identical regional economies reveals different growth rates, wages, and land rents, despite the fact that migration and trade have never been restricted.

The endogenous growth theory provides a credible response. The endogenous growth theory affirms that technology is not a residual effect of "spontaneous generation" from which the economy benefits miraculously. Instead, knowledge is created within the economy and the factors of production—labor, capital, and entrepreneurship—create and dissipate knowledge. The key input in producing current technology is the knowledge of past technologies. Private research (knowledge) can temporarily be a rival good protected by confidentiality agreements and patents. These are not universally and rapidly accessible because of obstacles such as language, distance, and political embargoes. But knowledge cannot be kept secret for long—eventually it becomes a pure public good.

New firms more rapidly adopt new technology. Older industrial areas lose their capability to innovate because of obsolescence and the presence of megafirms. The dominance of these large firms discourages new firm formation. Workers with entrepreneurial spirit are faced with an alternative: (1) work for the megafirm and abandon their ambitions for higher compensation and financial stability or (2) go elsewhere to realize their dreams.

The value of labor surpasses its numeric value because its greatest asset is the amount of human capital that it has or that it can acquire. A high level of human capital in a region facilitates the dissemination and diffusion of knowledge from firm to firm and from industry to industry. Human capital takes account of health, educational attainment, and length of time in the labor force or with a specific company. Human capital also includes social capital, which is the ability of individuals to rely on social networks and to understand the functioning of the bureaucracy.

Physical capital and entrepreneurship disseminate technology and create economic growth. When entrepreneurs invest in the latest capital, the latest technology is spilling over on the workplace. Schumpeter's theory of creative destruction maintains that the most important firms are driven by innovating entrepreneurs. At each period in history, the most recent capital is superimposed on the oldest. Layered on top of everything are the experimental prototypes. These different technologies are simultaneously competing for market dominance.

The old industrial areas are often victims of severe recessions because they do not have innovative entrepreneurs and because of their higher costs. But, the economic domination of behemoth firms creates a "modus operandi" that discourages an enterprising spirit.

To increase capital, some regions try to lure foreign direct investment. Foreign investment can take place either by developing a Greenfield site or acquiring existing facilities. According to the internalization theory, multinationals profit from advantages available in the host region. The network theory assumes that the locational advantages are preestablished production networks in the region.

Nonindigenous firms could either be a blessing or a curse. Multinationals are in what is called a virtuous cycle and provide long-term benefits if they encourage the formation of local agglomeration economies. However, when the external firms import their components and abandon existing supply networks, they are in a vicious cycle that may impede long-term growth.

We summarize the effect of technology on growth as follows: entrepreneurs compete by finding new technologies and new markets. At any given moment in history, past technologies are combined with cutting-edge technologies in a fierce whirlwind of competition. A competitive place is one where ideas churn relentlessly—a healthy place in which growth will continue unless governmental or labor union bureaucrats enforce inept regulations that preserve obsolete methods and techniques. Such policies are a death knell for suffering economies. Technological change combined with entrepreneurial dynamism is the condition *sine qua non* of economic growth.

Chapter Questions

1. According to the traditional neoclassical model, what is the impact on production of:
   a. 100 new machine presses.
   b. 200 workers entering the labor force.
   c. An increase in demand of $1.5 million new lawnmowers.
   d. Incorporating nanotechnology into production.
   e. An increase in taxes to benefit less fortunate regions.
2. According to the neoclassical model, a new lawnmower manufacturing firm locates in Tall Grass Prairie, despite that area's low unemployment rate. To be able to fulfill the $1.5 million contract for new lawnmowers, the firm is forced to increase wages by 30%.

According to the neoclassical model, how does this increase in wages affect:

a. The other employers in Tall Grass Prairie.
b. Employers in neighboring communities.
c. Employees in both Tall Grass Prairie and neighboring communities.

Research Assignments

1. From the National Center for Education Statistics Web site or from your state's Department of Education Web site, consult the **School District Profiles** or the census data (QT-P19; SF-3, School Enrollment) to determine the total number of students in school. Compare this number to the number of school-age children in your area according to the last census or population estimate to determine the enrollment rates in your area. (Check File QT-P2; SF-3. Single Years of Age under 30 Years and Sex: 2000.) Compare these with your state.
2. Check out the census Web site (for QT-P16 in SF 3) to determine the proportion of people in your county for which English is not the primary language spoken at home. What other languages are spoken regularly at home? How does your city or county compare with your state?
3. According to the last census, what was the median education level for people 25 years and over in your area? Are the better educated older or younger? How does this compare with your state? Compare also the median income of your county and state. Does there seem to be a correlation? (Check QT-P20; SF-3. Educational Attainment by Sex.)
4. Empirical evidence points out that a high proportion of engineers in an area boosts growth, but a large proportion of lawyers dampens growth. What is the proportion of lawyers (legal occupations) and engineers (drafters, engineering, and mapping technicians) in your county and state compared with the nation? (Check out QT-P27; SF-3. Occupation by Sex.) Compare your figures with the growth rates of each region. Why would the occupational mix be less likely to affect a county than a state or nation?
5. Does a strong entrepreneurial base portend local growth?
    a. From the CA05 data on the BEA Web page (http://www.bea.gov), what is the proportion of proprietors' earnings in your county compared with your state?
    b. From the County Business Pattern data (also through the Census bureau), what is the proportion of firms with fewer than 50 employees? Fewer than 500 employees?

    c. Small firms are defined by the Small Business Administration in the United States as those having fewer than 500 employees. What industries, if any, tend to hire more than 500 employees according to this definition? How do your figures compare with those of your state?

    d. Does this result conform to the results of others in the class?

6. Find the number of patents issued to companies or individuals in your state per 1000 employees in a site such as the state new economy index (http://www.neweconomyindex.org/state/2002/05_innovation_04. html). How does this compare with the nation?

References

About the Telecom Corridor®. http://www.telecomcorridor.com/tc/ (accessed on January 4, 2002, site now discontinued).

Aghion, P., and P. Howitt. 1992. A model of growth through creative destruction. *Econometrica* 60 (2):323–351.

Amable, B., and D. Guellec. 1992. Les théories de la croissance endogène (The theories of endogenous growth.). *Revue d'Économie Politique* 102 (3):313–377.

Andersson, A. E., and O. Persson. 1993. Networking scientists. *Annals of Regional Science* 27 (1):11–21.

Arrow, K. J. 2002 [1962]. Economic welfare and the allocation of resources for invention. In *Science Bought and Sold: Essays in the Economics of Science*, eds. P. Mirowski and E.-M. Sent, Chicago: University of Chicago Press, 165–180.

Ashcroft, B., and J. H. Love. 1992. External takeovers and the performance of regional companies: a predictive model. *Regional Studies* 26 (6):545–553.

Bacchetta, P. Regional investment and growth in the European community. WP 257.94. Departamento d'Economia i d'Història. Institut d'Anàlisi Económica CSLC Discussion paper, Universitat Autónoma de Barcelona, 1994.

Barro, R. J. 1991. Economic growth in a cross section of countries. *Quarterly Journal of Economics* 106 (2):407–443.

Batten, D. F., and K. Kobayashi. 1993. Product quality and regional accessibility to knowledge among Japanese manufacturing industries. *Annals of Regional Science* 27 (1):79–94.

Blaug, M. 1976. The empirical status of human capital theory: a slightly jaundiced survey. *Journal of Economic Literature* 14 (3):827–855.

Boudeville, J. R. 1966. *Problems of Regional Economic Planning*. Edinburgh: University Press.

Brandenburger, A. M., and J. B. Nalebuff. 1996. Co-opetition: a revolution mindset that combines competition and cooperation: the game theory strategy that's changing the game of business. *Japanese Economic Review* 50 (1):96–103, (As cited in Rossell, Marci and Craig Walker, 1999. Entry solicitation and deterrence in R&D competition with spillovers).

Brander, J. A. 1992. Comparative economic growth: evidence and interpretation. *Canadian Journal of Economics* 25 (4):792–818.

Browne, L., P. Mieszkowski, and R. F. Syron. 1980. Regional investment patterns. *New England Economic Review* 5–23.

Brusco, S. 1986. Small firms and industrial districts: the experience of Italy. *Economia Internazionale* 39 (2-3-4):85–97.

Butler, A. 1990. The trade-related aspects of intellectual property rights: what is at stake? *Federal Reserve Bank of St. Louis Review* 72 (6):34–46.

Camagni, R. 1986. The economics of industrial revitalisation in declining metropolitan areas. *Economia Internazionale* 39 (2–3–4):316–334.

Camagni, R. 1993. Inter-firm industrial networks: the costs and benefits of cooperative behaviour. *Journal of Industry Studies* 1 (1):1–15.

Canals, V., C. Diebolt, and M. Jaoul. 2003. Convergence et disparités régionales du poids de l'enseignement supérieur en France: 1964–2000. (Convergence and regional disparities of the weight of French higher education: 1964–2000). *Revue d'Economie Régionale Et Urbaine* 0 (4):649–669.

Carlino, G., and R. DeFina. 1995. Regional income dynamics. *Journal of Urban Economics* 37 (1):88–106.

Carlino, G. A. 2001. Knowledge spillovers: cities' role in the new economy. *Federal Reserve Bank of Philadelphia Business Review* 17–26.

Carlsson, B. 1994. Technological systems and economic development potential: four swedish case studies. In *Innovation in Technology, Industries, and Institutions: Studies in Schumpeterian Perspectives*, eds. Y. Shionoya and M. Perlman, Ann Arbor: University of Michigan Press, 49–69.

Coronado, R., and L. Vargas. 2001. Economic update on El Paso del Norte (Part 1). *Federal Reserve Bank of Dallas, El Paso Branch; Issue2.*

Coughlin, C. C., J. V. Terza, and V. Arromdee. 1991. State characteristics and the location of foreign direct investment within the United States. *Review of Economics and Statistics* 73 (4):675–683.

Crevoisier, O. 1994. Dynamique industrielle et dynamique régionale: L'articulation par les milieux innovateurs. *Revue d'Économie Industrielle* 0 (70):33–48.

Davidsson, P., L. Lindmark, and C. Olofsson. 1995. Small firms, business dynamics and differential development of economic well-being. *Small Business Economics* 7 (4):301–315.

De Long, J. B. 1988. Productivity growth, convergence, and welfare: comment. *American Economic Review* 78 (5):1138–1154.

Denison, E. F. 1985. *Trends in American Economic Growth, 1929–1982.* Washington, DC: The Brookings Institution.

Easterlin, R. A. 1981. Why isn't the whole world developed?. *Journal of Economic History* 41 (1):1–19.

Eberts, R. W., and E. Montgomery. 1995. Cyclical versus secular movements in employment creation and destruction. National Bureau of Economic Research, Inc., NBER Working Papers.

Fagerberg, J., and B. Verspagen. 1996. Heading for divergence? Regional growth in Europe reconsidered. *Journal of Common Market Studies* 34 (3):431–448.

Fielding, A. J. 1994. Industrial change and regional development in Western Europe. *Urban Studies* 31 (4–5):679–704.

Fischer, M. M., and A. Varga. 2003. Spatial knowledge spillovers and university research: evidence from Austria. *Annals of Regional Science* 37 (2):303–322.

Flap, H., et al. Measurement instruments for social capital of individuals. Questionnaire items as used in the 1999/2000 nation wide study "Social relations and networks in the neighborhood and at the workplace: the Social Survey of the Networks of the Dutch." (SSND)—a joint project of the universities of Utrecht, Groningen, and Amsterdam, http://www.xs4all.nl/~gaag/work/SSND.pdf, 1999/2000.

Flynn, P. M. 1993. *Technology Life Cycles and Human Resources*, Reprint edition London: University Press of America.

Ford, R., and P. Poret. 1991. Infrastructure and private-sector productivity. *OECD Economic Studies* 0 (17):63–89.

Fritsch, M. 2002. Measuring the quality of regional innovation systems: a knowledge production function approach. *International Regional Science Review* 25 (1):86–101.

Garofoli, G. 1994. New firm formation and regional development: the Italian case. *Regional Studies* 28 (4):381–393.

Gladstone, B., and J. L. Lee. 1995. The operation of the insolvency system in the U.K.: some implications for entrepreneurialism. *Small Business Economics* 7 (1):55–66.

Glickman, N. J., and D. P. Woodward. 1988. The location of foreign direct investment in the United States: patterns and determinants. *International Regional Science Review* 11 (2):137–154.

Goss, E., and G. S. Vozikis. 1994. High tech manufacturing: firm size, industry and population density. *Small Business Economics* 6 (4):291–297.

Grunwald, J. 1983. Re-estructuración de la industria maquiladora. *El Trimestre Económico* 50 (200):2123–2152.

Guesnier, B. 1994. Regional variations in new firm formation in France. *Regional Studies* 28 (4):347–358.

Gunderson, M. 1998. Regional impacts of trade and investment on labour. *Canadian Journal of Regional Science* 21 (2):197–225.

Gundlach, E. 1993. Empirical evidence for alternative growth models: time series results. *Weltwirtschaftliches Archiv* 129 (1):103–119.

Harris, A. H. 1987. Incoming industry and structural change: oil and the Aberdeen economy. *Scottish Journal of Political Economy* 34 (1):69–90.

Helsley, R. W., and W. C. Strange. 2002. Innovation and input sharing. *Journal of Urban Economics* 51 (1):25–45.

Higson, C., and J. Elliott. 1994. The incentive to locate a multinational firm: the effect of tax reforms in the United Kingdom. *International Tax and Public Finance* 1 (1):81–97.

Howland, M. 1984. Age of capital and regional business cycles. *Growth and Change* 15 (2):29–37.

Johansson, B. 1991. Regional industrial analysis and vintage dynamics. *Annals of Regional Science* 25 (1):1–18.

Johnson, T. G. 1994. The dimensions of regional economic development theory. *Review of Regional Studies* 24 (2):119–126.

Keeble, D., and S. Walker. 1994. New firms, small firms and dead firms: spatial patterns and determinants in the United Kingdom. *Regional Studies* 28 (4):411–427.

Khan, S. R. 1993. Underestimating aggregate rates of return to education. *International Journal of Manpower* 14 (8):17–22.

Kimmel, J. 1997. Rural wages and returns to education: differences between whites, blacks, and American Indians. *Economics of Education Review* 16 (1):81–96.

Kottman, S. E. 1992. Regional employment by industry: do returns to capital matter? *Federal Reserve Bank of Atlanta Economic Review* 77 (5):13–25.

Lacroix, R. 1984. Québec: les politiques et programmes gouvernementaux et la création d'emplois. (Quebec: Government policies and programs and job creation). *Canadian Public Policy* 10 (4):429–435.

Lagendijk, A. 1995. The foreign takeover of the Spanish automobile industry: a growth analysis of internationalization. *Regional Studies* 29 (4):381–393.

Lagendijk, A., and G. A. van der Knaap. 1993. Foreign involvement in the Spanish automobile industry: internalising versus networking. *Environment and Planning A* 25 (11):1663–1676.

Lazaric, N., and E. Lorenz. 1998. The learning dynamics of trust, reputation and confidence. In *Trust and Economic Learning*, eds. N. Lazaric and E. Lorenz, Cheltenham, U.K.: Elgar, 1–20, (distributed by American International Distribution Corporation, Williston, VT).

Leijonhufvud, A. 1986. Capitalism and the factory system, *Economics as a Process: Essays in the New Institutional Economics*, ed. R. N. Langlois, Cambridge: Cambridge University Press, 203–223.

Lucas, R. E. 1988. On the mechanics of economic development. *Journal of Monetary Economics* 22 (1):3–42.

Magee, S. P., W. A. Brock, and L. Young. 1989. *Black hole tariffs and endogenous policy theory: Political economy in general equilibrium.* Cambridge: Cambridge University Press.

Maillat, D., and L. Kebir. 1999. "Learning region" et systèmes territoriaux de production. ("Learning region" and territorial production systems.). *Revue d'Economie Régionale et Urbaine* 0 (3):429–448.

Malecki, E. J. 2000. Soft variables in regional science. *Review of Regional Studies* 30 (1):61–69.

McCombie, J. S. L. 1988. A synoptic view of regional growth and unemployment: I—the neoclassical theory. *Urban Studies* 25 (4):267–281.

Mulligan, C.B. and Sala-i-Martin, X. Measuring aggregate human capital, National Bureau of Economic Research, Inc., NBER Working Papers, 1995.

Murphy, K. M., A. Shleifer, and R. W. Vishny. 1989. Industrialization and the big push. *Journal of Political Economy* 97 (5):1003–1026.

Nakosteen, R. A., and M. A. Zimmer. 1987. Determinants of regional migration by manufacturing firms. *Economic Inquiry* 25 (2):351–362.

Nelson, R. R., and S. G. Winter. 1974. Neoclassical vs. evolutionary theories of economic growth: critique and prospectus. *Economic Journal* 84 (336):886–905.

Ó Huallacháin, B., and N. Reid. 1997. Acquisition versus Greenfield investment: the location and growth of Japanese manufacturers in the United States. *Regional Studies* 31 (4):403–416.

O'Farrell, P. N., and R. P. Oakey. 1992. Regional variations in the adoption of computer-numerically-controlled machine tools by small engineering firms: a multivariate analysis. *Environment and Planning A* 24 (6):887–902.

Pascallon, P. 1991. Introduction. *Economies Et Sociétés* 25 (8):5–19.

Peng, Y., Zucker, L.G. and Darby, M.R. Chinese rural industrial productivity and urban spillovers, National Bureau of Economic Research, Inc., NBER Working Papers, 1997.

Perroux, F. 1995 [1950]. Economic space: theory and applications. In *The Economics of Location. Volume 3: Spatial Microeconomics*, eds. M.L. Greenhut and G. Norman, Aldershot, U.K.: Elgar Reference Collection: International Library of Critical Writings in Economics, Vol. 42, Elgar, 211–226, (distributed in the U.S. by Ashgate, Brookfield, VT).

Podrecca, E. 1993. Recent growth theories: an assessment. *Rivista Internazionale Di Scienze Economiche e Commerciali* 40 (5):411–422.

Rallet, A. 1991. Théorie de la polarisation et technopoles (Growth pole theory and technopoles.). *Economies et Sociétés* 25 (8):43–64.

Renkow, M. 1996. Income non-convergence and rural-urban earnings differentials: evidence from North Carolina. *Southern Economic Journal* 62 (4):1017–1028.

Romer, P. M. 1986. Increasing returns and long-run growth. *Journal of Political Economy* 94 (5):1002–1037.

Romer, P.M. Human capital and growth: Theory and evidence, National Bureau of Economic Research, Inc., NBER Working Papers, 1989.

Romer, P. M. 1990. Are nonconvexities important for understanding growth?. *American Economic Review* 80 (2):97–103.

Romer, P. M. 1995. The growth of nations: comment. *Brookings Papers on Economic Activity* 1313–320.

Romer, P. M. 1996. Why, indeed, in America? theory, history, and the origins of modern economic growth. *American Economic Review* 86 (2):202–206.

Rondi, L., and A. Sembenelli. 1991. Testing the relationship between the growth of firms and the growth of the economy. *International Journal of Industrial Organization* 9 (2):251–259.

Rosenfeld, S. A. 2000. Community College/Cluster connections: specialization and competitiveness in the United States and Europe. *Economic Development Quarterly* 14 (1):51–62.

Rossell, M., and C. Walker. 1999. Entry solicitation and deterrence in R&D competition with spillovers. *Japanese Economic Review* 50 (1):96–103.

Sanchez, R. A. 1990. Health and environmental risks of the maquiladora in Mexicali. *Natural Resources Journal* 30 (1):163–186.

Savy, M., and P. Veltz. 1993. Les nouveaux espaces de l'entreprise, Paris. DATAR/-Editions de l'Aube, as cited in Guesnier, B. Regional Variations in New Firm Formation in France. *Regional Studies* 28 (4):347–358.

Schultz, T. W. 1963. *The Economic Value of Education*. New York: Columbia University Press.

Schultz, T. W. 1990. *Restoring Economic Equilibrium: Human Capital in the Modernizing Economy*. Cambridge: Blackwell.

Schumpeter, J. A. 1975[1942]. *Capitalism, Socialism and Democracy*. New York: Harper.

Schwalbach, J. 1994. Small business dynamics in Europe. *Small Business Economics* 6 (1):21–25.

Silverberg, G., and D. Lehnert. 1994. Growth fluctuations in an evolutionary model of creative destruction. In *The Economics of Growth and Technical Change: Technologies, Nations, Agents*, eds. G. Silverberg and L. Soete, Aldershot, U.K.: Elgar, 74–109, (distributed in the U.S. by Ashgate, Brookfield, VT).

Simon, C. J. 1998. Human capital and metropolitan employment growth. *Journal of Urban Economics* 43 (2):223–243.

Solow, R. M. 1991 [1956]. A contribution to the theory of economic growth. In *Growth Theory. Volume 1. Descriptive Growth Theories*, eds. R. Becker and E. Burmeister, Aldershot, U.K.: Elgar, 3–32, (International Library of Critical Writings in Economics, no. 10).

Stern, N. 1991. The determinants of growth. *Economic Journal* 101 (404):122–133.

Swamidass, P. M. 1990. Comparison of the plant location strategies of foreign and domestic manufacturers in the U.S. *Journal of International Business Studies* 21 (2):301–317.

Swan, T. W. 2001. Economic growth and capital accumulation. In *Landmark Papers in Economic Growth*, ed. R. M. Solow, Cheltenham, U.K.: Foundations of Twentieth Century Economics, Vol. 1, Elgar, 67–94, (distributed by American International Distribution Corporation, Williston, VT).

Tallman, E. W., and P. Wang. 1992. Human capital investment and economic growth: new routes in theory address old questions. *Federal Reserve Bank of Atlanta Economic Review* 77 (5):1–12.

Tansel, A., and N. D. Güngor. 1997. The educational attainment of Turkey's labor force: a comparison across provinces and over time. *Middle East Technical University Studies in Development* 24 (4):531–547.

Tether, B. S. 2000. Small firms, innovation and employment creation in Britain and Europe. A question of expectations. *Technovation* 20:109–113.

Tiano, S. 1990. Maquiladora women: A new category of workers? *Women Workers and Global Restructuring*, ed. K. Ward, Ithaca: Cornell International Industrial and Labor Relations Report series, no. 17, ILR Press, 193–223.

Tomaney, J. 1994. Alternative approaches to restructuring in traditional industrial regions: the case of the Maritime sector. *Regional Studies* 28 (5):544–549.

Vaessen, P., and D. Keeble. 1995. Growth-oriented SMEs in unfavourable regional environments. *Regional Studies* 29 (6):489–505.

Vargas, L. 1999. The binational importance of the maquiladora industry. *Southwest Economy* November/December:1–5.

Whittington, R. C. 1984. Regional bias in new firm formation in the UK. *Regional Studies* 18 (3):253–256.

Young, A. 1993. Invention and bounded learning by doing. *Journal of Political Economy* 101 (3):443–472.

Young, S., N. Hood, and E. Peters. 1994. Multinational enterprises and regional economic development. *Regional Studies* 28 (7):657–677.

Chapter 9

Core–Periphery Models: Distance Counts

So far in Part II, we have presented theories that follow the macroeconomic framework of regions without spatial dimensions. In these models, distance is inconsequential. However, in reality, proximity does matter. Growth does not occur randomly over space. This chapter evaluates growth within a region according to core–periphery models. These models describe the relation among the urban and the rural areas of a region. The periphery of a city is composed of the **periurban areas**—the rural areas that are contiguous to the urban area—and the **deep rural areas** which, despite the distance, considers the city as its central place for specialized purchases.

Because distance from some focal point is now significant, land rents become important in allocating land to its most profitable use. The central place model (Chapter 3) depends on the distance between cities of various sizes and underscores many of the core–periphery studies. This section introduces three models to complement the central place theory: von Thünen's concentric ring theory, Vernon's product life cycle theory, and Perroux's growth pole theory.

The concentric ring theory of von Thünen underlies current urban land-rent theories. The product life cycle theory evaluates the optimal proximity of a plant to the city center according to the degree of innovation and technology. Finally, the growth pole theory lays out the conditions according to which urban growth will stimulate the periphery or suffocate it.

Developed or Developing Countries: What's the Difference?

According to Lemelin and Polèse (1993), the factors that affect job location are the same in both developed and developing countries. The authors studied examples of locations in Canada and Mexico and concluded that urban size, economies of agglomeration, and distance are basic variables that determine firm location in both countries. Industries that benefit from agglomeration economies locate in the larger cities. The costs and benefits associated with distance reflect the differences in quality of the local transportation network and the efficiency of the financial sector. However, but these differences in the amounts of the costs and benefits do not change the decision-making formula.

For development, urbanization is a necessary but not a sufficient condition. Lemelin and Polèse find no systematic relation between urban size or urban form and levels of development. Policies that offset the natural tendency to decentralize economic activity may cost dearly if policy makers do not respect the factors that rest on the optimal location of firms.

Lemelin and Polèse (1993)

---

von Thünen's Concentric Rings

Johann Heinrich von Thünen's **Der isolierte Staat** (1826) was written during an agrarian age. This model justifies the location of different economic activities based on the cost of transporting their product to the center of the city. Today this model is the foundation of contemporary urban and rural land-use models. The original model assumes a homogeneous plain that is equally fertile everywhere. The marketplace is a one-dimensional city at the center of that plain. Costs of production are the same everywhere. Transportation costs are a linear function of distance. Under these circumstances, von Thünen wondered what goods will be produced and where. The answer to his question not only determines an optimal use for land as a function of distance to the city but also places a monetary value on land (i.e., land rent).

Bid-Rent Functions

The competitive market at the city center determines the product prices that the profit maximizing firms face. Total costs consist of production and transport costs. Production costs include a normal profit. The residual ($TR - TC$) potentially consists of supernormal profit and land rent. However, the entire residual will be absorbed by the cost of a location as close to the city as possible, thus eliminating all supernormal profit. The result of this competition for land is found in the **cost–distance function** in Figure 9.1. The cost–distance function determines how much rent a firm is willing to bid for land at a given distance from the market center. The maximum bid will be for land at the market center. In Figure 9.1, the farthest from the market center that a firm is willing to locate is 50 miles, and this is only if it pays nothing for land rent.

Land rent is calculated as follows: land rent per acre (residual) is equal to the Total Revenue per Acre less the Total Cost per Acre, or

$$\text{Land Rent} = TR - PC - tD \tag{9.1}$$

where TR is the total revenue, PC is the production cost (normal profit included), t is the marginal transportation cost per unit of distance, and D is the distance.

We assume, for example, that the total revenue per acre is $100, production costs are $50, and the marginal transportation cost is $1 per mile. At the market center where distance is 0, this firm will be willing to pay $50 for land rent. The amount that the firm is willing to pay will steadily decline until it drops to 0 at 50 miles from the center ($TR - PC - tD = \$100 - \$50 - (\$1 \times 50) = 0$) as in Figure 9.2.

Figure 9.2 depicts the bid-rent function associated with the cost–distance function in Figure 9.1. **Bid-rent functions** show the maximum amount of

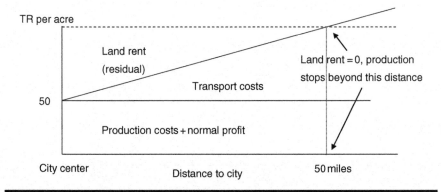

Figure 9.1 Cost–distance function.

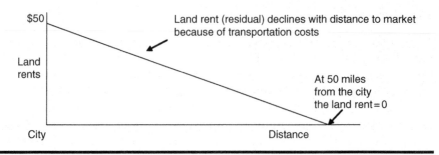

Figure 9.2 Bid-rent function.

rent that firms in a specific industry are willing and able to pay at each distance from the city.

To understand how the concentric rings are formed, we assume for now that only two products are grown—pumpkins and lettuce. We assume further that both goods provide the same total revenue per acre. We imagine that lettuce has lower production costs and because it is fragile, higher transportation costs per mile. In contrast, pumpkins have higher production costs, but because they do not bruise as easily, transportation costs per mile are low. The city is at the center of the plain and farmers must travel there to sell their produce. The resulting cost–distance functions (Figure 9.3) show that for land closest to the city center, lettuce producers can outbid the pumpkin producers. The two products have the same monetary return per acre regardless of the place of production. The difference between the cost–distance function and the line of total revenues per acre is the maximum amount that can be bid for land by these producers.

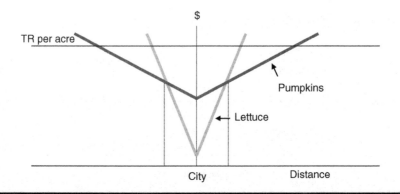

Figure 9.3 Cost–distance functions.

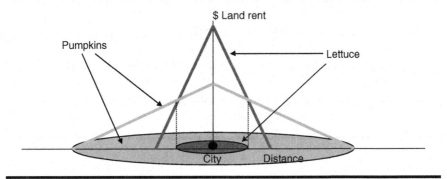

Figure 9.4   Bid-rent functions.

Inverting the cost–distance function creates the bid-rent functions for each. Each land use has a distinct cost–distance function, and therefore its own bid-rent function. Figure 9.4 depicts two bid-rent functions and the resulting land-use patterns. Lettuce producers are able to bid more for land located closer to the city, so lettuce is grown closer to the city (in *the smaller* concentric ring). Pumpkin producers can only afford land farther from the city; therefore, pumpkins will be grown in the *outer* concentric ring surrounding lettuce producers.

The resulting land-use pattern implicitly assumes that the goal of the hinterland is to serve the city. The most perishable goods and those most difficult to transport are produced closest to the city, and goods that are easiest to transport and least perishable are located away from the city. Land prices decline with distance from the city. Figure 9.5 illustrates these concentric rings.

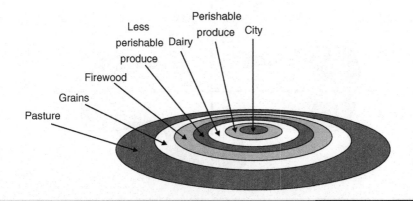

Figure 9.5   von Thünen's concentric circles.

Think About it...

As you travel through your city or from one city to the next, note how land uses change. What types of employment centers or jobs are provided in different areas of your community?

Land-Use Patterns

In reality, land uses will not be geographically concentric. Because transportation costs are more a function of time than distance, higher land rents are inversely related to the duration of a journey to the market center. Figure 9.6 depicts von Thünen's "concentric" rings with two roads intersecting the city center. Land rents are highest in light gray areas, moderate in the medium gray areas, and least expensive in the dark gray area. Here, physical distance does not matter as much as does the length of time to reach the city center.

Growth in a von Thünen Landscape

In von Thünen's landscape, growth proceeds as follows: increased demand for a product increases its price. If production costs are constant, the increased price results in higher residuals. Competition for space near the city turns these extra residuals into increased land rents and an expansion of the amount of land devoted to that sector. Say, for instance, that the economy consists of three sectors, A, B, and C. Assume further that the

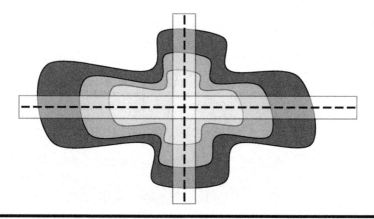

Figure 9.6 Concentric circles adjusted for intersecting routes.

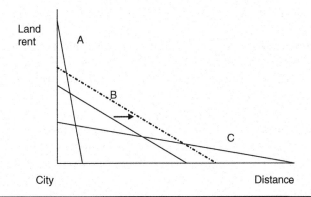

Figure 9.7   Bid-rent function showing growth of Sector B.

demand for goods produced by Sector B increases, but the demand for goods from Sectors A and C remains constant. Then, as depicted in Figure 9.7, the bid-rent function for Sector B expands and production of B will encroach on lands previously devoted to A and C. If the decrease in supply of goods A and C also results in their prices increasing proportionally, the final result will be an increase in the amount of the hinterland devoted to serving the city.

Product Life Cycles and Firm Location

Vernon's (1966) product life cycle argument gives another use for rural areas besides providing goods for the city. The product life cycle is the criterion that determines the location of a firm in an urban or a rural area. This model investigates the impact of technological change on investment decision making. It assumes that rural areas are limited to providing unskilled, low-income employment opportunities because they lack agglomeration economies needed to maintain or create an innovative milieu. Only the cities can provide jobs for highly skilled professionals. However, a secondary implication of the model is the troublesome concept of regional technological determinism.[1]

A Product's Three Stages

A product's life cycle evolves through three stages: the innovation stage, the transition (or maturity) stage, and the standardization stage. The

---

[1] Hekman (1985); Taylor (1986).

location in an urban or a rural area is decided according to the life cycle of the product.

In the ***innovation stage***, production runs are short with small amounts of output. The only locational advantages for these firms are the agglomeration economies at the urban core. The firms need frequent input from scientists and engineers to upgrade the products. High-tech industries locate near universities despite the accompanying higher land rents. Creating and introducing new products require (1) flexibility in obtaining inputs, (2) swift and accurate communications with suppliers, customers, and competitors, and (3) an affluent market that can afford these new and expensive products. These conditions are found only in metropolitan centers.

Location Quotients at the Core

Mack and Jacobson (1996) use location quotients to analyze core-periphery relationships in the European Union. They find that in the periphery, the location quotients for manufacturing are greater than 1 for low-tech goods and standardized production. Thus, the periphery specializes in these types of production. However, high-tech and large-scale manufacturing have location quotients less than 1.

A similar dualism exists among the service industries. The location quotient for wholesale trade, retail, communication, and educational services equals 1 in the periphery, whereas producer services have location quotients less than 1. For core areas, the location quotients for high-technology industries as well as small-scale manufacturing and producer services are greater than 1.

Mack and Jacobson (1996)

The ***transition (maturity) stage*** occurs with substantial investment in research and development and in production technology. The production technology is embedded in capital and can thus be easily transferred from one site to another. Firms are still linked to the research centers but the bonds between production and design are more relaxed. In this stage, firms flourish if they move outward to sites that offer lower production and land costs—perhaps to suburbs or counties contiguous to a major research center and a pool of skilled workers.

As product design becomes standardized, unskilled labor, and automation substitute for the skilled assembly workers needed in the early production stages. The need for flexibility in hiring inputs declines and the firm benefits from economies of scale due to mass production. At this ***standardization stage*** in the product cycle, production moves either to rural areas or overseas to places endowed with an abundance of low-paid, unskilled workers. This move is essential because a standardized product is routinely imitated. A fierce price competition for the product causes its demand to be more elastic.[2]

Is the Product Life Cycle Explanation Valid?

In general, the theory does a good job explaining which types of firms tend to locate in the periphery of an urban area. Mature high-technology manufacturing industries rely on specialized services and labor force characteristics that are only found in urban areas. These industries expand in counties that are adjacent to urban areas where land prices are lower and the skilled labor force resides. However, Sherwood-Call (1992) found little evidence of product cycle patterns in California's electronics markets, perhaps because the technology has not yet attained full maturity.

Technological determinism implies that ideas only flow down an urban hierarchy from the largest to the smallest city. Like the supposed flow of goods and services in the central place theory, the product life cycle theory claims that small cities or rural areas are unable to create and innovate; the metropolitan area is the presumed monopoly of these qualities. In reality, not all large cities generate innovation, and not all innovations come from large cities. People from small- and medium-size towns and rural areas also innovate.[3]

Innovation and Large Cities

Technological spillovers from localization and urbanization economies are responsible for the majority of innovations in a large city. Lucas (1988) argues that the opportunities to interact and learn from others, which are essential to a maximum productivity, are the only reasons to locate in a place

---

[2] Hekman (1985); Taylor (1986).
[3] Sherwood-Call (1992); Wojan and Pulver (1995).

where land rents are high. The key question concerning innovation is to know whether the spillovers from localization economies or urbanization economies cause greater innovation (Chapter 5).

Researchers who favor localization economies (***Marshall-Arrow-Romer*** or ***MAR Externalities***) point to the spying, imitation, and rapid interfirm movement of skilled labor as causing the most innovation as in Silicon Valley. Those who believe urbanization economies (***Jacobs Externalities***) create more innovation might point to Detroit's history. Detroit's automobile industry is the offspring of its history of shipbuilding. In the 1820s, Detroit mainly exported flour. Along the Detroit River, small shipyards developed to build and repair ships to use in the flour trade. The shipbuilding industry refined and adapted the internal combustion gasoline engine to power the boats on Michigan's waterways. A firm named Olds produced boat engines and a company named Dodge repaired these engines. Since the internal combustion engine was better suited to power automobiles than the steam engine, the internal combustion engine industry combined with the steel and machine tool industries to make Detroit the world's capital in automobile production.

Studies that analyze patent activity and employment data agree that urbanization economies are more economically stimulating than localization economies. For example, in 1956, the primary metals industry grew rapidly in Savannah, Georgia, where it was not concentrated, but declined in Fresno, California, where it was heavily concentrated. Furthermore, patent activity and employment grew faster in cities where the firms were smaller than the average firms in their industries.[4]

Nursery Cities

Not all large cities make good incubators for new firms. Chinitz (1961, 1964) compared the innovation potential of New York, where large firms do not dominate the economy, with the possibilities in Pittsburgh, Pennsylvania. At that time, Pittsburgh was heavily specialized in a few industries that were dominated by large plants and firms. New York, in contrast, offered more diversity in a competitive industrial structure. Because Pittsburgh had fewer entrepreneurs per capita, they produced fewer innovations than New York. In

---

[4] Jacobs (1969); Romer (1990, 1995); Crampton and Evans (1992); Carlino (2001).

general, most small-scale, highly competitive industries require outside services and facilities available only in areas with large agglomeration economies, but only few large-scale manufacturers need such services.

Crampton and Evans (1992), Carlino (2001)

Innovation in Peripheral Towns

Several studies have shown that small- to medium-sized firms in the periphery introduce almost as many successful innovations as their metropolitan counterparts. The expanding firms in the periphery surrounding London, for example, employ fewer research and development employees than those in the capital, but their total revenues are 29 percent higher. The faster growing firms on the periphery provide more external training programs for their employees than their counterparts in the metropolitan areas or their slower growing neighboring firms to maintain their levels of innovation.

In the Netherlands, because of congestion and the fact that research and development workers and entrepreneurs prefer to live in attractive areas, innovative entrepreneurs tend also to locate in the suburban rings and medium-sized towns. In the United States, Denmark, and France, empirical evidence supports the hypothesis that research and development jobs follow skilled workers to the suburbs and outskirts of the city. Thus, a theory that predicts greater amounts of innovation in the central cities is not valid for medium-sized firms.

Kleinknecht, Poot, and Reijnen (1991),
Barkley et al. (1995), Vaessen and Keeble (1995),
Henry and Schmitt et al. (1999)

Innovation in Rural Areas

"Common knowledge" alleges that firms in remote rural areas lag behind those in accessible rural areas in terms of innovation and adopting new technology. Firms in remote locations lack the possibilities for advanced training. The areas without well-developed telecommunication infrastructures decrease the potential for firms to innovate. Because firms in the more innovative sectors, like instrument and electronic engineering, research and development, and business and computer services, are less likely to locate in remote areas, deep rural areas lacking agglomeration economies do produce fewer innovations than those in accessible rural areas.

Innovation in Rural Europe

Vaessen and Keeble (1995) showed that in Great Britain, a rural environment stimulates a different kind of innovation because firms must be inventive to overcome local constraints. For instance, firms in the tourism industry become innovative by introducing products of the local artisans. If the rural firms have access to solid telecommunications infrastructures and can use external sources of information and expertise, there is little difference between the innovation and innovative ability of rural firms and similar firms in more accessible locations. In the Netherlands, the research and development of rural firms is more efficient in simplifying the production processes, even though urban firms invest more in their research and development.

Kleinknecht, Poot, and Reijnen (1991),
Vaessen and Keeble (1995)

Without innovation, rural areas are doomed to stagnation. Conditions once thought favorable to growth turned out to be millstones around the neck of the rural American South. Low taxes, low wages, unregulated environment, and second-rate schools may lead to high rankings on business climate indexes, but in reality, they are a handicap for high-growth industries. For high-tech industries, good schools, cultural amenities, and a skilled, intelligent work force are more important than proximity to markets. Firms prefer to pay higher taxes if they receive better schools or an efficient network of services.[5]

South Africa's Technology Clusters

Every country wants its own Silicon Valley. However, the high-tech clusters in low-income countries are fundamentally different from those in industrialized countries, according to Hodge (1998). This is because developing countries lack the technological and innovative capacity of multinational high-tech firms and because multinationals tend to locate components of their research and development and production in places most appropriate to accomplishing those tasks. Therefore, high-tech clusters in developing countries are usually less dynamic, less innovative, and tend to concentrate on process innovation for established products.

Midrand, South Africa, has a disproportionately large share of the nation's inputs for high technology sectors. The cluster includes a large group of high-tech multinationals and solid local firms. The cluster is not based on research and development, but on the head office, warehousing, and transport functions as well as manufacturing. South Africa's research and development activities locate instead near universities.

Hodge (1998)

Product Cycles in Brazil, Japan, Korea, and America

Henderson (1997) looked at the distribution of manufacturing activity within cities of different sizes in four countries. He found that the distribution of city sizes is

[5] Kleinknecht, Poot, and Reijnen (1991); Barkley et al. (1995); Vaessen and Keeble (1995); Henry et al. (1999); Fisher (2005).

stable over time and that medium sized cities are much more specialized in manufacturing activities than the metropolitan areas. Medium-sized cities specialize either in manufacturing or in services. For example, they can be a corporate headquarters, a college town, or a strong retail, repair, transportation, or banking and financial center. The medium-sized cities that are manufacturing centers concentrate on standardized goods such as textiles, food processing, steel, automobile parts or assembly, pulp and paper, or electrical machinery. This specialization occurs because of agglomeration economies and internal economies of scale. It persists despite the fact that half the manufacturing firms in countries as varied as the United States, Colombia, and Indonesia go out of business and are replaced by new plants every five years.

The large metropolitan areas are quite different from the medium-sized cities. They concentrate on more specialized services like finance, advertising, the arts, high fashion apparel, or publishing, but the rest of the manufacturing base is highly diversified. The physical output per worker is low due to an emphasis on administration and research and development activities. New products develop in the milieux of large metropolitan areas. Production of standardized products moves to the medium-sized cities. Japanese firms use low cost Thai labor to produce standardized electronics components. American firms tend to produce such components in Mexico.

Henderson (1997)

Growth Poles

The term "growth pole" is used in two broad ways. First, a **natural growth pole** is a dynamic element in the spatial structure of an economy. Second, a **planned** or **induced growth pole** is the cornerstone of a government-funded investment strategy that involves the spatial concentration of infrastructure and investment in plant and equipment. Using the growth pole as a locality's investment strategy requires artificially redefining the geographic space. A government could attract new firms (without knowing if they will be viable) into the urban centers of slow-growing regions with a combination of promises, such as construction of new infrastructure and monetary incentives. Usually, however, the expected spread effects into the rest of the region do not materialize with induced growth poles.

François Perroux (1956) used the concept of growth pole (***pôle de croissance***) to demonstrate that market forces do not guarantee the harmonious equilibrium in space predicted by the neoclassical growth theory. Economic activity does not necessarily spread evenly or equitably. Instead, activity will naturally cluster together, thus creating a dominance–dependency relationship among urban centers, regions, and nations. Perroux preferred the term "economic space" to "geographic space", because innovations launch new developments that influence firms and industries not just locally but in all parts of the world. He believed that the true growth poles of Latin America and Africa were actually in Europe and in the United States. The growth pole concept combines regional economic growth theory with the analysis of the spatial location of economic activity.

"Economic space" is a more precise term than "geographic space", because the concept of a growth pole is useless for planners unless they intend to plan and economically develop the entire world. To limit the geographic scale of analysis, Boudeville (1966) treated growth poles as urban centers and he envisioned the growth effects spreading over the periphery.[6]

Is There an Optimal Sized City for a Growth Pole?

Most urban and regional growth policies justify them-selves as being applications of the growth pole doctrine. In Japan, growth poles were vast industrial complexes requiring hundreds of millions of dollars of investment. In contrast, one study demonstrated that despite its population of 2.5 million, its universities, producer services, research centers, and high-tech industries, Montreal was too small to serve as the growth pole of Quebec. The competition from Toronto and U.S. cities was too strong. At the other extreme, the Economic Development Administration of the United States tried to create growth centers in isolated towns with as few as 500 people.

Higgins (1983)

---

[6] Parr (1973); Higgins (1983).

The main problem that researchers face when analyzing a potential "growth pole" is the lack of a consistent and usable description. Generally recognized characteristics include:

- The existence of what Perroux referred to as a motrice (stimulant, key, leading, or propulsive) firm or industry.
- A gathering of backward and forward linkages that will grow with the motrice firm.
- A potential for technical or administrative innovation.
- The capability to attain self-sustained growth.
- The capability for growth to spread over the pole's hinterland.

A common definition of a growth pole is that it is an urban center with a population greater than some threshold size. At a given time, this center displays a growth in population or employment at a rate greater than that of the regional benchmark economy. But this definition is in fact a tautology (true by definition) and impossible to test empirically: If an area's population or employment grows faster than its regional economy, then it is a growth pole. If, in contrast, it stops developing, it is no longer a growth pole even though the "conditions" remain unchanged.[7]

Spread and Backwash Effects and Growth

A typical region is composed of three elements: ***urban areas, periurban areas*** (i.e., rural areas that are adjacent to the urban area), and ***deep rural areas***. The labor force in the deep rural areas is generally more unskilled compared with that of the urban or periurban zone. Thus, a higher proportion of small firms are located there.

A ***spread (trickle-down) effect*** exists if growth at a pole extends to the hinterland and increases the demand for goods and services produced there. Alternatively, the ***backwash (polarization) effects*** predominate if growth at the pole siphons incomes, jobs, and employees from the hinterland. Whether a spread or backwash effect prevails depends on the size of the pole and the type of regional economic activity.

In total, five classifications of spatial association between a core and its periphery exist. First, ***spread through growth*** is produced if the hinterland growth is associated with growth in the metropolitan area. This scenario describes an agricultural or resource-based area surrounding a small city characterized by low incomes. A motrice firm that processes agricultural products or natural resources almost instantaneously creates a spread effect if it decides to locate in the city. The dynamic nature of this firm

---

[7] Parr (1973).

increases the demand for production in the hinterland and in the city itself. The increased demand for labor by the firm causes households to either migrate to the city or commute. The migration increases population density in the entire city, and the population density gradient (i.e., a graph of population per square mile) gets steeper.

Second, a **backwash** exists if a decline in rural population is associated with growth in the city. The city is recognized as a growth pole with moderate per capita income levels. An added motrice firm creates a backwash effect by creating agglomeration economies. Firms from the hinterland move to the city and a selective migration of population to the city creates **settlement sorting**: production workers move to smaller settlements whereas white-collar workers choose an urban area. In essence, people follow their jobs. The high cost of transporting freight centralizes firms and therefore jobs.

Spread, Backwash, or Nodes?

Washington State's core is the Seattle-Tacoma area. The state's two second-tier cities are Yakima in the south central and Spokane to the east. Using input–output analysis, Hughes and Holland (1994) concluded that the standard growth pole theory did not characterize Washington State's economy. Most of the core's growth industries were not strongly linked to the periphery. Even though, the periphery had strong linkages with the core, due mainly to the induced effects. Thus, the core felt a stronger effect from the economic growth in the periphery than the reverse. This characterizes a nodal response. Roberts (1998) had observed the same result for rural and urban interdependencies in Grampian, northeast Scotland.

Hughes and Litz (1996) also determined that the spillover effects from the periphery to the core are larger than any from the core to the periphery in Monroe, Louisiana. They studied the spillover effects from food and cotton processing industries in the core. The spread from the core to the periphery was not particularly small. However, because of small multipliers and the fact that these industries only represent a fraction of the Monroe economy, the absolute gain by which the periphery benefited was negligible. A substantial growth in the percentage of final demand for the industry at the core did not translate into large changes in output in either the core or the periphery.

Hughes and Holland (1994), Hughes
and Litz (1996), Roberts (1998)

Third, **spread-through decentralization** takes place if the growth of the hinterland is associated with declining metropolitan population. In this third scenario, per capita incomes are relatively high, but diseconomies of agglomeration are beginning to decentralize economic activity. The metropolitan population has declined except in the outer-ring suburbs, where the population levels have not yet hit their maximum. In this case, the jobs follow people—firms go to the outskirts of the metropolitan area.

Two other scenarios are also possible. A **nodal response** involves the reversal of the core and the periphery roles. This happens when increasing demand in a periphery generates the economic growth in the core. Finally, there is **independence** if growth in the hinterland is not associated with changes in the urbanized area.

Growth generally starts in the metropolitan core. Urban spread first affects rural places that have at least an average labor and population density. The spread effects increase with the size of these districts and then tumble down the urban hierarchy, spilling outward to the peripheries surrounding each individual urban center. Growth in the lower level cities lags behind that of the metropolitan areas. On the other hand, the backwash effects occur more frequently in rural places dependent on natural resources, endowed with low population densities, as well as in the periurban fringe where growth is weaker.[8]

Nodal Effects and Growth in Natural Resource-Based Economies

The types and amounts of resources in a region determine its growth. Industries that depend on natural resources provide more jobs and income in metro than nonmetro counties. Global and national economies, policies regulating natural resources and the environment, as well as technical changes affect the growth and stability of jobs and income in these industries. Lower incomes in the fishing industry and unemployment in

---

[8] Myrdal (1957); Parr (1987); Moriarty (1991); Hughes and Holland (1994); Barkley et al. (1995); Fritsch (1997); Parr (2001).

forestry, energy, and mining illustrate the instability of natural resource industry. The survival of these regions depends on the availability of alternative industries in the area.[9]

Similarly, regulations that affect the periphery also affect its core. Waters, Holland, and Weber (1994) found that when the spotted owl was listed as an endangered species, its protection affected the periphery's timber harvest in western Oregon and 31,620 jobs were lost, out of which 14% (4427) were lost in the metropolitan region, 40% (10,877) of total jobs in the periphery, and 80% of the lost metropolitan jobs were from the service sector (3542) because of the core–periphery trade in central place services.

Diversity in Resource-Based Economies and Community Vitality

Stabler and Olfert (1993) contrasted factors that contributed to the relative vitality of northern Saskatchewan to the south of the province. Even though most coal mines, petroleum, and natural gas production is in the south, large grain farms dominate that declining region. In contrast, relatively small but agriculturally diversified farms and more intensive land use characterize the north. Rather than concentrate on one or two crops, northern farms grow a diversity of products: oilseeds, specialty crops, bees, and livestock. Likewise, all of the forest activity and most of the tourism industry are located in the north.

Diversity requires a higher population density which supports more trade-center functions. The consolidation of farms is coupled with diversification and increased intensity of land use. Therefore, a greater population density allows communities to diversify into agricultural-related and other manufacturing activities linked to or independent of natural resources. To illustrate the importance of population density in the effort to diversify, consider the failure of this attempt in the south of the province. Because of the consolidation of farms (even family-owned farms), the south could not diversify because it lacks the threshold size population

---

[9] Hughes and Holland (1994); Barkley et al. (1995).

to make viable not only the commercial centers but also the social infrastructures (e.g., service stations, convenience centers, churches, schools, and city offices).

Stabler and Olfert (1993)

Staple Theory of Economic Development

The staple theory of economic development, formulated by Canadian economist Harold Innis (1956), affirms that regional economic growth (and hence, employment opportunities) are largely determined by the growth of the staple (resource-based) industries in each region. According to Innis, the prosperity of the staple industries determines regional prosperity, which attracts people from depressed regions.

Although abundant natural resources are an essential ingredient in world economic growth, they are neither necessary nor sufficient for a region's economic growth. Hong Kong, for instance, has few natural resources, but Hong Kong's per capita income is the highest in Southeast Asia. Alternatively, many countries in Africa, Latin America, and Asia have abundant natural resources but political instability and inefficient bureaucracies prevent their growth.

Yet, natural resources played an important role in the early development of many regions. Current literature concerning the staple theory deals with the history of economic development in western North America. Low-cost farmland, minerals, timber, oil, and fishing first brought people and economic development to this area.

The economies of regions that depend on natural resources are extremely volatile because they are at the mercy of the world market. The quantity of the resource extracted or harvested is more responsive to earlier investments in machinery than to current resource prices. An increase in the price of the resource, especially if it is expected to persist, signals an increased market value of that resource and therefore quite lucrative profits. Profit increases spur investment and employment growth, thus increasing incomes.

Over time, new industries surface to support primary resource industries by providing services or equipment (indirect effect). Increased wages and possibilities for wealth attract migrants who create a demand for consumption products and residential construction (induced effect). Resource-based industries cannot easily expand production, so wealth created in the industry diversifies through acquisitions. Symmetrically, when resource prices fall, migration and outside investment slows.

The sustainability of economies that depend on natural resources is precarious. First, the national income accounts list neither the natural resources as assets nor their extraction as a debit, and thus they only give a partial representation of potential future growth. For example, the value of pulpwood boosts gross regional product, but the value of the stand of timber that is cut down to produce pulp is not subtracted.

Second, as regions grow, they should diversify, creating industries independent of natural resources. However at the time, this strategy seems unsound because profit rates in the resource industries are close to their peak and significantly higher than any alternative investment. Nonetheless, those economies depending on natural resources that have the astuteness to diversify while the resource prices are high will become more stable. Ghost towns flourish in the desert.[10]

"I Promise Not to Blow It All This Time"

According to a *New York Times* article from December 2000, successive increases in natural gas prices promised to revive oil patches in Oklahoma. A bumper sticker on a truck in Oklahoma read, "Dear God, please give me another oil boom and I promise not to blow it all this time around."

Stories abound in extravagances from the oil boom 20 years earlier. For instance, one oilman reportedly flew friends to New Orleans for lunch because he wanted fresh oysters. Another brought 57 of his best friends to Las Vegas for a weekend.

Due to a lack of diversification, per capita income in Oklahoma grew from 83 percent of the U.S. average in 1969 to a high of 99 percent of the national average in 1982. By 2000, Oklahoma's per capita income had plummeted to 80 percent of the national average.

Yardly (2000); Per capita income figures from Bureau of Economic Analysis, REIS data set http://www.bea.doc.gov/bea/regional/reis/ accessed 30 October 2002.

---

[10] Foot and Milne (1984); Weber, Castle, and Shriver (1987); Schmidt (1990); Dowrick (1992).

Rural Economic Development

Recent literature tells a "tale of two cities" in evaluating prospects for future economic well-being in rural areas. The areas with the brightest prospects are: (1) rural counties adjacent to metropolitan areas, (2) those having acquired sufficient agglomeration economies to become regional centers, and (3) those endowed with scenic amenities. Conversely, the large numbers of deep rural, isolated counties that remain too dependent on agriculture and natural resource industries have a bleak economic outlook.

The causes of persistent poverty in rural areas result from some of the very solutions that are instituted to fight it. First, a shift from a heavy dependence on natural resources to low-skill and low-wage manufacturing and service industries makes rural areas particularly vulnerable to business fluctuations, international competition for the production plants, and technological obsolescence. Second, rural workers often lack education, training, and work experience. Earnings are lowest and poverty rates are highest among those with least education. Those who can leave to go to school do so. Those who cannot are condemned to vegetate in the less productive, low-wage jobs (if they could even find them). Third, a lack of formal childcare and dependable transportation inhibit employment prospects for traditional mothers as well as for female-headed households. Fourth, because nonmetropolitan counties have higher percentages of elderly and disabled people, the **labor force participation rate**, that is [(Employed + Unemployed)/Population], is low. Fifth, areas that depend on natural resources, governmental bureaucracy or foreign (outside) investment, or ownership of resource extraction industries encourage and perpetuate rural poverty (Chapter 8).

Volatile shifts in commodity demand in international markets cause boom–bust cycles. Rural residents who are victims of frequent market swings have few skills beyond their everyday work. They are often tied to their communities despite the adverse economic conditions. This lack of mobility results in cycles of temporary or long-term poverty. Depletion of nonrenewable resources, such as minerals or petroleum, the rate of renewable resource extraction in forestry and fisheries, as well as problems of weather and disease in agriculture and forestry cause a free-fall in local incomes for dependent regions.[11]

Summary and Conclusions

This section discussed three core–periphery models: von Thünen's concentric rings, Vernon's product life cycles, and Perroux's growth poles.

---

[11] Hirschman (1958); Rosenfeld (1988); Barkley and Wilson (1992); Leatherman and Marcouiller (1996).

The concentric ring theory assumes that the sole use of the periphery is to serve its city. The amount left after a firm pays production and transportation costs determines land rents. Because all trade only occurs at the city center, the land rent near the center is highest and land rents decrease with distance from the city center. All products needed by the city are produced in concentric rings surrounding the city. Growth increases the amount of hinterland serving the core city.

The product life cycle argument describes the city as an incubator for new firms that require the latest technology. As these firms mature and "leave the nest," they land just at the outskirts of the city. It is only when the product becomes standardized that firms move to rural areas or developing countries to take advantage of mass production techniques and economies of scale. In this model, the periphery still serves the city by mass producing goods at a lower cost than in the city core. However, this theory depicts an image of a rural periphery that cannot innovate. All innovation will take place in the city and trickle down to the periphery.

The growth pole concept echoes the myth of technological determinism. Growth poles are urban centers. As growth poles develop, the periphery will either grow or decline. The spread effect occurs when growth in the urban center stretches outward to the periphery, either (1) because of increased demand for its goods and services or (2) because of decentralization due to diseconomies of agglomeration in the urban center. However, if growth in an urban area siphons incomes, jobs, and employees from its periphery, the periphery will decline (backwash effect).

A nodal effect takes place when job growth in the periphery causes urban growth. This may exist because of the induced effect: rural workers shop in the city. The rural areas are dependent on agriculture or natural resources. If these areas do not diversify, they are doomed to volatile economic cycles influenced by world commodity prices. Low-skilled, rural labor competes with labor from low-income countries to attract assembly plants. Those who can leave to go to school do so, those who cannot leave or who do not have that ability are trapped in unproductive, low-wage jobs with no future.

Chapter Questions

1. Using the following hypothetical data on watermelon and bean production:
   a. Determine the equations for the bid-rent function of each product, and at what quantity, if any, the two bid-rent functions cross.
   b. Draw the bid-rent functions for these two products.
   c. Predict what crop will be grown 5 miles from the market center.

d. Give the maximum land rent per acre that will be paid at that location.
e. How far out will beans be grown for sale in the city?

	Income and Costs for an Acre's Produce (000) per Year		
Crop	Revenue from Sale at Market	Production Cost	Transport Cost per Mile
Watermelon	300	200	5
Beans	200	20	10

2. Answer the same questions as in problem number 1, assuming that revenue from selling beans jumps to $250 at the market, but everything else is the same.
3. What are the three stages of a product's life cycle?
   a. In which stage will a firm benefit from locating in the metropolitan area? How will the firm benefit?
   b. How does innovation differ between the deep rural areas and the metropolitan areas?

Research Assignments

1. Calculate location quotients from the detailed data in the **County Business Patterns**. Compare the types of manufacturing firms in the largest county in your state with (1) those in a first-tier county (one that is contiguous) to the largest county and (2) a second-tier county. Does your area seem to support or refute Vernon's product life cycle theory?
2. From census data, find the occupations of residents of your city and the surrounding minor civil divisions. (Check out QT-P27; SF-3. Occupation by Sex from the Census Bureau.) Is there any pattern of "settlement sorting" around your city?

References

Barkley, D. L., and P. N. Wilson. 1992. Is alternative agriculture a viable rural development strategy? *Growth and Change* 23 (2):239–253.

Barkley, D. L., M. S. Henry, S. Bao, and K. R. Brooks. 1995. How functional are economic areas? Tests for intra-regional spatial association using spatial data analysis. *Papers in Regional Science* 74 (4):297–316.

Boudeville, J. R. 1966. *Problems of Regional Economic Planning*. Chicago: Aldine.

Carlino, G. A. 2001. Knowledge spillovers: cities' role in the new economy. *Federal Reserve Bank of Philadelphia Business Review* 0 (0):17–26.

Chinitz, B. 1961. Contrasts in agglomeration: New York and Pittsburg. *The American Economic Review* 51 (2):279–289.

Chinitz, B. 1964. *City and Suburb: The Economics of Metropolitan Growth.* Englewood-Cliffs, NJ: Prentice-Hall, Inc..

Crampton, G., and A. W. Evans. 1992. The economy of an agglomeration: the case of London. *Urban Studies* 29 (2):259–271.

Dowrick, S. 1992. Technological catch up and diverging incomes: patterns of economic growth 1960–1988. *Economic Journal* 102 (412):600–610.

Fisher, P. 2005. Grading places. What do the business climate rankings really tell us? Economic Policy Institute, http://www.epinet.org/books/grading_places/ grading_places_(web).pdf accessed 24 August 2005.

Foot, D. K., and W. J. Milne. 1984. Net migration estimation in an extended, multiregional gravity model. *Journal of Regional Science* 24 (1):119–133.

Fritsch, M. 1997. New firms and regional employment change. *Small Business Economics* 9 (5):437–448.

Hekman, J. S. 1985. Rental price adjustment and investment in the office market. *American Real Estate and Urban Economics Association Journal* 13 (1):32–47.

Henderson, V. 1997. Medium size cities. *Regional Science and Urban Economics* 27 (6):583–612.

Henry, M. S., B. Schmitt, K. Kristensen, D. Barkley, and S. Bao. 1999. Extending Carlino–Mills models to examine urban size and growth impacts on proximate rural areas. *Growth and Change* 30 (4):526–548.

Higgins, B. 1983. From growth poles to systems of interactions in space. *Growth and Change* 14 (4):3–13.

Hirschman, A. O. 1958. *The Strategy of Economic Development.* New Haven, CT: Yale University Press.

Hodge, J. 1998. The midrand area: an emerging high-technology cluster? *Development Southern Africa* 15 (5):851–873.

Hughes, D. W., and D. W. Holland. 1994. Core–periphery economic linkage: a measure of spread and possible backwash effects for the Washington economy. *Land Economics* 70 (3):364–377.

Hughes, D. W., and V. N. Litz. 1996. Rural-urban economic linkages for agriculture and food processing in the Monroe, Louisiana, functional economic area. *Journal of Agricultural and Applied Economics* 28 (2):337–355.

Innis, H. A. 1956. The teaching of economic history in Canada. In *Essays in Canadian Economic History*, ed. Innis, M. Q. Toronto: University of Toronto Press, 3–16.

Jacobs, J. 1969. Strategies for helping cities. *American Economic Review* 59 (4, Part I):652–656.

Kleinknecht, A., T. P. Poot, and J. O. N. Reijnen. 1991. Formal and informal R&D and firm size: Survey results from the Netherlands, In *Innovation and Technological Change: An International Comparison*, eds. Acs, Z. J., and Audretsch, D. B. Ann Arbor: University of Michigan Press, 84–108.

Leatherman, J. C., and D. W. Marcouiller. 1996. Persistent poverty and natural resource dependence: rural development policy analysis that incorporates income distribution. *Journal of Regional Analysis and Policy* 26 (2):73–93.

Lemelin, A., and M. Polèse. 1993. La localisation de l'emploi est-elle si différente dans les pays en développement: modèles d'urbanisation et analyses comparatives des systèmes urbains canadien et mexicain. *Canadian Journal of Development Studies* 14 (1):73–102.

Lucas, R. E., Jr. 1988. On the mechanics of economic development. *Journal of Monetary Economics* 22 (1):3–42.

Mack, R. S., and D. S. Jacobson. 1996. Core periphery analysis of the European Union: a location quotient approach. *Journal of Regional Analysis and Policy* 26 (1):3–21.

Moriarty, B. M. 1991. Urban systems, industrial restructuring, and the spatial-temporal diffusion of manufacturing employment. *Environment and Planning A* 23 (11):1571–1588.

Myrdal, G. 1957. *Economic Theory of Underdeveloped Regions.* London: Duckworth.

Parr, J. B. 2001. On the regional dimensions of Rostow's theory of growth. *Review of Urban and Regional Development Studies* 13 (1):2–19.

Parr, J .B. 1973. Growth poles, regional development, and central place theory. *Papers of The Regional Science Association* 31 (2):173–212.

Parr, J. B. 1987. Interaction in an urban system: aspects of trade and commuting. *Economic Geography* 63 (3):223–240.

Perroux, François. 1956, 1957. *Théorie générale du progrès économique. Les mesures des progrès économiques et l'idée d'économie progressive. II. Les composants: 1. La creation. 2. La propagation: A. Modèles microéconomiques.* Paris: Institut de Science Economique appliquée.

Roberts, D. 1998. Rural-urban interdependencies: analysis using an inter-regional SAM model. *European Review of Agricultural Economics* 25 (4):506–527.

Romer, P. M. 1990. Are nonconvexities important for understanding growth?. *American Economic Review* 80 (2):97–103.

Romer, P. M. 1995. The growth of nations: comment. *Brookings Papers on Economic Activity* 0 (1):313–320.

Rosenfeld, S. A. 1988. The tale of two Souths, In *The Rural South in Crisis: Challenges for the Future*, ed. L. J. Beaulieu, *Rural Sociological Society, Rural Studies Series*, Westview Press in cooperation with the Southern Rural Development Center\ Mississippi State University: Boulder\ London, 51–71.

Schmidt, R. H. 1990. Natural resources and state growth, *FRBSF Weekly Newsletter*, 23.

Sherwood-Call, C. 1992. Changing geographical patterns of electronic component activity. *FRBSF Economic Review* 2:25–35.

Stabler, J. C., and M. R. Olfert. 1993. Farm structure and community viability in the northern great plains. *Review of Regional Studies* 23 (3):265–286.

Taylor, M. 1986. Product cycle model—a critique. *Environment and Planning A* 18 (6):751–761.

von Thünen, J. H. 1966 [1826]. *Isolated State; an English edition of Der isolierte Staat.* Translated by Carla M. Wartenberg. Edited with an introduction by Peter Hall. Pergamon Press, Oxford, New York.

Vaessen, P., and D. Keeble. 1995. Growth-oriented SMEs in unfavourable regional environments. *Regional Studies* 29 (6):489–505.

Vernon, R. 1966. International investment and international trade in the product cycle. *The Quarterly Journal of Economics* 80 (2):190–207.

Waters, E. C., D. W. Holland, and B. A. Weber. 1994. Interregional effects of reduced timber harvests: the impact of the northern spotted owl listing in rural and urban Oregon. *Journal of Agricultural and Resource Economics* 19 (1):141–160.

Weber, B. A., Castle, E. N., and Shriver, A. L. 1987. The performance of natural resource industries. In *Rural economic development in the 1980's: Preparing for the future*, ed. U.S. Department of Agriculture, Economic Research Service, Agriculture and Rural Economy Division, 5.1–37. ERS Staff Report series, no. AGES870724 Author, Washington, DC.

Wojan, T. R., and G. C. Pulver. 1995. Location patterns of high growth industries in rural counties. *Growth and Change* 26 (1):3–22.

Yardly, J. 2000. Oil patch comes back to life as natural gas prices climb, *New York Times*, Dec. 16.

Chapter 10

Regional Labor Markets and Migration

The local labor market is a major factor in determining the economic growth of an area, but even catastrophic changes in local labor demand could be just a ripple in the state or national labor market. Labor is called a ***derived demand*** because it is derived from the demand for the product it makes. Increases (decreases) in the demand for the product in turn boost (reduce) the demand for workers specialized in producing it. The demand for labor can also change because of changes in the training required to apply a new technology or because of the relocation of production.

A region's potential labor supply can influence growth. Firms hesitate to locate in an area where there is a presumed "labor shortage." This shortage is often due to the firm or firms offering wages lower than the equilibrium rate. A large enough increase in wages is a guaranteed remedy for chronic regional labor shortages. Increased wages boost (1) the population's labor force participation, (2) the maximum commuting distance, and (3) migration rates, and thus the quantity of labor supplied.

This chapter will introduce the study of regional labor markets by first reviewing the two types of labor market structures—perfect competition and monopsony. Next, we will explain why wages and unemployment rates differ among regions. Finally, we will analyze the three determinants of the local supply of labor: labor force participation rates, commuters, and migration.

What Comes First, the Chicken or the Egg?

What comes first, the demand or the supply of labor? Do jobs follow people or do people migrate toward jobs? The answer is "both." As shown in Chapter 9, people follow jobs and go to a city if urban economic growth creates a backwash effect; but when the spread effect causes decentralization, jobs follow people. If people follow jobs, an economy grows only by attracting new firms. However, if jobs follow people, the local amenities indirectly become the stimulant behind economic growth.

Empirical studies show that migration responds almost instantaneously to possibilities of new employment. Labor-intensive firms generally locate in amenity-rich areas where potential employees reside. The firms that do not do so must compensate their employees for the lack of amenities or for the additional cost of commuting. In this light, Partridge and Rickman (2003) determined that jobs tend to follow people in the Sunbelt states of the United States, but people from depressed regions will move toward jobs in the Rust Belt, the Farm Belt, and the Energy States.

Fik, Amey and Mulligan (1992), Kohler (1997), Partridge and Rickman (2003)

Labor Market Structure

Firms hire as long as the ***marginal revenue product of labor*** is greater than the ***marginal factor cost***, and they stop hiring as soon as the marginal revenue product equals the marginal factor cost. The marginal revenue product is the amount of extra revenue a firm can expect when it hires the next worker, and it is thus the firm's demand for labor. The marginal factor cost of labor is the increased cost incurred from hiring one more unit of labor. The sum of marginal revenue products of all firms becomes the market demand for labor. The supply of labor responds to the wage rate and the preferences for work and leisure.

Competitive Labor Markets

Large urban areas and their peripheries are often competitive markets, especially for unskilled or semiskilled labor. In a competitive labor market,

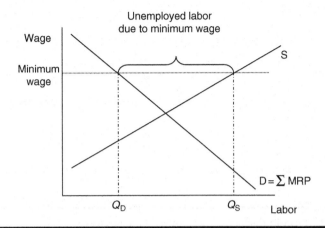

Figure 10.1   Minimum wage imposed on perfectly competitive labor market.

a firm can hire as many employees as it needs at the going wage, so the marginal factor cost is the wage rate determined by the intersection of the local supply and demand curves (Figure 10.1).

However, if the labor market is perfectly competitive and either a union or the government imposes a minimum wage, the number of workers hired is determined by the demand curve. At the higher wage more people will be willing and able to work, but firms will not be willing or able to hire as many workers as before. The result is higher unemployment, that is, a surplus of people who cannot find work at the recognized minimum wage. These unemployed people are generally those with the lowest marginal revenue products: the least skilled and youngest.

In a competitive market, the firm takes the market wage as given and hires that quantity of labor (L^*), where its own marginal revenue product equals the market wage (its marginal factor cost). See Figure 10.2.

Monopsonistic Labor Markets

The *monopsonistic labor model* dominates most nonmetropolitan areas as well as labor markets for youth in urban areas. Because information about employment travels through social networks, the place of residence influences the quality of this information. For example, the concentration of Black and Hispanic youth in the inner cities of urban areas limits their access to labor markets in the suburbs.[1] The lack of information limits employment alternatives and sustains monopsonies. When a firm must

---

[1] Ihlanfeldt (1993).

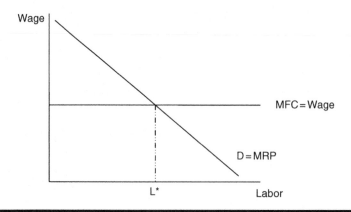

Figure 10.2 Firm in perfectly competitive labor market.

increase its wage to hire even one more worker, it is a ***monopsonist***. Its labor demand curve is the same marginal revenue product curve as if it were in a competitive labor market. However, because the firm must increase wages for its current employees as well as for the new hire, the marginal factor cost curve will be above the supply curve and twice as steep.

As Figure 10.3 shows, firms still hire the quantity L*, where the marginal factor cost equals the marginal revenue product. Once L* is determined, the firm uses the supply curve to establish the wage that is necessary to attract that quantity of labor. The result is a wage that is lower than the marginal revenue product.

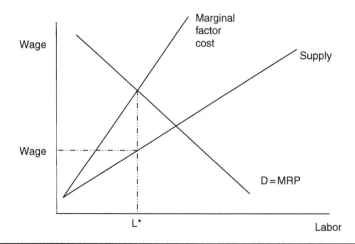

Figure 10.3 Monopsonistic labor market.

Think About It...

If you work, are you working in a perfectly competitive market, a monopsonistic market, or an oligopsonistic market?

How many local firms are hiring workers with skills that you possess?

What proportion of the total labor in your area works for the largest employer? What about for the largest five employers?

In a monopsonistic labor market, if the government or a union imposed a minimum wage, workers would all be better off. If the minimum wage is between the current wage and the marginal revenue product associated with L*, wages and employment both rise. A new marginal factor cost curve and a new supply curve are together and horizontal at the imposed wage (the *thick* lines in Figure 10.4) until the point where the line showing the minimum wage touches the supply of labor curve at L_2. At this point, supply slopes upward following the original curve. At the same time, the marginal cost of labor also jumps to its original curve. This is because the marginal factor cost of hiring an additional worker is simply the minimum wage. However, when the firm's

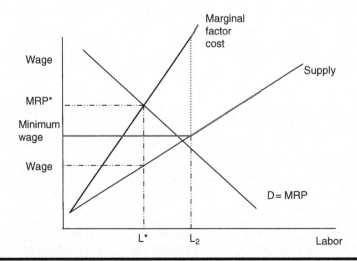

Figure 10.4   Minimum wage in monopsonistic labor market.

demand curve intersects supply at a quantity that is greater than L_2, hiring more workers again requires increased wages for everyone working there.

The predominance of nonunionized, monopsonistic labor markets in rural areas partly explains why rural wage rates are lower than urban wage rates. This market also explains some of the difficulty in empirically measuring the negative effects of minimum wages.

Regional Wage Differentials

The local market structure is just one element in explaining regional wage differences. The neoclassical growth theory (Chapter 8) maintains that a misallocation of resources causes regional wage differentials. Allowing capital or labor to migrate—and thus to profit from an increased rate of return—alleviates the resource allocation problem.

However, empirical studies consistently show that migration in fact exacerbates wage differentials.[2] The neoclassical view assumes that labor is homogeneous, but in reality, labor includes different skill levels. Migration rates are highest among the better educated. The skilled and productive workers move to urban areas that pay higher real wages (wages adjusted for the cost of living). Because of economies of agglomeration, an influx of highly productive people increases the growth potential in the receiving region and wages soar. On the other hand, the sending (source) region (affected by out-migration) becomes less specialized and less productive. This causes a stagnation of growth and a fall in real wages.

Wages in some areas will always be lower than in others. Nominal wages vary with city size, industry mix, and an area's amenities. In fact, when researchers account for local cost of living differences, they find little or no divergence in regional wages.[3] This is because the land and the housing markets are also affected by migration, as we will see in Chapter 12 and Chapter 13.

Nominal wage rates are positively correlated with *city size*. First of all, cities provide more jobs for highly skilled, highly productive workers. Technological spillovers from the intermingling of many skilled employees increase productivity. In addition, larger cities facilitate more advanced training than do rural areas. In rural areas, training is more costly because the employee must travel to the city or take correspondence courses. Finally, city workers require a higher nominal wage to compensate for the higher costs of urban living. The high costs reflect not only the land and

[2] See Greenwood (1985); Blackaby, Bladen-Hovell, and Symons (1991); Jackman and Savouri (1992b); Kottman (1992); Deller, Shields, and Tomberlin (1996) for instance.
[3] Blackaby Bladen-Hovell, and Symons (1991); Kottman (1992); Deller, Shields, and Tomberlin (1996) for instance.

housing costs, but also the inconveniences caused by congestion (e.g., traffic and crowds) and higher crime rates.

An area's *industry mix* also influences wages. Rankings of industries by average wage tend to be comparable everywhere. For example, if computer programmers earn the most in the United States, they will also be the highest wage earners in France or Japan. This consistency is associated with equal growth rates in industrial productivity, level of capital intensity, and labor unionization trends within each industry.

Finally, regional wages are negatively correlated with the presence of *amenities*. People migrate to maximize utility. If an area provides an agreeable climate, mountains, or seashore, people are willing to accept reduced wages or less stable jobs to live there. This tendency results in long-run equilibrium differences in both unemployment rates and wages across regions within the same country.[4]

Types of Unemployment

Not only wages but also unemployment varies by region. There are three categories of unemployment.

- *Demand deficient* unemployment, is solved by increasing the demand for goods that the region produces (Chapter 7).
- *Frictional* unemployment is a temporary state of unemployment that allows firms to hire and expand production. The unemployed people soon will find a jobs. This type of unemployment is healthy for an economy.
- *Structural* unemployment takes place when skills are no longer in demand locally. Long-run, regional, structural unemployment is exceptionally tenacious and difficult to remedy.

Three events could cause structural unemployment. First, the relocation or dissolution of a former employer creates pockets of skilled labor. Unemployment persists as long as the workers as well as potential employers have no knowledge of the others' locations.

Second, an unstable product market due to a fickle demand causes structural unemployment because labor is a derived demand. A decrease in the demand for a product reduces the demand for workers specialized in producing it.

---

[4] Greenwood (1975); Beeson and Groshen (1991); Blackaby, Bladen-Hovell, and Symons (1991); Jackman and Savouri (1992a); Kahn and Ofek (1992); Kottman (1992); Gittleman and Wolff (1993); Brown (1994); Deller, Shields, and Tomberlin (1996); Groenewold (1996).

Third, changes in ***product technology*** (Chapter 8) require employees to keep their skills up-to-date to remain competitive. On the other hand, ***process technology*** will decrease the demand for skilled workers and could cause the relocation of a firm in an area where nonskilled workers are plentiful.

Skills of the long-term unemployed depreciate. They cannot update their skills as easily as existing workers, which decreases their chance of finding a job. Unemployment duration increases the probability of migration, but if an unemployed worker waits too long, the chances of being hired elsewhere diminish. Employers use unemployment duration as a screening device and hesitate to hire the long-term unemployed. The failures discourage further job search and unemployment becomes the accepted norm in economically depressed areas.

The labor force includes the number of people who are currently working plus the number who are unemployed but actively seeking work. Those who have given up searching for a job, the ***discouraged workers***, are not included in the labor force. Access to information about the availability of distant jobs can help these people return to the labor force.[5]

Increasing a Region's Labor Supply

Firms hesitate to locate where there is insufficient labor. They generally focus on wage rates rather than the unemployment rate to accurately predict potential labor supply because high unemployment rates may signal nothing but a lack of usable skills. As the demand for labor increases, wage rates rise, boosting the quantity of labor supplied. The new workers can only come from three sources:

- Upsurges in the local labor force participation rate
- Commuting
- In-migration.

Think About It...

- Are you participating in the labor force?
- Are you 15 years of age or older?

---

[5] Meager and Metcalf (1987); Byers (1991); McHone and Rungeling (1993); Bradley and Taylor (1997).

- Do you work now? If not, have you actively looked for a job in the last two weeks?

You are in the labor force if you have responded "yes" to either of these questions.

Whether or not you are in the labor force, how are you spending your "free" time?

Labor Force Participation

The decision whether to work or not is a decision made to maximize household utility as much as it is to maximize an individual's own utility. According to the 1992 Nobel Prize winner Gary Becker, people spend their time doing one of the three activities: (1) work outside the household, (2) work within the household, or (3) consume leisure activities. Whether to participate in the labor force involves two decisions: whether or not to work and how many hours to work.

The determining factor in labor force participation is the educational level. If a low-skilled worker benefits the household more when he or she works at home, that person will probably stay out of the labor market. Labor force participation increases if skills increase, if market wages increase, as well as if the marginal benefit of working outside the home is greater than the marginal benefit of either working inside the household or consuming leisure activities. However, as household incomes increase, labor force participation may again decrease because of the propensity to consume more leisure.[6]

Cultural Values Influence Employment Decisions

The unemployment of Alaskan Natives closely follows the pattern of industrial concentration that dominates the economy of that region. Level of education is a determining factor in labor force participation decisions, and Native men have higher employment rates in regional centers than in the more rural areas of the state.

---

[6] Chalmers and Greenwood (1985); Martin (1988); Radakovic (1991); Henry (1993); O'Reagan (1993).

However, according to Lane and Thomas (1987), businesses that need unskilled workers for jobs that are neither challenging nor fulfilling drift to the Alaskan villages but risk not finding a sufficiently motivated workforce for this type of job. The more materialistic workers have already emigrated, and those who remain in their villages prefer a traditional way of life and are not motivated to earn more than that what is needed to purchase basic necessities. Cultural values, traditional subsistence activities, seasonal work, and government subsistence programs eradicate the fear of not having a job.

Lane and Thomas (1987)

Urban and Rural Choices: to Work or Not

In rural areas, the choice to "work at home" often includes working on a farm. Over 55 percent of all farm owners in the United States work off the farm. Factors that influence the off-farm labor force participation are proximity to an urban center, the local unemployment rate, the person's education level, going wage rates, and most importantly, the quality of health care benefits. Off-farm labor permits diversification and a reduction in the risks inherent in agriculture. Capital intensive farming techniques allow the farmer to work more hours in town. But, as expected, increases in farm revenue, the net worth of the farm, or the number of livestock reduce the off-farm labor force participation.

Female farmers choose outside employment more often than do urban women when their children are all of school age because child care is less of a problem. Manufacturing, which dominates the rural areas, allows couples to work alternate shifts. In addition, rural families are less mobile, so members of extended families help care for the children. If this presents a problem, the lower rural crime rates mean that latchkey children are safer. Finally, to decrease their own isolation, farm women work as a social activity. Compared to urbanites, their husbands earn less. Rather than work off-farm, some women have converted their household activities into market activities (selling fresh or canned produce) or in some cases, agrotourism.

Gunter (1990), Lass, Findeis and Hallberg (1991), Alwang (1992), Ventura (1994).

U.S. Department of Agriculture (2002)

Think About It...

Those of you who moved to attend school: why didn't you commute from home?

Those of you who commute to attend school: why didn't you move?

When a Commute Becomes a Migration

Close to the decision to participate in the labor force is the decision whether to commute or move. Households will decide to move rather than to commute if the marginal benefit of working in the urban area (greater compensation) is greater than the marginal cost of commuting stress. **Commuting stress** entails psychological costs such as the anxiety and frustration that result from traveling long distances. As the amount of commuting stress increases, the temptation to migrate grows—as long as the housing market and cost of living in the new community does not exclude that possibility.

Increased prices due to inefficiencies in local housing markets hamper migration and create more commuters. Specifically, higher housing prices encourage out-migration and discourage in-migration. Thus, workers change jobs without moving. Others may finally find satisfactory living arrangements and change residences but keep the same jobs. In Great Britain and places where the government supplies "affordable" public housing, people seldom move to change jobs because local residents have priority in their local public housing. At the same time, stringent planning and land-use controls restrict new housing development in the private sector, causing very high prices. The result is increased commuting.[7]

Migration

There are two concentrations within migration research: gross migration and net migration. Studies of ***gross migration*** ask why in-migrants move

---

Women Commute Patterns in Colombia and Columbus, Ohio

In Bogotá, Colombia, housing consumption and location as well as labor supply decisions vary across gender and household types. Married women who work outside the home have both a long journey to work and a heavier share of household responsibilities. They consistently earn lower wages and work longer hours at their jobs than the males do. Travel diary data from Columbus, Ohio, also shows that regardless of their employment status, women who work do more housework than men. The women who work full time also travel longer distances to work than the men do, even though they shoulder more of the household responsibilities.

Other studies confirm that women commute shorter distances to work than men when they have different labor market opportunities. When women's jobs are located in the suburbs or there is less spatial variation in women's wages, women have less reason to commute. Young children tend to increase the commuting journey of female household heads by eight minutes or 26 percent.

White (1986), Madden and Chiu (1990),
Assadian and Ondrich (1993), Kwan (1999)

---

[7] Blackaby and Manning (1990); Islam and Choudhury (1991); Smith (1991); Jackman and Savouri (1992b); Stabler, Olfert, and Greuel (1996); Bentolila (1997); Boyle, Flowerdew, and Shen (1998); Detang-Dessendre, and Molho (1999).

What are the Dimensions of a Labor Market Area?

The maximum distance that commuters find acceptable depends on the economic base of the city. In a study of Saskatchewan labor markets, commuters from the periphery were willing to travel 38.7 miles to work at a job in a primary-wholesale retail center. The average commute from the periphery to a secondary retail-wholesale center was 26.9 miles, whereas to a city with only a complete shopping center, the commute from the rural area was a maximum of 23.8 miles.

Stabler, Olfert and Greuel (1996)

into an area and out-migrants leave, whereas **net migration** uses aggregated data to see if the flow of in-migrants is larger than the flow of out-migrants. Net migration (in-migration − out-migration) is calculated by subtracting natural population change from the total change in population. Because

$$\Delta \text{ Population} = (\text{Net Migration}) + (\text{Births} - \text{Deaths}) \qquad (10.1)$$

then

$$\text{Net Migration} = \Delta \text{ Population} - \text{Deaths} + \text{Births} \qquad (10.2)$$

Population counts or estimates are determined by the Census Bureau or a state's Demographer's Office. Birth and death statistics are provided by a state's Department of Health or a Department of Vital Statistics.[8]

Think About It...

The last time you or your family moved, what drew you to your present location?

Do you plan on moving back to your initial city? Why or why not?

---

[8] Greenwood (1985); Greenwood et al. (1991).

Do you plan to stay where you are now until you retire? Will you leave and return after you retire? Why or why not?

Who Migrates?

Migration is selective not only in terms of age and level of human capital, but also in terms of personal characteristics. Those who are ready to move have greater drive, determination, and entrepreneurial abilities. People of different ages migrate for different reasons. Most migrants are young, just out of college and employed for the first time, or are in the military. Older workers and younger retirees look for amenity-rich places to live. Elderly migrants are more concerned with the proximity to caregivers or health services.

Traditionally, wives and mothers give up their jobs and employment status, if the husband has a job offer that requires migration. To the extent that they are both professionals, a dual-location decision for a couple is difficult. However, the choice of a larger metropolitan area will increase their chances of both finding employment.

The less educated are not as likely to move if they lack access to information about the labor market in another area or if the distant jobs offer the same wages they earn at home. Tendencies to migrate also differ by occupations. Locally licensed professionals and those who have built up practices or clientele are less likely to move than administrators. Similarly, workers and technicians are more stable than engineers or administrators.[9]

Human Capital Migration

In a 1991 study, Krieg discovered that the states of Arkansas and Vermont had a net in-migration of people but a net out-migration of human capital. This loss of human capital is accompanied by a loss of the

---

[9] Greenwood (1975, 1985); Cheung and Liaw (1987); Long (1988); Shields and Shields (1988); Kahley (1991); Krieg (1992); Payne, Warner and Little (1992); Rives and West (1992); Morrill (1994); Warnes and Ford (1995); Fokkema, Gierveld and Nijkamp (1996); Hsing and Mixon (1996); Kriaa and Plassard (1996); Greenwood (1997); Lin (1997); Jarvis (1999); Bound and Holzer (2000); Detang-Dessendre and Molho (2000); Millington (2000); Cooke (2001); Ritsilä and Haapanen (2003).

right to tax the higher incomes generated by the state's human capital investment. Conversely, Connecticut and Minnesota data showed a net out-migration of people but a net in-migration of human capital.

Krieg (1991)

Why Do People Migrate?

Labor market variables affect long-distance migration, but local moves are primarily related to housing. People will migrate to maximize their utility or the overall utility of their household. Specifically, they will migrate if they perceive that the marginal benefits of the move are greater than the marginal costs.[10]

Costs and Benefits of Migrating

Migration is generally a once-and-for-all decision involving a change in the location of one's job. Migration responds to information about job vacancies. Vacancy information is both informal (friends and relatives) and formal (employment bureaus, newspaper ads, and placement agencies).

Migration costs are a function of distance. The monetary cost of moving is low compared to the increased uncertainty and psychic costs of moving. Households have more knowledge about their own area (local human capital), but as distance increases, information about the new community and its quality of life decreases considerably. Because uncertainty is associated with distance, distance becomes a proxy for the psychic costs of migrating.

Pushing forces are those that drive households out of an area: a loss of employment or housing; a loss of quality of life, quality schools, or medical services; and life cycle changes such as divorce, bankruptcy, or change of occupations. In contrast, ***pulling forces*** attract migrants: high hourly wages and generous benefits; long-term or stable employment opportunities; recreational opportunities or scenic quality; and compatible social, religious, and political settings.

Three models explain migration: the ***human capital model*** of Sjaastad (1962), Rosen's (1974) model of ***amenity attraction***, and Tiebout's (1956) hypothesis that location decisions of households depend on the ***local fiscal policies*** of various jurisdictions.[11]

---

[10] Vanderkamp (1988); Groenewold (1997).
[11] Vanderkamp (1977); Greenwood (1985); Lonner (1987); Schachter and Althaus (1989); Clark and Hunter (1992).

Migration as an Investment in Human Capital

According to Sjaastad (1962), a person will migrate from the **sending region** to the **receiving region** only if the present value of increased income in the new region is greater than the increased costs of living there. People select a destination that maximizes the rate of return on their investment. The rate of return depends on the difference between both the current and the future incomes in both regions. Young adults have a longer time over which to recover the costs of migration and reap positive net benefits from that investment. The rate of return from migrating at age 30 is reduced by more than half given the same calculations for someone at age 20.

Migrants who respond to labor market incentives fall into three categories: (1) they already accepted a new job, (2) they are in hopes of obtaining employment, or (3) their job transferred. Those who are in the first category have compared several offers and will move to where the net present value of their migration investment is the highest. Those who are in the second category will move to where the possibilities of employment will bring the highest rate of return to their skill level.

Employee transfers are in a slightly different situation. Employers would like their most able and best-matched employees to transfer. These employees are older than other migrants (around age 37), and they have extensive professional experience that aids them in training new associates. For them, the transfer is a promotion.[12]

Greener Pastures to the North

Hanson and Spilimbergo (1999) examine illegal immigration from Mexico to the United States and find that attempted illegal immigration is highly sensitive to changes in Mexican wages. The purchasing power of the U.S. wages in terms of pesos and in terms of dollars predicts the number of border apprehensions. Thus, prospective immigrants expect to maintain links with Mexico through return migration or by supporting family members who stay home.

---

[12] Greenwood (1975); Greenwood (1985); Kahley (1991); Nakosteen and Zimmer (1992); Jackman and Savouri (1992a); Herzog, Schlottmann and Boehm (1993); Kilpatrick and Felminham (1996); Bentolila (1997); Boehm, Herzog and Schlottmann (1998); Bosco (1999); Hacker (2000).

Factors that reduce the United States/Mexico wage gap, such as NAFTA, will also reduce Mexican immigration. One striking feature is how tightly the United States and Mexican labor markets are linked. The effect of American and Mexican wages on apprehensions is immediate. Reducing the Mexican real wage or increasing the U.S. real wage leads to an increase in the number of apprehensions in that same month.

Hanson and Spilimbergo (1999)

Think About It...

If you commute or if you moved to attend university, think about your high school classmates who chose to stay in your home town. Do they ever plan to leave? What are they doing now? Project your life five and ten years from now and compare it with a projection of what they will be doing.

Youth Go Where Their Skills Are Valued

Youth in the 14 to 22 age group compare rates of return for their skills and locate in the state or region where they can earn the most money. In this way, young workers avoid mismatches between skills and rewards. The destination and skill composition depends on their comparative advantage.

The mismatch motivates the young to relocate, and the regions that offer the better salaries will attract the most qualified workers. In contrast, low-skilled or unskilled workers move to areas where—because of a temporary shortage of workers or because of the nature of the industry—the wages are higher than elsewhere.

Borjas, Bronars and Trejo (1992)

College Students and Migration

The lack of access to information contributes to even wider employment and earnings gaps for low-skilled workers. Within a given age group, the poorly-educated are likely to be involved with short-distance moves whereas the well-educated are more likely to move long distances. Education reduces the importance of tradition and family ties just as it increases a person's awareness of other localities in which to live.

Students choose to study out-of-state when they want to have a greater future return. The expected future income needs to compensate for tuition expenses, especially if these expenses are greater due to the prestige of the university. Both tuition and prestige vary from institution to institution. To attract top nonresident students in other regions, universities must pay attention to academic quality and the reputation of the faculty, they must to maintain a low student-faculty ratio, and they must offer a variety of programs including big-time college athletics programs.

Migration rates peak for those who have completed four years of college. Generally, students have left a region with low per capita incomes to study in places where education is a priority, where the population is better educated, and where the growth rates of employment are high. College students generally move twice. They move for training and then again to take their first job. Training mobility depends on the diversity of programs in the student's field of interest. The specific program will partly determine the eventual occupational choice and depends on the socio-professional category of the parents.

Long (1988), Mixon and Hsing (1994), Hsing and Mixon (1996), Kriaa and Plassard (1996), Greenwood (1997), Bound and Holzer (2000), Mak and Moncur (2003)

Brain Drains and Brain Gains

Zhao, Drew, and Murray (2000) found that the educated Canadians who migrate to the United States are being replaced by foreign workers with the same training. The better-paid Canadians immigrate to the United States. Among them are many physicians, nurses, engineers, scientists, and managers. Physicians leave Canada at a ratio of 19 out of every 20, nurses at 15 out of every 16, and engineers and managerial workers at 7 out of 8.

At the same time, immigration to Canada increased 15-fold among computer scientists, 10-fold for engineers, 8-fold for natural scientists and 4-fold among managerial workers. Permanent immigration to Canada fell for physicians, nurses, and teachers. However, according to the authors, depopulation is not a problem in Canada because the influx of immigrants is greater than the outflow to the United States.

Zhao, Drew, and Murray (2000)

Repeat and Return Migration

Until now, we focused on *primary migrants*—those who have for the first time left their initial places of residence for another location, but we have not examined those who relocate several times—the *repeat migrants*. Gender, education, and wages are determining factors in the initial decision to leave, but they are not relevant to successive migrations. Empirical studies show that frequent movers are less rooted because they have fewer children and do not belong to labor unions.[13] College-educated young adults have a greater probability of making an initial migration and a lower probability of migrating again to correct past migration mistakes.

There are two types of repeat migrants—*onward migrants*, who are moving again but not back to where they lived before, and *return migrants*, who move back to a previous place of residence or to their home town. *Onward migrants* expect a better salary. Unfortunately, a more distant move increases the probability of moving again because distance diminishes the reliability of information about the quality of life and the cost of living in the new place. The best educated are likely to move

---

[13] For example, Bailey (1993); Hou and Beaujot (1995); Bohara and Kreig (1996).

on quickly if their surroundings are not acceptable. Their opportunities are national if not international in scope and they can easily find a new job. The propensity to move onward could be caused by the expected duration of the job, job transfers, or the psychological profile of the individual.

Return migration could be preplanned, such as returning home after school or after a stint with the military. Most often, however, it is the result of an unsatisfactory first migration. Return migrants generally have fewer skills and less education than onward migrants. If unemployment is the motive for the initial move and financial pressures limit job searches, return moves are more probable.[14]

There's No Place Like Home

Demographic stability is achieved by maintaining a population core that does not immigrate. Studies on nonmigration suggest that the factors that anchor people to places may be different from those that push others to migrate. In the United States, the proportion of the population residing in the same county between 1985 and 1990 varies directly with the number of locally owned small-scale retail and manufacturing establishments, family farms, local civic associations, and the proportion of people who are active in the community.

Irwin, Tolbert and Lyson (1999)

Rural Emigration

Salaried jobs in rural labor markets pay less and generally offer few opportunities for upward mobility. However, they are more stable than the jobs in the urban labor market and the hiring is less anonymous. In anonymous labor markets, people with degrees are better paid because their degree signals a greater potential productivity, but a long period of unemployment constitutes a handicap.

If the markets are not anonymous, like in rural regions, employers have several sources of information about the applicants. To the extent that

---

[14] Greenwood (1985); Matsukawa (1991); Bailey (1993); Schmidt (1993); Lam (1994); Hou and Beaujot (1995); Jayet (1995); Bohara and Kreig (1996); Newbold (1996); Lin, Liaw and Tsay (1999).

employers know the applicant personally or by reputation, they can access criteria other than the degree. Further, a long period of unemployment is not a stigma. Although employment stability is a plus for current employees, the lack of turnover means job searchers need to find their first job in the city. A solid education enhances their possibilities.

Perils of Employment Stability

Rural jobs are most stable in the United States and in Europe. An office worker aged 40 with 10-year seniority in a small firm located in an urban area has a 61.9 percent probability of being in the same firm five years later. This probability increases to 68.3 percent for periurban workers and 71.6 percent for those in the deep rural areas. Rural employees are generally paid minimum wage. They are usually more loyal to their employers and rarely quit voluntarily. In return for their loyalty, employers prefer to recruit among the members of the same families. If it is necessary to lay people off, the employer takes into consideration the needs of each household.

As a result of the stability, the low turnover means that labor force entrants will have difficulty. Thus, 68 percent of the youth originating in deep rural areas of the United States find their first jobs in the city. For youth who come from the periurban areas, the figure is 79 percent.

Blanc and Lagriffoul (1996), Doeringer (1984)

Nonmetropolitan areas of the United States have recently experienced significant structural changes. The distinct spatial divisions of labor attract different types of new firms into rural areas. Urban employees migrate to the periphery because land prices are lower or because of the amenities offered. To the extent that the population invades the periphery, firms relocate to be close to their employees as well as to benefit from lower land rents. Periurban areas face a strong technological competition. Diseconomies of large cities, old and declining quality of private capital stock, and public infrastructure cause spread effects toward the periphery. In contrast, the firms that don't need skilled labor move to the deep rural areas, benefiting thus from lower land prices and even lower wages.

Despite strong and persistent migration toward the cities, the wage gap between rural and urban workers has widened. Recessions can persist in a rural community because (1) international market forces have eroded the economic base of agriculture, forestry, energy, and labor intensive manufacturing; (2) the trend toward a service-based economy and high-tech manufacturing is more of an advantage for metropolitan areas than for rural areas because of agglomeration economies; and (3) the increasing numbers of retirees who move to rural areas increase demand for services (generally for low-paying service jobs) and often oppose logging, resource extraction, or heavy manufacturing that would create high-wage jobs. In addition, the low turnover rates in employment hinder population renewal.[15]

Local Amenities

Migration linked to amenities, according to Rosen (1974), acknowledges the fact that a household's utility function includes more than a favorable bank balance. This utility function includes goods and services that can be purchased as well as those that cannot—amenities such as mountains, seashore, temperate climate, sunshine, and clean air. Changes in demand for amenities (due principally to life cycles) cause migration. To the extent that the value of the location-specific amenities will decrease wages and increase rents, migration cannot spatially equilibrate wages. Therefore, the households will only migrate if the value they place on amenities is greater than the lower "real" income resulting from decreased wages and increased rents.[16]

Amenities, Wages, and Land Rents

Both land and labor markets adjust to the presence or the absence of amenities. Prized regions are characterized by high rents or low wages. A survey of the migrants into 15 fast-growing wilderness counties showed that only 25 percent benefited from an increased income, but 50 percent had to accept income losses. Amenities and quality of life are thus factors that are more important than employment in their migration decision. Retired

---

[15] Doeringer (1984); Hodge and Whitby (1986); Barkley (1995); Broomhall (1995); Blanc and Lagriffoul (1996); Nord (1998); Detang-Dessendre and Molho (1999); Henry et al. (1999); Mills (2001).

[16] Graves and Linneman (1979); Rosen (1979); Greenwood (1985); Knapp and Graves (1989); Rasmussen, Fournier, and Charity (1989); Graves and Waldman (1991); Berger and Blomquist (1992); von Reichert and Rudzitis (1992, 1994); Thomas (1993); Potepan (1994).

people were attracted to places where the amenities are capitalized into wages.

von Reichert and Rudzitis (1992)

Heat at the Winter Olympics

The choice of Salt Lake City, Utah, for the Winter Olympics (2002) caused a controversy. Opponents feared that the international spotlight shining on the beauty of their area would cause undesirable immigration. Proponents, on the other hand, maintained that the Games would enhance the quality and quantity of local jobs, thus mitigating any undesirable effects.

In reality, the Olympic Games in the cities of North America caused economic expansions during the period of preparation rather than during the events themselves. The Olympic events may attract some jobs to an area, but the effect of this type of employment growth on per capita incomes is similar to any other type of tourism event.

Lybbert and Thilmany (2000)

Local Public Goods (Tiebout Hypothesis)

People are not only attracted by an area's natural amenities, but also by the local fiscal policy. Fiscal influences are stronger for short-distance moves than for long-distance migration. Local differences in taxes and public services encourage inter-community migration, according to the Tiebout (1956) hypothesis. For example, communities with higher than average state and local taxes, those that finance generous welfare spending, and those with high violent crime rates witness negative net migration.

Tiebout Hypothesis in Japan

Empirically, the Tiebout hypothesis should not apply to Japan because their regional and local governments are strictly controlled by the national government and lack the freedom to use tax and fiscal policies to promote their own economic growth. However, a study by Sakashita and Hirao (1999) of 117 cities around Tokyo and 72 cities around Osaka revealed that per capita public expenditures, per capita incomes, and population densities affect land prices. In effect, the authors concluded that public expenditures had a high statistical significance, meaning that individuals sort themselves according to even the slightest differences in patterns of public expenditures.

Sakashita and Hirao (1999)

Just as with natural amenities, local fiscal policies affect land values. If one jurisdiction taxes property at a higher rate than neighboring areas, *ceteris paribus*, the demand for land in that jurisdiction will decrease and with it, land prices will fall. In this way, a local tax is *capitalized* into the land values. However, if local spending is efficient and provides services that the residents prefer, those who want to benefit from these services migrate in, causing an increase in the demand for land in that jurisdiction and soring land values.[17]

Welfare Magnets

The human capital theory of migration applies to those who live on public assistance. Clinton's Welfare Reform Act of 1996 also guaranteed that the benefits welfare recipients receive remain the same as in the county where they first applied for assistance. The reason for this restriction was the large amount of empirical evidence showing that counties with generous welfare benefits attracted more recipients, *ceteris paribus*.

---

[17] Islam and Rafiquzzaman (1991); Day (1992); Assadian (1995); Westerlund and Wyzan (1995); Hsing (1996); Conway and Houtenville (2001).

It is a myth to believe that persistently poor families cannot move because they lack the financial resources or because they depend on locally administered welfare programs for their survival. Welfare benefits influenced migration decisions primarily for single mothers with small children or for women without recent labor market experience. Single women were more attracted by generous welfare payments than married ones. Therefore, when welfare benefits in one state were greater than in the others, that state attracted a large proportion of recipients. This influx caused an exodus of workers and the elderly.

Long (1988), Cebula and Koch (1989), Cebula (1991), Cushing (1993), Hsing (1995), Enchautegui (1997), Saving (1999)

Life Cycle Considerations and Migration

Amenities and local fiscal policies become more or less important with age. Jobs are most significant to migrants during their working years. For the 18 – 24 age group, amenities are just not a priority. In fact, this is the only group that is attracted to central city counties. With age, cultural and recreational amenities become more important, as long as tax rates do not increase. Between ages 45 and 64, workers tend to move into small cities rich in amenities and into periurban counties.

Housing costs influence the out-migration of retirees. Some postpone their out-migration from areas with soaring housing prices in the hopes of reaping a larger return from the sale. Others feel pushed out by the increased property taxes that accompany high housing prices. The elderly who stay where housing costs are high are more likely to live with a child or other relative for intergenerational support.

Morrill (1994), Lin (1997), Millington (2000)

Consequences of Immigration

The arrival of younger families can guarantee the survival of an aging host region. Natural population decreases (the birth rate less than the death rate) are no longer rare in the United States and in the industrialized countries. By 1989, 34% of all the United States counties experienced at least 1 year where the death rate was higher than the birth rate. This problem is most common in remote rural areas. To overcome a natural population decrease, some states such as Iowa actively seek foreign immigrants.

Most of the debates on migration policy concern international migration rather than internal migration. Because these disagreements affect localities, we are going to briefly review the arguments. What is striking about this literature is that studies from many nations come to similar conclusions.[18]

Problems for International Migrants

Questions raised by international migrants include (1) whether their human capital is transferable to a different country, (2) whether there will be a wage differential between themselves and otherwise similar local workers, and (3) the length of time before they will become assimilated into the new culture.

Human capital is imperfectly transferable from one country to another. The country where the individual received his or her education is crucial in determining its value. Besides quality of education, the ease of transfer depends greatly on the individual's linguistic ability and knowledge about the culture in the host country. The level of competence in reading the host country's language influences the wage rate received by the immigrant. In Germany, writing proficiency improves the migrant's earning potential. In Australia, English language fluency increased earnings by 9.3%; in the United States, 16.9%; and in Canada, 12.2%.

Wage Consequences of International Migration

The variations in the rate of return to foreign schooling reflect differences in quality and compatibility with the

---

[18] Johnson (1993).

host labor market, according to studies from Israel and Canada. In contrast, professional experience in the country of origin is generally insignificant. Estimates of wage differences between equally skilled immigrants and local workers range from 11.8 percent in the Netherlands to as high as 57 percent in Israel, but they are insignificant in Germany. These numbers suggest a purely arbitrary character.

The same wage discrimination does not hold for internal migrants, according to Borjas, Bronars and Trajo (1992). Young internal migrants may initially earn less than locals, but the wage differential disappears within a few years. The initial disadvantage depends on the distance moved (because of interstate differences in culture) and economic conditions in the new labor market.

Borjas, Bronars and Trajo (1992), Kee (1995), Schmidt (1997), Friedberg (2000), Li (2001), Weiss, Gotlibovski and Sauer (2003)

The level of schooling and the number of years in the host country will increase language fluency, but fluency comes slowly for the elderly immigrant. All else equal, fluency rates are lower if (1) the probability of return migration is large, (2) the language of origin belongs to a completely different type of writing, and (3) the immigrant is a refugee.

The rate of assimilation into the host culture will be more rapid for educated immigrants. Their children will have better educations, higher salaries, and will tend to marry someone from a different ethnic group. Even if the children are born in the host country, they will continue to have a wage handicap, but it will be only around 50–60% of the gap of their ethnic group.[19]

For Receiving Regions

Firms in the receiving region benefit from a fresh influx of skilled workers, but even in this case some organizations think that immigrants constitute a potential drain on the public coffers. In addition, these groups

---

[19] Kahley (1991); Borjas, Bronars, and Trejo (1992); Dustmann (1994); Chiswick and Miller (1995); Kee (1995); Schmidt (1997); Card, DiNardo and Estes (1998); Elhorst (1998); Friedberg (2000); Weiss, Gotlibovski and Sauer (2000); Li (2001).

estimate that competition between migrants and local workers will decrease salaries.We now investigate these hypotheses further.

Local Fiscal Impacts of Immigration

Much debate centers on local problems caused by immigration. Immigration opponents consider the United States and Europe as welfare magnets that attract the poor from elsewhere by the generous social programs. According to others, immigrants steal jobs from citizens. However, few studies support either of these complaints.

Immigrants arrive when they are young, strong, and healthy. They work and produce many years before they collect pensions and expensive public medical care. Empirical studies indicate that immigrants who pay less in taxes because of their low incomes also take less advantage of public benefits.[20] Even when children of immigrants were covered by Medicaid, they were less likely to use the public health care perhaps because of unfamiliarity with the system. Even expanded eligibility had negligible effects on Medicaid coverage among expanded children of immigrants.

Only the young, school-age children and elderly refugees systematically cost localities more than they get in tax revenues. An influx of immigrants into a local area puts a strain on local public services such as schooling.[21] In the schools, for example, the children of immigrants are often placed in classes for handicapped students or those with learning disabilities, diminishing considerably that student/teacher ratio. Additionally, if these students come from poor families, they are eligible to participate in federally financed "Chapter 1" programs, where the goal is to provide remedial education to disadvantaged children. Their participation in these programs reduces the spending per pupil. Elderly immigrants (as do elderly, internal migrants) tend to burden the receiving state's public assistance programs.

Some studies suggest that overall, immigrants pay more in taxes than they receive in services at the federal level, but they impose a net burden on state and local communities where they are concentrated. According to Betts (1998), high immigrant-receiving states receive a net of $3,178 (taxes minus spending) per household ($1996) while nonimmigrants paid a net sum of $1,178 per household. In effect, immigrant families have more school-age children than other families and require English as a Second Language (ESL) classes.

However, a snapshot of annual estimates does not capture the entire fiscal contribution of immigrants. Immigrants' incomes rise over time, as do their tax payments. The United States-born children of immigrants are not

[20] Akbari (1991); Straubhaar and Weber (1994); Currie (1995); Simon (1996).
[21] Espenshade and King (1994); Betts (1998).

counted as immigrants once they move out of the household and start their careers. The studies that focus on one point in time ignore the further benefits from immigrant children when they become taxpayers. Such studies also ignore the threefold increase in economic benefits that we discuss below.[22]

Are Domestic Workers Worse Off with an Open Migration Policy?

How domestic workers are affected by an open migration policy depends on whether the immigrant's occupation is a complement to or a substitute for that of the local workers. If the immigrants are complements in production, everyone is better off. According to the **complementarity hypothesis**, the immigrant possesses unique skills or works in niches that local workers avoid. As such, immigrants raise the productivity of other workers, raising wages, and lowering unemployment. The classic example is that of the immigrant domestic worker. A Canadian study by Grenier (1992) found that rather than expanding the earnings differentials between men and women, areas with a high proportion of immigrants lowered this differential. Thus, immigration has a positive impact on women's labor market by allowing women to take more full-time jobs.

The **substitution hypothesis** asserts that immigrants have the same training and skills as local workers. They therefore compete directly with local workers and will be responsible for a fall in their wages if not an increase in their unemployment. To protect American physicians from the competition of immigrants, the federal government enacted laws limiting international medical graduates from working in the United States by requiring that they take a four-step ECFMG (Educational Commission for Foreign Medical Graduates) clinical skills test that costs $1,200 and is only offered in Philadelphia. The assertion that international physicians are substitutes for American physicians is questionable because the foreign-born physicians regularly choose to locate in medically underserved localities with high poverty rates or with underserved minority populations.

Doesn't an Increase in the Supply of Labor Decrease Wages?

The answer is yes, but not significantly. Many studies have found that the fall in wages of local workers

---

[22] Akbari (1991); Espenshade and King (1994); Straubhaar and Weber (1994); Currie (1995); Simon (1996); Betts (1998); Fox Kellam and Vargas (1998a,b).

caused by immigration is slight. A simulation study of Hong Kong data (Suen 2000) estimated that if the number of immigrants increased by 40 percent, wages would decrease by no more than 1 percent. In the United States, Friedberg and Hurt (1995) determined that a 10 percent increase in the fraction of immigrants in the population reduces native wages by 0.1 percent overall. If the local workers are complementary, they lose nothing. In fact, everybody gains. But if they are substitutes, their loss is minimal.

However, a study by the National Research Council (1997) estimated that immigration caused a 15 percent increase in the supply of workers with less than a high school education. Competition reduced wages of this group by 5 percent, but the wage reduction was not statistically significant.

Friedberg and Hurt (1995), National Research
Council (1997), Suen (2000)

Most empirical evidence supports the complementarity hypothesis. In Austria for instance, native blue-collar workers in firms that hired immigrants earned approximately 14% more than workers in firms that employed only local workers. The immigrants were willing to take jobs at the bottom of the job hierarchy, which allowed local workers to be promoted to better positions.

Recent studies failed to support the substitution hypothesis. An Australian study by Chapman and Cobb-Clark (1999) concluded that in practically all circumstances, immigration increases the chances of employment for unemployed citizens. This is due in part to the number of jobs created by initial immigrant spending. To the extent that some immigrants specialize in new activities for the community, all consumers benefit from the variety of goods and services that generally are not costly.

According to a study by the National Research Council (1997), the economic benefits to the United States from immigration are between $6 and $20 billion annually. If the United States pursued an immigration policy that attracted skilled workers, these gains would be even larger. This study also found an insignificant relationship between the wages of local workers and the number of immigrants in a given region. This finding is true for all local workers: skilled and unskilled, male and female, minority and nonminority. Prior waves of immigrants face the greatest losses from the new immigrants—a 10% increase in the supply of new immigrants reduces wages of earlier immigrants by 2–4%.[23]

Immigration and its Effect on the Sending Region

A discussion concerning the impact of immigration on a sending region most often focuses on international immigration because data are more readily available, but it would also apply to rural areas in the same country. Immigrants contribute to the sending region when they send money home. In 1996, families and small businesses in Mexico received approximately $4.2 billion in monetary transfers from Mexican nationals in the United States and other countries. Unfortunately, it is impossible to track the amount of money sent from urban American workers to their rural families.

Nevertheless, the major effect of out-migration is the brain drain. Those who leave have the more potential, more drive, and more education—qualities that are needed for regional development. Furthermore, the government in the sending region, which subsidized part of the education of the migrants, cannot recuperate its investment.

For this reason, rural areas try desperately to entice former residents to return home before they retire and to bring their factories and skills with them. Of course, these reverse migrants often lack the agglomeration economies that would be able to sustain a new firm. In addition, the migrants that return home are generally older and look forward to the consumption activities of retirement.[24]

Summary and Conclusions

A region's labor supply is a function of the labor force participation rate and the willingness and ability of workers to commute or migrate. The decision to participate in the labor force and how many hours to work is determined by maximizing the household's utility function. Household members could choose (1) to work outside the home, (2) to work within the home or on the farm, or (3) to consume leisure activities. The choice will depend on whether activities inside the household yield greater marginal benefits than activities outside the household.

A decision to commute or to migrate depends on the marginal costs and benefits. Commuters compare the compensation package from a distant

---

[23] Grenier (1992); Pope and Withers (1993); Borjas (1995); Friedberg and Hunt (1995); Zweimuller and Winter-Ebmer (1995); National Research Council (1997); Stevans (1998); White and Liang (1998); Chapman and Cobb-Clark (1999); Suen (2000); Polsky (2002).

[24] Krieg (1991); Burda (1993); Ghosh (1996); Fox Kellam and Vargas (1998a,b); Irwin, Tolbert, and Lyson (1999); Iqbal (2000).

employer with the marginal costs of commuting. As commuting stress escalates, workers consider migrating. The costs of migrating are higher for older workers and people who have never moved before. According to the neoclassical growth theory, both the wage differentials and the spatial mismatch that results in regional structural unemployment will be eliminated by migration. High migration costs that stem from inadequate skills, strong locational preferences, a lack of information about distant jobs, or high physical costs of moving prevent spatial mismatch from self-correcting. In addition, regional differences in the cost of living and amenities also influence wages.

Young graduates with drive and ambition are most likely to migrate in response to labor market incentives. The elderly migrate in search of comfort and amenities. People in occupations that require local licenses or local clientele (e.g., doctors, lawyers, or small business owners) are less likely to migrate.

People migrate if the expected benefits of migrating are greater than the expected costs. Benefits include better working conditions, nicer amenities in a new location, or more favorable local public goods. Costs increase with distance, which becomes not only a physical barrier to moving, but also a barrier to adequate information. Distance is also a proxy for the psychic costs of leaving family and friends.

The most successful countries are nations of immigrants. However, an immigrant's human capital is not perfectly transferable due to differences in the quality and compatibility of education in the sending country. A lack of both language fluency and knowledge of the culture in the host country exacerbates the problem. Contrary to public opinion, immigrants pay more to public coffers than they receive from the government. Even though education expenses increase because of immigrant families, localities recuperate their costs when the immigrant children enter the labor force.

Usually, immigrant workers complement local workers in production and actually create even more jobs. To the extent that immigrants are substitutes for local workers, they decrease wages very slightly, and the results are statistically insignificant. Empirically, the earlier waves of immigrants lose the most to new immigrants.

Chapter Questions

1. Backwaters, Minnesota, is a town with a low population density. Backwaters Boats and Barges is the only manufacturing firm within 45 miles. To be able to hire ten more workers, the firm must increase wages from $4.00 to $4.25 per hour.

a. Draw a diagram that represents the industry structure for the labor market for this firm.

b. What would be the effect of a minimum wage set at $5.50? Show this on your diagram.

2. Urban Legends, Nebraska, is a city with high population density. The newspaper can get all the employees it needs at the going $5.00 wage.

a. Draw a diagram that represents the industry structure for the labor market for this firm.

b. What would be the effect of a minimum wage set at $5.50? Show this on your diagram.

3. Your job as economic advisor to the mayor of your city is to ascertain that there are enough workers for the four new employers who are considering a move to town.

a. Name three general ways that labor supply can increase.

b. Based on your answer to Question 3.a., what types of policies could you implement to increase your city's labor supply?

4. What costs do households face when they migrate? What benefits are they hoping to get? (That is, what are the three principal models in migration theory?)

5. What costs and benefits besides those you discuss in Question 4 are involved with international migration—to the migrant, to the sending region, and to the receiving region?

Research Assignments

1. Calculate the average annual wage (payroll/number of employees) by industry for 1990 and 2000 either through *County Business Patterns* (http://www.census.gov/epcd/cbp/view/cbpview.html) or find weekly wages by industry from the *Quarterly Census of Employment and Wages* (http://www.bls.gov/cew) from the Bureau of Labor Statistics. What industries consistently pay higher wages in your state? Adjust the data for inflation using a CPI Index from the Bureau of Labor Statistics.

2. For your county and either your state or an adjacent county:

a. Determine the net migration rate between 1990 and 2000. Using population figures for 1990 and 2000 from the census, find the population change. Sum the yearly birth and death data for your county from 1990 to 1999 from data provided by your state's department of health.

   b. Find average wage and salary disbursements from the Bureau of Economic Analysis *CA 30 Regional Economic Profiles* data for 1990 and 2000. Adjust the data for inflation using a CPI Index from the Bureau of Labor Statistics.

   c. How is your city's quality of life in such rankings as *Places Rated Almanac* and *Sperling's Best Places?*

   d. From your state's department of education, find out how schools in your city rank on standardized test scores compared to surrounding schools and the overall state's averages?

   e. Compare the tax collections of your region per $1,000 of personal income from the *Census of Government* or a taxpayer's association in your state. Find the effective property tax rate for your county from your state's department of revenue.

   f. Has the median age of your county's population changed between 1990 and 2000?

   g. Explain the net migration trend to or from your county with these statistics?

3. If a large firm were to locate in your county, would it have a labor supply problem?

   a. What is the labor force participation rate for your county? What is your unemployment rate? (The labor force figures are under Local Area Unemployment Statistics, http://www.bls.gov).

   b. Using data from the MCD/County-To-MCD/County Worker Flow Files, in the Journey to Work and Place of Work data sets (http://www.census.gov/population/www/socdemo/journey.html), determine from where people commute to your county to work and to where people in your county commute to work. What is the average travel time to work for workers in your county (From the QT-P23; SF-3 data from the census)?

4. Check the *Digest of Education Statistics* (http://nces.ed.gov/programs/digest/) to see if your state net imports or exports freshmen to universities. For 2003 data, this information was in Table 206 through Table 208 of Chapter 3.

References

Akbari, A. H. 1991. The public finance impact of immigrant population on host nations: some Canadian evidence. *Social Science Quarterly* 72 (2):334–346.

Alwang, J., and J. I. Stallmann. 1992. Supply and demand for married female labor: rural and urban differences in the southern United States. *Southern Journal of Agricultural Economics* 24 (2):49–62.

Assadian, A. 1995. Fiscal determinants of migration to a fast-growing state: how the aged differ from the general population. *Review of Regional Studies* 25 (3):301–315.

Assadian, A., and J. Ondrich. 1993. Residential location, housing demand and labour supply decisions of one- and two-earner households: the case of Bogotá, Colombia. *Urban Studies* 30 (1):73–86.

Bailey, A. J. 1993. Migration history, migration behavior and selectivity. *Annals of Regional Science* 27 (4):315–326.

Barkley, D. L. 1995. The economics of change in rural America. *American Journal of Agricultural Economics* 77 (5):1252–1258.

Beeson, P. E., and E. L. Groshen. 1991. Components of city size wage differentials 1973-1988. *FRB Cleveland Economic Review* 27 (4):10–24.

Bentolila, S. 1997. Sticky labor in Spanish regions. *European Economic Review* 41 (3–5):591–598.

Berger, M. C., and G. C. Blomquist. 1992. Mobility and destination in migration decisions: the roles of earnings, quality of life, and housing prices. *Journal of Housing Economics* 2 (1):37–59.

Betts, J. R. 1998. Educational crowding out: do immigrants affect the educational attainment of American minorities? *Help or Hindrance? The EconomicImplications of Immigration for African Americans*, eds. D. S. Hamermesh, and F. D. Bean, New York: Russell Sage Foundation, 253–281.

Blackaby, D. H., R. C. Bladen-Hovell, and E. J. Symons. 1991. Unemployment, duration and wage determination in the UK: evidence from the FES 1980-86. *Oxford Bulletin of Economics and Statistics* 53 (4):377–379.

Blackaby, D. H., and D. N. Manning. 1990. Earnings, unemployment and the regional employment structure in Britain. *Regional Studies* 24 (6):529–535.

Blanc, M., and C. Lagriffoul. 1996. Mobilité et marches du travail ruraux: une approche en termes de segmentation. *Revue d'Economie Régionale et Urbaine* 0 (2):329–342.

Boehm, T. P., H. W. Herzog, and A. M. Schlottmann. 1998. Does migration matter? Job search outcomes for the unemployed. *Review of Regional Studies* 28 (1):3–12.

Bohara, A. K., and R. G. Krieg. 1996. A Poisson hurdle model of migration frequency. *Journal of Regional Analysis and Policy* 26 (1):37–45.

Borjas, G. J. 1995. The economic benefits from immigration. *Journal of Economic Perspectives* 9 (2):3–22.

Borjas, G. J., S. G. Bronars, and S. J. Trejo. 1992. Self-selection and internal migration in the United States. *Journal of Urban Economics* 32 (2):159–185.

Bosco, L. 1999. Employment illusion, variable costs of migration and labour mobility. *Labour* 13 (3):711–736.

Bound, J., and H. J. Holzer. 2000. Demand shifts, population adjustments, and labor market outcomes during the 1980s. *Journal of Labor Economics* 18 (1):20–54.

Boyle, P. J., R. Flowerdew, and J. Shen. 1998. Modelling inter-ward migration in Hereford and Worcester: the importance of housing growth and tenure. *Regional Studies* 32 (2):113–132.

Bradley, S., and J. Taylor. 1997. Unemployment in Europe: a comparative analysis of regional disparities in Germany, Italy and the U.K. *Kyklos* 50 (2):221–245.

Broomhall, D. 1995. The influence of the local economy and the willingness to move on human capital accumulation in central Appalachia. *Journal of Agricultural and Applied Economics* 27 (2):488–499.

Brown, R. J. 1994. Do locational amenities equalize utility across states? *Journal of Economics (MVEA)* 20 (1):25–30.

Burda, M. C. 1993. The determinants of east-west German migration: some first results. *European Economic Review* 37 (2–3):452–461.

Byers, J. D. 1991. Testing for common trends in regional unemployment. *Applied Economics* 23 (6):1087–1092.

Card, D., J. DiNardo, and E. Estes. 1998. The more things change: immigrants and the children of immigrants in the 1940s, the 1970s, and the 1990s. National Bureau of Economic Research, Inc, NBER Working Papers.

Cebula, R. J. 1991. A brief note on welfare benefits and human migration. *Public Choice* 69 (3):345–349.

Cebula, R. J., and J. V. Koch. 1989. Welfare policies and migration of the poor in the United States: an empirical note. *Public Choice* 61 (2):171–176.

Chalmers, J. A., and M. J. Greenwood. 1985. The regional labor market adjustment process: determinants of changes in rates of labor force participation, unemployment, and migration. *Annals of Regional Science* 19 (1):1–17.

Chapman, B., and D. Cobb-Clark. 1999. A comparative static model of the relationship between immigration and the short-run job prospects of unemployed residents. *Economic Record* 75 (231):358–368.

Cheung, H. Y.-F., and K.-L. Liaw. 1987. Metropolitan out-migration of elderly females in Canada: characterization and explanation. *Environment and Planning A* 19 (12):1659–1671.

Chiswick, B. R., and P. W. Miller. 1995. The endogeneity between language and earnings: international analyses. *Journal of Labor Economics* 13 (2):246–288.

Clark, D. E., and W. J. Hunter. 1992. The impact of economic opportunity, amenities and fiscal factors on age-specific migration rates. *Journal of Regional Science* 32 (3):349–365.

Conway, K. S., and A. J. Houtenville. 2001. Elderly migration and state fiscal policy: evidence from the census migration flows. *National Tax Journal* 54 (1):103–123.

Cooke, T. J. 2001. 'Trailing wife' or 'trailing mother'? The effect of parental status on the relationship between family migration and the labor-market participation of married women. *Environment and Planning A* 33 (3):419–430.

Currie, J. 1995. Do children of immigrants make differential use of public health insurance? National Bureau of Economic Research, Inc, NBER Working Papers.

Cushing, B. J. 1993. The effect of the social welfare system on metropolitan migration in the U.S., by income group, gender and family structure. *Urban Studies* 30 (2):325–337.

Day, K. M. 1992. Interprovincial migration and local public goods. *Canadian Journal of Economics* 25 (1):123–144.

Deller, S. C., M. Shields, and D. Tomberlin. 1996. Price differentials and trends in state income levels: a research note. *Review of Regional Studies* 26 (1):99–113.

Detang-Dessendre, C., and I. Molho. 1999. Migration and changing employment status: a hazard function analysis. *Journal of Regional Science* 39 (1):103–123.

Detang-Dessendre, C., and I. Molho. 2000. Residence spells and migration: a comparison for men and women. *Urban Studies* 37 (2):247–260.

Doeringer, P. B. 1984. Internal labor markets and paternalism in rural areas, In *Internal labor markets*, ed., P. Osterman, Cambridge, Mass., and London: MIT Press, 271–289.

Dustmann, C. 1994. Speaking fluency, writing fluency and earnings of migrants. *Journal of Population Economics* 7 (2):133–156.

Elhorst, J. P. 1998. The nonutilisation of human capital in regional labour markets across Europe. *Environment and Planning A* 30 (5):901–920.

Enchautegui, M. E. 1997. Welfare payments and other economic determinants of female migration. *Journal of Labor Economics* 15 (3):529–554.

Espenshade, T. J., and V. E. King. 1994. State and local fiscal impacts of U.S. immigrants: evidence from New Jersey. *Population Research and Policy Review* 13 (3):225–256.

Fik, T. J., R. G. Amey, and G. F. Mulligan. 1992. Labor migration amongst hierarchically competing and intervening origins and destinations. *Environment and Planning A* 24 (9):1271–1290.

Fokkema, T., J. Gierveld, and P. Nijkamp. 1996. Big cities, big problems: reason for the elderly to move? *Urban Studies* 33 (2):353–377.

Fox Kellam, B., and L. Vargas. 1998a. Immigration and the economy—Part I. *FRB Dallas Southwest Economy* 4.

Fox Kellam, B., and L. Vargas. 1998b. Immigration and the economy—Part II. *FRB Dallas Southwest Economy* 5.

Friedberg, R. M. 2000. You can't take it with you? Immigrant assimilation and the portability of human capital. *Journal of Labor Economics* 18 (2):221–251.

Friedberg, R. M., and J. Hunt. 1995. The impact of immigrants on host country wages, employment and growth. *Journal of Economic Perspectives* 9 (2):23–44.

Ghosh, B. 1996. Economic migration and the sending countries, In *The Economics of Labour Migration* ed. J. van den Broeck, Cheltenham, U.K./Brookfield, VT: Elgar/distributed by Ashgate, 77–113.

Gittleman, M., and E. N. Wolff. 1993. International comparisons of inter-industry wage differentials. *Review of Income and Wealth* 39 (3):295–312.

Graves, P. E., and P. D. Linneman. 1979. Household migration: theoretical and empirical results. *Journal of Urban Economics* 6 (3):383–404.

Graves, P. E., and D. M. Waldman. 1991. Multimarket amenity compensation and the behavior of the elderly. *American Economic Review* 81 (5):1374–1381.

Greenwood, M. J. 1975. Research on internal migration in the United States: a survey. *Journal of Economic Literature* 13 (2):397–433.

Greenwood, M. J. 1985. Human migration: theory, models, and empirical studies. *Journal of Regional Science* 25 (4):521–544.

Greenwood, M. J., P. R. Mueser, D. A. Plane, and A. M. Schlottmann. 1991. New directions in migration research: perspectives from some North American regional science disciplines. *Annals of Regional Science* 25 (4):237–270.

Greenwood, M. J. 1997. Internal migration in developed countries, In *Handbook of Population and Family Economics. Volume 1B.*, eds. M. R. Rosenzweig, and O. Stark, New York and Oxford/North-Holland: Amsterdam/Elsevier Science, 647–720.

Grenier, G. 1992. L'immigration et les revenus relatifs des femmes, des jeunes et des personnes peu scolarisées au Canada. *L'Actualité Économique* 68 (4):697–713.

Groenewold, N. 1997. Does migration equalise regional unemployment rates? evidence from Australia. *Papers in Regional Science* 76 (1):1–20.

Gunter, L., and K. T. McNamara. 1990. The impact of local labor market conditions on the off-farm earnings of farm operators. *Southern Journal of Agricultural Economics* 22 (1):155–165.

Hacker, R. S. 2000. Mobility and regional economic downturns. *Journal of Regional Science* 40 (1):45–65.

Hanson, G. H., and A. Spilimbergo. 1999. Illegal immigration, border enforcement, and relative wages: evidence from apprehensions at the U.S.-Mexico border. *American Economic Review* 89 (5):1337–1357.

Henry, M. S. 1993. The rural economic gap: Fact or fiction?. In *Economic Adaptation: Alternatives for Nonmetropolitan Areas*, ed. D. L. Barkley in Rural Studies Series, Boulder and Oxford: Westview Press, 9–28.

Henry, M. S., B. Schmitt, K. Kristensen, D. Barkley, and S. Bao. 1999. Extending Carlino-Mills models to examine urban size and growth impacts on proximate rural areas. *Growth and Change* 30 (4):526–548.

Herzog, H. W. , A. M. Schlottmann, and T. P. Boehm. 1993. Migration as spatial job-search: a survey of empirical findings. *Regional Studies* 27 (4):327–340.

Hodge, I. D., and M. Whitby. 1986. The U.K.: rural development, issues and analysis. *European Review of Agricultural Economics* 13 (3):391–413.

Hou, F., and R. Beaujot. 1995. A study of interregional migration between Ontario and Atlantic Canada: 1981–1991. *Canadian Journal of Regional Science* 18 (2):147–160.

Hsing, Y. 1995. The impacts of welfare benefits and tax burdens on interstate migration. *Regional Science Perspectives* 25 (2):16–24.

Hsing, Y. 1996. Impacts of government policies, economic conditions, and past migration on net migration in the USA: 1992–93. *Applied Economics Letters* 3 (7):441–444.

Hsing, Y., and F. G. Mixon. 1996. A regional study of net migration rates of college students. *Review of Regional Studies* 26 (2):197–209.

Ihlanfeldt, K. R. 1993. Intra-urban job accessibility and Hispanic youth employment rates. *Journal of Urban Economics* 33 (2):254–271.

Iqbal, M. 2000. Brain drain: Empirical evidence of emigration of Canadian professionals to the United States. *Canadian Tax Journal* 48 (3):674–688.

Irwin, M., C. Tolbert, and T. Lyson. 1999. There's no place like home: Nonmigration and civic engagement. *Environment and Planning A* 31 (12):2223–2238.

Islam, M. N., and S. A. Choudhury. 1991. Self-selection and intermunicipal migration in Canada. *Regional Science and Urban Economics* 20 (4):459–472.

Islam, M. N., and M. Rafiquzzaman. 1991. Property tax and inter-municipal migration in Canada: a multivariate test of the Tiebout hypothesis. *Applied Economics* 23 (4A, Part A):623–630.

Jackman, R., and S. Savouri. 1992a. Regional migration in Britain: an analysis of gross flows using NHS central register data. *Economic Journal* 102 (415):1433–1450.

Jackman, R., and S. Savouri. 1992b. Regional migration versus regional commuting: The identification of housing and employment flows. *Scottish Journal of Political Economy* 39 (3):272–287.

Jarvis, H. 1999. Identifying the relative mobility prospects of a variety of household employment structures, 1981–1991. *Environment and Planning A* 31 (6):1031–1046.

Jayet, H. 1995. Marchés de l'emploi urbains et ruraux et migrations. *Revue Economique* 46 (3):605–614.

Johnson, K. M. 1993. When deaths exceed births: natural decrease in the United States. *International Regional Science Review* 15 (2):179–198.

Kahley, W. J. 1991. Population migration in the United States: a survey of research. *Federal Reserve Bank of Atlanta Economic Review* 76 (1):12–21.

Kahn, J. R., and H. Ofek. 1992. The equilibrium distribution of population and wages in a system of cities. *Review of Regional Studies* 22 (3):201–216.

Kee, P. 1995. Native-immigrant wage differentials in the Netherlands: discrimination? *Oxford Economic Papers* 47 (2):302–317.

Kilpatrick, S., and B. Felmingham. 1996. Labour mobility in the Australian regions. *Economic Record* 72 (218):214–223.

Knapp, T. A., and P. E. Graves. 1989. On the role of amenities in models of migration and regional development. *Journal of Regional Science* 29 (1):71–87.

Kohler, H.-P. 1997. The effect of hedonic migration decisions and region-specific amenities on industrial location: Could Silicon Valley be in South Dakota? *Journal of Regional Science* 37 (3):379–394.

Kottman, S. E. 1992. Regional employment by industry: do returns to capital matter? *Federal Reserve Bank of Atlanta Economic Review* 77 (5):13–25.

Kriaa, M., and J. M. Plassard. 1996. La mobilité géographique des diplômes de l'enseignement supérieur français: processus de double sélection et fonction de gains. *Recherches Economiques De Louvain* 62 (1):95–122.

Krieg, R. G. 1991. Human-capital selectivity in interstate migration. *Growth and Change* 22 (1):68–76.

Krieg, R. G. 1992. Internal migration and its influence on earnings of working husbands and wives. *Regional Science Perspectives* 22 (2):79–89.

Kwan, M.-P. 1999. Gender, the home-work link, and space-time patterns of none-mployment activities. *Economic Geography* 75 (4):370–394.

Lam, K.-C. 1994. Outmigration of foreign-born members in Canada. *Canadian Journal of Economics* 27 (2):352–370.

Lane, T., and C. K. Thomas. 1987. The labor force status of Alaska's native population, *Developing America's Northern Frontier*, ed. T. Lane, Lanham, MD: University Press of America, 63–89.

Lass, D. A., J. L. Findeis, and M. C. Hallberg. 1991. Factors affecting the supply of off-farm labor: A review of empirical evidence, *Multiple Job-Holding Among Farm Families*, eds. M. C. Hallberg, J. L. Findeis, and D. A. Lass, Ames: Iowa State University Press, 239–262.

Li, P. S. 2001. The market worth of immigrants' educational credentials. *Canadian Public Policy* 27 (1):23–38.

Lin, G. 1997. Elderly migration: household versus individual approaches. *Papers in Regional Science* 76 (3):285–300.

Lin, J.-P., K.-L. Liaw, and C.-L. Tsay. 1999. Determinants of fast repeat migrations of the labor force: evidence from the linked national survey data of Taiwan. *Environment and Planning A* 31 (5):925–945.

Long, L. 1988. *Migration and Residential Mobility in the United States*, The population of the United States in the 1980s Series. New York: Russell Sage Foundation for Research on the 1980 Census.

Lonner, T.D. 1987. Transient work forces as casualties in northern frontier development, In *Developing America's Northern Frontier*, ed. T. Lane, Lanham, MD: University Press of America, 181–197.

Lybbert, T. J., and D. D. Thilmany. 2000. Migration effects of Olympic siting: A pooled time series cross-sectional analysis of host regions. *Annals of Regional Science* 34 (3):405–420.

Madden, J. F., and L. C. Chiu. 1990. The wage effects of residential location and commuting constraints on employed married women. *Urban Studies* 27 (3):353–369.

Mak, J., and J. E. T. Moncur. 2003. Interstate migration of college freshmen. *Annals of Regional Science* 37 (4):603–612.

Martin, F. 1988. The influence of unemployment insurance benefits upon the social cost of labor in lagging regions, In *Regional Economic Development: Essays in Honour of François Perroux*. eds. B. Higgins, and D.J. Savoie, Boston: Unwin Hyman, 244–268.

Matsukawa, I. 1991. Interregional gross migration and structural changes in local industries. *Environment and Planning A* 23 (5):745–756.

McHone, W. W., and B. Rungeling. 1993. Replacement income, duration of unemployment and the migration of unemployed prime age males. *Applied Economics* 25 (7):905–909.

Meager, N., and Metcalf, H. 1987. *Recruitment of the long-term unemployed*, IMS Report no 138, Brington.

Millington, J. 2000. Migration and age: the effect of age on sensitivity to migration stimuli. *Regional Studies* 34 (6):521–533.

Mills, B. F. 2001. Unemployment duration in non-metropolitan labor markets. *Growth and Change* 32 (2):174–192.

Mixon, F. G. and Y. Hsing. 1994. The determinants of out-of-state enrollments in higher education: a Tobit analysis. *Economics of Education Review* 13 (4):329–335.

Morrill, R. 1994. Age-specific migration and regional diversity. *Environment and Planning A* 26 (11):1699–1710.

Nakosteen, R. A., and M. A. Zimmer. 1992. Migration, age, and earnings: the special case of employee transfers. *Applied Economics* 24 (7):791–802.

National Research Council. 1997. *New Americans: Economic, Demographic, and Fiscal Effects of Immigration.* http://books.nap.edu/books/0309063566/html/1.html.

Newbold, K. B. 1996. Income, self-selection, and return and onward interprovincial migration in Canada. *Environment and Planning A* 28 (6):1019–1034.

Nord, M. 1998. Poor people on the move: county-to-county migration and the spatial concentration of poverty. *Journal of Regional Science* 38 (2):329–351.

O'Regan, K. M. 1993. The effect of social networks and concentrated poverty on black and Hispanic youth unemployment. *Annals of Regional Science* 27 (4):327–342.

Partridge, M. D., and D. S. Rickman. 2003. The waxing and waning of regional economies: the chicken-egg question of jobs versus people. *Journal of Urban Economics* 53 (1):76–97.

Payne, D. M., J. T. Warner, and R. D. Little. 1992. Tied migration and returns to human capital: the case of military wives. *Social Science Quarterly* 73 (2):324–339.

Polsky, D. 2002. Initial practice locations of international medical graduates. *Health Services Research* 37 (4):907–928.

Pope, D., and G. Withers. 1993. Do migrants rob jobs? Lessons of Australian history, 1861–1991. *Journal of Economic History* 53 (4):719–742.

Potepan, M. J. 1994. Intermetropolitan migration and housing prices: simultaneously determined? *Journal of Housing Economics* 3 (2):77–91.

Radakovic, G. M. 1991. Identifying employment barriers in rural western Pennsylvania. Pennsylvania Economic Association: Proceedings of the Sixth Annual Meeting, May 23–25, University of Pittsburgh, Johnstown, 417–431.

Rasmussen, D. W., G. M. Fournier, and D. A. Charity. 1989. The impact of cost of living differentials on migration of elderly people to Florida. *Review of Regional Studies* 19 (2): 48–54.

von Reichert, C. and G. Rudzitis. 1992. Multinomial logistic models explaining income changes of migrants to high-amenity counties. *Review of Regional Studies* 22 (1):25–42.

von Reichert, C. and G. Rudzitis. 1994. Rent and wage effects on the choice of amenity destinations of labor force and nonlabor force migrants: a note. *Journal of Regional Science* 34 (3):445–455.

Ritsila, J., and M. Haapanen. 2003. Where do the highly educated migrate? Micro-level evidence from Finland. *International Review of Applied Economics* 17 (4):437–448.

Rives, J. M., and J. M. West. 1992. Worker relocation costs: the role of wife's labor market behavior. *Regional Science Perspectives* 22 (1):3–12.

Rosen, S. 1974. Hedonic prices and implicit markets: product differentiation in pure competition. *Journal of Political Economy* 82 (1):34–55.

Sakashita, N., and M. Hirao. 1999. On the applicability of the Tiebout model to Japanese cities. *Review of Urban and Regional Development Studies* 11 (3):206–215.

Saving, J. L. 1999. Migration, labor-leisure choice, and Pareto suboptimal redistribution. *Regional Science and Urban Economics* 29 (5):559–573.

Schachter, J., and P. G. Althaus. 1989. An equilibrium model of gross migration. *Journal of Regional Science* 29 (2):143–159.

Schmidt, C. M. 1993. Country of origin, family structure and return migration. Working paper. London School of Economics – Suntory Toyoto, Taxation, Incentives and Distribution of Income, London School of Economics – Suntory Toyota, Taxation, Incentives and Distribution of Income.

Schmidt, C. M. 1997. Immigrant performance in Germany: labor earnings of ethnic German migrants and foreign guest-workers. *Quarterly Review of Economics and Finance* 37 (0):379–397.

Shields, G. M., and M. P. Shields. 1988. Families, migration and adjusting to disequilibrium. *Economics Letters* 26 (4):387–392.

Simon, J. L. 1996. Some findings about European immigration. *International Regional Science Review* 19 (1–2):129–137.

Sjaastad, L. A. 1962. The costs and returns of human migration. *The Journal of Political Economy* 70 (5): 80–93.

Smith, B. H. 1991. Anxiety as a cost of commuting to work. *Journal of Urban Economics* 29 (2):260–266.

Stabler, J. C., M. R. Olfert, and J. B. Greuel. 1996. Spatial labor markets and the rural labor force. *Growth and Change* 27 (2):206–230.

Stevans, L. K. 1998. Assessing the effect of the occupational crowding of immigrants on the real wages of African American workers. *Review of Black Political Economy* 26 (2):37–46.

Straubhaar, T., and R. Weber. 1994. On the economics of immigration: some empirical evidence for Switzerland. *International Review of Applied Economics* 8 (2):107–129.

Suen, W. 2000. Estimating the effects of immigration in one city. *Journal of Population Economics* 13 (1):99–112.

Thomas, A. 1993. The influence of wages and house prices on British interregional migration decisions. *Applied Economics* 25 (9):1261–1268.

Tiebout, C. M. 1956. A pure theory of local expenditures. *The Journal of Political Economy* 64 (5): 416–424.

Vanderkamp, J. 1977. The gravity model and migration behaviour: an economic interpretation. *Journal of Economic Studies* 4 (2):90–102.

Vanderkamp, J. 1988. Regional disparities: a model with some econometric results for Canada, *Regional Economic Development: Essays in Honour of François Perroux*, eds. B. Higgins, and D. J. Savoie , Boston: Unwin Hyman, 269–296.

Ventura, F. Women in Italian agriculture: new roles new problems, In *Rural Gender Studies in Europe*, eds. P. Leendert van der, and M. Fonte European Perspectives on Rural Development series, Assen: Van Gorcum, 80–90.

Warnes, A. M., and R. Ford. 1995. Housing aspirations and migration in later life: developments during the 1980s. *Papers in Regional Science* 74 (4):361–387.

Weiss, Y., M. Gotlibovski, and R. M. Sauer. 2003. Immigration, search, and loss of skill. *Journal of Labor Economics* 21 (3):557–591.

Westerlund, O., and M. L. Wyzan. 1995. Household migration and the local public sector: evidence from Sweden, 1981–1984. *Regional Studies* 29 (2):145–157.

White, M. J., and Z. Liang. 1998. The effect of immigration on the internal migration of the native-born population, 1981–1990. *Population Research and Policy Review* 17 (2):141–166.

White, M. J. 1986. Sex differences in urban commuting patterns. *American Economic Review* 76 (2):368–372.

Zhao, J., D. Drew, and T. S. Murray. 2000. Knowledge workers on the move. *Perspectives on Labour and Income* 12 (2):32–46.

Zweimuller, J., and R. Winter-Ebmer. 1995. Internal labor markets and firm-specific determination of earnings in the presence of immigrant workers. *Economics Letters* 48 (2):185–191.

Chapter 11

Can Government Change a Region's Growth Path?

Some jurisdictions want to promote local economic growth, and thereby increase living standards in their community. Others do their best to limit it. Because trends to limit growth are more an urban phenomenon, we will analyze the effects of growth controls and the so-called "smart growth" in Chapter 15.

The theoretical role of government in promoting growth varies from one theory to another. According to the ***economic base model*** (Chapter 7), government spending is the one dependable exogenous variable that can pull an economy out of a recession. How government spending is increased and who receives the monetary injection is not directly discussed in this macroeconomic model. It is as if government distributes "spending" (perhaps by using cargo planes), equally across the region. Nobody pays for this injection; it rains down like manna from heaven.

In the ***neoclassical theory*** (Chapter 8), government spending either crowds out private investment, or helps boost one economy at the expense of the one that is taxed to pay for the injection in the first economy. Finally, ***endogenous growth theory*** (Chapter 8) asserts that the quality of education and the infrastructure, property rights enforcement, and access to information, ideas, and technology stimulate regional growth. To the extent that these are pure public goods, the market cannot provide an efficient quantity. This market failure suggests a possible role for the government to correct the inefficiency.

In this chapter, we will review the efficiency aspects of policies that stem from these theories. In the Appendix, we offer several welfare measures with which one can evaluate the merit of areas to receive such programs, or the effects of existing programs on economic welfare.

Think About It ...

Check your local newspapers or contact your chamber of commerce. What does your locality or your state do to promote local growth?

- Construct highways or improve existing transportation infrastructure
- Construct schools or programs to improve teaching
- Provide wireless Internet access
- Support university research programs
- Support continued professional education training programs

Or, does it instead:

- Promote tourism and recreational activities such as arts and culture, or sports stadiums
- Target publicity to attract retirees or others with guaranteed monthly incomes to move in
- Subsidize businesses or give tax breaks to firms if they relocate locally
- Create TIF districts or Enterprise Zones (EZ)
- Reduce interest rates on loans for businesses

If your city succeeded in attracting a large firm to your area, how much did the municipality pay for each expected job? Per actual job created?

What is the annual budget for the economic development efforts? How much tax revenue is foregone per year that the new businesses do not have to pay?

As you explore this chapter, try to determine whether the marginal benefit is equal to the marginal cost of the economic development efforts in your locality.

The impact of national aggregate spending on the long-run growth path is not clearly established by empirical studies. The potential impacts depend on what the spending is used for. Poot (2000) reviewed 123 studies of the effect of national spending on growth and categorized them as such: Eleven out of 12 studies support the hypothesis of a positive national impact for education expenditure on long-run growth, and 72% of the studies using national data showed that spending on public infrastructure had long-term positive effects. On the other hand, only 1 out of 41 found that defense spending had a positive impact on growth. Just over half of these studies determined that defense spending had significantly negative influences on long-run growth.[1]

However, two questions remain. Is the impact of the local government spending proportional to the summation of national government spending? Will the impact on rural regions differ from the impact on urban areas?

Why Government?

According to the classic public finance text by Musgrave and Musgrave (1989), government has three reasons for existence: redistribute income, provide public goods, and administer fiscal policy programs to curb unemployment and inflation. We will study in detail the redistribution and public goods aspects in Chapter 16 through Chapter 18.

Economists evaluate policy programs on the basis of the combined criteria of efficiency and equity. The concept of efficiency has three components.

1. ***Allocative efficiency*** means that consumers are paying the marginal cost of the last unit produced.
2. ***Technical efficiency*** means that consumers are paying the lowest price necessary. These programs can be evaluated by using a cost-benefit analysis or consumer and producer surplus framework (Chapter 6). Such evaluations must also determine the effect of the program on the incentives of the economic actors.
3. ***Distributional efficiency*** is founded on the principle of ***Pareto Optimality***. According to this principle, the optimal solution exists only when nobody can be made better off without making someone else worse off. Economists also ask about the incidence of specific policy programs: who benefits and who pays.

Public Goods

As we saw in Chapter 8, pure public goods are nonrival and nonexcludable. However, most goods provided by local government are ***club goods (quasi-***

---

[1] Poot (2000).

public goods), neither purely nonrival nor purely rival; neither purely nonexcludable nor purely excludable because they are subject to congestion.

The effectiveness of various government initiatives varies depending on whether they provide pure public goods, pure private goods, or club goods. Except for instances of market failure, economic theory asserts that private goods are most efficiently produced by the market. Because of the extra costs caused by a potential free rider, the government provides pure public goods most efficiently.

Club goods could be provided by either government or the private sector. Local governments provide police protection and public schools. However, those who want more police protection always have recourse to private security agencies. In the same way, those who think that private schools are better, do not have to send their children to public schools. In five North American jurisdictions — Massachusetts, British Columbia, Virginia, Texas, and Indianapolis — private sector firms maintain the highways.[2]

Investments in Public Capital

According to the endogenous growth theory, examples of club goods that will stimulate long-run growth include highways, education, telecommunications, and technology. However, the outcomes of these stimulus packages will not be the same in rural areas as in urban.

One question that permeates this analysis is whether new infrastructure investments (highways, water and sewer facilities, or communication capacity) are capable of stimulating growth, or if they only accommodate the growth that is already occurring. The response depends on the area. The urban areas and their periphery have a higher probability of benefiting from these investments because they will stimulate growth. For remote rural areas, the effect is indeterminate. If the remote areas do not invest, new firms or households will not come. If they do invest, migration of households or firms is not guaranteed.[3]

Which Comes First: Spending or the Residents?

Binet (2003) tests for this causality using data from 1987 to 1996 for 27 French cities around the city of Rennes. The study revealed two strategies. Seventeen localities

---

[2] Lisk (1998).
[3] Fox and Porca (2001).

invested in capital expenditures to attract new residents, while the others reduced their tax rates to increase the residential population. This study concluded that most of the time, government investments preceded migration.

Binet (2003)

Highways

Highway construction includes two phases, each with its own distinct economic impact. The impact associated with the **construction phase** depends directly on the local inputs used to construct the highway, along with their associated indirect and induced effects. These expenditures carry on indefinitely as the highway needs maintenance and improvements. The size of the multiplier depends on the existence and size of local interindustry linkages.

The **post-construction phase**, on the other hand, facilitates mobility and provides long-run advantages to the location. An improved transportation infrastructure shows mixed effects on growth because a road goes two ways. Highways facilitate the travel of firms and consumers from the urban core out to the periphery. They also assist rural consumers who want to shop and work in the core. In general, if an area has poor transportation infrastructure, new firms and households think that they are more isolated and are less tempted to migrate to the core. Merely improving transportation infrastructure does not guarantee that economic development will take place. In fact, such an improvement may hasten the demise of a rural area.

We can analyze changes in transportation costs between two regions by using international trade models. The results of the analysis depend on which of the two types of models are used: partial equilibrium and the more detailed general equilibrium. From a partial equilibrium perspective, decreased transportation costs lead to increased trade between the two regions. Say that when trade is limited, Area A (Adamsville) has higher product prices than Area B (Bakerstown). With improved transportation, Adamsville's consumers are better off purchasing the product from Bakerstown, increasing demand in Bakerstown to D' and reducing demand in Adamsville as shown in Figure 11.1. Area B's f.o.b. price will increase, while Adamsville's price falls until the two prices equilibrate.

The consumers in Adamsville benefit, but producers of the imported product in Adamsville are worse off. At the same time, employment in Bakerstown expands because of its increase in exports. Bakerstown's households and producers are better off. In essence, everyone but the

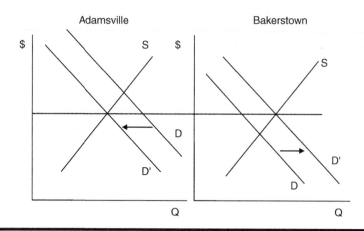

Figure 11.1   Effect of decreased transportation costs on trade in two cities.

high priced, inefficient producers in Adamsville is better off with improved transportation.

In a general equilibrium framework, we go a step or two further. Not all producers in Adamsville will be worse off. The decrease in the f.o.b. price of the traded good may allow Adamsville's consumers to purchase other goods from local manufacturers, thereby increasing profits of firms in the nonbasic sectors of Adamsville's economy. Similarly, if Bakerstown's labor market is tight and unemployment is not a problem, all of Bakerstown's firms may be forced to increase wages, decreasing profits even for producers of nonbasic goods in Bakerstown.

We could also analyze the changes in transportation costs between two regions by using two models of regional trade: the core–periphery model and the growth pole model. Core–periphery models shed a different light on the effect of lower transportation costs in a periphery region (Chapter 9). In von Thünen's model, for instance, improving transportation infrastructure decreases transportation costs of agricultural products, causing the bid-rent function for agriculture in that area to flatten out (Figure 11.2). Farmers who own fields around the new transport route will absorb the largest portion of economic benefits because the value of their land increases. The price of farmland closest to the market declines because of the drop in prices. The lower prices cause the intercept of the bid-rent function to slide downward because farmers located at the city center would face lower revenues and lower residuals with which to bid for land at the prime location. Urban residents benefit from the improved transportation networks only after the prices of agricultural products fall.

Finally, according to the growth pole theory (Chapter 9), the characteristics of the localities and the length of time after the highway is built

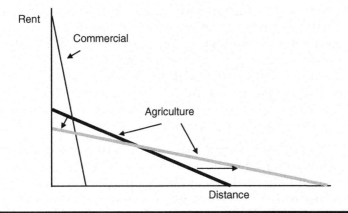

Figure 11.2 Bid-rent function with decreased transport costs for agriculture.

determine, in part, the economic impact. Remember from Chapter 9 that during the first and third phases, urban growth spreads to the periphery, whereas during the second stage, the backwash effects cause a flight of resources from the periphery to the urban center. In the first stage, improved transportation routes allow a wider area of the hinterland to provide inputs and intermediate goods to the motrice firm, thus spreading growth to a wider area. However, in the second stage, improved transportation systems increase the flow of commuters to the center city, exacerbating the backwash effect. The backwash effect allows the urban area to grow at the expense of the periphery because the resources are siphoned from the rural area to the urban area. Finally, in the third stage, the spread effect occurs first along transportation routes. Rural areas with poor roads will not benefit from the spread of economic activity. Those with good roads increase the probability of growth because of the in-migration of labor and firms, as well as expanded tourism.[4]

Highways as Mini-Growth Poles

The quality of the highways helps spread a dense urban population to less dense metropolitan counties. Empirically, because of the combined backwash and spread effects, employment growth due to highway investment is not guaranteed to spread to rural areas. Interstate highways increase the level of economic

---

[4] Rietveld (1989); Ambrose and Springer (1993); Rephann and Isserman (1994); Haughwout (1999); Chandra and Thompson (2000).

activity in counties that they pass directly through, but create a backwash effect in counties that are only adjacent to those that do. A quarter of a century after the opening of an interstate highway, the total increase in earnings to counties through which the highway passed ranged from 6 percent to 8 percent. Retail and service sectors grew between 5 percent and 8 percent because of the induced effects.

However, for counties that are adjacent to the highway counties, earnings in retail fell by 8–11 percent, even though total earnings fell by 1–3 percent. While initial access to interstate highways is important, additional highway infrastructure does not seem to contribute to a county's ability to attract firms.

Ambrose and Springer (1993), Haughwout (1999),
Chandra and Thompson (2000)

Education

Empirically, national levels of investment in education have a stronger and more predictable effect on output than investment in transportation infrastructure. Regionally, high-quality schools influence migration because of the ***parental migration effect***, a corollary of the Tiebout Hypothesis (Chapter 10).

The parental migration effect is stronger for K-12 education spending than for university spending, because students often attend university in cities other than where their parents live. The result of the parental migration effect is a growing number of families that value education. This expanded population increases both the supply of labor and the demand for local goods besides education.

However, if the goal of the locality is to create a large number of productive workers by expanded investment in education, it must wait, because education is a long-term investment. Improving the quality of higher education only begins to increase the productivity of a labor force 4 years later—after students graduate—assuming they do not leave to find work elsewhere. Elementary and secondary education will increase worker productivity also, but after a 4–9 year lag.[5]

---

[5] Quan and Beck (1987); Garcia-Milà and McGuire (1992); Strathman (1994); Carlino and DeFina (1995).

Some States Free-Ride on Higher Education

Nationally, the positive impact of quality human capital investment on growth is unambiguous. Similarly, states with inferior K-12 education face greater negative impacts on productivity levels, because workers with a diploma from a poor quality high school cannot easily find jobs elsewhere and their ability to pursue quality higher education is hampered.

On the other hand, states need to account for the spillover effects when they choose the optimal level of investment in higher education. Educated people are more mobile than others. Individuals educated in one state may migrate to other states, reducing the impact of local human capital investment on regional growth rates. States with poor quality colleges and universities can still employ high-quality graduates who were educated elsewhere.

Benefit spillovers from public higher education lead to lower appropriations from the state legislators. For each percentage point increase in out-migration, the appropriations per student tend to decline by about $100 and tuition rates increase.

Quan and Beck (1987), Strathman (1994)

Telecommunications and Utilities

Telecommunications is crucial for rural development. Nevertheless, some isolated regions do not even have basic telephone service. In 1999, more than 55% of all Native Americans living on reservations in the United States did not have a telephone. Replacing party lines, where from two to eight subscribers are connected to the same telephone exchange, with high-speed Internet or even private telephone service could boost rural development. Quality telecommunications can provide up-to-the-minute weather forecasts, disaster warnings, information on agricultural innovations, and current market prices. Such technology allows rural areas to share urban facilities through distance learning, conference calls, diagnoses, and sometimes treatment of heath problems. With links between rural school systems and universities, schools can offer a greater variety of courses to students than they could otherwise. The TeleCottage program offered in Scandinavian countries and in the United Kingdom, for example, provides ongoing training programs for the rural workforce at lower costs than bringing in teachers or sending workers away for training. Distance learning centers in the United States offer courses, certificates, and degrees for K-12 education, universities, and corporate training programs.

However, to the extent that deep rural areas improve communications infrastructure with their economic development funds to entice information technology firms, they may be "Waiting for Godot."[6] The industries will never come. Generally, rural residents have higher adoption rates for computers and other advanced telecommunications methods than urban areas, just as they did with electricity and telephone access in the early 20th century. However, because a required threshold level of demand is not met, some periurban residents and most deep rural residents lag behind the urban core in technological advances such as cable modems, fiber optics, and higher bandwidths.

Rural developers dream of luring potentially footloose, information intensive activities by investing more in telecommunications than in the more expensive transportation infrastructure. Rural developers face barriers that may be more important than poor telecommunications infrastructure: isolation, lack of human capital, lack of adequate services, and poor transportation infrastructure. Could improved telecommunications ameliorate these problems, too? No. In fact, telecommunications will increase the need for travel rather than decrease it. The two types of infrastructure are complements in production.

Those who dream that information technology activities can thrive in their rural area generally rely on several assumptions:

1. That information is both the major input and output of information technology production.
2. That information travels costlessly over telecommunication lines.
3. That superior telecommunications infrastructure is a perfect substitute for transportation infrastructure.
4. That all high-tech or information technology activities have similar needs.

Salomon and Schofer (1991) listed the needs of three types of telecommunications technology industries that might be candidates for rural development: high-tech manufacturing, manual information processing, and research centers. Each of these requires sound transportation infrastructure to accompany the telecommunications investment. High-technology

---

[6] This expression is the title of a play by Samuel Beckett and means "waiting in vain."

manufacturing and research centers also need cultural amenities and good schools to attract highly skilled professionals. Manual information processing and research centers require airports. Manual information centers do not require highly skilled workers, but to the extent that check clearing and credit card statements are increasingly processed electronically, such centers are no longer growth industries.[7]

Government Technology Programs

Governmental research and development and private research and development are complementary goods. Technical complementarity between government and private research and development efforts comes from funding, establishing "infratechnology," and sharing knowledge. Governmental research and development facilitates knowledge distribution outside the laboratory. ***Infratechnology*** includes standardized measurements and testing methods, data formats, and technical interface bases. This type of government involvement is effective only at a national or international level. State and local governments create massive inefficiencies when they standardize measurements or technical interfaces just for products sold in their jurisdiction. A myriad of such regulations creates nothing but chaos in the industry and stifles growth.

The key component of state and local technology programs is a research university. However, the optimal role of a research university may not be to collaborate with private industry. Link and Rees (1991) surveyed firms that were involved with research universities. These firms most highly praised their access to students as future employees. Because faculty needs to publish and teach, universities cannot guarantee that what companies want to use as their confidential research will, in fact, remain confidential.

Nonetheless, recent advances in academic research assist the development of approximately 10% of the new products and processes. This is especially true for the information technology and pharmaceuticals industries. The first page of more than one-third of all patent applications by private industry cites journal articles published by academicians. Spillovers of academic research are strongest in areas surrounding research universities (Chapter 8), which is why such facilities are essential in Pascallon's ***golden triangle***.[8]

---

[7] Bhalla and Jéquier (1988); Dillman, Beck, and Allen (1989); Schwartz (1990); Salomon and Schofer (1991); Rowley and Porterfield (1993); Rubin and Holsten (1999); Freshwater (2000).

[8] Leyden and Link (1991); Link and Rees (1991); Mattey (1998); Tassey (1998).

Club Sophia Antipolis

In April 1972, Sophia Antipolis, "city of science," was created in southern France to serve as a pole of attraction. By 1990, some 130 French and foreign firms employed 5000 people. The nucleus of this center was a major IBM research laboratory close to Nice. The area was perfect, with proximity to: an international airport, to a dynamic university, and to the French Riviera. Soon Texas Instruments located a research facility in the same area.

Although some successes are attributed to Sophia Antipolis, the complex is as much a pole of repulsion as it is a pole of attraction, according to Hansen (1990). Both IBM and Texas Instruments refused to share technologies and information with potential competitors. Relatively routine projects are subcontracted to small- and medium-sized firms, so that the two tenants can guard their industrial secrets. Further, because these projects have little high-tech content, the subcontractors are not high-tech firms, nor do they employ skilled labor. This atmosphere of distrust is basically a pole of repulsion: the small- and mid-sized high-tech firms have little to gain in this prestigious closed club that this economic development project has become, and in which land rents are excessive.

Hansen (1990)

Will Nonresident Consumer Spending Sustain Regional Prosperity?

If heavy investment in communications technology is ineffective, perhaps by investing in amenities or entertainment, an area could buy its prosperity. We keep repeating that areas need cultural amenities to entice skilled professionals to consider relocating. If these investments are such great ideas, where are the private entrepreneurs? If these goods are excludable or rival, what mandate does government have to be responsible for their provision? We will look at six alternative economic bases: tourism, arts, sports, casinos, outdoor recreation, and retirees.

Tourism

By definition, tourism brings in outside money and qualifies as an export industry (Chapter 7). Tourism has direct, indirect, and induced impacts, like any other increase in final demand. If local handicrafts are sold in souvenir shops, tourism could open up a new market for locally produced goods. In addition, renovation dictated by tourism creates a positive image for the locality, not only for current residents, but also for future residents, those who are tempted to relocate or invest in the area.

Nevertheless, there are negative impacts from tourism. First, tourism jobs are low paid with low productivity. Employees are part time, low skilled, seasonal, and predominantly female or workers from the secondary labor market. The **secondary labor market** is one where wages, job security, and benefits are at a minimum. These jobs are not ideal for the household's main wage earner.

Second, competition for tourists is intense. Without continuously adding new attractions, a tourism destination will not attract repeat visitors. Third, tourism requires that local governments expand budgets for the administration of investments, public transportation, police and fire protection, corrections, and parks and recreation. Fourth, what is the opportunity cost of tax money spent on tourism? What else could have been produced if the money were invested elsewhere? Finally, because tourism is at best a club good, if not a private good, why is government using tax money to invest in and produce tourist attractions? Where are the private entrepreneurs?[9]

Arts

Quality cultural industries improve the image of an area and may provide the advantage needed to attract professionals and skilled workers. Arts and culture fall under the category of "merit" goods or goods that government provides, because the private and nonprofit sector will not provide enough of them according to some opinions. Is this type of subsidy efficient for economic growth? Cultural industries generate employment multipliers between 1.3 and 1.5, but 27% of the employees in this industry belong to the secondary labor market and only work part time.[10]

Sports Teams and Stadiums

Empirical studies are unanimous in rejecting the construction or renovation of sports stadiums as motors of economic development. In effect, sports stadiums often impede development. The economic impact of a

---

[9] Wong (1996); Williams (1997).
[10] Williams, Shore, and Huber (1995).

professional sports franchise on an area is statistically insignificant. No appreciable amount of new spending is generated. Instead, spectators spend their entertainment budget in the sports stadiums and surrounding shops rather than in other local establishments. This is called a ***substitution effect***. Professional sports affiliates win big time, while other local business providers lose big time. Except for the superstar athletes and owners, the rest of the spending on economic development supports only labor-intensive, unskilled, low-wage, seasonal labor.

For example, in each of 15 studies that Noll and Zimbalist (1997) examined, the local economic impact of sports teams and stadiums was drastically less than proponents promise. In fact, a $10 million subsidy may promise $100 million in benefits, but produce actual benefits that are negative. The local multiplier of sports stadiums will be smaller if spending is filtered through the sports stadiums instead of through other local entertainment venues. This will happen if the alternative local recreation and entertainment choices have stronger backward linkages to the community (Chapter 5). Local governments subsidize stadiums only because of local politics. They are blackmail victims: professional sports teams will go elsewhere unless their new stadium is built.[11]

Casinos

In some areas, gaming facilities are an ideal economic development package, especially for economically struggling counties with few resources. Baby boomers who have more disposable income contribute to the increase in demand for games of chance. Casino gaming can be a successful development strategy. Aging baby boomers have more disposable income, so the demand for gaming is up. Overall receipts in casino counties grew 46% faster than in similar counties without casinos. The service sector alone grew twice as fast and per capita income increased by nearly 5%. State and local government spending did not increase proportionally for other activities.[12]

Casinos: Do They Attract New Revenues or Reshuffle Old Ones?

Casinos promote a modest amount of tourism, but it is difficult to determine whether the casinos are

---

[11] Baade and Dye (1990); Noll and Zimbalist (1997); Wassmer (2001).
[12] Rephann et al. (1997).

redistributing the entertainment budgets of residents away from other types of recreation. In South Korea, the finding answer is simple: only people with foreign passports are allowed in the casinos. For casinos in other countries, a rule of thumb is that when more than half the gamblers come from outside the area, the industry attracts new recreational expenditures.

The best locations for a casino are either relatively isolated areas close to large urban centers, or next to the border of a state that prohibits gaming. These locations also mitigate any negative social consequences of gaming because the area exports problems right back home with the gamblers. In fact, allegations that casinos would aggravate crimes such as prostitution or compulsive gambling and family problems have not been confirmed by empirical evidence. Such problems would exist in the absence of the casino.

Rephann et al. (1997), Eadington (1998),
Pearce (1999)

To function, casinos need to import enough trained gaming professionals. These professionals will benefit from the higher paying jobs, until the local employees can be trained. Many casinos are referred to as economic islands or economies within an economy. They provide restaurants, hotels, and live entertainment. They sell souvenirs and sometimes add other forms of recreation such as golf. Casinos have few backward linkages, and thus might undermine the impact of an existing entertainment industry. If an interstate highway leads directly to the casino, gamblers show up, spend money at the casino, and return home without visiting other businesses.[13]

Betting on a Winner

In Minnesota, the major effect of the Indian casinos has been to redistribute wealth from the more affluent

---

[13] Vinje (1996); Rephann et al. (1997); Eadington (1998); Pearce (1999).

urban centers to the state's poorer rural areas. Most casinos offer full-time, nonseasonal jobs that include health benefits. Wages are between $5 and $8 per hour, plus tips.

In the short run, tribal casinos stimulate local economies, create jobs, increase property values, and set a de facto higher minimum wage for rural workers who are not associated with them. They also reduce the number of people on public assistance. If the gaming proceeds are invested in tribal schools and educational scholarships, improved housing, medical clinics, and establishment of industrial parks, casinos can have a viable long-run impact.

Vinje (1996), Rephann et al. (1997)

Outdoor Recreation Activities

Wilderness recreation is a weak economic base because expenditures by visitors are not large enough to influence local county economies. Most campers carry their own supplies. In southern Utah, Keith and Fawson (1995) estimated that wilderness users contribute a maximum of 2.5% in any one county and less than 1% of total sales to most counties. In a study of 250 counties in the Intermountain West, Duffy-Deno (1997) found no evidence that supported the contention that a federal wilderness is associated either directly or indirectly with an increased population density or growth in employment density.

On the other hand, if agritourism is considered outdoor recreation, this industry has supplemented incomes in rural areas of the United States, the United Kingdom, and France. This type of tourist activity includes anything from bed and breakfasts to dude ranches (where tourists do work on the farm or ranch).[14]

Retirees and Income Transfers

Some rural areas have found that their incomes and the numbers of jobs increase with the arrival of relatively young, healthy retirees. This could be true, but in general, retirees are more of a Pandora's Box than a panacea.

---

[14] Keith and Fawson (1995); Duffy-Deno (1997); Disez (1999).

The fixed portion of the income of retirees could create stability in areas that are susceptible to employment gyrations from existing industries, but a large portion of retirement income fluctuates with the stock market. When the Federal Reserve System increases the money supply, thereby causing interest rates to drop, spurring an increase in aggregate demand in the national economy, a local economy heavily reliant on retirement income will suffer.

Jobs created by spending of the elderly are low paying, more often directed toward retail or service sectors. If localities do not offer an adequate mixture of retail or services, the elderly buy elsewhere. As they age, some elderly outlive their assets, increasing the demand for local income maintenance programs, meals-on-wheels, and in-home nursing care funded by local taxes.

Retirees generally live in periurban areas that provide access to quality health care. The quality of the schools does not concern them, but they do want more public transportation, grocery delivery services, and shuttle buses for the handicapped as well as meals-on-wheels programs.

So, can we spend our way to prosperity? The short answer appears to be: not often. The best that such programs do is siphon off taxes that would have increased jobs in secondary labor markets chosen by household spending—to create secondary labor market jobs chosen by government. So, if government cannot efficiently boost local demand, can it impact its aggregate supply curve?[15]

The Effects of Economic Development Policy

According to William Alonso (1988), most regional development policy resembles the cargo cults in the South Pacific, especially of New Guinea and the Melanesian Islands during World War II. The natives noticed the arrival of American troops who cleared and leveled oblong pieces of the jungle on nearby islands, placed lights along the full length of these strips, and after a while, a giant silver bird landed, carrying with it all sorts of valuable treasures. The cargo cults tried to attract the silver bird to their islands by imitating the Americans. Unfortunately, their lighted "landing strips" just could not attract these gift-laden silver birds. Regionally, modern "cargo cults" build industrial zones, enhance infrastructure, offer tax advantages, and then wait like a spider in a web for what Alonso calls the mysterious silver bird of industry to land. Sometimes it comes, but generally not.[16]

---

[15] Hoppe (1991); Debertin (1993).
[16] Alonso (1988); Wikipedia (n.d.).

Waves of Economic Development

State and local economic development programs in the United States started during the 1930s with Mississippi and other Southern states aggressively chasing smoke-stacks, that is, recruiting branch plants of northern firms. During this *first wave*, jobs were transferred, not created. Developers exclusively provided the necessary money. In this "beggar thy neighbor" strategy, the jurisdiction that provides enough incentives for a firm to relocate, benefits at the expense of the other.

In the mid-1980s, a *second wave* of programs targeted start-ups, small businesses, and existing businesses. Most of the economic development funds still took the form of financial assistance, but the second-wave programs also added special business services. Business incubators provided low-cost office space with common secretarial staff and office help for small firms, for example. The second-wave programs lacked accountability and the support of current businesses. Services were fragmented and poorly organized.

State and local economic development budgets were slashed in the late 1980s, and the "economic development industry" had to reinvent itself. The resulting *third wave* layers ideas such as market-based initiatives, public–private partnerships, and the use of quasi-public agencies to provide what is now termed a "holistic" approach to economic development. A reengineered local government offers a wider range of public services to "steer rather than row," and "empower rather than serve" local growth components. Whatever.

Lowery and Gray (1992), Bartik (1993)

Economic development programs leave a controversial legacy. First, government programs that try to eliminate regional disparities often have the opposite effect of what was intended. They create instead, slow-growth regions reliant on governmental transfer payments. Such programs either kill the entrepreneurial spirit or redirect it to chasing government funds rather than efficiently providing goods and services that the market wants.

Economic Development in the Black Belt

According to Bellamy and Parks (1994) the South's economic development strategy of "chasing smoke-stacks" was successful for a while in luring labor intensive industries, such as textiles and food processing industries, as well as women's clothing and shoes. The firms that came to the Black Belt counties were, in contrast, smaller, low-volume plants specialized in products such as catfish and fish byproducts.

The Black Belt is composed of 623 Southern rural counties for which at east a quarter of the popu-lation are minorities. These counties are characterized by high poverty levels, low education levels, and high unemployment rates. This results from an education system that does not provide skills necessary to be productive in very many industries. Areas with a lower-educated population can only attract manufacturing industries for routine jobs that rely on unskilled workers. They compete with workers in low-income countries for these positions. Wages from these jobs may be so low that living standards and quality of life do not improve. To remedy the hazards of this competition and to ensure that the Black Belt firms will remain, these firms are given generous subsidies and tax advantages. The result is an insufficient tax base that cannot provide a decent education, thereby creating a new generation of poverty. Thus, accor-ding to Joshi et al., tax abatement policies are among the major obstacles to alleviating poverty in these regions.

Bellamy and Parks (1994), Joshi et al. (2000)

Second, the empirical track record of local economic development incentives is difficult to judge, because it is difficult to compare the impact of the industrial policy of one state to another. Interstate analysis is tricky because it requires detailed knowledge of the tax system of each state. For example, Iowa can offer firms an exemption from paying property tax on machinery and equipment. Neither Pennsylvania nor Minnesota would ever offer such an exemption, because such property is not taxed to begin with.

Third, policies from the second wave have not replaced the first, but added to them. (See the box entitled *Waves of Economic Development*.) Likewise, the third wave merely added more to the established basket of development tools, so it is very difficult to determine with aggregate data the efficiency of each successive wave.

Finally, the traditional method of establishing whether some policy or other influenced firm location is to survey firms. However, the responses to surveys of this nature are questionable. Why would businesses ever admit that they would have chosen their locations even without the subsidy package?

Conventional wisdom of economists asserts that local incentives cannot change firm location decisions. These incentives amount to no more than "corporate welfare:"[17]

- Empirical studies consistently find that either local incentive programs are not cost effective, or the projects would have been completed even without the fiscal stimulus.
- Even if economic developers do succeed in increasing jobs or wages locally, in-migration or increased commuting from outside the area would quickly offset any advantages for the local labor market.
- Subsidized financing or reduced interest rates are not cost effective from the state–local government viewpoint.

A 1958 study of small business finance sponsored by the Federal Reserve concluded that the availability of financial capital and credit was not an obstacle to the development of new businesses or the expansion of existing ones, unless the business is extremely risky. This conclusion has never been disputed. Even risky enterprises can get capital, albeit at higher rates or perhaps by sharing equity with investors.

Decreasing the price of capital encourages an inefficient substitution of capital for labor. If the goal is to create jobs, subsidizing capital expenditure makes sense only if capital and labor are complementary inputs in production. Government subsidy of an unsuccessful firm merely prolongs its ultimate death. The cost of providing financial assistance to localities is large given the high-risk investments.[18]

---

[17] Netzer (1991); Bartik (1993); Wassmer (1994).

[18] Alonso (1988); Higgins and Savoie (1988); Netzer (1991); Lowery and Gray (1992); Bartik (1993); Wassmer (1994); Fisher and Peters (1997).

Rent-Seeking Behavior

Rent seeking is the attempt to capture excess profits (economic rents) bestowed by government. In Schumpeter's model (Chapter 8), profit-seeking entrepreneurs drive the creative destruction that leads to economic prosperity. Similarly, microeconomic theory asserts that individuals follow their self-interest and weigh the marginal benefits against the marginal costs of their actions. Those who attempt to receive economic rents will be those who expect that the marginal benefit of having this rent is greater than its marginal cost to them. The benefits of being awarded economic rents are large to the beneficiaries. The costs are diffused among all taxpayers, including firms that are in direct competition with the rent seeker for market share or for inputs.[19]

Economic Development Incentive Tools

We will now evaluate several components of the subsidy packages that local developers offer to new firms, including subsidies, tax abatement policies, tax increment financing (TIF), and enterprise zones (EZs).

Think About It …

Assar Lindback, the chair of the Nobel Prize in Economics selection committee, commented on Sweden's economic development policy.

"It is not by planting trees in a desert or subsidizing tree planting in a desert created by politicians that government can promote … industry, but by refraining from measures that create a desert environment."

In your opinion, does your locality plant trees in a desert or create and maintain an environment favorable to the growth of "trees" in the economy? Defend your argument.

Does Local Tax Policy Matter in Firm Location?

Empirically, differences in state fiscal policies do not explain differences in state growth. But that does not mean that the fiscal policies do not matter. States generally keep their overall tax rates in line with those in neighboring

---

[19] Hite (1993); Anderson and Wassmer (1995).

states: some states replace an income tax with higher sales taxes or extra high taxes on tobacco, alcohol or gasoline. However, the average taxpayer pays around the same percentage of income in taxes despite these differences. Because there is little variation in overall fiscal policies among the states, it would be difficult for any analysis to discern the actual impact of each individual nuance.[20]

Subsidy Games

Public investment could play a positive role in economic development. Government subsidies helped build railroads to the Pacific Northwest; Seattle was able to create a comparative advantage in national and international trade. Subsidies are reported to be the reason that nonfarm employment in southeastern states grew by 2.5% compared with 1.8% for the rest of the country.

However, for the most part subsidies are the rewards from a game played by the economic development industry and firms that attempt to sniff out economic development rents. We outline two types of these games here. In one game, a new firm will seem to pursue a community in which it could not survive and have that community offer a plump subsidy package. It then goes to a second community, the one in which it really wants to locate, and in which it would locate without any incentives at all. Then, it tries to persuade their local economic developer to match the package that the first community offered. The result is an unnecessary subsidy to that firm, and rewards to the firm that demonstrate sound strategic bargaining behavior.[21]

Oechessler (1994) describes a second type of game in which subsidy allocation decisions easily turn into a signaling game between the firm and the city (or state). The firm has done its own location analysis and knows its different relocation possibilities. But the city is not privilege to this information. A relatively large firm could use the relocation as a threat ("I will leave this city" or "I will not come to this city") if it does not receive a subsidy. For the city, this means an actual or potential loss of tax revenues, of jobs, and even prestige. The city needs to make two choices: it must assess the probability that the firm is bluffing and it must determine the amount of the subsidy package that the rival community can give.

How is this game played? Only the firm has its private information, so it must make the first move. It announces the possible relocation. Suppose that this firm is in the city of Springfield and that it is not doing as well as it would like to. It may claim that wages and taxes are too high, and it can no

---

[20] Wasylenko (1981); Mofidi and Stone (1990); Papke (1991); Yu, Wallace, and Nardinelli (1991); Netzer (1997).

[21] Schmidt and Sherwood-Call (1989); Farrell (1996).

longer compete in its own market. The firm announces that it will move to the city of Avon where it can prosper. The firm also leaks information that wages and taxes are lower in Avon and that Avon's economic developer promised very generous subsidies if it moves. (Subsidies from Avon are required, you see, because relocating is costly.)

The economic development team of Springfield now must determine whether the firm is bluffing or not. The firm's threat to move will not be credible unless it specifies its moving plans and actually starts negotiations with Avon. If the story is accurate, and Springfield does nothing, the city loses jobs and tax revenues. If, on the other hand, the employees also leave with their employer, housing prices will decline when large numbers of houses flood the market. Life in Springfield will be bleak.

Springfield must either offer or refuse to offer the subsidy. If the subsidy is granted, the firm will stay. However, if the subsidy request is refused, the firm must decide whether to stay or to leave. If the firm stays after the request for a subsidy is denied, it loses credibility in any subsequent games it wants to play.

The provision of such gifts to a new or existing firm may have detrimental effects for an existing firm that does not play the game. Hite (1993) summed it best by saying that much of the difficulty in using economic development incentives is a struggle between the new firms, who want artificially created economic rents, and the existing firms, who want to keep the rents that they were awarded.

Empirical Analysis of Regional Development Policies

Evidence has consistently found that regional policy instruments and financial assistance payments are ineffective.[22] Although local industrial policies had substantial effects on manufacturing employment and per capita income in the 1970s, subsidies had little impact in the 1980s.

Neither variations in taxes nor subsidies influenced location decisions of high-technology manufacturing or most services in metropolitan areas in the United States between 1977 and 1984. On the other hand, EZs and university research parks did have an influence because of the localization economies. Empirical analyses unanimously agree that firm location decisions are dominated by three essential elements:

1. The product market,
2. The quality of labor, and
3. The quality of the transportation networks.

---

[22] See for example, Wasylenko (1981); Wolkoff (1985); Mofidi and Stone (1990); Yu, Wallace, and Nardinelli (1991); Ó hUallacháin and Satterthwaite (1992); Wassmer (1992); Wren (1994); Anderson and Wassmer (1995); Kelly, Henderson, and Seaman (1997).

Thus, an economic development policy that consists of increased educational attainment and school quality as well as sound transportation infrastructure is the most effective recipe for regional growth.[23]

Firm Location Tendencies Transcend Culture

Polèse and Champagne (1999) compared location patterns of 16 industries in Canada and Mexico at two points in time. They determined that the principles of classic location theory apply identically to nations independent of their stages of development. Both the relative stability over time and the relative similarity of patterns in Canada and Mexico suggest that industrial location is more predictable than otherwise thought.

The spatial distribution of activity exhibits similar patterns in both nations. Urban industrial special-ization varies systematically with city size and distance. Moreover, location patterns resist the various attempts to change them. Policies that try to attract manufacturing to small peripheral cities or otherwise radically alter location trends are just as difficult to implement in both countries.

Polèse and Champagne (1999)

Tax Abatement Policies

To minimize production costs or to maximize profits, businesses choose locations that are close to input and product markets (Chapter 4). Some local jurisdictions provide location incentives to counteract either their high crime rates or their high taxes that might prevent firms from considering their areas as viable locations. Proponents of such policies never explain why these costs are not capitalized into land values as they are everywhere else. Proponents instead offer the cumulative causality argument (Chapter 5) according to which a dynamic agglomeration will produce localization or urbanization economies if enough firms respond.

Unlike investments in infrastructure, tax abatements can vary and are applied in smaller increments. Therefore, tax abatements are tools preferred

---

[23] ÓhUallacháin and Satterthwaite (1992); Carroll and Wasylenko (1994); Wren (1994).

by local developers. However, this practice results in inefficient tax price for resident taxpayers. The added costs to taxpayers are greater than the additional community benefits. The size of tax abatement packages varies with the amount of capital invested per job. Firm-specific tax abatements result in decreased home values, decreased local expenditures per capita, increased local property tax rates, and increased state subsidies to local governments. Often, taxpayers in rural, low-income parts of the state subsidize generous tax abatement packages in the urban center. The opportunity cost of funds is seldom included in the cost-benefit analysis of such programs.

A final problem with tax abatements is that they are awarded quite arbitrarily: it all depends on the firm demanding the abatement and the committee being addressed. Abatements are almost always awarded to the rent seekers upon request. These awards are costly, not only because of the loss of tax revenue, but also because the awards will go to firms that would have located in the jurisdiction anyway, or to firms that will generate few external benefits.[24]

When Incentives Are Not Popular

The popularity of economic incentives depends on the median household income and the effective property tax price of the local public services. The higher the median income, the longer a municipality will wait before granting manufacturing property tax abatements. This reflects increased resentment of citizens who recognize the inherent favoritism of these entitlements. Industrial development is an inferior good, and the residents with higher incomes are less interested in its financing.

Moreover the higher the property tax price of local public services, the lower is the probability that the municipality will grant tax abatement. Waiving tax payments for new firms will increase the congestion and thereby decrease the probability of residents being able to use the local services. This reduction increases the tax price of the services that they do use.

Anderson and Wassmer (1995)

---

[24] Wolkoff (1985); Wassmer (1992); Anderson and Wassmer (1995); Kelly, Henderson, and Seaman (1997).

Tax Increment Financing

Rather than offering a direct subsidy, some municipalities try to attract firms via tax increment financing (TIF). This financing allows a city to "capture" the additional tax revenue generated by a firm and use it specifically to fund public projects that directly benefit that firm. If TIF is a statewide program, then the residents of the entire rest of the state are affected by one city's use of it. As occurs with tax abatement policies, a program instituted in cities with above average per capita incomes is subsidized by low-income taxpayers living in another part of the state.

Essentially, any increase in tax revenues resulting from redevelopment in the TIF district goes into a TIF fund that is used to subsidize even more redevelopment activities for areas with high unemployment rates. The TIF is not a new tax; however, it does redirect the allocation of tax dollars. A municipality uses the increases in taxes (tax increments) that result from an area's redevelopment to subsidize its redevelopment costs. TIF allows cities to avoid the red tape and bureaucracy of intergovernmental aid, municipal debt limits, and the need for voter approval.

TIF creates many problems:[25]

- An area could become a TIF district even if unemployment problems are minor or nonexistent.
- Overlapping jurisdictions such as school districts lose tax money within the TIF district, and the affected taxing bodies lose all taxes that they would normally get.
- Because TIF is used as an urban revitalization tool, it offers nothing to existing businesses and residents, but their taxes reward property absentee owners or businesses that create their own problems by charging excessive rents, by not maintaining their property, or by being too inefficient to compete.
- Small businesses and households may be forced to relocate when their neighborhoods are destroyed to make way for the ambitious redevelopment projects that generate more taxes.
- If every town uses TIF to develop a shopping mall to try to attract shoppers from the neighboring town, neither the contiguous jurisdictions nor the state will see a net benefit (geographic substitution).

However, an empirical study by Man and Rosentraub (1998) shows that median owner-occupied housing values in cities that adopted TIF were 11% greater than in cities that did not adopt TIF, everything else being equal. If property values reflect an expanding economy, then a TIF program

---

[25] See for instance, Davis (1989); Dye and Sundberg (1998); Man and Rosentraub (1998); Dye and Merriman (2000).

potentially fosters growth and enhances both the property base and the economic returns for a community. Initially, there is no measurable effect because the growth in property values is measurable 2 years after implementation, but even in this case, cities that adopt TIF grow more slowly than those that do not. This is because the TIF reallocates capital to less productive locations. The blighted areas are growing, but at the expense of the rest of the city.[26]

Enterprise Zones

In most Western countries, the escalation in the cost of regulation and taxation during the post-World War II years coincided with the slowdown in economic growth and a gradual increase in average unemployment rates. Taxes and regulation distort incentives, introduce rigidities into adjustment processes, and result in inefficient uses of resources. Because of this, economists urge widespread deregulation or regulation reform. Deregulation throughout society eliminates the paternalistic governmental protection of consumers from incompetent or unscrupulous producers and leans more toward *caveat emptor*. In this light, some areas have created zones wherein firms located within the boundaries face fewer restrictions and lower taxes.

Zones of this nature have a long history. In the 1500s, the Hanseatic cities of northern Europe were once defined as zones of free trade and enterprise. They allowed the merchants, bankers, and craftsmen to carry on business free from the mercantilistic and guild policies.

Recently, Enterprize Zones (EZs) have been revived to rehabilitate older urban areas suffering from economic or physical decay. State governments can designate a specific number of "economically depressed areas" that may benefit from a vast array of subsidies and tax cuts. But what area would not benefit from tax cuts and subsidies? These zones were popularized in 1981 by Peter Hall, a British geography professor. While traveling in Asia, Professor Hall was impressed with the level of economic development in Singapore and Hong Kong. His mission was to create a little "Hong Kong" in a blighted corner of London or perhaps at the dockyards in Liverpool. Since then, many such zones have been initiated around the world.

The success of these zones is debatable. In England, the PA Cambridge Economic Consultants calculated that each job in the zones only cost £8500 ($13,934 US) of government revenues in 1989, whereas researchers with the Department for Transport, Local Government and the Regions (2001) found no significant impact on the unemployment of the distressed areas. The zones were placed on land that is mostly owned by the government or a

---

[26] Davis (1989); Wassmer (1994); Dye and Sundberg (1998); Man and Rosentraub (1998); Dye and Merriman (2000); Peters and Fisher (2002).

nationalized industry. Business properties do not pay property taxes. The Treasury reimbursed the cities for the lost revenue. Building and equipment could be fully depreciated in one year. However, only one deregulation affected the zoning: as long as the basic designs follow uncomplicated criteria, the building permits were issued quickly. Butler (1992) referred to EZs as nothing but urban industrial parks.

Usually, EZ incentives are available to businesses for a 10-year period and include exemptions from property taxes, accelerated depreciation allowances on buildings, rapid governmental action on planning, or other approvals and a simplification of the bureaucracy.

Firms within the EZs have lower production costs because they do not have to deal with regulators. The lax regulations and low taxes increase output per dollar of payroll. Because technological innovation involves risk (potential lawsuits with consumers, for example) and is often confronted with archaic regulations, government intervention is not as rigorous, promoting innovation. Free of some constraints, firms are free to innovate, leading to a greater variety of output which benefits consumers.

Nevertheless, social costs of EZs are many.[27] For instance, resources such as labor or firms that supply inputs (backward linkages) are diverted from an area that was initially viable toward the EZ when the large firm relocates. In addition, EZs decrease tax revenue and generate a need to raise other taxes, impose new taxes, or lower government spending. The main beneficiaries from EZs are landowners and the building contractors. The new and small enterprises gain nothing from being there.[28]

Measuring the Net Revenue Loss per Job Caused by Enterprise Zones

Peters and Fisher (2002) sampled 75 enterprise zones in 13 states between 1990 and 1998. They calculate that on average, state and local governments gain about $18,000 in revenue over a 20-year period for each job that was created in the zones. However, governments lose about $6,600 for every job that receives unnecessary incentives. More jobs siphon off revenues from

[27] Erickson and Syms (1986); Talbot (1988); Nissen (1989); Lever (1992); Papke (1993); Boarnet and Bogart (1996); Peters and Fisher (2002) cite other examples.
[28] Grubel (1984); Erickson and Syms (1986); Talbot (1988); Nissen (1989); Lever (1992); Zuckerman (1992); Papke (1993); Wassmer (1994); Boarnet and Bogart (1996); Peters and Fisher (2002).

the state and locality at a rate of $6,600 than are providing the gain of $18,000. All in all, the state and local governments lose about $59,000 for every job created.

Peters and Fisher (2002)

Enterprise Zones: Easy Come, Easy Go

Wherever they are found, enterprise zones seem to be at best an arbitrary industrial policy tool that provides no new investment and no measurable increase in employment. Any measurable employment change occurs because firms move in from outside the zone. The incentives offered in these enterprise zones tend to favor short-distance moves. This tendency generates considerable resentment between local authorities in and outside the enterprise zones. The Clydebank EZ, around Glasgow, Scotland employed 5400 workers, but only 31 percent of the jobs were directly attributable to the enterprise zone incentives. After adjusting for job losses due to short-distance moves, Lever (1992) calculated a cost to the government of £23,000 ($40,625 US) per job.

That the benefits from an enterprise zone are all capitalized in the value of the land within its geographic boundaries, significantly increasing rents of industrial buildings in the zone, while those in the periphery drop. Note also that innovation is not automatic for firms within the zone. In a study of Tyneside, United Kingdom, firms outside the zone were significantly more innovative than those within the zone.

Erickson and Syms (1986), Talbot (1988),
Nissen (1989), Lever (1992), Papke (1993),
Boarnet and Bogart (1996), Peters
and Fisher (2002)

In summary, economic development incentive tools do not deliver clear-cut evidence that they work. The section evaluated subsidies, tax abatement policies, TIF, and EZs. First, it is not clear that higher taxes repel firms. If they do, it is because of the types of aid that the tax money supports rather than the tax bill in and of itself. Firms look at the overall tax–expenditure picture. Potential subsidies create signaling games between the firm and the city developers. Empirically, variations in taxes and subsidies do not influence location decisions of firms.

Then why is this practice followed? Some policy makers assert that even if the policies are not always effective, it is necessary to do something (to help the poor). Sound bites for political campaigns favor politicians who "create jobs." Who could possibly be against helping a family to become independent? Sound bites ignore the following questions: who pays for these jobs, and how much? Bartik (1991) determined that economic development policies are not only costly, but that they have a negative effect on the lowest 20% of the income distribution, because many programs are funded by an increase in personal income taxes or a reduction in social programs.

In general, beneficiaries of such spending are easily identifiable and the amount by which they benefit is large to them. However, those who pay for these benefits have no idea how much they are paying—and the amount from each taxpayer is relatively small. Even with full disclosure and complete transparency, it is difficult to count the number of jobs created or lost, as well as their respective locations.

The only reason for the existence of these "economic development" tools is that they signal a "pro-business climate." Local leaders cannot "do nothing" because if they do not play the economic incentive game well, they will not have the possibility to parade their economic success and get reelected. The result is a competition between localities that fuels an "arms race" mentality.[29]

Is the Battle Worth It?

Competition among cities can be good, especially competition to see which city is most attractive, which has the best quality schools, or provides the best infrastructure. Such competition forces local governments to provide optimal levels of taxation and services. However, when this state or local competition includes subsidy packages and preferential tax treatment for firms, the efficiency of such competition is questionable.[30]

---

[29] Ellis and Rogers (2000).

[30] Netzer (1991); Mattey and Spiegel (1995); Barlett and Steele (1998); Klier and Johnson (2000).

Bribe or Blackmail? How Much Is Your Job Worth?

In 1980, Tennessee bid "only" $11,000 per job for the creation of a Nissan plant. In 1993, Indiana proposed $451 million to attract a 6300-employee United Airlines maintenance facility ($72,000 per job). This maintenance plant closed in 2003. Alabama captured a new Mercedes plant for an incentive package worth $169,000 per new job. In 1995, Kentucky used $350,000 per job in tax credits to attract a 400-employee steel plant and $125 million in expenditures to lure a Toyota plant to leave Missouri. In 1997, Pennsylvania gave $307 million in incentives to a Norwegian company to reopen part of Philadelphia's naval shipyard and hire 950 people at a cost of $323,000 per job. Wouldn't it be more efficient to give each person half the cost of their job and help them start a business?

Rio Rancho, New Mexico, attracted Intel Corporation, along with other firms, but it had problems providing adequate public services like schooling. Students had classrooms in trailers, played on dusty playgrounds, and had to use portable toilets.

Barlett and Steele (1998), Mattey and Spiegel (1995)

Arguments in Favor of Local Tax Competition

Local tax competition may enhance efficiency. First, if the tax competition is efficient, it could increase or create agglomeration economies in a locality, especially if the target firm purchases local inputs and supports spin-off firms. Second, if the per-unit cost of public goods falls, as in infrastructure, the marginal cost of providing a new firm and its workers with such services would be less than the revenue that these services would generate. In this instance, a government can move closer to the optimal level of provision by subsidizing firms and thereby increasing the use of public goods.

Finally, to the extent that a financial aid package succeeds in attracting a firm to relocate, a popular argument is that the new jobs will help the community retain its young adult population, and thus its human capital investment. A study by Klier and Johnson (2000) estimated that the presence of automobile plants had a significant and positive effect on migration patterns to the host counties and to the adjacent counties. The large plants that employ 1000 or more people had the most impact in migration to a specific county.

Arguments Against Local Competition

While tax competition can be good, competition directed at specific businesses leads to adverse consequences. First, such tax competition reduces revenues to localities and thus leads to inadequate levels of public goods and services. Such revenue losses are partly offset by increased taxes from other sources. In other words, the established residents and firms pay higher tax prices to receive the same amount of public benefits.

Second, states that involve themselves with tax competition most often end up with fewer jobs and smaller tax revenues than that expected from the target firm. In auction markets, the term *winner's curse* means that bidders have different perspectives about the quality of the good on which they are bidding. The "cursed" bidder is the one that is the most optimistic about the quality of the program, offers the highest bid, and is stuck with a potential boondoggle.

No Thanks, Saturn

General Motors' Saturn plant near Spring Hill, Tennessee, began producing automobiles in November 1990. Negotiations for that site were carried out by the state government with no local input. The firm announced it would provide 6,000 jobs, but subsequently hired only 3,200 people. General Motors specified from the start that only its present and past employees would be hired there, but many people moved to Spring Hill anyway hoping to find jobs. They were not hired. A large number of the migrants remained in Spring Hill, unemployed. Most new jobs went to former General Motors workers who were laid off from plants elsewhere.

A telephone survey of about 800 residents in June 1990, and again in June 1991, confirmed that few residents were happy about the new plant. Respondents felt that the Saturn plant would prompt better medical care and better roads. However, 84 percent feared an increase in property taxes and 35 percent thought that the plant was not paying its fair share of taxes. Most respondents agreed that Saturn caused crowded public schools, and that school quality would deteriorate. A substantial number of respondents also feared an increase in

> housing prices, which their own property tax bill would reflect, creating a burden for those on fixed incomes. They note also that the increased crime rates were caused by the plant and that Saturn made their community a worse place to live.
>
> Accountability: The Newsletter of Business
> Incentives Clearinghouse (1999),
> Bartik (1991a), Foltz et al. (1993)

Third, the arms race hypothesis postulates that states tend to increase their incentive offerings to new firms if such incentive programs are used in the states that are perceived to be direct competitors. The result is a prisoner's dilemma type of game playing among the states, like an arms race between enemy countries. When a state discovers that its neighbor actually attracted new investment, it is forced to offer tax reductions merely to stay in the game. The neighboring state then retaliates by decreasing their taxes even more. The result is an epidemic of tax decreases with little actual change in the stock of capital in the two states. Workers are worse off because they will be assessed higher taxes to pay for the public services.

If the arms race hypothesis is true, the escalating level of incentives erodes the associated marginal social benefits. Interstate competition provokes a continual increase in the costs of economic development, whereas the benefits remain essentially the same. Net benefits tumble. Public money spent on ***place-based programs*** where a handful of firms benefit, produced very low, and sometimes negative, rates of return on the investment. This money could give positive results if it financed ***people-based programs*** such as education or early childhood development, for which the expected rates of return are between 7 and 16%.

Rolnick (2000), for one, has called for a national ban on tax competition. He supported a bill that all economic development incentives be taxed at a 100% rate by the federal government. This law would reduce the spiraling inefficiencies caused by state and local economic development spending.[31]

Summary and Conclusions

This chapter investigates the government's role in altering the growth path for a regional economy. The role varies widely with the models used to analyze the economy.

---

[31] Mattey and Spiegel (1995); Jenn and Nourzad (1996); Rolnick (2000).

1. The economic base model anchored in Keynesian analysis states that government spending is one of the key dependable factors used to increase equilibrium employment.
2. Neoclassical theory suggests that government spending may have a positive effect if it does not crowd out private investment, but if the spending comes from taxes generated in another area, jobs are promoted in one area and reduced in another.
3. The endogenous growth theory provides a role for club goods, if not public goods, such as good quality schools and infrastructure, property rights enforcement, and stimulating technology and research.

Evaluating public policy is done by examining the efficiency and equity aspects of a policy. From the standpoint of production efficiency, we want to know whether the government or private sector would be the better provider of certain goods and services. From the standpoint of distributional efficiency on the basis of Pareto optimality, we ask ourselves if someone is made better off without making another worse off. The principle of equity considers the questions: Who pays? Who benefits?

We then looked at the efficacy of public investments in highways, education, telecommunications infrastructure, and technology. Depending on whether there are backwash effects or spread effects, highways could benefit a periurban area or impede its growth. If the urban area is growing because of increased demand for products made in the hinterland, or if the urban area is starting to decentralize, the spread effects will flow along good roads and highways. If, however, urban growth siphons resources from the rural area, good roads will intensify the backwash effect.

Investment in K-12 education has a solid impact on regional growth, not only in the parental migration effect, but also by increasing the productivity of future generations. Investment in universities has less impact because firms can hire educated workers coming from another state. However, if many states in a country try to free ride on the higher education investments of a few, the latter states will also decrease university funding. To the extent that states wish to accelerate local technology programs and lure high-tech industry, they must invest in research universities and have a source of highly skilled personnel. A good telecommunications infrastructure is required for growth, but it will not substitute for transportation infrastructure.

Many local and national governments have tried to create the perfect milieu for high-tech firms to survive, and they have successfully enticed the ingredients of such a milieu to locate in one place. However, they cannot legislate how far ideas in each firm spread to other firms. They cannot require that conversations take place freely and easily as they did in Silicon Valley in its heyday.

Some regional governments invest in tourism, the arts, sports stadiums, casinos, or wilderness recreation areas. Others renovate to attract retirees. These strategies may succeed in creating jobs, but the jobs that they create are low-wage, low-skill, part-time jobs. Less successful ventures such as sports stadiums and casinos will cause a redistribution of entertainment expenditures from industries that have larger multipliers to those industries with smaller local multipliers. Likewise, catering to retirees can decrease the possibility of generating higher paying jobs because logging, resource extraction, or large manufacturing facilities may destroy the amenities that enticed retirees to an area.

The results of economic development policies have not been stellar. Many initiatives merely relocate a firm from a few miles away, resulting in a "beggar thy neighbor" strategy. Other firms have every intention of locating where they did without the government subsidy, but because the incentives exist, they would be stupid to not take the role of a rent seeker. Subsidies or artificially reduced interest rates are an unnecessary enticement, because credit availability is not an obstacle to firm location. Likewise, tax abatement policies determined on a firm-by-firm basis are not fair to existing firms or residents who pay higher tax prices for their public goods. Firms have a relatively inelastic response to property tax rate differentials anyway. With respect to EZs, if such policies are good for some firms, why not make the entire country an enterprise zone?

Chapter Questions

1. On a dual continuum with rival–nonrival on a vertical axis and excludable–nonexcludable on a horizontal axis, categorize the following as public goods, private goods, or club goods.
   a. Chocolate chip cookies with nuts
   b. Public television
   c. Movie in an uncrowded theater
   d. Police protection
   e. Municipal golf courses
   f. Private golf courses
   g. Fishing in your state's largest lake
   h. National Guard
   i. Private marina
   j. Public marina
   k. Parking in a restricted parking lot
   l. Municipal liquor store
   m. Private liquor store
   n. Highways
   o. City streets

2. What types of projects are used to try to attract consumer spending? Who benefits and who loses because of this type of investment by a government entity?
3. Define rent-seeking behavior. Why is this type of behavior of interest in evaluating economic development policy?
4. Is the state better off or worse off if cities within the state compete for firms to relocate? Likewise, is the country better off or worse off if states compete for firms? Who wins and who loses when a firm relocates from one state to another?
5. Draw the bid-rent functions for three industries surrounding your city: commercial, industrial, and residential. Determine what will happen to land values and land use under the following scenarios:
    a. Say that the commercial sector expands, perhaps because of improved transportation and along with it, the demand for housing.
    b. Say that the low crime rates and superior schools increase the demand in your area for housing.
    c. Say that the property taxes on industrial property increased, resulting in an outflux of firms and lower demand for housing.

Research Assignments

1. Check in your local newspapers for local economic development activity by the local economic development authority in your area. What types of incentives have been given to potential firms starting in your area? What possibilities for government assistance in your area are available through the Small Business Administration or the Economic Development Administration according to their Web sites (http://www.sba.gov; http://www.eda.gov)?
2. From the *Census of Governments*, or an Internet search for the budget of your county, city and state, determine the local per capita expenditures on welfare, hospitals, health, highways, police protection, corrections, natural resources, park and recreation, sewerage and sanitation, and interest on general debt for your political entities. In what areas is your city or county spending a greater or lesser amount than that of your state?

Appendix: Measuring an Area's Economic Welfare

Economic development is designed to promote the economic welfare of a region. Several measures of welfare described below combine with shift-share analysis and location quotient analysis (Chapter 7) to help researchers and decision makers compare one area to another or identify potential regional trouble spots. We describe five of these measures.

1. The ***standard of living*** is a measure of relative spending power. To find it, divide per capita income by a cost of living index:

    $$\text{Standard of living} = \frac{\text{Per capita income}}{\text{Cost of living index}}.$$

    Per capita income for the United States is found in 10-year increments for almost every minor civil division (counties, cities, townships) from the Bureau of Census, http://www.census.gov. Estimates of local area per capita income are also found by county in CA 05 data set from the Regional Economic Information System (REIS) databank produced by the Bureau of Economic Analysis (http://www.bea.gov/bea/regional/reis). Regional CPI measures are available for some large metropolitan areas through the Bureau of Labor Statistics at http://www.bls.gov. The American Chamber of Commerce Research Associates (ACCRA) publishes data for cost of living indexes for 250 or so MSAs every quarter. Note that the calculation of the standard of living will be imprecise if one lives in a rural area of these MSAs or any area not included in the MSA.

2. A ***dependency ratio*** determines the proportion of people generally considered "unemployable" or dependent on others within the economy. The dependency ratio is found by dividing the number of children and elderly by the working age population, or

    Dependency ratio

    $$= \frac{\text{Population aged } 0-15 \text{ years} + \text{Population aged } 65+ \text{ years}}{\text{Population aged } 16-65}.$$

    A high dependency ratio points to a region with a larger population that is not of working age. The higher the dependency ratio, the fewer people are probably working or paying taxes and more people need to be looked after. Two variants of this ratio are the "child dependency ratio" which includes only people under 15, and the "old-age dependency ratio" which includes only those people 65 and older. Age distributions are available through the census Web site at http://www.census.gov.

3. The labor force participation rate calculates the proportion of people who are either working or looking for work, or

    Labor force participation rate

    $$= \frac{\text{Number employed} + \text{Number unemployed}}{\text{Population over age } 15}.$$

    Labor force participation rates can be calculated for the entire population (of a country, a state or a county) or for subsets of the population. In 2003, the male labor force participation rate in the United States was 68.9%. This means that 68.9% of the males over age 15 were working or looking for work. Female labor force participation rate for 2003 was 56.1%. Generally, this number varies indirectly with the dependency ratio.

A similar statistic is the **employment ratio**, or

$$\text{Employment ratio} = \frac{\text{Number of people employed}}{\text{Population over age 15}}.$$

In July 2004, the U.S. employment ratio was 62.5%, meaning that 62.5% of the people over age 15 were working.

The **unemployment rate** is calculated as the proportion of the labor force who are actively seeking employment, or

$$\text{Unemployment rate} = \frac{\text{Unemployed}}{\text{Employed} + \text{Unemployed}}.$$

These three measures are available by county and for some large cities through the Bureau of Labor Statistics Web site (http://www.bls.gov) under the Local Area Unemployment Statistics (LAUS) data set.

For several reasons, the changes in employment or unemployment over time (from January to January of the following year, for instance) are a better indicator of short-term economic difficulty than the actual unemployment rate. First, unemployment rate differences among jurisdictions may reflect both short-term differences in response to a recession and long-term differences in structural unemployment due to restructuring the local economy. Social factors like education or stigma about being unemployed may decrease the likelihood of residents in some localities to apply for unemployment compensation or to extend their job searches longer.

In addition, the discouraged worker phenomenon may be different in different jurisdictions. For instance, unemployed people in rural areas are more inclined to survive with multiple part-time jobs. If they lose one job, they are not officially unemployed because they are working. Finally, in sparsely populated areas, where turnover is rare, unemployed workers have a better chance of getting a job by commuting or moving to the larger city.

4. Gini coefficients are measures of income inequality. They vary from zero (complete inequality) to one (complete equality). Gini coefficients are generally calculated from individual-level data rather than grouped data. Methods of estimating Gini coefficients from grouped data call for the average income within each income group. Lacking a calculation for the mean, one can substitute the midpoint of each group, except for the highest income group, unless the researcher knows the top income in the region.

5. An alternative measure of income inequality using public data is **Sazama's index of inequality**, calculated using the following equation:[32]

$$IEQ_{it} = \sum_{q=1}^{5} \frac{(20 - P_{qt})^2}{5},$$

where t is the specific year, i is the category (e.g., gender, race, etc., if any), q is the income quintile, and P_{qt} is the percentage of people in each category of the income quintile q during year t. The smaller the index, the less is the inequality. To calculate this index:

1. Determine the proportion of people in each of the five income quintiles (by category) from census data from the CPS March Supplement.[33]
2. Subtract this percentage from 20. (Remember that the percentage is the proportion multiplied by 100.)
3. Square these differences and sum them.
4. Divide the totaled sum of squared differences by 5.

For the United States in 2003, the income distribution was as follows:

Quintile	Number of People	Step 1 Calculate %	Step 2 Subtract from 20	Find the Squared Differences and Sum them	Divide the Sum by 5
Lowest quintile	23,790,000	13.6	6.4	40.96	—
Second quintile	27,676,000	15.8	4.2	17.64	—
Third quintile	34,408,000	19.6	0.4	0.16	—
Fourth quintile	41,848,000	23.9	−3.9	15.21	—
Fifth quintile	47,452,000	27.1	−7.1	50.41	—
Total	175,174,000	—	—	124.38	24.876

If the Index of Inequality is larger in your area, your income distribution is more unequal than in the overall United States. Smaller IEQs mean that the area's income is more equal. Income distribution data by

[32] Sazama (1992).
[33] For instance, http://ferret.bls.census.gov/macro/032003/hhinc/new05_000.htm provides the distribution of households by selected characteristics within income quintiles.

income group for the United States is calculated for states, counties, and even down to zip-code level for *"Effective Buying Income"* or an estimate of disposable income by the Sales and Marketing Management's *Survey of Buying Power*, a yearly publication.

6. The Tiebout hypothesis suggests that people vote with their feet. To this end a net migration rate may hint at an area's quality of life. Populations will increase either because people move in or babies are born. Populations will decrease when people move away or when they die. Therefore, a change in population is the sum of the natural population change (births − deaths) and net migration. To find net migration, therefore, take the change in population (from a census or good inter-census population estimates) plus deaths minus births (during that time), or

$$\text{Net migration} = \Delta\text{Population} - \text{Births} + \text{Deaths}$$

The net migration rate is calculated by dividing net migration by total population at the beginning of the period.

The temptation to use yearly population estimates in addition to birth and death statistics available by county (and some cities) from the National Center for Health Statistics (http://www.cdc.gov/nchs/) and the state's department of health must be mitigated by the observation that the population estimates are just that. Estimating net migration over time using population estimates tests the validity of those estimates.

Other indicators of social well-being include statistics such as infant deaths (per 1000), serious crime (per 100,000), average years of education of the adult population, age of housing, or population density. These are available from the National Center for Health Statistics, the Federal Bureau of Investigation (http://www.fbi.gov/ucr/ucr.htm), and the Census Bureau.

Research Assignment

Compare indices of well-being for your area as described in the Appendix. Calculate and analyze the following ratios for 1990 and 2000, comparing your city with your state or with another city:

1. How does your standard of living rank with the state or another city?
2. Is your city more or less dependent on the working population than the state or another city? Which is the larger group of dependents in your city, children or the elderly?
3. Compare your labor force participation rate, employment rate, employment to population ratio, and unemployment rate to that of the state or the other area.

4. Compare the Gini coefficients or Sazama's index of inequality for your area to another area or to your state. Is your area homogeneous or heterogeneous with respect to income levels? How might this affect current and future policy proposals?
5. Another measure of quality of life is the net migration rate. Are more people coming to your area or leaving it?

References

Alonso, W. 1988. Population and regional development. *Regional Economic Development: Essays in Honour of François Perroux*, eds. H. Benjamin, and D. J. Savoie. Boston: Unwin Hyman, 131–141.

Ambrose, B. W., and T. M. Springer. 1993. Spatial variation of nonmetropolitan industrial location. *Journal of Real Estate Finance and Economics* 7 (1):17–27.

Anderson, J. E., and R. W. Wassmer. 1995. The decision to "bid for business": municipal behavior in granting property tax abatements. *Regional Science and Urban Economics* 25 (6):739–757.

Baade, R. A., and R. F. Dye. 1990. The impact of stadiums and professional sports on metropolitan area development. *Growth and Change* 21 (2):1–14.

Barlett, D. L., and J. B. Steele. 1998. Corporate welfare. *Time Magazine* 152 (19):2.

Bartik, T. J. 1993. Federal policy toward state and local economic development in the 1990s, In *Structuring Direct Aid: People versus Places*, ed. R. D. Norton. *Research in Urban Economics*, Vol. 9, Greenwich, Conn. JAI Press, pp. 161–178.

Bartik, T. J. 1991a. *Who Benefits from State and Local Economic Development Policies?* Kalamazoo, Mich. W. E. Upjohn Institute for Employment Research.

Bartik, T. J. 1991b. *The Effects of Metropolitan Job Growth on the Size Distribution of Family Income*, Upjohn Institute Staff Working Paper 91-06, March.

Bellamy, D. L., and A. L. Parks. 1994. Economic development in Southern Black Belt counties: how does it measure up? *Review of Black Political Economy* 22 (4):85–108.

Bhalla, A. S., and N. Jequier. 1988. Telecommunications for rural development. N *New Techologiesand Development: Experiences in "Technology Blending"*, eds. A .S. Bhallal., and D. James, Boulder, Colo: Rienner, 269–283.

Binet, M.-E. 2003. Testing for fiscal competition among French municipalities: granger causality evidence in a dynamic panel data model. *Papers in Regional Science* 82 (2):277–289.

Boarnet, M. G., and W. T. Bogart. 1996. Enterprise zones and employment: evidence from New Jersey. *Journal of Urban Economics* 40 (2):198–215.

Butler, A. 1992. Is the United States losing its dominance in high-technology industries? *Federal Reserve Bank of St. Louis Review* 74 (6):19–34.

Carlino, G., and R. DeFina. 1995. Regional income dynamics. *Journal of Urban Economics* 37 (1):88–106.

Carroll, R., and M. Wasylenko. 1994. Do state business climates still matter? Evidence of a structural change. *National Tax Journal* 47 (1):19–37.

Corporation for Enterprise Development. 1999. *Accountability: The Newsletter of Business Incentives Clearinghouse* 1(6), 1999. http://www.cfed.org/sustainable_economies/business_incentives/BI_newsletters/6_99_2.htm, (accessed on March 31, 2003; site now discontinued).

Chandra, A., and E. Thompson. 2000. Does public infrastructure affect economic activity? evidence from the rural interstate highway system. *Regional Science and Urban Economics* 30 (4):457–490.

Davis, D. 1989. Tax increment financing. *Public Budgeting and Finance* 9 (1):63–73.

Debertin, D. L. 1993. Rural development issues for agricultural economists to the year 2000: discussion. *American Journal of Agricultural Economics* 75 (5):1173–1174.

Department for Transport, Local Government and the Regions. 2001. *New Deal for Communities; National Evaluation Scoping Phase*, December 2001, http://www.renewal.net/Documents/RNET/Policypercent20Guidance/Newdeal-worklessness.pdf, (accessed on August 30, 2005).

Dillman, D. A. D. M. Beck., and J. C. Allen. 1989. Rural barriers to job creation remain, even in today's information age, *Rural Development Perspectives*, U.S. Department of Agriculture, Economic Research Service, Washington, DC, 5(2), 21–27.

Disez, N. 1999. Agritourisme: Logiques d'acteurs ou logiques de territoires? *Economie Rurale* 0 (250):40–46.

Duffy-Deno, K. T. 1997. Economic effect of endangered species preservation in the non-metropolitan West. *Growth and Change* 28 (3):263–288.

Dye, R. F., and D. F. Merriman. 2000. The effects of tax increment financing on economic development. *Journal of Urban Economics* 47 (2):306–328.

Dye, R. F., and J. O. Sundberg. 1998. A model of tax increment financing adoption incentives. *Growth and Change* 29 (1):90–110.

Eadington, W. R. 1998. Contributions of casino-style gambling to local economies. *Annals of the American Academy of Political and Social Science* 556 (0):53–65.

Ellis, S., and C. Rogers. 2000. Local economic development as a prisoners' dilemma: the role of business climate. *Review of Regional Studies* 30 (3):315–330.

Erickson, R. A., and P. M. Syms. 1986. The effects of enterprise zones on local property markets. *Regional Studies* 20 (1):1–14.

Farrell, C., 1996. *The Economic War among the States: An Overview*. Federal Reserve Bank of Minneapolis: *The Region*, June. http://minneapolisfed.org/pubs/region/96-06/reg966b.cfm.

Fisher, P. S., and A. H. Peters. 1997. Tax and spending incentives and enterprise zones. *New England Economic Review* 0 (0):109–130.

Foltz, D. H., L. Gaddis, W. Lyons, and J. M. Scheb, II. 1993. Saturn comes to Tennessee: citizen perceptions of project impacts. *Social Science Quarterly* 74 (4):793–803.

Fox, W. F., and S. Porca. 2001. Investing in rural infrastructure. *International Regional Science Review* 24 (1):103–133.

Freshwater, D. 2000. What can social scientists contribute to the challenges of rural economic development?. *Journal of Agricultural and Applied Economics* 32 (2):345–355.

Garcia-Milà, T., and T. J. McGuire. 1992. The contribution of publicly provided inputs to states' economies. *Regional Science and Urban Economics* 22 (2):229–241.

Grubel, H. G. 1984. Free economic zones: good or bad?. *Aussenwirtschaft* 39 (1-2):43–56.

Hansen, N. 1990. Innovative regional milieux, small firms, and regional development: evidence from Mediterranean France. *Annals of Regional Science* 24 (2):107–123.

Haughwout, A. F. 1999. State infrastructure and the geography of employment. *Growth and Change* 30 (4):549–566.

Higgins, B., and D. J. Savoie. 1988. *Regional Economic Development: Essays in Honour of François Perroux*, eds. B. Higgins., and D. J. Savoie. Boston: Unwin Hyman, 1–27.

Hite, J. 1993. Rural development, privatization and public choice: Substance depends upon process. *Journal of Agricultural and Applied Economics* 25 (1):89–98.

Hoppe, R. A. 1991. The elderly's income and rural development: some cautions. *Rural Development Perspectives* 7 (2):27–32.

Jenn, M. A., and F. Nourzad. 1996. Determinants of economic development incentives offered by states: a test of the arms race hypothesis. *Review of Regional Studies* 26 (1):1–16.

Joshi, M. L., J. C. Bliss, C. Bailey, L. J. Teeter, and K. J. Ward. 2000. Investing in industry, underinvesting in human capital: forest-based rural development in Alabama. *Society and Natural Resources* 13 (4):291–319.

Keith, J., and C. Fawson. 1995. Economic development in rural Utah: is wilderness recreation the answer? *Annals of Regional Science* 29 (3):303–313.

Kelly, T. M., J. W. Henderson, and S. L. Seaman. 1997. The efficiency of tax abatement in the market for jobs. *Journal of Economics (MVEA)* 23 (2):73–88.

Klier, T. H., and K. M. Johnson. 2000. Effect of auto plant openings on net migration in the auto corridor, 1980–97. *Federal Reserve Bank of Chicago Economic Perspectives* 24 (4):14–29.

Lever, W. F. 1992. Local authority responses to economic change in west central Scotland. *Urban Studies* 29 (6):935–948.

Leyden, D. P., and A. N. Link. 1991. Why are government R&D and private R&D complements? *Applied Economics* 23 (10):1673–1681.

Link, A. N., and J. Rees. 1991. Firm size, university-based research and the returns to R&D, In *Innovation and Technological Change: An International Comparison*, eds. J. A. Zoltan., and D. B. Audretsch. Ann Arbor: University of Michigan Press, 60–70.

Lisk, D., 1998. *Competing for Highway Maintenance: Lessons for Washington State*, September. http://www.washingtonpolicy.org/ConOutPrivatization/PBLisk-TransHiwayMaintenance.html, (accessed on March 30, 2003).

Lowery, D., and V. Gray. 1992. Holding back the tide of bad economic times: The compensatory impact of state industrial policy. *Social Science Quarterly* 73 (3):483–495.

Man, J. Y., and M. S. Rosentraub. 1998. Tax increment financing: municipal adoption and effects on property value growth. *Public Finance Review* 26 (6):523–547.

Mattey, J. Mattey, 1998. Reasons for public support of research and development. *FRBSF Weekly Letter* #98–16.

Mattey, J., and M. M. Spiegel. Mattey and Spiegel, 1995. Is state and local tax competition harmful? *FRBSF Weekly Letter* #95–26.

Mofidi, A., and J. A. Stone. 1990. Do state and local taxes affect economic growth? *Review of Economics and Statistics* 72 (4):686–691.

Musgrave, R. A., and P. B. Musgrave. 1989. *Public Finance in Theory and Practice*, 5th ed. New York: McGraw Hill Book Company.

Netzer, D. 1991. An evaluation of interjurisdictional competition through economic development incentives, In *Competition Among States and Local Governments: Efficiency and Equity in American Federalism*. D. A. Kenyon., and J. Kincaid. Washington, DC: Urban Institute Press in cooperation with the Advisory Commission on Intergovernmental Relations, 221–245 distributed by University Press of America, Lanham, MD.

Netzer, D. 1997. Metropolitan-area fiscal issues. In *Intergovernmental Fiscal Relations*, eds., R .C. Fisher. Recent Economic Thought Series, Boston: Kluwer Academic, 199–239.

Nissen, B. 1989. Enterprise zones as an economic development tool: the Indiana experience. *Regional Science Perspectives* 19 (2):3–20.

Noll, R. G., and A. Zimbalist. 1997. Sports, jobs, and taxes: the real connection,In *Sports, Jobs, and Taxes: The Economic Impact of Sports Teams and Stadiums*, eds., R. G., Noll, and Zimbalist, A. Washington, DC: Bookings Institute Press, 494–508.

ÓhUallacháin, B., and M. A. Satterthwaite. 1992. Sectoral growth patterns at the metropolitan level: an evaluation of economic development incentives. *Journal of Urban Economics* 31 (1):25–58.

Oechssler, J. 1994. The city vs. firm subsidy game. *Regional Science and Urban Economics* 24 (3):391–407.

Papke, L.E., 1993. *What Do We Know about Enterprise Zones?* National Bureau of Economic Research, Inc, NBER Working Papers.

Papke, L. E. 1991. Interstate business tax differentials and new firm location: evidence from panel data. *Journal of Public Economics* 45 (1):47–68.

Pearce, D. G. 1999. Assessing the impact of urban casinos on tourism in New Zealand. *Tourism Economics* 5 (2):141–159.

Peters, A. H., and P. S. Fisher. 2002. *State enterprise zone programs: Have they worked?* Kalamazoo, Mich.: W.E. Upjohn Institute for Employment Research.

Polèse, M., and E. Champagne. 1999. Location matters: comparing the distribution of economic activity in the Canadian and Mexican urban systems. *International Regional Science Review* 22 (1):102–132.

Poot, J. 2000. A synthesis of empirical research on the impact of government on long-run growth. *Growth and Change* 31 (4):516–546.

Quan, N. T., and J. H. Beck. 1987. Public education expenditures and state economic growth: Northeast and Sunbelt regions. *Southern Economic Journal* 54 (2):361–376.

Rephann, T. J., M. Dalton, A. Stair, and A. Isserman. 1997. Casino gambling as an economic development strategy. *Tourism Economics* 3 (2):161–183.

Rephann, T., and A. Isserman. 1994. New highways as economic development tools: an evaluation using quasi-experimental matching methods. *Regional Science and Urban Economics* 24 (6):723–751.

Rietveld, P. 1989. Infrastructure and regional development: a survey of multiregional economic models. *Annals of Regional Science* 23 (4):255–274.

Rolnick, A.J., 2000. *Winning Battles, Rather than the War, on Economic Development Subsidies.* Federal Reserve Bank of Minneapolis: Fedgazette, July. http://minneapolisfed.org/pubs/fedgaz/00-07/opinion.cfm, (accessed on December 8, 2002).

Rowley, T. D., and S. L. Porterfield. 1993. Removing rural development barriers through telecommunications: illusion or reality? In *Economic Adaptation: Alternatives for Nonmetropolitan Areas*, ed. D. L., Barkley. *Rural Studies Series*, Boulder: Westview Press, 247–264.

Rubin, R. and S.E., Holsten. 1999. *FCC Initiates Rulemakings Seeking to Promote Telecommunications Service in American Indian Tribal Lands and other Underserved Areas*, Greenberg Traurig Memorandum: Telecommunications. August 5. http://www.gtlaw.com/practices/telecom/memo/1999/080599.htm, (accessed on December 1, 2002; site now discontinued).

Salomon, I., and J. Schofer. 1991. Transportation and telecommunications costs: some implications of geographical scale. *Annals of Regional Science* 25 (1):19–39.

Sazama, G. W. 1992. Has federal student aid contributed to equality in higher education? A method of measurement. *American Journal of Economics and Sociology* 51 (2):129–146.

Schmidt, R. H., and C. Sherwood-Call. 1989. Why Do Regional Economies Differ? *FRBSF Economic Letter.*

Schwartz, G. G. 1990. Telecommunications and economic development policy. *Economic Development Quarterly* 4 (2):83–91.

Strathman, J. G. 1994. Migration, benefit spillovers and state support of higher education. *Urban Studies* 31 (6):913–920.

Talbot, J. 1988. Have enterprise zones encouraged enterprise? Some empirical evidence from Tyneside. *Regional Studies* 22 (6):507–514.

Tassey, G. 1998. *Comparisons of U.S. and Japanese R&D Policies.* March. http://www.jiaponline.org/specialreports/1998/march/sp3_1998.pdf (accessed on December 1, 2002; site now discontinued).

Vinje, D. L. 1996. Native American economic development on selected reservations: a comparative analysis. *American Journal of Economics and Sociology* 55 (4):427–442.

Wassmer, R. W. 2001. Metropolitan prosperity from major league sports in the CBD: Stadia locations or just strength of the central city? A reply to Arthur C. Nelson. *Economic Development Quarterly* 15 (3):266–271.

Wassmer, R. W. 1994. Can local incentives alter a metropolitan city's economic development? *Urban Studies* 31 (8):1251–1278.

Wassmer, R. W. 1992. Property tax abatement and the simultaneous determination of local fiscal variables in a metropolitan area. *Land Economics* 68 (3):263–282.

Wasylenko, M. 1981. The location of firms: The role of taxes and fiscal incentives. In *Urban government finance: Emerging trends*, ed. R. Bahl, Urban affairs annual reviews, vol. 20. Beverly Hills, CA: Sage Publications.

Wikipedia. n.d. Cargo cult. http://en.wikipedia.org/wiki/Cargo_cult, (Date accessed on 24 November 2004).

Williams, C. C. 1997. *Consumer Services and Economic Development*. London: Routledge.

Williams, A., G. Shore, and M. Huber. 1995. The arts and economic development: Regional and urban-rural contrasts in UK local authority policies for the arts. *Regional Studies* 29 (1):73–80.

Wolkoff, M. J. 1985. Chasing a dream: the use of tax abatements to spur urban economic development. *Urban Studies* 22 (4):305–315.

Wong, J. D. 1996. The impact of tourism on local government expenditures. *Growth and Change* 27 (3):313–326.

Wren, C. 1994. The build-up and duration of subsidy-induced employment: evidence from U.K. regional policy. *Journal of Regional Science* 34 (3):387–410.

Yu, W., M. S. Wallace, and C. Nardinelli. 1991. State growth rates: taxes, spending, and catching up. *Public Finance Quarterly* 19 (1):80–93.

Zuckman, J. 1992. Enterprise Zone alchemy: 90s-style urban renewal; in Washington, policy-makers debate whether the idea works, how many areas to target and which incentives to use. *Congressional Quarterly Weekly Report* 50 (32):2354–2357.

URBAN LAND USE AND URBAN FORM

Land rents and land-use patterns, the subject of Chapter 12, are the heart of urban economics. In this chapter we first define rent and we describe the different categories of the term "rent." Then, we will investigate the dynamics of the supply and demand for land. An analysis on agricultural land rents will lead us to the periurbanization phenomenon that we studied in Chapter 8. Periurbanization combines with urban land rent theory into what is called the "New Urban Economics." Finally, we will look at land rents and land-use patterns within the urban core. As cities grow, the traditional monocentric model derived from von Thünen's theory (Chapter 9) gives way to polycentric cities consisting of older central cities surrounded by suburbs and edge cities. Transportation systems and traffic arteries dictate city formation.

Residences make up the bulk of urban land use. In Chapter 13 we will provide analyses of housing supply and demand and study the effect of amenities and disamenities on housing prices. We will also examine the programs proposed to make housing more affordable.

Chapter 14 will concentrate on the supply and demand for transportation. Congestion is one of the components of the diseconomies of agglomeration that drives people and firms away from the metropolitan areas toward smaller communities. We will examine some of the ways that cities throughout the world have tried to allocate congestion costs. Highway safety issues and policies enacted to increase the efficiency of mass transit will also be part of our study. Finally, in Chapter 15 we will evaluate the economic impact and efficacy of growth controls, smart growth, and zoning.

Chapter 12

Land Rents and Land-Use Patterns

Land rents and intrametropolitan land use constitute the foundation of urban economics. "New Urban Economics" is the study of land rents and land-use patterns within the periurban and urban areas.[1] Some cities follow the traditional monocentric model but as they expand, a polycentric form takes shape following transportation arteries. Distance is a major determinant of land rent, but amenities and disamenities also influence land values.

Land Rent, Contract Rent, and Economic Rent

The term "rent" has several meanings. **Land rent** is the sum paid for using land as a factor of production. The purchase of land provides the buyer two inseparable attributes: location in proximity to other sites and physical space. Land rent is composed of two elements: (1) **site rent** (**ground rent**), which is a function of the earnings associated with an existing location, and (2) **improvement rents**, which is a function of the earnings due to the buildings or other improvements to the land. Because a site is unique, site rent earned the pejorative term "monopoly rent." One can improve land by using fertilizers or facilitating access.[2]

---

[1] Goffette-Nagot (1996a, 1996b); Duranton (1997a, 1997b).
[2] Evans (1991, 1993).

In contrast, the rent that tenants pay to their landlords is called ***contract rent***. Only a portion of that includes the payment of land rent.

Finally, ***economic rent*** is the difference between the actual payment for a factor of production and the minimum amount that is needed to keep it full-time in that occupation. For example, suppose that a young man named Michael Jagger decides to fund his studies at the London School of Economics by composing and interpreting his music.[3] We assume also that the diploma that he obtains allows him to teach economics if he desired. However, he preferred his career in entertainment, and as long as he was paid anything above X income, he devotes himself to music. We assume also that if his income falls below X, he could supplement his earnings by teaching part time. Sir Mick Jagger, lead singer and cofounder of the Rolling Stones, has an income of Y. The difference between what he currently earns (Y) and the minimum that he would need to continue his musical career ($Y-X$) is his economic rent.

The concept of economic rent appeased the moralists/scholars of the late 1800s who were convinced that collecting rent from land was immoral. According to them, God made land. Therefore, any income received by land was an unearned increment (something for nothing). The compromise that quelled the controversy was the notion that all production factors can earn economic rent if (1) they are better than average or more in demand, and if (2) an increase in demand for their services raises their income but not the quantity supplied.

Until the late 1800s, theorists maintained that there is a fixed amount of land on Earth. The Earth did not expand or contract as land prices fluctuated. Therefore, the total rent earned by land was a surplus; more than necessary to generate that amount of land. The land market for a specific use was characterized by a perfectly inelastic supply of land (Figure 12.1).

In this model, demand alone determines rent because supply is fixed. All land rent is therefore a residual, and confiscation of land rent would not change the quantity of land available for production. Because the same supply of land would exist even if it earned no rent, government can confiscate this "unearned increment" without affecting output. Thus, a tax confiscating some or all the land rents, as Henry George proposed, was considered a ***neutral tax***—it would in no way alter economic incentives.

However, the concept according to which economic land is a fixed resource is not realistic. If land rents increase, more land can be cleared, drained, or filled in. For example, land for Japan's Kansai Airport was made by filling in part of an inlet with compacted garbage. The Netherlands has

---

[3] London School of Economics and Political Science *Wikipedia, the Free Encyclopedia* (http://www.wikipedia.org/wiki/London_School_of_Economics).

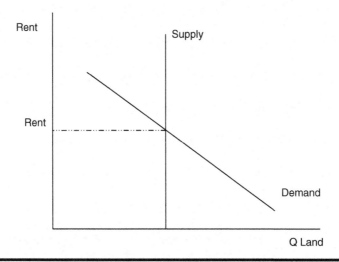

Figure 12.1 Land market with a perfectly inelastic supply of land.

reclaimed swampy land close to the Atlantic Ocean for centuries. If the price of land were not high enough to compensate for these improvements, the amount of land would not increase. In addition, local planning authorities affect the supply of economic land for particular purposes by permitting or denying its development. Thus, the supply of **economic land**, that is, land used in production of a good, is not perfectly inelastic, but partly upsloping (Figure 12.2).[4]

The rent concept depicted in Figure 12.2 consists of two types of rent. R_2 is the market price for land because this is the rent at which demand intersects supply. R_1 is the **tipping price** or the price at which the supply becomes perfectly inelastic. **Price-determined** rent or pure rent is the revenue generated from rents greater than R_1. After this point, increases in demand will only increase the land rent; the quantity supplied of land does not change. **Price-determining rent**, improvement rent, or quasi-rent is essentially the amount of producers' surplus below R_1 in Figure 12.2.

According to Euler's theorem, under constant returns to scale in a perfectly competitive market, the price of a good can be exactly allocated by paying each factor of production the value of its marginal product. Following this theorem, the payments that determine the price of land are treated no differently than payments for labor or capital. If the demand intersects the supply curve at or above R_1, the amount of rent due to the improvements is determined by the difference in the price of the factor of production and the sum needed to attract the maximum amount of that

---

[4] Kivell (1993); Ijichi and Shimbun (2000).

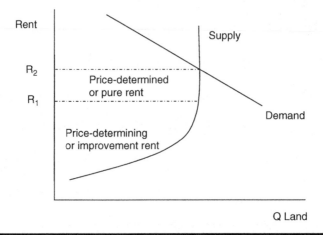

Figure 12.2 Land market showing pure rent and improvement rent.

factor into production. Pure rent is the amount going to the factor of production after the total quantity is already maximized.

The characteristics that increase the pure rent of a parcel of land depend on the sector using it:

- For agricultural land, more fertile land with easy access;
- For commercial property, locations close to the transport networks or locations closer to the central business district (CBD); and
- For industrial land, the greater the advantages of agglomeration economies and the proximity to backward and forward linkages.

Demand for Land

The demand for land includes both nonresidential land uses and residential uses. The demand for nonresidential land is a function of four components:[5]

1. The value of cleared agricultural land rent,
2. The cost of converting agricultural to urban uses, if necessary,
3. The value of accessibility, and
4. The present value of expected future rent increases as a growth premium.

The estimated present value of agricultural, commercial, and industrial land depends on its real rate of return. The demand for residential land

---

[5] Capozza and Helsley (1989).

depends on two components of a household's utility function: local amenities and distance to work or school. We will explore residential land use in detail in Chapter 13.

The present value is calculated by the following formula:

$$PV = \sum_{t=1}^{T} \frac{A}{(1+r)^t},$$

where A is the expected yearly net income generated in a specific location and r is the interest rate. The summation sign, Σ, means that we add up the present value for every year starting from year 1 and going through year T, the last year we expect to own the property. Thus, everything that affects the earnings potential of a site will affect the demand, and consequently the price of the site.

For instance, if the yearly net income of a parcel is expected to be $10,000, the interest rate is 6%, and the landowner expects to hold on to the land for 5 years, the present value would be

$$PV = \sum_{t=1}^{5} \frac{10,000}{(1.06)^t} = \frac{10,000}{(1.06)^1} + \frac{10,000}{(1.06)^2} + \frac{10,000}{(1.06)^3} + \frac{10,000}{(1.06)^4} + \frac{10,000}{(1.06)^5}$$

$$= 9433.96 + 8899.96 + 8396.19 + 7920.94 + 7472.58 = 42{,}123.64.$$

If the maximum return that an investor expects for a certain parcel is $42,123, the investor will not bid more than that amount for the parcel.

Agricultural Land Rent

Determinants of agricultural location have changed since von Thünen. Transportation costs for raw agricultural produce have decreased. Agricultural produce is no longer sold at a central market in a city, but to food processors located outside the city.[6]

The expected present value of future returns to **agricultural land** is determined by a few buyers and sellers of land at any given moment and is thus partly subjective. Land prices vary with local market forces. Because the change in ownership affects only a small proportion of land, buyers and sellers do not have perfect knowledge of the market. If a potential buyer wants to acquire agricultural land for a nonagricultural use, he or she must pay a premium to the seller. The sale of land above local prevailing prices will increase the value of all land because higher prices signal landowners to raise their expectations.[7] However, the value of agricultural land close to a city is not based entirely on the basis of the present value of future net

---

[6] Goffette-Nagot (1996).
[7] Elad, Clifton, and Epperson (1994); Shi, Phipps, and Colyer (1997).

income. The prices are a function of farm returns, the value after conversion to an urban land use, household incomes, population densities, and proximity to major metropolitan areas. If farmland owners anticipate a conversion, residential or commercial usage will be important determinants of farmland prices.[8]

Pricing Farmland

Studies of farmland prices in the Mid Atlantic states of the United States, Quebec, France, and Great Britain verify that farmland prices increase, perhaps more rapidly than the price of housing, as counties become more urban. Net migration toward peripheral communities has caused an increase in land rents because the land is being converted to a residential use. Iowa is one exception. Because of its low population densities, the impact of urban activities on its rural land rents is small.

Hodge and Whitby (1986), Cavailhes et al. (1994), Romain (1994), Shi, Phipps and Colyer (1997), Hardie, Narayan, and Gardner (2001).

Smaller land parcels close to a city have a higher value if they are not zoned. However, exclusive agricultural zoning increased agricultural land values for Wisconsin land parcels larger than 35 acres and at least 10 miles from a large city. This is because exclusive agricultural zoning, which is often strictly enforced, limits development. Without this zoning, residential spaces could be constructed, creating problems between the new residents and farmers. The presence of pig farms or feedlots imposes negative externalities on the transplanted urbanites who live downwind. Thus, the exclusive zoning arrangements represent a guarantee for the farmers by reducing the uncertainty of the future of their livelihood.[9]

Urban Land-Use Patterns

Chapter 9 introduced von Thünen's model of land use for a city and its hinterland. Urban economists have adapted this model for urban areas. The CBD is the primary employment and transactions center of a monocentric

---

[8] Shi, Phipps, and Colyer (1997).
[9] Henneberry and Barrows (1990).

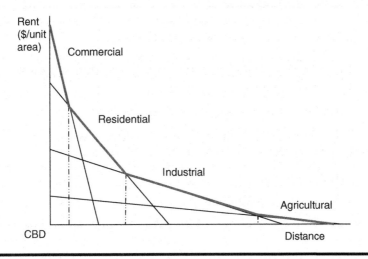

Figure 12.3   Rent gradient.

city. Other land uses radiate in a concentric fashion from the CBD (Figure 12.3). Each land use (commercial, industrial, residential, agricultural, etc.) has its own ***bid-rent function***, a graph of the amount of rent required from each type of user as a decreasing function with distance from the center city. This decrease in rents permits the user of land to maintain a normal profit at each distance from the CBD. Thus, the bid-rent functions are essentially equal profit functions.[10]

Non-residential bid-rent functions are steeper:

■ the higher the transportation cost per unit of distance for that particular land use,
■ the easier it is to substitute land for other inputs, and
■ the greater the frequency of face-to-face transactions needed to conduct business[11].

The bid-rent curve for residential land which is a function of the amount that buyers are willing and able to pay, depends on their incomes and commuting distance. The cross-section of the surface of bid-rent curves for land uses within a specific city is called the ***rent gradient*** (thick line, Figure 12.3). The bid-rent gradient shows the maximum amount of rent that landowners can receive regardless of the land use.

---

[10] Shieh (1983).
[11] McCann (1995).

Think About It ...

In your city, where are the tallest buildings? Downtown? Along a travel corridor?

What activities do these buildings house?

What land uses surround these buildings within three blocks, six blocks, twelve blocks, two miles,...?

What activities occur on the outskirts of your city?

Is your city an "edge city" or does it have one?

Intraurban Industry Location

In a monocentric city, the distance from a central focal point determines the nature of activities. In the 19th century, this point was generally a port or rail terminal. Residential areas form a circular ring around the central core where all employment opportunities are located. Because of agglomeration economies, proximity to the other firms leads to larger differences between revenues and costs, that is, a greater amount of "surplus" or "residual" with which firms bid for land.[12]

The bid-rent function for the commercial sector is steepest and highest because land used in these activities can easily be substituted for capital. The tall office buildings can pay more per square foot of land because each floor multiplies the surface of land. In contrast, agricultural activities cannot readily substitute land for capital. Farmers cannot easily grow corn on one story of a building while their cows graze on another. In contrast, because commercial transactions require face-to-face contact, the bid-rent function for commercial land use is quite steep, whereas for agricultural activities the bid rent is relatively flat.

Because the bid-rent function is highest and steepest for commercial land, the price paid for this usage increases as one approaches the CBD (Figure 12.3). Residential land would be in a concentric ring around the commercial center. Industrial areas would surround the residential, and finally agricultural areas surround the city.

---

[12] Anas (1987).

Monocentric Cities

The maximum price that a firm is willing and able to pay is the discounted sum of expected future net returns at a given location. The expected revenues depend in a large part on the ease of access for consumers. Attributes of a location influence its value. Land rents vary according to the location in the CBD. Firms choose their locations by taking account not only of the rent but also of the transport costs between them and their inputs, as well as to their market. Local amenities and disamenities increase or decrease land rents.[13]

Think About It ...

Where are the better jobs located in your city—downtown, in the central business district, in the suburbs or at the edge of the metropolitan area? What types of jobs are located in each area?

Wage Gradients and the Monocentric City

Locations close to the CBD offer both advantages and inconveniences. Wages tend to be highest in the center of a metropolitan area and fall with increasing distance from the center. For workers who resist relocating, the wage gradient becomes a compensating wage differential for commuters. Downtown firms must pay higher wages than suburban firms to compensate commuters, but they benefit from agglomeration economies for their industry.[14]

Wage Gradients and Commuting Choices

The monocentric model seems to predict wages very well in Des Moines, Iowa. A study by So, Orazem, and Otto (2001) based on 1990 Census data examined the commuting choices of 6214 adults residing in a 31-county region of central Iowa. They concluded that high housing price levels discourage in-migration, but

---

[13] Fujita (1989); Sasaki (1991); Ota and Fujita (1993).
[14] Leigh (1986); Welch (1989); Smith (1991).

high wages attract new residents and commuters. As a result, commuters have higher wages than do noncommuters, as the utility maximizing model predicts. Commuting is a negative function of distance, and approaches zero as a one-way commute approaches one hour. For Des Moines, the extent of the labor market is thus the distance that can be traveled in one hour. Reitsma and Vergoossen (1988) determined for the Netherlands, commuting stress reached a critical level after only 30 minutes.

Reitsma and Vergoossen (1988),
So, Orazem, and Otto (2001).

Spatial Specialists

Firms respond to the trade-offs by becoming spatially specialized. In the United States, clerical and administrative support jobs (back offices) tend to locate in the suburbs as soon as technology and transportation allow. In Europe, surveys show that the back offices relocate to the suburbs at a faster rate than other types of office employment. The corporate business (front) offices are in the CBD to benefit from agglomeration economies, especially contacts with the headquarters of other firms. In contrast, the back offices only contact their front offices.

Welch (1989), Clapp, Pollaowski,
and Lynford (1992).

International Consistency in Land-Use Patterns

Lee (1982, 1989, 1990) unambiguously concluded that the land-use patterns of Bogotá, Colombia, and Seoul, South Korea, correspond to those of the metropolitan areas in industrialized countries. Land-use patterns in low-income countries are explained by the same models with similar degrees of success.

Distance from the central urban core is a powerful predictor of industrial land use. Heavy industry that cannot easily substitute land for capital such as auto-mobile manufacturing, primary metals, and chemicals is concentrated in the outer rings and satellite cities. Publishing and apparel locate closer to the center. Similarly, Hansen (1990) found that in doubling the distance from Sao Paulo, Brazil, the productivity of a plant decreases by an average of 8.9 percent, and the labor costs decline by an average of 8.7 percent. Because of even the small difference in the two averages, some entrepreneurs relocated to the periph-ery of Sao Paulo. According to Hansen, the Brazilian industrialists located as they "should" in terms of their private costs and benefits. Without intervention, market forces will decentralize Brazilian manufacturing so that it will spread away from the large metropolitan regions onto the urban periphery similar to the urban exodus of manufacturing firms in developed countries.

Lee (1982, 1989, 1990), Hansen (1990).

Tests of the Monocentric Model: Wasteful Commuting and Housing Price Gradients

Hamilton (1982, 1989) suggested that urban workers would minimize their commutes if they chose their residence as a function of their work location as the monocentric model predicts. To test the model, he calculated that the minimum distance of a commute for the average worker in a group of cities in the United States was only 1.1 miles. He then compared the results to the actual average length of the journey to work for those workers (8.7 miles), and assumed that the difference between the two figures was "wasteful commuting." He found similar results for Japanese cities. According to Hamilton, either 90 percent of the commutes were unnecessary or the monocentric urban model in which workers take account of their commuting distance was flawed.

In defense of the monocentric model, White (1988) argued that time rather than distance is a more precise measure of commuting costs. Using the same cities, she calculated commuting in terms of time and found that only about 11 percent of the actual amount of commuting in urban areas was wasteful.

Hamilton (1982, 1989) and White (1988).

Intraurban Residence Location

A large part of urban land is reserved for residential neighborhoods. Households maximize their utility functions, which depend on housing, neighborhood amenities, and a composite good which includes everything but housing. The traditional monocentric model assumes that all households are identical in both incomes and preferences. Household income is spent on housing, the composite good, and transportation. The household bid-rent function is the maximum that households are willing and able to pay for land at each distance from the employment center (CBD) while still maintaining a fixed utility level.

Because of the time and income constraints faced by households, they must balance accessibility, space, and amenities. Accessibility includes the monetary expenses as well as the opportunity cost of the time involved with commuting, shopping, and traveling to recreational activities. Space consists of the size and quality of the lot and house. Natural amenities such as green space are important, as are neighborhood characteristics such as school quality, safety, and socioeconomic and racial composition of the residents.[15]

Challenging the Monocentric Model

The monocentric model worked for 19th century cities, but as employment decentralized, cities became more polycentric. The urban monocentric model has several weaknesses. First, it cannot explain the appearance of

---

[15] Fujita (1989); Anas (1990); Kivell (1993).

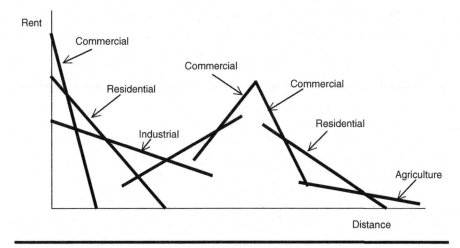

Figure 12.4   Bid-rent functions for a polycentric city.

complex urban structures with several centers or the emergence of secondary employment centers, edge cities, or other configurations (Figure 12.4). Second, the monocentric model does not explain how cities form, or how firms and households simultaneously determine optimal locations.[16]

Evolving Urban Forms

Polèse, Perez, and Barragan (1995) attempted to predict the evolution of the urban structure of Puebla, Mexico. The center city of Puebla is quite dynamic, and it is the historic social and cultural heart of the area. However, the need for space has pushed manufacturing and warehouses to locate close to the major Mexico-Veracruz freeway.

New householders who have more money than the preceding generation and who would like more spacious housing are also drawn toward suburbs as in the U.S. cities to the north. Most upscale tertiary firms also moved to suburban shopping centers, to the southeast and to the west of the heart of the city,

---

[16] Baumont and Huriot (1998).

> potentially creating for Puebla an "exploding" urban form and decaying inner city.
>
> Polèse, Perez, and Barragan (1995).

Finally, the monocentric model does not explain the periurbanization phenomenon very well. Many urban workers prefer rural residences. Periurbanization (the New Urban Economics) is essentially a model of residential choice within the periurban area. A large proportion of periurban land is reserved for recreation, second homes, prestige, nostalgia, or speculation. Eventually, employment centers and housing spread throughout the periurban area, changing the use of agricultural land.[17]

Land is converted to urban use whenever urban land values increase sufficiently to cause the sale of farmland. The monocentric urban land-use model ensures that land development takes place in a ring at the periphery of the city. This is not always the case, especially when unusually productive agricultural land is close to an urban area and less productive land remains idle short distances away. Urban expansion is likely to leapfrog past the more productive agricultural land, at least temporarily, to low-quality farm land. We will further discuss the implications of "urban sprawl" in Chapter 15.[18]

Some Owner's Treasures Are (Almost) Priceless

> When there is no direct measure of monetary income associated with land, economists must measure its nonmonetary or psychic income. This is difficult because land possesses unique attributes for someone who lives there. A nostalgic value exists for the seller, but not for the buyer. For buyers, one farm or house is much like another. The supposed sentimental value seldom merits a premium.
>
> Evans (1983), Shi, Phipps, and Colyer (1997).

---

[17] Goffette-Nagot (1996a, 1996b).
[18] McMillen, Jarmin, and Thorsnes (1992).

Portrait of a Periurban Household

Suburbanites and periurbanites have similar preferences. Periurbanites, who live in less populated areas,
simply prefer more green space. Studies based on both
U.S. and French data noted that the young couples and
moderate-income households with children choose to
live in periurban areas if they want to own their own
houses.

Periurban areas with good transport networks are also
preferred choices for dual career households. Households where both spouses are employed in a
professional or managerial occupation spend significantly more on housing for given income levels.
Couples who live in the outskirts of the city are prepared
to commute long distances to work, nearly always by car.

Anas (1987), Phillips and Vanderhoff (1991),
Margo (1992), Goffette-Nagot (1996a, 1996b), Green
and White (1997), Nelson, and Sanchez (1997).

Polycentric Cities

According to the *monocentric model*, housing price gradients decrease at an
increasing rate from the CBD outward. But, according to the *polycentric urban
model*, housing prices decrease not only with distance from the CBD, but also
with distance from secondary employment centers. A survey by Wachs (1993)
of employees working for a southern California health care provider
confirmed that choices of residential location depend on many factors.
Besides the home-to-work commutes, it is necessary to take into account
the amenities, school quality, and perceived safety of a neighborhood.[19]

Polycentric Land Value Surfaces

In Dallas County, Texas, housing price gradients are
significant not only from the CBD but also from

---

[19] Wachs et al. (1993); Waddell, Berry, and Hoch (1993); Clapp, Rodriguez, and Pace
(2001).

multiple employment centers. The influence of an employment center on land prices is fairly localized— extending no more than 10–15 miles. The prices of more distant houses are influenced by other employment centers.

However, in Washington, DC, demographics and technological innovations shape land values. People who work at home are attracted to areas with low structural density and high socioeconomic status as well as low land values. A large number of workers do not work in the closest employment center but in another center farther away. The resulting cross-commutes cancel out the bid-rent predictions of a polycentric urban model.

Waddell, Berry, and Hoch (1993), Clapp, Rodriguez, and Pace (2001).

Think About It ...

Is your city monocentric or polycentric?

If polycentric, what firms are located on the outskirts of town rather than at the center of the city?

What firms are in the central business district?

Why do you suppose that the city's subcenters were created in that part of the periphery?

Edge Cities

Garreau (1991) observed that the urban evolution that leads to edge cities is a progression of three events. First, residences migrate to the outskirts of the city. Second, shopping centers move close to the new residences. Third, factories and office complexes follow the residential developments. Edge cities are always located close to major highways. They rarely have a

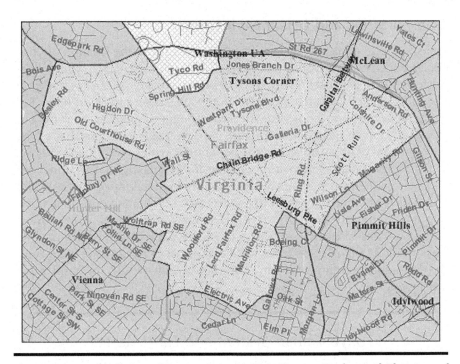

Figure 12.5   Boundaries of Tysons Corner, CDP (Census Designated Place) as of 2003. (From http://en.wikipedia.org/wiki/Image:TysonsCornerCDPmap.gif.)

mayor or city council, and they almost never have specific boundaries found on a map.

To be classified as an edge city, the area must have more than five million square feet of office space, over 600,000 feet. of retail space, and more jobs than homes. It must be a primary destination for entertainment, shopping, and recreation (activities that were totally absent 30 years ago).

Tysons Corner, Virginia (Figure 12.5) is a typical example. It is situated near the junctions of the Washington Beltway and the route to the Dulles International Airport. In 1970, Tysons Corner was a small, unincorporated community, but now has become the largest retail area on the East Coast south of New York City. Edge cities have been identified not only in the United States, but also an international phenomenon as automobile ownership becomes prevalent.[20]

---

[20] Garreau (1991); Lowe (2000); Gaschet (2002).

Transportation and Urban Land Use

Transportation costs play a significant role not only in the location of edge cities, but also in forming the shapes of traditional cities. The spatial organization of land uses determines the plan and characteristics of transport networks, and at the same time transport routes determine land uses. The evolution of transport modes from horse and buggy to streetcar to car and bus along with the necessary infrastructure improvements have also shaped the development of urban areas and the geographic patterns of urban land use.

The appropriate explanatory variable for estimating density functions and rent gradients is perhaps represented by the total transportation costs rather than distance from the CBD. Decreased commuting costs flatten the population density and land-rent gradients for housing. Lower transportation costs also increase the size of the CBD. Reduced commuting costs result in a larger periurban area. If the cost of commuting were zero, the population, employment, and land rent would be uniformly distributed.[21]

Tokyo Transit System and Land Values

Hatta and Ohkawara (1993) compared the population and employment structures of two metropolitan areas, Tokyo and New York. Tokyo is twice as large as New York in both population and in employment. The well-developed mass transit system in Tokyo was essential in supporting its size even before cars were mass produced.

The residential area of Tokyo is more spread out and the population density curve of its suburbs is flatter than that of New York. This is due in part to a well-developed suburban transit system that decreased commuting time and, in part, to an untaxed reimbursement of commuting expenses that the Japanese companies pay their employees. Relatively high land prices are accompanied by a relatively low employment density in the Tokyo CBD.

Hatta and Ohkawara (1993), Yamaga (2000).

---

[21] Berechman (1980); Krakover and Casetti (1988); Yinger (1993); Chen (1996); Pickrell (1999).

Capitalization Process

People and firms move to areas with pleasant amenities or to jurisdictions that provide a preferred number of public goods. The growing number of people who want to live and work in an area increases the supply of labor, which in turn, decreases wages or boosts the demand for land as well as the associated land values. The more the firms locate adjacent to others to take advantage of agglomeration economies, the greater is the increase in land values in that area. The relocation will continue until the total benefit from proximity is capitalized into the value of land. Likewise, land loses its value if it is adjacent to negative externalities or if it is located in jurisdictions with inadequate mixes of property taxes and public goods.[22]

Access Is Everything

In 1990, residential land values located within one-half mile of the transit station sites increased by 17 percent. The average annual rent of a residence increased by $24 while commercial space prices rose by $0.06 per square foot. The calculated monetary benefits, which vary between $0.50 and $1.50 per round trip, were capitalized into land values. This increase is due to the transit line that improved access to downtown Chicago. In New York City, a more efficient subway system slightly decentralizes residential locations away from Manhattan and toward the Bronx, Brooklyn, and Queens.

On the other hand, an improvement of 10 percent in highway travel yields aggregate benefits of about $4 per round-trip. Transportation improvements significantly decreased residential property values in the central area, but substantially increased the value of commercial space because highway improvements encouraged both commuting and shopping.

Anas (1995), McDonald and Osuji (1995).

---

[22] Polinsky and Shavell (1976); Cropper (1981); Guntermann (1997).

Hedonic Price Indices

The values of amenities and the costs of disamenities borne by land are often calculated using the method of ***hedonic prices*** detailed by Rosen (1974). Households migrate to areas that offer a variety of amenities, bidding up land prices in those areas. Thus the market prices of these attributes reflect the consumer preferences as well as the costs of maintaining such attributes. The hedonic price indices result from a competitive market process. The indices, which reflect a variety of attributes, are calculated using the hedonic regression method. The dependent variable is the price of the land (or the price of the house). The independent variables include indicator variables that describe not only the structure of the land, access to running water, sewer, and electricity, but also variables indicating the presence or distance from specific amenities and disamenities.[23]

Land values for nonresidential property are not only affected by micro-location, possibilities of development and neighborhood characteristics, but also by each parcel's interaction with the dominant structures of a city. Proximity to the place of employment is more important than proximity to the CBD for industrial and commercial firms. Office land values increase with proximity to either the CBD or the secondary employment centers. This result underscores the fact that office activities benefit more from agglomeration than do commercial or industrial activities.[24]

Summary and Conclusions

In this chapter, we first differentiated the concepts underlying the term "rent" and briefly described their evolutions. The great debate of the late 1800s centered on the following question: did land determine the prices of products or did those prices determine land values? The debate fizzled, but the most obvious conclusion was that both sides were right. A parcel of land that is usable after being transformed increases the price of the good produced on it if the owner's income reimburses the improvement cost. However, as soon as all of the land in an area is used, further growth in demand increases the land rent without increasing quantity. The increase in land rent independent of quantity represents the pure rent or the economic rent of land.

The demand for nonresidential land has several components: (1) its value as agricultural land, (2) the cost of converting it to an urban use, (3) a value based on accessibility or other amenities, and (4) a growth premium.

---

[23] See Cropper et al. (1993) for a comparison of the hedonic model and multinomial Logit model for estimating amenity attributes.

[24] Peiser (1987).

The demand for residential land is linked to the household's utility function, commuting time, and local amenities. Within a city, the bid-rent function is essentially an equal profit function. Bid-rent functions describe the rents that a firm in a specific industry is willing to pay while maintaining a normal profit.

The determination of agricultural land values has changed since the time of von Thünen (1826). The fields that surrounded a city 50 years ago now have a larger value if they are converted to residential or industrial usage. Prices for farmland are a function not only of farm returns, but also of the values of converted land nearby, local household incomes, population densities, and the proximity to major metropolitan areas.

The monocentric city model has adapted von Thünen's theory by making the CBD the sole market, and studying land-use patterns and land rents in relation to the distance from the CBD. All employment is in the city center in this model, and households locate in a ring surrounding the CBD. Firms that move to the suburbs or the periphery do not have to compensate their workers as much because they live nearby. Land values are lower, but firms risk giving up the face-to-face interaction and agglomeration economies that make the CBD attractive.

Households locate to maximize their utilities. Household utility increases with income, the amount of housing, local amenities, and the amount of discretionary budget of the household. However, it diminishes with commuting time. Many households prefer a rural residence and an urban job. Periurbanization is a model of residential choice within the periurban area, often referred to as the "New Urban Economics." Moderate-income households with children, who want to own their own homes, choose to live outside the city limits despite the commute.

The monocentric model cannot explain the emergence of complex urban structures that we find in modern cities with several centers, secondary employment centers, or edge cites. The result is a complex of housing, shopping, and employment centers that may or may not fit neatly within one jurisdiction's boundaries. Transportation costs and traffic arteries are essential in determining the shape of urban land areas and the slope of the bid-rent functions. Distance to some focal point is the main determinant of land prices. The place of work is not the only focal point that influences land prices; distance to amenities also counts.

Chapter Questions

1. Slicker is a growing, monocentric city surrounded by 500 miles of farmland in all directions.

Land Use	Amount of Rent Earned Per Acre/Year/Land-Use Type at the Market Center	Transport Cost Per Mile
Industrial	$750	$50
Commercial	$1000	$100
Residential	$500	$25

    a. From the figures listed in the above table, draw the bid-rent curves for the three industries.

    b. Determine the maximum distance from the market center that land will be used for commercial purposes. _____ (Remember to consult your diagram.)

    c. Determine the maximum distance from the market center that land will be used for industrial purposes. _____

    d. How far from the center of Slicker City will you expect the agriculture sector to start?

2. Consider two residential developers, Bonny and Clyde, who compete for land in a monocentric urban area. Bonny plans to build 20 units per acre, and Clyde, 1 unit per acre. Suppose that the prices that Bonny and Clyde will get per unit of housing services are equal, that both operate in the same labor and capital market, and that construction technologies and management efficiency are identical. Finally, suppose that unit transportation costs are uniform throughout the urban area.

    a. Who will locate closer to the city center? Why?

    b. Suppose that the local government passes land-use legislation that prohibits densities greater than 10 units per acre. Assuming that Bonny alone changes her plans, show what happens to the bid-rent curves and the rent gradient. Diagram the new bid-rent functions for Bonny and Clyde.

3. A tax on land is shown by a decrease in demand rather than shifting the supply curve inward. Draw a graph similar to Figure 12.1 and show the effects of the imposition of a new land tax on the diagram. Now draw the graph in Figure 12.2 and show the same land tax. Does anything change?

4. Say that you are considering the purchase of a 320-acre farm. You hope to earn revenues equaling $80,000 each year, and the interest rate looks like it will be approximately 6% for the foreseeable future. You plan to farm for 5 years before you retire. What is the maximum price you should pay for your farm?

Research Assignments

1. Find the amount of wetlands and woodlands in your county in 1997 and again in 2002 according to the *Census of Agriculture*

(http://www.nass.usda.gov/census/). Has the amount increased or decreased?

2. What is the average value of farmland per acre in your county? How does this compare with your state? Has the amount of land used in farming increased or decreased since the last census? (http://www.nass.usda.gov/census/).

References

Anas, A. 1987. *Modeling in Urban and Regional Economics.* Fundamentals of pure and applied economics series, regional and urban economics section no, Chur/Switzerland/London/New York/Melbourne: Harwood Academic.

Anas, A. 1990. Taste heterogeneity and urban spatial structure: the Logit model and monocentric theory reconciled. *Journal of Urban Economics* 28 (3):318–335.

Anas, A. 1995. Capitalization of urban travel improvements into residential and commercial real estate: simulations with a unified model of housing, travel mode and shopping choices. *Journal of Regional Science* 35 (3):351–375.

Baumont, C., and J.-M.Huriot. 1998. The monocentric model and after. *Recherches Economiques De Louvain* 64 (1):23–43.

Berechman, J. 1980. A general framework for the integration of a land-use model with a transportation model component. *Journal of Regional Science* 20 (1):51–69.

Capozza, D. R., and R. W. Helsley. 1989. The fundamentals of land prices and urban growth. *Journal of Urban Economics* 26 (3):295–306.

Cavailhes, J., C. Dessendre, F. Goffettee-Nagoa, and B. Schmitt. 1994. Change in the French countryside: some analytical propositions. *European Review of Agricultural Economics* 21 (3– 4):429–449.

Chen, H.-P. 1996. The simulation of a proposed nonlinear dynamic urban growth model. *Annals of Regional Science* 30 (3):305–319.

Clapp, J., H. O. Pollakowski, and L. Lynford. 1992. Intrametropolitan location and office market dynamics. *American Real Estate and Urban Economics Association Journal* 20 (2):229–257.

Clapp, J. M., M. Rodriguez, and R. K. Pace. 2001. Residential land values and the decentralization of jobs. *Journal of Real Estate Finance and Economics* 22 (1):43–61.

Cropper, M. L. 1981. The value of urban amenities. *Journal of Regeonal Science* 21 (3):359–374.

Cropper, M. L., L. Deck, N. Kishor, and K. E. McConnell. 1993. Valuing product attributes using single market data: a comparison of hedonic and discrete choice approaches. *Review of Economics and Statistics* 75 (2):225–232.

Duranton, G. 1997a. L'analyse économique du zonage urbain: une brève revue de la littérature. *Revue d'Economie Régionale et Urbaine* 0 (2):171–187.

Duranton, G. 1997b. Une approche alternative du zonage. *Recherches Economiques De Louvain* 63 (3):271–292.

Elad, R. L., I. D. Clifton, and J. E. Epperson. 1994. Hedonic estimation applied to the farmland market in Georgia. *Journal of Agricultural and Applied Economics* 26 (2):351–366.

Evans, A. W. 1983. The determination of the price of land. *Urban Studies* 20 (2):119–129.

Evans, A. W. 1991. On monopoly rent. *Land Economics* 67 (1):1–14.

Evans, A. W. 1993. On monopoly rent: reply. *Land Economics* 69 (1):111–112.

Fujita, M. 1989. *Urban Economic Theory: Land Use and City Size.* Cambridge; New York and Melbourne: Cambridge University Press.

Garreau, J. 1991. *Edge City: Life on the New Frontier.* New York: Doubleday.

Gaschet, F. 2002. The new intra-urban dynamics: suburbanisation and functional specialisation in French cities. *Papers in Regional Science* 81 (1):63–81.

Goffette-Nagot, F. 1996a. Choix résidentiels et diffusion périurbaine. *Revue d'Economie Régionale et Urbaine* 0 (2):229–246.

Goffette-Nagot, F. 1996b. Un modèle radioconcentrique pour l'analyse des espaces ruraux périurbains. *Revue d'Economie Régionale Et Urbaine* 0 (4):813–832.

Green, R. K., and M. J. White. 1997. Measuring the benefits of homeowning: effects on children. *Journal of Urban Economics* 41 (3):441–461.

Guntermann, K. L. 1997. Residential land prices prior to development. *Journal of Real Estate Research* 14 (1–2):1–17.

Hamilton, B. W. 1982. Wasteful commuting. *Journal of Political Economy* 90 (5):1035–1051.

Hamilton, B. W. 1989. Wasteful commuting again. *Journal of Political Economy* 97 (6):1497–1504.

Hansen, E. R. 1990. Agglomeration economies and industrial decentralization: the wage-productivity trade-offs. *Journal of Urban Economics* 28 (2):140–159.

Hardie, I. W., T. A. Narayan, and B. L. Gardner. 2001. The joint influence of agricultural and nonfarm factors on real estate values: an application to the mid-Atlantic region. *American Journal of Agricultural Economics* 83 (1):120–132.

Hatta, T., and T. Ohkawara. 1993. Population, employment, and land price distributions in the Tokyo metropolitan area. *Journal of Real Estate Finance and Economics* 6 (1):103–128.

Henneberry, D. M., and R. L. Barrows. 1990. Capitalization of exclusive agricultural zoning into farmland prices. *Land Economics* 66 (3):249–258.

Hodge, I. D., and M. Whitby. 1986. The U.K.: rural development, issues and analysis. *European Review of Agricultural Economics* 13 (3):391–413.

Ijichi, K., and M. Shimbun. 2000. Rail link for Kansai airport faces grounding. Mainichi Newspaper http://www.mainichi.co.jp/english/news/, (accessed 22 September 2003).

Kivell, P. 1993. *Land and the City: Patterns and Processes of Urban Change.* Geography and environment series, London and New York: Routledge.

Krakover, S., and E. Casetti. 1988. Directionally biased metropolitan growth: a model and a case study. *Economic Geography* 64 (1):17–28.

Lee, K. S. 1982. A model of intraurban employment location: an application to Bogotá, Colombia. *Journal of Urban Economics* 12 (3):263–279.

Lee, K. S. 1989. *The Location of Jobs in a Developing Metropolis: Patterns of Growth in Bogotá and Cali, Colombia.* World Bank research publication series New York; London; Toronto and Melbourne: Oxford University Press for the World Bank.

Lee, K. S. 1990. A model of intraurban employment location: estimation results from Seoul data. *Journal of Urban Economics* 27 (1):60–72.

Leigh, J. P. 1986. Are compensating wages paid for time spent commuting? *Applied Economics* 18 (11):1203–1213.

Lowe, M. S. 2000. Britain's regional shopping centres: new urban forms? *Urban Studies* 37 (2):261–274.

Margo, R. A. 1992. Explaining the postwar suburbanization of population in the United States: the role of income. *Journal of Urban Economics* 31 (3):301–310.

McCann, P. 1995. Journey and transactions frequency: an alternative explanation of rent-gradient convexity. *Urban Studies* 32 (9):1549–1556.

McDonald, J. F., and C. I. Osuji. 1995. The effect of anticipated transportation improvement on residential land values. *Regional Science and Urban Economics* 25 (3):261–278.

McMillen, D. P., R. Jarmin, and P. Thorsnes. 1992. Selection bias and land development in the monocentric city model. *Journal of Urban Economics* 31 (3):273–284.

Nelson, A. C., and T. W. Sanchez. 1997. Exurban and suburban households: a departure from traditional location theory? *Journal of Housing Research* 8 (2):249–276.

Ota, M., and M. Fujita. 1993. Communication technologies and spatial organization of multi- unit firms in metropolitan areas. *Regional Science and Urban Economics* 23 (6):695–729.

Peiser, R. B. 1987. The determinants of nonresidential urban land values. *Journal of Urban Economics* 22 (3):340–360.

Phillips, R. A., and J. H. Vanderhoff. 1991. Two–earner households and demand: the effect of the wife's occupational choice. *Journal of Real Estate Finance and Economics* 4 (1): 83–91.

Pickrell, D. 1999. Transportation and land use. In *Essays in Transportation Economics and Policy: A Handbook in Honor of John R. Meyer*, eds., J. A. Gomez-Ibanez, W. B. Tye, and C. Winston, Brookings Institution Press, Washington, DC, 403–435.

Polèse, M., S. Perez, and C. Barragan. 1995. Développement et forme urbaine: le déplacement de l'activité commerciale et industrielle dans la ville de Puebla. *Canadian Journal of Development Studies* 16 (1):105–130.

Polinsky, A. M., and S. Shavell. 1976. Amenities and property values in a model of an urban area. *Journal of Public Economics* 5 (1–2):119–129.

Reitsma, R. F., and D. Vergoossen. 1988. A causal typology of migration: The role of commuting. *Regional Studies* 22 (4): 331–340.

Romain, R. 1994. Les subventions des taux d'intérêt et le prix de la terre agricole au Québec. *Canadian Journal of Agricultural Economics* 42 (1):51–64.

Rosen, S. 1974. Hedonic prices and implicit markets: product differentiation in pure competition. *Journal of Political Economy* 82 (1):34–55.

Sasaki, K. 1991. An empirical analysis of the space rent and land rent within a central business district. *Environment and Planning A* 23 (1):139–146.

Shi, Y. J., T. T. Phipps, and D. Colyer. 1997. Agricultural land values under urbanizing influences. *Land Economics* 73 (1):90–100.

Shieh, Y. 1983. Location and bid price curves of the urban firm. *Urban Studies* 20 (4):491–494.

Smith, B. H. 1991. Anxiety as a cost of commuting to work. *Journal of Urban Economics* 29 (2):260–266.

So, K. S., P. F. Orazem, and D. M. Otto. 2001. The effects of housing prices, wages, and commuting time on joint residential and job location choices. *American Journal of Agricultural Economics* 83 (4):1036–1048.

Thünen, J. H. von. 1966 [1826]. The Isolated State; an English edition of Der isolierte staat. Translated by Carla M. Wartenberg. Edited with an introduction by Peter Hall. Oxford, New York, Pergamon Press.

Wachs, M., B. D. Taylor, N. Levine, and P. Ong. 1993. The changing commute: a case-study of the jobs-housing relationship over time. *Urban Studies* 30 (10):1711–1729.

Waddell, P., B. J. L. Berry, and I. Hoch. 1993. Residential property values in a multinodal urban area: new evidence on the implicit price of location. *Journal of Real Estate Finance and Economics* 7 (2):117–141.

Welch, W. P. 1989. Improving medicare payments to HMOs: urban core versus suburban ring. *Inquiry* 26 (1):62–71.

White, M. J. 1988. Urban commuting journeys are not "wasteful". *Journal of Political Economy* 96 (5):1097–1110.

Yamaga, H. 2000. The impacts of fare reimbursement and congestion charge on housing rent: the case of a commuter train line in Tokyo. *Review of Urban and Regional Development Studies* 12 (3):200–211.

Yinger, J. 1993. Around the block: urban models with a street grid. *Journal of Urban Economics* 33 (3):305–330.

Chapter 13

The Housing Market

Everyone needs shelter. According to psychologist Maslow's (1943) hierarchy of needs, it is only after we satisfy the physiological needs (i.e., health,
food, clothing, and shelter) that we worry about social needs such as safety,
love, self-esteem, or self-actualization. The Universal Declaration of Rights
of Man (1948), Article 25-1 states:

> Everyone has the right to a standard of living adequate for the
> health and well-being of himself and of his family, including
> food, clothing, housing, and medical care and necessary social
> services, and the right to security in the event of unemployment,
> sickness, disability, widowhood, old age or other lack of liveli-
> hood in circumstances beyond his control.[1]

Not only is housing essential for life, it is also one of the most regulated,
taxed, and subsidized goods in the world. It is subject to extensive
government intervention because of market failure. Market failure is due
to both positive and negative externalities that are inherent in the housing
market. These come about because residents simultaneously influence and
are influenced by their neighborhoods, their neighbors, and the decisions of
local government concerning the quality of schools and other public
services. The (sometimes questionable) tastes and decorating decisions of
previous owners and neighbors, as well as neighborhood amenities (or

---

[1] Office of the United Nations High Commissioner for Human Rights (1948).

disamenities), create a bundle of characteristics that cannot be separated from the physical quality of a house.[2]

The first question we answer is whether the supply and demand model is valid in the analysis of the inefficiency of the housing market. If it is, we must decide how to measure the price and quantity of housing before we are able to consider the effect of commuting, the decisions to buy or rent, as well as the questions of segregation and affordable housing.

Why Is the Housing Market Inefficient?

An efficient market has three components: (1) a large number of buyers and sellers, (2) homogeneous goods, and (3) the distribution of perfect information about the quality of the good. Some authors assert that traditional supply and demand models cannot explain the housing market because: (1) there is a limited number of buyers and sellers in a given period and for a particular market, (2) every house is a heterogeneous product, and (3) not even the sellers are always aware of hidden defects in their house.

But is there ever a perfectly efficient market? Evans (1995) calculated that the stock market comes closest at approximately 99% efficiency, but the housing market is only 90% efficient. An inefficient market means that the market does not completely determine the price. Psychology, search strategies, and negotiating ability of buyers and sellers are also important. To decrease search costs, sellers have recourse to real estate agents who work for commission. These agents help the seller determine the prices because they have information about comparable sales.

Despite the evident inefficiency of the market, economists continue to use supply and demand to explain fluctuations in prices. Houses are treated like any other asset. Rather than determined by the market, the "price" is in effect a distribution of prices, where the mean of the distribution represents the equilibrium for a specific house. One way to assess such a distribution is by using "thick" supply and demand curves (Figure 13.1). At each quantity, there is a bell-shaped distribution of potential prices. The middle of the distribution is the estimated value of the property. The tails of the distribution represent the most probable range of selling prices, according to whether the seller or the buyer is the better negotiator. A 10% margin of error on both supply and demand means that a property estimated at a value of $100,000 may sell at any price between $90,000 and $110,000.

Besides price, the expected quality of life and average after-tax real income are the most important variables in a regression equation used to estimate the aggregate demand for housing. Housing supply is influenced

---

[2] Minford, Ashton, and Peel (1988); Roberds (1992); Evans (1995); Archer, Gatzlaff, and Ling (1996).

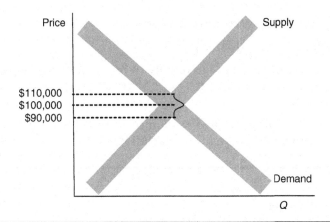

Figure 13.1 Thick supply and demand curves for housing.

primarily by construction costs and the supply of undeveloped land. There are in effect two housing markets: one market for housing stock and one for the flow of housing services (utility to consumers from the consumption of certain types of houses). Models of housing stock analyze either the median sales prices along with the total quantity of houses, or markets for specific types of housing (corner apartments facing south, two-bedroom ranch houses, mobile homes at the interior of a well-kept park, or Victorian-style houses at the urban fringe). In contrast, the models of the flow of housing services describe the opportunity cost of housing.[3]

Housing Services

Because of the inherent heterogeneity in the housing market, researchers use the nebulous concept of "housing services" as the "quantity." Conceptually, two units of housing services provide twice the utility as one unit of housing services.

Think About It...

Find the asking price of housing in your neighborhood.

Compare these prices with those in adjacent

---

[3] Case and Shiller (1987, 1989); Rothenberg et al. (1991); Arnott (1994); Evans (1995); Rouwendal (1998).

neighborhoods or jurisdictions.

Why is there a difference?

Because of the average quality of housing? The quality of the neighborhood? School quality? Incomes of residents?

Because of proximity to employment? To natural amenities? To recreational facilities?

Housing Prices

Reports of soaring real estate prices make eye-catching headlines. In reality, they mean very little. For residential properties, the most widely reported price trends are compiled by the National Association of Realtors. Their price trends consist of the median value of existing single family housing as reported by the transactions negotiated in a number of metropolitan areas. However, these sales prices are not standardized for any characteristics of the dwellings bought and sold. Real estate prices can "soar" merely because regions implemented more stringent housing codes.

Two concepts of the term "housing price" correspond to the two types of housing markets. For the **stock of housing**, price is the amount paid for the average dwelling. For owner-occupied houses, the price is simply the purchase price. For rental units, the monthly rent is the price.

The price for the **flow of services** is more difficult to estimate. Because a tar-paper shack represents fewer "housing units" than a 17-room mansion, for instance, we need some method of defining the price per unit of housing services. In fact, we have two principle techniques: repeated sales price index and the hedonic regression technique.

The **repeat sales price index** (Bailey, Muth, and Nourse 1963; Case and Shiller 1987) is one way to standardize changes in house prices. Researchers avoid the difficulty of specifying and measuring the various characteristics of homes by creating an index of average sales prices of homes sold more than once over a specific time. The increase in the price of one home over a given period more accurately measures housing inflation. This method eliminates properties that have only been sold once during a specific period as well as the houses resold after undergoing substantial renovations.

The method has some drawbacks. First, it ignores potentially valuable information when it excludes properties. In addition, although it excludes properties whose physical characteristics have changed between sales, very few datasets pinpoint neighborhoods endowed with a newly established crack house, a new golf course, or an improved school system. The market prices, on the other hand, will reflect these changes. Finally, according to Akerlof's (1970) Market for Lemons, houses that are sold repeatedly probably have structural defects. To the extent that the repeat sales price index is dominated by these "lemons," this index would give lower price estimates for structurally solid houses. Regardless of these drawbacks, the repeat sales price index may be the only viable way to estimate house price inflation within a community.[4]

The *hedonic regression technique* is the second way to statistically standardize the prices of both houses and housing services. This technique results in a distribution of prices for urban housing dependent on the amenities of the house and its surrounding area.

Think About It...

Determine the average wage for your (intended) occupation from http://www.bls.gov/bls/blswage.htm and multiply that by the number of years you plan to work. The average family spends 26 percent of its income on housing.

Plan the most basic single-family (starter) house: How many rooms? How many square feet does it have? How many floors? Basement? How many bedrooms? Bathrooms? Type of garage? How much yard space? Find a similar home in your area for sale. What is its price?

Use a mortgage calculator on the Internet to determine the total amount of interest you will pay at the current rate. Also check to determine the annual cost of homeowners' insurance in your area.

What proportion of your total earnings is your basic house (plus interest and total insurance)?

Now, how much would you pay to upgrade your basic home?

For one more bedroom?

For a fireplace?

For an increase of 100 sq. ft.

---

[4] Barnett (1985); Manning (1989); Case and Quigley (1991); Gyourko and Voith (1992); Muth (1996).

For 100 sq. ft. more of yard space?

For one more bathroom?

For central heating or air conditioning?

——————?

——————?

Housing Hedonics

The hedonic technique quantifies the effect of various housing and neighborhood characteristics on house prices. Market prices attributable to specific features reflect consumer preferences, as well as the installation costs. This technique uses regression analysis to explain variations in market prices for single-family homes. The dependent variable is the transaction price, or some other estimate of market value. Independent variables are features such as the square feet of living space, the lot size, the number of bedrooms, the age of the structure, the presence or absence of a swimming pool, a fireplace, a deck, a porch, or other characteristics. Researchers often add independent variables to account for the value of various neighborhood amenities.[5]

Amenities and Housing Values

Brueckner, Thisse, and Zenov (1999) identified three types of amenities that affect housing values: ***natural amenities*** (such as green spaces, proximity to bodies of water, or other scenic landscapes), ***historic districts***, and ***endogenous amenities*** (such as quality education and other publicly provided services, proximity to transit routes, and proximity to nice restaurants or other urban facilities). Changes in land prices due to natural amenities are surprisingly consistent across studies. Green space, waterfront, and landscaping all add a fairly consistent amount to home values.

Green Is Gold for Homeowners

Amenities include open spaces even without proximity to scenic waterways. Rural areas provide green space

---

[5] See Cropper et al. (1993) for a comparison of the hedonic model and multinomial logit model for estimating amenity attributes; Goodman and Thibodeau (1995).

and tranquility, easier access to recreational opportunities, and absence of urban disamenities. Proximity to small neighborhood parks can affect the value of a home up to 1500 ft. away, according to studies using data from both Greenville, South Carolina, and Portland, Oregon. Properties adjacent to golf courses around San Diego, California, sold at an average premium of 7.6 percent. Even if the residents do not play golf, they "bought" low population density, as well as privacy. Green spaces enhance residential land values, but they do not always affect the values of industrial or commercial land.

Peiser (1987), Do and Grudnitski (1995),
Bender et al. (1997), Espey and
Owusu-Edusei (2001) Irwin and Bockstael (2001),
Lutzenhiser and Netusil (2001)

Benefits of Cocooning

When a population ages, the people tend to "cocoon," that is, to spend more time and more money renovating their homes and yards. Des Rosiers et al. (2002) noted that cocooning activities can add significant value to a house.

Data from sales of 760 single-family homes in Quebec between 1993 and 2000 shows that the presence of trees between two properties increases their values, especially if there are many retired people in the neighborhood. Well-groomed lawns, flower gardens, rock gardens, and hedges also command a sizeable market premium. Hedges boosted housing values by 3.9 percent on average, a landscaped patio raised house values by 12.4 percent, and landscaped curbs, 4.4 percent.

Des Rosiers et al. (2002)

How Much Is Waterfront Worth?

The aesthetic and recreational advantage of waterfront properties falls rapidly with distance, becoming asymptotic to some minimum value. Lakefront properties in central Texas and in northwestern Wisconsin commanded prices 22 percent greater than otherwise equal properties. A view of the ocean in Bellingham, Washington, increased the market price of an otherwise comparable home by between 8 and 60 percent, depending on the quality of the view. The value of an ocean view decreased with distance from the water.

Land-use restrictions that limited residential development around Chesapeake Bay, Massachusetts, were adopted to protect the coastal environment and water quality, but they had a substantial effect on housing prices. These restrictions increased prices for houses with water frontage from 46 to 62 percent. Prices for housing without frontage increased from 14 to 27 percent. Prices for housing near but not in the critical areas increased from 13 to 21 percent because of the ecological restrictions.

Smith (1993), Landford and Jones (1995a, 1995b),
Doss and Taff (1996), Benson et al. (1998),
Spalatro and Provencher (2001)

Historic districts affect housing values if they change the demand. Current residents are tempted to move for the following reasons:

- The property that they were renting was converted to owner-occupied housing.
- A higher sale price for their homes makes selling more desirable.
- The consequent property tax increases drive older, fixed income residents from their neighborhoods.

Higher income people may move into historic districts, but unless these districts attract new residents to the city, the higher demand (and prices) for housing in this area only decreases demand (and prices) for housing outside the district. The creation of a historic district is generally accompanied by better public services in the district, such as greater police protection, more frequent garbage collection, and better maintained streets. Thus, it is difficult to distinguish whether the increased housing values are due to better services or because of the location within the historic district itself.

History Pays

Historic districts in many European cities generally increase land values but this does not always happen in the United States. Since the 1980s, cities in the United States have tried historic preservation of residential and commercial property to revive the declining metropolitan areas. The local housing market conditions and zoning rules determine whether an historic designation will increase or decrease property values.

For instance, a study of nine Texas cities determined that historic designation increased property values from 5 to 20 percent. Likewise, the designation in four of the six preservation districts in Sacramento, California, caused property values to rise. But the historic designation in Aurora, Illinois, only increased housing prices by about 6–7 percent, and the one in Elgin, Illinois, made no statistically significant impact on prices.

Coffin (1989), Clark and Herrin (1997),
Brueckner, Thisse, and Zenou (1999),
Leichenko, Coulson, and Listokin (2001)

School Quality and Property Values

The quality of public goods is capitalized into property values just as the Tiebout hypothesis predicts. Residents of Fresno County, California, value attributes of schools more than environmental quality. Property values around Dallas, Texas, reflect student test scores rather than school expenditures per pupil. In Ohio metropolitan areas, each percentage point increase in the number of ninth grade students who pass the statewide proficiency exam increased house prices by an average of 0.5 percent. Because pass rates ranged between 6 and 89 percent, estimated house prices varied greatly due to this variable alone. The fact that the better schools had a larger population of whites constitutes another reason. However, studies from Charlotte, North Carolina, and Los Angeles County, California, found that school quality and not race affected housing values.

Similarly, unpopular decisions taken by school district administrators decrease home prices and thereby the property tax base used to fund education. For example, a proposal to save costs by creating a 12-month school year in Las Vegas, Nevada, reduced home prices by about 5.2 percent. The expected savings did not compensate for the loss caused by the decline in property prices. Likewise, in 1987, an unpopular school redistricting plan in Shaker Heights, Ohio caused social and racial problems, disrupting neighborhood schools so much that within seven years, housing values had fallen by 9.9 percent or $5738 for the average value home.

Jud and Bennett (1986),
Haurin and Brasington (1996),
Hayes and Taylor (1996),
Clark and Herrin (2000),
Clauretie and Neill (2000)

Neighborhood Churches: A Blessing or a Curse?

Proximity to a neighborhood church affects housing prices. In Chula Vista, California, the presence of a church significantly decreased sales prices of houses up to 850 ft. away. However, this finding is not national. Property values were higher, all else equal within a half-mile radius of a church in Henderson, Nevada, a suburb of Las Vegas. Carroll, Clauretie, and Jensen (1996) quip that because residents of Henderson live so close to

"Sin City" (Las Vegas) they prefer a church be built on vacant lots rather than a neighborhood casino.

Do, Wilbur, and Short (1994),
Carroll, Clauretie, and Jensen (1996)

Crime Steals Housing Values

Reductions in the crime rate increased land values in Boston, Massachusetts, and Jacksonville, Florida. The Jacksonville study used data from fiscal year 1994–1995 and found that homes in high crime areas were discounted by about 39 percent compared to otherwise identical houses elsewhere.

Epple and Sieg (1998),
Lynch and Rasmussen (2001)

Disamenities and Land Values

The presence of a noxious or even potentially bothersome site decreases the demand for nearby land, causing prices to fall. Undesirable effects of neighboring land include health risks (such as pollution, allergens, and noise) and blots on the landscape by the presence of unaesthetic structures. These negative effects translate into lower values for adjacent property. This impact decreases with distance.[6]

Pollution Fouls Property Values

Air quality affects house values. In the Los Angeles basin, a 20 percent improvement in average visibility increased housing values by between $875 and $3178 per year. Proximity to hog farms in southeastern North Carolina reduced home prices by up to 9 percent

---

[6] Farber (1998).

depending on the distance from the house to the feeder lot and the size of the facility.

Noise also lowers land values, but the effects dissipate rapidly. A study of railroad proximity in Oslo, Norway, found that two identical houses, one situated 65 ft. from a railroad line and the other situated 328 ft. away, differed in price by about 182,000 NOK, or $26,093. In Kingsgate, a northern suburb of Seattle, Washington, the effect of highway noise vanished for houses 1000 ft. from the road.

The price of houses located 300 ft. from underground storage tanks (whether they leaked or not) decreased prices by 17 percent in Cuyahoga County, Ohio. Electric transmission lines also decrease property values because of the visual externalities of the transmission towers.

Palmquist (1992), Hamilton and Schwann (1995),
Palmquist, Roka, and Vukina (1997),
Simons, Bowen, and Sementelli (1997),
Beron, Murdoch, and Thayer (2001),
Strand and Vagnes (2001)

Amenities and Household Sorting

An airport can be an amenity or disamenity. Proximity to the Reno–Sparks airport (Reno, Nevada) had a significantly negative value on properties. The average home in areas where noise levels could reach 65 db or higher lost $2400 of its value compared to equivalent homes in quiet neighborhoods. Proximity to airports and airport noise decreases housing values by an average 0.65 percent. This number has been consistent for several decades and in a number of Western countries. In contrast, improved access and employment opportunities of living close to the airport increased residential values in Manchester, United Kingdom.

The proximity to a nuclear power plant could surprisingly create a premium. At Diablo Canyon, California, for example, there is a premium paid for houses within a radius of 23 miles from the plant. The area surrounding the plant is less urban and offers more green space. Negative impacts from perceived risks did not overwhelm the positive attributes of more green space.

Uyeno, Hamilton, and Biggs (1993),
Clark et al. Herrin (1997), Tomkins et al. (1998),
Espey and Lopez (2000)

Housing Supply Functions

Four features set housing supply apart from the supply of other goods:

1. Houses are costly to build and, therefore, a risky investment.
2. Housing is a durable good.
3. Two absolutely identical houses are still different because of their locations.
4. Once a house is produced, it is impossible to move it along with its neighborhood amenities.

In addition, housing supply comes from three types of economic actors, each of which reacts to different incentives: (1) builders of new home and rental agencies, (2) current homeowners, and (3) public agencies. New home builders and rental agencies are firms that maximize profits. Builders must provide the type and quality of housing that new-home buyers want under the existing building codes. Rental agencies decide the amount of maintenance on the basis of their expected rate of return and rental housing codes.

Homeowners respond to incentives that maximize either their incomes or their utilities. These homeowners may lease part of their houses, thereby increasing the supply of rental units. Homeowners also determine the optimal amount of maintenance or rehabilitation in which they should invest, and thereby influence the depreciation rates on existing housing. In fast-growing housing markets, homeowners are likely to spend more on the improvements because they are certain of an increased return on their investment. Between 1993 and 2002 for example, the funds devoted to home improvements totaled between 40 and 50% of the spending for new single-family and multifamily dwellings. We investigate the incentives of government in providing housing later in the chapter.[7]

---

[7] Bajic (1991); Montgomery (1992); Mayer and Somerville (1996); Hakfoort and Matysiak (1997); Blackley (1999); DiPasquale (1999); Fergus (1999); Pryce (1999); United States Bureau of Census (2002).

Housing Demand

Increases in the demand for housing come from one of two sources: in-migrants or new householders. Both of these components are affected by the city's business cycle and the age of the householder. During a recession, few migrate. Rather than form new households, many new householders choose cohabitation (sometimes with their parents). The reverse is true when jobs are more plentiful and higher paying.

Housing Elasticity

Housing supply is more price inelastic in the short run than the long run. Long-run elasticity estimates vary from between 1.6 and 3.9 in the United States, to 6.0 in The Netherlands. Supply is less elastic during economic booms than during economic slumps. New housing starts are as much a function of weather, land, and other input costs, credit availability and regulatory-imposed delays as they are of house prices.

The price elasticity estimates for owner-occupied housing range from -0.09 (Italy) to -0.73 (Tokyo metropolitan region). Price elasticities for the U.S. housing market range from -0.32 to -0.51. Income elasticities range from 0.31 to 0.65. However, the variance in income is also an important determinant of demand. A 10 percent increase in the variability of income reduces homeownership by the same amount as a 5 percent decrease in income.

Haurin (1991), Mayer and Somerville (1996),
Hakfoort and Matysiak (1997),
Haurin and Chung (1998), Blackley (1999),
Fergus (1999), Pryce (1999), Nese (1999),
Tiwari and Hasegawa (2000)

According to the **life cycle hypothesis**, age groups view changes in household formation differently. The 15- to 25-year-old people would rather not live with their parents or friends if the cost of housing and their incomes permit. Housing costs, race and ethnicity, health problems, and an urban or rural location also influence the need for independence. Likewise, decreases in marriage rates and increases in divorce rates increase the demand for housing.

The demand for low-density housing declines with family size but rises as age and incomes increase. High apartment rents increase the demand for owner-occupied single-family homes because these are substitute goods. Similarly, higher house prices increase the demand for high-density rental apartments.[8]

Think About It...

Do you own or rent? What influenced your housing decision? Do or did your parents own or rent?

What about your grandparents?

What would cause you to change your tenure choice?

Tenure Choice

Housing tenure refers to the contractual arrangement by which someone is allowed to inhabit a specific dwelling. The two main forms of housing tenure are owner occupancy and tenancy, where rent is paid to the actual owner or landlord. ***Tenure choice*** (choosing to rent or own) depends on a comparison of the net marginal benefits, and depends principally on the wealth of the family and the preferences of the household, which vary with age.

Owner-occupied housing is unique because it is both an investment good and a consumption good. As an investment, housing often comprises the largest portion of a household's asset portfolio. Consumption of and investment in housing are intricately related to a household's savings decisions. Nevertheless, only a small fraction (20%) of young people who leave their parents' home to live as a couple can start out by purchasing their own homes. Homeownership is greatest among older "nest leavers" with higher incomes, those whose parents are homeowners, and those who form a partnership. Those whose parents are homeowners are more likely to become homeowners themselves and to do so more quickly than those whose parents rented. The intergenerational effects favoring home ownership reflect the transfers of resources from parents to their adult children as well as the adult child's own tastes and ambitions.

---

[8] Mills (1991); Haurin, Hendershott, and Kim (1993); Skaburskis (1999); Harding, Miceli, and Sirmans (2000); Garasky, Haurin, and Haurin (2001).

Older people sell their homes and rent when they need to become more financially liquid, often so that they can leave a significant inheritance or pay their medical bills. Housing wealth is often treated as precautionary savings and is spent only after much of the other financial assets have been liquidated.

The amount of the down payment required by mortgage lenders constrains a household's tenure choice. In The Netherlands, people do not need to accumulate financial wealth before they purchase their homes because buyers do not need a down payment. Where there are no borrowing constraints, tenure choice affects the level of financial wealth; if people are not renting, they are investing more in home equity. In the United States, borrowing constraints are more important than potential earnings in the tenure decision. Borrowing constraints reduce the home ownership by as much as 10%–20%.

In 1940, when the United States federal income tax rates were much lower, only 40% of the dwellings were owned by the occupants. This percentage was 67% in 1999. This increase in home ownership is due to a change in borrowing costs and greater tax advantages. The Veterans Administration Mortgage Guarantee Program, started after World War II, brought down both the mortgage interest rates and the required down payments, thereby increasing the number of homeowners.[9]

Why Do Parisian Rents Rise with Unemployment?

Blondel and Marchand (1997) observed that apartment rent in exclusive neighborhoods in Paris is lower than in less elite neighborhoods. The discrepancy in rents reflects the risk of nonpayment. If the renter does not pay the monthly rent, the landlord cannot pay back the loan on the apartment and may lose that investment. The risk of nonpayment depends on the financial solvency of the household: employment status, average income, whether the tenant is foreign, and the probability of divorce. As the financial solvency of

---

[9] Sweeney (1974); Boehm, Herzog and Schlottmann (1991); Haurin (1991); Dusansky and Wilson (1993); Clark, Deurloo, and Dieleman (1994); Jones (1995, 1997); Gyourko and Linneman (1996); Muth (1996); Di Salvo and Ermisch (1997); Goss and Phillips (1997); Green and White (1997); Haurin, Hendershott, and Wachter (1997); Haurin and Chung (1998); Henley (1998); Withers (1998); DiPasquale and Glaeser (1999); Kan (2000); Green and Hendershott (2001); Hochguertel and van Soest (2001).

the households decreases, the rental rates increase.

In France, as in many states in the United States, insolvent tenants are difficult to evacuate. Even if a court trial favors the landlord, the landlord cannot eject a nonpaying renter during winter months. Because of the difficulty of expulsion, poor households pay relatively higher rents than the rich.

Blondel and Marchand (1997)

Renters' Stats

A total of 36 percent of U.S. households rent. Essentially, six groups constitute the demand for rental housing:

■ Families: 17 percent

■ Lifestyle renters: 21 percent

■ College graduates who are starting out: 26 percent

■ Black renters: 15 percent

■ Elderly life cycle renters: 10 percent

■ Struggling blue-collar workers: 11 percent

Renting attracts those under 25 years of age and those past 75 years old. Renter incomes average 54 percent of homeowners. The rental payments represent 27 percent of their income on housing, compared to 21 percent for homeowners with mortgages. Renter households are smaller than those of homeowners. 33 percent of the renters are single, compared with 20 percent of the homeowners. Single parents are more likely to rent than own.

Varady and Lipman (1994)

Home Ownership and Community Stability

The existence of a large proportion of homeowners has a positive effect on a community. Home ownership increases the stability of a household, reducing unemployment rates, and the mobility of the family. Homeowners vote more often, they are politically active, and thus they affect social changes over time. They also invest in local amenities and social capital, thereby improving the quality of life of their community. Statistically, children of homeowners stay in school longer and their daughters are less likely to have children as teenagers.

Public policy enthusiastically promotes home ownership because homeowners are civic-minded and contribute to the welfare of the community. Instead of moving, unemployed homeowners are more inclined to search for a job more intensely to make their monthly mortgage payments. This reduces unemployment duration. Because home equity increases the wealth of the homeowners, if necessary, they could borrow against the asset and wait for a better job.

Clark, Deurloo, and Dieleman (1994),
Goss and Phillips (1997),
Green and White (1997), Henley (1998),
DiPasquale and Glaeser (1999)

Think About It...

In your city, where do high-income people live—in the suburbs or near the central business district? Where do the poorest people live?

Compared with the suburbs, does the central business district offer more cultural or natural amenities? Historic places? Upscale dining establishments? Theater or other recreational activities?

Do people of the same ethnicity seem to congregate in the same areas? Which ethnic groups seem to cluster together?

Income Differences in Housing Location

In the United States, middle- and high-income households generally prefer the suburbs. However, in many European, Latin American, and Asian cities, luxury apartments and townhouses cluster near the urban center. Brueckner, Thisse, and Zenou (1999) theorize that the geographic distribution of different income groups depends on the location of amenities. If the center provides more amenities than the suburbs, the rich will prefer life in a central location. If, in contrast, the center has few amenities, the rich will prefer suburban life.

In Paris, London, and Amsterdam for instance, the incomes of the central city residents are higher than those in the suburbs. The same pattern holds for Lyon (the second largest metropolitan area in France), Caen, and Nancy, but most French cities conform to the United States pattern. Brussels, Belgium, replaced much of its historical center with new office buildings to house the European Union agencies, causing an exodus of the rich toward the suburbs, as in the United States.

Although the rich are attracted by low housing prices in the suburbs, everything else equal, they need to account for the high opportunity cost of time that significantly increases their per-mile commuting costs. Amenities are also normal goods, and the marginal value of amenities increases sharply with income. Thus, the affluent value accessibility to an amenity-rich CBD more than do the poor, to decrease travel time. When the CBD does not offer many amenities, it cannot attract high-income residents.[10]

Residential Succession

In models with both high- and low-income groups, housing is constructed at one distance for high-income consumers and at a distance closer to the CBD for low-income consumers. The high-income housing is first occupied by high-income consumers and then filters to low-income consumers before it is abandoned. Conversely, low-income housing is only occupied by low-income consumers before being abandoned.

Residential succession examines how occupancy of one housing unit passes from one income or demographic group to another. Two models explain this process. The ***filtering model*** (also known as the Natural Evolution Theory of Urban Expansion) relies on the fact that both housing quality and quantity are normal goods; that is, as incomes increase, households consume greater amounts of housing services. Over time, there is a decline in the quality of housing, which compels a higher income

---

[10] Fujita (1989); Madden and Chiu (1990); Braid (1991); Assadian and Ondrich (1993); Polèse, Perez, and Barragan (1997); Bruekner, Thisse, and Zenou (1999).

household to move to a nicer and more spacious house. A household from a lower income group will move into their house, which is in better shape than the one they left behind. This causes housing units to filter down to a lower income group. See Figure 13.2. Improved transportation arteries facilitate this trend as highlighted in the box entitled *Commuting, housing, and labor markets.*

Commuting, Housing, and Labor Markets

Commuting ties together urban land uses, labor markets, residential neighborhoods, and transportation networks. Households are willing to pay a premium for accessibility. According to Quigley (1985), to save 1 hour of commuting time by car per month, households were willing to pay about 62 percent of the average pretax hourly wage per month (about $2.29) in higher rent.

If a large proportion of suburban residents work in the CBD, these suburbs often provide good commuter rail access. These residents own fewer cars and pay 6.4 percent more for housing than similar neighborhoods without commuter rail access.

The introduction of a transit system increases density near the transit line and decreases density elsewhere. If the change in transportation system causes an expansion of the city beyond its former economic borders, the expansion will be only in areas near the transit line.

Quigley (1985), Steen (1986),
Voith (1991a, 1991b)

In contrast, the **externality theory** emphasizes the fiscal and social environments of city centers, the neighbors' income levels, and racial composition in explaining housing turnover. A neighborhood initially inhabited by high-income residents could, for example, experience an influx of low-income households as their incomes trend upward. These new households lower the perceived quality of the neighborhood, decreasing the number of people who are willing to bid for housing. Higher income groups "vote with their feet" for neighborhoods populated by households more to their liking. If the externality effect is strong enough, the neighborhood may "tip" from high income to low income.

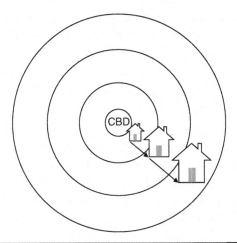

Figure 13.2   Filtering theory of residential succession.

If the tipping explanation holds, then the construction of low-income housing may be an efficient method of providing affordable housing. However, if the filtering model is correct; then housing policy specifically aimed at low-income households is less necessary.[11]

Segregation and Discrimination

DeRango (2001) noted that housing in the United States is more segregated now than it was in 1860, before the Civil War. If people could find more jobs by moving to the suburbs, why do they not move? Why does segregation persist? Is it the result of discrimination? Perhaps, but not necessarily.

Four hypotheses try to explain segregation:

1.   Interracial differences in income, perhaps due to discrimination in the labor market or inadequate schools, restrict the low-income residents (nonwhites) to inferior quality housing and neighborhoods, whereas higher income groups (whites) are able to move to new housing as the filtering hypothesis predicts.
2.   Different ethnic or cultural groups voluntarily sort themselves into specific neighborhoods.
3.   Racial steering by rental agents and realtors limits the choice of their clients in only showing them housing located in neighborhoods predominated by households of similar race and ethnicity.

---

[11] White (1986); Coulson and Bond (1990); Voith (1991a, 1991b, 2000).

4. Local housing and zoning regulations that (inadvertently) cause higher housing prices effectively bar low-income households from their jurisdictions.

Racial segregation could either help or hinder the economic achievement of minorities. According to Wilson (1987), racial segregation may ensure that minorities have middle-class role models live among them who serve as examples. The absence of these models deprives the young of a mentor who could encourage them. But on the other hand, segregation becomes an obstacle that impedes access to information, especially about employment opportunities. This isolation will lead to a geographic concentration of poverty and a tax base insufficient to provide quality schools, thereby encouraging illicit "trades."[12]

Dissimilarity Index

A dissimilarity (segregation) index measures the extent of residential segregation. It is computed thus:

$$D = \frac{1}{2} \sum_{i=1}^{n} \left| \frac{P_{iw}}{P_w} - \frac{P_{ih}}{P_h} \right| \times 100,$$

where: P_{iw} is the number of whites living in the ith census tract of the city; P_w is the total number of whites in the city; P_{ih} is the number of the specific racial/ethnic minority population k living in the ith census tract of the city; P_h is the total number of that specific population in the city; n is the number of census tracts in the city.

The dissimilarity index varies from 0 when the two proportions are equal (no segregation) to 100 (complete segregation). Using this index, Echenique and Fryer (2005) noted that in 2000, the most segregated city for Asians in the United States was Honolulu, Hawaii; for blacks, Detroit, Michigan; for Hispanics, McAllen, Texas; and for whites, Lowell, Massachusetts. They also noted that Los Angeles has the largest minority ghetto of Hispanics—17,909 contiguous blocks. Blacks in Detroit live in the second largest minority ghetto, but the largest segregated ghetto is located in Jackson, Mississippi. Table 13.1 provides a list of the ten most segregated cities in the United States for each of five racial groups and their associated dissimilarity index (*D*) using data from the 2000 Census.

---

[12] Cutler and Glaeser (1997); DeRango (2001).

Table 13.1 Top Ten Most Segregated Cities, by Racial Group

Whites		Blacks		Asians		Hispanics	
City	D	City	D	City	D	City	D
Lowell, Massachusetts	99.984	Detroit, Michigan	95.421	Honolulu, Hawaii	93.403	McAllen, Texas	95.85
Lawrence, Massachusetts	99.984	Monroe, Louisiana	94.912	San Francisco, California	80.56	Laredo, Texas	94.97
Nashua, New Hampshire	99.966	Milwaukee, Wisconsin	93.605	San Jose, California	71.692	Los Angeles, California	93.9
Sharon, Pennsylvania	99.952	Flint, Michigan	93.027	Los Angeles, California	65.878	El Paso, Texas	92.56
Boston, Massachusetts	99.949	Pine Bluff, Arkansas	92.744	Vallejo, California	63.447	San Antonio, Texas	90.48
York, Pennsylvania	99.947	Chicago, Illinois	92.060	Oakland, California	56.615	Brownsville, Texas	87.69
Barnstable, Massachusetts	99.947	Memphis, Tennessee	91.660	Anaheim, California	53.402	Tuscon, Arizona	86.54
Johnstown, Pennsylvania	99.944	Miami, Florida	91.513	Seattle, Washington	52.639	Anaheim, California	86.24
Providence, Rhode Island	99.943	Birmingham, Alabama	91.449	New York, New York	47.642	Corpus Christi, Texas	83.22
Springfield, Massachusetts	99.933	Gary, Indiana	91.418	San Diego, California	41.735	Albuquerque, New Mexico	82.46

Calculations performed using block-level data from all MSAs in the 2000 United States Census. The sample includes all census blocks in all MSAs. Racial categories are mutually exclusive. Asians include Pacific Islanders. *Source:* From Echenique, F. and Fryer, R.G. Jr., On the measurement of segregation, *NBER Working Papers*, National Bureau of Economic Research, Inc., 2005. With permission.

Inner-City Living and the Spatial Mismatch Hypothesis

According to the spatial mismatch hypothesis, structural unemployment is due to inadequate information about job availability or high costs of moving or commuting. Within an urban area, this hypothesis relates to structurally unemployed people who live in the inner city and who do not work in the suburbs. When the jobs move to the suburbs, the central city employees quit rather than commute. According to the *job access hypothesis* of Kain (1968, 1971), concentrations of minority populations within central cities limit the workers' access to the large number of job opportunities in the suburbs, and thus sustain structural unemployment. Wilson (1987) argued that out-migration of upwardly mobile blacks leaves fewer and weaker role models for the central city poor, and this influences the amount of structural unemployment.

Empirical tests of these hypotheses show mixed results regarding the validity of the spatial mismatch hypothesis. Researchers have used various models to attempt to capture the phenomenon. Weinberg (2004) reconciles the myriad of findings when he reported evidence of spatial mismatch only for residents of cities with a population greater than 500,000, but not for smaller urban areas. The evidence of spatial mismatch is strongest for youth, women, and elderly workers who do not have a college education.

Inner-city residents are dependent on a public transportation system that geographically limits the extent of their job search. As we will see in Chapter 14, public transportation systems are designed to transport workers from the suburbs to the CBD in the morning, and back home in the evening. Return trips carrying central city residents to the suburbs and back home are not common. However, even when transportation barriers are removed, spatial mismatch persists, not only because of the lack of information and inadequate schooling, but also because of the feeling of "not belonging" in the white suburbs. In addition, the long-term unemployed choose to remain in the inner city rather than move elsewhere and be subjected to racial profiling.[13]

Voluntary Sorting

Surprisingly little evidence supports the hypotheses that differences in income, wealth, or educational attainment significantly affect segregation levels. As incomes rise or fall, segregation levels do not vary by much. Racial

---

[13] McCormick (1986); Wilson (1987); Gordon, Kumar and Richardson (1989); Holzer (1991); Hughes and Madden (1991); Holzer, Ihlanfeldt and Sjoquist (1994); Taylor and Ong (1995); Coulson, Laing and Wang (2001); Gotlieb and Lentnek (2001); Smith and Zenou (2003).

segregation in housing does not seem to be a by-product of economic stratification. The hypothesis of voluntary sorting asserts that people want to live with people of their ethnic group. Farley, Fielding, and Krysan (1997) analyzed interview data from metropolitan Atlanta, Boston, Detroit, and Los Angeles and found that race remains significant in the choice of a neighborhood. Whites prefer to relocate in neighborhoods where few blacks live. Blacks prefer multiracial neighborhoods as long as there is a sizeable proportion of blacks.

Everything else equal, Gyourko, Linneman, and Wachter (1999) found no racial difference in ownership rates among those households capable of meeting the down payment and closing cost requirements required by the mortgage underwriters. However, over one-half of the sample of minorities did not have the money for a down payment, compared to approximately one-third of the white households. Nevertheless, whites who have trouble meeting the wealth requirements still own their own homes at higher rates than equivalent minority households. Minorities tend to own homes in the central city, whereas whites generally own in the suburbs.

Language and cultural attributes create neighborhood preferences. Residential succession tends to take place between households of the same ethnic group. Multi-ethnic neighborhoods, where the majority is nonwhite, attract foreign and native-born black and Hispanic households. Areas where the native language of most of the residents is not English attract immigrants with the same background.[14]

At What Price Culture?

Gonzalez (1998) calculated the price of Mexican culture using data for California and Texas from the 1990 Census. He found that the Mexicans who concentrated in "enclaves" earned less money and paid higher rents. In contrast, the non-Mexicans in these "enclaves" had higher earnings.

Mexican "islands" offer cultural amenities for which new immigrants are willing to pay a premium. If land rents there are higher, then workers without this cultural preference must be compensated with higher earnings to keep them from moving. The "price of

---

[14] Farley, Fielding and Krysan (1997); Gyourko, Linneman and Wachter (1999); Rosenbaum and Schill (1999); DeRango (2001).

Mexican culture" is highest for Mexican immigrants, slightly lower for Mexican–Americans, and statistically equal to zero for Asians, blacks, and whites.

Gonzalez (1998)

Racial (Geographic) Steering

According to the ***perceived preference hypothesis***, real estate agents or rental agents may discriminate to save the minority customer from moving to a potentially hostile neighborhood. Real estate agents are under the impression that the minority client would be more comfortable in a neighborhood that already has minorities of the same group. Agents only want to maximize the number of sales and their own profits (commissions). They profile their clients to save the time needed for a complete interview, or by only showing the clients the housing that they (the agents) think that the client would like. Real estate agents can also steer clients by providing positive and negative commentary on home locations and neighborhoods.

The practice of racial steering has been illegal in the United States since 1968, but only recently does the practice seem to have become less frequent. The Department of Housing and Urban Development (HUD) conducted fair housing audits in Cincinnati, Ohio, and Memphis, Tennessee, in 1989 and again in 2000. Black, Hispanic, and white auditors were sent to the firms posing as buyers to see if these groups of buyers were treated equally.

The 1989 study found that the six real estate firms that were studied engaged in some sort of steering during at least half the audited transactions. The firms did not systematically refuse to show specific neighborhoods to specific clients. However, if on demand, a black auditor wanted to see a house in a white neighborhood, the agents showed it to him. But in total, the black auditors were only shown a few of these residences. Similarly, the agencies did not show houses in the racially mixed areas to the white auditors unless they specifically asked to see them. Realtors often praised neighborhood amenities and quality schools to the white auditors, but seldom to black auditors. On the bright side, the 2000 study found almost no evidence of racial steering.[15]

Segregation by Local Regulations

Residential patterns due to income and race may result from local and federal regulations. Local land-use regulations that require minimum lot

---

[15] Galster (1990); Farley et al. (1993); Page (1995); Roychoudhury and Goodman (1996); South and Crowder (1998); Ondrich, Striker and Yinger (1999); Reade (2003).

sizes increase housing prices and tend to exclude low- and moderate-income households. Because of the correlation between income and race, such regulations tend to promote racial segregation.[16] We will study this phenomenon in detail in Chapter 15.

Affordability

The concern for equitable access to housing in the United States prompted the passage of the National Housing Act of 1934. The subsequent Housing Act of the United States (1949) established a national goal of "a decent home and suitable living environment" for all Americans. It was also the origin of the American housing and urban development policies.

How well has this 70-year-old program fared? Some say, "very badly," others say "very well." Advocates for even greater housing assistance who think that we are not close to meeting the goal point to the following problems:

- The number of young households has considerably decreased since the middle of the 1980s.
- First-time homebuyers must rely more on gifts from their families for the down payment for their first home. Those with no affluent relatives can only rent.
- Children graduate from high school or college and cannot afford a house in their old neighborhood.
- Increased housing costs have reduced the probability of home ownership for young, single mothers.

Middle-income households with low education levels have a disproportionately high housing budget. They lack the qualifications that would permit them to find a job that paid as well as the ones they had in manufacturing. We keep hearing about increases in homelessness, fewer rental units that the least prosperous members of society can afford, and other implications of growing income inequality.[17] Yet in 2000, 67.4% of Americans owned their own home and 80% of those were 55 years and older.

In contrast, those who think that the housing act policies are a success, use for their criteria the original definition of the term "affordability." In 1940, the definition included overcrowding, physical deterioration, and lack of private plumbing facilities. In the same year, over 20% of all dwellings were occupied by more than one person per room (overcrowded), but less

---

[16] Schill and Wachter (1995); Ondrich, Stricker and Yinger (1999).

[17] Linneman and Megbolugbe (1992); Winkler (1992); Mayer and Engelhardt (1996); Ziebarth and Meeks (1998); Somerville and Holmes (2001).

than 6% of all residences entered into this category in 2000. In 1940, 18% of all dwellings suffered from severe physical deterioration, whereas this number was less than 2% in 2000. In 1940, 45% of all dwellings lacked a complete set of plumbing fixtures in bathrooms and kitchens. Only 1% fit this category in 2000.

By 2000, almost all homes had refrigerators, and 86.8% are self-defrosting; 77% have washing machines, and 71% have clothes dryers. More than 50% have dishwashers. In 1940 the concern in some regions was lack of central heating. Now, because of local housing codes, 94% have some form of central heating. In 2000, 84% of the new single-family homes, and 45% of all homes in the United States had central air conditioning.

Over time, the bar defining a "decent house" keeps rising. To prove "lack of affordability," policymakers now look at prices rather than quality. The standard public policy indicator of housing affordability in the United States is the percentage of income spent on housing. Housing expenditures that exceed 30% of the household income signal an affordability problem. Rather than concentrating on the proportion of income spent on housing, a more logical measure would be based on the opportunity cost of housing. Unfortunately, that is seldom used.[18]

Using a ratio of median home prices to median income does not account for the following problems: (1) the actual financial restrictions or tastes of individual home buyers, (2) mortgage interest rates, (3) down payment requirements, (4) insurance rates, (5) property tax rates, (6) local disparities in median income, and (7) the mix of homes for sale. These are all extremely important factors in the estimation of the aggregate demand for housing.

A better definition of affordability takes account of the opportunity cost of housing. Does "unaffordable housing" mean that the household cannot pay or that they prefer to buy other goods instead of their rent? If housing prices are in line with production costs, the term "affordability" may well signal a lack of enough income to afford a standard home.

The escalations in real house prices are chiefly due to substantial improvements in the quality of the houses for sale. What level of quality is considered "good enough" for basic shelter? Quality improvements increase costs and prices. Higher housing costs do not differentiate between basic shelter requirements and increased tastes for more housing amenities such as the number of bathrooms, gadgets and appliances, and central heating or central air conditioning.

After analyzing construction cost data, along with census data and data from the American Housing Survey, Glaeser and Gyourko (2003) concluded that in general, home prices in the United States are close to construction

---

[18] Miron (1989); Linneman and Megbolugbe (1992); Salins (1998); U.S. Bureau of Census (2002).

costs. In some parts of the country, home prices are actually below the physical costs of construction (not necessarily on purpose). Land values take up close to 20% of the total value of the house. Zoning that requires a minimum lot size is responsible for the high housing prices where house prices diverge substantially from construction costs. Regulations slow the equilibration of supply and demand of housing. Once the developers decide to invest, they face delays in getting financing and securing both building permits and zoning variances.[19]

The Role of Government

Should access to inexpensive, high-quality housing be a government-guaranteed universal right? If the private housing market does not or cannot provide affordable housing, perhaps government could provide low-cost housing or enforce rent controls. In some states, provinces, and countries, governments have tried to provide decent, affordable housing for every household. However, changes in housing affordability are linked to the evolving household composition. Thus, programs that decrease housing costs increase the quantity demanded of housing and require even larger subsidies later.[20]

Proponents say that government has the moral dictate to intervene in the housing market. Opponents say that the government policies themselves are the cause for a lack of affordable dwellings. To effectively help low-income households afford housing, the government need only allow the private market to work with minimal interference. Instead, the government has only succeeded in reducing the quantity of low-cost housing. In earlier times, people without much money had a larger variety of housing choices than are currently allowed. However,

- Apartments in buildings with three or four stories now require elevators.
- Planners oppose mixed-use developments such as living quarters over shops or behind shops because they judge such living arrangements to be unsightly.
- Apartments over garages are forbidden because of potential carbon monoxide poisoning.
- Rooming houses, tenement houses, row houses, triplexes, fourplexes, and low-rent hotels are unseemly, and thus may be banned.

---

[19] Luger (1986); Miron (1989); Glaeser and Gyourko (2003); Somerville and Mayer (2003).

[20] Lambelet and Zimmermann (1991); Hancock (1993); Salins (1998).

The apartments above or behind stores or shops were often occupied by the shop owners themselves. Afternoon customers could smell the shop owner's dinner cooking. Other low-income dwellings were near noxious factories, stockyards, or rendering plants. These living quarters were by no means high-quality housing, but they served basic shelter requirements. The poor were not living in the street.

The Standard State Zoning Enabling Act of 1922 was a response to those who complained about negative externalities from commercial and industrial activity. This act became the model for zoning ordinances separating commercial and industrial activity from residential areas. The resulting separate single-use zoning impaired the affordability of housing.[21]

These programs that purported to create affordable housing in fact exacerbated the problems of poverty. For instance, by constructing public housing projects and concentrating the poor, the government amplified the spatial mismatch problem and structural unemployment. We will now consider three policies undertaken to eliminate the problems of affordability: public housing, rent controls, and housing vouchers.

Public Housing

In 1937, Congress established the Federal Housing Administration to provide more public housing. Most public housing projects were intended to be temporary and located according to the needs of the market. This governmental involvement replaced the competition of the private sector in the affordable housing market with its monopoly in "project homes." The lack of a profit motive for this monopolist to provide shelter resulted in an utter debacle.

In the 1950s, a second version of the Federal Housing Administration constructed stark high-rises such as the Robert Taylor homes in Chicago and the Pruitt–Igoe housing project in St. Louis. The Robert Taylor homes project was the largest public housing development in the world when it was completed in 1962. The development consisted of 4300 apartments in 28 buildings 16 stories high on a 2-mile-long stretch of South State Street in Chicago. Drivers passing by on the Dan Ryan Expressway called it the concrete curtain. Most of these high-rises have now been razed, and by April 2006, only one building remained.

Likewise, the $15 billion Pruitt–Igoe complex, completed in 1956, was razed 16 years later. That cost is equivalent to approximately $110 billion in 2006 dollars. The project, consisting of 33 11-story buildings on 55 acres in St. Louis, Missouri (Figure 13.3a–c), incurred a reputation as the worst example of public housing in the nation's history. Both of these

---

[21] Norquist (1998).

properties, and in fact, any of the "project homes" built during that time concentrated a large low-income population on an isolated site. "The projects" turned into a national icon of the backward philosophy of postwar public housing.[22]

Rent Controls

Rent controls represent a less costly solution to the affordable housing problem, and thus are more popular among local governments. Consult any principles of economics book to find the standard economic argument against rent controls. Rent controls are represented as a price ceiling in a standard supply and demand model (Figure 13.4). Rent controls discourage investment, cause arbitrary redistributions, and are nightmares to administer.

The rental housing stock deteriorates rapidly; landlords can neither afford to maintain their buildings, nor justify an investment in new rental units. The result is supposed to be a reduction in the quantity supplied and consequently, a rationing controlled by either the landlords or government. The rationing creates inequities and nurtures a black market in rental housing.

If rent controls are that problematic, why are they so pervasive, and why can they not be confirmed empirically? Price controls have been advocated back to the time of Hammurabi and the laws of Babylon (1792–1750 BC). Rent controls currently exist in some form or another in countries such as the United Kingdom, France, Italy, India, Hong Kong, and Egypt, and in all Canadian provinces during the 1970s. However, Alberta, British Columbia, and New Brunswick abandoned their rent controls at the end of the 1970s. The nature of rent controls no longer conforms to the standard model of the price ceiling imposed on a perfectly competitive market.

There were two generations of rent controls in New York City and many European countries after the Second World War. The first generation of "hard rent controls" confirmed the standard analysis. These rent controls did not apply to newly constructed or rehabilitated housing or to luxury units. The controls created a dual rental market. Households that could not rent in the controlled sector increased the demand and rents in the uncontrolled sector. The controls prevented the increases in price that accompany a general increase in demand from spreading evenly to all sectors. In 1968, the controls were lifted and rents in the controlled sector of New York City rose by 22%–26%, although rents in the uncontrolled sector fell approximately 22%–25%. The rent controls, therefore, increased rents in the unregulated sector.

---

[22] Chicago Housing Authority (2003). City of St. Louis Development Activity (2003).

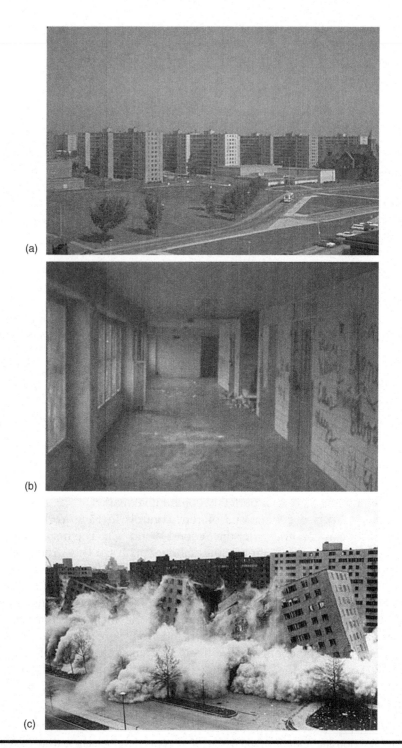

(a)

(b)

(c)

Figure 13.3 (Caption on facing page).

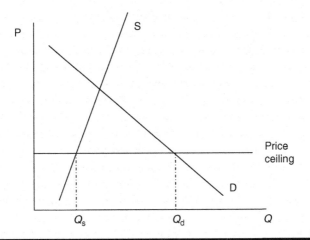

Figure 13.4 First-generation rent controls.

The second generation of "soft" rent control systems is systematically different. These new controls simply restrict the increases in annual rents. Landlords are required to maintain their buildings, but maintenance costs can be passed on to the renter.

The standard analysis asserts that rent controls cause a housing shortage, and thereby increase homelessness. However, most researchers conclude that rent controls are not a significant factor in explaining the problem. For example, a study by Quigley (1990) that used 1985–1988 data for 44 metropolitan areas in the United States, found that the existence of a rent control law increases a city's homeless shelter population by 0.03% and its street population by 0.008%—effectively zero.

If rent controls do not affect homelessness, do they decrease the housing supply or quality? The results depend on the wording of the legislation. In New York City, under the first-generation rent controls, yes. Landlords reduced housing maintenance and some required tenants to lease furniture. However, in 1990, the Cambridge Rent Control Board in Massachusetts found that in basically all the 200 controlled units examined, the tenants

Figure 13.3   (a) The Pruitt–Igoe housing project in St. Louis in 1956. (b) What communal spaces became. (c) The destruction of the Pruitt–Igoe housing complex 16 years later, in 1972. (From the photographs, a through c are excerpts from the report, creating Defensible Space, originally published by the United States Department of Housing and Urban Development, Office of Policy Development and Research, and is reproduced here with the Department's permission. The complete text can be found and downloaded for free at: (http://www.huduser.org/publications/pubasst/defensib.html or in printed form by calling 1-800-245-2691.)

themselves did the painting and plastering, major electrical system repairs, and kitchen renovations. In some buildings, tenants maintained the common areas as well as their own apartments.

In Brookline, Massachusetts, the rent control by-laws limit the return on improvements. Tenants can reject any capital improvement to avoid paying the incremental rent increase. Under these laws, tenants do not provide maintenance even if they pay a rent lower than market. In this case, rent controls discourage spending on maintenance and renovations; in the long run, controls led to the deterioration of housing.

Rent controls can actually improve economic efficiency by forcing oligopolistic landlords to behave more like perfect competitors. In small towns and specific neighborhoods, the rental housing market is often oligopolistic with immobile, low-income populations. Luger (1986) analyzed data from United States cities with fewer than 200,000 people, and concluded that those with relatively high populations of poor, large concentrations of students, and a high growth rate, have the highest concentration of rentals owned by monopolists or oligopolists in particular neighborhoods.

However, even the second-generation rent controls have negative side effects. Rent controls decrease mobility if the laws allow the landlord to increase rents for the new occupant. Tenants may compensate for this increase in rent by just not moving. This immobility leads to housing mismatches. An apartment that was adequate for a childless couple will be cramped after the children are born. In contrast, couples who rented while their children were young will find that their apartment has become too large after their children left. This mismatch alone leads to a deadweight loss in welfare in New York City of over $500 million annually (Glaeser and Luttmer 2003).[23]

Housing Vouchers

Housing vouchers are a third method that governments could use to make housing more affordable. According to this system, households can choose to rent in the private sector as long as the rental meets the standards set by the United States Department of HUD. This program allows households to rent at the current market rate and eliminate the inefficiencies of government-provided housing, as well as the complex bureaucracy associated with rent control.

---

[23] Luger (1986); Moorhouse (1987); Quigley (1990); Lambelet and Zimmermann (1991); Marks (1991); Ho (1992); Caudill (1993); Jackson (1993); Arnott (1995); Nagy (1995); Glaeser (1996); Anas (1997); Glaeser and Luttmer (1997); Grimes and Chressanthis (1997); Malpezzi (1998); Olsen (1998); Early and Phelps (1999).

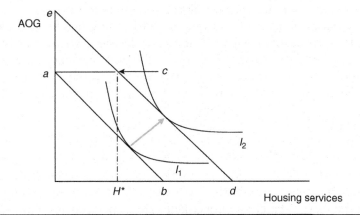

Figure 13.5 Housing vouchers when housing is a normal good.

The concept of housing vouchers can be analyzed with the indifference curves and budget constraints shown in Figure 13.5 and Figure 13.6. Let H^* be the minimum optimal quantity of housing services, as established by HUD. Without housing vouchers, individuals would be on some indifference curve tangent to budget constraint *ab*. The addition of a housing voucher increases the amount of housing that can be consumed, without necessarily decreasing the amount of all other goods (AOG) consumed, as long as the recipient chooses quantity H^* or larger. It is evident that with the voucher, the consumer will be on a higher indifference curve.

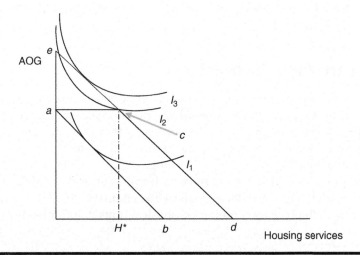

Figure 13.6 Housing vouchers when housing is an inferior good.

One of two scenarios will take place. If an indifference curve is tangent to the new budget constraint at a quantity of housing higher than H^*, as in Figure 13.5, the recipient will make the same decision, whether the benefit is in the form of a housing voucher or cash for the same amount.

Without a housing subsidy of $5000, for example, the consumer opts for an austere housing arrangement, given the tangency position of indifference curve I_1 to the budget constraint *ab*. With the housing voucher, the consumer is on budget constraint *cd* and indifference curve I_2, which is higher than I_1. Note, however, that I_2 is not tangent to the budget constraint *cd*; it pivots around that constraint at the corner point *c*. No tangency can exist at a corner, because the slope of the indifference curve is not equal to a slope of a budget constraint. However, two scenarios for **Pareto improvements** still exist. A Pareto improvement exists when someone can be made better off without making anyone worse off.

If the consumer just received the $5000 in cash with no required minimum housing requirement, either less money can be spent to keep the consumer on indifference curve I_2, or the consumer could be better off by having the voucher turned into cash and spent at the consumer's discretion. With cash, this recipient would be better off at the tangency of indifference curve I_3 on budget constraint *ed*. The consumer would choose a lower quality housing than the H^* required to get the housing voucher, and more of all other goods (AOG). At the same time, the cost of this program to taxpayers is the same, so they are no worse off—a Pareto optimal choice.

Of course, an award to the recipient of the amount of cash needed to remain on indifference curve I_2 would also be a Pareto improvement over a strict housing voucher. In this scenario, the recipient is no worse off, but taxpayers gain. In this instance, the householder could receive, say $4000 cash to spend at will, and society would have $1000 to spend elsewhere—also a Pareto optimal choice.[24]

Summary and Conclusions

This chapter investigated the nature of the housing market, as well as problems of segregation, discrimination, and affordability. Even though it's imperfect, the housing market is nevertheless 90% efficient. The perfectly competitive model may not provide one market-determined price for a specific dwelling, but it does provide a range of prices, with the median price close to the market-determined price. A housing market could include the supply and demand for a certain quality or a certain type of house, where the quantity is defined as the number of physical units that fit this description.

---

[24] Brennan (2002); United States Department of Housing and Urban Development (2003).

Alternatively, it could define Q as a measure of units of housing services or quality of housing, with P being the price that each level of housing quality goes for, according to a hedonic model or repeat sales index.

Housing supply functions must account for the incentives of the four components of housing supply: developers or speculative home builders, sales or rentals of existing homeowners, existing rentals of apartments controlled by rental agencies, and local government decision makers. Overall, housing demand in an area is primarily determined by household formation and migration patterns, as well as housing prices. Within a specific neighborhood, housing demand is a function of the accessibility to employment locations. Tenure choice is determined by the relative costs of owning and renting, the wealth of the householder, the age of the individual, and the probability of migration.

Housing being a normal good, people prefer to spend increases in their incomes on larger homes, which can only be had at the outskirts of the metropolitan area. The preference for amenities also increases with income. To the extent that higher-income people are employed in the CBD where the amenities are located, their preference will be to live in the center, rather than in the suburbs. However, if the center offers few amenities, as is true of most cities in the United States, the higher-income people will reside in the suburbs.

A hedonic price index is constructed to reflect the market price for specific attributes of a property: proximity to green spaces or bodies of water, historic districts, quality education, or transit routes. Because these amenities are immobile, their popularity is capitalized into the land values surrounding these sites. Similarly, negative externalities (air pollution, noise, or proximity to underground storage tanks) translate into lower land values for neighboring property. Improved school quality increases land values, but unpopular decisions imposed by school districts or zoning boards, or by other regulatory bodies, can decrease land values.

Two theories describe how polycentric cities are formed. The natural evolution theory suggests that development moves to the open tracks of land in the suburbs to escape the congestion in the center city. The higher income groups filtered out into the suburbs first and new firms located next to the skilled workers, creating secondary employment centers and a geographic income stratification.

The second theory focuses on the fiscal and social problems of the inner cites that drive higher income people to the suburbs. Residential concentration of the poor prolongs structural unemployment, according to the spatial mismatch hypothesis. The absence of information about the labor market outside that specific ethnic neighborhood is a greater problem than commuting costs. If segregation in a particular neighborhood increases unemployment and exacerbates the probability of a household falling into a poverty trap, why does segregation persist?

Income differences possibly play a minor role, especially when accompanied by increased housing prices due to regulations and zoning ordinances. Voluntary sorting allows immigrants to adapt more easily to a new cultural and linguistic environment. The fear of discrimination, perhaps exacerbated by racial steering, causes systematized segregation.

Affordability is a problem for people who do not want or cannot acquire housing of a certain quality. The quality of housing that was acceptable in 1940 or in 1960 is no longer acceptable today in the United States. We have, therefore, made progress in increasing the quality of housing available, but affordability remains a concern. The increased quality of housing is associated with increased prices. The majority of homes in the United States are priced close to construction costs. Solutions carried out by the government include building public housing, controlling rents, or providing housing vouchers.

The construction of housing projects caused the concentration of the poor into concrete warehouses, erased middle-class role models from their lives, and limited the access to information about jobs outside their enclave. Most projects were poorly maintained, notoriously crime ridden, and have since been razed or scheduled for demolition.

The term "rent control" makes economists bristle. However, second-generation rent controls are kinder to the market in the sense that landlords can recover the cost of maintaining their buildings. These controls may align housing prices from monopolistic or oligopolistic housing markets with those of the competitive solution. However, the administrative costs are high.

Housing vouchers can bypass some of the administration costs. However, they impose a minimum quality of housing on recipients, and regulating the quality of this housing could be costly. A program that offers cash, rather than a voucher that can only be used toward housing, would put the recipients on higher indifference curves, besides eliminating one more layer of administrative costs.

Chapter Questions

1. In some places, the higher-income people live farther from the CBD and lower-income people live closer. In other places, the reverse is true.
   a. Why? Explain using economic analysis.
   b. What can an inner city do to attract higher-income people?
   c. How might one measure the value of urban amenities?
2. List four groups that contribute to housing supply. What incentives are needed by each group to increase the quantity of housing supplied to the market?

3. What two main groups of people will increase housing demand?
4. If you plan to invest in multi-family housing rental property, which groups would likely be your tenants? What amenities could you provide to increase the desirability of your property for these groups?
5. How is the filtering theory dependent on income and distance? What implications would filtering have on segregation, spatial mismatch of jobs, and educational quality?
6. Governments have tried creating affordable housing by building housing projects, by creating and enforcing rent controls, and by providing housing vouchers. Given the assumption that the problem is not the lack of cheap housing, but the lack of sufficient income, explain who benefits and who is harmed for each of these three methods, compared to simply providing a cash transfer to the households.

Research Assignments

1. Does the filtering process describe housing patterns in your area?
   a. Note the median housing values for the major city in your area, along with small towns, suburbs, and townships directly adjacent to your city.
   b. Note the median income levels for these areas.
   c. Compare also the vacancy rates for housing in your area with the surrounding areas.
   d. In what way does your data conform or fail to conform to the filtering theory?
2. Calculate a dissimilarity (segregation) index for your city.

References

Akerlof, G. A. 1970. The market for 'lemons': quality uncertainty and the market mechanism. *Quarterly Journal of Economics* 84 (3):488–500.

Anas, A. 1997. Rent control with matching economies: a model of European housing market regulation. *Journal of Real Estate Finance and Economics* 15 (1):111–137.

Archer, W. R., D. H. Gatzlaff, and D. C. Ling. 1996. Measuring the importance of location in house price appreciation. *Journal of Urban Economics* 40 (3):334–353.

Arnott, R. 1994. Review of: Rothenberg, Jerome, et al. Review of: The maze of urban housing markets: theory, evidence, and policy. *Journal of Economic Literature* 32 (2):741–743.

Arnott, R. 1995. Time for revisionism on rent control? *Journal of Economic Perspectives* 9 (1):99–120.

Assadian, A., and J. Ondrich. 1993. Residential location, housing demand and labour supply decisions of one- and two-earner households: the case of Bogotá, Colombia. *Urban Studies* 30 (1):73–86.

Bailey, M. J., R. F. Muth, and H. O. Nourse. 1963. A regression method for real estate price index construction. *Journal of the American Statistical Association* 58 (304):933–942.

Bajic, V. 1991. The structure of production in urban housing: a multi-input cost function approach. *Applied Economics* 23 (3):447–458.

Barnett, C. J. 1985. An application of the hedonic price model to the Perth residential land market. *Economic Record* 61 (172):476–481.

Bender, A., A. Din, P. Favarger, M. Hoesli, and J. Laakso. 1997. An analysis of perceptions concerning the environmental quality of housing in Geneva. *Urban Studies* 34 (3):503–513.

Benson, E. D., J. L. Hansen, A. L. Schwartz, and G. L. Smersh. 1998. Pricing residential amenities: the value of a view. *Journal of Real Estate Finance and Economics* 16 (1):55–73.

Beron, K., J. Murdoch, and M. Thayer. 2001. The benefits of visibility improvement: new evidence from the Los Angeles metropolitan area. *Journal of Real Estate Finance and Economics* 22 (2–3):319–337.

Blackley, D. M. 1999. The long-run elasticity of new housing supply in the United States: empirical evidence for 1950 to 1994. *Journal of Real Estate Finance and Economics* 18 (1):25–42.

Blondel, S., and O. Marchand. 1997. Pourquoi les rendements locatifs parisiens augmentent-ils avec le chômage? *Revue d'Economie Régionale et Urbaine* 0 (5):737–752.

Boehm, T. P., H. W. Herzog Jr. and A. M. Schlottmann. 1991. Intra-urban mobility, migration, and tenure choice. *Review of Economics and Statistics* 73 (1):59–68.

Braid, R. M. 1991. Residential spatial growth with perfect foresight and multiple income groups. *Journal of Urban Economics* 30 (3):385–407.

Brennan, B. Background on MTO. 2005. *Moving To Opportunity Research*. Created August 30, 2000. Last modified 22 August. http://www.wws.princeton.edu/ ~kling/mto/background.htm (accessed on August 8, 2005).

Brueckner, J. K., J.-F. Thisse, and Y. Zenou. 1999. Why is central Paris rich and downtown Detroit poor? An amenity-based theory. *European Economic Review* 43 (1):91–107.

Carroll, T. M., T. M. Clauretie, and J. Jensen. 1996. Living next to godliness: residential property values and churches. *Journal of Real Estate Finance and Economics* 12 (3):319–330.

Case, B., and J. M. Quigley. 1991. The dynamics of real estate prices. *Review of Economics and Statistics* 73 (1):50–58.

Case, K. E., and R. J. Shiller. 1987. Prices of single-family homes since 1970: new indexes for four cities. *New England Economic Review* 0 (0):45–56.

Case, K. E., and R. J. Shiller. 1989. The efficiency of the market for single-family homes. *American Economic Review* 79 (1):125–137.

Caudill, S. B. 1993. Estimating the costs of partial-coverage rent controls: a stochastic frontier approach. *Review of Economics and Statistics* 75 (4):727–731.

Clark, D. E., L. Michelbrink, T. Allison, and W. C. Metz. 1997. Nuclear power plants and residential housing prices. *Growth and Change* 28 (4):496–519.

Clark, D. E., and W. E. Herrin. 1997. Historical preservation districts and home sale prices: Evidence from the Sacramento housing market. *Review of Regional Studies* 27 (1):29–48.

Clark, D. E., and W. E. Herrin. 2000. The impact of public school attributes on home sale prices in California. *Growth and Change* 31 (3):385–407.

Clark, W. A. V., M. C. Deurloo, and F. M. Dieleman. 1994. Tenure changes in the context of micro-level family and macro-level economic shifts. *Urban Studies* 31 (1):137–154.

Clauretie, T. M., and H. R. Neill. 2000. Year-round school schedules and residential property values. *Journal of Real Estate Finance and Economics* 20 (3):311–322.

Coffin, D. A. 1989. The impact of historical districts on residential property values. *Eastern Economic Journal* 15 (3):221–228.

Coulson, N. E., and E. W. Bond. 1990. A hedonic approach to residential succession. *Review of Economics and Statistics* 72 (3):433–444.

Coulson, N. E., D. Laing, and P. Wang. 2001. Spatial mismatch in search equilibrium. *Journal of Labor Economics* 19 (4):949–972.

Cropper, M. L., L. Deck, N. Kirshor, and K. McConnell. 1993. Valuing product attributes using single market data: a comparison of hedonic and discrete choice approaches. *Review of Economics and Statistics* 75 (2):225–232.

Cutler, D. M., and E. L. Glaeser. 1997. Are ghettos good or bad? *Quarterly Journal of Economics* 112 (3):827–872.

DeRango, K. 2001. Can commutes be used to test the spatial mismatch hypothesis? *Urban Studies* 38 (9):1521–1529.

Des Rosiers, F., M. Thériault, Y. Kestens, and P. Villenueve. 2002. Landscaping and house values: an empirical investigation. *Journal of Real Estate Research* 23 (1–2):139–161.

Di Salvo, P., and J. Ermisch. 1997. Analysis of the dynamics of housing tenure choice in Britain. *Journal of Urban Economics* 42 (1):1–17.

DiPasquale, D. 1999. Why don't we know more about housing supply?. *Journal of Real Estate Finance and Economics* 18 (1):9–23.

DiPasquale, D., and E. L. Glaeser. 1999. Incentives and social capital: are home-owners better citizens? *Journal of Urban Economics* 45 (2):354–384.

Do, A. Q., and G. Grudnitski. 1995. Golf courses and residential house prices: an empirical examination. *Journal of Real Estate Finance and Economics* 10 (3):261–270.

Do, A. Q., R. W. Wilbur, and J. L. Short. 1994. An empirical examination of the externalities of neighborhood churches on housing values. *Journal of Real Estate Finance and Economics* 9 (2):127–136.

Doss, C. R., and S. J. Taff. 1996. The influence of wetland type and wetland proximity on residential property values. *Journal of Agricultural and Resource Economics* 21 (1):120–129.

Dusansky, R., and P. W. Wilson. 1993. The demand for housing: theoretical considerations. *Journal of Economic Theory* 61 (1):120–138.

Early, D. W., and J. T. Phelps. 1999. Rent regulations' pricing effect in the uncontrolled sector: an empirical investigation. *Journal of Housing Research* 10 (2):267–285.

Echenique, F. and R. G. Fryer, Jr. 2005. On the Measurement of Segregation, *NBER Working Papers*, National Bureau of Economic Research, Inc.

Epple, D. and Sieg, H. 1998. Estimating equilibrium models of local jurisdictions, *NBER Working Papers*, National Bureau of Economic Research, Inc.

Espey, M., and H. Lopez. 2000. The impact of airport noise and proximity on residential property values. *Growth and Change* 31 (3):408–419.

Espey, M., and K. Owusu-Edusei. 2001. Neighborhood parks and residential property values in Greenville, South Carolina. *Journal of Agricultural and Applied Economics* 33 (3):487–492.

Evans, A. W. 1995. The property market: ninety per cent efficient? *Urban Studies* 32 (1):5–29.

Farber, S. 1998. Undesirable facilities and property values: a summary of empirical studies. *Ecological Economics* 24 (1):1–14.

Farley, R., C. Steeh, T. Jackson, M. Krysan, and K. Reeves. 1993. Continued racial residential segregation in Detroit: "Chocolate city, vanilla suburbs" revisited. *Journal of Housing Research* 4 (1):1–38.

Farley, R., E. L. Fielding, and M. Krysan. 1997. The residential preferences of blacks and whites: a four-metropolis analysis. *Housing Policy Debate* 8 (4):763–800.

Fergus, J. T. 1999. Where, when, and by how much does abnormal weather affect housing construction? *Journal of Real Estate Finance and Economics* 18 (1):63–87.

Fujita, M. 1989. *Urban Economic Theory: Land Use and City Size*. Cambridge: Cambridge University Press.

Galster, G. 1990. Racial steering by real estate agents: mechanisms and motives. *Review of Black Political Economy* 19 (1):39–63.

Garasky, S., R. J. Haurin, and D. R. Haurin. 2001. Group living decisions as youths transition to adulthood. *Journal of Population Economics* 14 (2):329–349.

Glaeser, E. L. 1996. The Social Costs of Rent Control Revisited, *NBER Working Papers*, National Bureau of Economic Research, Inc.

Glaeser, E. L., and J. Gyourko. 2003. The impact of building restrictions on housing affordability. *Federal Reserve Bank of New York Economic Policy Review* 9 (2):21–39.

Glaeser, E. L., and E. F. P. Luttmer. 2003. The misallocation of housing under rent control. *American Economic Review* 93 (4):1027–1046.

Gonzalez, A. 1998. Mexican enclaves and the price of culture. *Journal of Urban Economics* 43 (2):273–291.

Goodman, A. C., and T. G. Thibodeau. 1995. Age-related heteroskedasticity in hedonic house price equations. *Journal of Housing Research* 6 (1):25–42.

Gordon, P., A. Kumar, and H. W. Richardson. 1989. The spatial mismatch hypothesis: some new evidence. *Urban Studies* 26 (3):315–326.

Goss, E. P., and J. M. Phillips. 1997. The impact of home ownership on the duration of unemployment. *Review of Regional Studies* 27 (1):9–27.

Gottlieb, P. D., and B. Lentnek. 2001. Spatial mismatch is not always a central-city problem: an analysis of commuting behavior in Cleveland, Ohio, and its suburbs. *Urban Studies* 38 (7):1161–1186.

Green, R. K., and P. H. Hendershott. 2001. Home-ownership and unemployment in the U.S. *Urban Studies* 38 (9):1509–1520.

Green, R. K., and M. J. White. 1997. Measuring the benefits of homeowning: effects on children. *Journal of Urban Economics* 41 (3):441–461.

Grimes, P. W., and G. A. Chressanthis. 1997. Assessing the effect of rent control on homelessness. *Journal of Urban Economics* 41 (1):23–37.

Gyourko, J., and P. Linneman. 1996. Analysis of the changing influences on traditional households' ownership patterns. *Journal of Urban Economics* 39 (3):318–341.

Gyourko, J., and R. Voith. 1992. Local market and national components in house price appreciation. *Journal of Urban Economics* 32 (1):52–69.

Gyourko, J., P. Linneman, and S. Wachter. 1999. Analyzing the relationships among race, wealth, and home ownership in America. *Journal of Housing Economics* 8 (2):63–89.

Hakfoort, J., and G. Matysiak. 1997. Housing investment in The Netherlands. *Economic Modelling* 14 (4):501–516.

Hamilton, S. W., and G. M. Schwann. 1995. Do high voltage electric transmission lines affect property value? *Land Economics* 71 (4):436–444.

Hancock, K. E. 1993. 'Can pay? won't pay?' or economic principles of 'affordability'. *Urban Studies* 30 (1):127–145.

Harding, J., T. J. Miceli, and C. F. Sirmans. 2000. Do owners take better care of their housing than renters? *Real Estate Economics* 28 (4):663–681.

Haurin, D. R. 1991. Income variability, homeownership, and housing demand. *Journal of Housing Economics* 1 (1):60–74.

Haurin, D. R., and D. Brasington. 1996. School quality and real house prices: inter- and intrametropolitan effects. *Journal of Housing Economics* 5 (4):351–368.

Haurin, D. R., and E. C. Chung. 1998. The demand for owner-occupied housing: implications from intertemporal analysis. *Journal of Housing Economics* 7 (1):49–68.

Haurin, D. R., P. H. Hendershott, and D. Kim. 1993. The impact of real rents and wages on household formation. *Review of Economics and Statistics* 75 (2):284–293.

Haurin, D. R., P. H. Hendershott, and S. M. Wachter. 1997. Borrowing constraints and the tenure choice of young households. *Journal of Housing Research* 8 (2):137–154.

Hayes, K. J., and L. L. Taylor. 1996. Neighborhood school characteristics: what signals quality to homebuyers. *Federal Reserve Bank of Dallas Economic Review* 0 (4):2–9.

Henley, A. 1998. Residential mobility, housing equity and the labour market. *Economic Journal* 108 (447):414–427.

Ho, L. S. 1992. Rent control: its rationale and effects. *Urban Studies* 29 (7):1183–1189.

Hochguertel, S., and A. van Soest. 2001. The relation between financial and housing wealth: evidence from Dutch households. *Journal of Urban Economics* 49 (2):374–403.

Holzer, H. J. 1991. The spatial mismatch hypothesis: what has the evidence shown? *Urban Studies* 28 (1):105–122.

Holzer, H. J., K. R. Ihlanfeldt, and D. L. Sjoquist. 1994. Work, search, and travel among white and black youth. *Journal of Urban Economics* 35 (3):320–345.

Hughes, M. A., and J. F. Madden. 1991. Residential segregation and the economic status of black workers: new evidence for an old debate. *Journal of Urban Economics* 29 (1):28–49.

Irwin, E. G., and N. E. Bockstael. 2001. The problem of identifying land use spillovers: measuring the effects of open space on residential property values. *American Journal of Agricultural Economics* 83 (3):698–704.

Jackson, R. 1993. Rent control and the supply of housing services: the Brookline, Massachusetts experience. *American Journal of Economics and Sociology* 52 (4):467–475.

Jones, L. D. 1995. Testing the central prediction of housing tenure transition models. *Journal of Urban Economics* 38 (1):50–73.

Jones, L. D. 1997. The tenure transition decision for elderly homeowners. *Journal of Urban Economics* 41 (2):243–263.

Jud, G. D., and D. G. Bennett. 1986. Public schools and the pattern of intraurban residential mobility. *Land Economics* 62 (4):362–370.

Kain, J. F. 1968. Housing segregation, Negro employment, and metropolitan decentralization. *Quarterly Journal of Economics* 82 (2):175–197.

Kain, J. F. 1971. Housing segregation, Negro employment and metropolitan decentralization: rejoinder. *Quarterly Journal of Economics* 85 (1):161–162.

Kan, K. 2000. Dynamic modeling of housing tenure choice. *Journal of Urban Economics* 48 (1):46–69.

Lambelet, J.-C., and C. Zimmermann. 1991. Droit au logement ou économie de marché? Une analyse de L'immobilier en Suisse. Lausanne, Switzerland: Éditions Payot.

Landford, N. H. Jr., and L. L. Jones. 1995a. Recreational and aesthetic value of water using hedonic price analysis. *Journal of Agricultural and Resource Economics* 20 (2):341–355.

Lansford, N. H. Jr., and L. L. Jones. 1995b. Marginal price of lake recreation and aesthetics: an hedonic approach. *Journal of Agricultural and Applied Economics* 27 (1):212–223.

Leichenko, R. M., N. E. Coulson, and D. Listokin. 2001. Historic preservation and residential property values: an analysis of Texas cities. *Urban Studies* 38 (11):1973–1987.

Linneman, P. D., and I. F. Megbolugbe. 1992. Housing affordability: myth or reality? *Urban Studies* 29 (3–4):369–392.

Luger, M. I. 1986. The rent control paradox: explanations and prescriptions. *Review of Regional Studies* 16 (3):25–41.

Lutzenhiser, M., and N. R. Netusil. 2001. The effect of open spaces on a home's sale price. *Contemporary Economic Policy* 19 (3):291–298.

Lynch, A. K., and D. W. Rasmussen. 2001. Measuring the impact of crime on house prices. *Applied Economics* 33 (15):1981–1989.

Madden, J. F., and L. C. Chiu. 1990. The wage effects of residential location and commuting constraints on employed married women. *Urban Studies* 27 (3):353–369.

Malpezzi, S. 1998. Welfare analysis of rent control with side payments: a natural experiment in Cairo, Egypt. *Regional Science and Urban Economics* 28 (6):773–795.

Manning, C. A. 1989. Explaining intercity home price differences. *Journal of Real Estate Finance and Economics* 2 (2):131–149.

Marks, D. 1991. On resolving the dilemma of rent control. *Urban Studies* 28 (3):415–431.

Maslow, A. H. 1943. A theory of human motivation. *Psychological Review* 50:370–396.

Mayer, C. J., and G. V. Engelhardt. 1996. Gifts, down payments, and housing affordability. *Journal of Housing Research* 7 (1):59–77.

Mayer, C. J., and C. T. Somerville. 1996. Regional housing supply and credit constraints. *New England Economic Review* 0 (0):39–51.

McCormick, B. 1986. Employment opportunities, earnings, and the journey to work of minority workers in Great Britain. *Economic Journal* 96 (382):375–397.

Mills, L. 1991. Understanding national and regional housing trends. *FRB Philadelphia Business Review* September:15–23.

Minford, P., P. Ashton, and M. Peel. 1988. The effects of housing distortions on unemployment. *Oxford Economic Papers, N. S.* 40 (2):322–345.

Miron, J. R. 1989. Household formation, affordability, and housing policy. *Population Research and Policy Review* 8 (1):55–77.

Montgomery, C. 1992. Explaining home improvement in the context of household investment in residential housing. *Journal of Urban Economics* 32 (3):326–350.

Moorhouse, J. C. 1987. Long-term rent control and tenant subsidies. *Quarterly Review of Economics and Business* 27 (3):6–24.

Muth, R. F. 1996. Theoretical issues in housing market research,. *Regional and Urban Economics. Part 2*, ed. R. Arnott. In *Fundamentals of Pure and Applied Economics. Encyclopedia of Economics*, Vol. 1, Amsterdam: Harwood Academic; distributed by University of Toronto Press, 731–779.

Nagy, J. 1995. Increased duration and sample attrition in New York City's rent controlled sector. *Journal of Urban Economics* 38 (2):127–137.

Nese, A. 1999. Housing demand in Italy: a microeconometric analysis. *Giornale Degli Economisti e Annali Di Economia* 58 (1):63–94.

Norquist, J. O. 1998. How the government killed affordable housing. *American Enterprise* 9 (4):68–70.

Office of the United Nations High Commissioner for Human Rights. 1948. *Universal Declaration of Human Rights*, Geneva, Switzerland, http://users.skynet.be/sky35213/append3.htm (accessed on November 2003).

Olsen, E. O. 1998. Economics of rent control. *Regional Science and Urban Economics* 28 (6):673–678.

Ondrich, J., A. Stricker, and J. Yinger. 1999. Do landlords discriminate? The incidence and causes of racial discrimination in rental housing markets. *Journal of Housing Economics* 8 (3):185–204.

Page, M. 1995. Racial and ethnic discrimination in urban housing markets: evidence from a recent audit study. *Journal of Urban Economics* 38 (2):183–206.

Palmquist, R. B. 1992. Valuing localized externalities. *Journal of Urban Economics* 31 (1):59–68.

Palmquist, R. B., F. M. Roka, and T. Vukina. 1997. Hog operations, environmental effects, and residential property values. *Land Economics* 73 (1):114–124.

Peiser, R. B. 1987. The determinants of nonresidential urban land values. *Journal of Urban Economics* 22 (3):340–360.

Polèse, M., S. Perez, and C. Barragan. 1995. Développement et forme urbaine: le déplacement de l'activité commerciale et industrielle dans la ville de Puebla. *Canadian Journal of Development Studies* 16 (1):105–130.

Pryce, G. 1999. Construction elasticities and land availability: a two-stage least-squares model of housing supply using the variable elasticity approach. *Urban Studies* 36 (13):2283–2304.

Quigley, J. M. 1985. Consumer choice of dwelling, neighborhood, and public services. *Regional Science and Urban Economics* 15 (1):41–63.

Quigley, J. M. 1990. Does rent control cause homelessness? Taking the claim seriously. *Journal of Policy Analysis and Management* 9 (1):89–93.

Reade, J. 2003. Testing for housing discrimination: findings from a HUD study of real estate agents, *Communities and Banking, 2003*: 11–16. http://www.bos.frb.org/commdev/c&b/2003/spring/testing.pdf (accessed on 30 November 2004).

Roberds, W. 1992. Edge city: life on the new frontier: review essay. *Federal Reserve Bank of Atlanta Economic Review* 77 (3):53–56.

Rosenbaum, E., and M. H. Schill. 1999. Housing and neighborhood turnover among immigrant and native-born households in New York City, 1991 to 1996. *Journal of Housing Research* 10 (2):209–233.

Rothenberg, J., G. C. Galster, R. V. Butler, and J. R. Pitkin. 1991. *The Maze of Urban Housing Markets: Theory, Evidence, and Policy*. Chicago: University of Chicago Press.

Rouwendal, J. 1998. On housing services. *Journal of Housing Economics* 7 (3):218–242.

Roychoudhury, C., and A. C. Goodman. 1996. Evidence of racial discrimination in different dimensions of owner-occupied housing search. *Real Estate Economics* 24 (2):161–178.

Salins, P. D. 1998. Comment on Chester Hartman's "The case for a right to housing": housing is a right? Wrong! *Housing Policy Debate* 9 (2):259–266.

Schill, M. H., and S. M. Wachter. 1995. Housing market constraints and spatial stratification by income and race. *Housing Policy Debate* 6 (1):141–167.

Simons, R. A., W. Bowen, and A. Sementelli. 1997. The effect of underground storage tanks on residential property values in Cuyahoga County, Ohio. *Journal of Real Estate Research* 14 (1–2):29–42.

Skaburskis, A. 1999. Modelling the choice of tenure and building type. *Urban Studies* 36 (13):2199–2215.

Smith, B. H. 1993. The effect of ocean and lake coast amenities on cities. *Journal of Urban Economics* 33 (1):115–123.

Smith, T. E., and Y. Zenou. 2003. Spatial mismatch, search effort, and urban spatial structure. *Journal of Urban Economics* 54 (1):129–156.

Somerville, C. T., and C. Holmes. 2001. Dynamics of the affordable housing stock: microdata analysis of filtering. *Journal of Housing Research* 12 (1):115–140.

Somerville, C. T., and C. J. Mayer. 2003. Government regulation and changes in the affordable housing stock. *Federal Reserve Bank of New York Economic Policy Review* 9 (2):45–62.

South, S. J., and K. D. Crowder. 1998. Housing discrimination and residential mobility: impacts for blacks and whites. *Population Research and Policy Review* 17 (4):369–387.

Spalatro, F., and B. Provencher. 2001. An analysis of minimum frontage zoning to preserve lakefront amenities. *Land Economics* 77 (4):469–481.

Steen, R. C. 1986. Nonubiquitous transportation and urban population density gradients. *Journal of Urban Economics* 20 (1):97–106.

Strand, J., and M. Vagnes. 2001. The relationship between property values and railroad proximity: a study based on hedonic prices and real estate brokers' appraisals. *Transportation* 28 (2):137–156.

Sweeney, J. L. 1974. Housing unit maintenance and the mode of tenure. *Journal of Economic Theory* 8 (2):111–138.

Taylor, B. D., and P. M. Ong. 1995. Spatial mismatch or automobile mismatch? An examination of race, residence and commuting in US metropolitan areas. *Urban Studies* 32 (9):1453–1473.

Tiwari, P., and H. Hasegawa. 2000. Effective rental housing demand in the Tokyo metropolitan region. *Review of Urban and Regional Development Studies* 12 (1):54–73.

Tomkins, J., N. Topham, J. Twomey, and R. Ward. 1998. Noise versus access: the impact of an airport in an urban property market. *Urban Studies* 35 (2):243–258.

U.S. Bureau of Census. 2002. *Statistical Abstract of the United States.* Section 20. Construction and Housing, http://www.census.gov/prod/2002pubs/01statab/construct.pdf (accessed on October 27, 2003).

U.S. Bureau of Census. 2002. *Total Private Construction Data*, http://www.census.gov (accessed on October 27, 2003).

Uyeno, D., S. W. Hamilton, and A. J. G. Biggs. 1993. Density of residential land use and the impact of airport noise. *Journal of Transport Economics and Policy* 27 (1):3–18.

Varady, D. P., and B. J. Lipman. 1994. What are renters really like? Results from a national survey. *Housing Policy Debate* 5 (4):491–531.

Voith, R. 1991a. Is access to center city still valuable? *Federal Reserve Bank of Philadelphia Business Review* 0 (0):3–12.

Voith, R. 1991b. Transportation, sorting and house values. *American Real Estate and Urban Economics Association Journal* 19 (2):117–137.

Voith, R. 2000. Has suburbanization diminished the importance of access to center city. *Federal Reserve Bank of Philadelphia Business Review* 0 (0):17–29.

Weinberg, B. A. 2004. Testing the spatial mismatch hypothesis using inter-city variations in industrial composition. *Regional Science and Urban Economics* 34 (5):505–532.

White, M. J. 1986. Sex differences in urban commuting patterns. *American Economic Review* 76 (2):368–372.

Wilson, W. J. 1987. *The Truly Disadvantaged: The Inner City, the Underclass, and Public Policy.* Chicago: University of Chicago Press.

Winkler, A. E. 1992. The impact of housing costs on the living arrangements of single mothers. *Journal of Urban Economics* 32 (3):388–403.

Withers, S. D. 1998. Linking household transitions and housing transitions: a longitudinal analysis of renters. *Environment and Planning A* 30 (4):615–630.

Ziebarth, A. C., and C. B. Meeks. 1998. Public policy issues and financing for rural housing. *Advancing the Consumer Interest* 10 (1):11–19.

Chapter 14

Transportation

Transportation systems are the lifelines of a local economy. When poorly planned and maintained, they suffocate economic growth, but well-run transportation corridors allow goods and people to flow smoothly, thereby decreasing costs and increasing the well-being of everyone affected. However, between 1980 and 2001, the number of miles that vehicles traveled in the United States urban areas increased by 233%, although only 39% more urban road mileage (length of the urban roads×the number of lanes) was built.[1] This combination guarantees congestion. What can we do to unclog these transportation arteries? Engineers advise building even more roads. Economists have a better solution.[2]

In Part I of the text, we assumed that congestion was inevitable and one of the causes of diseconomies of agglomeration, but in this chapter we are going to study various ways to make congestion more bearable. To do this, we will first examine transportation demand in general and how transportation modes affect commuting patterns. Second, we will look at supply of transportation systems, both highway and mass transit. We will compare the effects of government incentives with those of the private sector to evaluate the privatization solution that intrigues economists.

Finally, we will set up a supply and demand analysis to calculate the costs associated with externalities such as pollution, road damage, highway safety, and congestion. Next, we will consider several solutions to decrease

---

[1] U.S. Department of Transportation (n.d.).
[2] Giuliano and Small (1995); Thomson (1998).

congestion: increasing parking costs, instituting gasoline taxes, and creating congestion tolls (or "decongestion" tolls). We will finish by exploring the experiments of four cities that have tried to reduce congestion.

Transportation Demand

Transportation demand varies according to residential location, household life cycle, gender, and cost. Compared to urban dwellers, rural residents have few public transportation alternatives and are thus more dependent on their automobiles. Families in various stages of their life cycle have different transportation demands as outlined in the box entitled *Life Cycle Travel Patterns*. To forecast demand, we must predict:

- Where trips will start (trip generation)
- The destinations and times of travel (trip distribution and trip scheduling)
- The mode and route of travel (modal choice and route assignment)
- How many in the vehicle (vehicle occupancy)
- How often the trips will be made (trip frequency)[3]

Think About It...

What is the weekly cost of your commute? What would it be if you used an alternative transportation mode?

If you drive (or were to drive):

Number of hours commuting per week _____ ✕ after-tax hourly wage _____	
Number of miles per week of commuting _____ ✕ 48.5¢ (or current business mileage reimbursement rate from IRS)	
Weekly parking fee	
Total:	

---

[3] Hills (1996).

If you use (or were to use) public transportation:

Number of hours commuting per week _____
  (include the time to walk to the train station
  or bus stop and the average length of wait)
  ×hourly wage_____	

Weekly fare	

Psychic costs (if any) of not being able to control
  who is traveling next to you, crowding,
  inconvenience of having to retrace your steps to do
  errands, and so forth	

Total:	

Life Cycle Travel Patterns

According to Goodwin (1990), dual-income households with no kids require good access to work for each person. Traditionally, the wife needs a more flexible transport system because she runs errands during her lunch time or follows "trip chains" to complete various household errands while returning home.

The presence of young children does not change the traditional husband's travel patterns, but working mothers pick the children up from day care in the course of doing other errands. Stay-at-home mothers need a dependable mode of transport for medical visits, errands, and other social functions. Whether the mothers work or not, until their children are old enough to drive, the "soccer mom" chauffeurs children to and from school and social activities. As soon as the teens obtain their drivers' licenses, they become more independent.

When the children leave the family nest, the parents return to the routine of the childless couple. At retirement age, these couples have substantial freedom of movement until health problems reduce their mobility.

Goodwin (1990)

The private commuting equilibrium is that quantity of trips where the private marginal benefit of the trip is equal to the private marginal cost. This quantity is optimal from the perspective of each driver, but not from a social perspective. Social costs of commuting include the marginal cost of road maintenance, highway patrol, and highway administration, as well as marginal costs due to air pollution, increased probability of accidents, and congestion.

Costs of transport are both internal and external in nature. Internal costs to the traveler include the cost of fuel and the loss of time. The value of travel time represents 60% of estimated internal costs. Because of long-haul economies, the marginal value of travel time is lower for travelers on a long journey than for those taking short trips. A 1% increase in commuting time is a sufficient incentive for 5% of the drivers to change their route, Merriman and Hellerstein (1994).[4]

Relative Social Costs of Transport Modes

The proponents of public transportation [e.g., bus, light-rail (or tramway), and subway (or metro)] assume that these transportation modes generate social benefits: reduced congestion, lower air pollution, less noise, and fewer road accidents. Boniver and Thiry (1994) studied the social costs generated via the car, the bus, light-rail and the metro for Brussels, Belgium. They then ranked the transport modes according to the marginal social costs for each of them during peak times and off-peak hours. As predicted, they found that external costs are highest for the automobile, and the lowest for the metro.

The total cost (private + social) of the automobile is 15 times higher than that of the bus during rush hour and 2.5 times more during off-peak hours. The marginal cost of congestion represents between 73 and 87 percent of the total cost during peak times. During off-peak hours, the largest social cost depends on the transport mode. For the automobile, congestion cost represents more than 40 percent of total cost. For the bus, light-rail, and metro, the marginal cost of accidents is most important. For light-rail, this marginal cost is

---

[4] Merriman and Hellerstein (1994); Calfee and Winston (1998); Hensher (2001).

highest because of accidents with pedestrians and bicyclists. For the bus, this cost is less than half that of light-rail, although, for the subway, it is less than one-third of that for light-rail.

Boniver and Thiry (1994)

Estimating Travel Demand

Most travel is a **derived demand**, derived from the benefits created by the movement from one location to another. Some travel, however, is without any concrete destination; people enjoy driving. The sense of speed and motion, being in control of oneself in a picturesque setting, induce some people to take the scenic route even for business trips. Taking the car out for a spin, cruising on Friday and Saturday nights, and Sunday drives are all leisure activities. However, joyriding is a spur-of-the-moment decision and, therefore, impossible to model precisely. The majority of studies that investigate trip generation limit themselves to the derived aspect of travel demand.[5]

Travel behavior is surprisingly similar across many countries. People average the same general daily costs, both in income and in time, regardless of whether they reside in urban or rural areas. Urban travelers who make at least one motorized trip a day spend on average one hour of time traveling daily. Urban households that rely totally on public transportation also average an hour in commuting, but they also spend 3%–5% of their incomes on travel. In contrast, households that own at least one automobile spend an average of 10%–15% of their income on travel.[6]

Short-run demand for both miles traveled and gasoline consumed varies by occupation and life cycle. The demand for gasoline is also a derived demand because it is a required input into the household production of transportation services. Occupations most clearly define these differences. Nuclear, white-collar families have the most price-elastic demand for gasoline. Households where the householder is retired or unemployed are least responsive to changes in gasoline price, but their demand for gasoline is most responsive to changes in disposable income.[7]

---

[5] Mokhtarian and Salomon (2001).
[6] Espey (1997); Schafer (2000).
[7] Greening et al. (1995); de Jong and Gunn (2001).

Modal Travel Elasticities

The "price" of private automobile travel is predominantly a function of travel time and gasoline prices. Elasticities of demand for automobile travel in the United States, Japan, France, Germany, Norway, Sweden, Denmark, and the United Kingdom, have different coefficients, but automobile travel demand is price and income inelastic in all eight countries. The elasticity of trips (or distance) with respect to travel time is larger than the elasticity with respect to changes in the cost of driving a car.

Price elasticities of demand for travel range from −0.41 for public transportation in general to −0.79 for rail travel. Automobile elasticity with respect to gasoline prices averages −0.48. A sustained 10 percent increase in real fuel prices will decrease traffic by about 1.5 percent in the short run and fuel consumption by about 3 percent. In the long run, traffic will diminish by 3–5 percent due to reduced car ownership and using other transport modes.

Elasticities with respect to time differ according to transport mode. For instance, rail elasticity averages around −0.87, and for automobiles it is about −0.47. This signifies that automobilists are the more patient of the two. The cross-price elasticity for car with respect to rail services is a minuscule 0.06. Because of rail's low share of the leisure market, rail demand is less inelastic than car travel in Great Britain.

Goodwin (1992), Espey (1997), Wardman, Toner, and Whelan (1997), de Jong and Gunn (2001)

Increases in gasoline prices have a greater impact on rural households than on urban ones because rural households have access to few, if any, forms of public transportation and travel longer distances to access required services. Rural households have more difficulty adjusting travel behavior in response to an increase in driving costs. The incidence of gasoline taxes hits rural households hardest, even though they generate the lowest overall congestion costs.[8]

---

[8] Roberts et al. (1999).

Commuting Patterns and Modal Choice

The economic study of commuting combines four subdisciplines of economics, each one asking slightly different questions. Regional (and labor) economists ask why a commute becomes a migration (Chapter 10). Urban economists analyze commuting patterns to test the robustness of the monocentric urban model and to modify the polycentric models (Chapter 12). To housing economists, the commuting theory explains the allocation of residences and employment centers (Chapter 13). Transportation economists focus on the modal choice of commuters. Modal choice (modal split) studies determine the proportion of travel by each transportation mode.[9]

Modal Choice Models

Economists use three main methods of forecasting trip generation and modal choice. The most generic technique is the ***trip rate model (cross-classification model)***. Researchers calculate the average number of trips per person in each subsample of the population using national survey data. They then multiply the national averages by the number of local people in the respective subgroup to estimate the number of local trips to expect.

Analysts who have a slightly higher budget may prefer the more accurate ***aggregate simulation models***. These models try to estimate the number of total "trips" using aggregate demand factors such as population, number of work centers within a certain distance of the destination, a competition index, the comparative duration of the commute by rail, by bus, and by automobile.

The most accurate but also most expensive procedure is the ***disaggregate mode choice model***, which uses a multinomial logit regression technique to analyze individual survey data. Surveys gather data on each individual's age, race, income, occupation, wages, and time savings attributed to their modal choice. These are combined with cost data to estimate the preferred mode for commuting. Only the last two methods provide separate estimates for work (peak) trips and nonwork (off-peak) trips.[10]

Public Transit Costs

The relative costs created by the marginal passenger (the last passenger) include delays that the passenger imposes on the system

---

[9] Evers (1989).

[10] Preston (1991).

and the discomfort that a passenger imposes on other travelers, especially during peak times. In general, the optimal price includes the transport provider's marginal cost plus a value for the marginal costs imposed on fellow passengers.[11]

The cost of time dominates modal choice, especially for commuters at rush hour. Travel uncertainty involves both the deleterious possibilities of being late for work or arriving at work earlier than necessary. Commuters generally modify the time of departures or their route to minimize the cost of travel time as well as the costs associated with delays. Solutions that reduce the variance in morning commute times will also minimize the expected costs for the travelers. One possible solution consists of informing commuters about traffic conditions and possible delays by using a telematics system such as the Advanced Traveler Information System (ATIS). Another is to give public transportation the right-of-way through intersections by automatically changing the traffic lights with the approach of the bus or light rail.[12]

We already studied commuter shopping behavior and multi-stop shopping from a firm location perspective (Chapter 2). **Trip chaining** is the term that transportation economists use to explain commuter shopping. Since commuters try to minimize the time budget necessary to accomplish the maximum number of activities, trip chaining, by its nature, is more convenient by automobile.[13]

───────────────────────────────

Explorers, Sheep, and Traffic Information

Downs (1962) classified commuters as either "explorers" or "sheep." Explorers are inventive and constantly search for a faster route. Sheep are docile and tend to travel the same route unless a major disruption occurs. One way of improving travel flow uses telematics. The explorers will be the first to use this technology once it is introduced while the sheep will wait and see.

However, the access to information can initially have adverse effects and negative consequences when a large number of drivers overreact, that is, if they all try to converge on the same route, and create a second bottleneck. This possible over-reaction depends on

---

[11] Jansson (1993).

[12] Noland (1997).

[13] Peters and MacDonald (1994); Hensher and Reyes (2000).

the number of people who access the information, as well as the quality of information itself. Eventually, habit and experience will aid the drivers to predict the reactions of others.

Downs (1962), Emmerink, et al. (1995)

Public Transport is Preferred in Zurich

The high level of public transport use in Zurich, Switzerland, is due to the quality as much as the frequency of the service, the extended network, and comfort. A continued increase in ridership since World War II is due to the introduction of *Regenbogenkarte* (literally, rainbow ticket)—which is transferable from one transport mode to another and also between people—and from the installation of automatic traffic-light signaling.

A computerized control center monitors both the transit timetables and the location of each vehicle. Loudspeakers inform drivers and passengers of the train's progress. If the light rail is delayed reserve buses are ready to be called up. Computer-controlled automatic light changes keep public transport modes from stopping at intersections. Average waiting times for public transport during the evening rush hour fell by 38 percent after the system was implemented in 1985.

FitzRoy and Smith (1993), Eidgenössische
Technische Hochschule Zürich (n.d.)

More parking spaces at commuter rail stations increase ridership. An increase of one parking space is associated with between 0.6 and 2.2 additional rail commuters depending on the hour. Expanding parking capacity creates positive social benefits by reducing congestion costs, but such public expenditures create unpleasant distributional effects. This type of public spending benefits higher income people. All taxpayers pay for expanded parking for these commuters, whose average incomes exceed the regional average.[14]

Telecommuting

Telecommuting—working from home and "commuting" via the Internet and telephone—has been touted as the cure-all for any and all commuting ills. Nevertheless, telecommuting is not a congestion panacea. A study by Balepur, Varma, and Moktarian (1998) analyzed survey data from California. They noted that the number of trips is about the same whether workers commute or telecommute.

In fact, telecommuters averaged one more trip each day even though the distance of their journeys decreased by 18 percent. Travelers also shifted from using public transportation to driving alone on telecommuting days. The length of their trips tended to be compressed into certain off-peak hours (which is a good thing), but the freedom that the telecommuters enjoyed of going to lunch, shopping, or enjoying social trips still causes congestion.

Balepur, Varma, and Moktarian (1998)

Carpooling

The amount of carpooling or ridesharing is a function of the cost of fuel, administrative costs, and the value of time, traffic congestion, air pollution, noise levels, and access to parking at the workplace. Compared to people who drive alone or who use public transportation, those who carpool save money and time. They share expenses, and eliminate the walk to, and the wait for, scheduled public transportation.

Commuters who use public transport spend 70% more time than the average carpool trip, but carpooling takes 17% more time than driving alone, according to Rietveld et al. (1999). Unfortunately, carpooling is inconvenient

---

[14] Merriman (1998).

for trip chainers, as well as for people who work flexible hours. Furthermore, the "social climate" of a carpool may be distasteful to some riders. In 2000, the share of commuters who carpool to work in the United States fell to 12.2%, compared to 19.4% in the 1980s.[15] Employers could promote the use of carpools if they increase parking costs for solo drivers.

Transportation Supply

It is difficult to estimate the marginal costs and marginal benefits of an additional mile of transport infrastructure. Since demand is a derived demand, the benefits of infrastructure supply cannot be isolated. It interacts with the entire economic system. The benefits accrue over an average period of 20 years, whereas most of the costs accrue during the construction phase.[16]

Highway Supply and Demand

The solution to the congestion problem is very simple for the transportation engineers: increase road capacity, perhaps to create "spaghetti junctions" such as Figure 14.1. But this is only a short-term solution. Downs (1962) adapted *Parkinson's Second Law* (the demand for a resource rises to meet its supply) to become *Parkinson's Second Law Applied to Traffic*: "On urban commuter expressways, peak-hour traffic congestion rises to meet maximum capacity." We will explain this statement later using Figure 14.3.

Figure 14.2 shows the supply (marginal costs) and demand (marginal benefits) for road space at both peak and off-peak hours. The marginal costs for off-peak road users are composed almost exclusively of private marginal costs (time and automobile maintenance). The marginal costs for peak highway users add the marginal social costs to the marginal private costs. Thus, the socially optimal quantity of road usage is less than the private choice because drivers are not paying the total cost of driving.[17]

The **trip unit** is the standard measurement of quantity. Trip units are the number of trips per time, and trips are generally measured in passenger car equivalents (PCE). Quantity is calculated as the number of PCE per lane per hour. The PCE is the number of passenger cars that correspond to a

---

[15] U.S. Bureau of the Census (n.d.); Rietveld et al. (1999); Huang, Yang, and Bell (2000).
[16] Lakshmanan et al. (2001).
[17] Newbery (1990); White (1990).

Figure 14.1 Freeway interchange of the 405 and 105 in Los Angeles, California. (From http://en.wikipedia.org/wiki/Image:Los_ Angeles_Freeway_Interchange.jpg).

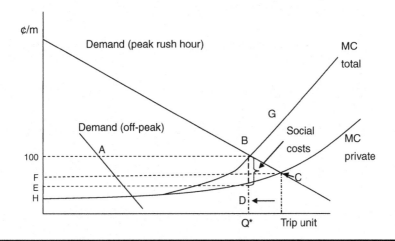

Figure 14.2 Transport demand and marginal cost.

single heavy vehicle of a particular type under prevailing road and traffic conditions.[18] Single unit trucks vary from 1.00 to 1.37 trip units, and combination trucks vary from 1.00 to 2.18, depending on traffic volume and speed. Point C shows the private marginal cost of commuting during rush hour. In off-peak hours, demand imposes little or no additional social cost. The social cost imposed per trip unit at peak times is BD.[19]

Adding more road mileage shifts the marginal cost curves outward, temporarily decreasing private transport costs at rush hour, and thus increasing quantity demanded and confirming *Parkinson's Second Law Applied to Traffic*. In Figure 14.3, the marginal cost curves associated with the new roads are MC total$_2$ and MC private$_2$. The optimal quantity of trips increases from Q_1^* to Q_2^*, with increased road capacity.

In the long run, the construction of new roads is necessary, but in the short run, economists prefer another solution: the imposition of a tax (or toll) equal to the amount of social cost that each driver inflicts on others. An efficient toll would change from zero during off-peak hours to a maximum of BD (in Figure 14.2) during peak road use. In this way, the user would pay the marginal social cost of each trip, and the quantity of road trips will fall to the optimal level. This optimal level is situated at the point where the combined marginal social, plus private cost, equals the marginal benefit.

---

[18] Akcelik and Associates (2003).
[19] Newbery (1990); Benekohal and Zhao (2000).

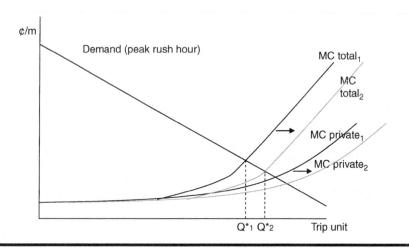

Figure 14.3 Transport demand and marginal cost with increased road capacity.

Privatization of Highways

The government owns and maintains most roads and bridges. When there is no congestion, transport infrastructure is a nonrival and nonexcludable good; the public sector should therefore be more efficient than the private sector in providing the good. However, when congestion exists, the transport infrastructure becomes a club (or quasi-public) good, and it is no longer clear that government is the most efficient provider.[20]

The quality of services provided by the public sector has not been optimal. As they are currently administered, subsidies discourage productivity, innovation, or initiative and lead to financial mismanagement. The imposition of variable tolls on roads that are "free" today may be politically incorrect, but it underscores questions of efficient management. However, privatization of specific toll lanes could increase efficiency.[21]

Private routes are not a new phenomenon in the United States. Back in 1802, the Little River Turnpike Company in Virginia constructed a paved road 34 miles long, exclusively financed by tolls. Currently, several forms of privatization exist:

■ Individual firms pay for the construction of new highway interchanges close to their plant.

---

[20] Winston (2000); Lakshmanan et al. (2001).
[21] Giuliano and Small (1995); Karlaftis and McCarthy (1999); Winston (2000).

- In some states, the private sector shares highway construction costs by purchasing the land for highways and donating it to the state.
- In Texas, road utility districts are groupings of landowners who take on the responsibility of building and maintaining public highways.
- Area residents rejected a proposal to put a bridge connecting northern residential areas of Fargo, North Dakota, with those of Moorhead, Minnesota, because it would increase traffic through a residential area. However, a private company built and operates a two-lane toll bridge in the place of the four-lane bridge that was originally planned.
- A popular form of privatization outside the United States is the "build-operate-transfer" (BOT) principle. Canadians refer to it as Build-Operate-Own-Transfer (or BOOT). The private sector builds the infrastructure, operates it for a fixed period, and then turns the facility to the public sector. Examples of BOT include the Italian Autostrade, the Anglo-French Chunnel, the Sydney Harbor Tunnel in Australia, the Oslo Tunnel, and two expressways in Malaysia and Singapore.[22]

Norwegian BOT Tunnels

Some European cities use toll tunnels to decrease the congestion in the center city. Constructed and operated by the private sector, these tunnels offer drivers the following advantages: peak/off-peak pricing (congestion pricing), nonstop electronic toll collection, and the absence of heavy trucks. Smaller-sized tunnels built exclusively for automobiles reduce the amount of capital investment.

In the 1980s, Oslo used tolls to finance an improved transport system and decrease congestion. Seventy percent of the new system in Oslo consists of 16 tunnels, totaling 8.7 miles. The largest component is a six-lane, two-mile-long tunnel that bypasses part of the downtown waterfront area.

Poole and Sugimoto (1995)

---

[22] Viton (1995).

Privatization of Public Transit Systems

Many studies analyzing data from several countries by a wide range of methods have examined the effects of government aid on the efficiency of public transportation. Specific results vary, but the conclusions unanimously link the increases in subsidies with reductions in performance and productivity.[23]

The first problem with rail construction projects is that the planning stage inevitably incorporates two serious errors: the overestimation of the number of users and the underestimation of capital and operating costs. For example, the 17.4-mile-long Los Angeles Red Line light rail system that opened in June 2000 cost more than $4.5 billion. Only after 5 years was it able to boast that it finally met its target of 100,000 users (in a county of ten million residents).[24] The planners have no incentive to ensure that riders actually use the new networks, so transit systems are rewarded for adding new routes regardless of whether there is a demand for them. The Transportation Equity Act for the 21st Century subsidizes empty buses (that produce zero social benefit) at almost the same rate that it subsidizes full ones. One solution would be to design an incentive structure to improve productivity and increase the number of users.[25]

Transit Subsidies Reroute Incentives

Researchers have established that operating revenues for the high-speed train in the Madrid-Seville corridor in Spain are far from covering total costs. This line is not justifiable in economic terms. Similarly, the current public transport subsidies in Adelaide, Australia, are significantly higher than can be justified based on the number of users.

Public transport subsidies in the United States fare no better. For example, the Los Angeles Blue Line was the first link of the $78.3 billion rail program. The blue line is a single light-rail line, extending 23 miles from downtown Los Angeles to the city of Long Beach. Constructed in 1991, it cost $877 million. The 1992 annual operating cost was $43 million, of which just 11 percent was

---

[23] For instance, Newbery (1990), Cromwell (1991), Obeng and Azam (1997), Tisato (1997), Karlaftis and McCarthy (1999), Winston (2000), and Schmidt (2001).

[24] Winston (2000) and Lightrailnow.org (2003).

[25] Schmidt (2001).

covered by fares. One passenger in three previously drove or rode in automobiles. The rest were former bus patrons or new travelers. The passengers who decided to switch from the automobile to take the Blue Line receive a subsidy of between $40 and $72 per one-way trip. The Blue Line is also subsidized by the inner city bus service, so these low-income riders subsidize the higher income suburbanites' commute.

Giuliano and Small (1995), De Rus and Inglada (1997),
Tisato (1997), Karlaftis and McCarthy (1999)

A second problem is that the subsidies from the federal government do not consider the total amount of monies available to each firm. Firms receive federal subsidies even if all their costs are covered from other sources. State and local governments have stronger incentives for monitoring public transit operations, and accordingly, greater potential to increase efficiency in the transit systems. Therefore, they have the incentive to monitor public transit operations and have them be even more efficient.[26]

Subsidies for new public transportation lines are for the most part cost ineffective. In effect, new public transport modes capture the pedestrians and cyclists, but few motorists are ready to abandon the convenience of their private vehicles to catch a bus or a train. To create an efficient transportation system, some economists think that it is necessary to eliminate subsidies and just privatize it. Profit maximization is a powerful incentive to reduce costs. The city of Indianapolis, Indiana, for example, started privatizing its transit operations in 1996, and since then, it has enjoyed an annual average reduction of 2.5% in operating costs.[27]

Finally, government subsidies have questionable distributional effects. For example, light rail subsidies benefit upper–middle-income rail riders, whereas subsidies for buses benefit lower- and middle-income riders. The average annual household income of bus commuters is less than $40,000, compared to $50,000 for those who take light rail. When the two modes of transport coexist, the lower- and middle-income bus riders help subsidize light rail.[28]

According to public choice theory, distortions take place when firms do not minimize costs because rent-seeking bureaucracies are always eager to

---

[26] Obeng and Azam (1997); Karlaftis and McCarthy (1999).
[27] Karlaftis and McCarthy (1999); Winston (2000).
[28] Winston (2000).

maximize their budgets. Distortions also come from principal–agent relationships when the agent (state or local agency) sets its own agenda, which differs from that of the principal (Department of Transportation). Private owners of transit capital equipment devote significantly more resources to maintenance of rail lines or buses than do public owners of similar capital. Because of inadequate maintenance, publicly owned capital deteriorates faster than similar private capital.[29]

Think About It...

How are you affected by traffic congestion?

- Do you suffer from air pollution?
- How often are potholes repaired? Are the roads well-maintained?
- How many traffic accidents occur per person per year in your city or neighborhood? Is that proportion trending upward or downward?
- What do you think can be done to efficiently decrease congestion externalities in your neighborhood?

Costing Out Externalities

Besides the cost of congestion, social costs of highways include pollution costs, road damage, and the risk of accidents. This section studies the components of these external costs and analyzes some policies created to diminish them.

Pollution Costs

Environmental impacts of road pollution range from local effects such as traffic noise, odor, vibration, lead, benzene, the rupture of a homogeneous community before a road is built through it, and visual intrusion, but also the global effects due to the emissions of nitrogen oxide (NOx) and carbon dioxide (CO_2). It is difficult to give a monetary value to these pollutants.

Nitrogen oxides, carbon oxides (CO), and hydrocarbons (HC) are a mix of various photochemical oxidants responsible for smog. Transport causes 50% of all NOx, 75% of all CO, and 40% of all HC. Traffic fumes blacken

---

[29] Cromwell (1991); Tisato (1997).

buildings. Acid rain, caused by nitrogen and sulfur oxides, threatens forests and woodlands. Transport only accounts for 3% of the sulfur oxides but it is largely responsible for the nitrogen. Carbon dioxide generates the "greenhouse effect" and transportation is responsible for 15% of the CO_2 emissions.[30]

Pollution costs caused by highway usage in the United States contribute less than 10% of total social costs from highways. Antipollution policies include mandating emission standards and differential taxes on the more polluting fuels, but such policies have not been economically efficient. Newbery's (1990) detailed cost-benefit analysis estimated that a $20 billion-per-year program designed to meet the stringent emissions standards act passed in 1984 cost an amount several times greater than the most optimistic estimates of the potential benefits of reducing pollution. A policy whose marginal cost is significantly greater than the marginal benefit is economically inefficient.

Road Damage Costs

Because most road damage is caused by heavy vehicles (trucks and buses), requiring additional axles on these vehicles reduces the damage. Even pouring a thicker road surface will increase the volume of traffic between repairs. The costs of maintenance due to vehicles depend on the climate, the strength of the road, and the interval between major repairs. In hot, dry climates, Newbery (1990) calculated that vehicles account for between 60 and 80% of the maintenance costs, but in regions where temperatures drop below 32°F, the cold is the principal cause because vehicles are responsible only for between 20 and 60% of total damage. Damage per trip unit, however, is negligible.

Accident Externalities and Highway Safety

Accident externalities cost as much as all other externalities combined. One hour spent in traffic is five times more dangerous than one hour at home. Traffic hazards are a function of traffic intensity, speed, road design, weather conditions, and driving habits. Because the number of accidents depends on distance as well as traffic, accident costs can be treated like congestion costs. The cost of an accident critically depends on the value of a life saved or the cost of a life lost.

According to the ***risk compensation explanation***, road users choose an acceptable level of perceived risk. Driving is boring when the risk is too low and frightening at high-risk levels. Improving road safety

---

[30] Rietveld and van Wissen (1991).

invites more reckless driving, but deteriorating road conditions (ice, snow, more traffic) encourage prudence.[31]

Universal Auto Insurance Increases Accident Rates

Quebec, Canada, introduced an Automobile Insurance Plan in March 1978 to govern accident compensation. The goal was to provide rapid and reliable compensation to victims, as well as to ensure low costs of car repairs and faster compensation for property damage. The legislators wanted to create a universal compensation for bodily injuries regardless of who was at fault. Just after the plan was instituted, the number of accidents increased significantly in Quebec.

There are two reasons for this phenomenon. First, the new insurance plan changed the mix of drivers. Statistical discrimination based on age and sex was abolished. Young drivers benefited from the lower insurance costs. Because males aged 16–24 years submit more claims, the number of accidents necessarily rose when more young males could afford insurance.

Second, the introduction of no-fault insurance did not encourage careful driving. A moral hazard problem emerged when the individual's unobservable attitudes and behavior affected the probability of an accident.

Boyer and Dionne (1987)

Speed does not kill, but a wide variance in speeds kills. Large variances in speed imply lane changing, passing, and tailgating—behaviors that adversely affect safety. However, higher speed limits cause larger differences in speed. This is because higher speeds accommodate larger traffic flows. At 130 mph, a six-lane highway can theoretically accommodate a traffic flow of 70,500 cars in an 18-hour travel day—much more than the average flow of a six-lane urban interstate. In reality, the traffic flow on highways also includes trucks, which are generally incapable of cruising at

---

[31] Newbery (1990).

130 mph. Older passenger cars cannot safely reach that speed either, and many drivers are unwilling or unable to take the risk. Thus, if the speed limit were set at 130 mph, the average speed would be lower than that limit, and there would be a wide dispersion of speeds around the mean. These are the gaps that increase the risk of an accident.[32]

Yet the 55 mph speed limit creates an average highway speed that is much too low. In reality, the actual highway speed depends on both the posted speed limit and the level of policing. Thus, local officials can increase highway speeds merely by reducing policing, without having to change the speed limit signs.[33]

Congestion

Several policies have been proposed and implemented to reduce the negative externalities of congestion. One solution is to increase the cost of parking the vehicles in the congested area. A second solution advocates an increase in the cost of driving (by raising the gasoline tax) or otherwise increasing the cost of owning vehicles (e.g., registration fees, higher insurance rates, and license plate charges). A third solution, which would have the least amount of unintended consequences, would be to implement a variable congestion toll.

Parking

The availability of parking at the workplace influences modal choice. In some Japanese cities, car owners need to purchase their own private parking spots because parking on city streets is forbidden. For eight hours a day, the commuter's car occupies space that could be used for other activities. This third method also frees up spaces that could be used during off-peak hours by shoppers and tourists to the downtown area. In the long run, an increase in the price of parking would permit a better use of land than just as an eight-hour warehouse for one car.[34]

Dutch Parking Solution

Dutch firms with more than 50 employees are required to have a transport plan. This plan describes current commuting patterns of their employees and spells out

---

[32] Lave and Lave (1999); O'Dea (2001).
[33] McCarthy (1989); Graves, Lee, and Sexton (1993).
[34] Rietveld and van Wissen (1991).

the firm's initiatives to reduce the number of commuting employees. A survey of employees of the Free University in Amsterdam showed that those who regularly drive to work strongly opposed policies that restricted parking, whereas users of public transport or alternative transport modes were in favor of them.

The time spent traveling, and perceived difficulties in finding a parking place, determine modal choice. The fixed characteristics of commuting behavior, such as distance and number of working days explain the different reactions toward parking policies. The study concluded that commuting behavior can be diverted into more favorable direction change if there are acceptable alternatives. A firm might use parking as a carrot rather than a stick if it guarantees a parking place to carpoolers.

Verhoef, Nijkamp, and Rietveld (1996)

In the preceding paragraph, we advocated an increase in the price of parking to use land more efficiently. We add, however, that this practice is inefficient when it tries to reduce congestion. First, an increase in the price of parking near the workplace causes parking demand to spill over to the neighboring residential neighborhoods. Second, there is not a strong correlation between parking and congestion. On the one hand, commuters who can park for free at work may increase the amount of traffic during peak times, but they may also reduce congestion by avoiding these hours. On the other hand, the lack of convenient, inexpensive parking increases cruising and creates an obstacle to punctuality. Once a parking place is found, the parking meter requires the driver to keep track of time, another inconvenience of a trip downtown. Finally, parking policies do not affect the amount of traffic that continues through the city.[35]

Commuter Parking

In Paris, 33 percent of the workers have access to free parking at their places of work. Of the employees who

---

[35] Giuliano and Small (1995); Verhoef, Nijkamp, and Rietveld (1996).

do not have this privilege, 8 percent use their car to commute. When the employer offers a parking place, 24 percent of the employees drive. In the United States, the federal tax policy considers employer-paid parking as a tax exempt fringe benefit, and a tax deduction for the employer. But neither the costs of parking, nor the expenses of commuting by automobile or any other transport mode, are tax deductions for the employee. Because providing parking spaces is a tax deduction for employers, 95 percent of the workers in the United States enjoy free parking.

Free parking at work encourages the commute by automobile. In 1992, in downtown Los Angeles, this privilege was equivalent to a subsidy of $3.87 per day, an amount much larger than the daily cost of gasoline. According to Giuliano and Small (1995), one solution is to require employers who offer free parking to offer a cash subsidy in lieu of free parking. If parking expenses average $150 per month, a subsidy of $150 per month could encourage the use of public transportation or other alternatives.

Giuliano and Small (1995), Aubert
and Tourjansky-Cabart (2000)

Because parking policies do not work well, let us see if one of the two other policies (taxation of gasoline or congestion tolls) is efficient in the fight against congestion.

Gasoline Taxes

Estimating the amount of the congestion externalities caused by one vehicle during rush hour is an inexact science. In 1989, the amount of this externality was between $.10 and $.23 on the United States urban freeways, but these pseudo-tolls consisted almost entirely of an excise tax on gasoline. In 2000, an average car got 20 miles per gallon of gasoline. The current average combined federal and state gas taxes in the United States is $.40 per gallon.[36] This translates into a "pseudo-toll" of

---

[36] Exxon/Mobile (2004).

2¢ per (or 2 cents per) mile, an amount much lower than most measurements of social costs generated per vehicle. Increasing the gas tax may be effective in controlling urban sprawl (Chapter 15), but it is an inefficient prescription for decreasing congestion. Gasoline taxes uniformly penalize all drivers, independent of the amount of congestion on the roads when they drive. A policy to discourage driving on congested routes would be a better solution.

Optimal Congestion Tolls

An optimal road toll should vary according to traffic density and its cost should be continuously transmitted to drivers. Invariable tolls have little influence on the amount of congestion during peak hours, but variable tolls can influence a driver's choice of the route and the time of travel. Individuals travel for various reasons during peak times and are affected differently by tolls imposed during these times. Some merely go to work; they do not have much flexibility. But others, who want to leave early on their vacation or shopping trip, will react to variable tolls.

Variable tolls are a regressive tax. Assembly-line workers, for example, who are required to start work at 7:00 am will most probably pay a large toll, because travel is during a highly congested period. If the value of their time is low, they have no interest in paying a toll that would save time. Alternatively, a professional with a high opportunity cost of time is very interested in paying a toll to reduce the duration of the commute. Where there is no toll, commuting times are rationed by queuing.[37]

But is it practical to impose different tolls at different times? Will peak, shoulder (intermediary), and off-peak rates allow policy-makers to create a toll such that each driver faces a trip price close to the marginal social cost? Several styles of toll roads have been used with varying degrees of success. We will investigate four of these: the Singapore experiment, the Hong Kong experiment, Norway's Cordon Toll Tunnels, and California's SR91.

Hong Kong's Experiment

Hong Kong's traffic congestion problem became severe in the early 1980s. Population density attained an average of 5070 people per square kilometer, peaking at 165,450 per square kilometer in the central business district.

The pilot stage of **Electronic Road Pricing (ERP)** operated between July 1983 and March 1985. The ERP used a variable toll to ensure

---

[37] Volmuller (1987); Arnott, de Palma, and Lindsey (1994); Arnott and Kraus (1995).

free-flowing traffic. Each vehicle was to be fitted with a pocket-sized radio transmission device about the size of a video cassette tape. Electronic loops installed under certain road surfaces signaled the passage of the vehicle to the control center, along with the time, date, and the electronic identification number. The control center then calculated the tolls and the owner received a monthly invoice similar to a long-distance telephone bill that detailed when each toll site was crossed. The average toll costs less than $2.86 (U.S.) per month.

The skepticism of Hong Kong residents stopped the adoption of this project. First, people did not find it necessary, given the projected traffic conditions and other congestion programs that had been implemented. In fact, the number of vehicles had been falling for several years before the ERP experiment. Only private vehicles (26% of the total volume during rush hour) were subject to the toll. Public transport (e.g, bus, minibus, and taxi) represented 54% of overall traffic; delivery vehicles represented the rest (20%) of the traffic during peak times. Besides, a mass transit railway was scheduled to open five years later, which, according to the city planners, was supposed to have been the congestion panacea. Finally, the average vehicle speed in the urban area increased by 40%—from 20 to 28 mph between 1979 and 1984. The residents, therefore, thought that the congestion was no longer a problem.

Second, Hong Kong residents took the ERP to be another scheme to increase government revenues. The ERP was supposed to lower if not eliminate license fees and decrease the gasoline tax. But the skeptical residents thought the contrary. Instead, they worried that a decrease in license fees would increase car ownership, which would create more congestion and thus lead to higher tolls, thereby replenishing the government's coffers.

Third, residents feared that this system would facilitate government espionage on private individuals, opening up possibilities for abuse. This was particularly bothersome because the Hong Kong government was to be under communist rule in 1997, that is, 13 years later. In addition, ERP required special arrangements for drivers who lived out-of-town or outside the principal island.

The objections underscored by the Hong Kong experience promoted the development of "***smart cards***," similar to telephone cards. The smart cards have an electronic purse that transfers money from the cardholder to the toll collector. The card is automatically debited until its funds are exhausted. Only after that would a central computer automatically send an invoice.[38]

---

[38] Fong (1986); Ho (1986); Hau (1990); Newbery (1990).

Singapore's Experience

In 1975, Singapore was the first city to adopt a form of congestion pricing, which included a license for the right of entry into the central city, variable parking fees, and a park-and-ride component. The right of entry is a simplified, but efficient form of marginal cost pricing.

This right of entry can be purchased by the day or by the month. Cars with at least four passengers, buses, and commercial vehicles were exempt of all charges, but not taxis. The initial impact of this project was spectacular—a 40% reduction in the volume of traffic in the restricted zone.

After implementation, three new travel patterns emerged: (1) drivers changed the time of their commute to just before or after the morning peak times (7:30 am–9:30 am) Monday through Saturday to avoid paying the fee, (2) during the morning rush hour, the congestion moved to new "escape corridors" that bypassed the CBD, and (3) because the toll was limited to morning commutes, drivers who avoided the center city on their way to work changed their itineraries on their way home, passing through the center city to reduce their mileage. To remedy the afternoon congestion, the toll was reinstated between 4:30 pm and 6:30 pm, Monday through Friday. Traffic volume fell by 38%. In 1991, the average speed was 22 mph compared to 6–7 mph in New York and 11 mph in London.

In 1990, the government of Singapore sought to reduce the sale of automobiles by initiating a quota system called the Certificate of Entitlement (COE). All buyers needed to obtain a COE before purchasing a vehicle. A limited number of COEs were auctioned off monthly. In 1991, the price of a new medium category car, including taxes and COE, was $44,800 (U.S.), but in 1994, the same car cost $88,300 (U.S.). To reduce the number of old vehicles, the COE permitted the owner to keep the car for ten years. After that, the COE could be renewed for a premium above the prevailing COE price. The approach penalized the owners of several vehicles or those who only used their cars on weekends.

Residents of Singapore were not opposed to these regulations, according to public opinion polls. It appears that many wanted to be among the few who owned private vehicles and they hoped to drive their vehicles on less congested roads.[39] The Singapore saga ended on September 1, 1998 when Singapore initiated an electronic road pricing system to supplement its COE system.

---

[39] Ho (1986); Hau (1990); Newbery (1990); Smith (1992); Toh (1992); Chu and Goh (1997); Noguchi. (n.d.).

Norwegian Cordon Tolls

The Norwegian toll is primarily a mode of financing, rather than a traffic control device. The tolls are therefore low and do not vary much during the day. The cordon toll is imposed at each entrance to the center of cities such as Oslo (since 1989) and Trondheim (since 1991). Tolls are required between 6:00 am and 5:00 pm. The prices are higher between 6:00 am and 10:00 am than between 10:00 am and 5:00 pm. Access is free during nights and weekends. Since its start, the system used the smart cards, so more than 90% of the vehicles pass the cordon without having to stop. Frequent travelers only pay once per hour, or 60 times per month.[40]

California Toll Roads

The California model is based on the belief in the free market, and an attempt for drivers to internalize the social costs due to externalities by way of taxes and congestion tolls. California State Route 91 has implemented congestion tolls since December 27, 1995. Riverside Freeway (SR91) is situated in Orange County, around Los Angeles. Times of peak congestion are between 4:00 am and 9:00 am and between 2:00 pm and 7:00 pm. They increased the volume of traffic by constructing two supplementary toll lanes in two directions, so that two lanes out of six (each way) are subject to congestion tolls and the other four lanes are not. The FasTrak was open to traffic in December 1995. The new lanes, maintained by a for-profit firm, cost $126 million and were entirely financed by tolls.

The toll and its structure are determined by the firm, but its profits are limited by the government of California. Except for motorcycles, zero-emissions vehicles, and vehicles with at least three occupants, users of the express lanes are subject to a toll. The express lanes are not open to trucks. The system used by SR91 flashes the current toll before motorists enter the toll lane, and at each of three entry points, the driver has one mile to choose between using the express lane or the nontoll lanes. Every six minutes in-road sensors adjust the toll according to traffic volume.[41] Tolls range from $1.10 to $8.50.

Thus, the two indirect methods of addressing congestion (parking restrictions and gasoline taxes) do not work well, and create unintended side effects that also need correcting. However, variable tolls directly affect congestion with few unintended consequences.

---

[40] Raux and Souche (2001).

[41] Liu and McDonald (1998); Raux and Souche (2001); Orange County Transportation Authority (2003) (2006); San Diego Association of Governments (2003).

Summary and Conclusions

Transportation problems can be studied using the traditional supply and demand analysis. The major issue of transportation deals with congestion and social costs. The analysis centers around variations of a cost-benefit comparison. A toll that varies by the calculated amount of externalities can optimize congestion and reduce the traffic density to acceptable levels.

Studies made on the supply and operation of transportation systems throughout the world consistently point to privatization as the only remedy to the inefficiency. Public subsidies from a number of countries and a variety of methods have never succeeded to provide the necessary incentives to induce efficiency. Even if such incentives would exist, they would be complicated to administer and enforce. Privatized transportation systems are more efficient because they need to satisfy their users by offering an optimal level of service at an optimal price.

To reduce road congestion, economists favor variable tolls. Drivers must be aware of the amount of the toll and have the option to change their route if the toll is too expensive. An electronic tracking system using refillable "smart cards" eliminates the stops and the inconvenience of fishing out the necessary change.

The negative externalities of commuting include time delays imposed on others, pollution costs, road deterioration, and increases in the risk of accidents. Measuring these costs is difficult for each roadway. Making sense of aggregated cost estimates is even more difficult. But nonetheless, the costs do exist.

Congestion remedies include parking fees, gasoline taxes, and congestion tolls. The parking fees and gasoline taxes do not change the incentives of people to drive during peak times. Free parking at the workplace encourages commuting by automobile. Charging prices for parking imposes a penalty on commuters regardless of when they show up to work, but it does not change the incentives of when to drive to work or what routes to use. Likewise, implementing a gasoline tax equally penalizes those who drive on noncongested roads at nonpeak times, as well as those who contribute to the peak congestion problem. Economists prefer an electronic toll that varies with congestion.

Chapter Questions

1. Draw a diagram similar to Figure 14.2 showing the marginal cost and the marginal benefit of a trip at 3:30 am (MB_a) and at 5:30 pm (MB_b).
2. Why would a constant toll of $.50 for everyone using the highway be inefficient? What type of toll will efficiently break up traffic jams?

3. Why do economists prefer congestion tolls to gasoline taxes or downtown parking fees? Who benefits and who is hurt in each case?

Research Assignments

1. What is the opportunity cost of traveling to work for the average person in your city, county, and state?
   a. Using census data, for your city, county, and state, determine average travel time to work. What proportion of people drive alone? During what times are the peak times in your city? Suggest a plan to decrease congestion in your area. Potential data sources for this project are:
   United States Bureau of Census. *Journey to Work: 2000*, http://factfinder.census.gov
   United States Bureau of Census. *Means of Transportation to Work for the United States: 1960–1990*, http://www.census.gov/population/socdemo/journey/mode6790.txt
   United States Department of Transportation. Federal Highway Administration, *Highway Statistics*, http://www.fhwa.dot.gov
   b. From REIS data, http://www.bea.gov/bea/regional/reis/ (CA30, line 300) find the average (annual) wage and salary disbursements per job. Divide that wage by 2000 (fifty weeks, five days a week, eight hours a day) to estimate an average hourly wage.

References

Akcelik and Associates. 1999–2003. Highway Capacity Manual (HCM), *Glossary of Traffic Terms*, http://www.aatraffic.com/HCMGlossary.htm (accessed on November 27, 2003).

Arnott, R., and M. Kraus. 1995. Financing capacity in the bottleneck model. *Journal of Urban Economics* 38 (3):272–290.

Arnott, R., A. de Palma, and R. Lindsey. 1994. The welfare effects of congestion tolls with heterogeneous commuters. *Journal of Transport Economics and Policy* 28 (2):139–161.

Aubert, J.-M., and L. Tourjansky-Cabart. 2000. L'allocation de la voirie dans les centres-villes. *Revue Française d'Economie* 15 (2):157–194.

Balepur, P. N., K. V. Varma, and P. L. Mokhtarian. 1998. Transportation impacts of center-based telecommuting: interim findings from the neighborhood telecenters project. *Transportation* 25 (3):287–306.

Benekohal, R. F., and W. Zhao. 2000. Delay-based passenger car equivalents for trucks at signalized intersections. *Transportation Research: Part A: Policy and Practice* 34 (6):437–457.

Boniver, V., and B. Thiry. 1994. Les coûts marginaux externes du transport public de personnes en milieu urbain estimations chiffrées pour la Belgique. *Cahiers Economiques De Bruxelles* 0 (142):203–240.

Boyer, M., and G. Dionne. 1987. Description and analysis of the Quebec automobile insurance plan. *Canadian Public Policy* 13 (2):181–195.

Calfee, J., and C. Winston. 1998. The value of automobile travel time: implications for congestion policy. *Journal of Public Economics* 69 (1):83–102.

Chu, S., and M. Goh. 1997. The price of car ownership in Singapore: an empirical assessment of the COE scheme. *International Journal of Transport Economics* 24 (3):457–472.

Cromwell, B. A. 1991. Public sector maintenance: the case of local mass-transit. *National Tax Journal* 44 (2):199–212.

de Jong, G., and H. Gunn. 2001. Recent evidence on car cost and time elasticities of travel demand in Europe. *Journal of Transport Economics and Policy* 35 (2):137–160.

de Rus, G., and V. Inglada. 1997. Cost-benefit analysis of the high-speed train in Spain. *Annals of Regional Science* 31 (2):175–188.

Downs, A. 1998 [1962]. The law of peak-hour expressway congestion, In *The Selected Essays of Anthony Downs. Volume 2. Urban Affairs and Urban Policy*, ed. A. Downs, Cheltenham, U.K. and Northampton, MA: Elgar; distributed by American International Distribution Corporation, Williston, VT, pp. 1–17.

Eidgenössische Technische Hochschule Zürich. 2004. *Public Transport.* http://www.dca.ethz.ch/info_verkehr_e.htm (modified May 11, 2004, accessed November 28, 2003).

Emmerink, R. H. M., K. W. Axhausen, P. Nijkamp, and P. Rietveld. 1995. Concentration, overreaction, market penetration and Wardrop's principles in an ATIS environment. *International Journal of Transport Economics* 22 (2):123–141.

Espey, M. 1997. Traffic jam: an international study of automobile travel demand. *Papers in Regional Science* 76 (3):343–356.

Evers, G. H. M. 1989. Simultaneous models for migration and commuting: macro and micro economic approaches, In *Migration and Labor Market Adjustment*, eds. J. van Dijk, H. Folmer, H.W. Herzog, Jr., and A.M. Schlottmann. eds., Norwell, MA/London: Dordrecht: Kluwer Academic, 177–197.

Exxon/Mobile. (n.d.) *U.S. Gas Prices in Perspective*, http://www2.exxonmobil.com/corporate/files/corporate/gpip.pdf (accessed on January 3, 2004).

FitzRoy, F. R., and I. Smith. 1993. Priority over pricing: lessons from Zurich on the redundancy of road pricing. *Journal of Transport Economics and Policy* 27 (2):209–214.

Fong, P. K. W. 1986. An evaluative analysis of the electronic road pricing system in Hong Kong. *Hong Kong Economic Paper* 0 (17):75–90.

Giuliano, G., and K. A. Small. 1995. Alternative strategies for coping with traffic congestion, In *Urban Agglomeration and Economic Growth*, ed. H. Giersch. In *Publications of the Egon-Sohmen-Foundation*, New York: Springer, 199–225.

Goodwin, P. B. 1990. Demographic impacts, social consequences, and the transport policy debate. *Oxford Review of Economic Policy* 6 (2):76–90.

Goodwin, P. B. 1992. A review of new demand elasticities with special reference to short and long run effects of price changes. *Journal of Transport Economics and Policy* 26 (2):155–169.

Graves, P. E., D. R. Lee, and R. L. Sexton. 1993. Speed variance, enforcement, and the optimal speed limit. *Economics Letters* 42 (2–3):237–243.

Greening, L. A., H. T. Jeng, J. P. Formby, and D. C. Cheng. 1995. Use of region, life-cycle and role variables in the short-run estimation of the demand for gasoline and miles travelled. *Applied Economics* 27 (7):643–656.

Hau, T. D. 1990. Electronic road pricing: developments in Hong Kong 1983–1989. *Journal of Transport Economics and Policy* 24 (2):203–214.

Hensher, D. A. 2001. Measurement of the valuation of travel time savings. *Journal of Transport Economics and Policy* 35 (1):71–98.

Hensher, D. A., and A. J. Reyes. 2000. Trip chaining as a barrier to the propensity to use public transport. *Transportation* 27 (4):341–361.

Hills, P. J. 1996. What is induced traffic? *Transportation* 23 (1):5–16.

Ho, L.-S. 1986. On electronic road pricing and traffic management in Hong Kong. *Hong Kong Economic Papers* 0 (17):64–74.

Huang, H.-J., H. Yang, and M. G. H. Bell. 2000. The models and economics of carpools. *Annals of Regional Science* 34 (1):55–68.

Jansson, K. 1993. Optimal public transport price and service frequency. *Journal of Transport Economics and Policy* 27 (1):33–50.

Karlaftis, M., and P. McCarthy. 1999. The effect of privatization on public transit costs. *Journal of Regulatory Economics* 16 (1):27–43.

Lakshmanan, T. R., P. Nijkamp, P. Rietveld, and E. T. Verhoef. 2001. Benefits and costs of transport: classification, methodologies and policies. *Papers in Regional Science* 80 (2):139–164.

Lave, C., and L. Lave. 1999. Fuel economy and auto safety regulation: is the cure worse than the disease? In *Essays in Transportation Economics and Policy: A Handbook in Honor of John R. Meyer*, eds. J. A. Gomez-Ibanez, W. B. Tye, and C. Winston. Washington, DC: Brookings Institution Press, 257–289.

LightRailNow.org. 2003. *Los Angeles: Rail Ridership Surges*. Revised July 10. http://www.lightrailnow.org/features/f_000004.htm (date accessed November 28, 2003).

Liu, L. N., and J. F. McDonald. 1998. Efficient congestion tolls in the presence of unpriced congestion: a peak and off-peak simulation model. *Journal of Urban Economics* 44 (3):352–366.

McCarthy, P. S. 1989. Accident involvement and highway safety. *Logistics and Transportation Review* 25 (2):129–138.

Merriman, D. 1998. How many parking spaces does it take to create one additional transit passenger? *Regional Science and Urban Economics* 28 (5):565–584.

Merriman, D., and D. Hellerstein. 1994. Compensations for commutes in the land and labor markets: some evidence from the Tokyo metropolitan area. *Journal of Regional Science* 34 (3):297–324.

Mokhtarian, P. L., and I. Salomon. 2001. How derived is the demand for travel? Some conceptual and measurement considerations. *Transportation Research: Part A: Policy and Practice* 35 (8):695–719.

Newbery, D. M. 1990. Pricing and congestion: economic principles relevant to pricing roads. *Oxford Review of Economic Policy* 6 (2):22–38.

Noguchi, N. (n.d.) *Multi-Lane Electronic Road Pricing System in Singapore*, http://www.its-taiwan.org.tw/memoir/memoir1/etc/etc5.htm (accessed on December 28, 2003).

Noland, R. B. 1997. Commuter responses to travel time uncertainty under congested conditions: expected costs and the provision of information. *Journal of Urban Economics.* 41 (3):377–406.

Obeng, K., and G. Azam. 1997. Type of management and subsidy-induced allocative distortions in urban transit firms: a time series approach. *Journal of Transport Economics and Policy* 31 (2):193–209.

O'Dea, W. P. 2001. Congestion pricing with an exogenously imposed speed limit. *International Journal of Transport Economics* 28 (2):229–248.

Orange County Transportation Authority. 2003. *91 Express Lanes Toll Schedules.* http://www.91expresslanes.com/tollschedules.asp?p=m3 (accessed December 28, 2003).

Peters, A. H., and H. I. MacDonald. 1994. The worktrips of rural non-metropolitan women in Iowa. *Growth and Change* 25 (3):335–351.

Poole, R. W., Jr. and Y. Sugimoto. 1995. Congestion relief toll tunnels. *Transportation* 22 (4):327–351.

Preston, J. 1991. Demand forecasting for new local rail stations and services. *Journal of Transport Economics and Policy* 25 (2):183–202.

Raux, C., and S. Souche. 2001. L'acceptabilité des changements tarifaires dans le secteur des transports: comment concilier efficacité et équité? *Revue d'Economie Régionale et Urbaine* 0 (4):539–558.

Rietveld, P., and L. van Wissen. 1991. Transport policies and the environment: regulation and taxation, in *Environmental Protection:* Public or Private Choice, eds. D. J. Kraan, and R. J. in't Veld. In Economy and Environment Series, Vol. 4, Norwell, MA: Kluwer Academic, pp. 91–110.

Rietveld, P., B. Zwart, B. van Wee, and T. van den Hoorn. 1999. On the relationship between travel time and travel distance of commuters: reported versus network travel data in The Netherlands. *Annals of Regional Science* 33 (3):269–287.

Roberts, D., J. Farrington, D. Gray, and S. Martin. 1999. The distributional effects of fuel duties: the impact on rural households in Scotland. *Regional Studies* 33 (3):281–288.

San Diego Association of Governments. 1998. *I-15 Express News.* http://argo.sandag.org/fastrak/pdfs/fall98.pdf (accessed November 28, 2003; site now discontinued).

Schafer, A. 2000. Regularities in travel demand: an international perspective. *Journal of Transportation and Statistics* 3 (3):1–31.

Schmidt, S. 2001. Incentive effects of expanding federal mass transit formula grants. *Journal of Policy Analysis and Management* 20 (2):239–261.

Smith, P. 1992. Controlling traffic congestion by regulating car ownership: Singapore's recent experience. *Journal of Transport Economics and Policy* 26 (1):89–95.

Thomson, J. M. 1998. Reflections on the economics of traffic congestion. *Journal of Transport Economics and Policy* 32 (1):93–112.

Tisato, P. 1997. User economies of scale: bus subsidy in Adelaide. *Economic Record* 73 (223):329–347.

Toh, R. S. 1992. Experimental measures to curb road congestion in Singapore: pricing and quotas. *Logistics and Transportation Review* 28 (3):289–317.

U.S. Bureau of Census. 2000. *Journey to Work: 2000.* http://factfinder.census.gov/servlet/QTTable?ds_name=D&geo_id=D&qr_name=DEC_2000_S-F3_U_QTP23&_lang=en (accessed November 28, 2003).

U.S. Bureau of Census. (n.d.) *Means of Transportation to Work for the U.S.: 1960–1990,* http://www.census.gov/population/socdemo/journey/mode6790.txt (accessed on November 28, 2003).

U.S. Department of Transportation. Federal Highway Administration. (n.d.) *Highway Statistics,* http://www.fhwa.dot.gov/policy/ohpi/qfroad.htm (accessed on November 28, 2003).

Verhoef, E., P. Nijkamp, and P. Rietveld. 1996. Regulatory parking policies at the firm level. *Environment and Planning C: Government and Policy* 14 (3):385–406.

Viton, P. A. 1995. Private roads. *Journal of Urban Economics* 37 (3):260–289.

Volmuller, J. 1987. Is road pricing a real contribution to urban transport policy? *International Journal of Transport Economics* 14 (1):7–18.

Wardman, M., J. P. Toner, and G. A. Whelan. 1997. Interactions between rail and car in the inter-urban leisure travel market in Great Britain. *Journal of Transport Economics and Policy* 31 (2):163–181.

White, M. J. 1990. Commuting and congestion: a simulation model of a decentralized metropolitan area. *American Real Estate and Urban Economics Association Journal* 18 (3):335–368.

Winston, C. 2000. Government failure in urban transportation. *Fiscal Studies* 21 (4):403–425.

Chapter 15

Growth Controls, Smart Growth, and Zoning

Until now, we have discussed the spread effects of urban growth as if they were always welcome. We have described the *new urban economics* (Chapter 12) as if urban expansion produces few ill effects. Not everyone agrees with this line of thought. In fact, the majority of cities in developed countries control the land uses within their jurisdictions in one way or another. They agonize over the best method to preserve scarce agricultural land for future generations and they worry about urban sustainability.

In this chapter we are going to study the term "urban sustainability" and discuss what it means in terms of property rights, land-use restrictions, and the implicit trade-off between the current property rights and the pursuit of a better world for tomorrow. Former Vice President Gore, for example, insisted that sustainable development will exist if future cites are compact and if we practice "smart growth." Smart growth (*the new urbanism*) will be the subject of the last section of this chapter.

Think About It...

What did your city look like 50 years ago?

How has it changed?

How do you envision it 50 years from now? How would you like it to become?

Urban Sustainability

Everyone agrees that there is no standard definition for the term "sustainable development." Nonetheless, sustainable development is a frequent concern in the implementation of economic policies. Contrary to popular belief, the term sustainability seldom means "no growth," and in reality, it does not ban continual use of industrial inputs or nonrenewable natural resources.[1]

Generally, the concept includes:

- a growth component,
- a distributional component, and
- an environmental component.

Everyone admits that economic growth is a necessary but insufficient condition for the overall improvement of quality of life and standard of living. Thus, sustainability must include growth. The distributional component needs to account for equity, both intragenerational equity (within the current generation), and intergenerational equity (with respect to future generations).

The environmental component is closely linked to intergenerational equity. A current definition popularized by the Brundtland Commission[2] ignores the intragenerational distribution and defines sustainable development as "meeting the needs of the present without compromising the ability of future generations to meet their own needs."

The promotion of compact cities or smart growth is common in Europe and Canada. This concept has also been adopted in 73 metropolitan areas of the United States. According to *Our Common Future*, the 1987 report of the World Commission on Environment and Development and Al Gore's (1992) book *Earth in the Balance: Ecology and the Human Spirit*, high-density compact cities will achieve the following two objectives: the creation of a more environmentally sustainable urban area, and an improvement in the quality of life. Smart growth theoretically favors environmental protection and resource conservation. This practice promises the creation of cleaner,

---

[1] Veeman (1991).

[2] The Brundtland Commission is formally known as the "World Commission on Environment and Development" chaired by Norwegian Prime Minister Gro Harlem Brundtland. The Commission's report, Our Common Future (1987), popularized the notion of sustainable development (Environmental Agency, 2003).

healthier, and more prosperous cities. However, there is a debate regarding whether compactness is all that it purports to be.[3]

Property Rights and Ownership

Property rights issues are at the heart of the analyses of zoning and other methods of controlling growth. Well-defined property rights increase economic efficiency because private property rights create incentives which lead to the most efficient use of resources. However, proponents of land-use restrictions believe deeply that the freedom of some land owners must be sacrificed to increase social welfare and achieve some "higher good." Opponents of these restrictions remind us that the political process used to reduce property rights is inefficient given the problems inherent in measuring social utility. This process would even be incapable of gathering a consensus that could be disguised as a "social mandate." Once such a mandate is instituted, rent seekers are eager to grab a large part of the "higher good" for themselves.

Other opponents suggest that the definitions of property rights underlying urban planning are rooted in Marxist or socialist traditions of community ownership rather than individual private ownership. They question both the equity and efficiency aspects embedded in communal ownership.

The three components of property rights are:

1. the right of use,
2. the right of exclusion, and
3. the right of transfer.

The right of use gives the owner the right of decision regarding the use or nonuse of a resource. The right of exclusion bans those who have no claim to the resource from benefiting from it. The right of transfer allows the asset holders to bequest, to give or to trade their property rights.

The government (federal, state, or local) and individuals share property rights to land in one combination or another. The structure that would give the most protection of these rights produces the highest value for each asset because owners have a greater incentive to use their resource the most efficiently. Usually, if land use is restricted, the value of that land decreases.[4]

---

[3] Breheny (1992); Satterthwaite (1997); Burby et al. (2001).
[4] Beck and Hussey (1989); Kivell (1993); Jaffe and Louziotis (1996); O'Toole (2000).

How to Control Growth

Jurisdictions have the authority to devise zoning and other land-use controls to promote the health, safety, and general welfare of the community. They also claim that these tools will improve the environment or maintain the charm of a community.[5]

Think About It...

What types of restrictions are currently used in your city?

Zoning?

Moratorium on utility connections?

Multiple permit systems?

Impact fees?

_____

_____

Land-Use Controls and Zoning

Zoning regulations constitute the first-generation land-use controls. After the passage of the Standard State Zoning Enabling Act in 1922, most states delegated that power to local governments. Local governments created an assortment of zoning ordinances, supposedly with the goal of promoting general welfare. Critics have, however, declared that zoning was more often used to promote local and fiscal interests of the city and to appease rent seekers.

By the late 1960s and early 1970s, many communities started to complain of the consequences and fallout from uncontrolled suburban growth. They reacted to an anticipated decline in their overall quality of life by instituting growth control programs—the second-generation land-use controls. Growth management programs tried to control environmental and fiscal

---

[5] Katz and Rosen (1987).

effects by declaring a moratorium on utility connections and collecting installation fees for providing services to new residences. During the 1980s and 1990s, growth controls, particularly in California and in Oregon, limited the construction of housing as well as all commercial and industrial development. The objective was to reduce the negative externalities and congestion to preserve the provincial character of communities.

Zoning laws can benefit a locality. Two reasons justify these controls: (1) they increase the certainty of how neighbors will use their land and thereby decrease the impact from negative externalities and (2) they increase the tax base by increasing land values in the zoned area. However, zoning could also be used to exclude certain social groups from the jurisdiction.[6]

Decreased Impact from Externalities

Zoning proponents assert that zoning minimizes the impact of negative externalities by banning incompatible land uses judged undesirable for the general welfare. If growth controls do reduce negative externalities or congestion costs, they produce amenities that are capitalized into the value of land. Many people would like to live in amenity-rich areas, increasing the supply of labor and reducing the wage. The reduction in the supply of land coupled with an increased demand leads inevitably to an increase in housing prices. It not only results in a larger tax base, but also a social selection of residents.

Similarly, zoning can influence the structure of a city and create optimal agglomeration economies. If the agglomeration economies are experienced equally throughout the city, the market allocation of land itself is optimal and minimizes transportation costs. Contrarily, if agglomeration economies are only localized in certain zones and transportation costs are high because of congestion, then the free market solution may not allow enough agglomeration.[7] However, most economists believe that while zoning pretends to fight negative externalities, in reality, it reflects objectives that have nothing to do with improving efficiency.

Increased Tax Base

Fiscal zoning takes place when a town forbids all development that does not guarantee an amount of tax revenue at least as large as the costs of adding service. For instance, if the school has attained its maximum

---

[6] Katz and Rosen (1987); Knaap and Nelson (1988); Navarro and Carson (1991); Gatzlaff and Smith (1993).

[7] Rolleston (1987); Mills (1990); Navarro and Carson (1991); Thorson (1996); Duranton (1997a).

capacity, the construction of new houses requires building new schools. If the revenues from the new houses do not cover the costs of constructing an additional school, current residents subsidize the newcomers through increased property taxes or suffer a reduction in school quality. Courts almost always decide that it is unreasonable for a community to establish a minimum dollar value on new homes, but communities can generally establish a minimum lot size or a minimum floor area. A minimum lot size is the most common form of fiscal zoning, for it reduces density and provides residents with a larger green space.

Fiscal zoning is rare in rural areas because these cities are most likely to have a public service capacity that exceeds their needs. To the extent that additional families bring in more revenues and thus help pay for the existing public services, the newcomers will be welcomed with open arms. Likewise, fiscal zoning is rare in central cites. In the central city, each resident has almost nothing to lose if a new development is projected. Developers, who choose a central city location, need to invest a large part of their resources to obtain authorization from the city. Suburbs, on the other hand, have public services that are more likely to be near or at capacity, and because of this they are more inclined to enact restrictive zoning measures.

However, minimum lot size does not resolve all suburban problems. First, the lot size does not predict the size of the house. Thus, this type of zoning limits a community's capability to extract sufficient revenues from its newcomers. In addition, if the intention was to attract well-heeled residents who pay high taxes but use a reduced number of services, fiscal zoning eliminates all possibilities of affordable housing. Finally, minimum lot sizes encourage urban sprawl. This unaffordability forces those who desire low-density housing but cannot pay a premium for it to move farther into the periphery.[8]

Exclusionary Zoning

Exclusionary zoning allows communities to build "invisible walls" that exclude certain land users who might disrupt the homogeneity. This practice is a subtle discrimination against low-income or minority groups. Land-use regulation increases the cost of new housing production and subsequently the housing prices. In some communities, this type of regulation maintains the price of housing at a level just high enough to preserve the social homogeneity.

Regulations that are explicitly discriminatory and overtly racist were abolished in the United States in 1948. However, if the courts cannot prove

---

[8] Fischel (1990); Miceli (1991); Pogodzinski and Sass (1991); Wheaton (1993); Thorson (1996).

that the intention of the zoning is discriminatory, the federal court allows it even if the impact on the poor or ethnic minorities is clearly negative.[9]

By definition, zoning limits the property rights of landowners and establishes collective rights to land use. If a community decides to preserve its agricultural heritage, and thus to forbid the conversion of a farm to a residential development, the community usurps the property rights from the farmer. Rather than confiscating the farmer's land, the community can try to reduce the choices the farmer has concerning the most efficient use of the property. The restriction of the use of land is a low-cost way to appropriate part of the property rights. When a local government decides to usurp all the property rights, in justifying this practice on the doctrine of eminent domain, it needs to provide "just compensation" to the owner (Fifth Amendment to the Constitution). Restrictive zoning requires no compensation.[10]

Think About It...

Under what conditions has your city practiced eminent domain?

Was the confiscated land blighted or did it discharge negative externalities on the neighborhood?

What did the government do with the confiscated land?

What distributional aspect is associated with the new land use compared to the old one?

That is, who is better off and who is worse off?

Eminent Domain

The doctrine of eminent domain permits governments to confiscate private property for public use. This right is granted because the sovereign government has given itself higher powers over all lands within its jurisdiction. Historically, governments have used eminent domain to take private property to build public roads, canals, military bases, national parks, and other public goods. Today, this principle is often used as a pretext for "economic development" to replace moderate-level residential

---

[9] Shelly v. Kraemer (334 U.S. 1, 1948); Village of Arlington Heights v. Metropolitan Housing Development Corporation (429 U.S. 252, 1977).

[10] Katz and Rosen (1987); Rolleston (1987); Clingermayer (1993); Lynch and Rasmussen (2004).

neighborhoods with commercial or industrial areas or a deluxe residential complex that would create jobs or expand the tax base.

The principle of eminent domain redistributes land. In June 2005, the Supreme Court of the United States decided that local governments can use this practice as an urban revitalization tool. The result is that communities can confiscate private property to give to other private individuals or firms if they could convince the local authorities that their use of land will generate more property taxes or that it will contribute to some "higher good" for the community. All private land—whether it is blighted or a quiet residential area—can be confiscated, according to the 2005 ruling.[11]

Proponents of eminent domain underline the need to avoid the strategic bargaining of individual property owners whose sole motive is to maximize their personal gain. For instance, one sole landowner refuses to sell property needed to build a road that would reduce the transportation costs between two cities. That one proprietor could dictate an exorbitant price or even threaten to halt the project altogether.

Opponents of eminent domain maintain that if the government cannot pay the price demanded, the land has a greater value to the private individual and therefore should remain private. These opponents think that it is inadmissible that private property rights could be sacrificed to save a few minutes of a commute.

The opponents think that an expanded definition of the term "public use" represents another danger. Rather than negotiating a land purchase with a private landowner, the buyer could persuade the local government to appropriate the land through eminent domain and then repurchase the land at a lower price.

Finally, the doctrine of eminent domain underscores the concerns regarding distributional equity. Public authorities generally overcompensate for expensive real estate or avoid taking it because the owners have the resources to fight the taking in court. However, governments tend to undercompensate for property whose owners do not have the wherewithal to litigate.[12]

Effects of Controlling Land Use

Controlling land use affects the demand and supply within and outside the controlled area. The control also influences the housing market and population density. To the extent that the zoning is inflexible, it affects the growth trajectory of the community because it freezes all development in some zones while encouraging leapfrog development in others. This

---

[11] Lane (2005).
[12] Munch (1976); McKenzie (1987); CBSnews.com (2003).

provokes migration into neighboring cities or into rural areas that are less strictly controlled.[13]

Land Market

Regulations that restrain the supply of land impose a minimum lot size. This reduces the density of new residential areas and thereby augments the cost of undeveloped land. If we consider the delays imposed by the administration for obtaining permits or for other regulatory compliance, the cost is even higher.

Industrial zoning can be used to decide if a specific area should be a "holding zone" in which all residential development will be prohibited to benefit other projects. Even if the authorities know that the demand for land for industrial development is nonexistent for the moment, the creation of this "holding zone" effectively keeps the land off the market. This practice of "overzoning" for industry reflects a "wait and see" policy that bans all development until a firm makes an acceptable offer to the government. To the extent that the amount of land that is zoned industrial is unrealistic for that jurisdiction, rather than boost economic development, such a practice thwarts development as the officials dream of "waiting for the Godot" that never comes.

Supply restrictions increase land prices. However, the effect of zoning on the demand for land is theoretically indeterminate. If growth controls create amenities by reducing negative externalities or decreasing congestion costs, the controls increase the local demand for land. Zoning may instead decrease the demand for land to the extent that individuals believe that the zoning laws are arbitrary and inefficient. Zoning diminishes the efficiency of real estate markets by preventing mutually advantageous trades between prospective buyers and sellers. These properties can no longer be used for activities that provide the highest rate of return. This encourages a suboptimal use of resources. If the zoning board is flexible and imitates the competitive market, the demand for land is unchanged when the controls are imposed. But if the goal of zoning is to replicate the competitive land market, why incur the cost of structuring, imposing, and implementing zoning restrictions?

Empirically, land prices are significantly higher as the arbitrary restrictions decrease supply. For instance, a study by Guidry, Shilling, and Sirmans (1999) used data between 1975 and 1990 for 26 United States cities and concluded that land values increased an average of 37% because of land-use controls.

---

[13] Turnbull (1991).

What are the equity implications of land-use restrictions? Land-use restrictions do not fulfill the intergenerational equity criterion. Intergenerational equity explores the multi-period social costs and social benefits of a particular policy. Regionally, intergenerational equity includes not only equity in relation to the children of residents but also equity in relation to in-migrants compared with long-term residents in an area. Current landowners gain from the increased price of land, but this is at the expense of future consumers. Think of resident landowners as renting land from themselves. Increasing land rents only benefits them when they sell their land. Until then, the only change that they encounter is a higher property tax bill. The higher taxes may force fixed-income landowners to move. Absentee landowners gain from increased rent in the city and thus this group most often favors more stringent controls.[14]

Housing Market

Growth controls decrease the supply of housing. The decreased supply drives up house prices and contract rents. Building codes and other regulations that designate minimum house size or require architectural changes increase the costs. Such regulations, as we have said, add uncertainty and costly delays. They also prevent the minimization of housing costs and decrease the probability of the community, offering a sufficient supply of affordable housing.

Using data from 44 United States metropolitan areas, Mayer and Somerville (2000) found that land use regulation significantly lowers the quantity of new construction. Metropolitan areas subject to extensive regulations witness significantly fewer (45%) housing starts. In addition, land-use controls create barriers to entry that facilitate monopoly power in the housing industry. Development restrictions provide an incentive to develop residential projects reserved for higher-income consumers.[15]

Inefficacy of Zoning

How does one determine the effect of controls that have been in place for over 80 years? Ideally, a researcher would do a "before" and "after" study to determine the effects of zoning in an urban environment. This is difficult given that more than 75 percent of

---

[14] Katz and Rosen (1987); Rolleston (1987); Clingermayer (1993); Brueckner, and Lai (1996); Guidry, Shilling, Sirmans (1999).
[15] Katz and Rosen (1987); Duranton (1997b); Mayer and Somerville (2000).

the population lives in a city that has had zoning since the 1920s and for which historical data does not exist. The city of Chicago constitutes an exception. McMillen and McDonald (1993, 2002) concluded that in 1921, two years before the first zoning ordinance, the geographically concentrated negative externalities were not pervasive enough to lower land values. However, negative externalities existed: they were particularly strong on the south side of Chicago close to the stockyards and the industrial sector. They also found that zoning corrected some externality problems, but it created others.

There is no reason to think that zoning affected land values 80 years ago. First, the competitive market would have already designated a particular use for each area. Land use was quite specialized in Chicago before the first zoning ordinance in 1923. Even now, Houston, Texas, which has never had recourse to zoning, presents land-use patterns curiously similar to cities subject to zoning. (See Figure 1.2.) Second, to the extent that zoning was flexible in the initial period, it completely mirrored the competitive market. Third, grandfather clauses permitted conflicting uses to continue indefinitely. In spite of these conditions, land values in Chicago increased with zoning—the landowners feared the intrusion of commercial activities would conflict with then-current land-use policies and were therefore in favor of controls.

Duranton (1997a), McMillen and McDonald (1993, 2002); City of Houston Planning and Development Department (2005).

Spillover Effects

Land-use controls affect the welfare of the residents of neighboring cities not subject to controls because they affect the population growth in these cities. Families who cannot enter into a zoned area relocate to another community, thus increasing demand for land and land prices there. To the extent that the land-use controls are implemented in suburban "bedroom communities" that are economically and culturally dependent on a larger metropolitan area, the restrictions imposed by even one suburb create spillover effects and encourage development in the uncontrolled communities and peripheral rural counties. The process of "leapfrogging" takes place when people move farther from the traditional employment centers. Such land-use controls increase the size of the total urban area, exacerbate congestion, and encourage urban sprawl.

Thus, land-use controls contest spatial equity. Spatial equity mandates that landowners in different cities or regions are treated equally. This is difficult to implement because of the law of unintended consequences. The land-use restrictions of one jurisdiction increase housing prices in uncontrolled areas and they increase congestion costs of commuters who work in the controlled city but prefer to live in a less controlled environment.[16]

Is There a Case for Controlled Growth?

The major problem with "urban sprawl" or unfettered growth is the uncertainty about the consequences of future growth for a community. The pejorative term "sprawl" has no precise definition and it is difficult to say that City A is affected and City B is not. Without the pejorative connotations, "sprawl" simply means low-density, noncontiguous development on the outskirts of a city.[17]

Urban sprawl creates four potential problems:

1. urban growth encroaches on agricultural land,
2. the cost of public services is higher when the population density is low,
3. the national consumption of nonrenewable resources is wasted by commutes, and
4. growth of suburbs drains the life from city centers.

To what extent are these indeed problems? A superficial study of the data can confirm these fears. For instance, between 1950 and 2000, the population in the United States increased by 86.5%. During the same time, urban population increased by 129.6%, while urban land area increased by 402.1%. Population density of urban areas fell from 5300 to 2400 per square mile.[18] Meanwhile, the total number of farms has been consistently decreasing and so has land devoted to farming. In only 20 years (1978–1997), the total number of farms in the United States plummeted by 18%, from 2,258,000 to 1,912,000. During the same period, farmland

---

[16] Brueckner (1990); Pollakowski and Wachter (1990); Navarro and Carson (1991); Helsley and Strange (1995); Cho (1997).

[17] Gatzlaff and Smith (1993).

[18] Demographia (2003); National Resources Conservation Service (2003).

diminished by 83 million acres or 8%.[19] Finally, given the growth of the urban population and urban land uses, the provision public services to a low-density population must be expensive.

Regarding energy consumption problems, consumption in the United States was 2433 thousand barrels per day in 1950, that is, 4.33 barrels per person per year. By 2000, consumption rose to 10.85 barrels per person per year.[20] The measurement of lost time because of traffic congestion is more difficult to calculate. In 2000, the average commute time was 25.5 min per day. In 1960, 64% of the United States working population commuted by car, truck, or van. In contrast, by 2000, the percentage rose to 87.5%, and three commuters of every four (75.7%) drove alone.

Finally, advocates of controlled growth compare the blighted center cities with the bustling suburbs to confirm that decentralization is harming the tax base of the inner city. New shopping centers, which are also employment centers, choose to locate in the suburbs rather than in a crime-ridden, congested central city. A central location requires that old buildings be razed before any construction is possible, so a location in the suburbs is evidently less costly. In addition, former fields and pastures seem to offer unlimited parking possibilities. All the problems cited above would be resolved, according to the promoters of smart growth, if urban residents would simply be content with living in smaller houses on smaller lots and either walking or taking public transit to work.

Opponents of managed growth, alternatively, assert that these problems have been exaggerated, and to the extent that they are real, they are caused by the policies of the local government itself. Remedies cause unintended consequences that in fact amplify the initial difficulties and create even greater problems.

Compact Cities

Compact cities or smart growth is proposed as the panacea. If we study each of the four "potential problems" in detail, we conclude that most of the premises are verifiable only if the study of the data is superficial. Most of the evidence falls under the logical fallacy known as *post hoc ergo propter hoc*, (after this, therefore because of this).

---

[19] U.S. Bureau of the Census (2002).
20 U.S. Department of Energy (2001).

Agricultural Land and Green Space

In truth, although urban areas have been growing since the beginning of time, according to the National Resources Conservation Service, in 2001, the total surface of large urban and built-up areas of greater than 10-acre parcels in the contiguous United States (77.6 thousands of acres) constituted 4% of the total land area of the country and the urban areas could all fit into the state of Nebraska. These urban and built-up areas include golf courses, parks, highway right-of-ways, and water control structures. In contrast, the amount of cropland has been decreasing in the United States since the 1930s, but the reduced cropland is not imputable to urban growth. It is due to the increases in agricultural productivity—less land is producing greater output.

According to the bid-rent models (chapter 12), good agricultural land close to the urban area will only be converted to residential or other nonagricultural uses if its conversion increases its value. If, in the name of "smart growth" planners limit the choices of periurban landowners, they restrain the freedom of landowners and halt their capability to allocate their asset to the most efficient and most profitable use.

Oregon's land-use planning program was started in 1973 to encourage urban economic development while protecting the farmland and natural resources from urban expansion. A study by Kline and Alig (1999) examined this program and concluded that concerning environmental protection, the program failed. There is no statistically significant change in the likelihood of development since the law was enacted. The same amount of development would have happened, according to their analysis, with or without land-use controls. To sidestep the restrictions, urbanites moved to the minimum-sized lots (40 acres) reserved for agricultural activity to start a small "hobby farm" which was in reality their residence.

This failure of land-use programs is not limited to the United States. For example, Sorensen (1999) examined the role of land conversion projects in the suburbs of Tokyo. He found that the projects stopped urban expansion into the protected areas but the workers who chose to live outside the controlled zones worsened the problems by their commutes.

Compact cities are supposed to be "greener" because of an increased numbers of parks, public gardens, playgrounds, walkways, meadows, and wilderness areas. The green spaces will allow for wildlife habitats as well as pollution filters and trees that will absorb carbon dioxide (CO_2) emissions. How will an expansion of the population density of a city be compatible with promoting green spaces? O'Toole (2000) reports that around Portland, Oregon, former golf courses, city parklands, and farmlands were targeted for high-density development to attempt to alleviate the housing problem. In addition to paving green space, some three dozen neighborhoods of single-family homes were bulldozed to make way for high-density housing.[21]

Efficient Public Service Provision

Contained cities are supposed to be cost effective because they do not have to bear the high cost of offering urban services to low-density areas. However, Ladd (1992), who studied the effects of population growth on local public spending, concluded that in the counties where the density is fewer than 250 people per square mile, the cost of providing public services was the lowest. This efficiency diminishes in areas with greater density. Thus, when the density is greater than 1250 persons per square mile, costs exceed those in the minimum-cost county by $334.82 per capita (in 2002 dollars), of which 13% is due to increased costs of public safety. In essence, an extremely high density is substantially more costly for a community.

For sparsely populated counties, the net impact on established residents is uncertain. Moderate increases in population could meet the minimum threshold size necessary to increase the range of public benefits provided. Of course, if the local governments do not adapt rapidly to the growth in demand, the result is a deterioration of public services.[22]

Compact Cities, Energy Consumption, and Congestion

The proponents of compact cities assert that they are the remedy for congestion and excessive consumption of energy, but this assertion does not hold up to analysis either. First, there is no precise correlation between efficient consumption of energy and urban form because such a relation is difficult to determine either theoretically or empirically. In fact, the **"commuting paradox"** (shorter commutes in a congested environment) has been observed in the "smart growth" regions, such as Amsterdam, Rotterdam, Leiden, Alkmaar, the Hague, Delft, Haarlem, and Utrecht, that constitute Randstad Holland, in the Netherlands, as well as in the urban areas of Southern California. This paradox is due to the clash between urban spatial restructuring and preferences for the private car.

Second, there is no evidence that the price elasticity of demand for travel is such that increased fuel prices result in substantially shorter trip lengths. On the contrary, the relocation of both residences and employment centers in the suburbs reduces both the distance of commutes and energy

---

[21] Breheny (1992); Kline and Alig (1999); Sorensen (1999); Gordon and Richardson (2000); O'Toole (2000); Burby et al. (2001).

[22] Ladd (1992).

consumption. The experiences of Randstad Holland confirm that the benefits of compact urban growth are indeterminate. The zoning that tried to curtail urban sprawl was only successful for the controlled area, but overall urban deconcentration continued, along with the associated use of automobiles and freeway congestion. Empirically, population density within a metropolitan area is highly correlated with fuel consumption. Consequently, the suburbs tend to have less fuel consumption because the commutes are from suburb to suburb on less congested roads.

Third, short journeys actually increase pollution. Catalytic converters are not efficient until they warm up. In addition, cars pollute less at higher speeds, which are not permitted in areas of high population density. Planners in Portland, Oregon, in fact, expected a 10% increase in smog when they proposed their smart growth initiative.

The supporters of compact cities count on telecommunications technologies to reduce travel expenses and congestion. In effect, the telecommuting allows people to work at home. Unfortunately, as we saw in the box in Chapter 14, some telecommuters take more frequent short trips than regular commuters. Besides, telecommunications cannot replace the spontaneity of face-to-face contacts and it cannot benefit from the other advantages offered by urbanization economies (Chapter 5). If each residence becomes a cubicle and human contacts are only made in public places, will all urbanization economies emanate from the neighborhood Starbucks®?[23]

Finally, compact cities are also supposed to provide greater sources of renewable energy. However, the large-scale operation of solar energy or wind power exists in wide-open spaces rather than in compact cities. By their nature, compact cities would create higher losses if a natural disaster were to happen.[24]

Suburbs Rob City Centers of Life

Compact cities could revitalize the core of the city, but at a very high cost. However, in Britain (where compact cities are not a recent phenomenon), the revitalized core deprives surrounding rural areas of the spread effects that could have sustained them. Because relocation in the periphery was not allowed, the restrictions resulted in an increase in land and housing prices.

What should be the goals of the city planners—to ensure utility maximization of the current residents or of future residents? Will either of these groups benefit?

---

[23] Starbucks is a registered trademark of Starbucks United States Brands Corporation.

[24] Breheny (1992); Clark and Kuijpers-Linde (1994); Dieleman (1997); O'Toole (2000).

According to Evans (1991), current residents prefer living in the suburbs rather than in extremely expensive "rabbit hutches on postage stamps." What will be the reaction of future residents? Those who prefer urban lifestyles will be satisfied, but what about the others?

Despite the obtrusive publicity promoting the virtues of living in a compact city (diversity and excitement of the urban center), surveys conducted by Fannie Mae (Federal National Mortgage Association, FNMA) have consistently shown that 80% of American households prefer to live in a single-family home.

Critics of compact cities are against this "town cramming." The urban core of many cites may be exciting and diverse, but most of the urban cores have been declining physically, economically, and socially for decades. When they can, residents flee from the "excitement" in these center cities to take refuge in a more humane environment. For many years, people have voted with their feet. Restricting their freedom of choice would also reduce their utility. If people want breathing space they relocate at the periphery, which involves longer commutes and exacerbates congestion problems.

Despite its critics, urban sprawl is in fact efficient (Gordon and Richardson 1998). Optimal land development requires dispersed, noncontiguous growth patterns that create polycentric nodes. In addition, controls create inequities. A community's intergenerational equity does not exist when it is beneficial for current residents at the expense of those who want to move into a compact city. Such controls also create distortions in the region's spatial equity, increase land values in neighboring jurisdictions and exacerbate congestion and pollution problems in areas where these would not be problems if the controls did not exist. Finally, the resulting increase in housing prices within the controlled city defies vertical equity, (equity among income groups)—affordable housing is incompatible with compact cities.

Planners who implement controlled growth are not maximizing the utility of those who prefer to live the "American dream". Instead, they appear to be intimidated by the power of local lobbyists and rent seekers. The traffic in influence deters the creative destruction process described by Schumpeter and resists all changes necessary for economic growth.[25]

Alternative Solutions for Curbing "Sprawl"

According to Brueckner (2001), the primary reason for government intervention is market failure. What market failures cause urban sprawl? Are

---

[25] Breheny (1992); Gatzlaff and Smith (1993); Mills (1999); Gordon and Richardson (1997, 2000); Power (2001).

there alternative remedies for these failures? One source of market failure may be the positive externality provided by large expanses of open land. However, it is difficult to estimate the total social benefit to urbanites of open space outside a city. Brueckner suggested that the creation of more parks inside the city might substitute for decreasing the number of red barns located close to town.

Mills (2001) suggests that sprawl can be curbed by taxation. He estimated that a gasoline tax of approximately $2.50 rather than 40¢ would put United States gasoline prices level with the average price in Europe. Using 1990 data for the United States, McGibany (2004) calculated that each penny added to gasoline taxes in the late 1980s translated into a reduction of nearly five square miles in the size of the average urbanized areas. However, despite Europe's high gasoline taxes, the efforts to prevent sprawl are largely unsuccessful. Congestion could be better addressed by congestion tolls. These could decrease the amount of travel time that consumers are willing to undertake so that they willingly move closer to their workplaces.

A new residential development for which the receipts do not cover the costs of providing the public services requires a remedy other than smart growth. Instead of banning such residential developments, jurisdictions could tax them an amount equal to the entire increased costs incurred by the growing municipality.

Finally, Graves (2003) believes that urban sprawl is caused by the insufficient provision of public goods provided by the cities. Tiebout (Chapter 10) asserted that people will choose the jurisdiction where the fiscal policy and the range of public goods offered are acceptable. Because urban centers generally do not have good schools and present problems of security, and pollution, the residents relocate to the periphery of the city, where each suburb has a unique mix of local goods and services. As Graves noted, not all externalities are sufficiently internalized in each market. The desire to maintain the value of their land and to keep costs of public services reasonable leads existing residents to prefer zoning because it excludes low-income households who cannot pay the taxes necessary to provide such services.[26]

Summary and Conclusions

This chapter studied various methods of complying with the amorphous concept of urban sustainability. Sustainability generally assumes that there is economic growth. It attempts to superimpose intergenerational equity over current distributional equity in an ecological context. To the extent that zoning decreases the uncertainty of neighboring land uses, it promotes growth.

---

[26] Brueckner (2001); Gordon and Richardson (2001); Mills (2001); Graves (2003).

If zoning, land-use regulations, and compact cities thwart optimal land use, they limit growth. Zoning, which gives priority to collective rights, determines the preferred land use to the detriment of private property rights. Under eminent domain, the government usurps the entire property rights to the land.

Jurisdictions want to control land use (1) to limit the impact of negative externalities, (2) to increase their tax bases so that current residents do not have to subsidize public services provided to newcomers, or (3) to exclude certain social or demographic groups (based on age, race, or income).

Controlling land use decreases the supply of land, thus increasing its price. Theoretically, it is impossible to determine how controls change the demand for land if in fact they do, but empirically, one can say that the land values in the controlled area increase approximately 37%. The household net worth may improve, but landowners only benefit when they sell—they see only an increased property tax bill in the meantime. Furthermore, housing prices will increase to the extent that building codes and other regulations drive up housing costs. The level of new construction drops and the supply of affordable housing dwindles.

Finally, the effects of growth controls in one city spill over to neighboring cities. Those denied residence in the first city or those who refuse to live in such a controlled environment will move to the neighboring cities or rural areas, increasing the land prices in those areas and commuting to work. The resulting leapfrog development is therefore the main cause of urban sprawl and traffic congestion.

Advocates for controlled growth want to preserve agricultural land and green spaces, diminish road congestion and the consumption of energy, offer public services efficiently, and guarantee the sustainability of the inner city. Compact cities would therefore be the panacea. Unfortunately, the reality is something else. Smart growth is supposed to provide cities with abundant green space, clean air, and smooth-flowing traffic while offering to its compact population all the attributes of a harmonious, dynamic, and frugal community. However, the majority of people want their own lot with a yard and a single detached house.

If Portland is the poster child for controlled growth, green spaces are in serious danger. Parks and golf courses are targets for high-density development. The promise of clean air does not hold. Cars that run short distances pollute more, solar or wind power generators require space, and people who refuse to live in such cramped quarters will commute from outside the planning district and thus create more traffic and congestion, as they do in Tokyo and Europe.

High-density compact cities are associated with substantially higher public spending than low-density areas. The optimal density to minimize public spending is fewer than 250 people per square mile. Finally, the rent seekers who thrive in this environment deter the creative destruction process that is essential in a vibrant, healthy economy.

Remedies for urban sprawl, if that is a social illness, would be (1) to create more parks inside the city, (2) to levy congestion tolls, (3) to impose on developers or their clients the responsibility for their own infrastructure costs, and (4) to abandon the rules concerning the density limitations or building height restrictions that artificially spread out urban areas.

Chapter Question

1. The concept of "urban sustainability" includes a growth component, a distributional component, and an environmental component. What are the impacts of zoning, eminent domain, and compact cities on urban sustainability?

Research Assignment

1. Identify in your area the jurisdictions that have or have not instituted controlled growth or smart growth plans. Also determine the date in which the plans took effect. Compare the planned and unplanned regions using "before-and-after" data (if they exist) to determine whether there are differences in terms of:
   a. Population
   b. Employment
   c. Journey-to-work data (between counties)
   d. Housing prices
   e. Income distribution patterns
   f. Pollution from vehicle emissions
   g. Ridership on public transit

Can you discern the difference between regulated and unregulated zones? Do you detect a spillover effect?

References

Beck, R. L., and D. Hussey. 1989. Politics, property rights, and cottage development. *Canadian Public Policy* 15 (1):25–33.

Breheny, M. J. 1992. The contradictions of the compact city: a review, In *Sustainable Development and Urban Form*, ed. M. J. Breheny. In *European Research in Regional Science Series, No. 2*, London: Pion, 138–159.

Brueckner, J. K. 1990. Growth controls and land values in an open city. *Land Economics* 66 (3):237–248.

Brueckner, J. K. 2001. Urban sprawl: lessons from urban economics. *Brookings-Wharton Papers on Urban Affairs* 0 (0):65–89.

Brueckner, J. K., and F. Lai. 1996. Urban growth controls with resident landowners. *Regional Science and Urban Economics* 26 (2):125–143.

Burby, R. J., A. C. Nelson, D. Parker, and J. Handmer. 2001. Urban containment policy and exposure to natural hazards: is there a connection? *Journal of Environmental Planning and Management* 44 (4):475–490.

CBSNews.com. 2003. 60 minutes http://www.cbsnews.com/stories/2003/09/26/60minutes/main575343.shtml, (accessed on 20 October 2003).

Cho, M. 1997. Congestion effects of spatial growth restrictions: a model and empirical analysis. *Real Estate Economics* 25 (3):409–438.

City of Houston Planning and Development. 2005. Open letter staring the lack of city zoning. http://www.houstontx.gov/planning/DevelopmentRegs/nozoning.pdf, (accessed on 19 August 2005).

Clark, W. A. V., and M. Kuijpers-Linde. 1994. Commuting in restructuring urban regions. *Urban Studies* 31 (3):465–483.

Clingermayer, J. 1993. Distributive politics, ward representation, and the spread of zoning. *Public Choice* 77 (4):725–738.

Demographia. (n/d) Urban population and economic growth: international context. http://www.demographia.com/db-1950200.pdf, (accessed on 20 October 2003; site now discontinued).

Dieleman, F. 1997. Planning compact urban form: Randstad Holland 1965–95: commentary. *Environment and Planning A* 29 (10):1711–1715.

Duranton, G. 1997a. L'analyse économique du zonage urbain: une brève revue de la littérature. (The economic analysis of urban zoning: A brief review.). *Revue d'Économie Régionale et Urbaine* 0 (2):(1997), 171–187.

Duranton, G. 1997b. Une approche alternative du zonage. *Recherches Economiques De Louvain* 63 (3):(1997), 271–292.

European Environmental Agency. 1993–2006. EEA glossary. http://glossary.eea.eu.int/EEAGlossary/B/Brundtland_Commission, (accessed on 20 October 2003).

Evans, A. W. 1991. 'Rabbit hutches on postage stamps': planning, development and political economy. *Urban Studies* 28 (6):853–870.

Fischel, W. A. 1990. Four maxims for research on land-use controls: introduction. *Land Economics* 66 (3):229–236.

Gatzlaff, D. H., and M. T. Smith. 1993. Uncertainty, growth controls, and the efficiency of development patterns. *Journal of Real Estate Finance and Economics* 6 (2):147–155.

Gordon, P., and H. W. Richardson. 1998. Prove it: the costs and benefits of sprawl. *Brookings Review* 16 (4):23–25.

Gordon, P., and H. W. Richardson. Gordon and Richardson, 1999 [1997]. Are compact cities a desirable planning goal? In *Environment, Land Use and Urban Policy*, eds. David, B., K. Button, and P. Nijkamp. In *Elgar Reference Collection. Environmental Analysis and Economic Policy*, Vol. 2 Elgar, Cheltenham, U.K. and Northampton, MA distributed by American International Distribution Corporation, Williston, VT, 516–527.

Gordon, P., and H. W. Richardson. 2000. Defending suburban sprawl. *Public Interest* 139:65.

Gordon, P., and H. W. Richardson. 2001. The sprawl debate: let markets plan. *Publius* 31 (3):131–149.

Gore, Al. 1992. *Earth in the Balance: Ecology and the Human Spirit*. Boston: Houghton Mifflin.

Graves, P. E. 2003. Nonoptimal levels of suburbanization. *Environment and Planning A* 35 (2):191–198.

Guidry, K., J. D. Shilling, and C. F. Sirmans. 1999. Land-use controls, natural restrictions, and urban residential land prices. *Review of Regional Studies* 29 (2):105–113.

Helsley, R. W., and W. C. Strange. 1995. Strategic growth controls. *Regional Science and Urban Economics* 25 (4):435–460.

Jaffe, A. J., and D. Louziotis Jr. 1996. Property rights and economic efficiency: a survey of institutional factors. *Journal of Real Estate Literature* 4 (2):137–159.

Katz, L., and K. T. Rosen. 1987. The interjurisdictional effects of growth controls on housing prices. *Journal of Law and Economics* 30 (1):149–160.

Kivell, P. 1993. *Land and the city: Patterns and processes of urban change, Geography and Environment Series*. London and New York: Routledge.

Kline, J. D., and R. J. Alig. 1999. Does land use planning slow the conversion of forest and farm lands? *Growth and Change* 30 (1):3–22.

Knaap, G. J., and A. C. Nelson. 1988. The effects of regional land use control in Oregon: a theoretical and empirical review. *Review of Regional Studies* 18 (2):37–46.

Ladd, H. F. 1992. Population growth, density and the costs of providing public services. *Urban Studies* 29 (2):273–295.

Lane, C. 2005. Justices affirm property seizures. http://www.washingtonpost.com/wp-dyn/content/article/2005/06/23/AR2005062300783.html, (accessed on 17 August 2005).

Lynch, A. K., and D. W. Rasmussen. 2004. Proximity, neighbourhood and the efficacy of exclusion. *Urban Studies* 41 (2):285–298.

Mayer, C. J., and C. T. Somerville. 2000. Land use regulation and new construction. *Regional Science and Urban Economics* 30 (6):639–662.

McGibany, J. M. 2004. Gasoline prices, state gasoline excise taxes, and the size of urban areas. *Journal of Applied Business Research* 20 (1):33–41.

McKenzie, R. B. 1987. *The Fairness of Markets: A Search for Justice in a Free Society*. Lexington, Mass., and Toronto: Heath, Lexington Books.

McMillen, D. P., and J. F. McDonald. 1993. Could zoning have increased land values in Chicago? *Journal of Urban Economics* 33 (2):167–188.

McMillen, D. P., and J. F. McDonald. 2002. Land values in a newly zoned city. *Review of Economics and Statistics* 84 (1):62–72.

Miceli, T. J. 1991. Free riders and distortionary zoning by local communities. *Journal of Urban Economics* 30 (1):112–122.

Mills, D. E. 1990. Zoning rights and land development timing. *Land Economics* 66 (3):283–293.

Mills, E. S. 2001. Urban sprawl: lessons from urban economics: comments. *Brookings-Wharton Papers on Urban Affairs* 0 (0):90–93.

Mills, E. S. 1999. Earnings inequality and central-city development. *Federal Reserve Bank of New York Economic Policy Review* 5(3): 133–142.

Munch, P. 1976. An economic analysis of eminent domain. *Journal of Political Economy* 84 (3):473–497.

National Resources Conservation Service. 2003. National resources inventory 2001 Annual NRI urbanization and development of rural land, July.

Navarro, P., and R. T. Carson. 1991. Growth controls: policy analysis for the second generation. *Policy Sciences* 24 (2):127–152.

O'Toole, R. 2000. Is urban planning "creeping socialism"? *Independent Review* 4 (4):501–516.

Pogodzinski, J. M., and T. R. Sass. 1991. Measuring the effects of municipal zoning regulations: a survey. *Urban Studies* 28 (4):597–621.

Pollakowski, H. O., and S. M. Wachter. 1990. The effects of land-use constraints on housing prices. *Land Economics* 66 (3):315–324.

Power, A. 2001. Social exclusion and urban sprawl: is the rescue of cities possible? *Regional Studies* 35 (8):731–742.

Rolleston, B. S. 1987. Determinants of restrictive suburban zoning: an empirical analysis. *Journal of Urban Economics* 21 (1):1–21.

Satterthwaite, D. 1997. Sustainable cities or cities that contribute to sustainable development? *Urban Studies* 34 (10):1667–1691.

Sorensen, A. 1999. Land readjustment, urban planning and urban sprawl in the Tokyo metropolitan area. *Urban Studies* 36 (13):2333–2360.

Thorson, J. A. 1996. An examination of the monopoly zoning hypothesis. *Land Economics* 72 (1):43–55.

Turnbull, G. K. 1991. A comparative dynamic analysis of zoning in a growing city. *Journal of Urban Economics* 29 (2):235–248.

U.S. Department of Energy. 2001. Annual energy review 2001 Table 5.12c Petroleum Consumption: transportation sector and end-use total, 1949–2001 http://www. eia.doe.gov/emeu/aer/txt/ptb0512c.html (accessed on 20 October 2003, site now discontinued).

World Commission on Environment and Development. 1987. *Our Common Future.* Oxford, New York: Oxford University Press.

Veeman, T. S. 1991. Sustainable agriculture: an economist's reaction. *Canadian Journal of Agricultural Economics* 39 (4, Part 1):587–590.

Wheaton, W. C. 1993. Land capitalization, Tiebout mobility, and the role of zoning regulations. *Journal of Urban Economics* 34 (2):102–117.

URBAN PROBLEMS AND POLICY

This final part will underscore urban problems such as poverty, the lack of a sufficient quality education, and crime. Such problems are intensified in urban areas simply because the city concentrates and amplifies all social maladies. Because of the very nature of metropolitan areas, solutions are not as evident as we would like to believe.

We will start this part with Chapter 16, which analyzes the extent to which a jurisdiction can provide various programs and public goods efficiently. We first highlight the difference between traditional public finance theory and public choice theory. Public choice theory, which assumes that public officials make decisions that maximize their own utility, is the primary lens through which we view public policy by accounting for the behavior of decision makers.

The main difference in the effect of a local provision of public goods and those that are nationwide is explained by the Tiebout hypothesis (Chapter 10). Chapter 16 will also examine the implications of this hypothesis on the decisions of local public goods and methods of financing them.

Interjurisdictional competition, as well as hierarchical governmental relationships, permits us to differentiate the topics relating to fiscal federalism and intergovernmental relations (Chapter 17). Externalities from local public goods provided in one jurisdiction often spill over onto other jurisdictions. People who live outside the community can enjoy the local goods provided by that community and pay nothing. On the other hand, because of intergovernmental grants, these same people could be required to pay for a local good but never benefit from it.

Chapter 18 will examine various definitions of income and poverty. It reviews the empirical literature that analyzes various forms, components and secondary effects of poverty. This chapter will also discuss tools to analyze the effectiveness and limitations of local poverty programs.

Education (human capital) is one means to escape poverty. If local schools do not adequately educate their students, the students will be the poor of tomorrow, for they will not be as productive. To this end, Chapter 19 will consider the various components of the demand for and supply of education. It will examine the various hypotheses regarding the causes of successful academic careers as well as the possible methods of improving school quality.

Chapter 20 will focus on a corollary of poverty—crime. The chapter first presents the economic theory of crime, in order to apply it to different types of crime: property crime, violent crime, organized crime, and victimless crimes, such as gambling and prostitution. We will then introduce the theory of "rational addiction" and its application to current smoking bans as well as prohibition of alcohol and illicit drugs. Finally, we will study the effectiveness of various crime reduction policies as well as the legalization of victimless crimes.

Chapter 16

Local Public Finance

Just as all politics is local, all economics is local. Voters theoretically have more contact with their local government officials than with the state or federal decision makers. The decisions of local government directly affect residents of that jurisdiction. Counties determine the welfare benefits for low-income households. Local governments finance, and thereby govern the quality of elementary and secondary education. They provide police and fire protection, road maintenance and public services (sewer, water, garbage, parks, and recreational facilities). They often oversee housing and community development projects.

This is why we pay taxes that permit the local governments to provide these goods and services. In the United States, local governments receive almost a third of their revenue from property taxes, sales taxes, or income taxes. Another third comes from intergovernmental grants and the remainder from user fees, fines, parking tickets, and other miscellaneous revenue sources.

This chapter will explore the nature of social decision making and the nature of local public goods before observing how the optimal quantity of these goods is determined and financed. We will devote Chapter 17 to the relations of government hierarchies and how local governments react to competition among jurisdictions of the same level.

Think About It

How do you and your roommates (or family) make decisions?

Are there some issues on which nobody can agree?

Who has standing in your decision-making process? A landlord or neighbor perhaps?

Did everyone in your household agree upon the last major decision that was made? If not, did you appease the disgruntled member, and how?

Have you had roommates leave because they couldn't agree?

Collective Choice and the Median Voter Model

Edgeworth boxes provide a better illustration of a person's utility by analyzing efficient and equitable distributions of a fixed quantity of goods between two individuals. (If necessary, please see the appendix to Chapter 16). What do we do when there are more than two protagonists? In a democratic society, social decision making is generally accomplished by majority rule. We use the **median voter model** to predict how majority rule works. If we could line up the electorate along a continuum, with the person the most emphatically for a project on one end and the person the most fervently against it on the opposite end, the wants of the median person on that continuum will prevail. (In a group of five people, the median person is the third.)

In the traditional public finance literature, the median voter wins. However, according to the Tiebout hypothesis (Chapter 10), the median voter's preferences can change over time because of migration. "Future generations" of a jurisdiction are not only the children of current residents. In fact, these children may not be the future of that locality.[1]

It is possible to predict the future policies of a jurisdiction by identifying the types of migrants the community attracts. For example, in areas where the majority of people have low incomes, a myopic fiscal policy tends to benefit them. Nevertheless, such policies may drive rich people out, because, like everyone else, the rich will relocate to where the fiscal policies

---

[1] Tullock (1971).

benefit them. Conley and Dix (2004) noted that is why higher-income neighborhoods get their streets plowed first. If households that pay higher taxes do not receive higher quality services, they would move, thereby decreasing the tax revenues of that municipality.

Affluent neighborhoods can impose minimum lot sizes to limit the number of low-income families in their jurisdiction. This would allow them to invest in and benefit from better quality schools, lower crime rates, and other "upscale" public goods. Without such restrictive measures, the poor in search of a satisfactory provision of public goods will relentlessly follow the rich from jurisdiction to jurisdiction playing what Hamilton (1975) called a game of "musical suburbs."

Whose Preferences Count?

To know how a jurisdiction makes its decisions, it is necessary first to identify who or which group has **standing**, that is, whose preferences should be included. For example, future generations (the young as well as those who have not yet migrated in) are among them, especially if they are responsible for paying the final bills.

But it is not always easy to determine who really has standing. City councils of college towns often try to persuade students to vote by absentee ballots at their parents' residence. Should students be able to vote in the jurisdictions where they pay sales taxes and their automobile registration? But have they the right to make decisions about the future of a community if they are going to leave in a few years?

Can transients influence local elections? South Dakota, for instance, allows people to call campgrounds and motels their "residence." Thus, in 2004, 46% of the voters in Todd County, South Dakota (close to Rosebud Indian Reservation) used absentee ballots.

What about the social standing of criminals? Should they be consulted when determining law enforcement issues? In some states, such as Minnesota, once convicted felons serve their time, they are again allowed to vote, and sometimes they are even informed of that right. Fourteen states (Alabama, Arizona, Delaware, Florida, Iowa, Kentucky, Maryland, Mississippi, Nevada, New Mexico, Tennessee, Virginia, Washington, and Wyoming) do not give felons the right to vote without special permission from the governor. Because most convicted felons are African–American, any racial discrimination intrinsic to the criminal justice system decreases the proportion of minorities who can vote.[2]

---

[2] Trumbull (1990); Sasaki (1991); Schwab and Oates (1991); Loomis (2000), Randall (2004), Schwan (2004); South Dakota Elections Information (2004).

How Does the Median Voter Model Explain Social Decision Making?

Alternatives to the median voter model (such as the Leviathan model or the bureaucratic model) describe the government as a revenue-maximizing organization composed of budget-maximizing bureaucrats to placate lobbyists. The median voter model rests on the hypothesis that public decision-makers behave as if they are maximizing the utility of the median voter, the voter that tips the majority in favor of a specific policy.

Baudry, Leprince, and Moreau (2002) used data from 1995 to 1997 on French jurisdictions (*communes*) with populations greater than 10,000. They tested the hypothesis that the local public decision-makers choose public spending that maximizes the utility of the median voter. Using both parametric and nonparametric tests, they concluded that both the supply of local public goods and the required income tax rate were chosen to satisfy the demand of the median voter.

Similarly, Ahmed and Green (2000) tried to determine the model that would best explain the spending of counties in New York State during 1970, 1980, and 1990. They determined that the median voter model has a slight edge over the others, but interest groups, as well as other institutional and redistributive factors, were equally important in public spending decisions.

Ahmed and Green (2000), Baudry, Leprince, and Moreau (2002)

Evaluating Social Utility

The second question concerning social decision making doubts the very existence of a **Pareto optimal improvement**. An improvement is Pareto optimal when at least one person gains and nobody is harmed from a change in policy. For example, the construction of a stadium financed by increased sales taxes will benefit middle- to high-income sports enthusiasts. However, because sales taxes are regressive, low-income households will be worse off. They will pay a greater proportion of their income in taxes to fund the stadium from which they are excluded because the ticket price is prohibitive. Such a solution is therefore not a Pareto optimal improvement. In fact, for most policy decisions some people win, but others lose.

The ***potential Pareto improvement*** criterion solves this problem. A potential Pareto improvement exists if the "winner" is able to compensate the "loser" and still have financial surplus left over. One can know if a decision is a potential Pareto improvement by determining a person's willingness to pay. The minimal payment that would compensate the "loser" is called the willingness to accept. According to the criterion of the potential Pareto improvement, if the amount that the "winner" will pay for a project is greater than the amount that the "loser" would pay to stop the project, society is better off if the project is realized.

It is preferable to estimate the amount that a person is willing to pay rather than to evaluate the amount of ***consumer surplus*** (Chapter 6). Estimates of consumer surplus calculate the subjective value placed on a good over and above the price paid for it. However, there is a problem. The consumer surplus measurement only accounts for the surplus of those who are willing and able to participate in the market of these goods or services. People who do not use the good have no standing in estimating its value. For instance, some people may benefit from advantages linked to the use or the existence of regular jazz or classical music concerts even if they do not often attend. Others value the existence of pristine mountains even though they are not hikers.

Willingness to pay, on the other hand, includes the amount that nonusers pay for the existence of the good. Researchers evaluate the willingness to pay by an opinion survey asking residents and visitors of an area how much they would be willing to pay to have a specific event or state of nature occur or not. The willingness to pay is therefore the sum of these hypothetical payments. The potential Pareto improvement criterion implies that the estimates of the willingness to pay not only have meaning, but they can also be compared between individuals even though the rich have more votes than the poor. Determining the social valuation of the event by adding the amounts that "society" is both willing and able to pay for it makes sense only if everyone has identical incomes and identical marginal utilities of money. Otherwise, people with higher incomes dictate "social" preferences.

If, for example, we could determine that Alan is better off in the state of nature A (state-of-the-art sports stadiums for professional teams) than Betty is in state of nature B (better schools and facilities for the elderly) we must be able to show (1) that Alan and Betty can agree that their utility functions are comparable, and (2) that their utility functions have a common measuring stick. If a third person, Chris, also has standing in the decision and is consulted, could we add up everybody's utility function to determine our choice between the state of nature A and state of nature B? Would a comparison of the subjective preferences of a person such as the Dalai

Table 16.1 Arrow's Voting Paradox

Voters/Projects	Alpha	Beta	Gamma
Alan	1	2	3
Betty	3	1	2
Chris	2	3	1

Lama with that of someone like Adolf Hitler for example, be useful in determining the optimal social policy for a jurisdiction?[3]

Arrow's Voting Paradox

To bypass the philosophical quicksand inherent in interpersonal utility valuation within a society, Arrow (1951) suggested majority voting as a potential model to analyze social decision making. Unlike the willingness-to-pay criteria, under majority voting, everyone gets one vote independent of their income. Arrow, however, admitted that majority voting was not flawless. Even though rational individuals have transitive preferences, even three individuals with diverse but well-defined preferences may constitute a society with intransitive preferences. Hence, the paradox.

For example, say that three individuals, Alan, Betty, and Chris, are going to vote on three projects: Alpha, Beta, and Gamma. Their preferences are shown in Table 16.1, where the numbers in the row show the preference rankings of each individual.

If they need to choose between projects Alpha and Beta, Alan and Chris prefer Alpha. Alpha therefore receives two votes, while Beta only has Betty's one vote. Between Beta and Gamma, Alan and Betty both vote for Beta: however, between Gamma and Alpha, Betty and Chris vote for Gamma. Thus, Alpha is preferred to Beta, and Beta is preferred to Gamma, but Gamma is preferred to Alpha. Taken together, social choices of rational individuals are not necessarily transitive and may seem irrational.[4]

Think About It...

If you share your living quarters with others, what goods are pure public goods for your household?

---

[3] Blackorby (1990); Trumbull (1990); Phipps (1991); Tinbergen (1991); Raux and Souche (2001).

[4] Blackorby (1990).

What goods are club goods? What goods are pure private goods?

Local Public Goods

Pure public goods provided by a central government, such as national defense, have distinct characteristics that local public goods do not have. First, the optimal level of pure public goods is determined by the majority voting process. For local public goods, citizens can vote with their ballot or with their feet in changing the jurisdiction if that migration will bring them a better mix of public goods. International migration is rare even in the case of unpopular national policies.

Second, people who live and work in another jurisdiction benefit from public highways, mass transit systems, parks, and libraries without having to contribute to their provision or maintenance. Municipalities are considered clubs and their local public goods are thus called club goods. Congestion diminishes the benefits of the good for each user, but exclusion is possible for most local public goods. For example, the use of a bridge or entrance into the center city could be restricted by imposing tolls or requiring right of entry licenses (Chapter 14). A fire department can refuse to offer its service outside of its district. Libraries and parks may charge a user fee. Because of congestion, public goods may become quasi-rival. The book you need may be checked out. A municipal fire station may have difficulty responding to several emergencies simultaneously.[5]

Privatization Creates Efficient Governments

In services where it is easy to monitor the enforcement of contracts (refuse collection, for example) a study of Dutch municipalities by Dijgkraaf, Gradus, and Melenberg (2003) found that private provision is superior. Outsourcing saves taxpayers in the United Kingdom about 20 percent without sacrificing quality of service (Domberger and Jensen 1997).

Blom-Hansen (2003) determined that road maintenance by the private sector in the county of Ringkøbing in

---

[5] Leuthold (1993); Oates (1994); Means and Mehay (1995); Shapiro and Deacon (1996); Loomis (2000); Brasington (2003).

western Denmark translated into in a savings of 2.5 percent of the budget. The private sector is more efficient because it uses employees more effectively. The county of Nordjylland in northern Denmark invited bids for seven road maintenance tasks. Subcontractors received four projects, while the county's own road division won three. This competition forced the public sector to reduce its costs.

Warner and Hebdon (2001) noted that the local governments in New York State used both private and public sectors. If privatization is not effective, the project reverts to the local government.

> Domberger and Jensen (1997), Warner and
> Hebdon (2001), Blom-Hansen (2003),
> Dijgkraaf, Gradus, and Melenberg (2003)

Private Provision of Public Goods

Because the majority of local public goods are club goods, their provision oscillates between the private sector and the public sector. The European Union, for instance, has been in favor of privatizing local goods and services to increase efficiency.[6]

Think About It...

If you have roommates, do you and your roommates have the same tastes and preferences? As your neighbors?

What change would you like to see in your roommate? Would you ever move out because of a roommate or a neighbor?

If you live alone, are there some people you would like as roommates?

What characteristics would be incompatible?

---

[6] Crowley (1994); Laffont and Tirole (1995); Fraser (2000).

Tiebout Hypothesis

The Tiebout model is the cornerstone of local public finance theory. This hypothesis affirms that people "vote with their feet" and move to that jurisdiction which offers what they judge to be an optimal mix of public goods at an acceptable tax price. The result is a sorting process: people with the same preferences move into the same jurisdictions. This sorting requires that we make several strong assumptions:

1. All residents can move costlessly.
2. Everyone has perfect knowledge about the qualities of each community.
3. Enough jurisdictions exist to provide a full range of public goods.
4. All communities, regardless of size, have the same cost functions for their services.
5. Public goods do not cause any positive or negative spillovers.
6. There is no social discrimination by jurisdictions.

Unfortunately, costless mobility (Assumption 1) seldom leads to an efficient economy because most local public goods suffer from congestion. To assume that enough jurisdictions exist to offer a full range of all possible combinations of public goods (Assumption 2 and Assumption 3) translates into urban sprawl (Chapter 15). Whereas most people despise urban sprawl, economists think that it is a false problem; more jurisdictions mean a higher probability that an individual will find the optimal jurisdiction.

Empiricists have analyzed the Tiebout hypothesis since the 1950s and have established that people do migrate in response to local public good provision (Chapter 10). Low-income households prefer areas that offer more public assistance, households with children are attracted to areas with superior schools, older people and those with high incomes desire areas with low property taxes and low income taxes. As we will see when we study interjurisdictional competition (Chapter 17), the Tiebout effect leads either to efficient provision of local goods or to a local government of an inefficient size, depending on the underlying theory.[7]

Think About It...

Who in your household makes the most decisions? Are the majority of decisions for the good of the household

---

[7] Oates (1981); de Bartolome (1990); Hochman (1990); Sass (1991); Teske et al. (1993); Hochman, Pines, and Thisse (1995); Page, Kollman, and Miller (1995); Glaeser (1996); Guengant, Josselin, and Rocaboy (2000); Caplan (2001); Pedone (2002).

or the good of that decision-maker? If you are not the person responsible for most of the decisions, are there any decisions that you would like to make because you do not trust the decision maker?

Public Finance Debates

Two fundamentally different theories of public finance are currently in use by economists: the ***neoclassical public finance theory*** originally formulated in Richard Musgrave's classic text, *The Theory of Public Finance* (1989), and the ***public choice theory*** that originated with Nobel laureate James Buchanan and Gordon Tullock's, *The Calculus of Consent* (1962). Only the nature of the objectives pursued by government officials differentiates these two theories. Because the goals ascribed to the officials differ, the prescriptions for an efficient government also differ.

Musgrave organized the different public finance models in existence before World War II, in what we now call the traditional public finance theory, Musgrave centered on the shortcomings of a market economy and examined how government might use its power to correct market failures and in this way achieve a "greater good" for society.

According to the Musgrave's view, government is a benevolent, omniscient dictator. Is there a problem? Government is here to help:

- Government efficiently allocates resources to provide optimal quantities of public goods.
- It redistributes income to create a more equitable and more just society.
- It is responsible for maintaining economic stability. Public officials select policies that maximize social welfare.

The public choice theorists, on the other hand, replace the assumption of a "benevolent dictator" with that of a group of purely self-serving civil servants who establish their own agendas and maximize their personal utility functions. Public choice theory also has roots in the neoclassical school of thought by proposing that the primary goal of civil servants is the pursuit of their own self-interest, just as it is for the private market participants. In this view, government officials cannot maximize the "common good" because such a thing is neither definable nor measurable. As Arrow's voting paradox shows, any social decision can become intransitive, irrational and unreliable.

Even if they try to maximize social welfare, the decision results in the maximization of benefits to the most zealous lobbyists, interest groups and rent-seekers. The true costs of these favors are impossible to accurately measure, and they are spread out over many taxpayers. This explains taxpayer inertia.

According to this view, government is at best a necessary evil that will inevitably become excessively large, unaccountable and untrustworthy. Public choice theorists assert that the goal of civil servants is to maximize their budgets to enhance their own prestige and their utility. The growth of government will thus be more rapid than that of the rest of the economy.

What incentive do public officials have to make the optimal decisions for social welfare? The principle-agent problem helps us to understand the choices of public decision makers. They are the agents of the voters within their jurisdiction. All of these officials have their own preferences and value judgments which color their perceptions. Consequently their decisions are not necessarily aligned with those of the majority of their electors.

To choose between the private sector or the public sector depends on which provides the club goods most effectively. Both have strengths and weaknesses. Market failures are due to externalities, imperfect competition, the presence of free-riders, the absence of precise information, the existence of excessive regulation, and absence of proper incentives to provide an adequate amount of the quasi-public good. Government failure stems from a poor interpretation of the electors' preferences or unreliable signals (for example, Arrow's voting paradox), the inertia inherent in bureaucracies, the tendency to mandate quick fixes (and its associated "law of unintended consequences"), and distributional inequalities.[8]

Think About It...

How do you share the expenses for your living quarters with your roommates? Do you use the benefit principle or the ability-to-pay principle? Was there a roommate who moved out because such a payment system was unfair?

---

[8] Scitovsky (1954); Oates (1978, 1989, 2001); Buchanan (1989); Forbes and Zampelli (1989); Zax (1989); Joulfaian and Marlow (1990); Lee and Wilson (1990); Nath and Purohit (1992); Crowley (1994); Malpezzi and Green (1996); Montgomery and Bean (1999); Mueller (2003).

Revenue Sources of Local Government

Providing public goods requires financial resources. Two conventional philosophies concerning the financing of pure public goods are based on the benefit principle and the ability to pay. The **benefit principle** suggests that the beneficiaries should pay. The benefit is difficult to measure when the public goods have positive externalities. For instance, residents who never leave their city still benefit from a highway that decreases the transport cost of merchandise. Employers benefit from the presence of good schools.

The ability to pay criterion centers on notions of equity and equal sacrifice. If everyone benefits equally from the provision of a pure public good, it is logical that each should contribute an equal amount. If the marginal utility of money is diminishing, those who have a greater means should pay more, and in so doing, total social welfare will increase. A reduction in the marginal utility of money is evident for anyone who was expected to pay for an impromptu celebration of a friend's birthday the day before payday. If funds are scarce the day before payday, the celebration will be simple but the day after payday, frugality falls by the wayside. Therefore, utility per penny is less important for the wealthy.

The community's concern about ability to pay determines whether it prefers taxes that are regressive, proportional, or progressive. But local taxes cannot be too progressive because the higher income people may move to a more advantageous area leaving the poorer, less mobile residents in an impoverished jurisdiction.

Loan Debt for Localities

Jurisdictions that rely on loans to provide durable goods reduce the potential of free riding caused by the arrival of new residents who do not pay for these goods. However, an indebted jurisdiction is less attractive for migrants and may cause out-migration if taxes increase to pay for the debt when it comes due.

Because one-third of a local government's revenues are from property taxes, the health and economic diversity of a locality determines its ability to contract debt. In 1992, when Hurricane Andrew destroyed Homestead Air Force Base, the city of Homestead, Florida, suffered. Even though the Air Base paid no taxes, the Base employees and local firms did. The municipal council of Homestead was quickly assured that the federal government would rebuild the air base.

In 1987, when Chrysler moved its headquarters from Highland Park, Michigan, to Auburn Hills, Michigan, Highland Park's property tax base shrunk by a third, and by twenty years after, its population dropped by 40 percent.

Schultz and Sjöström (2001),
Hildreth and Miller (2002)

An ideal tax is not only efficient, but also equitable. An efficient tax is predictable and does not alter economic activity. Such a tax is "neutral" because it has no influence on a worker's decisions. Few taxes fall into this category. A head tax (poll tax, or lump-sum tax) levied at a national level is relatively neutral, but this politically unpopular tax does not conform to the equity criteria because the amount is the same for all taxpayers, rich or poor.[9]

Can Communities Over Restrain a Leviathan Government?

Massachusetts Proposition 2½ was passed in November 1980. It limited property tax rates to 2½ percent of the assessed property value. Communities that had tax rates greater than 2½ percent needed to reduce their tax revenues by 15 percent per year until they complied with the law. Almost half of the communities had to cut taxes during the first year. Real per capita property taxes declined and remained almost 10 percent below the pre-Proposition 2½ level for eight years, despite a booming Massachusetts economy. Jurisdictions could raise their limit if the electorate voted to override these rates.

Lang and Tian (2004) found that the communities that passed overrides benefited from a faster growth in property values. This is because the communities were then able to provide an optimal level of services. Communities that followed the law could only offer an inadequate level of services.

---

[9] Sullivan (1985); Goodspeed (2000).

However, Downes and Figlio (1999) showed that California's Proposition 13 tax limits increased student–teacher ratios, decreased teacher salaries, and reduced test scores without affecting administrative spending. In addition, Figlio and O'Sullivan (2001) analyzed balance-sheet data from 5150 U.S. cities during the tax revolts of the 1970s and 1980s. They compared the spending on police and fire protection with spending on administration. Jurisdictions that passed overrides considerably decreased the ratio of teachers per administrator and police officers per administrator. However, when overrides were not possible, administrators reduced their own budgets.

Downes and Figlio (1999), Figlio and O'Sullivan (2001), Lang and Tian (2004)

Economists Favor Head Taxes, but Taxpayers Oppose Them

In 1990, Great Britain replaced its property tax with a poll tax (head tax) called the "Community Charge." This was a tax on every adult citizen. Only prisoners, mentally handicapped people, and religious orders were exempt. Fulltime students only paid 20 percent of the tax. Single households were better off under the poll tax, but households with two or more adults were worse off, as were households that paid low property tax rates. The losers were highly concentrated in the northern region where the average property tax rate was 60% that of the southeast around London.

Mair (1991) considered that this poll tax was "the single most unpopular fiscal reform in the country." Many taxpayers refused to pay, and riots led to over 300 arrests due to an epidemic of arson and looting. All this fuss was caused by a tax that was only slightly more regressive than the property tax.

Mair (1991), Smith (1991)

Tax Incidence

When they determine the impacts of tax rate changes, often officials mistakenly assume that the economic behavior is not affected. In their minds, doubling tax rates doubles tax revenue. Similarly, cutting the tax rate in half would decrease revenues by the same percentage. Unfortunately for these bureaucrats, tax rate changes undeniably influence economic behavior and are subject to the laws of supply and demand.

Tax incidence is the study of who is affected by the imposition of a tax. Those who pay a tax are not necessarily only those who write the check. The incidence of an excise tax is illustrated in Figure 16.1. An excise tax is a consumption tax, paid during the purchase of a particular product. Each unit sold is subject to the same amount of tax. Suppose that each unit is taxed $1.00. When demand slopes downward, a price increase of $1.00 decreases the quantity sold from Q_0 to Q_1. The total revenue to government is the shaded portion of the graph. The proportion of the $1.00 tax paid by consumers or producers depends on the relative elasticity of demand and supply. When supply is more elastic, consumers pay a greater proportion of the tax. When consumers have more alternatives (elastic demand), producers pay a larger proportion of the tax. In Figure 16.1, the relative elasticities are approximately equal; 50% of the tax is paid by the consumers (the upper half) and 50% by producers (the bottom portion of the shaded area).

To calculate the consumers' and producers' share of the tax, a partial equilibrium analysis is sufficient. However, we extend this to a general equilibrium analysis by specifying how producers react to the tax. When the quantity sold decreases, fewer workers are required and the excise taxes increases unemployment in the following industries:

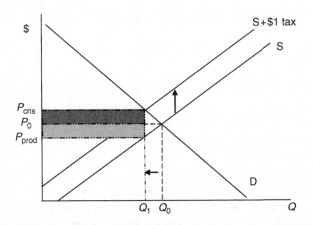

Figure 16.1   Incidence of an excise tax.

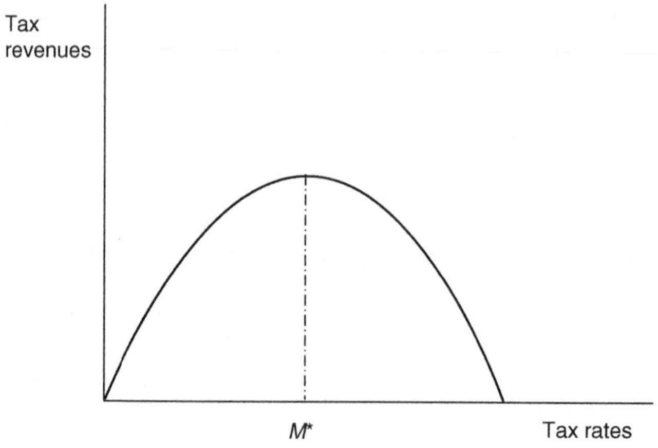

Figure 16.2 Laffer curve.

1. The taxed industry (direct effect).
2. The industries that supply products that the tax industry needs (indirect effect).
3. The industries that provide goods and services that the affected workers would use (induced effect).

Hsing (1996) estimated that the imposition of federal income tax rates above 36% causes revenues to decrease. This result is illustrated with an inverted-U-shaped Laffer curve, which compares tax rates to tax revenues (Figure 16.2). Income tax rates greater than M^* for example, lower the incentive to work, and encourage taxpayers to enjoy more leisure activities or to participate in the hidden economy by bartering, requiring cash payments, and engaging in other methods that avoid being taxed.

Local Taxes

Property taxes provide a large share of local government revenues in the United States. In 2000, property taxes constituted 23.4% of local government revenues; against 5% from sales taxes, 2% from income taxes, and 36% from intergovernmental revenues. Prescriptions for the optimal local tax policy depend on whether the advisor follows the traditional public finance theory of Musgrave or the public choice theory.

Tax studies based on traditional analysis assume that government is maximizing its tax revenue to provide sufficient quantities of public goods. In contrast, according to public choice theorists, the taxpayers exchange their money for an optimal amount of public goods. Public choice theorists also observe that politicians choose the mix of tax rates and fees that will minimize their political cost function. The political cost of tax policy decisions depends on the average tax burden for the jurisdiction as well as on the perceptions of social income groups and the various interest groups concerning their relative tax burdens.[10]

Property Taxes

Should local jurisdictions depend principally on property taxes? The subject is controversial. Proponents of this form of taxation remind us that property taxes permit governments to offer the services and amenities that the residents desire. With an optimal amount of public goods, property values increase as do the property tax revenues, which is equitable.

Conversely, property taxes are the most criticized of any local tax. First, they have nothing to do with either the ability to pay or the benefits received. Property is not necessarily connected to present income. Home-owners on fixed incomes are hurt when their property tax rates rise. In addition, the property tax supports services that have no relation to property. For example, badly maintained buildings with lower values are a burden for the city because these dilapidated structures present a serious fire hazard. All the same, their lower market value translates into a lower tax bill. On the other hand, well-maintained properties pay more in taxes but present a lower fire hazard. Finally, the property tax discourages investment in housing, and creates inefficient land use patterns especially in jurisdictions that try to receive a larger proportion of their revenues from the property tax than the neighboring jurisdictions.

There are three schools of thought regarding the incidence of a property tax: the traditional view, the new view, and the benefit view. The ***traditional view*** assumes that only one jurisdiction is raising its tax rate above those levied by other jurisdictions. This view acknowledges that the property tax is composed of two parts: (1) the landowner is entirely responsible for the land portion of the tax if the supply of land within a jurisdiction is essentially fixed (Chapter 12, Figure 12.1), and (2) the incidence of the tax on buildings is similar to that of the excise tax (Figure 16.1). Businesses and residents may avoid the tax by moving elsewhere.

Under the traditional view, the property tax is regressive because spending on housing is proportionally greater for the poor than for the rich. This regressive characteristic leads politicians to oppose attempts to increase property tax rates because the political cost to the politicians is high.

---

[10] Howard (2003).

Mieszkowski's (1970, 1972) ***new view of property taxation*** agrees with the traditional view, but it also analyzes what would happen if all jurisdictions would increase their property taxes by an equal amount. If this were to happen, *all* capital owners in the nation would bear the burden; it is essentially a profits tax and therefore progressive. Owners of taxed capital cannot move elsewhere, because the policy is national. The property tax decreases the rate of return of taxed property, causing property values everywhere to fall. The owners have an incentive to adjust their portfolios, substituting assets not subject to the property tax. The increase in demand for any type of untaxed asset will increase its price, thereby decreasing the rates of return in the same proportion as the increase in property tax rates.

According to the ***benefit view*** of Hamilton (1975), the property tax is a neutral charge paid by the user of local public services. To the extent that a jurisdiction offers an optimal amount and quality of local public services, households and firms will want to move there (Tiebout hypothesis). As they do, they will bid up the price of land by the value that they place on the services. In this way, landowners benefit as the value of these services is capitalized into the value of property. But the property taxes charged for the local services will decrease the value of property. If the amount of taxes equals the value of benefits, then the landowners both benefit from and pay for the local public goods. If the property tax works in this fashion like a user charge, there is no redistribution of income. Rather than being regressive or progressive, the tax is distributionally neutral.[11]

New View or Benefit View?

Empirical evidence supports both the excise tax and the profits tax hypotheses of the new view, but it does not (yet) favor the benefit view. However, results are inconclusive as to the nature of the property tax; is it a capital tax or a user fee? Wassmer (1993) used 1986 data for 62 U.S. cities to test the predictions of the various views. He concluded that variations in local property taxes affected local property values. Jurisdictions that rely too heavily on the property tax reduced the value of their property and drove out capital. He also found that the effects of property taxes on profits corroborated the new view.

---

[11] Heinberg and Oates (1970, 1972); Steen (1987); Harmon (1989); Schwab and Oates (1991); Fischel (1992); Slack (2002).

Homeowners are generally less mobile than firms. Thus, the excise tax effect of property taxation on homeowners is regressive. McDonald (1993) also found evidence of an excise tax effect. After studying data from 259 office buildings in Chicago, he determined that 45 percent of the property tax differences were shifted to the tenants, although 55 percent were borne by the property owners. The excise tax effects occurred even after taking into account the capitalization of benefits that followed property tax increases. Thus, the predictions of the pure benefit view were not substantiated in McDonald's analysis.

McDonald (1993), Wassmer (1993)

Site Value Tax

The site value tax (or land value tax) is an alternative to taxing buildings or movable capital. It is similar to the single tax proposed by Henry George (Chapter 12). Three Australian states (New South Wales, Queensland, and Western Australia), as well as some municipalities in New Zealand, only tax land. Honolulu, Hawaii, and 16 municipalities in Pennsylvania, including Pittsburgh, levy a two-rate tax by which the land (location) is taxed at a higher rate than the buildings. Plassmann and Tideman (2000) showed that the Pennsylvania cities that adopted a two-rate tax benefit from significantly higher levels of construction activity than they would have with traditional property taxes.

Under a site value tax, adjacent lots pay the same amount of tax, even if one is endowed with an enormous mansion and the second a tarpaper shack. Henry George asserted that a tax that usurped all land rents would be adequate to pay for all the efficiently supplied local public goods, but he refused to believe his tax resulted in the market price of land dropping to zero and hence, a nationalized land market. To date, no jurisdiction has tried surviving only on a land tax.

The single tax doctrine recently found a new life. The Henry George Theorem is based on the benefit view. This theorem states that the increase in land rents due to an efficient provision of local services will equal the decrease in land rents due to a tax that is just adequate to cover their cost.

Flatters, Henderson, and Mieszkowski (1974),
Plassmann and Tideman (2000)

Empirical Studies of Property Tax Incidence

Chawla and Wannell (2003) determined that even if property taxes are proportional to property values, they can be regressive if one considers family income. Using Canadian data, they found that families with incomes less than Can$20,000 paid 10 percent of their income in property taxes, although families with incomes over Can$100,000 paid an average of 1.8 percent. Between these two extremes, the proportion of income consumed by property tax decreases steadily with the increase in incomes.

Plummer (2003) examined the incidence of residential property tax in Dallas County, Texas, using data for 357,264 owner-occupied homes. After adjusting for federal income tax deductions of property taxes, Plummer showed that these taxes are more or less proportional. However, a further decomposition of the property tax showed that county and school taxes are proportional if not slightly progressive, but city taxes are moderately regressive because lower-income cities tend to have relatively higher tax rates. Because of the homestead exemption, city taxes are regressive and school taxes more progressive. Texas guarantees a tax ceiling for residents over age 65. This exemption increases the progressivity for all three jurisdictional taxes: elderly homeowners are disproportionately in the bottom of the income distribution.

Chawla and Wannell (2003), Plummer (2003)

Sales Taxes

Municipal sales taxes are essentially excise taxes. They decrease the quantity sold of the taxed products, thus creating deadweight losses. Reduced sales means that either some consumers do without the good or purchase it outside the jurisdiction. Because low-income households spend a greater proportion of their incomes on consumption goods, sales taxes are regressive. Nevertheless, the municipalities prefer these taxes because they are more exportable than property taxes or income taxes: nonresidents pay part of them.[12]

Local Income Taxes

Income taxes decrease the incentive to work. People will either substitute leisure for work, dabble in the hidden economy, or migrate to jurisdictions that do not tax incomes. Similarly, a local corporate income tax reduces the return on corporate capital, thereby increasing the incentive to relocate. Taxing corporate income is inefficient because it encourages firms to ignore some investment opportunities in favor of locations that might have lower pretax income, but higher after-tax returns.

Braid (2003) reported that many large cities in the United States tax wages or incomes. This is the case in San Francisco, California; Los Angeles, California; Newark, New Jersey; Birmingham, Alabama; Louisville, Kentucky; and Lexington, Kentucky, which tax the wages of workers in their jurisdiction, but they don't tax incomes of their residents who work elsewhere. The suburbs of these cities seldom tax wages, but if they do, their tax rates are lower than those of the central city. Baltimore, Maryland, taxes the income of its own residents.

Other cities (Detroit, Michigan; New York City, New York; Philadelphia and Pittsburgh, Pennsylvania; St. Louis and Kansas City, Missouri) levy an income tax on both the employees and the residents of their jurisdiction. The surrounding suburbs, if they tax, do so at a lower rate.[13]

Local Sales Tax Wedges

Man and Bell (1996) found that sales tax differentials in municipalities around Phoenix, Arizona, are capitalized into housing prices. The amount capitalized is

---

[12] Cutler and Strelnikova (2004).
[13] Stull and Stull (1991).

less than the municipal property tax differentials because some of the sales tax is exported. After studying 54 metropolitan areas in the western United States, Wassmer (2002) discovered that an increase in municipal sales tax revenues triggered retail activity just outside the city limits, and thus contributed to urban sprawl.

Cutler and Strelnikova (2004) used a computable general equilibrium (CGE) model to examine the impact of increased sales tax rates on the employment, output, size, and real incomes of Fort Collins, Colorado. An increase in the municipal sales tax rates translated into a decrease in population and economic activity. The less-mobile, lower-income households paid a greater share of the sales taxes than the higher-income households.

The migration effect was stronger in smaller cities that have fewer employment alternatives for low-skilled workers. In addition, because the retail sector is dominated by low-paying jobs, increasing the sales tax reduced employment opportunities for the poor causing these households to look for employment in other regions.

Man and Bell (1996), Wassmer (2002),
Cutler and Strelnikova (2004)

User Fees

User fees are prices for local services. To the extent that the local service is rival and excludable (a private good), pricing it at the marginal cost will lead to its efficient production and consumption. User fees are efficient for financing club goods that have few externalities, like water supply and sewerage. When the price is set at the marginal cost of production, residents will only consume a service if they value it equal to or greater than the price. This leads to efficient rationing because units of production will be allocated to consumers who value them the most as in the market for pure private goods.[14]

---

[14] Dewees (2002).

Tax Exporting

Discussions about tax exporting are based on interspatial incidence rather than interpersonal incidence. **Interspatial incidence** compares the areas that bear the burden of the taxes rather than areas from which the taxes are actually collected. For example, if tourists on vacation flock to resorts, these visitors shoulder much of the resorts' tax burdens. When nonresidents pay a portion of a tax, it is said to be "exported." Everyone wants a bargain. To maximize the utility of their own residents, jurisdictions have an incentive to levy taxes that raise the most revenue from nonresidents, and thereby subsidize the local goods and services.[15]

When a "User Fee" Becomes a Tax

Many local governments levy taxes on mobile tax bases. Their justification is that the taxes serve as user fees and reduce congestion. In Germany, this is the local business tax (*Gewerbesteuer*). Fuest and Riphahn (2001) analyzed data from 28 German municipalities over a period of 11 years. They found that the *Gewerbesteurer* was a source of revenue for general public expenditures. It is not a user fee.

Likewise, Borge (2000) noted that local governments in Norway increased utility charges when grants and taxes became more restricted. In principle, local governments could choose tax rates for income, wealth, and property within fixed limits. However, since the late 1970s, all local governments tax income at the maximum rate. Since 1980, user charges for utilities such as water supply, sewerage, garbage collection, and chimney sweeps grew from 6 to 12 percent and became the fastest growing component of Norwegian local government revenues. The use of these services is compulsory. In addition, these "user charges" are higher for small communities and for local governments with proportionately more employees.

Borge (2000), Fuest and Riphahn (2001)

---

[15] Inman (2001).

Exporting Taxes from Paradise

Act 340 passed by the Hawaii state legislature in 1986 imposed a 5.25 percent hotel room tax that started January 1, 1987. This is on top of the 4 percent sales tax. In 1990, the State of Hawaii collected $82 million, making the hotel tax the third largest source of state government revenues after the sales tax and state income tax. The sales tax collected from renting hotel rooms added $62 million to state coffers. Such a tax is popular because many people believe that the hotel room tax is largely exported to nonresidents with little effect on hotel operators.

Bonham et al. (1992) analyzed the effects of Hawaii's hotel room tax and confirmed that it did not have a significant negative impact on hotel rental receipts. The authors were not surprised because the 5.25 percent increase in room rates represents less than 1.5 percent of the total cost of a Hawaiian vacation. The authors caution that this extent of tax exporting may not be true for other travel destinations. If Hawaii weren't as isolated less of the hotel tax would be exported.

Bonham et al. (1992)

Tax Exports: Something for Nothing?

The most important components of local taxes for many countries are exportable taxes. In Germany, the *Gewerbesteur* is not only supposed to be a user tax, it is also exportable. A similar tax, *taxe professionnelle*, represents 38 percent of the revenues of French jurisdictions (*communes*). Because many business owners live outside of the jurisdiction, as do their employees, much of the tax paid to a given jurisdiction is perceived to be exported and borne by consumers, employees, and capital owners who live elsewhere.

Prud'homme (2000), and Jayet, Paty, and Pentel (2002)

Summary and Conclusions

Two main theories describe the interactions of governments among themselves and with their constituents: the traditional neoclassical theory and the public choice theory. Both theories follow neoclassical economic principles. The principal difference in the two theories is the assumed goal of the public officials. In the traditional neoclassical theory of public finance, the public officials maximize a social welfare function and act for the good of their jurisdiction. The public choice theorists assume, on the other hand, that these officials work to maximize their own utilities. The result of this debate leads economists to view government somewhere between an omniscient and benevolent dictator, if not a deity, and the devil incarnate, a Leviathan that must be controlled at every turn.

Local public goods suffer from congestion and thus are not pure public goods. Thus, there is no clear benefit by having the government provide them rather than the private sector. They are both imperfect. The Tiebout model is the cornerstone of local public finance theory, and characterizes a second problem: that of the optimal provision of local goods. Each of us has two ways to determine the quantity of local goods that we consume: we can either vote for the goods to be provided or we can move to a jurisdiction where the combination of goods and taxes is more favorable.

Local governments have several sources of revenues:

1. Residents of their jurisdictions pay property taxes, sales taxes, and sometimes income taxes as well as user fees.
2. Residents living in other jurisdictions could pay part of the taxes if those taxes can be exported.
3. Residents who never benefit from services provided to a specific locality still pay for the services in the form of intergovernmental grants provided by a higher level of government. From the federal government, these funds are often called "pork."

Tax incidence analysis determines who pays the tax. The taxpayers are not necessarily those who write the checks. Taxpayers could be consumers of the products made in jurisdictions that impose higher property taxes. Tax incidence analysis also reveals what social group pays more taxes, the rich or the poor.

The incidence of property taxes theoretically can be almost anyone. For example, they are borne in part by consumers, workers, and landowners because property tax incidence is similar to that of excise taxes. This tax is considered regressive when it is applied to residences or when it causes the layoffs of low-income workers. To the extent that all jurisdictions levy some type of property tax, owners of all capital pay the tax, thus the tax is progressive. Localities can intentionally make their property tax progressive, but if the higher income people can itemize deductions, the federal tax system makes it proportional.

Finally, if because of capitalization, property taxes decrease land values to the extent that local goods increase land values, the property tax becomes a user fee. The income tax is also capitalized into land values, as are high sales tax rates. The sales taxes are not capitalized to the same extent as property taxes and income taxes because a portion is exported and paid by residents of other jurisdictions.

Chapter Questions

1. Your city is composed of three groups: The Westenders, the East-enders, and the Centrists. Each has an equal number of voters trying to determine where to place the new library.

	Westside	Downtown	Eastside
Westenders	1	2	3
Centrists	3	1	2
Eastenders	2	3	1

   Explain using Arrow's voting theorem why these groups will not be able to reach a conclusion by voting.
2. List and describe four elements of government failure. If government is so prone to failure, why not abolish it and let the free market allocate all goods and services? (That is, when do markets fail?)
3. What is an ideal tax? Of the municipal taxes discussed in this chapter, which seems to best fit the ideal?

Research Questions

1. Obtain a copy of your city's budget. Divide the major expenditures by the number of people in the city. Compare that budget with the average budget for state and local governments per capita from http://www.census.gov/govs/www/index.html or from the *Statistical Abstract of the United States* at http://www.census.gov/compendia/statab/. How does your city differ?
2. From what sources does your city get its revenues? What proportions of revenues come from each source? How does this compare with proportionate state and local government sources for the United States? Compare with data from http://www.census.gov/govs/www/index.html or http://www.census.gov/compendia/statab/.

Appendix: Edgeworth Box and Pareto Optimality

Indifference curve analysis by itself assumes that each person exists independently. With a generous budget constraint, each person could purchase an infinite amount of all goods. The problem with this analysis is that the quantity of goods available is limited. The Edgeworth box diagram shows how to efficiently distribute goods between individuals. To show this analytical tool, we start with a point on a production possibilities curve such as point A in Figure 16A.1. At point A, society has produced 75 units of carrots (good X) and 50 units of grapes (good Y). Note that if the combination of the two goods were different, society would have a new combination of goods to distribute and a different Edgeworth box to analyze. Once the optimal combination is produced, the problem becomes how to efficiently distribute the output.

We use two sets of indifference curves to efficiently distribute the output between the two individuals. Figure 16A.2 shows the indifference curves for two people, Dick and Jane. Dick's indifference curves are dark gray, and Dick's origin is located at the lower left hand side of the diagram. Jane's indifference curves are light gray, and her origin is at the upper right hand side of the diagram. Utility increases the farther that each of our protagonists is from his or her origin. Again we will use two goods, carrots (*X*) and grapes (*Y*). The Edgeworth box shows that even if the entire output in society is allocated between our two individuals, it is sometimes possible to redistribute the goods and improve social welfare.

A key component of the Edgeworth box is a contract curve. The ***contract curve*** shows the entire set of all points where the two people's indifference curves are tangent to each other. When a distribution ends up

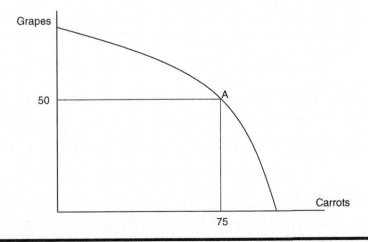

Figure 16A.1   Edgeworth box within a production possibilities curve.

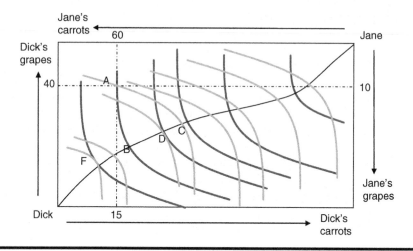

Figure 16A.2 Edgeworth box for Dick and Jane.

on the contract curve, that allocation cannot be improved on without making someone worse off.

Say that the initial endowment is at point A, where Jane starts with 60 carrots and 10 grapes, and Dick has 15 carrots and 40 grapes. In this instance, society can be made better off without increasing production of either commodity. If trade reallocates output from point A to point B, Jane's welfare improves, and that of Dick does not change because both points A and B are on his same indifference curve. At point C, Dick is better off, but Jane remains on the same indifference curve as she was at point A. Conversely, at point D, both Dick and Jane are on higher indifference curves and the curves are tangent to each other. If, however, the redistribution is from A to any point on the contract curve southwest of B, Jane benefits at Dick's expense; to the northeast of C, the reverse is true. A redistribution that makes at least one person better off without decreasing the satisfaction of another is called a ***Pareto optimal redistribution***.

The optimal distributions do not have to be in the middle. If Jane adores grapes and despises carrots and Dick strongly prefers carrots to grapes, the optimal distribution is a corner solution where Jane gets all the grapes and Dick all the carrots.

Pareto Optimality

The Edgeworth Box is one method used to apply the Pareto optimality rule to objectively evaluate whether a redistribution of output is efficient. Moving from a distribution, such as A in Figure 16A.2 to another allocation within the two indifference curves that include points B and C, is called a **Pareto improvement** because one or both people will be made better off without decreasing the utility of either. **Pareto optimality** occurs when the move ends up on the contract curve itself, because no further change is possible that will not harm one of the protagonists.

The Edgeworth box is not only an analysis of the distributions of goods, it also reveals equity concerns. If the original endowment is at Point F where Jane acquires most of both goods, a more equal redistribution would benefit Dick but harm Jane. Whether a "more equal" distribution is more "equitable" depends on the effort Jane put forth to produce the carrots and grapes relative to that of Dick. If redistribution affects the incentives to produce, such a policy may lead to a reduction in future production: the production possibilities curve will contract, *ceteris paribus*.[16]

Appendix Questions

1. Create an Edgeworth box for Tweedledum and Tweedledee that shows that Tweedledum has 80% of the oysters and 100% of the rattles. Be certain to label the axes and the origins for the two brothers.
   a. What would happen to the Edgeworth box in a second period if distribution of oysters and rattles depended on need rather than on productivity?
   b. Draw the production possibilities curve and the corresponding Edgeworth box after Tweedledum is forced to give 60% of his share to his lazy brother.
2. Jack Sprat can eat no fat, His wife can eat no lean.
   a. Given an Edgeworth box with fat on the horizontal axis and lean on the vertical axis, where is the optimal distribution point?
   b. Define Pareto optimality, and explain why your solution would be Pareto optimal.
   c. According to the Tiebout hypothesis, would Jack Sprat ever meet his wife? Why or why not?

References

Ahmed, S., and K. V. Greene. 2000. Is the median voter a clear-cut winner? Comparing the median voter theory and competing theories in explaining local government spending. *Public Choice* 105 (3–4):207–230.

---

[16] Ledyard (1987); Miyao and Kanemoto (1987); Tartarin (1987); Trumbull (1990); Phelan (2002).

Arrow, K. J. 2001 [1951]. An extension of the basic theorems of classical welfare economics. In *Welfare Economics. Volume 2.*, eds. W.J. Baumol, and C.A. Wilson *Elgar Reference Collection. International Library of Critical Writings in Economics*, Vol. 126, Cheltenham: Elgar, Mass; distributed by American International Distribution Corporation, Williston, VT, 45–70.

Baudry, M., M. Leprince, and C. Moreau. 2002. Préférences révélées, bien public local et électeur médian: tests sur données françaises. *Économie et Prévision* 0 (156):125–146.

Blackorby, C. 1990. Economic policy in a second-best environment. *Canadian Journal of Economics* 23 (4):748–771.

Blom-Hansen, J. 2003. Is private delivery of public services really cheaper? Evidence from public road maintenance in Denmark. *Public Choice* 115 (3–4):419–438.

Bonham, C., E. Fujii, E. Im, and J. Mak. 1992. The impact of the hotel room tax: an interrupted time series approach. *National Tax Journal* 45 (4):433–441.

Borge, L.-E. 2000. Charging for public services: the case of utilities in Norwegian local governments. *Regional Science and Urban Economics* 30 (6):703–718.

Braid, R. M. 2003. A three-input model of the spatial effects of a central-city wage tax. *Journal of Urban Economics* 54 (1):89–109.

Brasington, D. M. 2003. The supply of public school quality. *Economics of Education Review* 22 (4):367–377.

Buchanan, J. M. 1989. Richard Musgrave, public finance, and public choice: review article. *Public Choice* 61 (3):289–291.

Caplan, B. 2001. Standing Tiebout on his head: tax capitalization and the monopoly power of local governments. *Public Choice* 108 (1–2):101–122.

Chawla, R. K., and T. Wannell. 2003. Property taxes. *Perspectives on Labour and Income* 15 (3):7–14.

Conley, J., and M. Dix. 2004. Beneficial inequality in the provision of municipal services: why rich neighborhoods should get plowed first. *Southern Economic Journal* 70 (4):731–745.

Crowley, R. W. 1994. The Public Sector and public provision in economic theory Working Paper 94-08: Government and Competitiveness, School of Policy Studies, Queen's University.

Cutler, H., and I. Strelnikova. 2004. The impact of the U.S. sales tax rate on city size and economic activity: a CGE approach. *Urban Studies* 41 (4):875–885.

de Bartolome, C. A. M. 1990. Equilibrium and inefficiency in a community model with peer group effects. *Journal of Political Economy* 98 (1):110–133.

Dewees, D. N. 2002. Pricing municipal services: the economics of user fees. *Canadian Tax Journal* 50 (2):586–599.

Dijkgraaf, E., R. H. J. M. Gradus, and B. Melenberg. 2003. Contracting out refuse collection. *Empirical Economics* 28 (3):553–570.

Domberger, S., and P. Jensen. 1997. Contracting out by the public sector: theory, evidence, prospects. *Oxford Review of Economic Policy* 13 (4):67–78.

Downes, T. A., and D. N. Figlio. 1999. Do tax and expenditure limits provide a free lunch? evidence on the link between limits and public sector service quality. *National Tax Journal* 52 (1):113–128.

Figlio, D. N., and A. O'Sullivan. 2001. The local response to tax limitation measures: do local governments manipulate voters to increase revenues? *Journal of Law and Economics* 44 (1):233–257.

Fischel, W. A. 1992. Property taxation and the Tiebout model: evidence for the benefit view from zoning and voting. *Journal of Economic Literature* 30 (1):171–177.

Flatters, F., V. Henderson, and P. Mieszkowski. 1974. Public goods, efficiency, and regional fiscal equalization. *Journal of Public Economics* 3 (2):99–112.

Forbes, K. F., and E. M. Zampelli. 1989. Is Leviathan a mythical beast? *American Economic Review* 79 (3):568–577.

Fraser, C. D. 2000. When is efficiency separable from distribution in the provision of club goods?. *Journal of Economic Theory* 90 (2):204–221.

Fuest, C., and R. T. Riphahn. 2001. Is the local business tax a user tax? An empirical investigation for Germany. *Jahrbucher Fur Nationalokonomie Und Statistik* 221 (1):14–31.

Glaeser, E. L. 1996. The incentive effects of property taxes on local governments. *Public Choice* 89 (1–2):93–111.

Goodspeed, T. J. 2000. Tax structure in a federation. *Journal of Public Economics* 75 (3):493–506.

Guengant, A., J.-M. Josselin, and Y. Rocaboy. 2002. Effects of club size in the provision of public goods: network and congestion effects in the case of the French municipalities. *Papers in Regional Science* 81 (4):443–460.

Hamilton, B. W. 1975. Zoning and property taxation in a system of local governments. *Urban Studies* 12 (2):205–211.

Harmon, O. R. 1989. A new view of the incidence of the property tax: the case of New Jersey. *Public Finance Quarterly* 17 (3):323–348.

Heinberg, J. D., and W. E. Oates. 1970. The incidence of differential property taxes on urban housing: a comment and some further evidence. *National Tax Journal* 23 (1):92–98.

Heinberg, J. D., and W. E. Oates. 1972. The incidence of differential property taxes on rental housing: an addendum. *National Tax Journal* 25 (2):221–222.

Hildreth, W. B., and G. J. Miller. 2002. Debt and the local economy: problems in benchmarking local government debt affordability. *Public Budgeting and Finance* 22 (4):99–113.

Hochman, O. 1990. Cities, scale economies, local goods and local governments. *Urban Studies* 27 (1):45–65.

Hochman, O., D. Pines, and J.-F. Thisse. 1995. On the optimal structure of local governments. *American Economic Review* 85 (5):1224–1240.

Howard, B. 2003. Does the mix of a state's tax portfolio matter? An empirical analysis of United States tax portfolios and the relationship to levels and growth in real per capita Gross State Product. *Journal of Applied Business Research* 19 (3):97–109.

Hsing, Y. 1996. Estimating the Laffer curve and policy implications. *Journal of Socio-Economics* 25 (3):395–401.

Inman, R. P. 2001. Transfers and bailouts: institutions for enforcing local fiscal discipline. *Constitutional Political Economy* 12 (2):141–160.

Jayet, H., S. Paty, and A. Pentel. 2002. Existe-t-il des interactions fiscales stratégiques entre les collectivités locales? *Économie et Prévision* 0 (154):95–105.

Joulfaian, D., and M. L. Marlow. 1990. Government size and decentralization: evidence from disaggregated data. *Southern Economic Journal* 56 (4): 1094–1102.

Laffont, J.-J., and J. Tirole. 1995 [1987]. Auctioning incentive contracts. In *The Economics of Information Volume 2, eds.* D.K. Levine, and S.A. Lippman *Elgar Reference Collection. International Library of Critical Writings in Economics*, Vol. 53, Aldershot: Elgar; distributed in the U.S. by Ashgate, Brookfield, VT, 259–275.

Lang, K., and T. Jian. 2004. Property taxes and property values: evidence from proposition 2 ½. *Journal of Urban Economics* 55 (3):439–457.

Ledyard, J. O. 1987. Incentive compatibility. California Institute of Technology, Division of the Humanities and Social Sciences, Working Papers.

Lee, D. R., and P. W. Wilson. 1990. Rent-seeking and peak-load pricing of public services. *National Tax Journal* 43 (4):497–503.

Leuthold, J. H. 1993. A free rider experiment for the large class. *Journal of Economic Education* 24 (4):353–363.

Loomis, J. B. 2000. Vertically summing public good demand curves: an empirical comparison of economic versus political jurisdictions. *Land Economics* 76 (2):312–321.

Mair, D. 1991. The incidence of the property tax: a survey. *British Review of Economic Issues* 13 (31):1–27.

Malpezzi, S., and R. K. Green. 1996. What has happened to the bottom of the US housing market? *Urban Studies* 33 (10):1807–1820.

Man, J. Y., and M. E. Bell. 1996. The impact of local sales tax on the value of owner-occupied housing. *Journal of Urban Economics* 39 (1):114–130.

McDonald, J. F. 1993. Incidence of the property tax on commercial real estate: the case of downtown Chicago. *National Tax Journal* 46 (2):109–120.

Means, T. S., and S. L. Mehay. 1995. Estimating the publicness of local government services: alternative congestion function specifications. *Southern Economic Journal* 61 (3):614–627.

Mieszkowski, P. M. 1970. The property tax: an excise tax or a profits tax? Cowles Foundation, Yale University, New Haven, Cowles Foundation Discussion Papers.

Mieszkowski, P. 1972. Integration of the corporate and personal income taxes: the bogus issue of shifting. *Finanzarchiv* 31 (2):286–297.

Miyao, T., and Y. Kanemoto. 1987. *Urban dynamics and urban externalities.* Fundamentals of Pure and Applied Economics Series, vol. 11. Regional and Urban Economics Section. Chur, Switzerland: Harwood Academic.

Montgomery, M. R., and R. Bean. 1999. Market failure, government failure, and the private supply of public goods: the case of climate-controlled walkway networks. *Public Choice* 99 (3–4):403–437.

Mueller, D. C. 2003. *Public Choice III.* Cambridge: Cambridge University Press.

Musgrave, R. A., and P. B. Musgrave. 1989. *Public Finance in Theory and Practice,* 5th ed. New York: McGraw Hill Book Company.

Nath, S., and B. C. Purohit. 1992. A model of local fiscal choice. *Public Finance* 47 (1):93–107.

Oates, W. E. 1978. Decentralization, bureaucracy, and government: discussion. *American Economic Review* 68 (2):262–263.

Oates, W. E. 1981. On local finance and the tiebout model. *American Economic Review* 71 (2):93–98.

Oates, W. E. 1989. Searching for leviathan: reply. *American Economic Review* 79 (3):578–583.

Oates, W. E. [1994]. Federalism and government finance. In *The Economics of Fiscal Federalism and Local Finance*, ed. W.E. Oates *Elgar Reference Collection. International Library of Critical Writings in Economics*, Vol. 88, Cheltenham: Elgar; distributed by American International Distribution Corporation, Williston, VT, 10–40, 1998

Oates, W. E. 2001. Fiscal competition or harmonization? Some reflections. *National Tax Journal* 54 (3):507–512.

Page, S. E., K. Kollman, and J. H. Miller. 1995. A comparison of political institutions in a Tiebout model. California Institute of Technology, Division of the Humanities and Social Sciences, Working Papers.

Pedone, A. 2002. The importance of local public services. *Review of Economic Conditions in Italy* 0 (1):111–127.

Phelan, C. 2002. Inequality and fairness. *Federal Reserve Bank of Minneapolis Quarterly Review* 26(2) (Spring 2002):2–11.

Phipps, S. 1991. Equity and efficiency consequences of unemployment insurance reform in Canada: the importance of sensitivity analyses. *Economica* 58 (230):199–214.

Plassmann, F., and T. N. Tideman. 2000. A markov chain monte carlo analysis of the effect of two-rate property taxes on construction. *Journal of Urban Economics* 47 (2):216–247.

Plummer, E. 2003. Evidence on the incidence of residential property taxes across households. *National Tax Journal* 56 (4):739–753.

Prud'homme, R. 2000. Taxe professionnelle as an exportable local tax. *Environment and Planning C: Government and Policy* 18 (5):545–553.

Randall, K. Voting Rights Denied to 3.8 Million Americans due to Criminal Convictions. 8 November 2000, http://www.wsws.org/articles/2000/votes-N08.html, (accessed on December 3, 2004, site now discontinued, 2000).

Raux, C., and S. Souche. 2001. L'acceptabilité des changements tarifaires dans le secteur des transports: comment concilier efficacité et équité? (Acceptability of pricing changes in the transport sector: How to reconcile efficiency and equity?). *Revue d'Économie Régionale et Urbaine* 0 (4):539–558.

Sasaki, K. 1991. Interjurisdictional commuting and local public goods. *Annals of Regional Science* 25 (4):271–285.

Sass, T. R. 1991. The choice of municipal government structure and public expenditures. *Public Choice* 71 (1-2):71–87.

Schultz, C., and T. Sjöström. 2001. Local public goods, debt and migration. *Journal of Public Economics* 80 (2):313–337.

Schwab, R. M., and W. E. Oates. 1991. Community composition and the provision of local public goods: a normative analysis. *Journal of Public Economics* 44 (2):217–237.

Schwan, J. 2004. Republicans Resign over Questionable Absentee Ballot Applications. 11 October 2004, http://Keloland.com/NewsDetail2817.cfm?10_22,35221, (accessed on December 3, 2004, site now discontinued).

Scitovsky, T. 2002 [1954]. Two concepts of external economies, in *The Political Economy of Development. Volume 1. Development, Growth and Income Distribution,* ed. A. K. Dutt Cheltenham: Elgar, Mass; distributed by American International Distribution Corporation, Williston, VT, 230–238.

South Dakota Elections Information. 2004, http://www.sdsos.gov/2004/2004absenteenumbers.htm, (accessed on December 3, 2004, site now discontinued).

Shapiro, P., and R. T. Deacon. 1996. Estimating the demand for ublic goods: comments and extensions, *The Contingent Valuation of Environmental Resources: Methodological Issues and Research Needs,* eds. D. J. Bjornstad, and J. R. Kahn *New Horizons in Environmental Economics Series,* Cheltenham: Elgar; distributed by Ashgate, Brookfield, VT, 244–259.

Slack, E. 2002. Property tax reform in ontario: what have we learned?. *Canadian Tax Journal* 50 (2):576–585.

Smith, S. 1991. Distributional issues in local taxation. *Economic Journal* 101 (406):585–599.

Steen, R. C. 1987. Effects of the property tax in urban areas. *Journal of Urban Economics* 21 (2):146–165.

Stull, W. J., and J. C. Stull. 1991. Capitalization of local income taxes. *Journal of Urban Economics* 29 (2):182–190.

Sullivan, A. M. 1985. The pricing of urban services and the spatial distribution of residence. *Land Economics* 61 (1):17–25.

Tartarin, R. 1987. Efficacité et propriété. *Revue Économique* 38 (6) (November 1987):1129–1155.

Teske, P., M. Schneider, M. Mintrom, and S. Best. 1993. Establishing the micro foundations of a macro theory: information, movers, and the competitive local market for public goods. *American Political Science Review* 87 (3):702–713.

Tinbergen, J. 1991. On the measurement of welfare. *Journal of Econometrics* 50 (1–2):7–13.

Trumbull, W. N. 1990. Who has standing in cost-benefit analysis?. *Journal of Policy Analysis and Management* 9 (2):201–218.

Tullock, G. 1971. Public decisions as public goods. *Journal of Political Economy* 79 (4):913–918.

Warner, M., and R. Hebdon. 2001. Local government restructuring: privatization and its alternatives. *Journal of Policy Analysis and Management* 20 (2):315–336.

Wassmer, R. W. 1993. Property taxation, property base, and property value: an empirical test of the "new view." *National Tax Journal* 46 (2):135–159.

Wassmer, R. W. 2002. Fiscalisation of land use, urban growth boundaries and non-central retail sprawl in the western United States. *Urban Studies* 39 (8):1307–1327.

Zax, J. S. 1989. Is there a Leviathan in your neighborhood?. *American Economic Review* 79 (3):560–567.

Chapter 17

Intergovernmental
Relations

This chapter centers on the interactions and reactions of state and local governments to higher-level governments and to others at the same level. We first ask which level in a governmental hierarchy is best suited to provide which public services for its citizens. We then study the impact of one jurisdiction's decisions on its neighbors, as well as the attempts of a higher-level government to control the decisions of lower-level decision-makers.

We will also examine the optimal redistribution policies among governments and the effects of implementing them. Redistribution can take place between a city and its suburbs, from a wealthy area to a poor region, or from all taxpayers of a federal or state government for one city's public works projects. When a local government can overspend its budget and count on the central government to pay the difference, the central government revenues become a common property resource to which all local governments have access. The smaller governments lack the incentive to use that resource prudently.

Finally, we will observe two games that decision-makers and voters of several rival jurisdictions play: yardstick competition (the comparison of amenities among jurisdictions) and fiscal mimicry.

Think About It ...

What types of governmental services are available in your area? Are they provided by your local government? The state (or provincial) government? The federal government?

Do you think that a government of a different level could provide these goods more efficiently taking account of the market areas and scale economies?

Fiscal Federalism: Who Provides What and for Whom?

The multiple layers of government within a federal system raise the question: what level should have the responsibility to finance and provide for a particular public good? Usually, the questions of financing and provision are the same. According to the **theory of fiscal federalism**, it is the jurisdiction that decides to provide such service and decides to impose a tax on its citizens. The **principle of subsidiarity** stipulates that only the smallest jurisdiction capable of financing a public good for which it is the only beneficiary, will do so, thus internalizing all externalities. This rule of thumb assumes that the decision-makers whose constituents bear the costs of the services will make more efficient decisions. Therefore, the theory of fiscal federalism opens up a debate about the efficiencies of decentralization.

The opponents to decentralization point first to the economies of scale realized by everyone if the central government provides projects uniformly for all regions. The costs of pure public goods are generally fixed, so the per capita costs vary inversely with population. Decentralization leads to a fragmentation and an inefficient duplication of efforts furnished by similar, but autonomous, jurisdictions.

A second critique of decentralization rests on the existence of spillovers. Spatial spillovers exist when effects of fiscal policies of one city affect citizens of other jurisdictions. An ideal provision of a public good minimizes the spatial spillovers onto neighboring jurisdictions. The fiscal policies of one municipality can therefore affect the land and labor markets in other jurisdictions, and thus extend their effects beyond the jurisdictional boundaries. When one jurisdiction gets tough on crime, for instance, criminals move. Children educated in one community will benefit other communities when they relocate as adults. Generous local welfare systems of one city attract the poor. Because of positive or negative spatial spillovers, larger governments most efficiently provide these goods.

An unequal distribution of public resources represents a third problem when it is a lower-level government that furnishes the public goods. First, central governments can easily channel resources from a rich area to a poor one. In addition, these inequalities in the quality of education, public health, or sanitation can perpetuate poverty in jurisdictions. Finally, decentralization may encourage the proliferation of jurisdictions that compete to attract firms by offering fiscal advantages. These fiscal advantages for the firms translate into a reduction of public goods for the local community.

Big Government: Laudatory or Leviathan?

Empirical research from Ontario, Canada does not support the hypothesis that, compared to small cities, a regional metropolis supplies environmental and municipal services at a reduced cost. If "bigger is better," according to Jerrett, Eyles, and Dufournaud (2002) one should find substantial economies of scale. Instead, they find that environmental programs actually produce diseconomies of scale and that municipal services produce no measurable economies of scale.

The amalgamation of existing cities into larger ones is only efficient when economies of scale exist. But because there is none, such an amalgamation is purely political.

Jerrett, Eyles, and Dufournaud (2002)

Conversely, proponents of decentralization affirm first that local services produce no economies of scale. (See the box entitled *Big Government: Laudatory or Leviathan?*) Because of congestion (crowds and traffic), club goods produce a positive marginal cost.

Second, proponents firmly believe that "one size fits all" does not apply everywhere or to everyone. Local governments can more easily cater to local needs. For example, a given quality of a local good can be provided with different costs depending on the income of the population. Higher-income people tend to have fewer children, and they give them more time. The result is that, *ceteris paribus*, their children can be educated more efficiently. Crime rates in rich areas tend to be negligible and their neighborhoods are better protected with private security systems, so the city spends much less to obtain the same level of public safety as other jurisdictions. Rich districts have a different production function for local goods than poor districts.

Third, jurisdictions have a joint interest to negotiate among themselves for the provision of goods with interregional spillovers without the assistance of higher levels of government.

Fourth, public choice theorists have shown that regional disparities are minimized in decentralized regions because interjurisdictional competition forces local jurisdictions to provide services at the lowest cost.

Fifth, although central governments often favor jurisdictional equity, they can as easily, for political reasons, siphon funds from the peripheral regions to benefit the densely populated jurisdictions. As the power of the central government diminishes, it will increase in the peripheral jurisdictions, both politically and economically.

Finally, proponents of decentralization maintain that interjurisdictional competition induces governments to adopt the most efficient methods to satisfy the public service needs of their residents. Competition discourages favoritism (rent seeking).[1]

Decentralization in Developing Regions

Decentralization is popular the world over. Devolution, the transfer of powers from a central government to a local authority, is the goal in the European Union as much as the recognition of state's rights in the Tenth Amendment to the Constitution of the United States. During the last 20 years, the problems of the transition from communism to capitalism and the economic debates concerning the emerging economies of Latin America, Africa, and Asia have revolved around the question of decentralization. In China and India, decentralization was the principal cause of exceptional industrial growth of the 1990s. It reduced the role of the government by fragmenting central authority and introducing more intergovernmental control. It defused

---

[1] Oates (1978, 1981, 2001); Chernick (1992); Grosskopf and Hayes (1993); Hochman, Pines, and Thisse (1995); Gérard-Varet and Thisse (1997); Bordignon, Manasse, and Tabellini (2001); de Mello (2001); Fuest and Riphahn (2001); Hettler (2001); Perroni and Scharf (2001); Prieto and Zofio (2001); Chao and Yu (2002); Keen and Kotsogiannis (2002); Lulfesmann (2002); Besley and Coate (2003); Gil Canaleta, Pascual Arzoz, and Rapun Garate (2004); Wildasin (2004).

social and political tensions in regions of the world with rampant ethnic conflicts and separatist movements by giving political autonomy to localities.

Bardhan (2002) pointed out two types of federalism: "Coming together federalism" exists in the United States and other places where previously sovereign entities give up part of their autonomy to improve efficiency. "Holding together federalism" is what one finds in multiethnic, multilingual, and multinational democracies of India, Belgium, Switzerland, and Spain where the redistribution and compensation encourages collaboration between rival political organizations.

The decentralization literature of developing countries cautions against the dangers of possible disparities: because of agglomeration economies, the central governments attract superior human capital, and from this fact, rural government workers risk having training that their geographic isolation renders obsolete.

Bardhan (2002)

Spanish Decentralization Increases Municipal Accountability

Decentralization gained relevance for researchers and Spanish administrators after Franco's death in 1975. The Spanish Constitution, implemented in 1978, grants a certain degree of autonomy to the state and local governments in providing for education, health care, and security. From 1985 through 1995, state and local public spending grew by 44 percent.

This significant growth necessitated a system to evaluate the performance of the municipalities. According to Spanish law, 7/85 *Ley de Bases de Regimen Local*, municipalities must ensure an acceptable living standard for their residents. For instance, a suitable flow of drinking water, sewerage, and purification of wastewater need to be available. They must pave and light public thoroughfares and provide recreation centers. The infrastructure must be of high quality, and conform to specific norms from one municipality to another. Small municipalities that lack the financial means must request a subsidy from the state. Cost-benefit analysis and data envelopment analysis (DEA) are often used to determine whether a given spending has met its objectives.

Prieto and Zofio (2001)

Duret and Ventelou (1999) suggested a middle ground: that there is a Laffer-type curve (Figure 17.1) of decentralization that will arbitrate between the positive effect of proximity of public decision-makers to their constituents and the effects due to an absence of coordination between localities that are too small.

Governmental Hierarchies and Game Theory

Principal–agent theory defines local decision-makers as being simultaneously the agent for their constituency and an agent for higher government levels. As the agent for their constituency, local officials have the incentive to not increase taxes and to provide acceptable public goods. At times their role will be to find a compromise between these two functions. But also their role will be to obey the injunctions of the higher

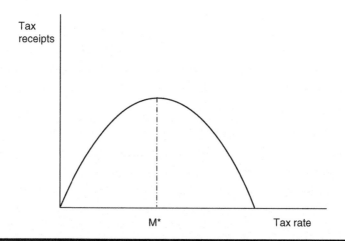

Figure 17.1 Laffer curve.

government levels, even if these injunctions are unpopular among the local constituency.[2]

Think About It ...

Search the Internet for the key words government, mandates, and the name of your state. How many mandates are in recent news? What mandates are funded? Which are unfunded? Which are popular and which are not?

Mandates

Governmental programs are often required by one level of government, but financed by taxes or fees provided by another governmental level. This system gives to the higher level of government the possibility to exploit the revenue-raising potential of the lower-level government. For instance, a central government can control local policy by providing grants (funded mandates) that are "earmarked" for certain goods such as welfare services.

According to the principle-agent model, the agents who control the expenditures generally pursue personal goals that are not always the same as the goals of those who provide the funds. In the United States, lower-level governments use up to 70% of federal aid for other things.

Centralized levels of government (federal or state government) often impose on lower government levels the obligation to operate programs that they do not finance. These unfunded mandates are almost impossible to enforce.[3]

Intergovernmental Grants

An ideal fiscal policy for hierarchical governments would be to permit local governments to provide public goods and services to their constituents, financed by efficient and equitable revenue systems. Traditional public

---

[2] Dudley and Montmarquette (1993); Bordignon, Manasse, and Tabellini (2001); Van Puyenbroeck (2001); Hofmann and von Wangenheim (2002); Schaltegger and Küttel (2002).

[3] Baicker (2001); Gillette (2001); Fenge and Meier (2002); Bates and Santerre (2003); Walden (2003).

finance theory assumes that intergovernmental grants are motivated by criteria of efficiency and equity. Such grants encourage localities to provide an optimal quantity of goods that have positive spillover benefits.

A large theoretical literature examines optimal redistribution among individuals, but few researchers have studied the optimal redistribution among governments. This redistribution is complicated because the local governments are themselves in a principal–agent relation with their citizens. The design of the redistribution policy must consider both the incentive to distort facts concerning local tax capacity, as well as the political repercussions regarding their choice of local tax rates. Because there are relatively few local governments that answer to each next highest layer of government, strategic behavior of competing local governments affects transfers paid or received by each of them.[4]

Local Jurisdictions Will Do it Their Way

Does competition between local governments make them more efficient at collecting taxes, allocating transfers, or enforcing regulations than a central government? Cai and Treisman (2004) suggest that interjurisdictional competition may itself erode the capacity of the central government to apply its national policy when it differs from regional interests. Local jurisdictions can compete for foreign direct investment by shielding firms from the central tax collectors, bankruptcy, or regulators, thus weakening the central government.

For instance, in the mid 1990s, Russia experienced a tax fraud epidemic. Tatneft, the fifth largest oil company, based in the Republic of Tatarstan on the Volga River, claimed insolvency. The president of this republic, Mintimer Shaimiev, used his influence and local financial resources to neutralize local and federal courts in favor of the firm Tatneft. Since Tatarstan is geographically isolated, it was easy to detour public funds earmarked for regional infrastructure.

---

[4] Hamilton (1983); Barnett, Levaggi and Smith (1991); Trionfetti (1997); Bordignon, Manasse, and Tabellini (2001); Heyndels (2001); Van Puyenbroeck (2001); Bahl Martinez-Vazquez and Wallace (2002).

During this same period, the creation of many economic zones in China increased net foreign direct investment (FDI) to $37 billion. Competition between local and provincial governments for FDI was carried out in three ways: (1) the reform of local laws, regulations, and taxes in favor of businesses, (2) the improvement of infrastructure, and (3) the possibility to evade customs duties.

Lai Changxing, currently a resident of Vancouver, British Columbia, smuggled more than $6 billion worth of goods (petrochemical products, construction material, pornography, watches, and luxury automobiles) into his native Fujian province. He also smuggled rubber and plastics for the relocated Taiwanese shoe and umbrella factories. He did the same with oil, selling it at half price. Between 1990 and 1996, the amount of FDI increased from 9.3 percent to 13 percent of the national total. The Fujian provincial government sees him as a hero. China sees him as public enemy number one.

Beech (2002), Cai and Treisman (2004)

Intergovernmental Aid Undercompensates

Major new urban shopping malls erode the sales tax base in the surrounding counties. This reduction erodes their tax capacities. The counties thus affected should, therefore, receive supplementary aid. From 1990–1991, two new shopping malls in middle Tennessee were responsible for an increase of $100 million in sales in that area. The neighboring jurisdictions thus lost an important part of their fiscal capacity because their residents preferred to shop at the new malls. The increase in aid to education in these counties only defrayed 14 percent to 18 percent of the lost sales revenue.

Chervin, Edmiston, and Murray (2000)

Revenue-sharing funds are collected by a higher-level government and shared among the lower levels of government according to a predetermined formula. These funds allow local governments to finance a greater volume of expenditures by shifting the cost to residents of other jurisdictions. This type of intergovernmental grant does not encourage local government efficiency. On the contrary, local governments not only have the incentive to underuse their own tax bases, but also to artificially inflate their budgets so that they can claim their share of revenues. This inefficiency is described in Figure 17.2 adapted from Inman (2001).

Optimal provision of a public good exists when the marginal benefit equals the marginal cost. In the absence of revenue sharing, the jurisdiction will choose the optimal quantity, Q^*. With revenue sharing, the marginal cost to the locality decreases such that the chosen quantity becomes Q_1. This results in an economic inefficiency of area BCD, because of overprovision. The marginal benefit enjoyed by the community at Q_1 is less than its true marginal cost.

Fiscally, localities tend to be less prudent when they receive transfers and subsidies because they have an incentive to undertax or overspend to gain from the redistributive system at the expense of the other regions. The central government, therefore, should require that the transfers are awarded based on data that the governments cannot manipulate. But is this possible?

To the extent that a higher-level government is obliged to rescue an extravagant local government that cannot pay its debts, ***vertical imbalances*** (the difference between expenditures and receipts) trigger fiscal transfers and create fiscal illusion because the benefits of providing local services are greater

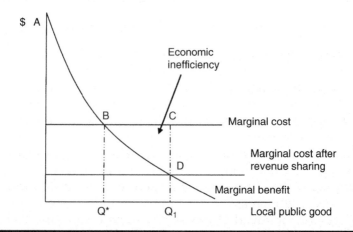

Figure 17.2 Inefficiency due to revenue sharing. This figure was originally published as Figure 1 in an article by Robert P. Inman., (2001). (From Transfers and bailouts: institutions for enforcing local fiscal discipline. *Constitutional Political Economy,* 12(2): 141–160. With permission of Springer Science and Business Media.)

than the costs. ***Fiscal illusion*** means that the voters/taxpayers have no idea of the cost of the public goods because it is invisible.[5]

Teriyaki "Pork"

The term "soft budget constraint" describes the inefficiency and the dependence of local governments. According to Ihori and Itaya (2004), the Japanese government annually spends about 5 percent of the national GDP to bail out local governments. They lobby the central government heavily for transfers, mainly in the form of local public works (pork). This results in a growing deficit for the Japanese government, especially since the 1990s.

An intergovernmental transfer program of this nature makes the national budget a common property resource that permits local governments to free ride. Political decision-makers have discretionary power in allocating grants. Ihori and Itaya think that the Japanese central government is so weak that it seldom denies these region-specific projects.

In Japan, the local governments cannot set their own tax rates (which are determined by the central government), and therefore they depend on these grants. Thus, the entire country pays. According to the authors, Japan needs an intergovernmental tax and transfer policy that reduces the marginal benefit of providing region-specific privileges.

Ihori and Itaya (2004)

Is There a Remedy for Fiscal Disparities?

Traditional theory maintains that redistribution should be a central government responsibility. This is because, first, the benefits of redistribution spill

---

[5] de Bartolome (1990); Charney (1993); de Mello (2001); Gemmell, Morrissey, and Pinar (2002); Hendrick (2002); Buettner (2003); Chu (2003); Dahlby and Wilson (2003); Levaggi and Zanola (2003); Boadway (2004); Gil Canaleta, Pascual Arzoz, and Rapun Garate (2004).

beyond jurisdictional boundaries. Redistribution policies of regional and local governments will be compromised by the in-migration of poor families attracted by higher benefits and the out-migration of rich families who move to escape the higher taxes.

However, the budget policies of state and local governments are responsible for delivery of health, welfare, and educational services, all of which are essentially redistributive. The collection of taxes on sales, income, and property involves the following choices:

> What will be the marginal income tax rate?
> What goods will be exempt under the sales taxes?
> What is the maximum proportion of a household's income that will serve as the base for property taxes?

The optimal redistribution among governments is a lump-sum distribution, under the following conditions:

■ Complete transparency
■ Absence of any budget constraint
■ Absence of interregional spillovers

Unfortunately, these conditions do not exist. First of all, the higher-level government is never committed. For a "benevolent government," the optimal solution would be an equality of local government receipts independent of all differences. However, this solution creates a moral hazard problem because the local government can change its behavior to the determent of the higher-level government as we see happens in the box entitled *Fiscal Equalization Problems*.

Fiscal Equalization Problems

Almost all nations with multiple government levels use fiscal equalization programs to equalize differences in tax revenue between regions. Fiscal equalization transfers aim to diminish the gap between actual tax revenues of a state and the national average. In Canada, fiscal equalization depends on the measured tax base, for which the rate is chosen by the local government. By raising rates on elastic tax bases, Canadian provinces depress the base and receive larger transfers that overcompensate the regional deadweight loss.

In Germany, the *Länder* (regional jurisdictions similar to America's states) cannot set their tax rates, but because they are responsible for collecting taxes, they can influence the degree of tax enforcement and the effort spent on regional economic development (*Standortpolitik*). Because these efforts are difficult to observe or verify, fiscal equalization policies in Germany also introduce moral hazard.

Smart and Bird (1996), Smart (1998),
Fenge and von Weizsacker (2001)

The goal of fiscal equalization is horizontal equity, which means that the government policy does not change household incomes and there is equity throughout the entire country. This concept of horizontal equity may conflict with the ideal of social welfare: it requires the suppression of all spatial disparities, depriving local authorities of the power to change tax rates.

In addition, there is a problem of asymmetric information. Exogenous regional characteristics change continuously over time, and central governments cannot access all the information available at the local level. This becomes an adverse selection problem: because the information is asymmetric between the two agencies, local governments cannot make optimal choices. A local government fixes the tax rates and chooses the quantity of local public goods relative to its own tax base. Central government's only role is to design and implement a policy for horizontal regional redistribution. Unfortunately, the central government cannot measure the seriousness of regional governments in collecting taxes or fighting tax evasion. It also cannot know the true market value of properties within their jurisdictions. This permits localities to manipulate the measurement of their tax bases.[6]

Central City and Suburban Relations

Fiscal disparities exist between the central city jurisdiction and its suburbs. According to some researchers, the central cities should receive more transfers because they have a high population density and the public goods, paid for by their residents, spill over to citizens of neighboring jurisdictions. For example, crimes are often concentrated in densely populated areas. Empirically, safety is a pure public good. For low numbers of inhabitants, the marginal cost of providing security for large cities with transient populations is often greater than the marginal benefit.

---

[6] Guengant (1993); Marchand (1997); Chervin, Edmiston, and Murray (2000); Fenge and von Weizsacker (2001); Fenge and Meier (2002); Ruggeri (2002); Bates and Santerre (2003); Buettner (2003); Johansson (2003); Levaggi and Zanola (2003); Boadway (2004); Gil Canaleta, Pascual Arzoz, and Rapun Garate (2004).

(See the box entitled *Equalizing the Central City and Its Suburbs.*) Thus, without extra revenues, cities cannot generally provide an optimal quantity of local public goods. Interregional transfers between the suburbs and the central city should correct for these spillover effects.

Equalizing the Central City and Its Suburbs

Philadelphia, Pennsylvania, like most of the older central cities, faces burdens and responsibilities that benefit the suburban commuters. It has:

- 70 percent of the region's poor, but 39 percent of the total population.

- 1465 violent crimes per 100,000 population, compared with 286 per 100,000 population in its suburbs.

- 5855 property crimes per 100,000 population compared with 2503 per 100,000 population in the suburbs.

As a result, in Philadelphia homeowners pay up to 14.4 percent of the family income in local taxes although this rate is about 9.5 percent for the average suburban homeowner. The tax rate differences and lower quality public services undermine agglomeration economies. Populations, incomes, and house values fall in the suburbs, as in the center city. Not only the central city, but the entire region loses. Inman proposes a commuter wage tax to revitalize the coffers of the central city to help both Philadelphia and the entire metropolitan region.

Inman (2003)

To the extent that firms benefit from local agglomeration economies, the increase in the demand for land in and around the CBD drives up land rents. This increase forces some residents to move to the suburbs, which reduces the tax base and will increase the taxes that the remaining downtown residents must pay. This is especially true if the city granted tax abatement for firms to locate there.

Opponents of subsidizing central cities pointed out that the advantages of agglomeration are limited anyway by congestion and other diseconomies of agglomeration. Diseconomies of agglomeration contribute to increasing wages and land rents and population density. The high per capita cost of public provision is due to the higher population density in the city. The densely populated cities do not need to be subsidized because they are beyond their optimal level of agglomeration.[7]

Electoral Carrots

Traditionally, intergovernmental grants were created to promote equity and efficiency among local jurisdictions. However, this is not the only reason. Intergovernmental grants are used to win votes.

Gavin Wright (1974) found that inequalities in federal spending in the United States were largely consequences of vote maximizing behavior of the president. Stromberg (2001) analyzed the impact of the radio on the Federal Emergency Relief Administration (FERA) during the great depression of the 1930s. He found that the U.S. counties with many radio listeners received more relief funds per capita.

Case (2001) determined that grants in Albania also had a political flavor to them. Johansson (2003) arrived at the same conclusion when he analyzed data from 255 Swedish municipalities and found that from 1981 to 1995, jurisdictions where the electors were indecisive received larger grants.

Wright (1974), Case (2001), Stromberg (2001), Johansson (2003)

Stopping Fiscal Unequalization

Systems of fiscal equalization among jurisdictions exist in many countries where transfers between jurisdictions of the same level are used to equalize

---

[7] Bahl (1994); Fenge and Meier (2002).

government budgets. The high costs of local pubic goods justify these transfers.

But Fenge and Meier (2002) maintained that cities should not be subsidized. They noted that that small jurisdictions with high income per capita tend to receive transfers from larger jurisdictions that are not as wealthy. In Germany, for instance, city-states of Berlin, Bremen, and Hamburg receive transfer payments from geographically larger states of Bavaria or Hesse because the current system assumes that all three city-states have 35 percent greater requirements per person, than do the larger *Bundesländer*. The same preferential treatment is found in the populous regions of Austria, Australia, and Canada. In Austria, cities with more than 50,000 in population receive 133% more grant money per person than smaller cities.

Fenge and Meier (2002)

Think About It ...

Besides the federal government, does your state or locality also tax incomes? If so, what is the total proportion of their income would someone who makes $25,000 pay in taxes? $50,000? $75,000? $100,000?

In your jurisdiction, are there any other tax bases that different levels of governments tax?

Overlapping Tax Bases

There is a **vertical fiscal externality** when the taxes or expenditures of one level of government affect the budget constraint of another level of government. When two levels of government impose taxes on the same tax base, the governments may end up on the downward sloping sector of the Laffer curve (Figure 17.1). The tax base overlap represents the exploitation of a common property resource by the public sector. This may become an overexploitation of the shared tax bases, equivalent to the overexploitation of common fishing grounds, which can reduce the tax revenues.[8]

Fiscal Externalities, Poverty, and Overlapping Taxes

Horizontal externalities result when the choices of one local government are influenced by choices made by another local government. There are vertical externalities when the same tax base is simultaneously exploited by different levels of government. Empirically, there is an interaction between (1) higher and lower levels of government, and (2) the lower levels of government.

Goodspeed (2000) examined the impact of horizontal and vertical externalities on the tax structure of a central government. He concluded that a higher national income tax rate and lower poverty rates lead to lower local income tax rates. For example, a one percentage increase in the national government income tax rate lowers the local income tax rate by about 0.17 percent in OECD countries. Taking account of the demographic mobility, an increase of 1 percent in the income earned by the poorest 20 percent of the population decreases local government income taxes by 0.59 percent.

Goodspeed (2000)

Think About It ...

In what ways does your jurisdiction compete with its neighboring jurisdictions? How does each jurisdiction promote itself on its homepage on the Internet to attract businesses or households?

---

[8] Aronsson and Wikström (2001); Dahlby and Wilson (2003).

Interjurisdictional Competition

Two theories account for spatial interaction among governments. First is a ***traditional spillover*** or ***externality model***. According to this model, expenditures on local public services may produce positive or negative externalities in the neighboring jurisdictions. For example, some counties spend more on police services than their neighbors, but because criminals are mobile, the need for police services in neighboring counties will also need to increase.

In the spillover models, each jurisdiction chooses a specific level of public good, but it is affected by the levels of that good that other jurisdictions choose. This suggests the presence of spillovers. Residents of Maine benefit from spending on roads in New Hampshire. Because of their geographic location, if New Hampshire's road quality was extremely poor, drivers from Maine would have to go into Canada to visit the rest of the United States.

There are ***horizontal fiscal externalities*** when tax competition is among governments of the same level. The literature on this subject examines the effect of one jurisdiction's taxes on the welfare of people in other jurisdictions. For instance, when one jurisdiction increases its taxes on a mobile tax base, capital (firms) will move from that jurisdiction and increase the next jurisdictions' tax bases.

Competition among Belgium Municipalities

Richard, Tulkens, and Verdonck (2002) studied panel data from the Belgian's 589 *communes*. They found that there was interdependence between municipalities in the choice of property tax rates and income tax rates for data from 1983 to 1997. In addition, they noted that lagged adjustments triggered by the differences in the rates of other *communes* take place slowly; 6 percent per year for the income tax rates and 10 percent for property tax rates.

Richard, Tulkens, and Verdonck (2002)

The traditional neoclassical view may be either for or against the benefits of interjurisdictional competition. The Tiebout (1956) argument maintains that tax competition leads to an efficient provision of local public goods when individual households can move costlessly among jurisdictions. Tax competition can effectively reduce the taxing power and desire of a local government and in this way competition promotes welfare. The result is the best of all possible worlds because the amount of local taxes paid and local goods consumed will be exactly what each resident wanted.

It is curious that neoclassical economists would argue against competition. However, that is exactly what happens in the public finance literature. The argument against local tax competition is that local officials will hold down tax rates and adopt lax environmental regulations to attract new businesses and new jobs. However, tax competition reduces welfare. To attract new firms, jurisdictions risk creating distortions by taxing capital at too low a rate and by underproviding public services. Thus interjurisdictional competition results in a "race to the bottom." These distortions explain the decline in public services and lower standards for environmental quality in some states or local jurisdictions.

On the other hand, the public choice theorists create a picture of a utility maximizing manager within the public sector bureaucracy. The bureaucracy is modeled as a perfect price-discriminating monopoly that usurps the entire amount of consumer surplus. Managers derive utility from status. Because the importance of status is proportional to the size of their budget, their payroll, or the number of employees, this bureaucracy tends to produce a quantity of public goods that is larger than the socially optimum level. Such management by managers within governmental bureaucracies goes against all definitions of efficiency, but because the government is a monopoly, they can do so with impunity.

Racing to the Bottom?

Are jurisdictions "racing to the bottom" to impose a minimal tax even if it results in inadequate services? We only have anecdotal evidence to support an affirmative response, for there is no systematic evidence to confirm that jurisdictions are bottoming out. Quite the opposite, empirical evidence supports a negative response. Millimet and List (2004), for example, studied the "new federalism" environmental policy of President Reagan in the early 1980s, which supposedly induced states to lower environmental standards. They find no evidence of a "race to the bottom." In fact, industrial pollution, the cost of equipment, and emissions of sulfur or nitrogen oxides at the state level either did not change or continued to decline.

Millimet and List (2004)

The incomes and wealth of residents affect the incentives of both politicians and taxpayers to monitor expenditures because income and wealth determine the fiscal capacity of municipalities. A greater capacity to generate revenues may increase the on-the-job leisure of politicians and public managers (meetings on the golf course or conferences in the Caribbean), which decreases the incentives to operate efficiently. On the other hand, given their high opportunity cost of time, the citizens of prosperous municipalities tend to neglect to effectively monitor spending.

Intergovernmental competition causes jurisdictions to evaluate the impact of their taxing and spending policies on economic growth, and to concentrate on economic development activities.[9]

Yardstick Competition

If there is a correlation between public spending levels and local property tax rates among local jurisdictions, researchers suggest that this interdependence among local governments is attributed to a *mimicking behavior* in setting local property taxes. A spatial pattern in public spending can be caused by a common shock affecting neighboring local governments or by a genuinely interdependent policy. In effect, neighboring jurisdictions pursue interdependent policies because of tax competition, or because voters compare their jurisdiction with adjoining ones.

Because information is costly, according to the *yardstick competition model*, voters in a local jurisdiction save time by using the performance of another jurisdiction as a yardstick to evaluate their own regime. Politicians therefore try to create policies that are similar to those of their neighbors. Local authorities thus mimic the policies of one another. The yardstick competition model fits within the spillover framework. Voters compare the public services and taxes of other jurisdictions to determine whether their government is wasting resources (by being inefficient or by catering to rent seekers) and should be reelected or not.

Mimicking the Neighbors

Jayet, Paty, and Pentel (2002) analyzed data from 1995 for the communes of the Nord Pas-de-Calais, a *département*

---

[9] Dye (1990); Hoyt (1991, 2001); De Borger (1994); Brueckner (2000, 2004); Rieber (2000); Brueckner and Saavedra (2001); Varone and Genoud (2001); Blankart (2002); Bretin, Guimbert, and Madiès (2002); Cebula (2002); Revelli (2002); Besfamille (2004); Wildeson (2004).

in France, and were able to confirm the hypothesis of fiscal mimicry for the Lille metropolitan area, the coast, and the Valenciennois—Cambrésis region. In effect, local authorities in these zones fixed the rate for their *taxe professionnelle* on those of the neighboring localities. Urbanization influences the degree of fiscal mimicry and the strategic interactions.

Jayet, Paty, and Pentel (2002)

The yardstick competition theory provides insights about the structure of government in democratic countries. Yardstick competition assumes that:

■ Citizens can observe the fiscal choices in jurisdictions other than their own.
■ The economic and institutional conditions in the neighboring jurisdictions are comparable.
■ The electoral behavior is the main tool that citizens have to punish inept incumbents.
■ Politicians react strategically to voters' behavior.

If politicians are conscious of the calculations of their constituents, they will make fiscal choices favorable to the voters. Yardstick competition therefore permits us to distinguish behavioral differences between (1) incumbent politicians and candidates preceding an election, and (2) those politicians who are leaving. Those who are not candidates for reelection will be less responsive to the decisions of other jurisdictions. This same detachment exists for incumbents who are confident of being reelected.[10]

Evidence of Italian Yardstick Competition

In Italy, the theory that decentralization and jurisdictional competition are motors in the production of local services has determined the fiscal reform of 1997

---

[10] Ricordel (1997); Boarnet and Glazer (2002); Jayet, Paty, and Pentel (2002); Schaltegger and Küttel (2002); Revelli (2002); Richard, Tulkens, and Verdonck (2002); Bordignon, Cerniglia, and Revelli (2003); Brueckner (2003); Buettner (2003).

and the constitutional reform that followed. Bordignon, Cerniglia, and Revelli (2003) tried to distinguish yardstick competition from tax mimicry using a sample of 143 adjacent *Comuni* (municipalities) in the Province of Milan with populations greater than 4000 residents. The key to distinguishing whether tax mimicry stems from tax competition or yardstick competition requires an analysis of the electoral system.

Their results favor a form of yardstick competition. A jurisdiction's property tax rates are positively correlated with its neighbors only when the mayor is running for reelection and the electoral outcome is uncertain. But there is no correlation in jurisdictions where either the mayor is at the end of the term limit, if the mayor is not running for reelection, or where the mayor is backed by a large majority.

Bordignon, Cerniglia, and Revelli (2003)

Summary and Conclusions

The interactions between local jurisdictions and among different levels of government form a large part of the local public finance literature. Efficient systems of government exist when a public good causes the smallest amount of spillovers and corresponds optimally to the needs of the constituents. Higher levels of government can provide grants to certain jurisdictions to promote fiscal equalization (or the political careers of the grantors). Higher government levels also require that minimum standards of local goods be provided by lower-level jurisdictions. Sometimes adequate funding accompanies these mandates, but not always.

When localities receive revenues from outside their jurisdictions to finance local public goods, there is fiscal illusion for the residents who demand too much of the local good because the marginal costs are artificially low.

The interaction of various governments can cause vertical and horizontal fiscal externalities. Vertical externalities exist when revenues decline because another level of government is taxing the same base. Horizontal externalities come about when the taxes or expenditures of one jurisdiction affect neighboring jurisdictions.

Tax mimicry exists when one jurisdiction imitates its neighbors. The tax mimicry results from fiscal shocks common to the entire region. It can also result from interjurisdictional tax competition, when each locality tries to attract more firms by charging lower taxes than its neighbors. Finally, it can result from the residents monitoring the quality of their own jurisdiction by the actions of the neighboring ones.

Chapter Questions

1. Which level of government would be better at providing or subsidizing the following government services? Assume that scale economies do not exist and that every jurisdiction has the same per capita incomes. Base your response on a market-area analysis and spillover effects:
   a. Elementary education
   b. Secondary education
   c. University education
   d. Street repair in your city
   e. Road repair for a major interstate going through your city
   f. Police protection
   g. Fire protection
   h. Defense against foreign invaders
   i. Regulating food processing
   j. Public health
   k. Sewerage
   l. Water
   m. Garbage
2. Different government levels can make decisions that lead to a moral hazard or an adverse selection. Give examples.
3. Describe two common property resource problems in relation to the revenues of different levels of government.
4. Does the "race to the bottom" exist? Base your argument in terms of the median voter theorem and the Tiebout hypothesis.

Research Questions

1. Check out the amount of intergovernmental revenues (total federal aid) that flow into your state (or city) from the *Statistical Abstract of the United States* (http://www.census.gov/prod/2004pubs/04statab/stlocgov.pdf). Also find out the amount of taxes paid from your state or city to the federal government http://www.census.gov/prod/2004pubs/04statab/stlocgov.pdf). Is your state collecting more or less in federal aid than it is spending in taxes? Is your state receiving a greater amount of federal aid per capita than the

average? That is, are the other residents of the United States subsidizing your state's projects, or are you subsidizing theirs, on balance?

2. Refer to the *CA30 Regional economic profiles* at http://www.bea.gov/bea/regional/reis/ Graph over time the per capita personal income with the per capita current transfer receipts for your state, your county or city and the adjacent jurisdictions. Are these figures for your county higher or lower than the state average? How do they compare with those in neighboring counties? Search the Internet for keywords: intergovernmental aid, counties (or cities), and the name of your state. Compare the amount of intergovernmental aid per capita for your county or city and the adjacent jurisdictions. Do you see evidence of lessening fiscal disparities over time?

3. Look under Factfinder at http://factfinder.census.gov/home/saff/main.html?_lang=en for the Fact Sheet for your city and the neighboring communities. Compare per capita incomes. From the city budgets, compare the per capita expenditures and tax revenues. Do jurisdictions with the highest per capita income pay the most in taxes per capita? Do high-income jurisdictions receive larger or smaller amounts of per capita expenditures from local governments?

References

Aronsson, T., and M. Wikström. 2001. Optimal taxes and transfers in a multilevel public sector. *FinanzArchiv* 58 (2):158–166.

Bahl, R. 1994. Metropolitan fiscal disparities. *Cityscape: A Journal of Policy Development and Research* 1 (1):293–306.

Bahl, R., J. Martinez-Vazquez, and S. Wallace. 2002. State and local government choices in fiscal redistribution. *National Tax Journal* 55 (4):723–742.

Baicker, K. 2001. Government decision-making and the incidence of federal mandates. *Journal of Public Economics* 82 (2):147–194.

Bardhan, P. 2002. Decentralization of governance and development. *Journal of Economic Perspectives* 16 (4):185–205.

Barnett, R. R., R. Levaggi, and P. Smith. 1991. Does the flypaper model stick? A test of the relative performance of the flypaper and conventional models of local government budgetary behaviour. *Public Choice* 69 (1):1–18.

Bates, L. J., and R. E. Santerre. 2003. The impact of a state mandated expenditure floor on aggregate property values. *Journal of Urban Economics* 53 (3):531–540.

Beech, H. 2002. Smuggler's Blues. http://www.time.com/time/asia/covers/1101021014/story.html Oct. 14. (accessed 28 February 2005).

Besfamille, M. 2004. Local public works and intergovernmental transfers under asymmetric information. *Journal of Public Economics* 88 (1-2):353–375.

Besley, T., and S. Coate. 2003. Centralized versus decentralized provision of local public goods: a political economy approach. *Journal of Public Economics* 87 (12):2611–2637.

Blankart, C. B. 2002. A public choice view of tax competition. *Public Finance Review* 30 (5):366–376.

Boadway, R. 2004. The theory and practice of equalization. *CESifo Economic Studies* 50 (1):211–254.

Boarnet, M. G., and A. Glazer. 2002. Federal grants and yardstick competition. *Journal of Urban Economics* 52 (1):53–64.

Bordignon, M., F. Cerniglia, and F. Revelli. 2003. In search of yardstick competition: a spatial analysis of Italian municipality property tax setting. *Journal of Urban Economics* 54 (2):199–217.

Bordignon, M., P. Manasse, and G. Tabellini. 2001. Optimal regional redistribution under asymmetric information. *American Economic Review* 91 (3):709–723.

Bretin, E., S. Guimbert, and T. Madiès. 2002. La concurrence fiscale sur le bénéfice des entreprises: théories et pratiques. *Economie et Prévision* 0 (156):15–42.

Brueckner, J. K. 2000. A Tiebout/Tax-competition model. *Journal of Public Economics* 77 (2):285–306.

Brueckner, J. K. 2003. Strategic interaction among governments: an overview of empirical studies. *International Regional Science Review* 26 (2):175–188.

Brueckner, J. K. 2004. Fiscal decentralization with distortionary taxation: Tiebout vs. tax competition. *International Tax and Public Finance* 11 (2):133–153.

Buettner, T. 2003. Tax base effects and fiscal externalities of local capital taxation: evidence from a panel of German jurisdictions. *Journal of Urban Economics* 54 (1):110–128.

Brueckner, J. K., and L. A. Saavedra. 2001. Do local governments engage in strategic property-tax competition? *National Tax Journal* 54 (2):203–229.

Cai, H., and D. Treisman. 2004. State corroding federalism. *Journal of Public Economics* 88 (3–4):819–843.

Case, A. 2001. Election goals and income redistribution: recent evidence from Albania. *European Economic Review* 45 (3):405–423.

Cebula, R. J. 2002. Net interstate population growth rates and the Tiebout-Tullock hypothesis: new empirical evidence, 1990–2000. *Atlantic Economic Journal* 30 (4):414–421.

Chao, C.-C., and E. S. H. Yu. 2002. On property tax coordination. *Journal of Real Estate Finance and Economics* 25 (1):67–79.

Charney, A. H. 1993. Migration and the public sector: a survey. *Regional Studies* 27 (4):313–326.

Chernick, H. 1992. A model of the distributional incidence of state and local taxes. *Public Finance Quarterly* 20 (4):572–585.

Chervin, S., K. Edmiston, and M. N. Murray. 2000. Urban malls, tax base migration, and state intergovernmental aid. *Public Finance Review* 28 (4):309–334.

Chu, H.-Y. 2003. The dual-illusion of grants-in-aid on central and local expenditures. *Public Choice* 114 (3–4):349–359.

Dahlby, B., and L. S. Wilson. 2003. Vertical fiscal externalities in a federation. *Journal of Public Economics* 87 (5–6):917–930.

de Bartolome, C. A. M. 1990. Equilibrium and inefficiency in a community model with peer group effects. *Journal of Political Economy* 98 (1):110–133.

De Borger, B. 1994. Explaining differences in productive efficiency: an application to belgian municipalities. *Public Choice* 80 (3–4):339–358.

de Mello, L. R. 2001. Fiscal decentralization and borrowing costs: the case of local governments. *Public Finance Review* 29 (2):108–138.

Dudley, L. and Montmarquette, C. 1993. "Fit or Fat?" Government and productivity growth, Discussion Paper no. 93-06, Government and Competitiveness, School of Policy Studies, Queen's University.

Duret, E., and B. Ventelou. 1999. Décentralisation financière, fédéralisme et croissance: Une approche par la qualité de gouvernance. *Revue d'Economie Régionale et Urbaine* 0 (4):709–736.

Dye, T. R. 1990. The policy consequences of intergovernmental competition. *Cato Journal* 10 (1):59–73.

Fenge, R., and V. Meier. 2002. Why cities should not be subsidized. *Journal of Urban Economics* 52 (3):433–447.

Fenge, R., and J. von Weizsacker. 2001. How much fiscal equalization? A constitutional approach. *Journal of Institutional and Theoretical Economics* 157 (4):623–633.

Fuest, C., and R. T. Riphahn. 2001. Is the local business tax a user tax? An empirical investigation for Germany. *Jahrbücher für Nationalökonomie und Statistik* 221 (1):14–31.

Gemmell, N., O. Morrissey, and A. Pinar. 2002. Fiscal illusion and political accountability: theory and evidence from two local tax regimes in Britain. *Public choice* 110 (3–4):199–224.

Gerard-Varet, L. A., and J.-F. Thisse. 1997. Local public finance and economic geography. *Annales d'Economie et de Statistique* 0 (45):19–35.

Gil Canaleta, C., P. Pascual Arzoz, and M. Rapun Garate. 2004. Regional economic disparities and decentralisation. *Urban Studies* 41 (1):71–94.

Gillette, C. P. 2001. Funding versus control in intergovernmental relations. *Constitutional Political Economy* 12 (2):123–140.

Goodspeed, T. J. 2000. Tax structure in a federation. *Journal of Public Economics* 75 (3):493–506.

Grosskopf, S., and K. Hayes. 1993. Local public sector bureaucrats and their input choices. *Journal of Urban Economics* 33 (2):151–166.

Guengant, A. 1993. Equité, efficacité et égalisation fiscale territoriale. *Revue Economique* 44 (4):835–848.

Hamilton, B. W. 1983. The flypaper effect and other anomalies. *Journal of Public Economics* 22 (3):347–361.

Hendrick, R. 2002. Revenue diversification: Fiscal illusion or flexible financial management. *Public Budgeting and Finance* 22 (4):52–72.

Hettler, P. 2001. Spillover effects of local fiscal policy. *Atlantic Economic Journal* 29 (4):406–419.

Heyndels, B. 2001. Asymmetries in the flypaper effect: empirical evidence for the Flemish municipalities. *Applied Economics* 33 (10):1329–1334.

Hochman, O., D. Pines, and J.-F. Thisse. 1995. On the optimal structure of local governments. *American Economic Review* 85 (5):1224–1240.

Hofmann, E., and G. von Wangenheim. 2002. Trade secrets versus cost benefit analysis. *International Review of Law and Economics* 22 (4):511–526.

Hoyt, W. H. 1991. Property taxation, Nash equilibrium, and market power. *Journal of Urban Economics* 30 (1):123–131.

Hoyt, W. H. 2001. Tax policy coordination, vertical externalities, and optimal taxation in a system of hierarchical governments. *Journal of Urban Economics* 50 (3):491–516.

Ihori, T., and J. I. Itaya. 2004. Fiscal reconstruction and local government financing. *International Tax and Public Finance* 11 (1):55–67.

Inman, R. P. 2001. Transfers and bailouts: institutions for enforcing local fiscal discipline. *Constitutional Political Economy* 12 (2):141–160.

Inman, R. P. 2003. Should Philadelphia's suburbs help their central city? *Federal Reserve Bank of Philadelphia Business Review* 0 (2):24–36.

Jayet, H., S. Paty, and A. Pentel. 2002. Existe-t-il des interactions fiscales stratégiques entre les collectivités locales. *Economie et Prévision* 0 (154):95–105.

Jerrett, M., J. Eyles, and C. Dufournaud. 2002. Regional population size and the cost of municipal environmental protection services: empirical evidence from Ontario. *Canadian Journal of Regional Science* 25 (2):279–300.

Johansson, E. 2003. Intergovernmental grants as a tactical instrument: empirical evidence from Swedish municipalities. *Journal of Public Economics* 87 (5–6):883–915.

Keen, M. J., and C. Kotsogiannis. 2002. Does federalism lead to excessively high taxes? *American Economic Review* 92 (1):363–370.

Levaggi, R., and R. Zanola. 2003. Flypaper effect and sluggishness: evidence from regional health expenditure in Italy. *International Tax and Public Finance* 10 (5):535–547.

Lulfesmann, C. 2002. Central governance or subsidiarity: a property-rights approach to federalism. *European Economic Review* 46 (8):1379–1397.

Marchand, M. J. 1997. La nouvelle donne des comportements budgétaires régionaux depuis la décentralisation. *Revue d'Economie Régionale et Urbaine* 0 (2):215–233.

Millimet, D. L., and J. A. List. 2003. A natural experiment on the 'race to the bottom' hypothesis: testing for stochastic dominance in temporal pollution trends. *Oxford Bulletin of Economics and Statistics* 65 (4):395–420.

Oates, W. E. 1978. Decentralization, bureaucracy, and government: discussion. *American Economic Review* 68 (2):262–263.

Oates, W. E. 1981. On local finance and the Tiebout model. *American Economic Review* 71 (2):93–98.

Oates, W. E. 2001. Fiscal competition or harmonization? Some reflections. *National Tax Journal* 54 (3):507–512.

Perroni, C., and K. A. Scharf. 2001. Tiebout with politics: capital tax competition and constitutional choices. *Review of Economic Studies* 68 (1):133–154.

Prieto, A. M., and J. L. Zofio. 2001. Evaluating effectiveness in public provision of infrastructure and equipment: the case of Spanish municipalities. *Journal of Productivity Analysis* 15 (1):41–58.

Revelli, F. 2002. Testing the tax mimicking versus expenditure spill-over hypotheses using English data. *Applied Economics* 34 (14):1723–1731.

Richard, J. F., H. Tulkens, and M. Verdonck. 2002. Dynamique des interactions fiscales entre les communes belges 1984–1997. *Economie Et Prévision* 0 (156):1–14.

Ricordel, P. 1997. La gestion publique locale: partenariat et performance. Une étude empirique sur 20 communes—centres d'agglomérations françaises. *Revue d'Economie Régionale et Urbaine* 0 (3):425–447.

Rieber, A. 2000. Intégration régionale, mobilité du capital et concurrence fiscale. *Economie Internationale* 0 (81):21–42.

Ruggeri, J. 2002. Fiscal restraint and subsidies to businesses: regional dimensions. *Canadian Journal of Regional Science* 25 (1):135–144.

Schaltegger, C. A., and D. Küttel. 2002. Exit, voice, and mimicking behavior: evidence from Swiss cantons. *Public Choice* 113 (1–2):1–23.

Smart, M. and R. Bird. 1996. Proceedings of the Eighty-Ninth Annual Conference on Taxation held under the auspices of the National Tax Association at Boston, Massachusetts, November 10–12, 1996 and minutes of the annual meeting held Sunday, November 10, 1996: 1–10.

Smart, M. 1998. Taxation and deadweight loss in a system of intergovernmental transfers. *Canadian Journal of Economics* 31 (1):189–206.

Stromberg, D. 2004. Radio's impact on public spending. *Quarterly Journal of Economics* 119 (1):189–221.

Tiebout, C. M. 1956. A pure theory of local expenditures, *The Journal of Political Economy* 64 (5):416–424.

Trionfetti, F. 1997. Public expenditure and economic geography. *Annales d'Economie et de Statistique* 0 (47):101–120.

Van Puyenbroeck, T. 2001. Bribing the grantee: asymmetric information and the enforcement of local minimum-provision levels through grants-in-aid. *Environment and Planning C: Government and Policy* 19 (3):443–460.

Varone, F., and C. Genoud. 2001. Libéralisation des services publics de réseau et jeux croises de la régulation: le cas de l'électricité. *Annals of Public and Cooperative Economics* 72 (4):481–506.

Walden, M. L. 2003. Dynamic revenue curves for North Carolina taxes. *Public Budgeting and Finance* 23 (4):49–64.

Wildasin, D. E. 2004. The institutions of federalism: toward an analytical framework. *National Tax Journal* 57 (2):247–272.

Wright, G. 1974. The political economy of new deal spending: an econometric analysis. *Review of Economics and Statistics* 56 (1):30–38.

Chapter 18

Income Inequality and Poverty

What does poverty and income inequality have to do with economic development? The answer is everything. The goal of economic development is to increase living standards by bringing jobs and income to a community. For this reason, in one way or another, the object of our course so far has been the fight against poverty.

Not only does poverty create a *raison d'être* for economic development, but the very subjects of regional and urban economics weave through the literature on poverty and income distribution. First, many programs designed to help the poor are often locally financed. The determination of who is poor in a community depends on the average incomes of that locality, as well as those of the neighboring jurisdictions. Second, according to the filtering theory (Chapter 13), people tend to congregate by income groups. Thus, low-income people tend to cluster together in one area of a municipality. Finally, jurisdictional competition (Chapter 17) encourages localities to attract high-income people by lower taxes and lower welfare funding. With that in mind, is it possible to eliminate the poor, not by driving them away, but by creating circumstances in which they are no longer impoverished? Not always. It depends on what the people themselves want, how poverty is defined, and the budget constraints that lower-income people face.

Economists assume that we make choices that maximize our utilities subject to various constraints. The constraints can be a lack of money or time, as well as constraints imposed by society and by ourselves. People in

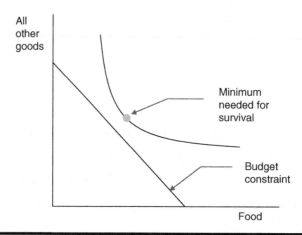

Figure 18.1 Budget constraint for a low-income household.

poverty have an insufficient command over resources, which keeps them from acquiring a minimum of required goods and services (Figure 18.1).

For many, a healthy labor market is the remedy for poverty. In 2005, 70% of aggregate personal income came from wages, salaries, and benefits. A good understanding of firm location theory can help to create a milieu conducive to attracting new firms to a region. Such a milieu can encourage regional economic growth and raise living standards.

Researchers have cited various causes of poverty: (1) side effects of deliberate choices of individuals to maximize their utilities, (2) the myopic behavior of dysfunctional individuals, (3) limited opportunities, and (4) antipoverty programs themselves. In addition, some prescriptions that can help one person could exacerbate the problem for others.

Unfortunately, some people are incapable of participating in the labor market or cannot do so efficiently. Children, frail elderly, and those with severe disabilities are not generally employed. Many poor people do not have sufficient human capital (education, training, or health). Those who choose alternative lifestyles maximize their psychic income (utility) to the detriment of pecuniary incomes. For example, some religious orders take the vow of poverty. What about artists who choose a bohemian lifestyle over financial stability? It is the same for members of the Peace Corps, Americorps*Vista, or other philanthropic organizations. "Beach bums" would rather surf than work, and thus gladly exchange fulltime employment for leisure. In addition, substance abuse may cause an individual's supply curve for labor to bend backward at relatively low wages; once they are paid, they stop working.[1]

---

[1] Bossert (1990); Blank (2003).

Limited opportunities can be caused by a disadvantaged socioeconomic environment, by becoming a mother too young, or again, by substance abuse. We already mentioned that poorly conceived antipoverty programs can create welfare dependency and dysfunctional behavior. For example, until March 29, 1996, Social Security Insurance (SSI) in the United States offered a program designed to reinforce the self-esteem of alcoholics and drug addicts. The working premise was that low self-esteem itself is the basis of substance abuse. Because higher incomes boost self-esteem, addicts in the program could receive as much as $600 per month depending on where they lived. The money was supposed to encourage sobriety. Unfortunately, if individuals chose to be rehabilitated and embrace sobriety, they no longer needed their monthly check because they were "cured." In essence these SSI payments compensated these individuals to continue the life of an addict.[2]

This chapter studies several definitions of income before researching the causes of income inequality. We will then evaluate different methods of measuring income inequality and analyze the ramifications of using an absolute or a relative measure of poverty. Next, we will examine the effects of poverty on children, women, and ethnic minorities. Finally, we will analyze policies that were designed to improve the lives of low-income people.

Definition of Income

Variations in wages and the number of hours of work are the principal causes of income differences among households. Hourly salaries and hours of work are essentially a function of the labor market and of the individual's human capital investment (Chapter 10). The demand for labor is a function of the marginal product of labor and this productivity is influenced by the worker's investment in human capital.

Wages represent the largest proportion of personal income. In the United States, employee compensation and proprietors' income constituted 69.3% of total personal revenue in 2003. Personal transfers from unemployment, retirement, and income maintenance checks added to 14.6%, and dividends, interest and rents constituted the rest (16.1%). The average annual wage per job in the United States was $38,798 in 2004 with a minimum of $27,721 in Montana and a maximum of $63,751 in Washington, DC.

Think About It...

Refer to the *CA 30, Regional Economic Profile* for your state and county (http://www.bea.gov/bea/regional/reis/

---

[2] Treatment Action Network (1996).

default.cfm#a). Determine the proportion of personal income that comes from:

1.   Employee compensation and proprietors' incomes (wage and salary disbursements+supplements to wages and salaries+proprietors' incomes)

2.   Personal current transfer receipts

3.   Dividends, interest, and rent

What is your county's average wage and salary disbursement per job?

How does your county compare to your state? To the nation?

The supply of labor is a function of personal preferences concerning work and leisure and other activities (generally household). Discrimination may cause persistent wage differences despite an acceptable investment in human capital. In addition, family structure, as well as changes in taxes and transfer payment policies, increase income inequality.

How Did the Wealthiest Australians Get So Rich?

Siegfried and Round (1994) wanted to pierce the secret of some wealthy Australians. They found that outside of monopoly profits, 75 percent of the rich were specialized in competitive industries, such as property development, sheep ranching, mineral exploration, newspapers, and construction. Other lucrative industries included clothing manufacturing and retailing, wholesale housewares, accounting, and car washing; this is in spite of the fact that the competitive model implies a normal rate of return in the long run.

Innovation and product differentiation create disequilibrium, that is, price has not yet adjusted to a new equilibrium level. This can be a source of some very nice profits. How does this work? To start, if one firm's costs are lower because they adopted a new technique, it will sell the improved product at a higher price. Similarly, if one firm has a monopoly in a niche market before its rivals intrude, that firm could make supernormal profits for a while. Besides showing good business acumen, compensation for risk when the adventure succeeded, as well as economic rents due to location and competent managers, also padded some nest eggs.

Siegfried and Round (1994)

Income Distributions

There are two ways to characterize income distributions. (1) A ***functional distribution*** of income is based on the allocation of a firm's revenue toward wages, interest, land rents, and profits. In a competitive market, these allocations are determined by the value of the marginal product of the inputs (Euler's theorem). (2) The ***size distribution of income*** the proportion of "income units" in each income group. In this chapter, we will study the second mode of distribution because it is directly linked to the problem of poverty.

Income gives a certain amount of control over resources. Individual lifetime earnings and wealth (salaries, interest, rent, profits, inheritance, etc., adjusted for inflation) have a more narrow distribution than income at a given time, generally because of age differences. Earnings generally peak before retirement. A temporary lack of financial resources for students, for example, may occur because the capital market fails to recognize their potential. Similarly, elderly people in good health who have already paid their mortgages may live quite well on an income that would be insufficient for a young household.

To understand the various (sometimes contradictory) results from income distributions, the variations of four components of the income concept need to be identified:

1. The income unit (individual, family, or household).
2. The definition of income.
3. The appropriate time length.
4. How to adjust for income units of different sizes.

Income Units

Income units may be individuals or groups of individuals. People grouped together may be related (family) or unrelated (household). According to the United States Census Bureau.

> "A ***family*** consists of two or more people, one of whom is the householder, related by birth, marriage, or adoption and residing in the same housing unit. A ***household*** consists of all people

who occupy a housing unit regardless of relationship. A household may consist of a person living alone or multiple unrelated individuals or families living together."[3]

Keeping the "income unit" in mind may clear up some of the seemingly conflicting reports on poverty trends.

- A single mother who cohabits with her boyfriend constitutes two income units within one household. The mother and her children make up one family. The boyfriend as an individual is a second income unit. Together they constitute one household.
- An elderly person living alone is considered an income unit. The same is true of his well-to-do, single daughter. If the elder's income declines dramatically, the number of households in poverty increases by one. However, if the elder moves in with his daughter, the household poverty count decreases by one unit. But, if the income unit is the individual rather than the household however, the poverty counts do not change when the two households combine.
- If you share an apartment with seven other roommates, together you all make up a household.
- Over time, family income distributions show different patterns than distributions using household data, primarily because of the increase in singles and retired couples as well as older people who can live alone past 90 years old.

Components of Income

The difficulty in defining what exactly to include as income creates a second problem in understanding income distributions. For example, the Bureau of the Census ignores imputed rent in their definition of income. ***Imputed rent*** is the opportunity cost of living in one's own home, measured by the income forgone if one were to rent it to someone else. Economists view homeowners as having a dual role. Homeowners own an asset: their homes. If they choose to live in their homes, in essence, they are renting the home to themselves rather than to someone else, and thus they pay themselves an imputed rent.

Official income measures also ignore inheritances, insurance payments, and the amount of capital gains received from selling assets. Likewise, household production (e.g., baking bread, raising children, canning, gardening, backyard mechanic work) has no value in the official income measure. Finally, although the amount paid in taxes is not subtracted from official measures of income, the value of in-kind transfers

---

[3] http://www.census.gov/population/www/cps/cpsdef.html

(food stamps, housing vouchers, and government-provided medical insurance) is ignored. If the value of in-kind transfers was included as income, what would be the optimal method of evaluating these transfers? Surveys consistently say that market value of in-kind transfers is greater than the recipient value.

Once we decide on the appropriate measurement for nominal income, we need to measure real income (spending power). Poverty thresholds in the United States are updated annually using the CPI-U (Consumer Price Index for all Urban Consumers). But these numbers do not have a comparable regional variation. Using the CPI as the deflator creates two problems. First, the cost of living depends on the cost of a specified market basket of goods, the contents of which vary with income. The prices of the market basket of goods that low-income households purchase do not increase at the same rate as those of goods that the medium- and upper-income households purchase. Therefore, using the CPI-U will not accurately estimate the purchasing power for every income group.

Second, the "law of one price" predicts that competitive forces will equalize the prices of identical commodities throughout the world. In reality, however, such prediction does not hold, especially not for housing. The amount of income necessary to live modestly in Springfield, South Dakota (population 792), where the average home value in 2005 was $86,209, will scarcely sustain someone in Springfield, Massachusetts, 90 miles from Boston (population 152,082) with an average home value of $147,000. Thus, people on public assistance or fixed incomes who live in smaller cities and rural areas have greater spending power. Unfortunately, their place of residence is often one with fewer job opportunities and often, a monopsonistic labor market (single buyer of labor).[4]

Appropriate Time Length

Income is a flow variable. What length of time is appropriate for this flow to be measured? Weekly? Monthly? Annually? Over the person's lifetime? Professors who are paid on a 9-month contract may be considered temporarily impoverished if their income were measured weekly or monthly over the summer, but probably not with an annual income measure. Studies that estimate lifetime earnings show more equal income distributions. Actual lifetime incomes would be more accurate, of course, but that amount is unknown with certainty until after the person's funeral. If today's poor will one day be the rich, few people would sympathize with

---

[4] Bell, Rimmer, and Rimmer (1992); Piachaud (1993); Cox and Alm (1995); Wilkie (1996); Motley (1997); Renwick (1998); Sharpe and Abdel-Ghany (1999); Qizibash (2003).

their plight. We are therefore more concerned with long-term and intergenerational poverty rather than some temporary phenomenon.[5]

Income Mobility: A Predictable Stability

Income distribution in a single year would be less important if households could freely move up and down the income distribution. Income mobility does exist, however. Cox and Alm (1995) analyzed 14,000 United States tax returns between 1979 and 1988. They found that 86 percent of the households that were in the lowest quintile in 1979 climbed up one or more quintiles ten years later, and 15 percent rose to the top quintile. Similarly, 35 percent of those who were in the top quintile in 1979 fell down by one or more quintiles.

Maurin and Chambaz (1996) reported the same phenomenon in France. During the period from 1988 to 1993, between 45 and 50 percent of households considered poor in one year had not been poor the year before. One year later, about 6 percent of the poor households had a standard of living more than 25 percent above the poverty line. On the other hand, 33 percent of the households which were not poor fell to 25 percent below the poverty line.

Close to 67 percent of the Dutch households considered poor in 1986 were not poor two years later. Each year, more than 10 percent of the households changed their category of income. Deleeck et al. (1991) determined that more than 70 percent of the Belgian households considered poor in 1985 were not poor three years later. These changes in income categories reflect discontinuities in the professional life or family life of the households.

Cox and Alm (1995), Maurin and Chambaz (1996), Deleeck et al. (1992)

---

[5] Piachaud (1993); Cox and Alm (1995).

Measuring Income Inequality and Poverty

Income inequality can be measured in several ways. The most often-used graphical method depicts a Lorenz curve. The Lorenz curve measures the cumulative proportion (between 0 and 100% of the population) on the horizontal axis and a cumulative measure of income or wealth (0%–100%) on the vertical axis. To create an income distribution, the Bureau of the Census sorts households by income from lowest to highest. They then divide the households into equal-sized population groups, typically quintiles. The 20% of the population with the lowest income are in the lowest quintile; the 20% of the population with the highest income are in the top quintile.

Figure 18.2 shows three Lorenz curves. The 45° line shows an economy with perfect income equality. Ten percent of the population has 10% of the income, for example. Everyone in this economy has the same income. The second extreme case is the "backward L" which constitutes the base and the right axis of the diagram. This curve shows an almost total inequality. About 99.99% of the population has no income, while 0.01% have it all. Finally, the "middle" Lorenz curve shows a reality common to many regions. For example, in the United States, the lowest quintile of households had 3.4% of the total income; the two lowest quintiles, 12.2%; and the three lowest quintiles, 27.1% in 2002. Meanwhile, the lowest 80% of the

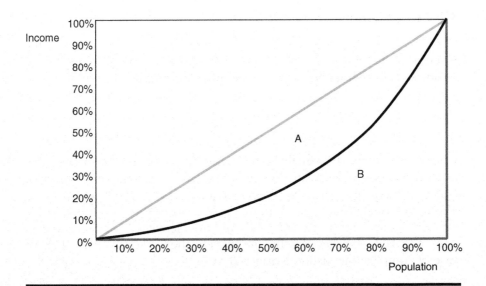

Figure 18.2 Lorenz curves.

households earned 50.3%, leaving 49.7% of the aggregate household income of the United States for the top quintile.[6]

What Caused the Shrinking Middle Class?

Burkhauser et al. (1996) studied the "shrinking" middle class in the United States during the 1980s. When we hear about a smaller middle class, we generally assume that the shrinkage is due to pauperization. However, these researchers determined that it is the inverse: the vanishing middle class ascended into the upper-income groups.

Having defined the middle class as those with incomes between two and five times the poverty line, the authors estimated that between 1970 and 1980, 92 percent of the lost middle class shifted to higher incomes, whereas only 8 percent fell into the lower income groups. The 8 percent comprised families where the household head was older than 62 years and families that depended on social assistance.

Burkhauser et al. (1996)

Gini Coefficients

The Gini coefficient is derived from the Lorenz curve, and it measures the extent to which the income distribution differs from the 45° line. A Gini coefficient for the middle Lorenz curve in Figure 18.2 is

$$G = \frac{A}{A + B},$$

where A is the area between the line of perfect equality and the Lorenz curve itself. B represents the area below the Lorenz curve but above the curve of complete inequality. The Gini coefficient takes on a value between 0 and 1. The more equal the income distribution, the closer is area A to 0 and the smaller is the Gini coefficient. The Gini coefficient=0 for the curve of perfect equality (because $A=0$). Alternatively, the Gini coefficient=1 in the case of complete inequality (because $B=0$).

---

[6] DeNavas-Walt, Cleveland, and Webster (2003).

Analyses that compare Gini coefficients tend to congratulate the region with the lowest coefficient. This implies that more equality is optimal. The optimal income distribution is a subject that goes back to the debates between Plato and Aristotle. Plato argued that because people should have equal status in society, nobody is worth more than another, and consequently, nobody should have more income or wealth. Aristotle, a rebellious student of Plato, insisted that if everyone were guaranteed the same income there would be no incentive for excellence.

The preference for greater income equality also implies a diminishing social marginal utility of income—that is, the fear that the financial betterment of a minority will be due to the detriment of the majority. However, Feldstein (1998) determined that the recent increase in higher incomes in the United States and other countries is accounted for by increased productivity, entrepreneurial success, longer workdays (highly paid professionals are now typically working 70 or more hours per week), and a vibrant stock market.

Each of these sources of higher incomes is Pareto optimal because it does not reduce incomes of others. The problem of a widening income distribution is thus not solved by punishing the wealthy, but by helping the poor.[7]

Asset Rich but Money Poor

Lerman and Mikesell (1988) asked what would happen to the poverty statistics if income included the annualized value of the net wealth of individuals. Wealth is not included as income, even though greater wealth implies a greater command over resources. The correlation between income and wealth is quite low, and wealth is much more unequally distributed than income. The Gini coefficient for American families in 1983 was 0.42 for income and 0.74 for net wealth.

The authors compared data from the *1983 Survey of Consumer Finances (SCF)* to the official poverty line for 1982 to obtain each family's poverty threshold according to its size and number of children. Of the 3509 families studied, they found that 87 percent would remain in poverty had the census used the wealth-adjusted income. The remaining (13 percent) of the families had enough assets that they would not be considered poor. The poor defined by the official income measure have different

---

[7] Feldstein (1998).

characteristics from those who are poor after accounting for their wealth. These 13 percent includes many farmers, retired persons, those who are ill, and residents of suburbs and periurban areas of large cities.

Lerman and Mikesell (1988)

How Do We Set Poverty Lines?

"What income level constitutes poverty?" The answer to this question varies from one region to another. Normative judgments are inherent in all measures of poverty, especially the choice of a poverty line. Thus setting these lines is consistently subject to perpetual debate. There are two approaches to establishing a poverty line: absolute measures and relative measures.

An ***absolute measure*** establishes that one is poor if the income is insufficient to cover the most elementary survival needs. This means that it is necessary to define "survival need," which is not easy, but this approach allows one to compare the extent of poverty over time or space. The definition of survival need leads to an uncertainty of knowing the exact income that separates the poor from those who are not poor. This approach implies that it makes sense to refer to an exact cutoff point that will be applicable everywhere; that being poor is not a matter of degree, but rather an answer to a true–false question.

Relative poverty measures, on the other hand, arbitrarily define the lowest percentage of the income distribution or of median income as the poverty line. This concept considers that a person's needs are relative to what others in their society have: a "need" in a wealthy region may be an extravagance in a low-income area.

Setting the Absolute Poverty Line

Setting an absolute poverty line requires the determination of what is absolutely necessary for survival. The United States determined the absolute minimum for survival in the mid 1960s using analyses from the United States Department of Agriculture (USDA). Economists within the USDA estimated the degree of thermal protection of clothing to ward off hypothermia. They also calculated the minimum cost of an adequately nutritious diet for the entire country, regardless of any local cost of living. At first, they defined "adequate nutrition" only in terms of the caloric content. As time went on, other vitamins, minerals, and proteins were added.

In 1965, Molly Orshansky of the Social Security Administration estimated the cost of a minimal diet adjusted for household composition based on the 1955 USDA Food Survey. She used this cost as a benchmark in her study of poverty, but had not any intention for this calculation to be used in an official capacity. Her estimate, nevertheless, became the basis for the official poverty line. The cost of the minimal diet was multiplied by three to account for all other expenses (rent, clothing, medical care, etc.), because expenditure surveys in the mid 1960s showed that poor people spent one-third of their incomes on food.

Absolute poverty lines present many problems:

1. There is no "one-size-fits-all" when it comes to minimum required caloric intake. The minimal amount of nutrition varies with body weights, metabolic rates, age, and physical activity.
2. The multiplier of three is still used over 40 years later even though surveys show that individuals in poverty are spending lower proportions of their incomes on food. Thus, the poverty cutoff is too low.
3. Threshold income levels are periodically adjusted for inflation, but components of these threshold levels have not changed since 1965.

It's All in the Definition

The United Kingdom has no official poverty line. The number of individuals whose income is less than half the average income is the most often cited statistic. This relative measure of poverty depends on the prosperity of the entire society, rather than on the sum of money needed to purchase a fixed market basket of goods. This market basket is measured before housing costs (BHC) and after housing costs (AHC). The deduction of housing costs (rent, mortgage payments, etc.) from income provides a figure that corrects for one of the most important regional differences in costs of living. For a household, it is equivalent to discretionary income. The AHC measure of income is more unequally distributed than the BHC.

How does using the relative or the absolute definition change the poverty trend in the United Kingdom? By the BHC measure, Burgess and Propper (1999) estimated that 10 percent of the population during the 1960s was poor in the United Kingdom. By 1977, that proportion fell to 6 percent, only to climb to over 20 percent in the early 1990s, and to fall back to 18 percent by 1995. However, if the United Kingdom had followed the fixed standard, poor households are those whose income is half of the average income for the country (equalized income in 1979 adjusted for inflation), absolute poverty would have fallen during the 1960s and 1970s. In 1961, almost 24 percent of the population was poor, falling to 8 percent in 1979. By 1994–1995, the number of people in absolute poverty in the United Kingdom fell to 5 percent using an absolute standard.

Burgess and Propper (1999)

A Century of Change in Dietary Assessment Methods

In 1899, Roundtree (1901) used nutritional studies from York, United Kingdom, that tried to quantify the dietary requirements for a physically active individual. He then calculated the lowest possible cost of an adequate diet that was simple but varied. The diet—which included a large proportion of bread, porridge, dumplings, and drippings—was just as appetizing then as it is today. But because it was based on a professional study about nutritional adequacy, it was considered "scientific."

McFarlane and Tiffin (2003) used linear programming to determine the minimum cost in 1995 of adequate nutrition that would include locally available products in the 14 countries studied. They calculated that an adequate diet composed of locally preferred foods would cost between $.10 and $.20 per capita per day almost anywhere in the world. For the United States and Canada, such a diet would consist of cereal, milk, and fruit—specifically, oranges in the United States; in the United Kingdom, cereal, sugar, milk, and potatoes; and India's minimum cost diet would entail cereal, sugar, milk, fruit, and beans.

Rowntree (1901), McFarlane and Tiffin (2003)

As we can imagine, the cost of such a minimum diet is neither simple, straightforward to implement, nor credible. Starches have been a staple of poor diets for centuries, but prices for potatoes varies depending on whether one needs to peel, wash, and prepare them or if they only need 2 min. in the microwave. Which price should we use? Besides, because the poverty line is a national cutoff, do we use the price of raw potatoes from a rural market or an urban supermarket? In summer, fall, winter, or spring? Finally, because two could live almost as cheaply as one, and small children are even cheaper, many researchers tried to determine an appropriate ***equivalence scale*** or the incremental cost of maintaining various sizes of income units. Table 18.1 is a table showing the equivalence scale used in the United States.[8]

Equivalence Scales

Most researchers agree that income figures must be adjusted for the size of the household or family. If we treat all members equally and allow the same amount of income for each person we will generate a much higher standard of living for larger households than for smaller households. Other researchers think that having a child is a matter of choice, and that people increase their utilities when they have children. A system that rewards poor people by giving them a monthly allocation for each child unjustly treats the households who decided to acquire a certain financial stability before starting their families.

Think About It...

Where do you fit in with respect to Table 18.1? How does your current household compare with that of your family?

Australian Poverty Line

Any measure of poverty is necessarily subjective, imperfect, and subject to continuing debate. The Commission of Inquiry into Poverty (1975) adopted the Henderson Poverty Line, named after Ronald

---

[8] Sharpe and Abdel-Ghany (1999).

Henderson, a pioneer of Australia's research on poverty in the 1960s. Henderson estimated poverty in Melbourne using a poverty line for a reference family of two adults and two-children. He set the poverty threshold based on an income equal to the value of the basic wage plus a family allowance.

The Henderson Poverty Line is a measure of per capita disposable household income adjusted for inflation and updated to reflect rising standards of living. The updates have raised it for a couple with two children from AUS$3,260.40 in 1973 to AUS$31,106.92 in 2005, an 854 percent increase. These sums are equivalent to $2,195.56 and $23,717.47 in USD, respectively. Some say that this threshold is too generous and likely to encourage welfare dependency. Others say that it is not high enough to allow people to live decently. In the United States, for a couple with two children, the poverty line was $4,540 in 1973 and $19,350 in 2005, an increase of 326 percent.

Fisher (1992), Hughes (2001), Dalaker (2001),
Brotherhood of St. Laurence (2005)

Defining "Relative Need"

For many, defining the poverty line as being three times the value of a minimum cost diet is a coldhearted method of determining the extent to which the less fortunate need assistance. Even Adam Smith (1776) insisted that people's needs are determined by the society in which they live. It is possible to define "relative need" in two ways. A first method is easy for it arbitrarily defines some proportion (say 60%) of median income as the poverty line.

A second method is based on a series of questions of which the responses determine society's concept of the term "need." Researchers associated with the University of Leidan (Belgium) asked two specific questions. This method includes variations in living costs, as well as differences in ordinary lifestyles to influence the estimated cutoff line.

The Minimum Income Question is as follows:

"What do you consider as an absolute minimum net income for a household such as yours? We should like to know an income amount below which you would not be able to make ends meet."

Table 18.1 Poverty Thresholds for 2005 by Size of Family and Number of Related Children Under 18 Years

Size of Family Unit		Related Children Under 18 Years							
	None	*One*	*Two*	*Three*	*Four*	*Five*	*Six*	*Seven*	*Eight or more*
One person (unrelated individual)									
Under 65 years	10,160								
65 years and older	9,367								
Two persons									
Householder under 65 years	13,078	13,461							
Householder 65 years and older	11,805	13,410							
Three persons	15,277	15,720	15,735						
Four persons	20,144	20,474	19,806	19,874					
Five persons	24,293	24,646	23,891	23,307	22,951				
Six persons	27,941	28,052	27,474	26,920	26,096	25,608			
Seven persons	32,150	32,350	31,658	31,176	30,277	29,229	28,079		
Eight persons	35,957	36,274	35,621	35,049	34,237	33,207	32,135	31,862	
Nine persons or more	43,254	43,463	42,885	42,400	41,603	40,507	39,515	39,270	37,757

Source: From United States Census Bureau. http://www.census.gov/hhes/www/poverty/threshld.html (Date accessed on November 26, 2006).

About _____ per week/month/year.

Please underline the length of time you refer to.

A similar Income Evaluation Question is worded:

In the circumstances of your household, which monthly disposable income would you regard as

Very bad   _____
Bad   _____
Insufficient _____
Sufficient   _____
Good   _____
Very good   _____

Municipalities could thus compare the average of the Minimum Income Question with the averages for each level of the Income Evaluation Question to determine a poverty threshold as it is conceived locally.[9]

Source: Questions originally printed in Flik, R. J., and B. M. S. van Praag. 1991. Subjective poverty line definitions. *De Economist* 139 (3): Income evaluation question, page 314, and Minimum Income Question, page 320. Reprinted with the kind permission of Springer Science and Business Media.

Think About It…

Given your answers to the Minimum Income Question and the Income Evaluation Question, are you in poverty?

Compare your poverty status (if any) here with your status based on the poverty thresholds in Table 18.1.

In 1995, the United Nations included in the definition of poverty, not only income, but also access to social services. In reaction to this definition, Gordon et al. (2000) and Pantazis, Gordon, and Levitas (2006) from the University of Bristol administered a national survey using an approach that conformed to the United Nation's definition. For them to be poor is to lack three (or more) unaffordable necessities. "Necessities" are goods that 50% of

---

[9] Flik and van Praag (1991); Van den Bösch (1996, 2001).

the population considered affordable and vital for adults. According to this method, 14% of the British households were living in poverty in 1963. However in 1999, 26% fit this description, even though only 17% live in "absolute poverty" as defined by the United Nations.

Table 18.2 shows that the goods considered necessary by at least 50% of the population ranged from everyone having their own bed and bedding to everyone having an outfit to wear for social occasions. Owning a car was not considered a necessity. The same survey administered in North America will rank items differently; similarly, rural areas would provide a different ranking than urban areas.

But from this, how do we estimate a consistent cost of major repairs such as a damp-free home and replacing or repairing broken electrical goods? One number to summarize the cost of cooking two meals a day for children would be different for babies than if the children were teenagers.

A relative poverty line is problematic. It does not provide statistics to measure the progress in fighting poverty that are comparable from one year to another or from one region to another. Even if each resident in a jurisdiction were "awarded" $100 million in addition to their existing income, the region will still have a portion of the population with incomes in the lowest 20% of the distribution. This leads to a paradox: poverty will always exist unless the region's Gini coefficient is 0 and everyone receives identical incomes.[10]

Think About It…

Take the survey in Table 18.2. By this method, would you be "poor?" (Do you lack three or more of the items that 50 percent or more of the survey respondents feel are necessities?)

What other goods would you consider necessary? What "necessities" could you easily do without? Is there a "necessity" relative to the procurement of employment, education, or training that the survey omitted or that at least 50 percent of those surveyed did not think was vital?

---

[10] Levernier, Partridge, and Rickman (1998); Martin and Taylor (2003).

Table 18.2 Percentage of Respondents Perceiving Adult Item/Activity as Necessary

	Items Considered Necessary
Beds and bedding for everyone	95
Heating to warm living areas of the home	94
Damp-free home	93
Visiting friends or family in hospital	92
Two meals a day	91
Medicines prescribed by doctor	90
Refrigerator	89
Fresh fruit and vegetables daily	86
Warm, waterproof coat	85
Replace or repair broken electrical goods	85
Visits to friends or family	84
Celebrations on special occasions such as Christmas	83
Money to keep home in a decent state of decoration	82
Visits to school, for example, sports day	81
Attending weddings, funerals	80
Meat, fish, or vegetarian equivalent every other day	79
Insurance of contents of dwelling	79
Hobby or leisure activity	78
Washing machine	76
Collect children from school	75
Telephone	71
Appropriate clothes for job interviews	69
Deep freezer/fridge freezer	68
Carpets in living rooms and bedrooms	67
Regular savings of $18 for rainy days or retirement	66
Two pairs of all-weather shoes	64
Friends or family round for a meal	64
A small amount of money to spend on self weekly not on family	59
Television	56
Roast beef, pork, or lamb/vegetarian equivalent once a week	56
Presents for friends/family once a year	56
A vacation away from home once a year not with relatives	55
Replace worn-out furniture	54
Dictionary	53

(continued)

Table 18.2   (Continued)

	Items Considered Necessary
An outfit for social occasions	51
New, not secondhand, clothes	48
Attending place of worship	42
Car	38
Coach/train fares to visit friends/family quarterly	38
An evening out once a fortnight (every 2 weeks)	37
Dressing gown	34
Having a daily newspaper	30
A meal in a restaurant/pub monthly	26
Microwave oven	23
Tumble dryer	20
Going to the pub once a fortnight (every 2 weeks)	20
Video cassette recorder	19
Holidays abroad once a year	19
CD player	12
Home computer	11
Dishwasher	7
Mobile phone	7
Access to the Internet	6
Satellite television	5

Source: From Pantazis, Gordon, and Levitas (2006); Table 4.1. with permission.

Poverty Indices

Poverty indices measure the distribution of income among income units in an area. For most uses, the ideal poverty index must have two characteristics. First, it must allow a comparison of the progress in the fight against poverty over time or over space. Second, if all incomes changed in the same proportion (perhaps to adjust by a regional price index), the regional cost of living index should not be affected.

The **head count** is the most obvious measure of poverty. It represents the proportion of people living below the poverty line. Therefore, with this statistic, one can measure changes over time. The head count increases or decreases as incomes fall below or rise above the poverty line. However, this measure does not indicate the **depth of poverty**. "Depth" measures the additional income necessary to boost an income unit up to the poverty line. For example, assume that the poverty line is set at $100 per week. The head count will not tell us if a family earns $1 less than the poverty line, or if its income is $90 below the poverty line. If the region's goal is to improve the head count, the most cost-effective remedy would be to give to the least poor just enough money to pull them just above the line. It would not be cost-effective to assist the most destitute because doing so would not decrease the poverty head count by as large a figure.[11]

In 2005, an estimated 12.7% of the population of the United States was below the official poverty level, up from 11.7% in 2001. The official poverty rate has declined steadily from a high of 15.1% in 1993 to 11.3% in 2000, but it has increased steadily since then.

The depth of poverty is most often measured by the poverty gap. The **poverty gap** is the aggregation of individual differences between each one's income and the respective poverty line. The aggregation represents the exact amount of income needed to boost every poor family just up to the poverty line and not a penny more. In 1999, the poverty gap in the United States was $65 billion. This gap was the same as it was in 1995 despite a drop of 3.4 million poor people between these same years. The decline in the number of low-income people was offset by an increase in the depth of poverty among those who remained poor. The poverty gap does not reflect the severity of the poverty problem in terms of the number of victims. Say that the annual poverty line is $21,000. An $80 billion poverty gap could result if either 80 billion people had incomes equal to $20,999, or if 40 million people had incomes equal to $1000.[12]

Two other common measures of depth of poverty are the **welfare ratio**, a ratio of a family's income to its poverty threshold, and the **income deficit (surplus)**, which tells how many dollars a family or household's income is below (above) its poverty threshold. These figures illustrate how the low-income population varies by level of poverty.

Deprivation indices measure the size a locality's disadvantage relative to that of some benchmark (county, state, or nation) that includes that locality. There is no standard method for measuring deprivation. Fieldhouse and Tye (1996), for instance, measure deprivation for cities in Britain by a survey composed of the following three groups of questions. The authors assigned a value of 1 to persons who responded affirmatively to one of the questions in the group. (The maximum figure assigned to any person is the value 9.) Group 1:

1. Lacking access to bath or shower.
2. Lacking access to an inside toilet.
3. Living in non-self-contained accommodations.

---

[11] Johnston, McKinney, and Stark (1996).

[12] Piachaud (1993); Davidson, Khan, and Rao (2000); Greenstein, Primus, and Kayatin (2000); Tentschert, Till, and Redl (2000).

Group 2:

1. Lack of access to car.
2. Living in a household where no person is in paid work.
3. Living in a rented accommodation.
4. Living in a house with no central heating.

Group 3:

1. Living in a household with more than one person per room (measures overcrowding).
2. Being unemployed, or for economically inactive persons and children, being in a family whose head is unemployed.

Source: Permission granted from *Environment and Planning A*, 1996, 28, 237–259, Pion Limited, London.

The authors counted the number of people who fall into one group, two groups, and in all three groups to determine the severity of individual deprivation. In Great Britain, 46.2% were in no group, 45.2% were in one group, 8.3% in two groups, and 0.3% were in all three groups. They calculated locality-specific deprivation indices by using aggregate data for the same nine characteristics. They then compared these measures to the average of each individual surveyed in the same region. They determined that deprived people lived everywhere in the country. A large proportion is urban, but that does not mean that the majority of urban dwellers are deprived. Similarly, whites have the lowest deprivation rate, but constitute the majority of poor people.

Think About It...

Calculate Fieldhouse and Tye's deprivation index for your class.

1. What proportion is not deprived? What proportion is deprived based on one group? Two groups? All three groups?

2. Take the average score (between 1 and 9) of the class based on the responses to the nine questions.

3. Create a z-score to evaluate the percentage of each category of poor and add up the percentages.

4. Divide the class into different categories based on major or place of residence (residence halls, on or

off campus, etc.) Are there differences in the deprivation distribution based on these criteria?

Poverty Spreads Like Cancer in East Montreal

Kitchen (2001) proposed a model of urban deprivation for East Montreal, Quebec, using data from the 1986, 1991, and 1996 Canadian Censuses: male and female unemployment rates; male, female, and youth labor force participation rates; percentage of lone female parent families; percentage of the population with less than a ninth grade education, or with some high school but no diploma; percentage of housing built before 1946; the average value of dwellings; the percentage of families with incomes less than "LICO"; and the percentages of males and females with incomes less than CAN$10,000.

Canada has no official poverty level, but most Canadian researchers use the low-income cut-off (LICO) developed by Statistics Canada. The LICO counts the number of families or individuals who spend 54.7 percent or more of their pretax income on food, clothing, or shelter as an estimate of the number of people in "strained circumstances."

Compared with other large Canadian urban areas, Montreal has one of the highest rates of unemployment and one of the lowest median family incomes. One-third of these families have income less than the LICO and live in the city's most disadvantaged neighborhoods. Thousands of jobs disappeared from the closing of its canneries, shoe factories, rail yards and shipyards in the 1990s. Kitchen found that deprivation spread through much of the central city and into the first-tier suburbs. The most affected areas are those that lost the most jobs and suffered out-migration.

Kitchen (2001), Ross, Shillington,
and Lochhead (1994)

Who Are the Poor?

So far we have described in detail various methods used to understand the income distributions and the degree of regional poverty problem. Understanding poverty involves taking account of the linkages between the labor market, household formation, and the current welfare system. This section will put a face on the poverty problem and provides a framework with which to evaluate regional and urban policies.

Child Poverty

The poverty rate for children under 18 in the United States increased from 16.7% in 2002 to 17.8% in 2004. Because children are viewed as innocent victims, child poverty raises emotions that poverty among adults does not. This is especially true if the exposure to poverty at a young age creates insurmountable barriers and predestines yet another generation to a life of deprivation.

Many studies have tried to determine the extent of lifetime damage created by child poverty. The consensus is in the long-run, childhood poverty affects the health and educational attainment. The economic success of adults is more closely related to their parents' education and family structure than family income. Income itself has no direct effect on a child's educational achievement as long as there is sufficient cognitive stimulation in the home. Still, the physical environment at home (structural defects such as a leaking roof, signs of rats, uncovered wires, and flakes of lead paint) combine with a crime-ridden neighborhood to create a setting that increases the probability of serious illness (physical or mental) that is not conducive to scholarship.[13]

Economic Development as Remedy Against Child Poverty

According to Friedman and Lichter (1998), the direct causes of child poverty are the chances that parents have to obtain paid employment and the amount of their salaries if they work. Thus, successful economic development programs (e.g., national, regional, statewide, or urban) are the remedy of choice. These researchers also determined that local differences in industrial composition account for the greatest amount of differentiation in child poverty across regions.

---

[13] Barham et al. (1995); Friedman and Lichter (1998); Blau (1999); Currie and Yelowitz (2000); Guo and Harris (2000); Kornberger, Fast, and Williamson (2001); Clark-Kauffman, Duncan, and Morris (2003); Jackson (2003); Oreopoulos (2003).

The Fight Against Child Poverty in Europe and in the United States

Bergmann (1997) asked why the child poverty rate is only 6 percent in France, while in the U.S. it soars to 22 percent. Both countries have similar proportions of births to single women and the same proportions of ethnic minorities. She determined that the differences are linked to dissimilarities in social programs for families with children. The French program, like those in other Western European countries, includes government provision of child care, health insurance, and cash support with no means testing. The goal is to encourage married couples to have big families, for children are the future of the nation. These programs are widely popular: both low- and middle-income families benefit. On the other hand, the goal of the U.S. program is to keep jobless families from sheer destitution, but there is a social stigma attached to families that take advantage of it.

Child rearing payments and parental or paternity leaves were enacted in France and Germany over 100 years ago. Today, many European countries provide child rearing payments until the child is three years old. Finland pays 80 percent of prior earnings for 105 days, for instance. The leaves are paid for by government programs rather than by the employer.

In France, the government provides free, high-quality public nursery schools (*écoles maternelles*) for all children between ages 3 and 6, and to about one-third of children between ages 2 and 3. Parents can arrange for before- and after-hours care for low fees. In Germany, the ministry of education offers universal care for all children aged 3–6 years, but the parents are required to pay between 16 and 20 percent of the costs. Eighty-five percent of the children participate. The teachers must have 3–4 years of postsecondary education.

The Head Start programs and public kindergartens in the United States concentrate on child development of low-income children, but they are half-day programs of inconsistent quality, and thus provide little help for working parents. However, Head Start programs have never been funded sufficiently to serve all eligible children or to offer programs of constant quality.

Bergmann (1997), Witte and Trowbridge (2004)

Family Structure

Empirically, most of the regional differences in poverty are explained by lone mothers, large families, young children, and a large proportion of nonwhites. Lone-parent families have the highest probability of being poor, especially if the mother is head-of-house. Divorce creates poverty for both men and women, but particularly for women because they traditionally have custody of the children.

The number of children in a family can cause poverty not only for the present generation but also for the next. Children from large families accumulate less wealth than do those from small families, all else equal. Siblings divide both the financial and the nonfinancial resources of a family, thus causing a reduction in income transfers and an environment that is less conducive to their scholarly success. Besides, large families do not have the time and energy to help with homework or to provide positive reinforcement for each child. In addition, they have fewer resources available for cognitive stimulation (books, computers, dance and music lessons, and foreign travel) than do families with fewer children.

In general, the more siblings one has, the lower the likelihood that each will receive a trust account or inheritance. Larger families have smaller savings portfolios themselves, so children have fewer opportunities to learn about the various investment avenues (banking services or stock markets), all else equal. Families that save, teach children the dangers of instant gratification. As a result, their children have sufficient financial transfers to cover their own college costs, purchase of automobiles, or the down payment on a home, creating even greater financial stability when they enter the labor market.[14]

As Ye Sweep so Shall Ye Weep

Dunifon, Duncan, and Brooks-Gunn (2001) noted that cognitive ability only accounts for about 20 percent of

---

[14] Becker and Murphy (1988); Kumazawa and Seeborg (1996); Albelda (1999); Chuang and Lee (2003); Keister (2003).

the variation in earnings. Parents' cognitive ability adds another 20 percent to the children's success. Noncognitive factors must account for the remaining 60 percent of the variation in adult earnings. What noncognitive factors are important? Jencks (1979) demonstrated that a person's industriousness, perseverance, and leadership qualities, as well as measures of self-esteem, increase subsequent earnings and occupational status.

Orderly surroundings mirror self-esteem. Cleanliness requires organizational skills, perseverance, industriousness, and if the dwelling is shared with others, leadership skills. Clean homes reflect a desire to maintain and create a sense of order. This desire for order may also extend to working and parenting. Organizational skills necessary for a well-functioning, organized home are prized in the labor market. Thus, children raised in organized households may be more successful in school and later in the adult world.

The Panel Study of Income Dynamics is a longitudinal data base that tracks the same individuals and families since 1968. Along with a great many other questions, interviewers need to assess the cleanliness of the respondent's dwelling at the time of the survey. After analyzing data from 1968 to 1995, Dunifon, Duncan, and Brooks-Gunn concluded that people who grew up in clean households had higher earnings 25 years later.

Dunifon, Duncan, and Brooks-Gunn (2001)

Does Cohabitation Contribute to Child Poverty?

By 1995, 49 percent of women in the United States ages 30–34 had cohabited at some time in their lives, and 53 percent had lived with partners before their first marriage. In the early 1990s, 41 percent of nonmarital births (12 percent of all births) occurred to cohabiting couples. Officially, cohabiting partners in the United States are considered separate family units. Unlike in some European countries, an unmarried parent who lives in a consensual union is counted by the United States Census Bureau as a single-parent family. The cohabitant is treated as a separate, unrelated unit.

Carlson and Danziger (1999) analyzed PUMS (Public Use Micro Sample) data from the 1990 United States Census of Population to calculate what poverty rates would be if cohabitants were treated as if they were married couples. The authors found that the official definition of "family" in this manner overstates the extent of poverty among all children by only about 3 percent. The impact is negligible because only 3.2 percent of all children live in cohabiting unions. In addition, many families would remain poor despite this change in measurement procedure because many cohabitants have little or no earnings. The propensity to cohabit is highest among high school dropouts, those who did not grow up in a nuclear family, and those whose parents depended on welfare. In conclusion, it seems that poverty contributes to cohabitation more than cohabitation contributes to poverty.

Carlson and Danziger (1999)

Teenage Pregnancy

Teenage pregnancy is almost a guarantee that a young woman and her child will fall into multigenerational poverty. Behaviors and choices that lead to pregnancy for younger teens are different from those for older teens. Family stability and those with higher incomes are the best defense against younger teen pregnancies. But for the older teens, the decision to have children is not necessarily irrational, even though, in general, teens tend to have a "high time preference for the present" (that is, they myopically want immediate gratification). The 18–19 years old are approaching high school graduation if they have not already graduated. Those who are in high school and earning good grades are less likely to get pregnant or become mothers. Many unmarried teens decide to have babies after taking account of the prevailing economic conditions and the local job market.

For the teen mothers, the long-term opportunity costs include chronic unemployment, low-paying jobs and maybe a lack of a high school diploma, but the older teens may already perceive that this is their fate, pregnant or not. If motherhood is a handicap for the young women and their children, local policies that reduce early childbearing will benefit the future income stream of these young families. However, if teen parents are just "different" from the others (that is, they belong to a social underclass, engage in risky behavior, are more rebellious), poor outcomes will surface regardless of the local policies.

Studies from the United Kingdom and the United States have confirmed that teenage childbearing decreases the probability of finishing high school by as much as 24%. Having a reduced human capital investment, the young mothers will work 3 years less on average, and earn from 5 to 22% less; teenage motherhood limits their professional development and increases the risk of transmitting poverty to the next generation. Thus, an efficient intervention rests on three priorities: teen mothers should (1) finish high school, (2) have access to low-cost child care, and (3) learn to balance work and family.[15]

Feminization of Poverty

People are poor because they have limited earnings capabilities. Family earnings depend on potential hours worked. These hours depend on the family structure: the number and gender of adults, whether or not children are present, and the age and gender of the head of household. Data from the United States and eight other industrialized countries confirm, all else equal, this international observation: families where a single-mother is head of the household have lower earnings potentials. Although the term "feminization of poverty" is the term applied to this situation, Albelda (1999) prefers the term "pauperization of motherhood," because women without children have a longer professional life and higher incomes.

For all women, the decision to work depends on the needs of the family. If they decide to stop working to take care of their families, their skill levels decrease and their confidence diminishes to the point where their salary can depreciate from 2.6 to 26.5%. The ability to enter the labor market is strongly linked to finding dependable child care, the costs of which can be as much as 25% of the earnings of single mothers working at minimum wage. If we add the necessity to find a means of transportation for commutes between daycare, work and home, many single mothers have strong incentives to avoid reentering the labor market if possible.[16]

---

[15] Ounce of prevention fund (1987); Kumazawa and Seeborg (1996); Tomal (1999); Chevalier and Viitanen (2003); Levine and Painter (2003).

[16] Phipps, Burton, and Lethbridge (2001).

Racial Differences

African–Americans and Hispanics have, on average, lower wages compared to Caucasians. In 2001, the median household income in the United States was $42,228. White, non–Hispanic households enjoyed a median income of $46,305; Hispanic households, $33,565; and black households $29,470. Carneiro, Heckman, and Masterov (2005) analyzed data from the National Longitudinal Survey of Youth 1979–2000 and determined that except for black males, most of the variations in wages are due to ability differences rather than discrimination. Ability differences include a lack of cognitive skills (low IQ scores) and noncognitive skills (persistence, self-discipline, reliability).

Deficits in cognitive and noncognitive skills among minority children are detectible early and widen over time. Differences in school and neighborhood quality as well as peer effects may account for some gap but not all. Hispanic children as well as African–American children start with cognitive and noncognitive deficits. They grow up in similar neighborhoods and attend similar schools. However, by the time they reach adulthood, Hispanics average higher test scores than blacks. The wage difference between whites and Hispanics with the same IQ is nonexistent but they are negative and statistically significant between Hispanics and blacks. One factor influencing wage differences could be differences in occupational choice affected by labor market discrimination.[17]

Discrimination

A person could do everything "right": come from a good family with educated parents who supplied abundant cognitive stimulation, graduate from a good school, and in spite of all that, earn a lower income because of discrimination. Discrimination exists if a person receives lower wages than others who have the same experience, education, and training. Several types of discrimination exist: employer discrimination, employee discrimination, customer discrimination, and statistical discrimination.[18]

Less Discrimination in Korean Urban Labor Markets

According to Kim (1987), urban demographic characteristics and employment conditions explain why

---

[17] Carneiro, Heckman, and Masterov (2005).
[18] Carlstrom and Rollow (1998).

unemployment and labor force participation rates vary by city size. Discrimination against women is less pervasive in larger cities than in smaller ones. The larger labor market means more vacancies in different occupations and industries, less sexual prejudice, and more support facilities such as daycare.

Kim (1987)

Employer Discrimination

Becker's (1957) analysis of the economics of discrimination affirms that, everything else equal, a competitive market structure eliminates any wage differences from discrimination because the firm has no control over price. Firms that do discriminate must have some market power, and they are willing to forgo some profits to exercise their "taste for discrimination." In urban areas with many different employment opportunities (that is, perfectly competitive labor markets), discrimination is less than in rural areas where labor markets are characterized by monopsony (single buyer of labor). See Chapter 10.

The reason can be explained using Figure 18.3. Panel A shows the demand and supply for an occupation (auto mechanics). To the extent that an unwritten social law excludes a "Group B" from working at this occupation that is traditionally held by "Group A," the wage for auto mechanics is kept artificially high because of the decreased supply (Panel A). If "Group B" is excluded from these higher paying jobs, they are forced into lower paying occupations (Panel B). The decreased demand (due to lower marginal revenue product of the "Group B") and increased supply for

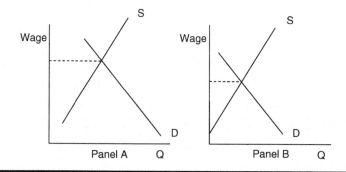

Figure 18.3 Employer discrimination.

nondiscriminatory jobs results in lower wages and lower prices paid by the nondiscriminatory consumer.

A mechanics shop that is willing to hire members of "Group B" at a wage slightly higher than that in Panel B, can repair cars at a lower cost than those who are paying the high wage required by "Group A." A perfectly competitive market for auto mechanics will be in equilibrium when both groups of auto mechanics receive the same wage. This solution assumes that the employers discriminate. The same solution may not work if employees or customers are at fault.

Employee Discrimination

Employee discrimination occurs when employees perceive that a certain group of potential workers are incompetent. For example, if a woman firefighter lacks the upper-body strength to do the job, not hiring her is not being discriminatory. However, if the male firefighters refuse to work with any woman, regardless of her strength, the employer may feel forced to no longer consider the applications of women due to employee discrimination.

Mines: Not Just for Men Anymore

In the 1970s, women took jobs at the Taconite mines in northern Minnesota because they were by far the best paying jobs in the area. The male miners tried to drive them out—making them feel guilty for taking a job away from a male who had a family to feed, and submitting them to constant sexual harassment, for instance. The women who stayed never had a chance at promotion for fear the male workers would not work under a woman supervisor. The women sued the mine and won. Their experiences are portrayed in the 2005 movie *North Country*.

Hemphill (2005)

Consumer Discrimination

Customer discrimination exists when a firm's customers refuse to be served from a certain type of employee. For example, few women work in hardware stores or auto parts stores. Fewer are auto mechanics. Because mechanics and electronics are traditionally male occupations, many customers prefer to deal with a male rather than a female. This reaction diminishes the productivity of the female, but reinforces the marginal revenue product of her male counterpart. Establishments that choose to cater to the "discriminatory" customers do so at higher prices.[19]

Statistical Discrimination

Not all discrimination is based on hatred, ignorance, fear, or prejudice. Employers invest in training programs, not only to advance their skills, but also to strengthen the culture of the company. They hire people to perform specific tasks, and when the people cannot perform the tasks adequately the team as well as the entire company suffers. The goal of an employer is to find the best, most reliable person for the job.

Gender and race are easy screening devices. For example, women between ages 15 and 44 years probably want to have children. Female employees with children, especially single mothers, have higher absentee rates because sick children cannot go to daycare. Their assignments may suffer. Mothers are less flexible than other employees. Because the rate of return for the training is lower for women with children, it would seem more profitable for a firm to hire a less-qualified, but more dependable and flexible male.

Firms that are willing to "take a chance on" the female employee may be willing to do so only if her salary is lower than that of a corresponding male. Although it might seem prudent for firms to judge people by these signals, Title VII of the Civil Rights Act of 1964 makes it illegal in the United States, to compensate, limit, segregate, or in other ways classify employees because of statistical discrimination.[20]

Urban Underclass

Wilson (1987) popularized the theory of the underclass, which asserts that some people are poor because they choose a way of life that keeps them poor. This dysfunctional behavior is passed from one generation to another. It includes not only voluntary joblessness, but also criminal behavior and welfare dependency. Coming from single-parent families, the underclass live isolated from the rest of society and they have weak labor force participation. The spatial isolation occurs because of the out-migration of middle-class role models leaving the "hard core" poor segregated together.

---

[19] Crofton (2003).

[20] Haagsma (1993); Jacobsen (1993).

Wilson argued that global economic pressures reduced blue-collar production jobs and replaced them with high-technology service jobs. Because African–Americans disproportionately occupied production jobs, the loss of these well-paying jobs produced many persistently unemployed people who will not take the low-wage jobs for which they qualify, leading to spatial mismatch (Chapter 10). The next generation will be the underclass.

However, the very existence of an underclass is controversial. How do we define or measure it, or even how do we explain why it mainly pertains to African–American males? Massey and Denton (1993) provided the strongest statistical challenge to Wilson's hypothesis when they concluded that racial discrimination in the housing market was the most important factor isolating the African–American poor in urban areas.

Sánchez-Jankowski (1999) could not support the hypothesis that an underclass, as Wilson described it, even exists. He conducted an ethnographic study (popular in sociology literature) of low-income communities in New York, Los Angeles, and Detroit between July 1989 and May 1995. At the start of his research, at least 20% of residents in each neighborhood were below the poverty line, but significant numbers of working-class and middle-income people lived in these areas also. Over the period of study, the proportion of low income families increased in all three areas to well over 40% as the higher-income groups moved out.

Sánchez-Jankowski found that labor market discrimination, housing market discrimination, and internal community dynamics are all important in segregating low-income African–Americans. It was the out-migration of workers, not of middle-income households that decreased socioeconomic mobility. Workers provided information about jobs. They financially supported individuals in distress and were the basis of a secure neighborhood. There was no sense of hopelessness even as isolation increased, but the new strategies for attaining the good life changed: manual labor was replaced by a combination of secondary labor markets and an illicit underground economy.[21]

Northern Ireland's Catholic Underclass

Leonard (1998) confirmed the hypothesis that Catholics represent an underclass in West Belfast (Northern Ireland). King James I established Belfast in 1613 so

---

[21] Massey and Denton (1988, 1993); Sánchez-Jankowski (1999); Ihlanfeldt (2002); Dore and Kulshreshtha (2003); Kain (2004).

that he could secure a Protestant majority. The potato famine of the mid 1800s caused the exodus of many Catholics from the Republic of Ireland who settled close to the Catholic minority in West Belfast. By 1901, one-third of the population of West Belfast was Catholic. Women worked in the textile industry, and men worked in construction. After World War II, the Northern Ireland government supported the traditional Protestant industries, but let the small-scale Catholic firms in West Belfast suffer. Between 1950 and 1976, 70 percent of the jobs in West Belfast disappeared.

The situation of the Catholics is comparable to that of the urban African–Americans in the United States. In 1994, 7 percent of the working-age population suffered long-term illness or disability. West Belfast had the highest rate of infant mortality in Northern Ireland and one found in this area alone, 23 percent of all gravely ill children in the country. In some neighborhoods of West Belfast, unemployment rates were almost ten times higher than the working-class Protestant parts of the city. Middle-class and working-class Catholics left the ghetto, but the long-term unemployed did not have that option. According to Leonard, their self-defeating attitudes and life-styles were their adaptation to a history of discrimination. Residents mentioned the negative reactions of employers to West Belfast addresses on the application forms was the principal cause of thus the above-average unemployment rate of Catholics.

When most of Belfast enjoyed full employment, 75 percent of the Catholic males had no stable job in the formal labor market. During the 1990s, the popular view was that the generous welfare benefits eroded the sense of self-reliance and the will to work creating a culture of dependency among the Catholics.

However, Leonard's ethnographic studies showed a preference to be employed rather than face the boredom and frustration of unemployment. Half the males who were entitled to welfare benefits also had some type of informal employment. "Doing the double" permitted some households to afford modest luxuries. The informal labor market demands a very strong work ethic. Unsatisfactory performance results in immediate dismissal. There is no sick leave or paid holidays, but in spite of these hard conditions, the workers recovered a certain dignity. Leonard found no evidence to confirm fatalistic attitudes or a lack of commitment to the work ethic from the youth or their parents.

Leonard (1998)

Attitudes, Self-Worth, and Incentives

Not everyone who grows up in a poor neighborhood remains poor. Not everyone with less than ideal parents turns out badly. Some who attend poor quality primary and secondary schools continue on to complete certification or degrees. We have all experienced things that we wish never happened. Some overcome, others succumb. Some disabled people are obsessed with what they are unable to do, whereas others concentrate on what they can do. How do some succeed in shaping their own destinies against all odds?

Akerlof and Kranton (2000) asserted that identity, or a person's sense of self, is the key element that will explain success or failure. Thus, those who lack self-confidence impose undue constraints on themselves that keep them poor. This sense of self may also explain the existence of an "underclass."

People's utility functions depend on their own self image, on their own actions, and the actions of others. Women who choose nontraditional jobs may be harassed or baited by their male coworkers because the women do not conform to their colleagues' definition of "what women do." Such women are a challenge to the men's definition of masculinity: if a woman is capable of doing a man's job, she hurts their machismo.

Besides the sense of identity, an interdependent utility function is also important. Interdependent utility functions exist when one person chooses to link his or her welfare the action of others. For example, the utility to some parents increases or falls depending on the success or failure of their child: these parents have interdependent utility functions. Another example: some students harass their classmates for getting good grades, because the classmates' success devalues the harassers' utility.

In general, suppose that a minority is composed of two groups of people. Group A identifies with a dominant culture whereas Group B rejects the A culture and the identity that the A's assign to the B's. Group A views Group B as inept, whereas Group B claims that if one of the minority tries to mimic the dominate culture, he or she creates negative externalities for all other Bs. This renegade who rejects, the "pure sub-culture B" will be taunted and banished from the group. Similarly, all members of Group A or Group B who succeeds by Group A's rules in identifying with the dominant culture will be viewed as a threat by the less successful in the dominant culture.[22]

Poverty Dynamics

Poverty can be temporary or long term. Temporary poverty can be caused by regional business cycles. Permanent poverty can stem from long-term illness and disability or structural unemployment, especially if it coincides with a stage of life when further human capital investment is not possible or practical. Long-term poverty can also come from discrimination or one's attitudes and concepts of self-worth.

Many poverty studies use cross-sectional data, and concentrate on poverty at a given moment. Studies that use longitudinal data sets test hypotheses concerning the causes and potential interventions regarding poverty over time. If income mobility were rare, cross-sectional analyses would be appropriate. But because income mobility is not rare, an analysis of poverty dynamics assists local decision-makers to determine appropriate policies to help others escape poverty.

Reentry into Public Assistance

Reentry to public assistance roles occurs because of changes in household composition, marital status, or employment status. Reentry often signals an unstable household unable to be self-sufficient. However, in a positive light, it shows that the recipient at least tried to leave the program, and may need to be on public assistance just a little while longer.

Bruce, Barbour, and Thacker (2004) examined 128,775 Tennessee families that left their Families First program between October 1996 and April 2001. One-third of these families returned to the program at least once.

---

[22] Akerlof and Kranton (2000).

> Those were most likely families with younger, female, or black heads of household or with many children. Most reentry occurs fairly quickly. The households that left the program because they met the 18-month time limit imposed in the program were also more likely to return.
>
> Bruce, Barbour, and Thacker (2004)

Half of all individuals that end a spell in poverty in a given year will be poor again within 4 years. Whether poverty is temporary or permanent largely depends on the characteristics of individuals and their families.

Individuals in male-headed households experience the most short-lived poverty. The educational attainment and the race of heads of households are also good predictors of the length of stay below the poverty line. Impoverished households headed by black, less-educated males will be poor for approximately 4 out of the next 10 years. Households headed by whites with at least a high school education that become poor will stay poor on average for 2.5 of the next 10 years. If the head-of-household is a single female or has less than a high school education, poverty is relentless; between 26 and 64% will live below the poverty line for 6 or more of the next 10 years. In contrast, for children in these female-headed households, the figures would increase to 47% and 90%.[23]

Obstacles to Income Mobility

The principal barriers to income mobility come from either the education system or the labor market. An education system that funds schools based on the property values within its own district can decrease the academic quality of schools within impoverished areas. For example, students from a poor district may not have the necessary computers. They can be at the top of their class, but have lower skill levels than the graduates of higher-income school districts. In addition, even if they want to continue their studies, borrowing constraints could stop them. Without the advanced training, they cannot qualify for the high paying jobs that will help them out of poverty.

Business Cycles and Regional Growth

Long-run economic growth, both at the state and at the national level, is an effective antipoverty tool. A strong macroeconomy reduces both the number of

---

[23] Stevens (1999).

families living in poverty and the average size of the poverty gap. Poverty is an integral part of the business cycle. When the economy is not dynamic, unemployment rates rise, wages fall, and poverty levels increase.

However, the impacts of dynamic economies do not fall uniformly across all families or racial groups. Nor are they uniform over time or space. During the 1980s and 1990s, lower unemployment rates and employment growth rates decreased poverty among married couple families and families with white heads of household. It was not until the high-growth economy of the 1990s increased the median wage that the extent and depth of poverty among female-headed households and minority families diminished.[24]

The Fight Against Poverty

The current welfare system in the United States has four main components: food stamps, medical assistance, Temporary Assistance for Needy Families (TANF), and Earned Income Tax Credit (EITC), a program similar to the negative income tax. Income distribution is classified as a public good, because of a potential free-rider problem that requires government intervention. Individuals vote with their feet and migrate toward jurisdictions whose public policies maximize their own wellbeing (Tiebout hypothesis). Thus, jurisdictions that decide to attempt to help "their" poor discover that they have many new poor people moving there. Thus, in the United States, the Personal Responsibility and Work Opportunity Reform Act (PRWORA) of 1996 (the Clinton Welfare Reform Act) assigned to anyone on welfare, the benefits initially offered by the county in which they first registered for public assistance regardless of where they currently live.[25]

Although helping the poor may be a public good, public giving is not optimal. First, public redistribution efforts have been shown empirically to crowd out private giving. In addition, public giving provides smaller psychic benefits to the taxpayer-donor than private giving. People get a "warm glow" when they themselves help the less fortunate. The same "warm glow" does not come from hearing how much government programs have gone to finance the fight against poverty.

Secondly, Okun (1975) claimed that government transferred income from the rich to the poor using a "leaky bucket." How much income "leaks" out of Okun's bucket? The marginal cost of government reducing income inequality is substantial. It takes $9.51 from the pockets of rich taxpayers to increase the disposable income of a poor person by $1

---

[24] Gundersen and Ziliak (2004).
[25] Wheaton (2000); Hu (2001); and Horowitz (2002).

according to Browning and Johnson (1984). It seems in conclusion, that the government is less capable of aiding the poor than the private sector.

Social Assistance in Europe: Public–Private Welfare Partnerships

Oberti (2000) compared antipoverty strategies of 13 cities in four European countries and highlighted the resulting local configurations. Each city had different arrangements and relationships between public institutions, intermediate organizations, the church, family, and local community.

The characteristics of poverty and welfare strategies varied considerably, depending on whether the city was hard hit by deindustrialization with a high unemployment rate and a marginal group of insecurely employed workers, or whether the city is dominated by the tertiary sector and public services.

The government is never alone in intervening to combat poverty. Relations between church and state are quite varied. The church may be an equal partner or only intervene in the most urgent cases. It may limit itself to traditional charity work (Lisbon) or function as a quasi-social service, with professional staff and a genuine organizational and financial structure (Milan). The Swedish cities of Gothenburg and Helsingborg are the most heavily regulated by the public sector. In Rennes and Saint-Etienne, France, welfare provision is highly institutionalized and charities play a minimal role.

In Bremen, Germany, the public powers coordinate a network of intermediate organizations such as trade unions and occupational or religious organizations. However, the programs in Halle (situated in the former East Germany) are still influenced by the former bureaucratic system, which marginalized informal and religious associations.

Turin, Italy, along with Vitoria and Barcelona, Spain, tightly integrated private associations and voluntary services with the public sector, while Milan, Italy, follows a more traditional concept of charity for the most deprived poor. Lisbon and Oporty (Portugal) have abandoned the traditional model of charity by mixing bureaucratic centralism with strong interventions by religions institutions. Income support provision of Lisbon is managed by a religious body (*Santa Casa da Misericórdia*), which is officially controlled by the state but is actually self-sufficient. Portugal's cultural heritage is centered on a culture of poverty more than a culture of citizenship, which according to Oberti leads to assistance relationships based on fatalism and passivity. There is no stigma associated with the widespread poverty in Portugal and the welfare assistance levels are low. The Portuguese concept of welfare tied to charity from religious institutions allows a passive acceptance of the arbitrary bureaucratic decisions.

Oberti (2000)

A substantial part of public expenditures associated with poverty are financed from local resources. Poverty rates of the inner cities are consistently larger than those in the suburbs of American cities as predicted from the filtering theory (Chapter 13). Although the inner cities contain a disproportionate number of low-income people, they also finance a substantial part of the public expenditures associated with poverty. The largest poverty-related expenditures come from indirect poverty expenditures: additional spending for police, fire, courts, general administrative functions, health, and hospitals. The primary poverty functions of local governments are generally financed by intergovernmental revenues, but the indirect expenditures receive little or no intergovernmental assistance. Cullen and Levitt (1999) used panel data from the 59 largest United States cities and found that crime differences between top and bottom quartile cities translated into an additional $30 per capita annually in police expenditure. Not only are public education costs greater for low-income children, but also the poor are less likely to be covered by private health insurance, which places added stress on public health insurance programs.

Local provision of welfare services fits into models of tax competition (Chapter 17). Households migrate to where they receive the greatest benefits to them for the lowest tax price. If localities want to attract a solid tax base, they will decrease the expenditures on programs that benefit low-income people. This policy will attract higher income households who will demand either other public programs or lower taxes. At the same time, such a policy will repel lower-income households either because of the lack of programs to fit their preferences or because of the high land rents. Thus, interjurisdictional competition could result in a "race to the bottom" in welfare benefit provision.[26]

Income Distribution and Welfare-to-Work Programs

Aid to Families with Dependent Children (AFDC) grew out of the Great Depression. It began with the Social Security Act of 1935. In the early 1960s, welfare in the United States was controlled completely by the states. "State Public Assistance" was a locally funded and regulated system of assisting the poor and unemployed. During the mid 1960s, the federal government "nationalized" the welfare system by creating two programs: AFDC and Unemployment Insurance (UI). This intervention of the central government standardized minimum benefits and eligibility requirements. The PRWORA of 1996 returned welfare to state control, with partial federal funding through largely unrestricted block grants and various types of welfare-to-work policies. The PRWORA also emphasized marriage and child support to discourage out-of-wedlock pregnancies and to encourage formation of two-parent families.

Welfare-to-work policies have also been set up in the United Kingdom, Australia, and New Zealand. The policies are in reaction to prevailing explanations of the causes of poverty and unemployment: welfare dependency, low motivation, and inadequate training. The rationale is simple: if you pay people to be inactive there will be more inactivity. However, people need suitable incomes, so society should help them earn their incomes by getting and keeping jobs. The main question is the impact of a severe recession on the work requirements of low-income families. Not enough time has elapsed to do such analyses yet.[27]

As Table 18.3 shows, high poverty rates describe both large and small metropolitan areas. In fact, depending on the definition, poverty rates from outside metropolitan areas often equal or exceed the rates from inner cities of the United States.

Will poverty alleviation programs that require parents to work end up harming the children? Not necessarily. Research suggests that it depends on the stage of the child's life cycle. Programs that increase the hours of work and income of the parents could have a neutral or positive effect for preschool-age children, but they may cause problems in adolescents. The increased incomes of the parents could lead to more books for the child and

---

[26] Pastor and Adams (1996); Pack (1998).

[27] Browning and Johnson (1984); Lee and McKenzie (1990); Tanner, Moore, and Hartman (1995); Bauer, Braun, and Olson (2000); Layard (2000); Peck and Theodore (2000); Saavedra (2000); Dadres and Ginther (2001); Saunders (2003).

Table 18.3 Percent of People in United States Metropolitan Areas Who Live Below Poverty Level in the Past 12 Months, 2004

Rank	Place	Percent
1	Detroit, MI	33.6
2	El Paso, TX	28.8
3	Miami, FL	28.3
4	Newark, NJ	28.1
5	Atlanta, GA	27.8
6	Long Beach, CA	26.4
7	Milwaukee, WI	26.0
8	Buffalo, NY	25.9
9	Philadelphia, PA	24.9
10	Memphis, TN	24.6
11	Baltimore, MD	23.9
12	Cleveland, OH	23.2
12	New Orleans, LA	23.2
14	Stockton, CA	23.0
15	St. Louis, MO	21.6
16	Fresno, CA	21.2
17	Chicago, IL	21.1
18	Dallas, TX	20.8
19	New York, NY	20.3
20	San Antonio, TX	19.8
21	Oakland, CA	19.7
22	Cincinnati, OH	19.6
22	Houston, TX	19.6
24	Tucson, AZ	19.5
25	Minneapolis, MN	19.1
26	Boston, MA	19.0
27	Washington, DC	18.9
28	Pittsburgh, PA	18.8
29	Tulsa, OK	18.5
30	Lexington-Fayette, KY	18.1
31	Los Angeles, CA	18.0
32	Sacramento, CA	17.8
33	Tampa, FL	17.7
34	Fort Worth, TX	17.6
34	Kansas City, MO	17.6
36	Seattle, WA	17.3
37	Corpus Christi, TX	16.8
37	Nashville-Davidson, TN	16.8

(continued)

Table 18.3 (Continued)

Rank	Place	Percent
39	Columbus, OH	16.7
40	Portland, OR	16.5
40	Toledo, OH	16.5
42	Phoenix, AZ	15.9
43	Louisville-Jefferson County, KY	15.7
44	Austin, TX	15.4
45	Denver, CO	15.1
46	Santa Ana, CA	15.0
47	Albuquerque, NM	14.9
48	Raleigh, NC	14.7
49	St. Petersburg, FL	14.2
50	Omaha, NE	13.9
50	St. Paul, MN	13.9
52	Jacksonville, FL	13.5
53	Colorado Springs, CO	13.4
54	Indianapolis, IN	13.1
55	Bakersfield, CA	13.0
55	Charlotte, NC	13.0
55	San Diego, CA	13.0
58	Oklahoma City, OK	12.7
59	Honolulu CDP, HI	12.4
60	Riverside, CA	12.2
60	Wichita, KS	12.2
62	Mesa, AZ	12.1
63	Las Vegas, NV	11.6
64	San Jose, CA	11.4
65	Aurora, CO	11.2
66	Arlington, TX	10.2
66	San Francisco, CA	10.2
68	Anaheim, CA	8.2
69	Virginia Beach, VA	7.7
70	Anchorage, AK	7.4

Source: U.S. Bureau of the Census, 2004.

Do Welfare-to-Work Systems Work?

What constitutes an efficient and equitable social service system? Each of the 50 states in the United States has been allowed to function as a laboratory since 1981 because the federal government allowed applications for waivers to test the results of different innovations. The definition of an optimal system depends on the state's goals regarding its low-income population. Greenberg, Mandell, and Onstott (2000) reported on three of these programs.

California provided considerable latitude in methods counties used for their welfare systems. Riverside, one of the six evaluation counties, strongly emphasized the need for welfare recipients to take jobs—any job as quickly as possible. They reduced AFDC benefits to sanction recipients who did not comply. Only when a program participant was initially unable to find a job did the person receive training. The other five evaluation counties emphasized training before job search. Riverside's version was more positive early in the program, but total program spending in Riverside was similar to, if not more than, spending at the other five sites. It spent quite a bit on training those that did not find immediate employment, and on case management and job search for those who found employment.

The participants in Florida's Project Independence were required to apply for a job with at least twelve employers. If they did not find a job, they joined a "job club," which was in essence a two- to three-week course on job hunting. Those who still could not find a job were labeled "not job-ready," and were then provided education and training services. The results of this project were positive in terms of cost: the resulting increase in tax revenues from the project exceeded the cost of providing the services. However, welfare recipients did not gain: the reduction in their welfare receipts was greater than the increase in their earnings.

New York's Child Assistance Program (CAP) was a voluntary program that induced AFDC recipients to find a job and to obtain child support court orders. Under CAP, cash transfer benefits were reduced by only 10 cents for each dollar of earnings up to the poverty level and by 67¢ for each dollar of earnings above the poverty level. CAP also removed restrictions on the amount of assets that the program participants may own. To qualify for the program, however, the recipients had first to obtain child support court orders. The program resulted in cost savings for the government because CAP's cash transfer benefits were offset by a dollar for each dollar of child support payments, but unfortunately, the effects on poverty via public assistance receipts to mothers were small and statistically insignificant.

Greenberg, Mandell, and Onstott (2000)

cognitive stimuli in the household as well as child care outside the family. Structured child care can aid cognitive development in children. Likewise, higher math scores have been attributed to children of working mothers, even if their employment is irregular.

Younger children of working poor families test at higher levels of verbal development than children from welfare dependent families. The differences in family background may explain this result. Children of parents who have at least a high school education also have higher levels of verbal development because this group of parents will more easily find a job. If, on the other hand, the system requires parents to look for jobs when they themselves lack sufficient education and already suffer from depression, the stress of working, the parents may erode their own well-being, exacerbate preexisting problems and thereby, stunt the child's cognitive development.

Unsupervised adolescents, on the other hand, may have difficulties if they are suddenly alone after school: a lack of supervision increases the tendency to find mischief and neglect homework. Also, if adolescent children may be asked to take care of younger siblings while their single mothers work, this responsibility could decrease the child's own academic performance.[28]

The Luck of the Draw

Loeb et al. (2003) noted that among children of about two years of age whose mothers participated in the

---

[28] Kornberger, Fast, and Williamson (2001); Clark-Kauffman, Duncan, and Morris (2003).

new welfare-to-work program, instead of the traditional program, had a modest gain in early learning and cognitive growth. To evaluate the effects of Jobs First, Connecticut's new welfare-to-work program, between 1996–1997 the welfare agencies in Manchester and New Haven randomly assigned eligible welfare applicants to either the program group or a control group that followed the old AFDC rules and benefit levels.

A child whose mother was assigned to the Jobs First program scored moderately higher (about 25 percent of a standard deviation) on the MacArthur Communicative Development Inventory than one whose mother was assigned to the traditional welfare program. Why the improvement? In the first place, the mothers in the new program were substantially more likely to be employed and have higher earned income, while the traditional program encouraged passivity. Second, the fact of having been placed in the reform group produced optimism among the case workers and the recipients that spread to the children.

Loeb et al. (2003)

Education and Training

The disconcerting part of a focus on working as soon as possible can, in the long run, have negative effects. The hours working at a menial job can be an obstacle to earning a degree. Without an investment in human capital the chances of moving up the social ladder are greatly reduced. Studies have disclosed that the lack of funds is not the sole reason that individuals from low-income households do not pursue higher education, or do not finish.[29] A study of the clients who were then receiving AFDC in Stearns County, Minnesota, during the late 1980s showed that 10% had completed a bachelor's degree, and a fair number even earned Master's degrees, mostly in elementary education or social work, two fields that prepare the clients for low wages and public assistance, two fields for which local employment is scarce and which predispose graduates to an uncertain future.

---

[29] Sazama (1992); Donni and Lejeune (1997).

It's Not Just the Money

Yorke and Thomas (2003) noted that in the United Kingdom, in 1997, 80 percent of the young people whose parents were professionals entered higher education compared with only 14 percent of those whose parents were unskilled workers. Unfortunately, because of confidentiality, the authors could not compare their respective progress.

Stinebrickner and Stinebrickner (2003) analyzed admissions data from Berea College in Kentucky. This establishment offers a full tuition subsidy as well as generous room and board subsidies to all entering students regardless of family income. All students work ten hours per week in off-campus jobs in addition to their studies. This common situation rules out the probability that attrition of low-income students is because they attempt to work excessively outside their academics. The authors control for college entrance exam scores, elementary and high school ratings, race, distance from home, and size of family. On average, family income is strongly negatively correlated with the students' grades. Something else within the family environment is hampering the ability of low-income students to succeed in academia.

Yorke and Thomas (2003), Stinebrickner and Stinebrickner (2003)

A Perverse Robin Hood, or Betting on the Future

Florida and Georgia finance public education through lotteries. Florida Bright Futures (FBF) scholarships are funded with about 19 percent of these proceeds. The scholarships provide partial or full tuition to students who graduate with a 3.5 GPA and 1270 SAT or 28 ACT score.

Georgia's lottery also funds a merit-based scholarship: Help Outstanding Students Educationally (HOPE). Besides the scholarships, that state's lottery also funds voluntary prekindergarten for four-year-old, student loans, capital improvements, costs of providing training to teachers and expenses of repairing instructional equipment.

Who pays and who wins? Empirical studies unanimously find that lottery sales are regressive. Low-income people, minorities, urban residents, and those with no college education purchase a majority of lottery tickets. Georgia's earmarking of education funds to its low-income areas mitigates the regressivity of that program. However, the lottery funded, merit-based scholarship program in Florida has a reverse Robin Hood effect. It essentially transfers wealth from lower-income groups to higher-income groups. Lower-income groups can expect to receive $700, although higher income groups can expect benefits of $2,250.

Lauth and Robbins (2002),
Garrett and Sobel (2004), Dee (2004),
Stranahan and Borg (2004)

Summary and Conclusions

In this chapter, we defined income as the command over resources, and poverty as insufficient command over resources. Because the definition of "scarcity" is unlimited wants but limited resources, under such a definition even the most affluent could claim poverty. To be more specific, one must specify the allowable needs. Absolute poverty lines are determined by the minimum cost of survival and provide measures that are comparable over time and over distance. Relative poverty lines define needs as dependent on social customs.

Income inequality is not a sign of a dysfunctional economy nor is increased inequality a sign of an infirmed economy. It could be merely the result of an abnormal age distribution or as in the 1980s and 1990s, it could be due to an increase in the productivity levels and hours worked by highly paid professionals.

Child poverty is a consistent social rallying point. Few people would favor more child poverty (as a character-builder, for instance). However, research based on detailed longitudinal data sets has suggested that any long-term effects from childhood poverty are not directly linked to income. However, a poor physical environment (increased levels of lead or unsanitary living conditions) could lead to chronic health problems. Young children of working parents who have been placed in a quality childcare facility have higher levels of verbal development and do better on standardized tests than children whose parents are on welfare. Similarly, higher education levels of parents regardless of the family's income level are associated with an increase in the cognitive ability of the children. Along with child poverty, family size, parental education, and family structure (teen mother, lone-mother families) are also correlated with inter-generational poverty.

Poverty means a lack of sufficient earnings. A lack of earnings has many potential causes such as illness and disability, a bad economy, lack of local legitimate employment, discrimination, and an individual's attitudes, feelings of self-worth, and identification.

Income redistribution has been considered a public good because of the free-rider problem. Altruism exists, but some people want to see the poverty problem addressed—by somebody else. However, studies have found that public giving does, in fact, crowd out private donations. In addition, government-sponsored income distribution programs use a "bucket" that "leaks" $8.51 for each $1.00 received by a poor person. Local provision of social services promises a "race to the bottom" for localities that engage in a form of "tax competition." Jurisdictions may be tempted to provide benefits that attract high-income, relatively low (public) maintenance households at the same time they decrease spending for programs that benefit low-income households.

Current poverty policies in the United States have four major parts: food stamps, medical assistance, TANF, and EITC. The TANF is primarily known as a welfare-to-work program, and by most measures is a significant step forward for alleviating poverty. The EITC is similar to a negative income tax for families with children.

Low incomes are theoretically due to insufficient human capital, but students from low-income households are constrained by more than just the ability to meet costs of tuition, room and board, and books. Even when these costs are accounted for, the poor quality of their former schools and their scores on college entrance exams still undermine students from low-income households who tend to earn lower grades on average.

Chapter Questions

1. Differentiate between functional distributions and size distributions of income. What would be the effect on either distribution of a decrease in the proportion of revenues going to wages?

2. What differences may occur by describing income distributions using families as income units and using households as the income unit? How does a family differ from a household?

3. In 2001, the Gini coefficient for the United States was 0.466, although in 1967 it was 0.399, according to *Annual Demographic Supplements to the Current Population Survey* (http://www.census.gov/hhes/www/income/histinc/ie1.html). What do these figures tell us about income distributions in the United States?

4. Canada's LICO is a count of the number of families or individuals who spend 54.7% or more of their pretax income on food, clothing, or shelter. Although it was not created to be a poverty line, it has become the de facto poverty line. Is this a measure of absolute poverty or relative poverty? Why?

5. Distinguish between employer, employee, consumer, and statistical discrimination, and give examples of each.

Research Questions

1. Refer to the *Small Area Income and Poverty Estimates (SAIPE)* website, http://www.census.gov/hhes/www/saipe/saipe.html, and find overall poverty data and child poverty data for your county for years 1989, 1993, and 1995 to present. On a spreadsheet such as Excel, plot the data over time using a scatter plot of poverty rates against time.

2. For the class, compare the relative poverty rate from the Minimum Income Question, the Income Evaluation Question. If possible compare your answers to those from a different class, perhaps from a different department or college within your university.

3. Administer the survey instrument from the University of Bristol used to determine what are considered adult necessities. How does the response from your class compare with that from the University of Bristol?

4. How does your city or county rank in terms of poverty and characteristics of poverty? Check the ACS (*American Community Survey*) Rankings Tables at http://factfinder.census.gov.

References

Akerlof, G. A., and R. E. Kranton. 2000. Economics and identity. *Quarterly Journal of Economics* 115 (3):715–753.

Albelda, R. 1999. Women and poverty: beyond earnings and welfare. *Quarterly Review of Economics and Finance* 39 (0):723–742.

Barham, V., R. Boadway, M. Marchand, and P. Pestieau. 1995. Education and the poverty trap. *European Economic Review* 39 (7):1257–1275.

Bauer, J. W., B. Braun, and P. D. Olson. 2000. Welfare to well-being framework for research, education, and outreach. *Journal of Consumer Affairs* 34 (1):62–81.

Becker, G. S. 1957. *The Economics of Discrimination.* Chicago: U of Chicago Press.

Becker, G. S., and K. M. Murphy. 1988. The family and the state. *Journal of Law and Economics* 31 (1):1–18.

Bell, D. N. F., R. J. Rimmer, and S. M. Rimmer. 1992. Poverty among young Australians. *Australian Economic Review* 0 (99):5–18.

Bergmann, B. R. 1997. Government support for families with children in the United States and France. *Feminist Economics* 3 (1):85–94.

Blank, R. M. 2003. Selecting among anti-poverty policies: can an economist be both critical and caring? *Review of Social Economy* 61 (4):447–469.

Blau, D. M. 1999. The effect of income on child development. *Review of Economics and Statistics* 81 (2):261–276.

Bossert, W. 1990. Population replications and ethical poverty measurement. *Mathematical Social Sciences* 20 (3):227–238.

Brotherhood of St. Laurence. 2005. Poverty line update, http://www.antipovertyweek.org.au/documents/poverty_line_update_May05.pdf. (Date retrieved 5 September 2005).

Browning, E. K., and W. R. Johnson. 1984. The trade-off between equality and efficiency. *Journal of Political Economy* 92 (2):175–203.

Bruce, D., K. Barbour, and A. Thacker. 2004. Welfare program reentry among post reform leavers. *Southern Economic Journal* 70 (4):816–836.

Burgess, S., and C. Propper. 1999. Poverty in Britain. In *The State of Working Britain,* eds. P. Gregg and J. Wadsworth, Manchester University Press; distributed by St. Martin's Press, Manchester, New York, 259–275.

Burkhauser, R. V., A. D. Crews, M. C. Daly, and S. P. Jenkins. 1996. Income Mobility and the Middle Class as cited in Daly, Mary C. 1997. The 'Shrinking' Middle Class? *FRBSF Economic Letter* 97-07 March 7. http://www.FRBSF.org/econrsrch/wklylrt/el97-07.html, (accessed on 30 July 2004), AEI Press, Washington, DC.

Carlson, M., and S. Danziger. 1999. Cohabitation and the measurement of child poverty. *Review of Income and Wealth* 45 (2):179–191.

Carlstrom, C. T., and C. D. Rollow. 1998. Regional variations in white–black earnings. *Federal Reserve Bank of Cleveland Economic Review* 34 (2):10–22.

Carneiro, P., J. J. Heckman, and D. V. Masterov. 2005. Labor market discrimination and racial differences in premarket factors. *Journal of Law and Economics* 48 (1):1–39.

Chevalier, A., and T. K. Viitanen. 2003. The long-run labour market consequences of teenage motherhood in Britain. *Journal of Population Economics* 16 (2):323–343.

Chuang, H.-L., and H.-Y. Lee. 2003. The return on women's human capital and the role of male attitudes toward working wives: gender roles, work interruption, and women's earnings in Taiwan. *American Journal of Economics and Sociology* 62 (2):435–459.

Clark-Kauffman, E., G. J. Duncan, and P. Morris. 2003. How welfare policies affect child and adolescent achievement. *American Economic Review* 93 (2):299–303.

Cox, W. M., and Alm, R. 1995. By our own bootstraps: economic opportunity and the dynamics of income distribution. http://www.dallasfed.org/fed/annual/index.html#1995.

Crofton, S. O. 2003. An extension on the traditional theory of customer discrimination: customers versus customers. *American Journal of Economics and Sociology* 62 (2):319–343.

Cullen, J. B., and S. D. Levitt. 1999. Crime, urban flight, and the consequences for cities. *Review of Economics and Statistics* 81 (2):159–169.

Currie, J., and A. Yelowitz. 2000. Are public housing projects good for kids? *Journal of Public Economics* 75 (1):99–124.

Dadres, S., and D. K. Ginther. 2001. Regional research and development intensity and earnings inequality. *Federal Reserve Bank of Atlanta Economic Review* 86 (2):13–26.

Dalaker, J. 2001. United States Census Bureau, Current Population Reports, Series P60-214, *Poverty in the United States:* 2000, United States Government Printing Office, Washington, DC. http://www.census.gov/prod/2001pubs/p60-214.pdf, (retrieved on 14 September 2005).

Davidson, B., S. A. Khan, and P. D. S. Rao. 2000. Child poverty in rural regions of Australia in 1990. *Australasian Journal of Regional Studies* 6 (1):47–65.

Dee, T. S. 2004. Lotteries, litigation, and education finance. *Southern Economic Journal* 70 (3):584–599.

Deleeck, H., B. Cantillon, B. Meulemans, and K. van den Bösch. 1992. Some longitudinal results of the Belgian socio-economic panel. *Journal of Income Distribution* 2 (2):211–231.

DeNavas-Walt, C., R. W. Cleveland, and B. H. Webster, Jr. 2003. Income in the United States: 2002. http://www.census.gov/prod/2003pubs/p60-221.pdf.

Donni, O., and B. Lejeune. 1997. Origine sociale et réussite scolaire: un modèle en chaîne de Markov estime sur données individuelles belges. *Recherches Economiques de Louvain* 63 (4):421–446.

Dore, M. H. I., and S. Kulshreshtha. 2003. The labor market and rural–urban differences among first nations: the case of Saskatchewan. *Journal of Socio-Economics* 32 (2):147–159.

Dunifon, R., G. J. Duncan, and J. Brooks-Gunn. 2001. As ye sweep, so shall ye reap. *American Economic Review* 91 (2):150–154.

Feldstein, M. 1998. Income inequality and poverty, National Bureau of Economic Research, Inc., NBER Working Papers.

Fieldhouse, E. A., and R. Tye. 1996. Deprived people or deprived places? Exploring the ecological fallacy in studies of deprivation with the samples of anonymised records. *Environment and Planning A* 28 (2):237–259.

Fisher, G. M. 1992. The development and history of the poverty thresholds. *Social Security Bulletin* 55 (4):3–14.

Flik, R. J., and B. M. S. van Praag. 1991. Subjective poverty line definitions. *De Economist* 139 (3):311–330.

Friedman, S., and D. T. Lichter. 1998. Spatial inequality and poverty among American children. *Population Research and Policy Review* 17 (2):91–109.

Garrett, T. A., and R. S. Sobel. 2004. State lottery revenue: the importance of game characteristics. *Public Finance Review* 32 (3):313–330.

Gordon, D., P. Townsend, R. Levitas, C. Pantazis, S. Payne, D. Patsios, S. Middleton, et al. *Poverty and Social Exclusion in Britain*, Published by the Rowntree Foundation, 2000, http://www.rouncefield.homestead.com/files/rowntree_2000.html.

Greenberg, D., M. Mandell, and M. Onstott. 2000. The dissemination and utilization of welfare-to-work experiments in state policymaking. *Journal of Policy Analysis and Management* 19 (3):367–382.

Greenstein, R., W. Primus, and T. Kayatin. 2000. Poverty Rate Hits Lowest Level Since 1979 as Unemployment Reaches a 30-Year Low, October 10th, 2000, Center on Budget and Policy Priorities.

Gundersen, C., and J. P. Ziliak. 2004. Poverty and macroeconomic performance across space, race, and family structure. *Demography* 41 (1):61–86.

Guo, G., and K. M. Harris. 2000. The mechanisms mediating the effects of poverty on children's intellectual development. *Demography* 37 (4):431–447.

Haagsma, R. 1993. Is statistical discrimination socially efficient? *Information Economics and Policy* 5 (1):31–50.

Hemphill, S. 2005. It's all about respect, Minnesota Public Radio September 20. http://news.minnesota.publicradio.org/features/2005/09/19_hemphills_hibtacsidebar/, (accessed on 9 October 2005).

Horowitz, J. B. 2002. Income mobility and the earned income tax credit. *Economic Inquiry* 40 (3):334–347.

Hu, W.-Y. 1999. Child support, welfare dependency, and women's labor supply. *Journal of Human Resources* 34 (1):71–103.

Hughes, H. 2001. The politics of envy: poverty and income distribution. *Policy* 17 (2):13–18.

Ihlanfeldt, K. 2002. Spatial mismatch in the labor market and racial differences in neighborhood crime. *Economics Letters* 76 (1):73–76.

Jackson, A. P. 2003. Mothers' employment and poor and near-poor African–American children's development: a longitudinal study. *Social Service Review* 77 (1):93–109.

Jacobsen, J. P. 1993. The use of earnings variance in testing the invisibility hypothesis. *Applied Economics* 25 (7):911–917.

Johnston, R., M. McKinney, and T. Stark. 1996. Regional price level variations and real household incomes in the United Kingdom, 1979/1980–1993. *Regional Studies* 30 (6):567–578.

Kain, J. F. 2004. A pioneer's perspective on the spatial mismatch literature. *Urban Studies* 41 (1):7–32.

Keister, L. A. 2003. Sharing the wealth: the effect of siblings on adults' wealth ownership. *Demography* 40 (3):521–542.

Kim, W. B. 1987. Urban unemployment and labor force participation in Korea. *Annals of Regional Science* 21 (1):44–55.

Kitchen, P. 2001. An approach for measuring urban deprivation change: the example of East Montréal urban community, 1986–1996. *Environment and Planning A* 33 (11):1901–1921.

Kornberger, R., J. E. Fast, and D. L. Williamson. 2001. Welfare or work: which is better for Canadian children? *Canadian Public Policy* 27 (4):407–421.

Kumazawa, R., and M. C. Seeborg. 1996. Teen mothers and their educational attainment: some evidence from the national longitudinal survey of youth. *Journal of Economics (MVEA)* 22 (1):95–104.

Lauth, T. P., and M. D. Robbins. 2002. The Georgia lottery and state appropriations for education: substitution or additional funding? *Public Budgeting and Finance* 22 (3):89–100.

Layard, R. 2000. Welfare-to-work and the new deal. *Schweizerische Zeitschrift für Volkswirtschaft und Statistik/Swiss Journal of Economics and Statistics* 136 (3):277–287.

Lee, D. R., and R. B. McKenzie. 1990. Second thoughts on the public-good justification for government poverty programs. *Journal of Legal Studies* 19 (1):189–202.

Leonard, M. 1998. The long-term unemployed, informal economic activity and the 'underclass' in Belfast: rejecting or reinstating the work ethic. *International Journal of Urban and Regional Research* 22 (1):42–59.

Lerman, D. L., and J. J. Mikesell. 1988. Impacts of adding net worth to the poverty definition. *Eastern Economic Journal* 14 (4):357–370.

Levernier, W., M. D. Partridge, and D. S. Rickman. 1998. Differences in metropolitan and nonmetropolitan United States family income inequality: a cross-country comparison. *Journal of Urban Economics* 44 (2):272–290.

Levine, D. I., and G. Painter. 2003. The schooling costs of teenage out-of-wedlock childbearing: analysis with a within-school propensity-score-matching estimator. *Review of Economics and Statistics* 85 (4):884–900.

Loeb, S., B. Fuller, S. L. Kagan, and B. Carrol. 2003. How welfare reform affects young children: experimental findings from Connecticut–A research note. *Journal of Policy Analysis and Management* 22 (4):537–550.

Martin, P., and J. E. Taylor. 2003. Farm employment, immigration, and poverty: a structural analysis. *Journal of Agricultural and Resource Economics* 28 (2):349–363.

Massey, D. S., and N. A. Denton. 1988. The dimensions of residential segregation. *Social Forces* 67 (2):281–315.

Massey, D. S., and N. A. Denton. 1993. *American Apartheid: Segregation and the Making of the Underclass*. Cambridge, MA: Harvard U Press.

Maurin, E., and C. Chambaz. 1996. La persistance dans la pauvreté et son évolution: une évaluation sur données françaises. *Economie et Prévision* 0 (122):133–152.

McFarlane, I. and R. Tiffin. 2003. *The minimum cost of adequate nutrition using locally available food items*, http://www.apd.rdg.ac.uk/AgEcon/research/workingpapers/dam_poster.pdf.

Motley, B. 1997. Inequality in the United States. *FRBSF Economic Letter* No 97-03, January 31.

Oberti, M. 2000. Diversity and complexity in local forms of urban anti-poverty strategies in Europe. *International Journal of Urban and Regional Research* 24 (3):536–553.

Okun, A. M. 1975. Inflation: its mechanics and welfare cost. *Brookings Papers on Economic Activity* 2 (75):351–401.

Oreopoulos, P. 2003. The long-run consequences of living in a poor neighborhood. *Quarterly Journal of Economics* 118 (4):1533–1575.

Ounce of Prevention Fund. 1987. Child Sexual Abuse: A Hidden Factor in Adolescent Sexual Behavior. Findings from a Statewide Survey of Teenage Mothers in Illinois. An Ounce of Prevention Study. Chicago, Illinois: The Ounce of Prevention Fund.

Pack, J. R. 1998. Poverty and urban public expenditures. *Urban Studies* 35 (11):1995–2019.

Pantazis, C., D. Gordon, and R. Levitas, eds. 2006. *Poverty and Social Exclusion in Britain: The Millennium Survey.* Bristol: Policy Press.

Pastor, M., and A. R. Adams. 1996. Keeping down with the Joneses: neighbors, networks, and wages. *Review of Regional Studies* 26 (2):115–145.

Peck, J., and N. Theodore. 2000. Commentary: 'work first': workfare and the regulation of contingent labour markets. *Cambridge Journal of Economics* 24 (1):119–138.

Phipps, S., P. Burton, and L. Lethbridge. 2001. In and out of the labour market: long-term income consequences of child-related interruptions to women's paid work. *Canadian Journal of Economics* 34 (2):411–429.

Piachaud, D. 1993. The definition and measurement of poverty and inequality. In Current Issues in the Economics of *Welfare, eds.* B. Nicholas and W. David *Current Issues in Economics series.* New York: Martin's Press, 105–129.

Qizilbash, M. 2003. Vague language and precise measurement: the case of poverty. *Journal of Economic Methodology* 10 (1):41–58.

Renwick, T. J. 1998. Basic needs budgets revisited: does the United States consumer price index overestimate the changes in the cost of living for low-income families? *Feminist Economics* 4 (3):129–142.

Ross, D., E. R. Shillington, and C. Lochhead. 1994. A working definitions of Statistics Canada Low Income Cut-offs (LICOs), http://www.ccsd.ca/pubs/archive/fb94/fs_povbk.htm, (accessed on 9 October 2005).

Rowntree, S. S. 2000 [1901], *Poverty: A study of town life*, Macmillan, London, Republished *Poverty: A study of town life: Centennial edition*, The Policy Press, Bristol. (http://www.bris.ac.uk/Publications/TPP/Pages/at036.htm).

Saavedra, L. A. 2000. A model of welfare competition with evidence from AFDC. *Journal of Urban Economics* 47 (2):248–279.

Sánchez-Jankowski, M. 1999. The concentration of African–American poverty and the dispersal of the working class: an ethnographic study of three inner-city areas. *International Journal of Urban and Regional Research* 23 (4):619–637.

Saunders, P. 1996. Special Article—Poverty and Deprivation in Australia. *Year Book Australia.* http://abs.gov.au/Ausstats/abs@.nsf/Lookup/5D709B83B7F7C25ECA2569DE00221C86#Links, (accessed on 14 September 2005).

Saunders, P. 2003. Turning back the tide: welfare lessons from America. *Policy* 19 (1):8–14.

Sazama, G. W. 1992. Has federal student aid contributed to equality in higher education? A method of measurement. *American Journal of Economics and Sociology* 51 (2):129–146.

Sharpe, D. L., and M. Abdel-Ghany. 1999. Identifying the poor and their consumption patterns. *Family Economics and Nutrition Review* 12 (2):15–25.

Siegfried, J. J., and D. K. Round. 1994. How did the wealthiest Australians get so rich? *Review of Income and Wealth* 40 (2):191–204.

Statistics Canada. Private Households in Non-farm, Non-reserve Dwellings by Household Type, Showing Number and Average Shelter Costs and Tenure, for Canada, Provinces and Territories, 1996 Census.

Stevens, A. H. 1999. Climbing out of poverty, falling back in: measuring the persistence of poverty over multiple spells. *Journal of Human Resources* 34 (3):557–588.

Stinebrickner, R., and T. R. Stinebrickner. 2003. Understanding educational outcomes of students from low-income families: evidence from a liberal arts college with a full tuition subsidy program. *Journal of Human Resources* 38 (3):591–617.

Stranahan, H. A., and M. O. Borg. 2004. Some futures are brighter than others: the net benefits received by Florida Bright Futures scholarship recipients. *Public Finance Review* 32 (1):105–126.

Tanner, M., S. Moore, and D. Hartman. 1995. The Work Versus Welfare Trade-Off: an Analysis of Total Level of Welfare Benefits by State, *Cato Policy Analysis No.* 240, (September 19, 1995), http://www.cato.org/pubs/pas/pa-240.html, (accessed on 21 July 2004).

Tentschert, U., M. Till, and J. Redl. 2000. Income poverty and minimum income requirements in the EU 14, Paper prepared for the VIth Bien Congress, Berlin October 5. http://www.etes.ucl.ac.be/bien/Files/Papers/2000 TenschertTill.pdf, (accessed on 14 July 2004).

Tomal, A. 1999. Determinants of teenage birth rates as an unpooled sample: age matters for socioeconomic predictors. *American Journal of Economics and Sociology* 58 (1):57–69.

Treatment Action Network. 1996. Changes in Social Security Law: people diagnosed with substance abuse disability will no longer receive Social Security benefits, June 4, 1996, http://www.projinf.org/news/96_06ssa.html, (accessed on 3 October 2005).

United States Bureau of the Census. 2004. Current Population Survey (CPS)— Definitions and Explanations, (January 20, 2004). http://www.census.gov/ population/www/cps/cpsdef.html, (accessed on 16 October 2005).

United States Bureau of the Census. 2004. Poverty Thresholds. http://www.census. gov/hhes/poverty/threshld/03prelim.html, (accessed on 8 April 2006).

United States Bureau of the Census. 2004. *Income, Poverty, and Health Insurance Coverage in the United States.* http://www.census.gov/prod/2005pubs/p60-229. pdf, (accessed on 11 August 2004).

United States Bureau of the Census. 2004. Table 700. People Below Poverty Level and below 125% of Poverty level by Race and Hispanic Origin: 1980 to 2001, 2003 Statistical Abstract of the United States. http://www.census.gov/prod/ 2004pubs/03statab/income.pdf, (accessed on 11 August 2004).

United States Bureau of the Census. 2004. Detailed Income Tabulations from the CPS. http://www.census.gov/hhes/www/income/dinctabs.html, (accessed on 12 August 2004).

van den Bösch, K. 2001. *Identifying the Poor: Using Subjective and Consensual Measures.* Sydney: Ashgate.

van den Bösch, K. 1996. Equivalence scales based on subjective income evaluations: Are children really cheap? *Recherches Economiques de Louvain* 62 (2):203–227.

Wheaton, W. C. 2000. Decentralized welfare: will there be underprovision? *Journal of Urban Economics* 48 (3):536–555.

Wilkie, P. J. 1996. Through-time changes in family income inequality: the effect of non-synchronous regional growth. *Applied Economics* 28 (12):1515–1527.

Wilson, W. J. 1987. *The Truly Disadvantaged: The Inner-City, the Underclass and Public Policy*. Chicago: University of Chicago Press.

Witte, A. D., and M. Trowbridge. 2004. The structure of early care and education in the United States: historical evolution and international comparisons, National Bureau of Economic Research, Inc., NBER Working Papers.

Yorke, M., and L. Thomas. 2003. Improving the retention of students from lower socio-economic groups. *Journal of Higher Education Policy and Management* 25 (1):63–74.

Chapter 19

Optimal Local Education Policies

Investment in education is a crucial policy for the growth of a community, a region, and a national, or even the global economy. Education that augments technological skills improves the chances of economic growth according to the endogenous growth theory (Chapter 8). High-tech firms are more willing to locate in areas that have an educated labor force (Chapter 5), thus increasing the tax base (Chapter 17). Families look for good quality schools, as evidenced by increased house values for surrounding residences (Chapter 13). Educated people are more productive and less likely to be on welfare or in prison.

But who pays? Should education be a place-based or person-based expense, or some combination of the two? Small- to medium-sized places that funnel large amounts of taxes into education do not necessarily benefit because well-educated people most often migrate to larger cities with a dynamic labor market, more diverse amenities, and a richer quality of life. First-rate high school students go on to university, and may never return. Thus, logic suggests that the investment should be person-based, perhaps funded by the private sector or the federal government. However, the less prepared students, either because they neglected their studies, or because they are the product of poor quality schools, are less productive. They have few possibilities elsewhere, and will have little chance to relocate (Chapter 10). For these reasons, an optimal investment strategy is in place-based education, at least at a basic level.

In this chapter, we will review the effects of human capital investment on the economic growth of a community and a region. We will then study the production function for education, and based on this model, we will analyze suggestions for creating an educated labor force. Finally, we will investigate a community's willingness to pay for education, as well as appropriate financing alternatives for local education policies.

Education and Growth

In Chapter 8 we saw the impact on regional growth due to increased human capital. Education is the economic engine needed for innovation and new technology. Endogenous growth studies no longer aggregate all workers into a "generic labor," but rather classify them by skill level.

Think About It...

Does the city that you are studying seem to attract or repel people with college degrees? How could the city attract more educated labor?

According to the 2000 Census, only 24.4 percent of the adults in the United States have earned at least a bachelor's degree. A four-year degree separates the "knowledge workers" from the manual laborers. In Chapter 10 we referred to a "chicken and egg" effect when we asked what comes first to a region, jobs or people. Educational attainment in an area creates a similar conundrum. Firms hesitate to locate in an area that lacks educated labor. Poor schools thus limit the tax base and the potential funding for K-12 education. If the K-12 education is not high quality, parents who value education also will locate elsewhere (Chapter 10). The brain drain continues when young people who succeeded in enriching their human capital decide not to return home.

Cities that have a higher than average level of educational attainment did not just send more students to college. They are also able to attract workers who already held advanced degrees. The attraction came because that's where the jobs are (as in Washington, DC), because the city is teaming with natural amenities (as in San Francisco), or because a dynamic economy is linked to cutting-edge technology (as in Seattle, Washington, and Atlanta, Georgia).

However, placing high-tech firms in a region does not guarantee that the populace as a whole is, or will become, better educated. North Carolina has a significant investment in its world-renowned Research Triangle Park, started in 1959. Hansen (1995) bemoaned the following paradox: North Carolina had more functionally illiterate adults than in the entire country of Japan. Over half of the employers had difficulty in finding workers who could read well enough, and 70 percent could not find workers with the right technical skills.

Technology Attracts Few Students

A study by de Grip and Willems (2003) of Dutch students 14–15 years of age determined that the choice of a speciality in technology or science was only slightly affected by economic motives. Poor school grades in math and sciences and a lack of interest in the field were more important predictors.

Females who earned high grades in math and science just shied away from a technological field. Individuals who were good in science but felt that "getting along with people" was the most important characteristic of a future occupation chose medicine or caregiving fields over technology

de Grip and Willems (2003)

Wage Inequality: The Next Pandemic

Gottlieb and Fogarty (2003) studied 75 large U.S. metropolitan areas and concluded that higher proportions of residents with at least a bachelor's degree in 1980 were associated with higher per capita income and employment levels 17 years later. Because of knowledge spillovers (Chapter 5 and Chapter 8), the most educated metropolitan areas in the United States had average per capita incomes 20 percent above the average, whereas the least educated had incomes 12 percent below the average.

The authors define "educational attainment" as the proportion of adults 25 years and older with four or more years of college. The average educational attainment was 25 percent for the top metropolitan areas: (Atlanta, Georgia; Austin, Texas; Boston, Massachusetts;

Denver, Colorado; Minneapolis/St. Paul, Minnesota; New York, New York; Raleigh-Durham, North Carolina; San Francisco-San Jose, California; Seattle, Washington; and Washington, DC). At the bottom of the list with an average proportion of 0.126 we found [Allentown and Scranton (Pennsylvania); Bakersfield, Fresno and Stockton (California); El Paso, Texas; Greenville-Spartanburg, South Carolina; Las Vegas, Nevada; Toledo and Youngstown (Ohio)].

Jacobs (2004) studied the progress of the wage inequality over time between skilled and unskilled workers in the Netherlands. He found that the number of well-educated women increased substantially, boosting the supply of skilled workers relative to unskilled workers. However, the steady advance in labor supply is more than offset by a soaring relative demand for skills, worsening the wage inequality.

The causes of this inequality are (1) the growth in skill-biased technology that requires highly educated workers, (2) the expansion of international trade with low-wage countries, (3) skilled workers complement capital better than unskilled ones, and (4) changes in labor market institutions that increased wage inequality. Such institutional changes include freezing minimum wages, welfare, unemployment and disability benefit reforms, and the growing amount of part-time jobs and flexible labor contracts. Jacobs predicted that wage differences between skilled and unskilled labor could reach between 10 percent and 55 percent by the year 2020.

Gottlieb and Fogarty (2003); Jacobs (2004)

If education increases human capital, and if enriching human capital generates economic growth and combats poverty, then we can say that a good quality education would be the key for individuals to escape poverty. It is also the key that will allow cities and regions to prosper. Most states subsidize postsecondary education. However, without a solid, basic education, resident-students will not be able to successfully complete advanced degrees.[1]

---

[1] Hansen (1995); Dellas and Koubi (2003); Gottlieb and Fogarty (2003); Jorgenson, Ho, and Stiroh (2003); Mykerezi, Mills, and Gomes (2003); Self and Grabowski (2003); Carlino (2005).

Production Function for Education

Economists model education as an output from a production function. Most education production functions, starting from Coleman (1966), have four basic factors that explain variations in school achievement scores: student's personal effort, parental inputs, school quality, and peer group effects. In turn, each of these factors influences the others. Studies that determine the effects of parental inputs concentrate specifically on early childhood development. We will examine school quality measures and peer group effects when we appraise primary and secondary school systems.[2]

Think About It...

What were your primary and secondary educational experiences like? What made your school good? What would you have changed?

What are the components of school achievement? In your opinion, do they include things other than test scores? What factors would you include in a model of the other qualities that make a successful school?

Causal Relations between Education and Growth

Does economic growth cause (allow) more people to pursue education or does an educated populace cause (create) economic growth? Causality is often tested by a procedure developed by 2003 Nobel laureate, Clive Granger. In essence, the method involves a regression analysis of one variable (say educational attainment) on past lags of itself and past lags of a potential causal variable (GDP), possibly including other variables. If the lagged values of the causal variable are significant (according to a Chow test), that variable "causes" (or "Granger causes") the dependent variable. Reverse

---

[2] Eberts and Kehoe-Schwartz (1990); Wößmann (2003).

causality is tested by exchanging the dependent and causal variables from the first regression.

Self and Grabowski (2003, 2004) studied causality between education and economic growth with data from Japan and India. From Japanese time-series data that ranged from 1888 to 1995, they determined that before WWII, increased proportions of adults with primary education "caused" economic growth. Secondary and university educational levels were also significant, but the effects of primary education dominated. After WWII, although primary, secondary, and university education continue to "cause" growth, increases in growth also explained the demand for all levels of education. However, they found no causal impact on growth due to vocational education.

Indian data from 1966 to 1996 showed that increased primary education of males had a strong impact on growth. However, this impact was not as robust as female education in primary, secondary, and tertiary levels. Overall, the causal linkage between primary and secondary education and growth suggests that these might be optimal candidates for place-based investment local funding.

Self and Grabowski (2003, 2004)

Student-Specific Education Production Functions

Bali and Alvarez (2003) asked if educational production functions differ for students from various races and ethnicity. Using data from the Pasadena Unified School District (PUSD) in southern California for the 1999–2000 school year, the authors tried to predict the variation in math and reading scores on California's mandatory Stanford Nine tests. Regarding family factors, they found that if the family had two parents, reading scores increased by 2.5 points for Hispanics, 3.3 points for African–Americans, and 1.3 points for Asians and whites. Students from a lower socioeconomic category (enrolling in free lunch programs or living in lower-valued homes) corresponded to lower scores in all groups.

The authors also found that a 10 percent increase in full credentials for teachers increased reading scores by almost one point and math scores by over one point for all ethnic groups. Increasing the number of computers from two per 100 students to 22 per 100 students helped Hispanic reading scores by over three points, but it had no effect on other students or on the math scores. The African–Americans in their sample did not benefit from smaller class sizes, but a decrease of 10 students in class size increased Hispanic reading and math scores by two points and Asian and white reading scores by over three points. An increase of 10 percent in the proportion of Hispanic and African–American teachers increased Hispanic and African–American math scores and Hispanic reading scores by about one point, but it decreased Asian and white scores by that amount.

Bali and Alvarez (2003)

Creating an Educated Labor Force

The two principal channels for acquiring human capital are on-the-job training and formal schooling. Extensive on-the-job training is costly for employers, especially because their newly trained employees can take a higher paying job with a competitor who does not bear the training costs. Creating an educated labor force through formal education requires that two components work together: (1) provision of good quality schools, and (2) students who are willing and able to invest in education. We will now scrutinize both the supply of school quality and the demand (willingness to pay) for education.

How to Improve School Quality

Colleges and universities predict the probability of students' success by observing how well they did in secondary school. Secondary schools predict the success of students by their achievements in primary schools, which rely on the quality of kindergarten and preschool experience. Quality preschools depend on the family as the main input. But the stable families are most often those with well-educated parents. How does a community extend this circle? How can an education system counteract the negative effect of dysfunctional families? How can a school district reallocate its funds to improve school quality?

Spending money to improve educational facilities, to decrease student/ teacher ratios, or to develop more appropriate curriculum will be a sound investment if nurture (training, upbringing) is the main cause of success at school. However, if nature (heredity, genetics) is the primary determinant of success, early intervention is essential.

Parental Human Capital Spillovers

Parents with higher educational levels have children who follow their example. Plug and Vijverberg (2003) used longitudinal data of biological and adopted children in Wisconsin. The IQ transfers from parent to child can be either genetic (nature) or environmental (nurture), but the authors conclude that about 55–60 percent of the parental ability is genetically transmitted. The study also determined that family income can improve a student's ability by as much as 15 percent.

Plug and Vijverberg (2003)

Carneiro and Heckman (2003) showed that the rate of return to investment in human capital is a monotonically decreasing function: preschool programs show the highest rate of return, formal schooling, a lower return, and post-school job training for those who did not finish high school very small. *Ceteris paribus*, the rate of return per dollar of investment made is higher while a person is young. Early investments are harvested over a longer horizon. They increase the productivity or lower the costs of later investments because of the synergy imbedded in human capital. Cognitive and noncognitive skills acquired early create a synergy for an increased capacity to learn, and the more one has learned, the more quickly one can learn.

Successful families generally have children who succeed in their studies and in turn, these children influence school quality. Schools work with what parents give them. They are more effective if parents encourage their children. It is difficult for schools to remedy years of trauma and neglect from dysfunctional families. The Coleman Report (1966) from the U.S. Office of Education suggests that the difference in quality only played a small part in pupil achievement. Many studies since Coleman (1966) have examined the efficiency of schools and school districts. Hanushek (1996) catalogued the results from 90 publications on the effect of various measures of school resources on student performance. Usually, the estimated effects of school inputs (number of teachers, administrators, and support staff), teacher salaries, quality of facilities, or overall expenditures per student are statistically insignificant and do not explain differences in average test scores among schools. When the variables were significant, the signs were not consistent from one study to another. Such inconclusive results are often interpreted as evidence of inefficient school systems when the results could in fact be due to poorly measured data, unmeasurable factors, or misspecified functions.

Current studies concur with the original Coleman Report: the family's influence and peer effects are the major determinants of school success. The most cost-effective methods for improving the quality of the labor force begin at home. What makes an optimal home environment? Differences in cognitive ability seem to be caused by the socioeconomic background of the child at early ages, specifically the mother's education, family structure, and the number of books the child has. Of course, just having books in the child's bedroom does not put small children on the road to becoming geniuses, but it is an indicator of the underlying parental attitudes toward the child's education. These attitudes, difficult to measure directly, substantially affect differences in cognitive ability.[3]

Pre-Preschool

Differences in ability are detectable at early ages, and persist over a person's lifetime. The literature on the early care and education (ECE) of small children leads us to the same literature that we cited under the rubric of child poverty (Chapter 18). Children start life with different endowments of health and attitudes because of genetics and the prebirth environment as well as their milieus after they are born. Attitudes and behavior of parents, especially mothers, affect the educational achievement of their children. The amount and type of stimulation as well as their sensitivity and interaction between the parent and the child affect the success in school. There are also other important factors: the parents' own physical and mental health, their ability, and the number of other family members.

---

[3] Carneiro and Heckman (2003); Carneiro, Hansen, and Heckman (2003); Currie and Moretti (2003); Mazumder (2003); Zhan and Sherraden (2003); Waldfogel (2004).

Think About It...

If you were to write a novel, how would you depict the early childhood experiences of a future administrator or company chairperson? Would these experiences be different for a future car thief or drug addict?

Cognitive ability is more easily shaped early in a child's life, and IQ is pretty much set by age eight. Feinstein (2003) determined that scores on tests given to youngsters at 22 months could predict educational qualifications at age 26. Scores on the standardized PIAT-Math and Peabody Picture Vocabulary Test (PPVT) tests given to children three and four years of age are already influenced by the family background, the environment and the mother's IQ [usually measured by the Armed Forces Qualification Test (AFQT)].

Cognitive ability explains differences in educational success and wages. However, noncognitive ability is also important. Noncognitive ability includes character traits such as attitude, motivation, persistence, self-discipline, and trustworthiness. Cognitive ability is important, but not all intelligent people can of finish projects, get along with people, or even pass a job interview. Determination, dependability, and consistency are the most important predictors of grades in school. These qualities are also prized by employers. Differences in mother's ability, mother's IQ, and family structure also affect the child's noncognitive abilities.

Hufnagel (2003), for example, used the German Socio-Economic Panel data and concluded that success at school is primarily a function not only of the parents' own education and the mother's IQ, but also of the care given to the child from birth to 36 months of age. Carneiro and Heckman (2003) asserted that if dysfunctional families are the major causes of poverty, crime and social problems, government intervention is mandatory. This intervention does not have to be draconian, however.

Parental leave programs are one way to permit parents to spend more time with their infants. European ECE programs begin with subsidized leave. Forty-one countries offer 52 weeks or more of paid leave. Eleven countries subsidize parental leave until the child is three years of age. The funds come from various federal programs such as unemployment insurance and disability. Subsidies could attain between 70 and 90 percent of the parent's prior earnings.

Under the Family and Medical Leave Act (FMLA) of 1993, new parents in the United States are entitled to 12 weeks of job-protected (unpaid) leave if they work for a firm with 50 or more employees, and if they worked

1250 hours or more in the previous year. Trzcinski (2005) reported that among women with no paid leave benefits, the average duration of leave was 6.6 weeks—the minimum period necessary for the mother to convalesce. This allowed no time to adjust the stress and fatigue that follow childbirth.

For children ages one and two, the quality of care is crucial. Good quality care can be given by either a parent or a nonparent caregiver. To be sensitive and responsive to the toddler's needs is essential. Such care is difficult to measure, and studies often use caregiver-to-child ratios or caregiver education to proxy this interaction. Loeb et al. (2003) used the Arnett Scale of Caregiver Behavior to measure the attention, interaction, and tenderness that the child received. The Arnett Scale also measures the ability of the caretaker to explain why certain actions are wrong and practice strategies required for the child to resolve problems. This type of interaction with an adult decreases the child's aggression and problem behavior.

The care given to children at the age of one or two produced cognitive gains without negatively affecting behavior. The most lasting gains include reduced delinquency and crime, as well as reduced teen births. The Infant Health and Development Program (IHDP) was an early intervention program implemented in eight U.S. cities between January 1985 and June 2000 for low-birth-weight children. This program provided center-based care for children at least a year old. It boosted IQ at age three by 20 points for children whose mothers dropped out of high school and ten points for children of mothers with only a high school education. It did not appreciably increase the measurable IQ of children whose mothers had earned a college degree.

Preschool

Much research has confirmed that mothers working outside the home have no negative effect on children aged three to five years as long as children are placed in a good quality daycare. High quality preschool programs for disadvantaged children produce substantial gains in terms of school readiness. Such preschool programs also have the advantage to give mothers the time necessary to possibly invest in their own education or employment.

The Perry Preschool Program, for example, was established to remedy dysfunctional families. Between 1962 and 1967, 123 disadvantaged African–American children with low IQs in Ypsilanti, Michigan, were randomly assigned to the Perry Preschool program at ages three or four. The parents of these children were taught parenting techniques where they were encouraged to be involved in their child's studies. A randomly assigned control group received no preschool program and their parents received no parental instruction. After one or two years of preschool, researchers followed the participants until age 27. According to Barnett (1992), the Perry Preschool Program returned $5.70 for every dollar spent, and the estimated return rises to $8.70 when projected over the lives of the program participants. The recent estimates of the rate of return to the Perry Preschool of 13 percent may have been even higher if the experiment included children of normal intelligence. The Perry Preschool intervention did not alter the IQ of the children, (which contradicts the conclusions of Feinstein (2003) mentioned above). But it did increase their noncognitive abilities and social skills. Compared to the control group, the Perry Preschool students gained more than a full grade level, which lasted throughout their academic careers.

The United States currently has three programs concerning ECE: child care vouchers, Head Start, and pre-K programs. These programs are funded from three different sources coming from different agencies. Thus, they each have different goals, standards, policies, evaluation criteria, and administration. It is difficult to evaluate them either as a unified whole, or even separately, but most of the evidence demonstrates that the marginal social benefits of the programs are lower than the marginal social costs. Not only are these programs not efficient, they also fail equity criteria.

The ***child care voucher program*** is partially funded by the Child Care Development Fund (CCDF) and partially from Temporary Assistance to Needy Families (TANF) funds. The CCDF funds come partially out of the federal budget and partially from state expenditures. The vouchers can be used with any child care provider, including faith-based providers.

These subsidies aid children from low-income families, but according to Witte and Trowbridge (2004) only 45 percent of the needy children between three and five years old are enrolled in preschool through this program, whereas 75 percent of those from higher income families also benefit from preschool; thus the child care voucher program violates the vertical equity criterion.

Head Start is supposed to become more accountable, in preparing children to read and to succeed in school, according to George W. Bush's 2002 *Good Start Grow Smart* initiative. Besides the emphasis on reading, Head Start also provides immunizations, as well as physical and dental exams. The quality of this program as a whole does not equal the Perry Preschool program. However, we must note that the 2700 Head Start Programs are not implemented identically everywhere. They are not as well funded as the Perry Preschool programs, and they do not include parental education.

Researchers have found short-term gains in test scores for all participating children, but most of the gains from this program were only temporary. However, Currie and Neidell (2003) noted that Head Start centers are of higher average quality than other child care available to low-income parents. They also found that test scores were higher and the rate of grade repetition diminished, but it does not boost children of poor families up to the average levels of achievement found in children from higher income families. The authors also remarked that fewer crimes were committed by young adults who attended Head Start programs as children, and that all else equal, these programs may be cost effective in the long run.

Concerning the impact on racial and ethnic groups, Currie and Neidell (2003) also determined that counties with a poverty rate greater than 11 percent (the national median) receive lower levels of Head Start funding than richer counties. African–American and Hispanic families are generally concentrated in poor counties, so on average, black and Hispanic children attend larger and more poorly funded Head Start programs than white and Asian children, which violates the horizontal equity criterion.

Pre-K programs are created by state and local governments to serve four-year-olds. California began its pre-K program in the mid 1960s, and 30 years later 23 other states had established their own programs. These programs are, depending on the state, offered by the public schools, contracted out to private or nonprofit organizations, or controlled by the private sector. Georgia and Oklahoma provide pre-K services to all four-year-old children, but most states only provide this service to children of low-income families.

There exist few evaluations of the child voucher program or the pre-K programs, but that is because of the wide variety of programs and the short amount of time they have existed. As a whole, evaluations of eight-hour programs that last all year for two years or more show long-term net benefits. However, the jury is out regarding which programs are cost effective.

Compared to the United States, most European governments invest substantially more funds to aid education of preschool children and their parents. In 1999, the United States was tied with Finland, Italy, Netherlands, Peru, Spain and the United Kingdom for 13th place out of 30 OEDC countries in the percentage of GDP devoted to early care and development. The United States spent 0.4 percent on ECE. Norway, Hungary, and Denmark spent 0.8% of GDP. France and Jamaica pay 0.7 percent. At the same time, the United States is second only to Denmark with the proportion of the population under three years of age in formal child care centers, but it is tied with Ecuador and Surinam for 39th in enrollment for three-to-five-year olds (57 percent).[4]

---

[4] Barnett (1992); Ladd (2002); Carneiro and Heckman (2003); Feinstein (2003); Hufnagel (2003); Loeb et al. (2003); Plug and Vijverberg (2003); Fryer and Levitt (2004); Heymann (2004); Black, Devereux, and Salvanes (2005).

Primary School

How do we define quality primary schools and what contributes to success of children in their elementary education? We encountered arguments

---

Are they Ready for School

Corman (2003) asked what will keep children from repeating a grade. The author tested (1) variations in overall school expenditures by state, (2) special education enrollments of students between 6 and 15 years of age, (3) handicapped preschool enrollments, and (4) Head Start allocations. The study found that none of these interventions significantly influences the probability of a child repeating a grade. The relative age of the student has the largest impact on his or her academic success or failure. Individual family and neighborhood characteristics are also significant determinants of success or failure.

Corman (2003)

Think About It...

Who was your favorite primary school teacher? What did you admire about this person? What would you have changed in the personality of your least favorite teacher?

---

supporting the spatial mismatch hypothesis according to which poor school quality in low-income neighborhoods creates intergenerational poverty. If so, what specifically is different among unsuccessful schools and successful ones?

The effect of teachers on learning is impressive, but difficult to measure. A good teacher can give students an education equivalent to $1\frac{1}{2}$ grade levels, but a bad teacher only provides a half year's education, according to Hanushek et al. (2003). Researchers have tried to measure teacher quality by number of years teaching, educational level, and number of homework assignments that the teacher gave and/or corrected. One reason that teacher quality may be difficult to measure is because good and poor students respond to various characteristics of teachers differently. The new teacher's enthusiasm can capture the attention of poor students, whereas good students prefer the challenges and ready answers provided by more experienced teachers. The number of homework assignments may not be as effective as the quality of the assignments, but the overall "assignment quality" measure is difficult to measure.

Effects of War on Children's Education and Earnings Potential

Ichino and Winter-Ebmer (2004) studied the effects of war on the educational attainment and earnings of 10-year-olds growing up in Austria and Germany during World War II. These individuals received less education compared to their counterparts in neutral Sweden and Switzerland, and their earnings potential decreased by about 20 percent per year of schooling lost due to the war. The Swedish and Swiss cohorts followed a smooth upward educational trend with no war disruption. The long-run effect of the war on earnings persisted even forty years after the conflict in magnitude of 0.8 percent of the GDP of Germany and Austria. No comparable loss in earnings or decrease in GDP took place in Sweden and Switzerland.

Ichino and Winter-Ebmer (2004)

Class size has no decisive influence on student performance even though most authors on the subject favor smaller classes. Krueger (2003) estimated that the internal rate of return of a reduction from 22 to 15 students is approximately six percent. However, small classes only benefit students in the first year, which is more consistent with the role of socialization rather than increased teaching effectiveness. Large class sizes may decrease student achievement because of discipline problems or because of the smaller amount of time teachers spend with individual students. Teachers can produce either public goods (lectures) or private goods (tutoring individual students). Smaller classes allow the teacher to devote more time to private tutoring, an advantage for low-achieving students, but a disadvantage for good students.

Effect of Class Size on Student and Parental Effort

Using Norwegian data from the eighth through tenth grades (lower secondary school) Bonesrønning (2003) determined that male students are significantly and positively affected by smaller classes but only when the teacher grades hard. No such correlation is found for female students except those from small families. The author measured student effort by asking the number of minutes that students spent daydreaming during a typical mathematics lesson. Thirty-one percent admitted that they were preoccupied for more than ten minutes per hour of class. Class size did not significantly affect their attention span. In addition, Bonesrønning (2004) noted that, paradoxically, parents tended to be less involved in their child's classes and school work as class size increases, but they increased their efforts when class sizes were smaller.

Bonesrønning (2003, 2004)

School District Decisions Support Public Choice Theory

Larger school districts seem to hinder student performance. They often limit the autonomy of individual schools, thereby restricting the ability of schools to adapt to the particular needs of the students. Fiscal controls may constrain innovation in program choice or use of resources. Poor coordination between schools not only reduces accountability, but also the influence that parents have in the education process.

VanderHart and Ransom (2003) studied public school districts in Ohio and estimated that 80 percent of the school districts chose combinations of educational inputs designed to increase test scores of their students. However, the rest of the school districts invested in educational inputs inefficiently. The inefficient school districts could improve matters by increasing the amount of capital expenditure and support staff, while decreasing the number of administrators and office personnel. Thus, administrators seem to have engaged in self-serving behavior by choosing to invest in inputs that made their own jobs easier, without adding to the students' scholastic achievement. This behavior, as public choice theory suggests, will result in an excessively large school bureaucracy, potentially producing negative marginal returns in terms of student achievement.

VanderHart and Ransom (2003)

Think About It...

What are your friends from primary and secondary school doing? Are they also in university or did they choose another life path? Did those who did not attend university support your decision to do so?

How do your peers now influence the classroom environments?

Hanushek et al. (2003) discovered that in elementary school, the achievement level of peers has a positive effect on that of the individual student. The role of peers is complex. Peer composition depends on the parent's choice of residence, the school itself, and the school administration's decisions on attendance rules. Of course, students affect their peers as much as they are influenced by them.

Peer groups can have an influence, not always negative, on the teacher. To better understand the role of peers, one needs data on specific friendships within classrooms as well as attributes of these friends and their families' socioeconomic status. Such data sets are difficult to obtain. Studying "peer effects" in elementary is therefore limited to information available on the aggregation of students within the entire grade or school.[5]

---

[5] Eberts, Kehoe-Schwartz and Stone (1990); Bonesrønning (2003); Coates (2003); Driscoll, Halcoussis, and Svorny (2003); Hanushek et al. (2003); VanderHart and Ransom (2003); Wößmann (2003); Fryer and Levitt (2004).

Incentive Systems

What types of intervention policies will help to improve elementary and secondary schools? Economists often suggest *incentive systems*, through which teachers are financially rewarded when "production" of student test scores increases. A link between the salary and academic success of the class forces the teachers and the schools to place a higher priority on the performance of students.

The incentive systems also have a positive effect on the students. The proponents of standardized tests assert that if students are required to demonstrate their basic competencies, they will have a greater incentive to learn. To justify their opinion, they cite the case of the cumulative exams required by schools in Europe that determine if the student will pass to the next grade or not. The adoption of such a system in the United States is a very controversial subject.

Opponents of standardized tests fear the types of incentives that these tests provide to teachers and administrators. For one thing, this system will keep instructors from teaching skills or topics not on that test. Second, these incentives tempt teachers and administrators to cheat. Such cheating was uncovered in Chicago Public Elementary schools (Jacob and Levitt 2003), and it has been documented in other schools in the United States and in Great Britain. Evaluators noticed that every answer sheet in some classrooms answered the same string of questions correctly and apparently the answer sheets had been altered after the student finished the examination. Some other teachers were accused of writing the answers on the blackboard. Obtaining accurate exam scores therefore requires the hiring of honest evaluators.

Economists also suggest increasing *competition* among schools. This could come about through school vouchers that parents may use for the school of their choice. This would eliminate the preestablished "market area boundaries" and permit parents and students the school of their choice. The administrators of these schools will thus be required to satisfy the demands of their clients.[6]

School Choice

In 1987, Minnesota implemented a system that allows students to enroll in any public school in the state as long as seats are available. In the mid 1990s, Boston, Massachussets, divided the city into three autonomous zones. Elementary and middle school students could attend any school within

---

[6] Neal (1997); Grogger and Neal (2000); Hanuchek (2000); Schwab (2000); Jacob and Levitt (2003).

their zones, if seats are available. Publicly-funded voucher programs also exist in Milwaukee, Wisconsin (1975); Cleveland, Ohio (1995); Washington, DC (2004); as well as Florida (1999); Utah (2005); and Maine and Vermont (since the 1800s). Privately funded programs provide vouchers for qualified students in New York City, Dayton, Ohio, and Washington, DC. The Children's Scholarship Fund, founded in 1998, expanded the private voucher program to the entire country. Most studies of these programs concluded that there are not enough data to determine the net effect of vouchers on test performance, school access, or racial integration.

Dangerous Incentives

New Zealand adopted a system of reform in 1989, Tomorrow's Schools, which transferred operating responsibility from the Department of Education to each school's newly elected government board of trustees. In 1991, New Zealand introduced freedom of choice for the parents thus establishing a competitive environment for all schools in the state. Because religious schools were integrated into the public school system in the 1970s, the reforms extended parental choice to all schools except non-religious private schools. The public financing of these schools is based on the number of students.

Schools can supplement their budgets with fund-raising activities, noncompulsory fees from parents, and foundation grants. When a school reaches its maximum number of students, the Ministry of Education permits it to specify its own selection criteria.

Since 1995, the Ministry of Education has ranked schools based on its ethnic mix as well as measures of socioeconomic status such as parent education level and the proportion of parents on welfare. The result was that students tended to drift toward the schools that served more economically and socially advantaged students because they were considered better. This tendency decreased the size of schools that served the ethnic minorities and students from low-income families.

"Successful" schools are those that easily attract students. However, this definition of success is not necessarily correlated with teaching quality. Students in the unsuccessful schools had a significantly lower chance of earning grades of A or B on the schools' standardized exams, according to Ladd and Fiske (2001). In addition, the average performance of these schools deteriorated between 1992 and 1997 as the percentages of their students receiving D or F increased. The reverse is true in successful schools. Instead of closing the gaps in school quality, this system of competition increased the disparities.

Ladd and Fiske (2001)

The Carrot or the Stick?

Figlio and Lucas (2004), as well as Figlio and Rouse (2006), studied Florida housing data ranging from the mid 1980s through early 2002. The Florida Department of Education assigned letter grades from A to F to each school in the middle of the year. Grades were based on curriculum, the students' attendance records, and their scores on standardized tests (reading, writing, and math). Independent of their personal performance, students who attended F schools could receive vouchers entitling them to attend better schools.

Figlio and Lucas observed the housing sales that occur in the months just before and just after the issuance of grades. After the first year, the difference between an A and a B translated into an increase in housing prices of 19.5 percent, *ceteris paribus*. The difference between a B and a C was valued at 15.6 percent. However, because school grades fluctuated substantially from year to year, the housing market capitalized the school grades less and less. After the third year, the difference between an A and a B was only 8.7 percent, and the difference between a B and a C had become negligible. The improved quality of instruction seemed to come from changes in the quality of the students themselves. Improved instruction was due more to the stigma of

receiving low grades from the Florida Department of
Education and the attraction of performance bonuses
to schools and teachers rather than to the threat of
having students choose better schools.

Figlio and Lucas (2004); Figlio and Rouse (2006)

The voucher program is designed to create a form of market for schools
by dissolving their monopoly and forcing the schools to provide instructional quality that matches the demands of consumers of public education.
Greater competition among schools leads to better schools.

Critics of these initiatives fear that such policies will harm public schools.
Their arguments rest on two opposing scenarios. The first assumes that public
schools are of high quality and most students are educated in public schools.
The second assumes that public schools are of low-quality and most students
are educated in the private sector. Both scenarios result in a stable equilibrium, but any cutback in public school funding could lead to a rapid
deterioration of public school quality and an exodus to private schools.

Critics also fear that greater choice of schools will increase inequality and
impede the ability of school systems to serve handicapped students or those
from low-income families. Families who value education and have the
means to either transport their children to schools elsewhere, or move to
other neighborhoods will do so, simultaneously skimming off the scholas-
tically able and motivated students (bright flight) and concentrating the
weakest and least motivated students. Because of housing or employment
discrimination, this practice will increase racial and economic segregation in
the elementary and secondary schools.

Other critics admit that vouchers will directly benefit families whose
children are enrolled in private schools. However, vouchers will affect
property values around the good and the poor schools. They make
private schools affordable and eliminate the need to live near a good
school. Property values in these neighborhoods will drop. Because families
can live where they want and still send their children to a good school,
paradoxically, housing values close to the inferior public schools will
increase merely because residents are no longer required to send their
children to the closest school. Note that this argument assumes that the cost
of transportation in terms of time or distance is not as important in choosing
a school as it is in choosing a place of work or a shopping center.

The subsidies that allow students from low-income families to attend
private schools constitutes another means of encouraging competition. Six
states (Arizona, Florida, Illinois, Iowa, Minnesota, and Pennsylvania) offer

either tax credits for private school tuition or tax deductions for education expenses. There are two types of private schools: Catholic schools and non-Catholic schools. Those that are not affiliated with the National Catholic Educational Association (NCEA) belong to the National Association of Independent Schools (NAIS). The difference in the types of private schools is significant. Hanushek (2000) corrected for different family backgrounds and found that non-Catholic private schools performed no differently than public schools and significantly worse than Catholic schools, despite the fact that they charge tuition.

Most studies document that students who attend Catholic secondary schools perform better on standardized exams, have greater high school graduation rates, and later, larger college graduation rates, which lead to higher future earnings.

The positive result from Catholic schools is particularly notable on the inner city students, especially ethnic minorities. But, differences in the quality of Catholic schools and suburban public schools are negligible. A consensus of studies concluded that Catholic schools were not superior to public schools in general, but they are similar in quality to suburban public schools. They are significantly better than urban public schools in poor neighborhoods.

What is the secret of the Catholic schools? Most of their students are placed in academic tracks and are required to take a rigorous set of academic courses. Teachers enforce strict discipline in the classrooms. The religious training stresses the importance of a shared sense of community.[7]

International Preoccupation with School Quality

Institutional features of schooling systems are positively related to differences in how schools are organized rather than differences in available resources. Wößmann (2003) studied international school systems in 39 countries using the Third International Mathematics and Science Study (TIMSS) database. After controlling for family background and the effect of resource differences, he studied the effects of national examinations, the level of school autonomy, and the amount of competition from private schools. He determined that students in schools facing national

---

[7] Wyckoff (1991); Couch, Shughart, and Williams (1993); Lee (1997); Hanushek (2000); Lankford and Wyckoff (2001); Peterson (2005).

exams scored an average of 16.1 points more in mathematics and 10.7 points more in science.

Dutch schools have the highest autonomy, while Greek, Norwegian, and Portuguese schools have the least in his data set. School autonomy allows better use of specialized knowledge and ability to meet the special needs of particular clusters of students, but unfortunately, a greater freedom carries with it a greater potential for local opportunistic behavior. Wößmann determined that a centralized curriculum and a list of approved textbooks increased student scores in mathematics and science. Schools that were free to allocate their own budget produced students with lower math and science scores (by 5.9 points and 3.5 points). However, test scores in schools that had autonomy in hiring teachers were significantly higher (12.7 and 5.2 in mathematics and science). It is the same for the schools that set teacher salaries (10.6 and 15.2). Students performed better when each teacher influenced curriculum (by 12.0 and 10.8), compared to those where teachers were unionized, (-32.3 in mathematics and -18.4 in science).

In all countries, the public sector is in charge of basic education, but countries differ considerably according to the degree of competition from private institutions. Only 25 percent of Dutch students attend public schools. The Japanese have the largest share of privately managed schools that are also independent of public funding. At the other extreme Australia, France, Germany, and Sweden have almost no financially independent private schools. Private schools are subject to monetary incentives to use resources efficiently. They also offer a choice to parents and thus introduce competition into the public education system. Wößmann determined that students in countries with larger shares of enrollments in private schools scored on average 10.3 points higher on mathematics tests for every increase in one standard deviation in private enrollment.

Wößmann (2003)

654 ■ *Regional and Urban Economics and Economic Development*

Where Have All the Teachers Gone?

Clotfelter et al. (2004) studied the potential side effects of the No Child Left Behind Act of 2001. This act puts added pressure on states to use standardized test scores as an accountability measure. Each state must test students in math and reading in grades three through eight and measure each school's yearly progress. The goal is to improve the performance of students in the worst schools.

Increased accountability is politically popular. In North Carolina, for example, the proportion of students in grades three through eight scoring at or above grade level in reading increased from 63 percent in 1992–1993 to 77 percent in 2000–2001. In math the scores increased from 61 percent to 81 percent.

Unfortunately, there is an unforeseen byproduct of the Act: low-performing schools have a hard time retaining and attracting high-quality teachers. The authors measure teacher quality by amounts of experience and by the university from which they were graduated. They found, for instance, that the percentage of beginning teachers in the 7th grade in low performing schools fell by four percent before the accountability period 1995–1995 to 1997–1998, but rose by three percent afterward. Similarly, proportions of 7th grade teachers from uncompetitive colleges and universities fell by seven percent before 1997/1998 but rose by five percent from 1997/1998 to 2000/2001.

Transparency hurts. Personnel in "successful schools" are respected as being effective and compensated. Those in "failing schools" are publicly examined and sanctioned. Thus, the "poor schools" attract the inexperienced and those who graduate from uncompetitive colleges and cause higher rates of teacher turnover. The schools that serve mediocre students cannot attract or retain quality teachers when stringent accountability requirements are imposed.

Clotfelter et al. (2004)

Secondary Schools

In addition to the problems common to primary schools, secondary schools risk losing students who can legally refuse to continue their education. What causes this decision? According to Stull (1995), high school students in the United States belong to one of three groups. The smallest group consists of students planning to attend competitive colleges or universities when they graduate. The second group is the students who plan to attend noncompetitive colleges and universities. The third group is the largest, consisting of students who have no intention of pursuing higher education in any form.

Stull's **rational apathy model** asserts that the absence of a reward system in high school is designed to generate apathy because most students do not see why they need to take their studies seriously. Stull tests his model using the *High School and Beyond* data set. The results suggest that neither the skills learned nor the grades earned in high school have an important influence on wages for those who do not go to college. Student apathy is therefore a rational reaction to an educational system that they believe is unable to prepare them for their future.

Think About It...

Think about your high school classmates who chose to not continue their education. What reasons did they give for quitting? What are they doing now? Have they returned to school? Are they thinking about doing so?

Time, Time, Time

Behavior models of adolescent delinquency are based on complex choices between labor and leisure. Adolescents do not only choose between market work and leisure, but also between school and delinquent activities. According to Healey, Knapp, and Farrington (2004), children who were identified at an early age as "troublesome" by peers and teachers, and who subsequently engaged in delinquent behavior during adolescence, spent significantly longer periods of time out of the workforce, unemployed, or in low-paying jobs before age 32. According to longitudinal data from the United Kingdom, the unstable employment for males, linked with low noncognitive skills are due to poor educational attainment in secondary school and higher rates of criminal convictions in early adulthood.

Using data from the Montreal Longitudinal Study, Leung (2003) showed that institutions such as family, church, school, and peers can affect the decisions of an adolescent to spend time between delinquency, schooling, and work. Teens who intend to pursue post-secondary education are less likely to be delinquent. Family support also helps deter delinquency. Teens that grow up in stable, two-parent households tend to choose more socially acceptable behavior

Healey, Knapp, and Farrington (2004); Leung (2003)

Usually, the lure of "big money" draws a student's attention away from coursework. This is one of the reasons for which a proposal to increase the minimum wage is controversial. Students who work part time are often myopic: at age 16 or 17 years, they often overvalue present consumption and instant gratification. Tyler (2003) calculated that if the average amount of time that students were allowed to work was reduced by ten hours per week, the average 12th grade math score for the United States students would rise by approximately 2.0 points. Given (1) a return to test scores of 20 percent for each standard deviation increase, (2) a discount rate of three percent, and (3) a retirement age of 65, Tyler estimated that the benefit to a 17-year-old student who worked ten hours per week less in the 12th grade increases the present value of lifetime earnings by approximately $30,000. If the student earns a wage of $10 per hour, the decrease in hours worked would only cost the student $3600 in lost wages during the school year.

Teens often drop out because they have imperfect information about labor markets. A labor force survey of Central Minnesota residents by Edwards and Partridge (2001) asked respondents if they felt that their job made full use of their skills, that is, did they think that they were underemployed. The majority of the self-identified underemployed workers were still in high school. A study by Oreopoulos (2003) using data from the United States, Canada, and the United Kingdom determined that if dropouts had stayed in school one more year, the present value of their income would have increased more than ten times the amount of the earnings that they sacrificed to stay in school, and more than two times the maximum lifetime annual wage.

Education and Earnings up in Smoke

Fersterer and Winter-Ebmer (2003) underlined the importance of the choice between instant gratification and academics for older teens. Time-preference rates correlate positively with smoking habits even after adjusting for income.

The results concluded that students who were born after 1952 and started to smoke at age 16, on average, invest in two quarters less schooling than nonsmokers. This cohort would have decided to smoke at about the time information on smoking risk became widespread. Smokers are not more absent from work than nonsmokers, but they earn between four percent and eight percent less, according to data from the National Longitudinal Survey of Youth.

Fersterer and Winter-Ebmer (2003)

In some cases family problems cause students to drop out. The physical and mental health of the parents influences this probability, especially for females. Female students are more likely to drop out if their mothers are battling depression or abusing alcohol. Fathers with clinical depression can also have the same effect. Male students are less affected by these negative influences. Depression or alcoholism limits a mother's ability to serve as a role model or to closely monitor the child's progress. When the mother is incapacitated, the daughter takes over. Such burdens on an adolescent decrease the time spent on academics, and increase the probability of failure.

Dropouts in the United States and in Australia

Those who leave school early often face difficulties in their transition from school to post-school education or training and are often unemployed. Rumberger and Lamb (2003) compared the future of dropouts in Australia and in the United States. Dropouts constitute just over 20 percent of the number of high school students in both countries. The risk of dropping out is higher for low-achieving students from poor families, from rural areas, and from public schools.

In the United States, most dropouts leave after completing the 10th grade. Those who earned GEDs often found jobs in skilled trades rather than clerical jobs. In contrast, Australian dropouts can still enter apprenticeships or other forms of vocational education without even having finished the 10th grade. Half of the Australian dropouts left school during their 10th year of school. Half of the U.S. dropouts complete high school before age 20, whereas fewer than 10 percent of the Australian dropouts ever complete high school. In spite of this, two-thirds of the male and one-third of female dropouts in Australia participated in apprenticeships and vocational education.

At age 20, or four years after they drop out, 45 percent of all dropouts in the United States are neither employed nor enrolled in any type of training program, whereas only eight percent of the graduates are in the same predicaments. In Australia, comparable proportions are 17 percent for dropouts and five percent for graduates.

Rumberger and Lamb (2003)

The possibility of earning a GED is an incentive for some to not finish school. However, the market does not always value the GED as equivalent to a traditional high school degree. Controlling for measured cognitive ability, GED recipients have lower hourly wages and obtain lower levels of schooling than other high school dropouts. This characterization does not hold for females who dropped out of school because of pregnancy. White females who earn the GED earn the same as other high school dropouts, *ceteris paribus*.

What are the effects of intervention programs for adolescents? Early intervention has the highest payoffs due to improved social skills, increased motivation, improved homelife of the child and longer time horizon from which to benefit. Adolescent intervention programs such as Big Brothers/Big Sisters pair youth with an adult mentor. On average, after 18 months of guidance, the teens are less likely to have started substance abuse, engaged in violent behavior, been truant, and are more honest with their parents. Their grades improved and they seemed to have an easier family life. A mentoring program such as Philadelphia's Sponsor-A-Scholar (SAS), which lasted longer than 18 months, increased college enrollments of at-risk students by between 16 and 22 percent.

Programs for dropouts, however, are less successful. Analyses of various youth training programs in Sweden, the United Kingdom; France; Quebec, Canada; and the United States all show that such policies have negative rates of return and are inefficient investments in the training of low-skilled workers. After accounting for the social costs of taxation required to finance these programs, the negative benefit-cost analysis is even more negative.

The United Kingdom instituted a two-year Youth Training Scheme (YTS). Dolton, Makepeace, and Treble (1994) found that disadvantaged youth gained little from their participation in YTS. The young people whose only training was YTS typically earned less than comparable individuals with no formal training. They found evidence of discrimination against apprentices with a YTS background. Participation in YTS signaled to employers a low potential productivity and a bad hire. Pénard and Sollogoub (1995) found identical results for training and community jobs programs for teens in France and Quebec, Canada. The Job Corps program in the United States has the same disappointing results (Carneiro and Heckman 2003). A direct monetary cost to participants of zero did not encourage the enthusiasm of the participants who not only suffered disutility from being in the program, but who may have also sacrificed their participation in a more lucrative activity (legal or illegal).[8]

Willingness to Pay for the Costs of Education

Education is a club good. To what extent is it a public good or a private good? Some argue that the free market leads to an inefficient investment because of the externalities associated with education (more productive and technologically savvy workers, more informed voters, less crime, and lower teen pregnancy rates, for instance). The lower crime rates do not result directly from education because it decreases the willingness to engage in criminal activity, but because most crime is committed by adolescent males who, if required to pass most of the day in school, are less exposed to influences of the street.

In addition, education increases income tax payments to the extent that educated people pay more taxes. Because housing is a normal good, the increased incomes lead to higher property values, a larger tax base, and potentially lower tax rates.

---

[8] Dolton, Makepeace, and Treble (1994); Calmfors and Skedinger (1995); Pénard and Sollogoub (1995); Stull (1995); Cameron and Heckman (1998, 2001); Edwards and Partridge (2001); Carneiro and Heckman (2003); Farahati, Marcotte, and Wilcox-Gök (2003); Nechyba (2003); Rosenthal (2003); Tyler (2003); Tyler, Murnane, and Willett (2003); Ahituv and Tienda (2004).

Finally, educated people are less likely to receive public assistance. They are probably in better health and in other words, the benefits to society are greater than the private benefits to the students.

Besides ignoring the social benefits of education, markets fail because of the uncertainty and transactions costs associated with education. Young children cannot commit to repaying educational loans used for their primary and secondary school education, but, according to Becker and Murphy (1988), if the family can finance the development of the child's human capital, the children could reimburse their elderly parents (by funding social security, for instance). Thus, both the parents and the children benefit.

Finally, society feels compassion toward disadvantaged children. Educational transfers satisfy society's taste for charitable giving, and they are a means of redistributing wealth and equalizing future incomes. The recipients would prefer cash, as we noted in Chapter 13 and Chapter 18, but society wants them to consume what it believes is optimal, not what the recipients think is good for them.

The price for public goods is difficult to determine. There is no market in which an individual's demand can be observed. To find the value of education it is necessary to use surveys to see if households are satisfied with schools (or other public goods), hedonic methods (Chapter 13), or median voter models (Chapter 17). According to the median voter model, families reveal their preferences by either voting or by choosing to live in a place that offers a particular mix of taxes and educational services.

The appropriate funding source for a public good depends on the size of the spillover of its associated externality (Chapter 17). Poor quality primary and secondary schools will create local spillover effects because the recipients will have few chances to better themselves by moving. In addition, a good quality basic education could eventually generate national or even global benefits.

Those who received a poor quality education will not earn large salaries and will add little to the local tax base, thus lowering the quality of schools through insufficient financing and will produce continuing generations of poor families. High-skilled workers will live in areas that respond better to their needs and those of their children. Thus the disparity between quality of education and job readiness will continue. For this reason, the principle of social equity mandates that federal or state government provide aid to low-income communities.

The federal government in the United States is commonly viewed as a compensator that counterbalances social inequities and promotes equality of opportunity. Through programs such as Title I, the federal government aids low-income schools and school districts.

However, such a policy may be a double-edged sword. To the extent that federal and state intergovernmental aid improves the local school system, such aid is capitalized into the price of housing in that locality. This is true even if the community substitutes state aid for its own tax revenues. Figlio, Husted and Kenny (2004) found that between 50 and 100 percent of the interjurisdictional variations in property taxes were capitalized into the housing values. The higher housing prices boost the cost of living for newcomers and harm the low-income residents who either wanted to purchase a home or whose property tax bill became unaffordable. School financing increases the capital gains for apartment owners near good quality schools because demand is higher. In contrast, the higher property taxes, which also affect multifamily dwellings, are borne by the renters who are obliged to pay more for rent. To the extent that vouchers do not place a premium on locating near a specific school, these instruments may meet the efficiency and equity criterion more effectively than does interjurisdictional aid. [9]

Through tax deductions and tax credits, the federal government subsidizes higher-income school districts. People in the 28% federal income tax bracket, who include $1000 in state and local taxes for schools as an itemized deduction, reduce their federal tax bill by $280. Loeb and Socias (2004) found that these deductions more than double the federal contribution to schools. If we add the Title 1 expenditures, the federal government paradoxically subsidizes high-income school districts more than the low-income districts.

Political Power Affects Spending on Education

Colburn and Horowitz (2003) used a demand for local public goods model to isolate the interest group pressures on educational spending in the Commonwealth of Virginia. The dominant interest groups for increased spending on public education are the primary beneficiaries (number of teachers and students), as well as the proportion of Democrats and the percentage of employees of the federal government. Larger proportions of African–Americans and higher income residents reduce this demand. Federal government employees might be more likely to

---

[9] Feldman and Beguin (1978); Bogart and Cromwell (1997); Crone (1998); Taylor (1999); Brunner and Sonstelie (2003); Kane, Staiger, and Samms (2003).

support greater spending because such policies lead to an increase in teacher salaries. Via the collective bargaining process, an increase in teachers' salaries may help augment the salaries of federal employees.

Colburn and Horowitz (2003)

Swedish Demand for Education

Using data from Swedish surveys, Ahlin and Johansson (2001) estimated the demand for local public school expenditures. Investment in primary and secondary schools constitutes the largest single item of local government expenditures. In spite of a minimum standard of education mandated (and financed) by the national government, local variations in per capita spending on schools are significant. The authors found that the proponents of increased school spending tend to be in the following categories: female, between 20 and 50 years of age, parents of school-age children, and municipal employees.

Municipal employees have different budget constraints than private employees. Suppliers of public goods are in part their own demanders. Private sector employers see an increase in taxes and will demand a lower quantity of services. Public employees also anticipate higher taxes, but more importantly, they see an increase in their salaries. Thus the price elasticity of demand for education will be less elastic for public employees than for private ones, and the income elasticity will be higher.

On average, the tax price and income elasticities for educational spending in Sweden are −1.09 and 1.14. Similar American studies reveal tax price elasticities ranging from 0 to −0.70 and income elasticities (from 0.10 to 0.23). The authors speculate that education is more necessary in the United States than in Sweden because the returns to education in Sweden are relatively low. Swedes know that they will do relatively well regardless of their education because of a guaranteed income floor. In addition, they are penalized by high tax rates if their incomes increase. The result is that education is more of a luxury good than a necessity.

Ahlin and Johansson (2001)

Summary and Conclusions

In this chapter we reviewed the literature on the effects of education on regional and metropolitan growth. Education is the impetus for regional growth. Without good quality labor, firms do not locate, tax bases and income levels stay low, as does the spending for elementary and secondary schools. This insufficient spending can create a downward spiral for future generations. To reverse this tendency, it is necessary to invest in quality teachers. Areas increase their pool of educated workers not only by sending their own children to the university, but mostly by attracting educated labor. If an area cannot attract these workers, then local amenities or dynamic, state-of-the-art entrepreneurial activity may be a sufficient magnet.

The production of education requires four main ingredients: student effort, parental inputs, school quality, and peer group effects. Consistently, the results of empirical studies suggest that parental inputs and peer groups are the most influential determinants: so much for increasing scholastic attainment by increased school financing alone.

Successful educational programs produce both cognitive and noncognitive abilities. Intelligence can explain wage differences, but noncognitive attributes such as attitude, motivation, self-discipline, and trustworthiness also affect earning abilities. Educational attainment is a function of parental inputs and family structure, school quality, and peer group effects. Time-on-task within a classroom results in improved test scores for the subject. Large class sizes may decrease student achievement because teachers have less time for private tutoring. Peer effects are important in determining academic success of a student. Classes with larger numbers of students from "good homes" create an environment that will foster learning by students from less than optimal backgrounds.

Creating an educated labor force requires students for whom an investment in education provides positive rates of return, and good quality schools starting from early day care facilities. Cognitive ability in a child is set by age eight. Scores on tests given children who were not yet two years old can predict educational attainment at age 26. The high correlation between education levels of parents and students is due to inherited ability (nature) and environment and cognitive stimulants at an early age (nurture).

Cognitive and noncognitive abilities develop faster when adults spend more time with the child.

Students in secondary schools have to allocate their time between school, working for wages, and leisure. If they do not think that high school experience could prepare them for their (blue-collar) career choice, they may decide to drop out. Besides the lure of independence associated with "big money," students decide to drop out also because of family problems, and because they have imperfect information about the conditions required by the labor markets. Intervention programs an effectively aim at improving the noncognitive skills of adolescents. Successful programs pair students up with a mentor over a period of about 18 months. Alternatively, youth training programs for dropouts seem to have a negative result because they signal to employers that the job applicant is a bad hire. Former participants generally earn less than those who had not participated.

Economists suggest two ways to improve school quality. The first is an incentive system that ties teachers' salaries to student performance. Students who, at the end of the year, do not demonstrate sufficient proficiency will be held back. Teachers as well as schools will be rewarded if larger proportions of students do well. However, critics fear that such a plan will limit the subjects presented in class. They also think that schools populated with mediocre students will have difficulty hiring and retaining good quality teachers. Further, the accountability requirements can be a temptation for teachers and administrators to alter students' answer sheets.

The second means is to increase competition among schools, which will eliminate the current monopoly of most school districts. Better schools are possible because they exist. A growing number of states and jurisdictions have experimented with school vouchers. However, we do not have enough data to empirically address their effects. Adjusting for family background of the students, Catholic schools are similar to public suburban schools, but they outperform public schools in the inner city as well as the private non-Catholic schools in the suburbs. Catholic schools place most of their students on academic tracks with rigorous academic courses in a disciplined environment. These traits create a work ethic in students that leads to increased human capital and increased earnings.

Financing education is a delicate subject. Spillover effects of a good education could be national or even global. However, poorly educated individuals are more likely to remain home, and to contribute meager amounts of taxes, thus perpetuating the existence of inefficient schools. Equity-of-chance considerations mandate a role for intergovernmental aid. However, if such aid results in increased school quality, the surrounding residences will increase in value. Poor families will have more difficulty settling there and the increased rents for multifamily dwellings will chase away some families that the governmental aid was designed to help.

Because vouchers have no such impact on the housing market, they may meet both the efficiency and equity criterion more effectively than inter-jurisdictional aid given directly to specific schools.

Chapter Questions

1. What are the inputs of an education production function? Which are variable inputs? Which are fixed?
2. According to the filtering theory, where within a city would the lower funded schools exist? Where would the better schools exist?

Research Questions

1. What proportion of adults 25 and older have advanced degrees? What proportion have at least a bachelor's degree? A high school diploma? What proportion did not finish grade school or high school? Check the educational attainment for people in your city, county, and state through American Factfinder at http://www. census.gov. Compare the educational attainment with the average per capita income for the area. Do you see a clear correlation with your data?
2. What types of incentive systems or school choice initiatives are being discussed in your city? What are the pros and cons of these as discussed in the local news?
3. How are the schools in your district funded? Most publications that include school funding data are called "School District Profiles" or something similar. Consult the School District Profiles for your state and your city, and compare the expenditure per pupil, staff/pupil ratio, and other measures of education inputs. Also check with the website for your Department of Education (or Department of Children, Families, and Learning in Minnesota) for a list of schools by test scores. Do you see a relationship between inputs and achievement in your data?

References

Ahituv, A., and M. Tienda. 2004. Employment, motherhood, and school continu-ation decisions of young white, black, and Hispanic women. *Journal of Labor Economics* 22 (1): 115–158.

Ahlin, A., and E. Johansson. 2001. Individual demand for local public schooling: evidence from Swedish survey data. *International Tax and Public Finance* 8 (4): 331–351.

Bali, V. A., and R. M. Alvarez. 2003. Schools and educational outcomes: what causes the "race gap" in student test scores? *Social Science Quarterly* 84 (3): 485–507.

Barnett, W. S. 1992. Benefits of compensatory preschool education. *Journal of Human Resources* 27 (2): 279–312.

Becker, G. S., and K. M. Murphy. 1988. The family and the state. *Journal of Law and Economics* 31 (1): 1–18.

Black, S. E., P. J. Devereux, and K. G. Salvanes. 2005. Why the apple doesn't fall far: understanding intergenerational transmission of human capital. *American Economic Review* 95 (1): 437–449.

Bogart, W. T., and B. A. Cromwell. 1997. How much more is a good school district worth? *National Tax Journal* 50 (2): 215–232.

Bonesrønning, H. 2003. Class size effects on student achievement in Norway: patterns and explanations. *Southern Economic Journal* 69 (4): 952–965.

Bonesrønning, H. 2004. The determinants of parental effort in education production: do parents respond to changes in class size? *Economics of Education Review* 23 (1): 1–9.

Brunner, E., and J. Sonstelie. 2003. Homeowners, property values, and the political economy of the school voucher. *Journal of Urban Economics* 54 (2): 239–257.

Calmfors, L., and P. Skedinger. 1995. Does active labour-market policy increase employment? Theoretical considerations and some empirical evidence from Sweden. *Oxford Review of Economic Policy* 11 (1): 91–109.

Cameron, S. V., and J. J. Heckman. 1998. Life cycle schooling and dynamic selection bias: models and evidence for five cohorts of American males. *Journal of Political Economy* 106 (2): 262–333.

Cameron, S. V., and J. J. Heckman. 2001. The dynamics of educational attainment for black, Hispanic, and white males. *Journal of Political Economy* 109 (3): 455–499.

Carlino, G. A. 2005. The Economic Role of Cities in the 21st Century. *Business Review, Federal Reserve Bank of Philadelphia* Q3: 9–15.

Carneiro, P., K. T. Hansen, and J. J. Heckman. 2003. Estimating distributions of treatment effects with an application to the returns to schooling and measurement of the effects of uncertainty on college choice. *International Economic Review* 44 (2): 361–422.

Carneiro, P. and J. J. Heckman. 2003. Human capital policy. In *Inequality in America: What Role for Human Capital Policies?*, eds. J. J. Heckman and A. B. Krueger, Edited with an introduction by B.M. Friedman, Alvin Hansen Symposium on Public Policy series, MIT Press, Cambridge and London, 77–239.

Clotfelter, C. T., H. F. Ladd, J. L. Vigdor, and R. A. Diaz. 2004. Do school accountability systems make it more difficult for low-performing schools to attract and retain high-quality teachers? *Journal of Policy Analysis and Management* 23 (2): 251–271.

Coates, D. 2003. Education production functions using instructional time as an input. *Education Economics* 11 (3): 273–292.

Colburn, C. B., and J. B. Horowitz. 2003. Local politics and the demand for public education. *Urban Studies* 40 (4): 797–807.

Coleman, J. S., E. Campbell, and C. J. Hobson. 1966. *Equality of Educational Opportunity.* Washington, DC: Superintendent of Documents, U.S. Government Printing Office.

Corman, H. 2003. The effects of state policies, individual characteristics, family characteristics, and neighbourhood characteristics on grade repetition in the United States. *Economics of Education Review* 22 (4): 409–420.

Couch, J. F., W. F. Shughart, and A. L. Williams. 1993. Private school enrollment and public school performance. *Public Choice* 76 (4): 301–312.

Crone, T. M. 1998. Housing prices and the quality of public schools: What are we buying? *Federal Reserve Bank of Philadelphia Business Review* (September/October): 3–14.

Currie, J., and E. Moretti. 2003. Mother's education and the intergenerational transmission of human capital: evidence from college openings. *Quarterly Journal of Economics* 118 (4): 1495–1532.

Currie, J. and M. Neidell. 2003. Getting inside the "black box" of head start quality: what matters and what doesn't? National Bureau of Economic Research, Inc., NBER Working Papers.

de Grip, A., and E. Willems. 2003. Youngsters and technology. *Research Policy* 32 (10): 1771–1781.

Dellas, H., and V. Koubi. 2003. Business cycles and schooling. *European Journal of Political Economy* 19 (4): 843–859.

Dolton, P. J., G. H. Makepeace, and J. G. Treble. 1994. The wage effect of YTS: evidence from YCS. *Scottish Journal of Political Economy* 41 (4): 444–453.

Driscoll, D., D. Halcoussis, and S. Svorny. 2003. School district size and student performance. *Economics of Education Review* 22 (2): 193–201.

Eberts, R. W., E. Kehoe-Schwartz, and J. A. Stone. 1990. School reform, school size and achievement. *Federal Reserve Bank of Cleveland Economic Review* 26 (2): 2–15.

Edwards, M., and Partridge, M. 2001. Region 7W Labor-Force Assessment: Workforce Availability, Prepared for the St. Cloud Area Economic Development Partnership, Stearns-Benton Employment Training Council and the Minnesota Department of Commerce.

Farahati, F., D. E. Marcotte, and V. Wilcox-Gök. 2003. The effects of parents' psychiatric disorders on children's high school dropout. *Economics of Education Review* 22 (2): 167–178.

Feinstein, L. 2003. Inequality in the early cognitive development of British children in the cohort. *Economica* 70 (277): 73–97.

Feldman, R., and J. Beguin. 1978. The effect of a differential add-on grant: title 1 and local education spending. *Journal of Human Resources* 13 (4): 443–458.

Fersterer, J., and R. Winter-Ebmer. 2003. Smoking, discount rates, and returns to education. *Economics of Education Review* 22 (6): 561–566.

Figlio, D. N., and M. E. Lucas. 2004. What's in a grade? School report cards and the housing market. *American Economic Review* 94 (3): 591–604.

Figlio, D. N., and C. E. Rouse. 2006. Do accountability and voucher threats improve low-performing schools? *Journal of Public Economics* 90 (1–2): 239–255.

Figlio, D. N., T. A. Husted, and L. W. Kenny. 2004. Political economy of the inequality in school spending. *Journal of Urban Economics* 55 (2): 338–349.

Fryer, R. G. , and S. D. Levitt. 2004. Understanding the black-white test score gap in the first two years of school. *Review of Economics and Statistics* 86 (2): 447–464.

Gottlieb, P. D., and M. Fogarty. 2003. Educational attainment and metropolitan growth. *Economic Development Quarterly* 17 (4): 325–336.

Grogger, J., and D. Neal. 2000. Further evidence of the effects of Catholic secondary schooling. *Brookings-Wharton Papers on Urban Affairs* 0: 151–193.

Hansen, N. 1995. Addressing regional disparity and equity objectives through regional policies: a skeptical perspective. *Papers in Regional Science* 74 (2): 89–104.

Hanushek, E. A. 1996. Measuring investment in education. *Journal of Economic Perspectives* 10 (4): 9–30.

Hanushek, E. A. 2000. Further evidence of the effects of Catholic secondary schooling: comment. *Brookings-Wharton Papers on Urban Affairs* 0: 194–197.

Hanushek, E. A., J. F. Kain, J. M. Markman, and S. G. Rivkin. 2003. Does peer ability affect student achievement? *Journal of Applied Econometrics* 18 (5): 527–544.

Healey, A., M. Knapp, and D. P. Farrington. 2004. Adult labour market implications of antisocial behaviour in childhood and adolescence: findings from a U.K. longitudinal study. *Applied Economics* 36 (2): 93–105.

Heymann, J., Earle, A., Simmons, S., Breslow, S., and Kuehnhoff, A. *The Work, Family, and Equity Index: Where Does the United States Stand Globally?* Harvard School of Public Health, Boston, MA, 2004, Available at: http://www. hsph.harvard.edu/globalworkingfamilies/ (accessed on October 25, 2005).

Hufnagel, R. 2003. The impact of domestic child care on school performance. *Schmollers Jahrbuch: Zeitschrift für Wirtschafts- und Sozialwissenschaften. Journal of Applied Social Science Studies* 123 (1): 189–197.

Ichino, A., and R. Winter-Ebmer. 2004. The long-run educational cost of World War II. *Journal of Labor Economics* 22 (1): 57–86.

Jacob, B. A., and S. D. Levitt. 2003. Catching cheating teachers: the results of an unusual experiment in implementing theory. *Brookings-Wharton Papers on Urban Affairs* 0: 185–209.

Jacobs, B. 2004. The lost race between schooling and technology. *De Economist* 152 (3): 47–78.

Jorgenson, D. W., M. S. Ho, and K. J. Stiroh. 2003. Growth of U.S. industries and investments in information technology and higher education. *Economic Systems Research* 15 (3): 279–325.

Kane, T. J., D. O. Staiger, and G. Samms. 2003. School accountability ratings and housing values. *Brookings-Wharton Papers on Urban Affairs* 0: 83–127.

Krueger, A. B. 2003. Economic considerations and class size. *Economic Journal* 113 (485): F34–F63.

Ladd, H. F. 2002. School vouchers: a critical view. *Journal of Economic Perspectives* 16 (4): 3–24.

Ladd, H. F., and E. B. Fiske. 2001. The uneven playing field of school choice: evidence from New Zealand. *Journal of Policy Analysis and Management* 20 (1): 43–63.

Lankford, H., and J. Wyckoff. 2001. Who would be left behind by enhanced private school choice? *Journal of Urban Economics* 50 (2): 288–312.

Lee, K. 1997. An economic analysis of public school choice plans. *Journal of Urban Economics* 41 (1): 1–22.

Leung, A. 2003. Delinquency, schooling, and work: time allocation decision of youth. *Applied Economics Letters* 10 (15): 943–949.

Loeb, S., and M. Socias. 2004. Federal contributions to high-income school districts: the use of tax deductions for funding K-12 education. *Economics of Education Review* 23 (1): 85–94.

Loeb, S., B. Fuller, S. L. Kagan, B. Carrol, J. Carroll, and J. McCarthy. 2003. Child care in poor communities: early learning effects of type, quality, and stability, National Bureau of Economic Research, Inc., NBER Working Papers, 2003.

Mazumder, B. 2003. Family resources and college enrollment. *Federal Reserve Bank of Chicago Economic Perspectives* 27 (4): 30–41.

Mykerezi, E., B. Mills, and S. Gomes. 2003. Education and socioeconomic well-being in racially diverse rural counties. *Journal of Agricultural and Applied Economics* 35 (2): 251–262.

Neal, D. 1997. The effects of Catholic secondary schooling on educational achievement. *Journal of Labor Economics* 15 (1): 98–123.

Nechyba, T. 2003. Public school finance and urban school policy: general versus partial equilibrium analysis. *Brookings-Wharton Papers on Urban Affairs* 0: 139–170.

Oreopoulos, P. 2003. Do dropouts drop out too soon? International evidence from changes in school-leaving laws, National Bureau of Economic Research, Inc., NBER Working Papers.

Organisation for Economic Co-operation and Development. *International Direct Investment Statistics Yearbook/Annuaire des statistiques d'investissement direct international: 1980–2000*, Author, Paris and Washington, DC, 2002.

Pénard, T., and M. Sollogoub. 1995. Les politiques françaises d'emploi en faveur des jeunes. Une évaluation économétrique. *Revue Economique* 46 (3): 549–559.

Peterson, K. 2005. *School Vouchers Slow to Spread.* http://www.stateline.org/live/ViewPage.action?siteNodeId=136&languageId=1&contentId=29789 (accessed on October 30, 2005).

Plug, E., and W. Vijverberg. 2003. Schooling, family background, and adoption: is it nature or is it nurture? *Journal of Political Economy* 111 (3): 611–641.

Rosenthal, L. 2003. The value of secondary school quality. *Oxford Bulletin of Economics and Statistics* 65 (3): 329–355.

Rumberger, R. W., and S. P. Lamb. 2003. The early employment and further education experiences of high school dropouts: a comparative study of the United States and Australia. *Economics of Education Review* 22 (4): 353–366.

Schwab, R. M. 2000. Further evidence of the effects of Catholic secondary schooling: comment. *Brookings-Wharton Papers on Urban Affairs* 0: 197–200.

Self, S., and R. Grabowski. 2003. Education and long-run development in Japan. *Journal of Asian Economics* 14 (4): 565–580.

Self, S., and R. Grabowski. 2004. Does education at all levels cause growth? India, a case study. *Economics of Education Review* 23 (1): 47–55.

Stull, W.J. 1995. Is high school economically relevant for noncollege youth? Federal Reserve Bank of Philadelphia, Working Papers.

Taylor, L. L. 1999. Government's role in primary and secondary education. *Federal Reserve Bank of Dallas Economic Review* 0: 15–24.

Trzcinski, E. 2005. No infant left behind: public finance arguments for mandated leave and income supports for parents. *Public Finance and Management* 5 (1): 1–59.

Tyler, J. H. 2003. Using state child labor laws to identify the effect of school-year work on high school achievement. *Journal of Labor Economics* 21 (2): 381–408.

Tyler, J. H., R. J. Murnane, and J. B. Willett. 2003. Who benefits from a GED? Evidence for females from high school and beyond. *Economics of Education Review* 22 (3): 237–247.

VanderHart, P. G., and J. K. Ransom. 2003. Not enough capital and too much bureaucracy: an analysis of the input choice efficiency of Ohio secondary schools. *Journal of Economics (MVEA)* 29 (1): 77–92.

Waldfogel, J. 2004. Social mobility, life chances, and the early years. http://sticerd. lse.ac.uk/dps/case/CP/CASEPaper88.pdf (accessed on October 25, 2004, site now discontinued).

Witte, A. D. and M. Trowbridge. 2004. The structure of early care and education in the United States: historical evolution and international comparisons, National Bureau of Economic Research, Inc, NBER Working Papers.

Wößmann, L. 2003. Schooling resources, educational institutions and student performance: the international evidence. *Oxford Bulletin of Economics and Statistics* 65 (2): 117–170.

Wyckoff, P. G. 1991. A new case for vouchers. *Journal of Policy Analysis and Management* 10 (1): 112–116.

Zhan, M., and M. Sherraden. 2003. Assets, expectations, and children's educational achievement in female-headed households. *Social Service Review* 77 (2): 191–211.

Chapter 20

Fighting Crime

Between 1960 and 1980, the total reported crime per 100,000 people in the United States rose by 215%; but between 1990 and 2000, crime rates plummeted by 29% (from 5802.7 per 100,000 population down to 4124.8). Murder rates are at their lowest levels in 35 years. The FBI's violent and property crime indexes fell 34 and 29%, respectively, between 1990 and 2000. Crime rates per 100,000 population vary greatly from city to city. For example, in 2001, Camden, New Jersey (population 79,904), ranked the second deadliest city (at 2118.7 violent crimes per 100,000) while Orem, Utah (population 84,324), was ranked the safest city for having 73.5 violent crimes per 100,000, and the overall violent crime rate in the United States was 504.4 per 100,000.

In this chapter we will first define "crime" and attempt to determine the potential causes of the abrupt change in crime rates over time, as well as the cause of the wide variance in crime among cities. To determine causes, we first will introduce the economic theory of crime and compare that to theories from other disciplines. We will look at the effects of deterrence and see what types of policies work to reduce which types of crime. We will also review the literature on substance abuse in light of the rational theory of addiction.

The graph in Figure 20.1 is prepared from the FBI's *Uniform Crime Reports* (UCR). These data go back as far as 1929 and consist of all crimes that are *reported* to state and local law enforcement agencies. The two major categories of reported crimes are:

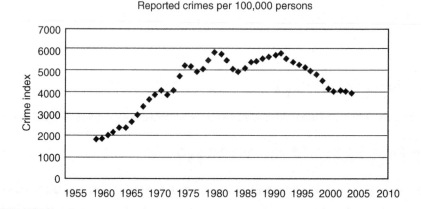

Figure 20.1 Reported crimes per 100,000 persons.

- Violent crime (murders, non-negligent manslaughter, forcible rape, robberies, aggravated assaults)
- Property crime (burglaries, larceny, theft, motor vehicle theft)

All data have limitations, and crime data are no exception. The major limitation of the UCR data is that the data only includes reported crimes. Not all crime is reported. People report crime if the marginal benefit to them in doing so meets or exceeds the marginal cost. Individuals in higher income groups, especially the elderly, tend to have more insurance and are thus more likely to report an incident. Individual attitudes also influence perceptions of the marginal cost and marginal benefit and thus help to determine the reporting behavior.

However, victims who perceive the police to be incompetent or those who lack positive experiences with the police are less likely to contact them about an incident. Likewise, if the victims think that they are partly responsible for the incident (the door was unlocked) they are also less likely to report the incident.

In addition, illegal drug users are less willing to involve the police if they are either a victim of property crime or a person involved in poor quality narcotics purchases. Whether or not someone will report a crime depends on the seriousness of the crime, the perceived threat from the incident, and when the incident occurred. If the incident is one of a series, the victim is less likely to report it. However, if it occurred at night or on the weekend or if the victim was injured, the incident has a higher probability of being reported.

A second group that tends to underreport crimes is the local police departments. Because they compile the statistics, departments that want to show reductions in crime may systematically underreport them.

Finally, crime rates are consistently underreported because of the nature of the system. A hierarchical method of counting crimes consists of only accounting for the most serious act for each incident. For instance, if a woman is raped and robbed before she was murdered, only the murder would be counted—not the rape or the robbery.

Constant Inconsistencies in Crime Data

Simons Jenkins, a British commentator for the Times of London, characterized crime statistics as positive proof that "with a bit of art, you can fool all the people all the time." MacDonald (2002) showed that the inconsistency in British data between crime rates projected from victimization surveys and crime rates from official statistics is primarily a result of victims underreporting and police under recording.

According to the 2000 British Crime Survey, only 39 percent of all crime incidents were reported. What victims believe to be a crime is not always recorded by the police as such. The official crime figures vary from the number of crimes reported because of police inefficiency and bureaucracy. This variance is also due to differences in the way crimes are recorded in the 43 regional police districts.

These inconsistencies can lead to biased results depending on whether the under-reporting (or under-recording) of crime is random or due to systematic variations. The consensus in the literature is that the crime rate is positively correlated with the unemployment rate in the short run. However, individuals who are unemployed are significantly less likely to report an incident than those who work. Thus, it seems that property crime rate varies procyclically with the unemployment rate, but the reporting rate varies counter-cyclically.

MacDonald (2002)

The FBI is compiling a new data set called the National Incident-Based Reporting System or NIBRS. Under this system, details about each crime, the victim, the offender, and the weapon used will be compiled for over 50 offenses. The NIBRS will include all rape victims—males and females. The goal of this complex database is to allow 16,000 separate law enforcement agencies to use it.

The other primary source of crime data in the United States is from the **National Crime Victimization Survey** (NCVS), conducted by the Bureau of Justice Statistics. The survey has been administered annually to approximately 50,000 households since 1973. The NCVS counts violent crimes (rapes, sexual assaults, robberies, and assaults) and property crimes (thefts, household burglaries, and motor vehicle thefts) reported by residents aged 12 years and older. This survey is more reliable than the UCR, but it is still not perfect. Most surveys conducted are telephone surveys. Victims of domestic violence may be afraid to report incidents when their batterer is in the room with them while they answer the survey questions or if they might take longer to answer the survey than their assailant did. Others may have forgotten that they were victims of minor crimes or they might think that a stolen object was simply misplaced. Neither the UCR nor the NCVS measures victimless crimes such as prostitution and drug activity.[1]

A Crime by Any Other Name

Comparisons of crime rates between cities of different countries are difficult because definitions of crime vary. For instance, the standard definition of intentional homicide is the "intentional killing of a person," including assault that results in death, euthanasia, and infanticide but excluding assisted suicide. However, some countries exclude assault leading to death in their data for intentional homicide and others exclude euthanasia. Norway, for instance, excludes infanticide but includes assisted suicide as intentional homicide.

In English law, domestic burglary is "any incident in which someone enters or tries to enter a dwelling as a trespasser with the intention of committing theft, rape, grievous bodily harm, or unlawful damage." That dwelling can be a house, an apartment, or any connected outbuilding or garage. In Greece and the

---

[1] DiIulio (1996); Boggess and Bound (1997); Barry (2004).

Netherlands, the domestic burglary count includes non-domestic premises such as shops, garages, and hotels. The Swedes include not only the attempts but also preparation and conspiracy as burglary.

Data about motor vehicle theft also varies. Generally, the definition includes theft of all land vehicles with engines—if the vehicle can run on the road and is used to carry people, it is included. Greece includes boats. Hungary only includes cars and New Zealand excludes motorcycles. In several European countries, joyriding in someone's vehicle is not counted as motor vehicle theft because the thief had no intent of keeping the vehicle.

MacDonald (2002); Council of Europe (2003)

Categorizing Crimes

The definition of the word "crime" is neither obvious nor consistent even within countries. In some areas of the United States, for example, gambling is perfectly legal; in other places it is unlawful unless the government is sponsoring it. Prostitution is legal and regulated in some jurisdictions but not in others. Some counties are "dry"—meaning that no alcohol can be sold there—but the bar just over the county line does a brisk business. Fireworks are unlawful in some states and perfectly acceptable in others. The same is true for abortions, which are illegal in one place and subsidized in another. Other "crimes" are on the books but only enforced at the discretion of the police and courts. Crimes are committed against:

■ Persons (homicide, rape, kidnapping, and assault).
■ Property (theft, larceny, burglary, vandalism, arson, embezzlement, and fraud).
■ The state (treason, counterfeiting, terrorism, tax fraud, regulatory violations, failure to pay parking meters, tearing labels off of a mattress, feeding wild ducks and geese in St. Cloud, Minnesota, and selling the military under-breaded shrimp) (*United States vs. Hartley*).[2]

---

[2] The under-breading of shrimp resulted in 33 counts of conspiracy, mail fraud, violations of the National Stolen Property Act and Racketeer Influenced and Corrupt Organizations (RICO) Act, according to G. Terwilliger, Commercial and Federal Criminal Law: Risks of Over-Criminalizing Commercial Regulation, June 13, 2002, http://www.fed-soc.org/pdf/Terwilliger.pdf, (accessed on 21 August 2004).

- Rent-seekers (selling lemons smaller than the legal size [in California], volunteering to "help" the USPS deliver Christmas cards [violates a monopoly reserved for the Postal Service], and selling gasoline below statutory minimum gasoline prices).
- One's self (prostitution, consumption of illegal drugs, and sodomy). Economists call these "victimless crimes."

Calendar Crimes

Crime is a seasonal activity. Gorr, Olligschlaeger, and Thompson (2003) reviewed urban crimes and concluded that crimes against property (burglary, robbery, and theft) are high in the fall and winter, especially around the holiday shopping season. Crowded shopping malls during Christmastime are dream locations for thieves because they have a lower risk of getting caught.

Crimes of aggression (assaults, homicides, and rape) are lowest in January and peak in midsummer. This seasonality supports the **temperature aggression hypothesis** in the environmental criminology literature: hot temperatures arouse anger, which leads to violence.

Gorr, Olligschlaeger, and Thompson (2003)

Economic Theory of Crime

Economists do not view criminals as deviants nor do they suggest that their physiology is different from that of model citizens. To an economist, crime is a question of labor supply. People choose to "work" in legal or illegal occupations. Following Becker's (1968) **rational choice theory**, individuals choose crime if the marginal benefit of committing a crime is greater than the marginal cost. People become criminals not because their basic motivation is different, but because their benefits and costs differ. Individuals allocate time to market work, crime, and leisure to maximize their utilities. Benefits from criminal behavior are the same as those behind everyday legitimate activities: the pursuit of pleasure, profit, gain, status, power, and for some, the satisfaction of rebelling against authority.

Circadian Rhythms of Crime

Crimes vary by hour. Felson and Poulsen (2003) note that a "day" in forecasting crime starts at 5:00 am, not at midnight. Around midnight, many people straggle home using public transportation or drive home from urban bars or parties in private homes. High blood alcohol levels make them likely offenders or prime targets of crime. By 5:00 am, most substance abusers and partiers are at home. Daylight and morning commuters curtail crime for a few hours.

The **median minute** is that minute of the day when exactly half of the daily robberies occur. The **quartile minutes** allow researchers to study the hourly dispersions of crime. Twenty-five percent (seventy-five percent) of the crimes per day are committed in the first (third) quartile minutes. Older offenders have different patterns of crime than younger offenders do. Entertainment districts differ from working and residential areas. High school students have an early median minute of crime (at the end of their school day) and a narrow daily span of crime involvement. Cities populated by older residents also have earlier median minutes and narrower time spans. However, cities where individuals tend to consume greater amounts of alcohol and cites where the bars are open late have later medians and wider time spans.

Felson and Poulsen (2003)

The marginal cost/marginal benefit diagram in Figure 20.2 clearly demonstrates the economic theory of crime. The **marginal benefit curve** for crime slopes downward. The criminal maximizes the net benefits from non-violent crimes at each period. The criminal essentially faces two problems: (1) Criminals will first execute the crime that they think will pay the most. The remaining opportunities provide lower returns. (2) As the supply of stolen goods increases, the prices their fences are willing to pay diminish. Because the criminal faces diminishing returns to crime, the marginal benefit curve slopes downward.

The **marginal cost curve** slopes upward because a person who commits more crime has to devote more resources to do so. Stealing

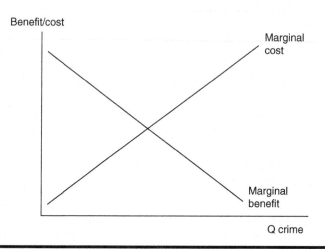

Figure 20.2   Market for crime (Criminal's perspective).

purses or cigarettes from unlocked cars in parking lots or even "borrowing" office supplies from one's employer does not require as many resources as creating and organizing an international gang of shoplifters, for instance. The costs of criminal activities also result from internal and external deterrents. Internal deterrents signify the self-restraint of the person. For most people, internal deterrents are sufficient to make crime a passing temptation. External deterrents are calculated by estimating the probabilities of getting caught, convicted, and sentenced.

Following Ehrlich (1973) Table 20.1 on page 682 shows, the calculations involved in committing a burglary would be as follows for two individuals, Tracy and Pat: Let's say that Tracy is better-educated than Pat and earns $30,000 per year. Pat has less investment in human capital and earns $10,000 per year. Both face a 30% probability of getting caught, and if they are caught, we assume that they will serve the same prison sentence (two years). Their opportunity cost is equal to the amount of legitimate earnings foregone during imprisonment. Their foregone legitimate earnings equal the expected length of punishment in years (the probability of being apprehended and convicted multiplied by the duration of imprisonment) multiplied by the earnings in a legitimate job.

From these basic calculations, it is clear that Tracy will not commit the burglary because the expected net benefits are negative; but for Pat, the temptation is greater. A large enough increase in the probability of apprehension and conviction or a long enough sentence, however, could deter Pat.

For most people, jail time will carry an extra cost of embarrassment and it will carry a decreased probability of finding a comparable job and even a respectable place to live afterward. These disadvantages force the criminal into the underground economy once the sentence is finished. But for others, jail time may provide bragging rights and respect. In addition, while in prison, they have the chance to network with others of their "profession" and perfect their skills. The result for both of these groups is a high *recidivism rate* (the rate at which criminals are convicted again).[3]

Higher Wages—Lower Crime Rates

In April 1999, the labor market in the United Kingdom adopted a national minimum wage. The minimum wage was set at £3.60 for people over age 21 and £3.00 for workers between 18 and 21 years of age. Hansen and Machin (2002) argue that this wage boost may have altered individual incentives to participate in crime. Minimum wages could increase unemployment, but the authors note this possibility existed only for workers in care homes.

The authors used data from 43 police precincts in England and Wales between April 1998 and March 2000. They uncovered a statistically significant negative relationship showing relative crime reduction in areas that had larger numbers of low-wage workers. Thus, increasing wage rates lowers the crime rates.

Hansen and Machin (2002)

Crime Does Pay After All

Measuring the actual supply of criminal activity is difficult. Extrapolating the tendencies of all criminals based on surveys of prisoners is misleading—these subsamples include only those who were caught, convicted, and sentenced.

Household telephone surveys are another way to determine who participates in crime. The 1980 National Longitudinal Survey of Youth (NLSY) asked a battery of questions about time spent in criminal activities.

---

[3] Deutsch, Hakim, and Spiegel (1990); CBS News.com (2004).

A surprisingly large number of young men, especially from inner city neighborhoods, voluntarily revealed the extent of their criminal involvement. Freeman (1996) found that 41 percent of these young men stated that they committed crimes in the previous year.

It is difficult to estimate how well crime pays. Freeman (1996) combined the 1980 NBER Inner City Youth Survey with a 1989 Boston Youth Survey and determined that between those two years, the proportion of youths who admitted they could earn more money "on the street" than in a legitimate job rose from 41 to 63 percent in Boston. In 1980, youth reported average annual criminal earnings of $1807; in 1989 the figure was $3008. After adjusting for inflation, the increase is about 5 percent. Transformed into hourly earnings, this amount equals $10.00 per hour for criminal activity during a time when legal work paid $5.00–$6.00 after taxes. Similarly, a 1990 survey of drug dealers in Washington, D.C., revealed that their average earnings translated into $30 per hour. This amount exceeded legitimate earnings by enough to make it financially worthwhile to spend one year in jail every two years.

Freeman (1996)

The routine activity approach developed by sociologists Cohen and Felson (1979) expanded on the rational choice theory by listing three minimal elements for direct contact predatory crime: a likely offender, a potential victim, and the absence of protection. In economic terms, the absence of a potential victim cancels out the benefit for possible offenders, whereas the absence of protection (efficient police) decreases the cost of committing a crime.

Glaeser and Sacerdote (1999) added that criminals in large cities enjoy higher monetary benefits, and the higher rewards from crime explain 25% of the association between city size and crime rates. The anonymity of committing urban crime explains, at most, 20% of that association. The presence of more female-headed households in the city explains between 33 and 50% of the urban crime effect.

Cities seem to attract crime-prone individuals because of the agglomeration economies of doing crime. For instance, larger cities have more pawn shops in which to pawn stolen merchandise. Commercial and residential breaking-and-entering incidents are distributed proportionally to family density and to areas close to highways.[4]

Competing Theories of Crime

Before the 18th century, "the devil made me do it" was an acceptable explanation for deviance. For the puritans, "bad souls" caused criminal tendencies. However, emphasis on rational behavior and free will brought on by the Enlightenment combined with the "Hedonistic Calculus" techniques of Jeremy Bentham (1789) created the ***deterrence theory***, which is at the base of the economic theory of crime. Of course, economists are not the only researchers who study crime. Other theories of crime exist, and many of these theories echo the rational choice theory of economists. Others are merely descriptive and do not speak to causes and effects. For sociologists, the individual's environment is responsible. For the biologist, anatomy is destiny, whereas psychologists point to childhood events. Geographers map "hot spots" of criminal activity.

Sociological Explanations of Crime

A sociologist and an economist can look at the same results from an empirical model of crime and exclaim to each other, "See? I told you so." Davis's (1959) ***theory of relative deprivation***, Agnew's (1983) ***strain theory***, and Shaw and McKay's (1942) ***social disorganization theory*** explain that social problems stem from income inequality. According to the theory of relative deprivation, the poor feel dispossessed (deprived of homes, possessions, and security) compared to wealthier people. Envy (unfair disadvantage) leads the poor to seek compensation any way that they can, including committing crimes against the rich and poor alike. The ***strain theory*** argues that the failure and frustration of unsuccessful individuals causes them to turn to crime. Without equal means to achieve society's goals, some people turn to deviant behavior. The greater the inequality, the more strain the people are subject to. Thus, envy goads these individuals to commit crime. However, under the rational choice theory, income inequality and poverty merely signals different net benefits associated with doing crime. Economists predict more crime from low-income individuals merely because of their low rate of return from market activity. As we saw in Table 20.1, Tracy, who has a higher "legal" income,

---

[4] Liu and Brown (2003).

Table 20.1 Expected Marginal Benefits and Marginal Costs of Committing a Burglary

	Tracy	Pat
Expected benefits from burglary	**$10,000**	**$10,000**
(a) Expected probability of apprehension and conviction	0.30	0.30
(b) Expected length of sentence served if convicted	Two years	Two years
(c) Earnings/year (legitimate)	$30,000	$10,000
Expected costs (a×b×c)	**$18,000**	**$6000**
Expected net benefits (Expected benefits — expected costs)	**−$8000**	**+$4000**

faces steeper penalties if caught and imprisoned than Pat, so Pat will be tempted to commit crimes that Tracy would not consider doing.

According to the ***social disorganization theory***, crime occurs when the mechanisms of social control are weak. The factors of social disorganization are poverty, racial heterogeneity, residential mobility, and family instability. Inequality is associated with crime because of its link to poverty.

Empirically, population density and large numbers of transient people are robust determinants of criminal activity. More crime per 100,000 people occurs in urban areas than in rural areas. The social disorganization theory would attribute this to feelings of alienation and anomie (lacking social values). Economists interpret the same findings as evidence of a lower probability of recognition and arrest in densely populated areas—that is, lower costs of committing crime, which cause greater quantities of crimes being committed. In a large city, a description of a white male of average build in blue jeans, a tee shirt, and a baseball cap does not narrow down the list of suspects. In a smaller town, people generally know most others in the town, and the description might be:

> That looks like one of the Anderson boys. What is he doing going into Mrs. Carlson's house while she is out? I'll bet that kid is up to no good.

Thus, criminals in a small town have higher probabilities of being caught.[5]

---

[5] Kelly (2000); Fajnzylber, Lederman, and Loayza (2002).

Biology and Crime

According to Italian physician Cesare Lombroso (1836–1909), criminals were an accident of evolution. This debate asserts that nature, not nurture or free choice, causes criminality.[6] Lombroso assured us that criminals could be identified by facial features and body types such as large jaws, high cheekbones, and bony arches above deep-set eyes. Mesomorphs, muscular body-types with action-loving, aggressive personalities, most often describe prison inmates. This group of people needs little sleep, suffers from hypertension, and is easy to anger. They love to gamble and take risks. They have a chronic need for excitement due to genetic differences in their autonomic nervous systems.

Current biologists add chromosomal abnormalities to the biological list of criminal traits. Most males have XY chromosomes, but a large proportion of prisoners have XYY chromosomes. Chronic offenders are thought to exhibit brain dysfunction that leads to extreme dyslogia (an inability to verbally express one's self) due to neurochemical imbalances. They lack empathy for animals or people. Incapable of abstract thought, they lack insight and foresight and they are incapable of learning from experience or predicting the consequences of their actions. They lack fear or remorse and have low anger thresholds; they are impulsive and antisocial.

Complications during birth and during their first months influence the tendency toward crime. Among males, neonatal complications increase the risk of juvenile delinquency by 300%, the risk of offending as an adult by 200%, and the risk of committing a violent crime by 250% (Hodgins, Kratzer, and McNeil 2002). Females, however, are not affected by neonatal complications.

Twins raised apart seem to be ideal subjects for testing the roles of nature vs. nurture. Such studies have concluded that an identical twin is two times more likely to have an arrest record if the other twin had one than if a fraternal twin did. The criminal role of a biological father influences the child more than that of the adoptive father.

Biology can be a predisposition, but it does not predestine one to crime. Genetic changes in a population happen over long periods. These biological explanations clarify neither the large expansion in crime rates from 1960 to 1980 nor the downward trend in crime in the United States since 1990. Biology does not predestine criminal behavior. The application of biological theories to the fight against crime would lead to unthinkable measures, like the elimination of all newborns with these characteristics.[7]

---

[6] Fadaei-Tehrani and Green (2002); Gado (n.d.).

[7] http://www.crime-times.org/; Mednick, Gabrielli, and Hutchings (1984); Hodgins, Kratzer, and McNeil (2002).

Psychological Theories of Crime

Originating from psychoanalytic theory, the psychological explanations of crime blame nurture for distorting a criminal's thinking process. Freud's only contribution to the theory of crime is that criminals constantly feel extreme guilt and want to get caught and be punished in order to temporarily lessen their guilt. However, neo-Freudians suggest that a childhood without loving parents or a broken home with too little or too much discipline creates a criminal personality.

Media violence is statistically correlated with aggressive people, but do violent TV programs cause aggressive tendencies in normal individuals or do aggressive people merely prefer violent entertainment? Japan enjoys a very low crime rate, but Japanese TV and movies often show extreme, graphic violence.

Like biology, nurture may predispose, but it does not predestine. Not all children of unstable families become criminals. Yochelson Samuel and Stanton E. Samenow (1976, 1984), psychiatrist and a clinical psychologist, studied "mentally ill" criminals at St. Elizabeth's Hospital in Washington, D.C., and determined that there was no difference between these criminals and the others. They concluded that criminals freely choose to commit crimes and that the "mental illness" tag allowed the person to avoid jail.

How does one decide what to believe? Good theories must be internally logical and consistent. They must be more consistent with facts than the rival theories and they must be consistent with a general theory. Economic theory of crime is consistent with the economic optimization theory that fits most other situations. People will engage in an activity as long as the marginal benefits are greater than the marginal cost. The economic theory of crime implies credible policies to reduce crime without recourse to the utopias present in some other theories.[8]

Keep the Barbarians at Bay

Helsley and Strange (1999) studied the effect of gated communities on the economic geography of crime. By denying access to the general public, these walled residential developments offer safe environments for the residents. Gated communities are found the world over: from South Africa, China, the Philippines, Brazil, and Mexico to Canada, Poland, and the United

---

[8] Reynolds (1985); New Hampshire Civil Liberties Union, Freedom of Expression in the Arts and Entertainment (no date).

Kingdom. In 2000, eight million people in the United States lived in these communities. Gated communities are a form of private government. The profit-maximizing developer typically governs the community until most of the lots are sold. A board composed of residents, builders, and representatives of the developer is elected. This board sets the maintenance fees, enforces design guidelines or other regulations, and hires security and maintenance personnel.

Helsley and Strange determined that more spending on gated communities in an area reduces the number of active criminals there, but increases them elsewhere, *ceteris paribus*. The increased crime in neighboring communities increases the demand for more gating. Gating lowers the payoff to criminals, thus resulting in fewer crimes committed as long as the community continues to have an active labor market.

Helsley and Strange (1999)

Social Costs of Crime

One way to infer the cost of crime is by estimating the differences in property values in high vs. low crime areas using hedonic analysis (Chapter 13). High crime rates in a neighborhood depress property values. People are willing to pay for safe homes or gated communities. They are also willing to pay high property taxes for a good police force. Still, this method does not give a precise estimate of the cost of an individual crime. Such estimates are generally limited to actual out-of-pocket costs. Without crime-specific cost estimates, the cost-benefit analysis of policy alternatives is impossible. For example, longer prison sentences may have a deterrent effect on the rate of crime, but is the decreased crime rate worth the increased costs associated with longer incarcerations?

The cost for victims consists of three components: (1) direct, out-of-pocket costs (lost wages, medical expenses, or stolen property), (2) the risk of death, and (3) the costs of pain, suffering, and fear. Direct costs are relatively straightforward to calculate. The monetary value of the risk of death, according to Cohen (1990), is the probability of death multiplied by the value of life. Table 20.2 shows the costs of crime as estimated by Cohen (1990), adjusted for inflation. In 2005 dollars, estimates of the value of life ranged from $1.85 million to $4.6 million, with a mean of $3.23 million.

Table 20.2 The Cost of Crime to Each Victim, Including Attempted Crimes (2005 Dollars)

Crime	Direct Losses	Pain and Suffering	Risk of Death	Total
Rape	$8530	$80,483	$5321	$94,335
Robbery	$2058	$13,781	$7429	$23,269
Assault	$780	$9092	$12,351	$22,223
Car theft	$5670	$0	$107	$5777
Burglary	$1735	$586	$214	$2535
Larceny				
Personal	$331	$0	$4	$334
Household	$320	$0	$0	$320

Source: Cohen (1990). Reproduced with permission of the publisher. Journal is available at http://www.tandf.co.uk/journals/titles/10799893.asp.

However, the probability of death is relatively small and similar to the probability of death in a work-related accident. Jury awards are higher than the costs of pain and suffering endured by the average accident victim. Cohen estimated the average pain and suffering for several types of crime by multiplying the probability of being a victim of a specific crime by the average jury award for pain and suffering.

Social costs of crime do not end with costs incurred by individual victims. First, crime could be thought of as a regressive tax levied more or less randomly. A narrow look at the redistribution effects would conclude that society is no worse off by a theft. The victim is worse off, true, but the criminal gains by the same amount. However, low income people are more often victims because they are less able to purchase self-protection systems. Second, to the extent that potential victims have low incentives to accumulate personal property if it can be stolen, crime will decrease the country's GDP. Third, a large proportion of homeless people are ex-felons. To the extent that ex-felons are stigmatized and barred from working in well-paying jobs or living in relatively comfortable housing, they may have few legal alternatives but to participate in the underground economy.

Victims

The quantity of crime committed in a city is determined by three groups of economic actors: criminals, potential victims, and the criminal justice system. Societies have two types of laws: civil law and criminal law. ***Civil law*** settles disagreements among private parties. The plaintiff initiates an action against a defendant. ***Criminal law*** deals with a wrong against "the state." Only the state can prosecute, arrest, and punish. The immediate victim or family can only pursue legal action in civil court. As government's role increases in importance, the victims become less important. If a criminal is freed early, the former victims are not necessarily informed.

Crime victims are partly self-determined. Not all stores have electronic technology to catch shoplifters. Not all homes have working security systems, and those that have elaborate systems may be inadvertently signaling would-be thieves that they have something worth stealing. Some people forget to (or just don't) lock their doors and windows. Students regularly come to night class without their personal bodyguards.

Victimization rates for women and the elderly are lower than rates for men and young adults. Because of fear, women and the elderly tend to stay in at night, hire private security guards, or move to gated communities. In essence, fear causes potential victims to place themselves "under house arrest" while criminals move about freely.

How Well do Consumers Protect Themselves from Identity Theft?

Milne (2003) published the results of a survey of 61 college students and 59 non-students on 13 ways to protect against identity theft. He discovered that less than 25 percent of both groups order a copy of their credit report once a year. More than 70 percent have boxes of blank checks mailed to their homes and dorms rather than to the banks as the FTC suggests. Students freely give merchants personal identification information, but 56 percent of the non-students surveyed carry social security cards in their wallets or purses—many older people think that they needed their social security card to pick up their medications.

Milne (2003)

Think About It...

Researchers have used standard questions from the British Crime Survey to measure fear of victimization.

These questions include:

How safe do you feel walking alone in your neighborhood (or on campus) after dark?

How safe do you feel in your home after dark?

How safe do you feel walking alone in your neighborhood (or on campus) during the day?

How worried are you about the following:

- Having your home broken into and something stolen?
- Being mugged and robbed?
- Having your car stolen?
- Having things stolen from your car?
- Being raped?
- Being physically attacked by strangers?
- Being insulted or pestered by someone in a public place?
- Being physically attacked because of your skin color, ethnic origin, or religion?

Source: Adapted from British Crime Survey, Crime and Fear of Crime, 2004, http://www.statistics.gov.uk/about/data/harmonisation/downloads/S9.pdf (accessed on 11 November 2005). Used with permission from the Office of Public Sector Information.

Analysis of Fear

The expected probability of becoming a victim and the actual probability do not coincide, according to the **risk-worry paradox**. Wiles, Simmons, and Pease (2003) analyzed 33,000 interviews from the British Crime Survey data from 2001 to 2002 and found that the wealthy seem to be the most vulnerable to being attacked by strangers: 2.1 percent of those with a household income of $45,500 or more were victims at least once compared to 1.6 percent of those with an income less than $7000 and 0.9 percent for those who earned between $7000 and $15,200. Yet, only 8 percent of the highest income group felt fairly or very likely to become a victim in the next year compared to 14 percent to 15 percent of the lower income groups.

The elderly, even though they have by far the lowest rate of victimization, worry more about crime than others. Nine percent of the men and 33 percent of the women over age 60 feel unsafe walking alone in their own neighborhoods after dark, compared to 3 percent of men and 15 percent of women under age 30. The relative risk of being attacked by a stranger or mugged is the inverse of feeling safe. About 8.5 percent of young men were victims of such attacks compared to 1.9 percent of young women. The elderly suffered such attacks at a rate of less than 0.1 percent.

Wiles, Simmons and Pease (2003)

Some neighborhoods turn to voluntary crime watch groups or Guardian Angels. Chapters of Guardian Angels are found throughout the United States, Japan, the United Kingdom, and Brazil. These types of programs increase the probability that a criminal will get caught. Neighbors get to know one another so they can more easily spot a stranger. Time is the largest cost of providing such a program, and despite the warnings, the inexperienced amateur heroes may forget that they have not had police training.[9]

Figure 20.3 shows the crime problem from a victim's perspective: the market for crime protection. The marginal benefit (demand) for protection is downsloping. Potential victims will first invest in an activity that brings the greatest increase in security to them. Such an activity might be just locking doors and windows. The marginal benefit function is equal to the probability of being victimized multiplied by the anticipated values of losses. The potential victim will stop investing in crime protection measures when the marginal benefit is equal to the marginal cost.

Offending Victims and Serial Victims

There is one gap in the victimization literature: victims and offenders appear to be from separate social

---

[9] Angels around the world (no date) http://www.guardianangels.org/chapter_overview.html, (accessed on 22 August 2004).

groups. According to Deadman and MacDonald (2004), offenders are more likely to become victims of violent crime for several reasons. (1) Some violent subcultures believe in the adage "an eye for an eye." (2) When young offenders are incarcerated, they are often victimized (assault, theft) by other inmates or their friends who are still free. (3) This is the most important—the routine activity theory suggests that if several offenders share similar lifestyles and frequent the same hangouts, the probability of committing crimes or being victims will increase.

In addition, an analysis of data from four British Crime Surveys showed that an average of 41 percent of property victimizations (excluding vehicle offenses) were associated with 2 percent of respondents who were serial victims (they reported 4 or more victimizations). At the same time, 84 percent of respondents reported no property offenses against them. For violent crime, just 1 percent of the respondents suffered 59 percent of the total number. In contrast, 92 percent of the respondents reported no experience of personal (violent) crime. Those who repeatedly victimize the same target are seasoned criminals—they know how to identify "easy targets."

Deadman and MacDonald (2004)

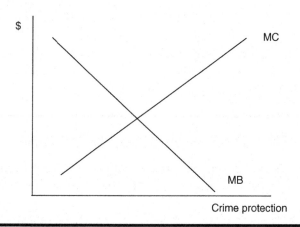

Figure 20.3 Market for crime protection (Victim's viewpoint).

Serial property crimes suggest that if a residence has been burgled, it may be burgled again by the same thief once goods have been replaced. Serial victimization is a function of individual lifestyle factors rather than the nature of the neighborhood.

Searching for Safe Environments

The fear of becoming a victim influences people's shopping choices and recreation choices. Thomas and Bromley (1996) analyzed the influence of safety on shopper anxiety in the traditional shopping centers of Cardiff and Swansea, South Wales. They surveyed the intensity and the nature of these anxieties: shoppers do not feel safe if they have to park in deteriorated or isolated areas. The retailers and the local government remedied this problem by enhancing security.

Similarly, outdoor enthusiasts simultaneously enjoy nature but fear the paths used for walking, cycling, horse riding, and jogging. Enclosures with dense vegetation offer cover for the individual, but also for potential assailants. Ravenscroft, Uzzell, and Leach (2002) used the findings from eight focus groups concerning five recreation routes in the United Kingdom and found that despite encountering very few disagreeable situations, the fear of assault stopped some from walking along the periurban trails.

Ravenscroft, Uzzell, and Leach (2002) and
Thomas and Bromley (1996)

What creates fear? Fear is a function of perceived vulnerability, previous experience as a victim or as a witness of victimization, the nature of the social environment, the quality of support networks, attitudes toward the police, and self-defense capabilities. People assess their risk of victimization from violent crime or property crime. They also stereotype the criminal intent of other individuals or groups and become fearful when these groups are nearby. Additionally, people feel physically vulnerable in the proximity of a larger and stronger potential perpetrator. Finally, the environment where a crime may take place—walking alone on a deserted street at night in a run-down neighborhood—will probably induce fear. Alternatively, familiarity affects risk perception. For instance, tourists perceive their risk levels to be higher than those of residents who frequent an area. In essence, tourists overestimate the risks along a route whereas commuters often underestimate these same risks.

Economic Theories of Hate, Passion, Violence, and Drugs

The economic theory of crime is easiest to explain when the criminal receives monetary rewards for the "work" performed (property crimes, dealing drugs). However, economic theory also explains other crimes that are prevalent in urban areas: hate crimes and riots, domestic violence, and crimes of passion, as well as victimless crimes such as prostitution and substance use.

Hate Crimes

According to the Hate Crime Statistics Act of 1990, hate or bias crimes:

> manifest evidence of prejudice based on race, religion, sexual orientation, or ethnicity, including where appropriate, the crimes of murder, non-negligent manslaughter, forcible rape, aggravated assault, simple assault, intimidation, arson, and destruction, damage, or vandalism of property.[10]

It would seem that the rational choice model would not apply to types of behavior in which the victim's only "mistake" is belonging to a certain hated group. Perpetrators of hate crimes generally do not know their victims whereas that is not the case with other assault victims. Hate crimes are exceptionally brutal and often they are carried out by people with no prior criminal history. These people generally commit the crime near the residence of the victim and must go to unfamiliar areas to find their prey.

Adam Smith (1776) assumed there was a spark of goodness in each individual, but history is crowded with hate-filled individuals who gladly incur personal costs to harm others. Hate is everywhere—Black Separatists, the Christian Identity, the Ku Klux Klan, Neo-Confederates, Neo-Nazis, and Racist Skinheads, to name a few.

Think About It...

The types of hate groups and the cities in which they are located can be found at the interactive website

---

[10] The full text is available through http://www.fbi.gov/hq/cid/civilrights/hate.htm.

http://www.tolerance.org/maps/hate/. Are there any hate groups in your city or surrounding cities? To what do they attribute their formation? What steps have your law enforcement agencies taken with respect to their activities?

Cultivating Hate

Sociological and psychological literature concentrates on the individual and asks what type of personality or what individual circumstances pushes a person to join a hate group. It turns out that in a small group, individuals may gain a higher reputation or a better relative income position by harming others. Of the 3,066 counties in the United States, only 316 counties have hate groups. What conditions favor the existence of such groups?

Jefferson and Pryor (1999) classified the location of these groups as identified by the Southern Poverty Law Center (SPLC). They determined that historical and extrinsic conditions explain more of the variations in hate crimes than sociological or economic variables. A county has a higher probability of containing a hate group if it was part of the Confederate States of America or if it is in a large urban center.

Jefferson and Pryor (1999)

Empirically, hatred (non-remunerative violence) is linked to vengeance. Those who hate believe that they are victims of an injustice (or at least that is their excuse). Bullies, wife beaters, tyrants, and other violent people tend to think that their victims attack or belittle them or at least have an unfair social advantage. Most murders are between acquaintances, especially spouses, and they almost always have an element of revenge. Similarly, gang wars and riots are often motivated by retribution.

Humans punish cheaters. Behavioral and experimental economic literature has documented that some people sacrifice their own welfare to punish those who are unkind or who do not play fairly. In repeated experiments, anonymous individuals sacrifice their earnings to hurt those who act opportunistically—we call such an action **negative reciprocity**. A taste for reciprocity implies that if an aggressor harms a victim then the victim will want to harm the aggressor. However, we need to go a step further to explain why members of the victim's group who are not themselves victims will start to hate members of the aggressor's group who are not themselves aggressors.

Glaeser (2005) used supply and demand to explain the existence of hatred. In this model, political gains determine the supply of hatred. If an individual spends enough time hearing about the past (or future) atrocities of the offending group, they will join the hate movement. The demand for hatred is based on the consumers because they can choose whether or not to listen to the hate-mongers. However, economic and social interactions make hatred costly because it is difficult to do business with people you detest. Those who have no connections with a minority group have no problem hating them. Segregation favors isolation and ignorance as well as a willingness to listen to hate messages.

Why do people listen to hate speech (demand hatred)? First, such propaganda seems to contain potentially useful information about the crimes committed by the hostile groups. Second, hate messages are often subsidized. For example, Glaeser reports that Osama Bin Laden helped the people of Afghanistan against Soviet oppression and thereby secured access to that country. Finally, hate messages make titillating headlines.

Recall this important point: in a national context, hate crimes are committed by those who consider themselves victims when the minority groups acquire civil or political rights that threaten the superiority of their social status. Hatred is therefore encouraged (supplied) by certain politicians or ringleaders whose goal is to increase support for policies that hurt minorities. According to a model by Nobel Prize winner George Akerlof and Rachel Kranton (2000) (Chapter 18), two criteria are needed so that individual hatred becomes collective hatred: (1) other members of the "victim's" group must both identify with the victim and (2) they must decide that all members of the targeted group are collectively guilty. The targeted group needs to have an intrinsic characteristic: they come from another race, another nationality, another religion, or another sexual orientation and these differences cause the crime, not the circumstances. All members of the targeted group are guilty and all members of the group that considers itself a victim are hurt. In this perspective, it is "us vs. them." There is no empathy for the individual victim: "if one of them hurt us, let's get them."

The rational choice approach assumes that individuals who commit hate crimes maximize their utility. The utility function for these perpetrators is a function of hate behavior and a composite of all other goods. Hate and consumption goods are not perfect substitutes. The consumption of hate takes more time and it cannot be purchased in the market. Hate needs to be self-produced using market goods and services along with one's own time. The utility functions of the haters depend negatively on the well-being of the target group. The haters are ready to reduce their own consumption of the composite goods if the consumption of their "target" is reduced even more.

What can society do to counter hate crimes? One safeguard is to build a case to hate the haters. By showing the atrocities of the haters (bigots), the haters become the hated. Dharmapala and McAdams (2005) suggested a model based on the "esteem theory" as an economic theory of persuasion. This theory posits that the esteem (admiration) of others, like conventional consumption goods, affects an individual's utility function. The opinion of others is important. When individuals care about esteem, speech will influence their conduct by providing information about what behavior others respect or do not respect and what they expect of the individual. When extremists overtly admire certain crimes, they increase the expected benefits of engaging in these crimes, causing a new wave of terror.

When people care about the esteem they receive from others, publicity allows the perpetrator to achieve the desired fame. The greater the probability that a crime is be publicized, the higher will be the potential offender's expected utility from the crime. For example, in live sports events, the camera generally ignores any incident caused by a spectator to deny the person fame and thereby decrease the expected utility from such behavior. Thus, restrictions on reporting hate crimes may reduce the incentives to commit these crimes.[11]

Riots

According to the media, "disaffected youth" caused the French riots in the fall of 2005. Joblessness, discrimination, and ostracism from French society supposedly created a tinderbox that was ready to explode at any time. However, the economic theory of riots predicts that only the private costs and benefits should determine whether individuals participate. If the benefits of the group (of rioters) are important, it is because of a link between them and private benefits to each rioter.[12]

The opportunity costs of time and the likely costs of punishment influence the eruption and intensity of the riots. Large, urban centers host more riots than smaller ones, perhaps because it is easier to organize political unrest in large cities than in small, rural towns. Cities offer the following advantages to rioters: reduction in the mobility of law enforcement because of congestion, rapid access to information, and ease of strategic coordination.

---

[11] Gale, Heath, and Ressler (2002).
[12] Carreyrou (2005).

In the ***economic theory of rioting***, DiPasquale and Glaeser (1998) assumed a population receives a range of net benefits from rioting, which include all the benefits and costs of rioting except those specifically linked to financing the police. The desire to participate in a riot comes primarily from individual benefits (stolen goods and merchandise), but also from the political benefits reaped by the group and internalized by individuals within the group. One could rank individuals by the benefits they receive from rioting and assign a higher index to individuals with fewer net benefits to derive a downward sloping benefits curve (Figure 20.4). Personal benefits from rioting are a function of the individual's cost of time and the probability of gaining monetary and nonmonetary rewards, as well as their share of group rewards from the riot. The benefit curve for rioting slopes downward because larger numbers of rioters reduces the benefits that the marginal rioter receives from joining in.

When the number of rioters is low, the costs are constant and higher than the benefits because it is easier to be identified and apprehended. In general, the marginal benefit curve slopes downward because there is protection in numbers—a large number of rioters means that the marginal rioter has a lower risk of being arrested because of anonymity and congestion for law enforcement. The shapes of the marginal cost/marginal benefit curves in Figure 20.4 lead to three possible equilibria: the first A represents the absence of a riot where there is no violence and the probability of being apprehended is large. The marginal costs per individual are greater than the marginal benefits. There will be no riot.

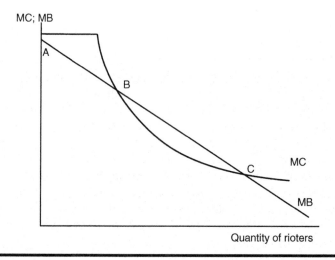

Figure 20.4 The costs and benefits of rioting. (Reprinted from *Journal of Urban Economics*, 43, DiPasquale and Glaeser, The Los Angeles riot and the economics of urban unrest, Pages 52–78, Copyright (2001), With permission from Elsevier.)

B and C are the points of intersection of marginal cost and benefit curves. These are equilibria and the individual observes that the costs and benefits of violence are equal. At Point B, the equilibrium is associated with a lower level of violence and a moderate probability of being arrested. This Point B determines the minimum size of the riot. This equilibrium is, however, unstable. If the initial size of the riot increases by even one more rioter, the riot will soon converge toward C because the marginal benefits are greater than the marginal costs to each potential individual. However, if the initial size of the riot is reduced by even one, the marginal costs will be greater than the marginal benefits to rioters and the riot will converge to Point A, the equilibrium without a riot. At Point C, the equilibrium requires a large number of rioters who each have a low probability of being arrested.

The equilibrium C is stable because a small number of rioters will increase the net benefits and attract other participants. Thus, Figure 20.4 shows that a riot requires an initial event that would bring the number of rioters to a critical size larger than Q_2. The higher probability of being arrested or an increase in costs resulting from apprehension will shift the marginal cost curve upward and reduce the likelihood and the extent of the riot. In addition, individuals with lower values of time (the unemployed, for instance) enjoy more benefits, increasing both the likelihood and extent of rioting. Finally, better information, more media coverage, and better Internet access are favorable to rioters.

Ethnic minorities have recourse to riots to acquire a larger share of the national wealth, political rights, or political power. Different ethnic groups have different behavioral norms. Actions acceptable to one group may be seen by another group as a violation of the social contract. These violations may again lead to vengeance or other hate crimes.

This explains why rioting is rational for an ethnic group as a whole, but why would rioting be rational for any one individual? The leaders may themselves internalize ethnic gains, and in turn, compensate or punish members of their group. In addition, tastes for hatred may anger individuals to willingly avenge any offenses against their group. If community variables trigger a taste for rioting, then these variables will shift the marginal benefits curve in Figure 20.4 outward and increase both the number and intensity of riots. Greater police expenditures increase the marginal cost curve. In addition, according to DiPasquale and Glaeser (1998), a greater proportion of homeowners decreases the probability of rioting because of the disincentive to burn down one's own neighborhood.

Domestic Violence

Violence within the family greatly contributes to the urban crime problem. In the United States, the number of victims of murder committed by an intimate partner was 1830 in 1998. Of this number, 75% of these victims are women. Thirty-three percent of all females murdered were killed by their intimate partners, while for men the figure is only between 3 and 4%.

For all demographics, women experience a higher rate of victimization for domestic violence than men. In 1998, for example, 1.5 per 1000 men were victimized, whereas the figure for women jumped to 7.5 per 1000. Women aged 16–24 years experienced the highest per capita rates of intimate violence: 19.6 per 1000 women. Young, urban African American women who are divorced or separated, earning low incomes, and renting their homes experienced the highest rates of victimization. Similarly, men implicated in this type of violence were for the most part young, black, divorced or separated, and renters.

Witte (1996) confirms that domestic violence may be more common in low-income households, but it also exists in high-income households. A man assaults his partner more frequently if she is of a different race or ethnicity, if she earns higher income, or if she is better educated, *ceteris paribus*.

The benefit/cost analysis also applies to domestic violence, both on the part of the assailant and on the part of the victim who has to choose between reporting the crime and potentially incarcerating the family's breadwinner. Some men seem to derive direct benefits from violence. They can release frustration and vent stress, but most importantly, they exercise control over their partner's behavior. Domestic violence tends to result from economic stress in a household, when the assailant lacks self-esteem, and when he clings to traditional gender roles.

The provision of legal services to victims and improving the women's economic status reduces domestic violence. Economic theory predicts that domestic violence declines when women have more choices—when they know that a legal support structure is available or when they have higher incomes. They will then be more confident and they will not hesitate to report the crimes, thus increasing the costs to the batterer. Because working women enjoy a certain amount of financial autonomy, the marginal cost of reporting the crime.

Unfortunately, a change in the economic status of women is difficult in the short run. Between 55 and 65% of all women on public assistance are victims of domestic violence. In fact, the 1996 Personal Responsibility and Work Opportunity Reconciliation Act (PRWORA) represents a potential danger for many women. The participation in employment and training activities can escalate violence, but not participating in a training program condemns her (and her children) to live in poverty and constant abuse. Abusers who demand total control of their partner can sabotage her efforts—they can shut off the alarm clock on the morning of the job interview, inflict visible bruises that force the woman to cancel the interview, or threatening to endanger the children if she is hired. The harassment and intimidation at the workplace are often means of efficient dissuasion—the newly hired victim will lose her job.

The time limits of services and the obligation to work places the victim in danger. She needs to reveal the identity the father of the children so the state can contact him for child support. If she does, the abuser can find her again. If she does not, public assistance is denied and she will be forced to return to the abuser for financial support. To remedy this situation, a large number of states have adopted the Family Violence Option (FVO) that was added to the 1996 reform bill (Wellstone–Murray Amendment). The FVO requires that the jurisdictions that adopted this option screen for potential victims of domestic violence and offer services and referrals to battered women's organizations. This option permits jurisdictions to exempt the victims from the five-year lifetime limit, from work participation requirements, and from paternity-related child support requirements. Forty-one states have adopted the FVO. Colorado and Ohio allow counties to adopt it if they so choose. Maine, Mississippi, Oklahoma, South Dakota, and Virginia have alternative domestic violence policies. As of 2005, Wisconsin and Illinois had no specific policies in place.[13]

Broken Windows, Abortion, and Murder Rates

Besides capital punishment being used as a standard instrument of deterrence, researchers have recently used the "broken window hypothesis" and a 20-year lag of the date that jurisdictions legalized abortions to explain changes in murder rates. The broken windows hypothesis states that there is a hierarchy of lawlessness starting with graffiti and continuing through vandalism to murder. If a broken window is not fixed, it seems that no one cares or that no one is in charge of the building and vandals will continue to break the windows. If still nothing is repaired, then no one cares about the street or that building. Law-abiding citizens fear walking down these streets, abandoning them to miscreants. In this way, the hierarchy of crime starts in a neighborhood.

Hierarchy of Crime

An economy that accepts broken windows will tolerate crime. Corman and Mocan (2005) tested the broken window hypothesis by regressing the monthly number of murders between 1974 and 1999 in New York City on

---

[13] Tauchen, Witte, and Long (1991); Hetling (2000); Farmer and Tiefenthaler (2003).

economic variables (unemployment rate and real minimum wage), deterrence variables (number of arrests, size of the police force, and the size of the prison population), as well as the number of misdemeanor arrests as a proxy for the broken windows hypothesis. They found that lagged values of the number of arrests, larger numbers of prisoners, and the current minimum wage adjusted for inflation are statistically significant in reducing murders. Lagged values of the number of misdemeanor arrests were inversely correlated with murder rates, but they were statistically insignificant.

However, a 10 percent growth in misdemeanor arrests decreased motor vehicle thefts by between 1.6 and 2.1 percent, robberies by between 2.5 and 3.2 percent, and grand larcenies by between 0.5 and 0.6 percent.

Corman and Mocan (2005)

Abortion laws may affect future murder rates, according to a controversial article by Donohue and Levitt (2001). Joyce and Mocan (1990) and Gruber, Levine, and Staiger (1999) showed that legalized abortion significantly decreased the number of adolescent childbearing and illegitimate births. Donohue and Levitt (2001) and Levitt (2004) concluded, after performing multiple statistical tests, that 20 years after abortions were legalized, criminal activity significantly declined. The five states that allowed abortion in 1970, three years before Roe v. Wade, experienced declines in the crime rates earlier than the rest of the nation. Between 1985 and 1997, the states where there were many abortions experienced a 25.9% decrease in homicide rates while homicide rates in low-abortion states increased by 4.1%. Unwanted, neglected children, perhaps raised by adolescents, are at greater risk for becoming criminals. The abortion theory also holds when researchers use data from Canada and Australia and it applies equally to other social problems such as drug abuse. Legalized abortion decreases the number of unwanted births, according to Levitt, who asserts that his study is not an expression for his personal political position. From a pro-life perspective, if abortion is murder, the million murders a year that happen through abortion only stop a few thousand murders 20 years later.[14]

---

[14] Lott and Whitley (2001); Hilsenrath (2005).

Victimless Crimes

Crime-against-self exists when people willingly become involved in activities that some groups in society determine to be harmful or immoral. We call these activities as victimless crimes. The criminalization of these activities aims to protect the consumers from themselves or to protect society from externalities created by these "victimless" crimes. Externalities include increased property crime to maintain habits for drugs and gambling, increased DUIs, increased health risk (AIDS and STDs, for instance), and other problems with the family, friends, or neighbors whose utility functions depend on the behavior of the "victim." We are going to study two forms of victimless crimes common to all large cities: prostitution and the consumption/distribution of mood modifying substances.

Prostitution

Prostitution is a multibillion-dollar industry employing many women worldwide. Lim (1998) estimated that the sex sector accounts for between 2 and 14% of the GDP of Southeast Asian countries of Indonesia, Malaysia, the Philippines, and Thailand. Prostitution is also well-rooted in developed countries. According to data from the 1992 ***National Health and Social Life Survey*** of the United States, 18% of men have ever paid for sex and 2% of women have ever been paid by a man for the same favors.

Big Money for Low-Skilled Women

Prostitution is a labor intensive occupation that requires no particular training and pays very well. Swedish prostitutes in 1998 earned the equivalent of $1,750 per day, which is the same as a month's salary for an average unskilled worker. In the same year, prostitutes in the Gulf States made $2000 per night and a Latvian prostitute claimed to earn $5000 per month—20 times the average monthly earnings. According to Edlund and Korn (2002), who analyzed a sample of 1024 female street prostitutes of Los Angeles in 1990–1991, determined an average income for prostitutes of $36,342 (in $1998). In the same year, the average income of females in the (legal) service sector was $28,000.

The "common knowledge" that prostitutes are victims of economic or emotional slavery is not always true.

Less than 6 percent of the street prostitutes of Los Angeles in 1990 and 1991 had to share their earnings with a pimp. The pimp fees in Malaysia amount to less than 2 percent of the prostitute's earnings, not including tips. Prostitution pays well even when it is legal. This is one of the only occupations where males earn less than females. The prostitute's career is short, however, because they earn the most when they are young.

Edlund and Korn (2002)

Prostitution is legal but highly regulated in several counties in Nevada, in Switzerland, in the Netherlands, and in several states in Australia. A brothel in Melbourne, Australia, even lists its shares on the Australian Stock Exchange. In other countries, prostitution is tolerated by varying degrees. For example, in Sweden, it is legal to sell sex but not to buy it. In Great Britain, selling sex is legal, but solicitation and living on "immoral earnings" is not. Similarly, curb-crawling (driving slowly around the red light district looking for action) is illegal. In some Muslim countries, prostitution carries the death penalty.

Edlund and Korn's (2002) ***theory of prostitution*** considers the supply of prostitutes just as the supply of labor for any other occupation. A woman without any particular training who does not plan to further her investment in human capital does not give up many future career options by a stint in prostitution. The opportunity cost to the woman is in terms of marriage market opportunities. If men do not want to marry former prostitutes, then the opportunity cost is the probability that a potential spouse will find out about the woman's background. The compensating wage differential falls with the probability of being discovered. This model predicts, therefore, that large numbers of prostitutes migrate. Foreign prostitutes need a lower compensating wage differential because they enjoy greater anonymity. Of course, the less lucrative market for homosexual prostitutes is more complex and does not figure into this discussion.

Married men take up most of the prostitutes' time and thus constitute the largest part of demand, even though in absolute numbers, single men are the majority of their clients. Edlund and Korn formulated the following hypothesis: some men place a premium on variety or prefer sex with younger women. Because young married women are generally not interested in extramarital relationships with older males, these males seek the services of prostitutes. In addition, a local surplus of males can increase the demand for prostitutes. Such was true for the medieval crusaders, frontier towns, mining and logging camps, military bases, and sex tourist destinations.

Both the supply and demand for prostitutes is sensitive to the risk of discovery and the social stigma associated with arrest and conviction. In many cities, citizen groups use "name and shame" techniques of deterrence. Photos and license plate numbers identifying both accomplices are posted on the Internet. The risk of discovery is greater for the street-based prostitution services. In the United States, for instance, street-walkers constitute between 80 and 90% of all prostitutes arrested.

Cities that implement a zero-tolerance initiative aimed at eliminating street crime in one neighborhood do nothing but change the location of the market. On the other hand, cities that tolerate red light districts where police do not intervene create a NIMBY (Not in My Back Yard) phenomenon. Prostitutes want to work in a safe place, but neighboring homeowners want them elsewhere.[15]

Hide and Seek for Finnish Prostitutes

Tani (2002) noted that in the 1990s, at the peak of street prostitution in Helsinki, there were between 1,000 and 2,000 prostitutes, about 15 percent of which were foreign. Most foreign prostitutes were streetwalkers, which led to the conclusion that the prostitution problem was created by foreigners. The Vagrancy Act controlled prostitution in Finland until 1986 when it was repealed. In the years that followed, prostitution was tolerated as long as it did not disturb the peace. During the summer of 1994, some civic groups in Helsinki undertook an anti-prostitution campaign because of the negative externalities imposed on the residents—they did not feel safe walking to their doors at night and curb crawlers were eyeing them even when they were carrying bags of groceries.

To counter this activity, the license plate numbers of the curb crawlers were published in the local newspaper. For others, telephone calls to their wives and employers exposed the identity of the johns. These efforts succeeded in shifting the market but only one block away.

In December of 1999, the city of Helsinki prohibited prostitution in public places. Prostitutes could be fined for soliciting in Helsinki even though prostitution was

---

[15] Cameron, Collins, and Neill (1999); Edlund and Korn (2002).

legal in Finland. Many prostitutes moved to the neighboring city, Vantaa. In the spring of 2000, Vantaa
adopted the same municipal ordinance as Helsinki.
Three years later, all of Finland prohibited prostitution
in public places—the prostitutes are now behind doors.

Tani (2002)

Mood Modifying Substances

Jurisdictions have tried to regulate the consumption of cigarettes and
alcohol and other mood modifying substances for more than a century. In
North America, cigarette bans peaked in the early 1900s. In 1903, Canadian
Parliament passed a resolution to prohibit the manufacture, importation,
and sale of cigarettes. Fifteen states in the United States banned the sale of
cigarettes and 37 states adopted the prohibition of alcohol as part of an
active Progressive Movement.

By 1905, three states in the United States banned alcohol sales, and by
1916, 23 other states followed. Nationally, alcohol prohibition started in 1917
as an emergency wartime measure. It was made permanent when the 18th
Amendment went into effect in January 1920 and continued until 1933 when it
was repealed with the 21st Amendment. Dry counties still exist, but that just
means that consumers drive a bit farther to purchase alcoholic beverages.

There are no official data on alcohol consumption during Prohibition,
but death rates from cirrhosis of the liver and from other diseases
attributable to alcoholism, as well as the drunkenness arrest rates and the
number of new patients admitted to mental hospitals for alcoholic psychosis
all point to the same story—Prohibition did not reduce the amount of
drinking, it merely pushed drinkers underground. At the start of Prohibition,
consumption declined sharply to about 30% of the pre-Prohibition level, but
in the 1920s, it increased significantly, rising close to between 60 and 70% of
the pre-Prohibition level. The marginal cost of enforcement was much larger
than the marginal social benefit of trying to force everyone to drink water.

Two arguments defend the prohibition of any type of mood modifying
substance: (1) irrational consumers and (2) negative externalities associated
with consumption. If consumers are irrational, they are not well informed
about the potential dangers of the substance. They either don't understand
the long-term repercussions of their behavior or they are myopic. Those
who believe in negative externalities assert that others are harmed by the
consumption of the good. Much research has outlined the negative health
risks of consumption and the costs of the negative externalities.

Arguments against prohibition assert that the consumption of an
addictive good is rational. The prohibition of these substances violates

freedom of choice. Researchers who oppose prohibition ask about the extent to which government should dictate healthy behavior. Smoking may include negative health risks, but so do lack of exercise and poor diet. If a community promotes the health of its residents by banning cigarettes, for instance, should the same communities require 30 min. of physical exercise daily? Should they ban french fries and all fast-food restaurants?[16]

Rational Addiction

Addiction defies the central economic assumption that humans rationally pursue their own self-interest. Addiction is defined as a habit where past consumption influences the utility of present consumption. Some addictions (habits) are positive. Time invested in music lessons, working out, or cultivating efficient work/study habits can increase future utility. The problem with harmful addiction is that many addicts claim that they want to change their behavior, but cannot. Their actions (revealed preferences) do not match their words (stated preferences). Economic theory is grounded in free choice, so how can standard economic theory explain addictive behavior?

According to Becker and Murphy (1988), addictive behavior is rational, but it is more complex than other behaviors because it involves a past consumption that the authors call reinforcement and tolerance. Current utility depends on current consumption of the addictive good, current consumption of a nonaddictive good, and the stock of the addictive capital (the summation of all the quantities of the addictive good consumed in the past). ***Tolerance*** decreases the utility from consumption because it requires greater quantities to achieve the same level of utility. Larger amounts consumed today will decrease future satisfaction because this will increase the amount of future consumption needed for the person to "feel good."

Reinforcement means that greater past consumption increases the desire for present consumption. For rational utility maximizers, reinforcement requires that today's pleasure outweigh the harm expected in the future. People who become addicted are those who pay less attention to future consequences than they do to present benefits—that is, they heavily discount the future.

For the consumer, the total cost of an addictive good is the sum of the good's price plus the dollar value of future adverse effects on health and well-being. Increasing the monetary price of a good or increasing the amount of information about future hazards reduces both short-run and long-run consumption. Because low-income and younger consumers tend

---

[16] Alston, Dupré, and Nonnenmacher (2002).

to be myopic (they value the present more than they value the future), they are more responsive to changes in the monetary price than to potential future health problems. As people age or as their incomes increase, the inverse is true: consumers are more concerned about their future health and are more responsive to the information.[17]

Cigarette and Alcohol Consumption

Before the 1960s, cigarettes were not considered dangerous. Doctors often suggested patients smoke cigarettes to calm their nerves, and cigarette advertisements pointed out that their brand was recommended by more physicians. Currently, rather than prescribe the cigarette, physicians proscribe cigarette and nicotine of any kind. Cities, counties, states, and even countries try to reduce consumption by taxation or the imposition of smoking bans.

The health risks of secondhand smoke preclude this from being a victimless crime, according to supporters of smoking bans and tobacco taxes. Policy analyses often weigh the private and social benefits and costs of banning or taxing cigarettes:

- Financial costs of longevity (higher nursing home costs and retirement pensions).
- Higher life insurance costs.
- Decreased gateway effects to using marijuana or other illegal drugs.
- Reduction of secondhand smoke.
- Loss of personal freedom.
- Lost utility of smokers who are victims of the prohibition.
- Potential loss of customers for restaurant and bar owners adjacent to jurisdictions that do not prohibit smoking—cigarettes and alcohol are complementary goods.

Not-so-Slippery Slope of Addiction

According to the "gateway theory," cigarettes and alcohol lead to the use of marijuana, which itself leads to cocaine and heroin. Beenstock and Rahav (2002) tested this hypothesis with data from the Israel Anti-Drug Authority for the years 1989, 1992, and 1995. Although no geographical differences in cigarette

---

[17] Becker and Murphy (1988); Becker, Grossman, and Murphy (1991); Becker (1992); Herrnstein and Prelec (1992).

prices exist in Israel, the real price of cigarettes has varied significantly over time.

People who grew up when cigarettes were cheap are more likely to smoke than people who grew up when cigarette prices were high. The lower prices attracted younger ages to start smoking. These cohorts were also more likely to be introduced to marijuana at a young age and to have continued smoking it. On the other hand, Beenstock and Rahav found no causal link between marijuana and cocaine or heroin.

Pudney (2003) combined data from the Youth Life-styles Survey and the 1998 British Crime Survey to construct a time path for drug users from a sample of 3901 respondents. Over 75 percent of those who use illegal substances generally started with marijuana or amyl nitrate before age 16. Those who experimented with crack, heroin, amphetamines, LSD, mushrooms, and tranquilizers did so by age 18. The average age for those who continue to use methadone, ecstasy, and cocaine was about 20 years. However, the gateway effects were slight. Pudney estimates that legalizing soft drugs would only increase the prevalence of cocaine and ecstasy by 3 percent.

Beenstock and Rahav (2002), Adbel-Ghany and
Wang (2003) and Pudney (2003)

States and cities in the United States impose an average tax of 69.5¢ per pack of cigarettes. As of January 1, 2005, cigarette taxes range from 3¢ per pack in Kentucky to $3.00 in New York City. Taxes on cigarettes ideally follow a Pigouvian tax (Chapter 17), which means that the tax is equal to the cost of the negative externalities imposed on others. Estimates of the negative externalities range from 25¢ to 76¢ a pack (Gruber and Kőszegi, 2004). However, the effect of an increase in taxes on cigarettes or alcohol by one jurisdiction may lessen consumption for the marginal smoker, but if the tax rates are high enough, smugglers will purchase their products through the Internet or from jurisdictions that tax less.[18]

---

[18] Hammar and Johansson-Stenman (2004).

Marijuana

The policies concerning marijuana (cannabis) vary widely by country. In the United States, even medical marijuana is illegal, while in the Netherlands cannabis is sold in "coffee shops." Australia has adopted a policy that tries to minimize the total harm from drugs—they identify programs that affect the incidence of heavy marijuana use as well as total consumption.

Williams (2004) analyzed the Australian National Drug Strategy's Household Survey to determine the price elasticity of demand for marijuana as well as the impact to changes in criminal status on demand. He found significant differences in the price elasticity of demand across age groups, and similarly, the effect of legalizing marijuana varied by age and by gender. Specifically, decriminalizing marijuana delayed the age at which males over the age of 25 gave up using the substance. However, legalizing marijuana did not increase its use by young males or females nor did it increase the frequency of use. If the response is symmetric, criminalizing marijuana has limited capability to reduce the harm associated with this drug.

Because of the possible gateway effect, advocates for banning marijuana would like even more severe laws. In contrast, advocates for legalizing marijuana suggest that legalization would eliminate the suppliers—marijuana would be sold in stores like alcohol is now. The government could then control trade and tax it as it does for cigarettes and alcohol.

Heroin

In 4000 BC, the Sumerians already knew of the pain-relieving effects of heroin and they called the opium poppy *hul gil*, or the "flower of joy." Currently, heroin is seldom prescribed to relieve pain, but it is a widely consumed illegal opiate. With tolerance, the user needs more of the substance to achieve the same intensity, but the pleasure associated with its use is quickly dominated by the worry about a painful withdrawal. As with other mood modifying substances, the economic viewpoint analyzes heroin use as an individual choice associated with negative externalities.

If it were not for negative externalities, prohibition would not be economically efficient because supply and demand policies reduce both consumer and producer surplus (Chapter 6). The social cost of abstinence includes the lost consumer and producer surplus plus the costs involved in enforcement. Supply-based policies increase prices, which lead to more crime when addicts need more money for their fix.

External costs of heroin consumption include health problems such as the spread of infectious diseases (e.g., HIV), if the users share needles. The Australians resolved this problem by providing inexpensive syringes.

Boccaccio and de Bonis (1999) list the following externalities of drug consumption:

1. Social distress (family disruption and urban decay)
2. Loss of productivity and workers
3. Asocial (if not criminal) behavior
4. Conversion of entrepreneurial activities and talent to the underground economy
5. Corruption of public officials
6. Bandwagon effects
7. Increased public health expenditures because of the negative consequences on public health

Are these externalities unique to heroin? No. A similar list exists for alcohol consumption. For instance, lower productivity (2 in the list) is reflected in wages and thus becomes a pecuniary externality. Public officials willing to be bought (5) do not need the excuse of illegal drugs to do so. The definition of asocial behavior is subjective. Drug consumption is blamed for spreading AIDS (7), which affects expenditures on public health, but perhaps the illegality of consumption is the cause of careless behavior. Alcohol abuse causes death as well as higher public health expenditures. If drug consumption raises such moral condemnation, society could refuse to finance remedies for personal consequences of such behavior, thus eliminating these expenses. Great Britain has chosen this path: people who smoke, drink, or have a body mass index over 30 (who are obese) are denied surgeries.

Prohibition creates inefficiencies by generating environments in which monopolistic or oligopolistic profits could finance investments that some legal sectors will oppose, leading to market distortions. In economic terms, strict prohibition may be warranted if the external marginal costs are so great that no consumption can be tolerated—that is, if the y-intercept of the total marginal cost curve in Figure 20.5 were at 10 or above on the y-intercept of the demand function. However, if the major externality is social disapproval, one has to in some way account for that disapproval in a cost-benefit analysis on drug prevention programs.[19]

Should We Legalize Drugs?

The War on Drugs is exacerbating the crime problem. Figure 20.6 illustrates the supply and demand diagram for drugs. Policies to decrease the supply raise the price of the drug. Addicts become more desperate to get money,

---

[19] White and Luksetich (1983); Clarke (2003).

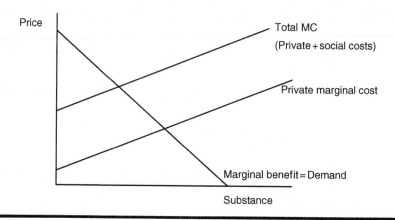

Figure 20.5   Externality analysis of mood modifying substances.

especially if demand is relatively inelastic. The result is not only larger quantities of crime, but also more violent crime. The dealers who are not apprehended benefit because the increase in prices under conditions of inelastic demand leads to an increase in total revenues. The increased prices also encourage "cost savings" when users combine benzodiazepines and alcohol with the hard drugs. These combinations interact to create a deadly, synergistic "cocktail." Finally, high prices encourage entry of new suppliers, who now face higher transactions costs. Because of the greater risk of apprehension, prices remain high.

Economists prefer demand-based policies to ones that decrease supply because decreases in demand do not raise prices. However, demand-based

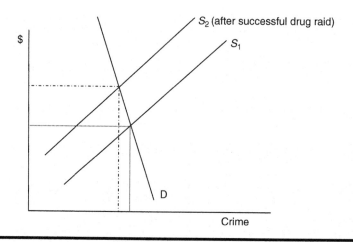

Figure 20.6   Effect of supply-based drug policies.

policies are not "politically correct" because, in the eyes of the public, they punish the addicts—the innocent victims of the dealers. These programs are also an attack on personal liberty. For the campaign to reduce demand, it requires arbitrary drug tests in schools, in universities, and in the workplace, which leads to the incarceration of addicts.

If the War on Drugs is not working, perhaps society would be better off calling a truce and legalizing drugs. This suggestion elicits strong differences of opinion. If we legalize drugs, the retail price of drugs would drop because of increased competition among suppliers. The supply curve for drugs would shift outward: with this, both sides agree.

Where the disagreement comes is in predicting how legalization will affect demand. Those who think that the majority of drug users are rebelling against authority predict the demand for drugs to decrease once they are decriminalized because the thrill of rebellion no longer exists. Others fear that legalization will increase demand—people may try the legalized drugs that would not dare touch them if they were illegal. Proponents of this legalization remind us that when opium was legal in the United States (before 1914), the proportion of opium addicts was negligible; there is no reason to believe that today the situation would be any different. Yet, any argument favoring the prohibition of illegal drugs must answer the question: why not also prohibit alcohol (again) and tobacco?

What is the effect of one jurisdiction alone relaxing its drug laws? Decriminalization in one country inevitably leads to spillovers in other countries. In 1976, the Netherlands decriminalized the possession of limited quantities of cannabis products but continued to prohibit harder drugs such as heroin, cocaine, and LSD. The Netherlands is now a center for drug tourism.

Organized Crime

Organized crime groups are quasi-governments, similar in structure and economic impact to predatory states, and they emerge from a power vacuum created by the absence of state enforcement. The lack of police protection could be geographic, social, ethnic, or due to prohibition. It could also reflect an ineffective law enforcement institution. Mafias and gangs follow a traditional hierarchical organization. Economic costs are higher than those that are typically associated with a government. Organized crime is found in almost every country. Japan has the yakuza; Hong Kong has triads; Colombia and Mexico have their drug cartels.

In the last half of the 1800s, the Sicilian Mafia started offering private protection to a variety of people pursuing both legal and illegal occupations. The American Mafia (La Cosa Nostra or LCN) started from the Sicilian Mafia and expanded rapidly between 1920 and 1933, during Prohibition. By the end of Prohibition, the Mafia controlled many labor unions from construction workers to fur manufacturers. In the 1960s, the Mafia's reputation that they could/would deliver on threats was strong enough to sell services such as contract insurance and dispute settlement.

Since the 1920s, the Mafia had many police commissioners and city councils in their pockets. Until 1980, mayors of Boston, Philadelphia, Chicago, and New York were tightly associated with the local Mafia. Since then, other ethnic organizations such as Nuestra Familia (a Mexican American youth gang) have taken over much of the Mafia's former business.

Organized crime essentially creates a monopoly for criminal activity out of a perfectly competitive market. The result is similar to the effect of monopolizing any other activity. As seen in Figure 20.7, the quantity of crime decreases but the crimes committed are substantially more severe and their social price is higher. The perfectly competitive solution takes place where the marginal cost equals demand (marginal benefit) and victims become essentially a common property resource for the criminals. In Figure 20.7, the quantity of crime is Qc at a price Pc. The effect of organization is similar to the monopolization of a fishery. The quantity of crime (number of victims) diminishes to Qm, although at a higher price (Pm). The severity of crimes committed by the mafia on other criminals is so harsh that the petty (perfectly competitive) criminals go elsewhere.

Urban gangs are essentially mercenary organizations that offer security or protection for their "clients" (Anderson and Tollison 1991). Youth gangs are found in most low-income areas throughout the world. The core ideology of youth gangs (in North America and Europe at least) rests on their belief that their ethnic group has been discriminated against. In addition to their economic role, youth gangs play an important social and cultural function for the members. They are generally less hierarchical and

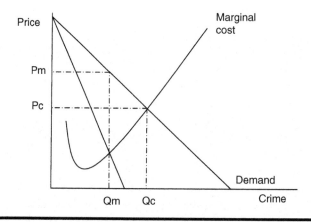

Figure 20.7 Organized crime and the market for crime.

more dependent on their communities. The primary reason is to provide justice for their community if neither the police nor the justice system can guarantee it.

Anti-gang laws try to limit the paramilitary activities (training and wearing uniforms) of any mercenaries because besides urban gangs, they also aim to neutralize other subversive groups (KKK, Aryan Nation, Passe Comitatus, etc.). Anti-gang laws, gun restrictions, and other regulations ensure that all drug dealers, big and small, established and new, compete on a level playing (killing) field.[20]

What Works to Reduce Urban Crime?

The cost of crime is a function of the probability of apprehension multiplied by the probability of conviction multiplied by the probability of punishment. Jurisdictions that want to reduce crime can increase the probability of apprehension by improving their police systems or private law enforcement agencies. Getting tough on crime also includes a total reform of the system of punishment and deterrence.

Police Systems

Each time, the criminal must choose where to commit the next offense and then continuously monitor the risks of that decision. The greater the certainty and severity of punishment, the lower is the likelihood of crime. If potential targets and victims are unevenly distributed across time and space, the expected utility and probability of success varies from one jurisdiction to another and the criminal will specialize where the net benefits are greater.

A change in police strategies creates spillover effects if they push the criminal to work elsewhere. To decrease the quantity of local crime, police can act so that the criminal believes the probability of being apprehended has increased considerably. To avoid spillovers, the police must change their activities without the criminals knowing about it. However, if criminals were using the original location as automotive "chop shops" or fences, such enforcement will reduce the return to theft in surrounding communities, thereby decreasing crime throughout the region.

The goal of an optimal police system is to minimize the total cost of crime, which is equal to the direct costs of crime plus the expenses of crime

---

[20] Anderson and Tollison (1991); Moselle and Polak (2001).

prevention. This does not translate into eradicating all crime unless the marginal cost of prevention is zero. Suppressing all crime would require all citizens to have a "guardian angel" following them constantly, and even the angels would need guardians.

Given their budget constraints, police departments must prioritize the crimes. If the goal is to maximize social welfare and 10% of the population is murdered, no police department should concentrate its resources on ticketing illegal parking. To minimize the total crime damage, it would make sense to resolve high-cost crimes such as murder, rape, and robbery. It would also be beneficial to clear crimes for which criminals are sensitive to the probability of arrest and conviction as well as the crimes that are easy to solve. The same people commit the same types of crimes often, so these would also rank as a high priority.[21]

To improve police performance, economic theory would suggest a system of incentives for the police officers. However, as discussed in the box entitled *Local Drug Enforcement Agencies as Entrepreneurs*, the incentives need to be well thought out. From a public choice perspective, individuals within bureaucracies make decisions, and these decisions are made to maximize their welfares given their constraints. Information is scarce and costly; citizens and their representatives have a limited ability to monitor and control bureaucracies. This leaves the bureaucrats with considerable discretion, at least in the short term. If police officers are rewarded with monetary benefits (for example, a 1% increase in wages for every 3% decrease in crime), then actual crime may decrease—but officers may be tempted to just not report as many crimes.

Local Drug Enforcement Agencies as Entrepreneurs

Mast, Benson, and Rasmussen (2000) noted that the ratio of drug arrests to total arrests in 1989 varied between of 0.266 in San Diego and 0.031 in Indianapolis. This ratio is high in areas where police can retain seized assets. Per 10,000 population, Atlanta's police made 232.8 drug arrests, but those in Indianapolis only arrested 23.3, San Antonio 47.2, and Phoenix 52.9. Why do some localities give priority to the War on Drugs?

[21] Polinsky and Shavell (2000).

Statutes governing the distribution of proceeds from seized assets vary considerably. Some states allow police to retain the proceeds while others mandate they go into a general fund. Many allow police agencies to keep only a part of the proceeds. Mast, Benson, and Rasmussen determined that legislation permitting police to keep a portion of seized assets raises drug arrests and a portion of total arrests by about 20 percent. Like market entrepreneurs, entrepreneurial bureaucrats respond to relative prices. When the price they expect to be "paid" for one activity increases relative to others, they readjust their priorities.

Mast, Benson, and Rasmussen (2000)

Specific vs. General Deterrence

Two types of deterrence exist:

- **Specific deterrence** acts on the individual criminal. A murderer in prison is essentially neutralized. Incarceration is a specific deterrence because it is more difficult for the prisoners to commit crimes on the outside from their prison cell.
- **General deterrence** acts on all potential criminals for they need to reevaluate their cost-benefit calculations when the probability of getting caught increases or when the average prison sentences are lengthened.

Economic theory determines that the optimal deterrence, taking account of the budget constraints, is found when the impact on crime per dollar spent on each different type of deterrent is equal. This is when $\dfrac{\text{Effect of jails}}{\$1}$

$= \dfrac{\text{Effect of patrols}}{\$1} = \dfrac{\text{Effect of crime labs}}{\$1} = \dfrac{\text{Effect of...}}{\$1}$

If patrols are more effective than building more jails, it makes sense to hire more patrol officers rather than build another jail. But how do we determine the most profitable detterence. It is almost impossible to accurately guess the amount of general deterrence that is attributable to jails, patrols, or crime labs. Besides, criminals will not react to longer jail time if they think that they are so good at their craft that they will never be caught or if they are unaware of the likely punishments for their contemplated crimes.

Are Harsher Punishments the Solution

In the late 1700s, picking pockets was a capital offense in England. Nevertheless, pickpockets routinely worked the crowds at public hangings. Based on 278 interviews of male inmates in North Carolina and Kentucky, Anderson (2002) examined the premise that criminals make informed and calculated decisions. Their results reported that 76 percent of ordinary criminals and 89 percent of the most violent criminals either did not conceive of the possibility that they would be caught or they did not know the likely punishments for their crimes.

Of those who habitually committed nonviolent crimes (robbery, burglary, drugs, DUI, and forgery), between 21 and 43 percent of them knew exactly what the punishment would be. In contrast, only between 4 and 16 percent of perpetrators of violent crimes knew what punishment to expect. Among them, 72 percent of violent offenders claimed that no punishment—no matter how severe—would have deterred them.

Why does increased punishment not deter some criminals? Except in assault cases, criminals do not think they will be caught. To get the criminals' attention, it is necessary to do more than make a minor change in the punishment. Even though the Constitution prohibits cruel and unusual punishment, many punishments have substantially increased. This impact is insignificant because, as Anderson demonstrates, would-be lawbreakers don't research penalties in law books as they research their cost-benefit analyses.

Anderson does not argue for decreasing existing punishments because they deter an unknown number of potential criminals, but he argues that few of the remaining crimes could be eliminated by harsher punishments.

Anderson (2002)

Think About It...

What is the punishment for speeding 5 (10? 20?) miles per hour over the speed limit?

What is the penalty for students who park in unauthorized lots? What about for parking past the time permitted?

What is the typical punishment of copying software?

What is the typical punishment for photocopying more than a "fair share" of a book? For sharing music? For jaywalking? For underage drinking or furnishing alcohol to a minor?

What proportion of offenders gets caught for these crimes?

Have the penalties become more or less severe in the last five years?

Do these penalties deter anyone you know from committing these crimes?

Deterrence generally originates within a person. Anyone would choose to commit crime given the right cost-benefit calculations, but a sense of morality keeps most people honest. Religions discourage immoral or illegal behavior because the system of rewards and punishments promises divine or supernatural sanctions even if the delinquent does not get caught in "this life." Freeman (1996) noted that church attendance is a better indicator of who escapes poverty, drug addiction, and crime than income, family structure, or other variables. However, Medoff and Skov (1992) expected that Christian Fundamentalism would successfully decrease deviant behavior because these groups practice their religion more intensely. Their results signaled that Fundamentalism significantly decreased abortion rates, but it had no impact on divorce, murder, or suicide rates.[22]

Punishment and Deterrence

The cost per year of maintaining someone in a state prison in the United States in 1996 averaged $20,100 ($55.18 per day), ranging from a high of

---

[22] Cloninger (1982, 1987, 1991, 1992); Legge and Park (1994); DeFina and Arvanites (2002); Garoupa and Klerman (2002).

$37,800 in Minnesota ($103.63 per day) to a low of $7987 in Alabama ($21.88 per day).[23] Federal prisons are the most costly, at $23,500 per year ($68.38 per day). Is there a more effective and less costly method of deterrence than prison? That depends on society's goals.

There are three rival philosophies of punishment. A ***pragmatic philosophy of deterrence*** proposes that society should choose the most efficient and least expensive means possible. If fines work, use them. Lengthen prison sentences and make prisons less pleasant if need be. Some adherents to this philosophy might insist that because it costs between $20,000 and $23,500 on average to warehouse prisoners, efficiency could allow us to pay (bribe) prisoners $15,000 as long as they do not commit crimes. However, this prescription ignores the incentive effects from those who are not currently criminals.

The second philosophy asserts that justice requires ***vengeance and retribution***. Execution and whipping are acceptable in this light. This concept is based on "eye for an eye" philosophy, and it further asserts that the punishment should fit the crime. This type of justice assumes that the prisoner is guilty without any doubt and that the person is not a victim of false charges. Besides, the punishment can be a consolation for the victim even if it has little impact on the rate of crime (see the box entitled *Are Harsher Punishments the Solution?*).

The third philosophy rests on ***rehabilitation***. The hope is that therapy will alter the internal deterrents of the criminal so much that the marginal cost of committing crime becomes prohibitive. This philosophy proposes a personalized treatment, and at the extreme, the abolition of all incarceration. With enough time and patience, psychologists and criminologists could transform the criminals into model citizens. One problem, among others, is that to be rehabilitated, a person must agree that he or she has antisocial behavior.

Imprisonment and Overcrowding

Prisons increase the cost of doing crime and thus lead to general deterrence. To a large extent, they also incapacitate individuals from pursuing their preferred activities. If we follow the incapacitation rationale, we arrive at an extreme point of view—the incarcerated population is spiraling upward. Individuals who represent a potential danger to society need to be incapacitated. Rapists and sexual offenders fall into this category and in this view they need to be imprisoned for life because of their propensity to recidivate.

Imprisonment works. Criminals are banished from the community (specific deterrence) so that they can only harm other inmates or prison

---

[23] Fadaei-Tehrani and Green (200IU2).

employees. Unidentified offenders are (we hope) deterred (general deterrence) if they think that the risk of confinement is too great given the expected gains from crime. In addition, society is exacting retribution. If a stay in prison is disagreeable, the ex-convicts will not be tempted to return.

However, managing prisons is costly. Prisons become human warehouses. A stay in prison can provide prisoners time to reflect on their past behavior, but it also constitutes a "school" where criminals can learn from one another. Costs of incarceration include not only the costs of construction and maintenance, the salary of directors, counselors, and guards, but also the losses in worker productivity and employability.

Statistically, age and maturity (which do not always go together) constitute the most effective deterrents. Many long-term prison sentences create "nursing homes surrounded by razor wire" with an aging, sickly inmate population. If the potential to commit crimes actually does decrease with age, it would be practical to liberate the older prisoners to make room for the young ones.[24]

Hang Them All?

Friedman (1999) reasoned that we are too squeamish about efficient punishments suggested by the pragmatists. If one were to (1) replace a punishment with another more severe and less costly option and (2) reduce the probability of conviction while maintaining the same degree of deterrence, society could reduce the costs of deterrence and enforcement. Execution is less costly than imprisonment and the recidivism rate is zero, but fines are even less costly. So why not either hang them or fine them? The budgetary deficits from which all jurisdictions suffer would be avoided. Societies use prisons simply because the entire judicial system profits from convictions.

In Becker's (1968) model, punishment is analyzed as a Pigouvian tax intended to make criminals internalize the externalities that they impose on others. If an offender has a 0.9 probability of receiving a 25-year prison term, this would be equivalent to some lower probability of being executed (say, 0.167).

Say that the criminal gives a value associated with each year of prison, A. This value is discounted over time. Thus,

---

[24] DiIuloi (1996).

the present value of a future life can be determined by the formula $\sum_{t=1}^{T}(A)/(1+r)^t$, where r is the discount rate and t is the time between 1 (current year) and T (the end of the life). Risk-neutral criminals (Chapter 5) can assign a current sum (say \$1 million) to their present value equation to find the specific probability of an execution ($t=0$) that would equal the largest probability of receiving a 25-year prison sentence:

$$(0.9)\sum_{t=1}^{25}\frac{A}{(1+r)^t} = \$1,000,000 = (0.167)\sum_{t=0}\frac{A}{(1+r)^0}.$$

Each time a criminal is convicted, society throws a die. Roll a number from 1 to 5 and the criminal goes free. Roll a 6 (a probability of 0.167) and he will be hung. The risk neutral criminal is as satisfied with prison or a certain probability of execution. The victims of the lucky criminal might be frustrated, but the deterrence is the same and prisons can be eliminated.

No efficient legal system uses prisons. Defendants with money will pay because fines are more efficient than execution. Those who don't pay their fines will be executed, with a probability based on the seriousness of the offense. The rules of the game can be changed, introducing, for example, the possibility of throwing one of two numbers (so that the probability increases from 0.167 to 0.33). In essence, no penalty would be used if another, more severe and more efficient penalty exists. Any existing prisons that do not pay for themselves are as unpleasant as possible to produce the maximum quantity of punishment per taxpayer dollar. It is evident for Becker and Friedman that the penal system leaves much to be desired.

Becker (1968) and Friedman (1999)

Three-Strikes Laws

In the 1990s, some states in the United States started to mandate a life sentence without the possibility of parole for 25 years for recidivists with three (or more) felony convictions. The thought is that anyone guilty of more than two felonies is a chronic criminal and should be permanently imprisoned. Washington State was the first to enact this law in 1993. California followed one year later, and by 2004, 26 states adopted three-strikes laws.

Strange results have occurred. In California, shoplifting is a felony if the person has a prior conviction for any form of stealing. Defendants have been sentenced to 25 years to life in prison for stealing golf clubs or even a slice of pizza. Defendants could be charged with and convicted of two "third strikes" simultaneously and be given two separate consecutive sentences (50 years or more). This happened to a Californian who stole some videotapes. Georgia even voted in a "two-strike" law and reinstated chain gangs and striped uniforms for prisoners.

One result of the tough-on-crime laws is that prison populations are up. In addition, the three-strikes laws are associated with 10%–29% more homicides. The criminals can reduce their anticipated costs by decreasing the risks of apprehension or conviction—they can re-locate to another jurisdiction, commit crimes that are not punished by the three-strikes law, bribe police, or eliminate the victims and witnesses to reduce the possibility of being identified.

Murder is tempting if the penalty for homicide is the same for the "third strike," as long as we assume that the risk of being caught in a homicide case is the same for the other crimes. Twelve states adopted three-strikes laws in 1994 and one more state adopted it a year later. The homicide rate in the United States declined nationwide during and after these years, but it declined by a smaller amount in the three-strikes law states.

In practice, there is no significant evidence that these laws reduced the crime rate. Instead, they give a slight advantage to some criminals, who once apprehended will receive substantial prison terms anyway, but at the discretion of the judge. These myopic criminals greatly discount the value for their future life when a prison term takes place and thus face a small deterrent from incarceration.

Fines

Monetary sanctions are less costly means of deterrence than prisons. In addition, they can be a source of income for the jurisdiction. Victims can receive compensation from the proceeds. In contrast, prisons only provide victims (and society in general) with higher tax bills. However, fines are not a perfect solution either because they become the monetary price for committing the offenses. High-income criminals could easily buy their liberty, but those who cannot would be jailed even for petty offenses because they cannot pay the fine. Fines could be levied as a proportion of income, but true income is difficult to ascertain if a large part of a criminal's income comes from crimes that remain unsolved.

Unfortunately, monetary sanctions are ineffective—inmate populations are overwhelmingly composed of people with little income before being arrested. If the probability of apprehending criminals is low, relying on stiff monetary sanctions alone will not deter crime. The probability of punishment for stealing a motor vehicle in the United States equaled the probability of arrest (0.076 in 1994) multiplied by the probability of an arrest resulting in conviction (0.19) or 0.014. If the probability of punishment has not changed and the value of a vehicle to the thief is $500, then to deter this crime, the fine would need to be $500/0.014 = $35,714, an amount much higher than people with few assets are able to pay.

Rehabilitation

Rehabilitation increases the depreciation rate of criminal energy, according to Meier (2001). Therapy may reduce the impulse but it cannot exclude the possibility of recidivism. In some situations, therapy can reduce the recidivism rate but this evidence could also be attributed to cream skimming by judges who allow therapy only for "good risks"—the individuals who are most apt to be rehabilitated. Although therapy reduces the probability of recidivism by increasing the depreciation on criminal energy, it is associated with a higher cost per period than simple incarceration. Does therapy last for the entire incarceration? Generally it does not, for therapy is more costly than simple imprisonment. The practice of using rehabilitation is at least irrational if it is not inefficient.

Alternative Crime Prevention Strategies

What works besides the very expensive solution of locking them up and throwing away the key? According to Witte (1996), there are two types of programs that affect urban crime in the long run. Social programs (for drug treatment, child welfare, and jobs) affect crime directly or indirectly. These programs offer meaningful activities (jobs, schools, and education) for youth and prevention or support strategies directed to young children and their families. Community-oriented and value-centered schools could improve educational performance and lower incidents of juvenile delinquency. Early child development intervention programs (Chapter 19) and intensive programs for at-risk youth (Chapter 18) are most successful, but even keeping the young people busy with legal activities is also efficient. For instance, McConnell and Glazerman (2001) estimated that Job Corps netted benefits of $2.02 for every dollar of program expenditures in 1995.

Of the $16,829 net benefits to society, 7%, or $1240, were due to reductions in crime.

Numerous empirical studies have provided evidence for the controversial hypothesis that in the short run, jurisdictions that legalized the sale and allow citizens to carry handguns permitted potential victims to better defend themselves. Thus, guns act as a general deterrence against rape, burglary, and homicide. The studies that contradict the benefits of carrying handguns argue primarily about the conclusions of the studies that come out in support of concealed handgun laws rather than with the economic models or statistical analyses themselves.[25] Restrictions on carrying handguns such as safe storage requirements and one-gun-a-month purchase rules are statistically associated with increases in crime rates. A prohibition of hand gun possession by juveniles has only an insignificant effect on decreasing gun homicides, but in fact, could increase the total number of homicides.[26]

Summary and Conclusions

Crime rates are not constant over time. This chapter focused on the causes of variations in crime by applying economic theory to the study of crime and criminal behavior. The two primary sources of crime data in the United States are the FBI's UCR and the BJS's NCVS. The primary problem with the UCR is that it only lists reported crimes, whereas the NCVS allows individuals to acknowledge that they were recent crime victims.

Rather than considering criminals as deviants, economists see the criminal act as a result of a rational decision. Criminals will commit crimes as long as their expected marginal cost is less than their perceived marginal benefit. The costs of crime include the probability of apprehension multiplied by the probability of conviction multiplied the expected length of sentence and the individual's legitimate earnings per year. For any given offense, everything else equal, lower income people will commit more crimes.

A large body of social science literature questions the rationality of criminals by trying to attribute the deviant behavior to some combination of nature, nurture, or social environment. The nature proponents describe a criminal's body type as one that is large and muscular, resembling a Neanderthal. This conforms to the economic theory because a strong muscular male with an aggressive personality would enjoy a decreased

---

[25] Moody (2001); Parker (2001); Rubin and Dezhbakhsh (2003).

[26] Lott and Mustard (1997); Bronars and Lott (1998); Benson and Mast (2001); Marvell (2001); Miron (2001); Lott (2001); Plassmann and Tideman (2001); Bice and Hemley (2002).

cost of doing crime. Victims will not hesitate to turn over their wallets. On the other hand, those in favor of nurture or social environment see the criminal as a victim of society in general. Everyone else is to blame for the criminal's impulses.

The quantity of crime is the result of interactions among three groups of actors: criminals, victims, and those involved with law enforcement systems. Victims respond to a marginal benefit-marginal cost calculus when they determine the quantity of crime prevention devices and activities in which to invest. Thus, victims are partly self-determined. Unfortunately, to be perfectly safe from crime requires that victims incarcerate themselves in fortified palaces. Miscreants would have complete freedom.

Economic theory can explain several types of crimes. For example, Glaeser (2005) describes hatred from a supply/demand perspective. Consumers demand hate because they can choose whether or not to listen to politicians or agitators who are persuaded that society is better off when certain ethnic minorities are neutralized. To safeguard its victims of hate, a city can show the atrocities of the haters so that they become the object of hate. Alternatively, restrictions on reporting hate crimes decrease the utility of the haters who are hoping to increase the esteem of other haters.

DiPasquale and Glaeser's (1998) economic theory of riots concluded that the rioters are also sensitive to marginal cost-marginal benefit analysis. Benefits of rioting can come from goods stolen during the riot or from the expectations of rewards from benefits gained by the overall group. Costs of rioting (incarceration) are higher when the number of rioters falls. A small number of rioters decreases the intensity of the riot.

Domestic violence also follows a cost-benefit analysis. The assailants release frustration, vent stress, and solidify their control over their partners through violence. However, with greater amounts of legal service provided and increased financial independence, the victim can leave the abuser. The risk of losing the partner as well as the increased probability of intervention by the legal system will decrease the equilibrium level of violence in a household.

Edlund and Korn's (2002) theory of prostitution explains why women prostitutes are paid more than men and why women would require such high levels of compensation for labor-intensive work that does not require special training. The economic theory of prostitution asserts that women must be compensated significantly more for being prostitutes because their probability of marriage and security is lower than if they took an alternate profession.

Consumption of mood modifying substances (both legal and illegal) is rational and it involves reinforcement and tolerance, according to Becker and Murphy (1988). With greater past consumption comes an increased desire for future consumption (reinforcement), but at the same time, the utility level of consuming a certain quantity of the good declines over time as more of the good is needed to achieve the same utility (tolerance). Reinforcement for rational utility maximizers requires that the benefits of consumption today are greater than the anticipated future harm. Addicts heavily discount the future and place great emphasis on the present.

Economists are in the minority in the promotion of the legalization of drugs. If drugs were legal, prices would decrease, the amounts of property crime committed to pay for the drugs would decrease, and fewer deaths would occur from unsafe substitutions. Opponents to legalizing drugs might also point to the rational theory of addiction for support—when prices decrease, people consume more of a harmful, addictive substance, and the reinforcement and tolerance effects come into play. Those who are most likely to be affected are poor people and youths because of their emphasis on present benefits over future pain.

The economic theory of crime emphasizes that criminals respond to punishment and deterrence in their decision to commit crimes. The goal of specific deterrence is to reduce the probability that the individual being punished will reoffend. The general deterrence angle dissuades other criminals from committing crime because they readjust their subjective probabilities with increased arrest rates, convictions, and punishments.

Individual jurisdictions can decrease crime locally by stepping up law enforcement, but criminals will just work in other locations. To decrease the spillover effects from a local tough-on-crime policy, law enforcement officials can disrupt the source of funds benefiting the criminals. Witte (1996) suggests that investing in social policies and early intervention programs for at-risk teens will increase the costs of doing crime for this group. Other economists think that relaxing gun control laws for handguns will increase the marginal cost of crime for criminals.

Chapter Questions

1. Refer again to Table 20.1.
   a. What increase in probability of apprehension and conviction would Pat need to reconsider committing the burglary?
   b. Keeping the probability of apprehension and conviction at 0.30, what length of sentence would keep Pat from expecting positive net benefits from the burglary?
2. Draw a supply and demand diagram for identity theft protection. What factors would increase the demand for such protection? What costs would be involved to incur the protection?
3. If one goal of organized crime is to decrease competition, then by organizing, criminals are acting as though they are monopolists.

Draw the demand, marginal revenue, and marginal cost curves for crime from the criminal's viewpoint.

In a perfectly competitive market, the supply curve is the summation of the marginal cost curves, so it is routine to compare the effects of perfect competition and monopoly by treating the marginal cost curve as if it were a supply curve.

Compare the optimal amount of crime in a perfectly competitive market with that of a market dominated by organized crime. What is the difference in "price" imposed on society in each of the markets? Is society better off with organized crime or many criminals working in a perfectly competitive environment?

Research Assignments

1. Consult the Crime and Justice Data Online for your area at http://bjsdata.ojp.usdoj.gov/dataonline/. What types of crime are more prevalent in your locality than elsewhere in the country?
2. If your city has a population of 250,000 or more, compare homicide trends in your locality with those for the country as a whole from the Crime and Justice Data Online at http://bjsdata.ojp.usdoj.gov/dataonline/. Given your knowledge of this locality, why would you think such trends differ?
3. How active are crime watch groups in your city (or neighborhood)? If there are not any, would your city be ripe for starting such a group given your analysis of Research Questions 1 and 2?

References

Abdel-Ghany, M., and M. Q. Wang. 2003. Contemporaneous and intertemporal relationship between the consumption of licit and illicit substances by youth. *Journal of Family and Economic Issues* 24 (3):281–289.

Agnew, R. S. 1985. A revised strain theory of delinquency. *Journal of Social Forces* 64 (1):151–167.

Akerlof, G. A., and R. E. Kranton. 2000. Economics and identity. *Quarterly Journal of Economics* 115 (3):715–753.

Alston, L. J., R. Dupre, and T. Nonnenmacher. 2002. Social reformers and regulation: the prohibition of cigarettes in the United States and Canada. *Explorations in Economic History* 39 (4):425–445.

Anderson, D. A. 2002. The deterrence hypothesis and picking pockets at the pickpocket's hanging. *American Law and Economics Review* 4 (2):295–313.

Anderson, G. M., and R. D. Tollison. 1991. The war on drugs as antitrust regulation. *Cato Journal* 10 (3):691–701.

Angels Around the World. (n.d.), http://www.guardianangels.org/chapter_overview.html (accessed on August 22, 2004, site now discontinued).

Barry, E. America's Best and Worst Cities for Crime Atlanta Chief Calls His City The Most Dangerous in Nation, 21 February 2004, http://www.bestplaces.net/crime02/crime_study6.asp (accessed on August 21, 2004, site now discontinued).

Becker, G. S. 1997 [1968]. Crime and punishment: an economic approach, In *Law and Economics, Volume 2, Contracts, Torts and Criminal Law,* eds. A. Richard Posner and F. Parisi, *Elgar Reference Collecto.International Library of Critical Writings in Economics,* Vol. 81, Elgar; distributed by American International Distribution Corporation, Williston, VT, Cheltenham, U.K. and Lyme, N.H, 427–475, 1997 [1968].

Becker, G. S. 1992. Habits, addictions, and traditions. *Kyklos* 45 (3):327–345.

Becker, G. S., M. Grossman, and K. M. Murphy. 1991. Rational addiction and the effect of price on consumption. *American Economic Review* 81 (2):237–241.

Becker, G. S., and K. M. Murphy. 1988. A theory of rational addiction. *Journal of Political Economy* 96 (4):675–700.

Beenstock, M., and G. Rahav. 2002. Testing gateway theory: do cigarette prices affect illicit drug use? *Journal of Health Economics* 21 (4):679–698.

Benson, B. L., and B. D. Mast. 2001. Privately produced general deterrence. *Journal of Law and Economics* 44 (2):725–746.

Bentham, J. 1907 [1789]. *Introduction to the Principles of Morals and Legislation.* Oxford: Clarendon Press.

Bice, D. C., and D. D. Hemley. 2002. The market for new handguns: an empirical investigation. *Journal of Law and Economics* 45 (1):251–265.

Boccaccio, M., and V. de Bonis. 1999. Economic notes on prohibition. *Journal of Public Finance and Public Choice/Economia Delle Scelte Pubbliche* 17 (1):45–62.

British Crime Survey, Crime and Fear of Crime, 2004, http://www.statistics.gov.uk/about/data/harmonisation/downloads/S9.pdf (accessed on November 11, 2005).

Boggess, S., and J. Bound. 1997. Did criminal activity increase during the 1980s? Comparisons across data sources. *Social Science Quarterly* 78 (3):725–739.

Bronars, S. G., and J. R. Lott. 1998. Criminal deterrence, geographic spillovers, and the right to carry concealed handguns. *American Economic Review* 88 (2):475–479.

Cameron, S., A. Collins, and T. Neill. 1999. Prostitution services: an exploratory empirical analysis. *Applied Economics* 31 (12):1523–1529.

Carreyrou, J. 2005. Culture clash, Muslim groups may gain strength from French unrest. *The Wall Street Journal,* 246 (98) (November 7):A1,A15.

CBS News. 60 Minutes Boosting for Billions, July 11, 2004, http://www.cbsnews.com/stories/2004/02/20/60minutes/main601396.shtml (accessed on August 21, 2004).

Council of Europe. 2003. European sourcebook of crime and criminal justice statistics, http://www.europeansourcebook.org/

Clarke, H. 2003. Economic analysis of public policies for controlling heroin use. *Australian Economic Papers* 42 (2):234–252.

Cloninger, D. O. 1992. Intercity variations in the police use of lethal response. *Journal of Economic Behavior and Organization* 17 (3):413–422.

Cloninger, D. O. 1991. Lethal police response as a crime deterrent: 57-city study suggests a decrease in certain crimes. *American Journal of Economics and Sociology* 50 (1):59–69.

Cloninger, D. O. 1987. Capital punishment and deterrence: a revision. *Journal of Behavioral Economics* 16 (4):55–57.

Cloninger, D. O. 1982. Moral and systematic risk: a rationale for unfair business practice. *Journal of Behavioral Economics* 11 (2):33–49.

Cohen, M. A. 1990. A note on the cost of crime to victims. *Urban Studies* 27 (1):139–146.

Crime Times Linking Brain Dysfunction to Disordered/Criminal/Psychopathic Behavior, http://www.crime-times.org/ (accessed on August 22, 2004).

Corman, H., and N. Mocan. 2005. Carrots, sticks, and broken windows. *Journal of Law and Economics* 48 (1):235–266.

Davis, J. A. 1959. A formal interpretation of the theory of relative deprivation. *Sociometry* 22 (4):280–296.

Deadman, D., and Z. MacDonald. 2004. Offenders as victims of crime? An investigation into the relationship between criminal behaviour and victimization. *Journal of the Royal Statistical Society: Series A (Statistics in Society)* 167 (1):53–67.

DeFina, R. H., and T. M. Arvanites. 1971. The weak effect of imprisonment on crime: 1971–1998. *Social Science Quarterly* 83 (3):635–653.

Deutsch, J., and G. S. Epstein. 1998. Changing a decision taken under uncertainty: the case of the criminal's location choice. *Urban Studies* 35 (8):1335–1343.

Deutsch, J., S. Hakim, and U. Spiegel. 1990. Learning by criming: theoretical analysis and empirical evidence. *Public Finance* 45 (1):59–69.

Dharmapala, D., and R. H. McAdams. 2005. Words that kill? An economic model of the influence of speech on behavior (with particular reference to hate speech). *Journal of Legal Studies* 34 (1):93–136.

DiIulio, J. J. 1996. Help wanted: economists, crime and public policy. *Journal of Economic Perspectives* 10 (1):3–24.

DiPasquale, D., and E. L. Glaeser. 1998. The Los Angeles riot and the economics of urban unrest. *Journal of Urban Economics* 43 (1):52–78.

Donohue, J. J., and S. D. Levitt. 2001. The impact of legalized abortion on crime. *Quarterly Journal of Economics* 116 (2):379–420.

Edlund, L., and E. Korn. 2002. A theory of prostitution. *Journal of Political Economy* 110 (1):181–214.

Ehrlich, I. 1973. Participation in illegitimate activities: a theoretical and empirical investigation. *Journal of Political Economy* 81 (3):521–565.

Fadaei-Tehrani, R., and T. M. Green. 2002. Crime and society. *International Journal of Social Economics* 29 (9–10):781–795.

Fajnzylber, P., D. Lederman, and N. Loayza. 2002. Inequality and violent crime. *Journal of Law and Economics* 45 (1):1–40.

Farmer, A., and J. Tiefenthaler. 2003. Explaining the recent decline in domestic violence. *Contemporary Economic Policy* 21 (2):158–172.

Federal Bureau of Investigation. *Uniform crime reports*, 2002, http://www.disastercenter.com/crime/uscrime.htm (accessed on August 20, 2004).

Federation of Tax Administrators. State Excise Tax Rates on Cigarettes, http://www.taxadmin.org/fta/rate/cigarett.html (accessed on November 21, 2005).

Felson, M., and E. Poulsen. 2003. Simple indicators of crime by time of day. *International Journal of Forecasting* 19 (4):595–601.

Freeman, R. B. 1996. Why do so many young American men commit crimes and what might we do about it? *Journal of Economic Perspectives* 10 (1):25–42.

Friedman, D. 1999. Why not hang them all: the virtues of inefficient punishment. *Journal of Political Economy* 107 (6):S259–S269.

Gado, M. (n.d.) *All About Criminal Motivation*, Chapter 6, Bodyshaping the criminal, http://www.crimelibrary.com/criminal_mind/psychology/crime_motivation/6.html?sect=19.

Gale, L. R., W. C. Heath, and R. W. Ressler. 2002. An economic analysis of hate crime. *Eastern Economic Journal* 28 (2):203–216.

Garoupa, N., and D. Klerman. 2002. Optimal law enforcement with a rent-seeking government. *American Law and Economics Review* 4 (1):116–140.

Glaeser, E. L. 2005. The political economy of hatred. *Quarterly Journal of Economics* 120 (1):45–86.

Glaeser, E. L., and B. Sacerdote. 1999. Why is there more crime in cities? *Journal of Political Economy* 107 (6):S225–S258.

Gorr, W., A. Olligschlaeger, and Y. Thompson. 2003. Short-term forecasting of crime. *International Journal of Forecasting* 19 (4):579–594.

Gruber, J., and B. Kőszegi. 2004. Tax incidence when individuals are time-inconsistent: the case of cigarette excise taxes. *Journal of Public Economics* 88 (9–10):1959–1987.

Gruber, J., P. Levine, and D. Staiger. 1999. Abortion legalization and child living circumstances: who is the "marginal child"? *Quarterly Journal of Economics* 114 (1):263–291.

Hammar, H., and O. Johansson-Stenman. 2004. The value of risk-free cigarettes—do smokers underestimate the risk? *Health Economics* 13 (1):59–71.

Hansen, K., and S. Machin. 2002. Spatial crime patterns and the introduction of the U.K. minimum wage. *Oxford Bulletin of Economics and Statistics* 64 (0):677–697.

Helsley, R. W., and W. C. Strange. 1999. Gated communities and the economic geography of crime. *Journal of Urban Economics* 46 (1):80–105.

Herrnstein, R. J., and D. Prelec. Herrnstein and Prelec, 1992. A theory of addiction. In *Choice Over Time*, eds. G. Loewenstein and J. Elster, Russell Sage Foundation, New York, 331–360.

Hetling, A. H. 2000. Addressing domestic violence as a barrier to self-sufficiency: the relationship of welfare receipt and spousal abuse. *Journal of Public and International Affairs* 11 (0):21–35.

Hilsenrath, J. E. 2005. 'Freakonomics' Abortion research is faulted by a pair of economists. *Wall Street Journal* A2.

Hodgins, S., L. Kratzer, and T. F. McNeil. 2002. Obstetrical complications, parenting practices and risk of criminal behaviour among persons who develop major mental disorders. *Acta Psychiatrica Scandinavica* 105 (3):179–188.

Jefferson, P. N., and F. L. Pryor. 1999. On the geography of hate. *Economics Letters* 65 (3):389–395.

Joyce, T. J., and Mocan, N. H. The impact of a ban on legalized abortion on adolescent childbearing in New York City, National Bureau of Economic Research, Inc., NBER Working Papers, 1990.

Kelly, M. 2000. Inequality and crime. *Review of Economics and Statistics* 82 (4):530–539.

Legge, J. S., and J. Park. 1994. Policies to reduce alcohol-impaired driving: evaluating elements of deterrence. *Social Science Quarterly* 75 (3):594–606.

Levine, P. B., Staiger, D., Kane, T. J., and Zimmerman, D. J. Roe v. Wade and American fertility, National Bureau of Economic Research, Inc., NBER Working Papers, 1996.

Levitt, S. D. 2004. Understanding why crime fell in the 1990s: four factors that explain the decline and six that do not. *Journal of Economic Perspectives* 18 (1):163–190.

Levitt, S. D. Interview with Scott Simon on National Public Radio, 2005, http://www.npr.org/templates/story/story.php?storyId=4583937 (accessed on November 12, 2005).

Lim, L. L. 1998. *The Sex Sector: The Economic and Social Bases of Prostitution in Southeast Asia.* Geneva: International Labour Office; distributed by ILO Publications Center, Waldorf, Md.

Liu, H., and D. E. Brown. 2003. Criminal incident prediction using a point-pattern-based density model. *International Journal of Forecasting* 19 (4):603–622.

Lombroso, C. 1903. Why criminals of genius have no type. *International Quarterly* VI:229–240.

Lott, J. R. 2001. Guns, crime, and safety: Introduction. *Journal of Law and Economics* 44 (2):605–614.

Lott, J. R., and D. B. Mustard. 1997. Crime, deterrence, and right-to-carry concealed handguns. *Journal of Legal Studies* 26 (1):1–68.

Lott, J. R., and Whitley, J. E. Abortion and Crime: unwanted Children and Out-of-Wedlock Births (April 30, 2001), Yale Law and Economics Research Paper No. 254, 2001, Available at SSRN: http://ssrn.com/abstract=270126orDOI:10.2139/ssrn.270126

Luksetich, W. A., and M. D. White. 1982. Crime and public policy. *An Economic Approach.* Boston, MA: Little, Brown and Company.

MacDonald, Z. 2002. Official crime statistics: their use and interpretation. *Economic Journal* 112 (477):F85–F106.

Marvell, T. B. 2001. The impact of banning juvenile gun possession. *Journal of Law and Economics* 44 (2):691–713.

Marvell, T. B., and C. E. Moody. 2001. The lethal effects of three-strikes laws. *Journal of Legal Studies* 30 (1):89–106.

Mast, B. D., B. L. Benson, and D. W. Rasmussen. 2000. Entrepreneurial police and drug enforcement policy. *Public Choice* 104 (3–4):285–308.

McCarthy, P. S. 1999. Public policy and highway safety: a city-wide perspective. *Regional Science and Urban Economics* 29 (2):231–244.

McConnell, S., and S. Glazerman. 2001. *National job corps study: the benefits and costs of job corps*, U.S.; District of Columbia.

Mednick, S. A., W. F. Gabrielli, and B. Hutchings. 1984. Genetic influences in criminal behavior: evidence from an adoption cohort. *Science* 224 (4651):891–894.

Medoff, M. H. 1999. Allocation of time and hateful behavior: a theoretical and positive analysis of hate and hate crimes. *American Journal of Economics and Sociology* 58 (4):959–973.

Medoff, M. H., and I. Lee Skov. 1992. Religion and behavior: an empirical analysis. *Journal of Socio-Economics* 21 (2):143–151.

Meier, V. 2001. On prison and therapy. *European Journal of Law and Economics* 12 (1):47–56.

Milne, G. R. 2003. How well do consumers protect themselves from identity theft? *Journal of Consumer Affairs* 37 (2):388–402.

Miron, J. A. 2001. Violence, guns, and drugs: a cross-country analysis. *Journal of Law and Economics* 44 (2):615–633.

Moody, C. E. 2001. Testing for the effects of concealed weapons laws: specification errors and robustness. *Journal of Law and Economics* 44 (2):799–813.

Moselle, B., and B. Polak. 2001. A model of a predatory state. *Journal of Law, Economics, and Organization* 17 (1):1–33.

New Hampshire Civil Liberties Union. N.D. Freedom of Expression in the Arts and Entertainment, http://www.nhclu.org/publications/artistic_freedom.html (accessed on August 21, 2004).

Parker, J. S. 2001. Guns, crime, and academics: some reflections on the gun control debate. *Journal of Law and Economics* 44 (2):715–723.

Plassmann, F., and T. N. Tideman. 2001. Does the right to carry concealed handguns deter countable crimes? Only a count analysis can say. *Journal of Law and Economics* 44 (2):771–798.

Parker, J. S. 2001. Guns, crime, and academics: some reflections on the gun control debate. *Journal of Law and Economics* 44 (2):715–723.

Polinsky, A. M., and S. Shavell. 2000. The economic theory of public enforcement of law. *Journal of Economic Literature* 38 (1):45–76.

Pudney, S. 2003. The road to ruin? Sequences of initiation to drugs and crime in Britain. *Economic Journal* 113 (486):C182–C198.

Ravenscroft, N., D. Uzzell, and R. Leach. 2002. Danger ahead? The impact of fear of crime on people's recreational use of nonmotorised shared-use routes. *Environment and Planning C: Government and Policy* 20 (5):741–756.

Reynolds, M. O. 1985. *Crime by Choice, an Economic Analysis.* Dallas, TX: A Fisher Institute Publication.

Reynolds, M. O. 1990. *Crime Pays, but so does Imprisonment.* .

Reynolds, M. O. National Center for Policy Analysis. (1997) Crime is Down Because Punishment is Up, 1997, http://www.ncpa.org/ba/ba247.html (accessed on November 21, 2005).

Roebuck, M. C., M. T. French, and M. L. Dennis. 2004. Adolescent marijuana use and school attendance. *Economics of Education Review* 23 (2):133–141.

Rubin, P. H., and H. Dezhbakhsh. 2003. The effect of concealed handgun laws on crime: beyond the dummy variables. *International Review of Law and Economics* 23 (2):199–216.

Shavell, S. 1991. Specific versus general enforcement of law. *Journal of Political Economy* 99 (5):1088–1108.

Shavell, S. 1993. The optimal structure of law enforcement. *Journal of Law and Economics* 36 (1):255–287.

Shaw, C. R., and H. D. McKay. 1942. *Juvenile Delinquency and Urban Areas*. Chicago, IL: University of Chicago Press.

Shepherd, J. M. 2004. Murders of passion, execution delays, and the deterrence of capital punishment. *Journal of Legal Studies* 33 (2):283–321.

Skaperdas, S. 2001. The political economy of organized crime: providing protection when the state does not. *Economics of Governance* 2 (3):173–202.

Soares, R. R. 2004. Development, crime and punishment: accounting for the international differences in crime rates. *Journal of Development Economics* 73 (1):155–184.

Tani, S. 2002. Whose place is this space? Life in the street prostitution area of Helsinki, Finland. *International Journal of Urban and Regional Research* 26 (2):343–359.

Tauchen, H. V., A. D. Witte, and S. K. Long. 1991. Domestic violence: a nonrandom affair. *International Economic Review* 32 (2):491–511.

Terwilliger, G. Commercial and Federal Criminal Law: Risks of Over-Criminalizing Commercial Regulation, June 13, 2002, http://www.fed-soc.org/pdf/Terwilliger.pdf (date accessed on August 21, 2004).

Thomas, C. J., and R. D. F. Bromley. 1996. Safety and shopping: peripherality and shopper anxiety in the city centre. *Environment and Planning C: Government and Policy* 14 (4):469–488.

U.S. Bureau of Justice Statistics. Crimes and Victims Statistics, http://www.ojp.usdoj.gov/bjs/cvict.htm#summary (accessed on August 21, 2004).

U.S. Bureau of Justice Statistics. Effects of NIBRS on Crime Statistics, http://www.ojp.usdoj.gov/bjs/pub/pdf/enibrscs.pdf (date accessed on August 7, 2004).

U.S. Bureau of Justice Statistics. National Incident-Based Reporting System (NIBRS) Implementation Program, http://www.ojp.usdoj.gov/bjs/nibrs.htm (accessed on August 7, 2004).

U.S. Bureau of Justice Statistics. Homicide trends in the U.S. Intimate homicide, http://www.ojp.usdoj.gov/bjs/homicide/intimates.htm (accessed on November 16, 2005).

U.S. Bureau of Justice Statistics. Intimate Partner Violence. May 2000. Revised 31 January 2002, http://www.ojp.usdoj.gov/bjs/pub/pdf/ipv.pdf (accessed on November 10, 2005).

U.S. Bureau of Justice Statistics. Crime and Justice in the United States and in England and Wales, 1981–1996, http://www.ojp.usdoj.gov/bjs/pub/html/cjusew96/jsc.htm#table (accessed on November 21, 2005).

Viscusi, W. K. Viscusi, 1995. Cigarette taxation and the social consequences of smoking. In *Tax Policy and the Economy*, ed. J. M. Poterba, Vol. 9, MIT Press for the National Bureau of Economic Research, Cambridge, 51–101.

White, M. D., and W. A. Luksetich. 1983. Heroin: price elasticity and enforcement strategies. *Economic Inquiry* 21 (4):557–564.

Wiles, P., J. Simmons, and K. Pease. 2003. Crime victimization: its extent and communication. *Journal of the Royal Statistical Society: Series A (Statistics in Society)* 166 (2):247–252.

Wilkins, A. Domestic Violence, Welfare Reform. National Conference of State Legislatures, http://www.ncsl.org/statefed/welfare/famvioopt.htm (accessed on November 17, 2005).

Williams, J. 2004. The effects of price and policy on marijuana use: what can be learned from the Australian experience? *Health Economics* 13 (2):123–137.

Williams, J., and R. C. Sickles. 1958. An analysis of the crime as work model: evidence from the Philadelphia birth cohort study. *Journal of Human Resources* 37 (3):479–509.

Witte, A. D. 1996. Urban crime: issues and policies. *Housing Policy Debate* 7 (4):731–748.

Yochelson, S., and S. E. Samenow. 1976. The criminal personality, Vol. I. *A profile for change*. New York: Jason Aronson.

Yochelson, S., and S. E. Samenow. 1977. The criminal personality, Vol. II. *The change process*. New York: Jason Aronson.

Index

H

Harley–Davidson, 117
Hate crime, 692–695
Hazards and transportation, 467–469
Head counts, 591
Head Start, 642
Hedonic price indices, 394
Hedonic regression, 405–406
Heroin, 706, 708–709
Hershey, Milton, 126
Hexagons, 54–57, 59–60
Hierarchies
    city systems, 20, 57–65
    crime, 699–700
    governments, 548–559
Higher education, 225–232, 335, 619
Highways, 459–469
    privatization, 462–466
    public capital investment, 331–334
    safety, 467–469
Historic districts, 406–407
History and agglomeration economies, 124–126
Homeownership, 417–418
Home working, 292–293
Hong Kong, 472–473
Horizontal fiscal externalities, 560
Horology, 116–117
Hotelling, Harold, 27–34
Hotel room taxes, 532
Housing
    amenities, 406–413
    costs, 307, 583–584
    location/income differences, 419
    markets, 401–439
        affordability, 427–429
        commuting, 420
        demand, 402–403, 414–421
        discrimination, 421–427
        government, 429–436
        hedonic regression, 405–406
        inefficiency, 402–403
        labor, 420
        land-use controls, 492–493
        prices, 405–410, 428–429
        public housing, 430–431, 432, 433
        rent controls, 431–434
        residential succession, 419–421
        segregation, 421–427
        services, 403–404
        supply, 413–421
        supply and demand, 402–403, 414–421
        supply functions, 413–421
        vouchers, 434–436

migration, 307
    monocentric cities, 383–384, 385–386
    poverty lines, 583–584
    prices, 383–384, 385–386, 405–410, 428–429
    primary school quality, 650–651
    services, 403–404
    supply functions, 413–421
    tenure, 415
    values, 405–413, 428–429
    vouchers, 434–436
    see also Land rents
Housing Act of the United States (1949), 427
Human capital
    education, 631–665
    investment, 618–620, 631–665
    migration, 296–297, 298, 306–307
    poverty, 618–620
    supply-based regional growth, 223–236
    technical change, 223–236
Human rights, 401

I

Identity theft, 687
Illegal immigration, 298–299
Imitation, 119
Immigration
    consequences, 308
    economic benefits, 312–313
    fiscal impacts, 310–311
    labor supply, 298–299, 308, 310–313
    local fiscal impacts, 310–311
    sending region impacts, 313
    welfare, 310–311
Imports, 177–178
Imprisonment, 718–721
Improvement rents, 375
Imputed rents, 576
Incentives
    economic development, 346, 347–356
    poverty, 607–608
    primary school quality, 648, 649–651
Income
    components, 576–577
    data sources, 15
    deficits, 592
    definition, 573–578
    distribution, 575, 613–618
    housing location, 419
    housing markets, 419, 427–428
    inequality, 571–622
    measurements, 576–578, 579–594
    mobility, 578, 609
    multipliers, 169, 179

CPSIA information can be obtained
at www.ICGtesting.com
Printed in the USA
LVOW13*0040020917

547313LV00013B/370/P